Creeds

and

Scripture Scales

Creeds and Scripture Scales

By

John Fletcher

Compiled and edited by
Jeffrey L. Wallace

ISBN-10: 0615813372
ISBN-13: 978-0615813370

A *Heritage of Truth* Book
Reclaiming the Wisdom of the Past

Heritage of Truth
Reclaiming the Wisdom of the Past

Published by:
Apprehending Truth Publishers
Brookfield, Missouri
2013

Buy the Truth and sell it not. ~Proverbs xxiii, 23
http://www.ApprehendingTruth.net

AT 10 9 8 7 6 5 4 3 2 1
051613

Jean Guillaume de la Flechere

The Works

of

John Fletcher

Volume Two

Creeds and Scripture Scales

Apprehending Truth Publishers

Brookfield, Missouri

2013

CONTENTS

SCRIPTURE SCALES   - 311 -

EDITOR'S PREFACE

In this second volume of John Fletcher's Works, he continues his assault on the perversions of Calvinism and its insubstantial misrepresentation of those they label Arminians and Pelagians. An examination of established creeds, both false and genuine, becomes necessary in any serious debate of the issue and his exhibition and comparison of Scripture with Scripture set forth in parallel scales, brings truth to the forefront when the false way of Reformed Theology would just as well keep it obscured.

Fletcher's genius is embedded in his genial comportment with the principles and precepts of the Scriptures. With such a grasp on Biblical injunctions of inward piety and superficies coupled with the necessity of proper hermeneutic, Fletcher belies the tendency of Calvinism's undermining of spiritual nutrition inherent in the Word of God. Never has there been a time of greater need for dogmatic insistence on the veracious handling of the Scriptures than now. With men waxing worse and worse, deceiving and being deceived, the importance of clinging to proper doctrine is essential.

Hence, Apprehending Truth Publishers presents for your consideration, *The Works of John Fletcher, Volume 2: Creeds and Scripture Scales.*

THE

FICTITIOUS AND GENUINE CREED:

BEING

"A CREED FOR ARMINIANS,"

COMPOSED

BY RICHARD HILL, ESQ.

TO WHICH IS OPPOSED

A CREED

FOR THOSE WHO BELIEVE THAT

CHRIST TASTED DEATH FOR EVERY MAN

BY THE AUTHOR OF THE

CHECKS TO ANTINOMIANISM

In doctrine show uncorruptness, gravity, sincerity, sound speech that cannot be condemned:
that he who is of the contrary part may be ashamed, Ttius ii, 7, 8.

The Works of John Fletcher

PREFACE

TO FICTITIOUS AND GENUINE CREED.

In which the author gives an account of Mr. Hill's new method of attack, and makes some reconciling concessions to the Calvinists, by means of which their strongest arguments are unnerved, and all that is truly Scriptural in Calvinism is openly adopted into the anti-Calvinian doctrine of grace.

WE should be deservedly considered as bad Protestants if we were not "ready always to give an answer with meekness to every man, [much more to Mr. Hill, a gentleman of piety, learning, reputation, wit, and fortune,] who asketh us a reason of the hope that is in us." We confess, that after the way which our opponents call the heresy of the Arminians and Perfectionists, we worship the God of our fathers; believing what is written in the Scriptures concerning the extent of redemption by price and by power.

Concerning the extent of Christ's redemption *by price*, we believe, that "he, by the grace of God, tasted death" to procure initial salvation "for every man," and "eternal salvation for them that obey him:" and concerning the extent of his redemption *by power*, we are persuaded that, when we come to God by him, he is able and willing to "save to the uttermost" our souls from the guilt and pollution of sin here, and our bodies from the grave and from corruption hereafter.

With regard to our extensive views of Christ's redemption by price, Mr. Hill calls us Arminians: and with respect to our believing that there is no perfect faith, no perfect repentance in the grave; that the Christian graces of repentance, faith, hope, patience, &c, must be perfected here or never; and with respect to our confidence that Christ's blood fully applied by his Spirit, and apprehended by perfect faith, can cleanse our hearts from all unrighteousness before we go into the purgatory of the Calvinists, or into that of the Papists; that is, before we go into the valley of the shadow of death, or into the suburbs of hell; — with respect to this belief and confidence, I say, Mr. Hill calls us Perfectionists: and appearing once more upon the stage of our controversy, he has lately presented the public with what he calls, "*A Creed for Arminians and Perfectionists*," which he introduces in these words: — "The following confession of faith, however shocking, not to say blasphemous, it may appear to the humble Christian, must inevitably be adopted, if not in express words, yet in substance, by every Arminian and Perfectionist whatsoever; though the last article chiefly concerns such as are ordained ministers in the Church of England." And as among such ministers, Mr. J. Wesley, Mr. W. Sellon, and myself, peculiarly oppose Mr. Hill's Calvinian doctrines of absolute election and reprobation, and of a death purgatory; he has put the initial letters of our names to his creed; hoping, no doubt, to make us peculiarly ashamed of our principles. And indeed so should we be, if any "blasphemous" or "shocking" consequence "inevitably" flowed from them.

But how has Mr. Hill proved that this is the case? Has he supported his charge by one argument? No: but among some consequences of our doctrine, which are quite harmless and Scriptural, he has fixed upon us some shocking consequences, which have no necessary connection with any of our doctrines of grace. We apprehend, therefore, that by this method Mr. Hill has exposed his inattention more than our "heresy."

If Mr. Hill had said, before a thousand witnesses, I hold *ten* guineas in my right hand, and *ten* in my left, could the author of the Checks wrong him, or expose his own candour, if he insisted upon the truth of this consequence: "Then Mr. Hill holds *twenty* guineas in *both* his hands?" And if Mr. Hill protested ever so long that he holds but *fifteen* in all, and that I am a "*calumniator*," for saying that he holds twenty; would not all the witnesses, who are impartial, and acquainted with the proportion of numbers, clear me of the charge of *calumny*, and accuse Mr. Hill of *inattention*? Again: if I had said, before the same witnesses, that I have *two* guineas in my right hand, and *two* in my left; and if Mr. Hill, to keep his error in countenance, by bringing me in guilty of as great a mistake as his own, fixed the following consequence upon my assertions: "Then you hold seven guineas in both your hands!" would he not expose himself more than me? And would not all the candid spectators declare, that although I have a right to maintain that *ten* and *ten* make *twenty*, my opponent cannot reasonably assert that *two* and *two* make *seven*. The justness of this illustration will appear to the reader, if he cast a look upon the creed which I have composed for an Antinomian, with Mr. Hill's principles. The doctrines that it contains are all his own, and they are expressed chiefly in his own words, as appears from numerous quotations, in which I refer the reader to the pages where he has publicly maintained the tenets which I expose. But Mr. Hill has not produced in his Arminian creed one line out of my Checks, from which any shocking or blasphemous doctrine flows by "unavoidable" consequence. If he had, I protest, as a lover of truth, that I would instantly renounce the principle on which such a doctrine might be justly fathered; being persuaded that the pure light of a pure doctrine can never be *necessarily* productive of a gross darkness: although it may accidentally be obscured by occasional difficulties, as the sun may be darkened by interposing clouds.

Some readers will probably think that I have made the Calvinists too many concessions in the following pages: but I am persuaded that I have granted them nothing but what they have a Scriptural right to; and God forbid that any Protestant should grant them less! At the synod of Dort, the Arminians being sensible that a *gratuitous election* can be defended by reason and Scripture, would debate first the doctrine of *gratuitous, Calvinian reprobation*, which is flatly contrary to reason and Scripture. The Calvinists, on the other hand, being conscious that the strength of their cause lay in maintaining a gratuitous election, and hoping that the gratuitous reprobation would naturally skulk under that election, insisted that the doctrine of election should be debated first. The Arminians would not consent to it, so that nothing was properly discussed: and the Calvinists, having numbers, and the sword on their side, deposed their opponents as obstinate heretics. While we disapprove the severity of the Calvinists, we blame the Arminians for provoking that severity by refusing to clear up the doctrine of election. And improving by the mistakes of both parties, we make the reconciling concessions which follow: —

1. We grant that there is an election of distinguishing grace: but we show that this election is not Calvinian election; thousands being partakers of the partial election of distinguishing grace, who have no share in the impartial election of distributive justice; two distinct elections these, the confounding of which has laid the foundation of numberless errors. See Scripture Scales, sec. 12.

2. We grant the Calvinists that initial salvation is merely by a decree of Divine grace through Jesus Christ. But we assert that eternal salvation is both by a decree of Divine grace and of distributive justice; God rewarding in Christ, with an eternal life of glory, those believers who "by patient continuance in well doing seek for glory, honour, and immortality."

3. We grant, that although God, as a judge, "is no respecter of persons;" yet, as a benefactor, he is, and of consequence has a right to be, so far a "respecter of persons," as to bestow his favours in various degrees upon his creatures; dealing them to some with a more sparing hand than he does to others.

4. We grant, that although God punishes no one with eternal death for original and necessary sin; yet when sin, which might have been avoided by the help of creating or of redeeming grace, has been voluntarily and personally committed; God does punish (and of consequence has a right to punish) with eternal death some offenders more quickly than he does others; his showing, in such a case, mercy and justice upon Gospel terms to whom he pleases, and as soon or late as he pleases, being undoubtedly the privilege of his sovereign goodness or justice: an awful privilege this, which is perfectly agreeable to the evangelical law of liberty, and with which the Calvinists have absurdly built their twin doctrines of finished salvation and finished damnation; not considering that such doctrines stain the first Gospel axiom, and totally destroy the second.

The nature of this concession may be illustrated by an example. Two unconverted soldiers march up to the enemy. Both have unavoidably transgressed the third commandment: the one by calling *fifty* times for his damnation; and the other *five hundred* times. Now, both have personally forfeited their initial salvation, and continuing impenitent, God, as a righteous avenger of profaneness, may justly suffer the *fifty pence debtor* to fall in the battle and to be instantly hurried to the damnation he had madly prayed for: and, as a long-suffering, merciful Creator, he may suffer the *five hundred pence debtor*, I mean the soldier who has sinned with a higher hand, to walk out of the field unhurt, and to be spared for years; following him still with new offers of mercy, which the wretch is so happy as to embrace at last. Here is evidently a higher degree of the distinguishing grace which was manifested toward Manasses, as it has also been to many other grievous sinners. But by this peculiar favour, God violates no promise, and he acts in perfect consistency with himself: for, when two people have personally forfeited their eternal salvation by one avoidable sin, of which they do not repent when they might: he does no injustice to the fifty pence debtor, when he calls him first to an account; and he greatly magnifies his long suffering, when he continues to reprieve the five hundred pence debtor.

By this sparing use of astonishing mercy, God strongly guards the riches of his grace. This *inferior* degree of forbearance makes thoughtful sinners stand in awe: as not knowing but the first sin they shall commit will actually fill up the measure of their iniquities, and provoke the Almighty to swear in his righteous anger that their day of grace is ended. To justify, therefore, God's conduct toward men in this respect, we need only observe, that if distinguishing grace did not make the difference which we grant to the Calvinists, perverse free will would draw amazing strength from the unwearied patience of free grace. Suppose, for instance, that God had insured to all men a day of grace of four-score years, would not all sinners think it time enough to repent at the age of three-score years and nineteen? Therefore. through the clouds of darkness which surrounds us, reason sees far into the propriety of the partiality with which distinguishing grace dispenses its *superior* blessings. But all the partiality which that grace ever displayed, never amounted to one single grain of Calvinian reprobation. Because God, as a righteous judge, lets every man have a fair trial for his life. Nor will all the sophisms in the world reconcile the ideas, which the Scriptures and rectified reason give us of Divine justice, with a doctrine which represents God as condemning to eternal torments a majority of men, for the necessary, unavoidable consequences of Adam's sin: a sin this, which, upon the scheme of the absolute predestination of all events, was also made unavoidable and necessary. To return: —

5. We grant, that although Christ died to purchase a day of [initial] salvation for all men, yet he never died to purchase ETERNAL salvation for any adults, but "them that believe, obey," and are "faithful unto death." And that of consequence the redemption of mankind by Jesus Christ is general and unconditional with respect to INITIAL salvation; but particular and conditional with respect to ETERNAL salvation; except in the case of infants, who die before actual sin: these, and only these, are blessed with unconditional election and finished salvation in the Calvinistical sense of these phrases: — These are irresistibly saved, and eternally admitted into one of the many mansions of our heavenly Father's house: free grace, to the honour of our Lord's meritorious infancy, absolutely saves them, without any concurrence of their free will. Nor is it surprising that God should do it unavoidably; for as they never were personally capable of working *with* free grace, i.e. of "working out their salvation;" so they never were in a capacity of working against free grace, or of beginning to work their damnation. Having never committed any act of sin, God can, consistently with the Gospel, save them eternally without any act of repentance. In a word, infants having *no unrighteousness* but that of the first Adam, reason, as well as Scripture, dictates that they need *no righteousness* but that of the *second* Adam.

6. From the preceding concessions, it follows that obedient; persevering believers are God's elect in the particular and full sense of the word, being elected to the reward of eternal life in glory: a reward this, from which they who die in a state of apostasy or impenitency have cut themselves off, by not making their calling and conditional election sure.

7. We grant that none of these peculiar elect shall ever perish. though they would have perished had they not been faithful unto death' and we allow, that, with respect to God's foreknowledge and omniscience, their number is certain. But we steadily assert, that, with regard to the doctrines of general redemption, of God's covenanted mercy, of man's free agency, of Divine justice, and of a day in which the Lord will "judge the world in righteousness:" we steadily assert, I say, with regard to these doctrines, the number of the peculiar elect might be greater or less, without the

least exertion of forcible grace or of forcible wrath. For it might be greater, if more wicked and slothful servants improved instead of burying their talents: and it might be less, if more good and faithful servants grew faint in their minds, and "drew back to perdition," before they had "fought their good fight out, kept the faith, and finished their course."

8. And lastly, we grant, that, according to the election of distinguishing grace which is the basis of the various dispensations of Divine grace toward the children of men, Christ died to purchase more privileges for the Christian Church than for the Jews, more for the Jews than for the Gentiles, and more for some Gentiles than for others: for it is indubitable that God, as a sovereign benefactor, may, without shadow of injustice, dispense his favours, spiritual and temporal, as he pleases: it being enough for the display of his goodness, and for the exciting of our gratitude, (1.) That the least of his heathen servants had received a talent, with means, capacities, and opportunities of improving it, even to everlasting happiness. (2.) That God never desires to reap where he does not sow, nor to reap a hundred measures of spiritual wheat where he only sows a handful of spiritual barley. And, (3.) That the least degree of his improvable goodness is a seed, which nothing but our avoidable unfaithfulness hinders from bringing forth fruit to eternal life in glory.

By making these guarded concessions, I conceive we rectify the mistakes of Arminius; we secure the doctrine of grace in all its branches, while Calvinism secures only the irresistible grace by which infants and complete idiots are eternally saved: we turn the edge, and break the point of all the arguments by which the Calvinian doctrines of grace are defended; and tear in pieces the cloak with which the Antinomians cover their dangerous error.

Had Arminius, and all the ancient and modern semi-Pelagians, granted to their opponents what we grant to ours, Calvinism would never have risen to its tremendous height. If you try to stop a great river, refusing it the liberty to flow in the deep channel which nature has assigned it, you only make it foam, rise, rage, overflow its banks, and carry devastation far and near. The only way to make judicious Calvinists allow us the impartial remunerative election, and the general redemption which the Gospel displays, is to allow them, with a good grace, the partial, gratuitous election, and the particular redemption which the Scriptures strongly maintain also. (See the Scales, sec. xi, xii, xiii.) For my part, I glory in going as near the Calvinists as I safely can. Zelotes is my brother as well as Honestus: and, so long as I do not lose firm footing upon Scripture ground, I gladly stretch my right hand to him, and my left hand to his antagonist; endeavouring to help them both out of the opposite ditches, which bound the narrow way, where truth frequently takes a solitary walk.

I conclude this introduction by thanking Mr. Hill for coming a little closer to the knot of the controversy in his *Fictitious Creed*, than he has done in his *Finishing Stroke*; for by this mean he has stirred me up to dig deeper into the Scriptures, — those inexhaustible mines of truth which God has set before us. I would not intimate that I have dug out new gold. No: the oracles of God are not new; but I hope that I have separated a little dross from some of the richest pieces of golden ore which the Arminians and the Calvinists have dug out of those mines: and I flatter myself that the judicious and unprejudiced will confess that some of those pieces which Calvinian and Arminian bigots have thrown away as lumps of dross or of arsenic, contain, nevertheless, truths more precious than thousands of gold and silver. Should these sheets in any degree remove the prejudice of professors, and prepare them for a reconciliation upon the Scriptural plan of the doctrines of grace and justice, or of the two Gospel axioms, I shall humbly rejoice and thankfully give God the glory.

J. FLETCHER.

MADELEY, DEC. 14, 1774.

THE

FICTITIOUS AND THE GENUINE CREED.

THE FICTITIOUS CREED,

BEING A CREED FOR ARMINIANS.

Composed by Richard Hill. Esq. and published at the end of his " Three Letters writtento the Rev. J. Fletcher, vicar of Madeley."

ARTICLE I.

"I BELIEVE that Jesus Christ died for the whole human race, and that he had no more love toward those who now are, or hereafter shall be, in glory, than for those who now are, or hereafter shall be, lifting up their eyes in torments; and that the one are no more indebted to his grace than the other."

THE GENUINE CREED,

Being an anti-Calvinian confession of faith, for those who believe that "Christ tasted death for every man;" and that some men, by "denying the Lord that bought them, bring upon themselves swift destruction."

ARTICLE I.

We believe that Jesus Christ died for the whole human race, with an intention, first, to procure absolutely and unconditionally a temporary redemption, or an initial salvation for all men universally: and, secondly, to procure a particular redemption, or an eternal salvation conditionally for all men, but absolutely for all that die in their infancy, and for all the adult who obey him, and are "faithful unto death."

We believe that, in consequence of the general and temporary redemption procured by Christ for all mankind, every man is unconditionally blessed with a day of grace, which the Scripture calls "the accepted time," and "the day of salvation." During this day, (under various dispensations of grace, and by virtue of various covenants made through Christ, David, Moses, Abraham, Noah, or Adam,) God, for Christ's sake, affords all men proper means, abilities, and opportunities to "work out their own salvation," or to make "their calling and *conditional* election" to the eternal blessings of their respective dispensations "sure;" and as many do it, by keeping "the free gift which is come" unto all men, or by recovering it through faithful obedience to re-converting grace: or, in other terms, as many as know, and perseveringly improve "the day of their visitation," are, in consequence of Christ's particular redemption, entitled to an eternal redemption or salvation: that is, they are eternally redeemed from hell, and eternally saved into different degrees of heavenly glory, according to the different degrees of their faithfulness, and the various dispensations which they are under. While they that bury their talent, and "know not [i.e. squander away] the day of their visitation," forfeit their initial salvation, and secure to themselves God's judicial reprobation, together with all its terrible consequences.

We believe, moreover, that although Christ "tasted death for every man," yet, according to his covenants of peculiarity or distinguishing grace, he formerly showed more love to the Jews than to the Gentiles, and now shows more favour to the Christians than to the Jews, and to some Christians than to others; bestowing more spiritual blessings upon the Protestants than upon the Papists; more temporal mercies upon the English than upon the Greenlanders, &c. We farther believe that this special favour is not only national, but also, in some cases, personal: thus it seems that God showed more of it to Jacob than to Esau; to Esau than to Shechem; to David and Solomon, than to Jonathan and Mephibosheth; to St. Paul than to Apollos; and to Peter, James, and John, than to Judas, Bartholomew, and Matthias. We likewise believe that God (*according to his prescience*) has a regard for the souls who (he foresees) *will* finally yield to his grace, and this regard he has not for the souls who (he foresees) *will* finally harden themselves against his goodness: thus, with respect to Divine foreknowledge, we grant that Christ had a respect for fallen Peter which he had not for fallen Judas: for, when they were both lying in the guilt of their crimes, he could not but prefer him who had not yet sinned out his day of grace to him who had: him who had done the Spirit of grace a *partial, temporary* despite, to him who had done that Spirit a *total* and *final* despite. And, in a word, him who *would* repent, to him who absolutely would *not*. However, this peculiar regard for some men, this lengthening or shortening a sinner's day of grace arbitrarily, and this bestowing more talents, i.e. more temporal and spiritual blessings upon one man than upon another, according to the sovereign prerogative which God claims in his covenants of peculiarity; this peculiar regard for some men, I say, never amounts to a grain of partiality in judgment: much less to a rape committed by overbearing grace, or infrustrable wrath, upon the moral agency of two men (suppose Peter and Judas) to bring about, in an unavoidable manner, the final *perseverance* of the one, and the final *apostasy* of the other. For had the covetous traitor humbly repented when he could have done it, he yet would have gone to heaven; and had the lying, perjured apostle put off his repentance as obstinately as Judas did, he would have gone to the place of impenitent apostates: for God having "put life and death before" the sons of men; and having appointed eternal rewards for those who "finally choose life" in the rectitude of their conduct, and eternal punishment for those who "finally choose death in the error of their ways," he can no more *finally* turn the scale of their will than he can *deny himself*, and turn the solemnity of the great day into the pageantry of a Pharisaic masquerade.

The end of the first article of Mr. Hill's *Fictitious Creed* is not less contrary to all our principles than the middle part. For, according to all our doctrines of grace, persons who are in glory like Peter, are infinitely more indebted to Christ's grace than persons who lift up their eyes in torments like Judas. This will appear, if we consider the case of those two apostles. Although they were both equally indebted to Christ for his redeeming love, which put them in a state of initial salvation; and for his distinguishing favour, which raised them to apostolic honours; yet upon our scheme Peter is infinitely more beholden to free grace than Judas; and I prove it thus: Christ, according to his remunerative election, which draws after it a particular redemption, and eternal salvation; — Christ, I say, according to that remunerative election, has chosen Peter to the reward of a heavenly throne and a crown of glory. Now this election, in which Judas has no interest, springs from God's free grace, as well as from voluntary perseverance in the free obedience of faith. It was of free grace that God designed to give to all penitent, persevering believers, and of consequence to Peter, a crown of glory in his heavenly kingdom: for he might have given them only the conveniences of life in a cottage on earth: he might have dropped them into their original nothingness, after having blessed them with one single smile of his approbation: nay, he might have demanded their utmost obedience, without promising them the least reward. Therefore Peter and all the saints in glory are indebted to Christ, not only for their rewards of additional grace on earth, but also for *all* their *eternal* salvation, and for *all* the heavenly blessings which flow from their *particular* redemption. Infinitely *gracious* rewards these, which God does not bestow upon Judas, nor upon any of those who die impenitent! Infinitely *glorious* rewards! which nothing but God's free grace in Christ could move his distributive justice to bestow upon persevering believers. Hence it is evident that Mr. Hill has tried to make our fundamental doctrine of *general redemption* appear ridiculous, by absurdly clogging it with an odious consequence, which has no more to do with that comfortable doctrine, than we have to do with Mr. Hill's uncomfortable tenet of *absolute reprobation*.

THE FICTITIOUS CREED.

ARTICLE II.

"I believe that Divine grace is indiscriminately given to all men; and that God, foreseeing that by far the greater part of the world will reject his grace, doth nevertheless bestow it upon them, in order to heighten their torments, and to increase their damnation in hell."

THE GENUINE CREED.

ARTICLE II.

We do not believe that Divine grace is *indiscriminately* given to all men. For although we assert that God gives to all at least *one* talent of *true* grace to profit with; yet we acknowledge that he makes as real a difference between *man* and *man*, as between an *angel* and an *archangel*, giving to some men *one* talent, to others *two* talents, and to others *five*, according to the election of *distinguishing grace*, maintained in the Scripture Scales, sec. xii. But the least talent of grace is saving, if free will do not bury it to the last.

And we believe that although God foresaw that in some unhappy periods of the world's duration the greater part of adults would reject his grace, he nevertheless bestows it in different measures upon all; but not (as Mr. Hill says) "in order to heighten the torments, and increase the damnation of any in hell." This is a horrid conceit, which we return to those who insinuate that God gives *common* grace (that is, we apprehend *unsaving, graceless grace*) to absolute reprobates, i.e. to men for whom (upon Mr. Hill's scheme of absolute reprobation) there never was in God the least degree of mercy and saving goodness. This shocking consequence, fixed upon us by Mr. Hill, is the genuine offspring of Calvinistic non-election, which supposes that God sends the Gospel to myriads of men from whom he absolutely keeps the power of believing it; tantalizing them with offers of free grace here, that he may, *without possibility of escape*, sink them hereafter to the deepest hell, — the hell of the Capernaites.

According to the Gospel, the reprobation that draws eternal damnation after it springs from our own personal free will doing a final despite to free grace, and not from God's eternal free wrath. And if Mr. Hill ask, "Why God gives a manifestation of the Spirit of grace to men, who (he foresees) will do it a final despite, as well as to those who through that grace will work out their own salvation:" we reply: —

1. For the same reason which made him give *celestial* grace to the angels who became devils by squandering it away; *paradisiacal* grace to our first parents; expostulating, Gentile grace to Cain; Jewish, royal grace to Saul; and Christian, apostolic grace to Judas. If Mr. Hill says he does not understand what that reason is; we answer: By the same reason which induced the master who corrected Mr. Hill for making a bad exercise at Westminster school, to give his pupil pen, paper, ink, and proper instruction, before he could reasonably call Mr. Hill to an account for his exercise. And by the same reason which would make all Shropshire cry out against Mr. Hill as against a tyrannical master, suppose he horse-whipped his coachman and postilion for not driving him, if he had taken away from them boots, whips, spurs, harness, coach, and horses; and if he had contrived himself the fall of their apartment, that all their bones might be put out of joint when the floor gave way under them.

2. If Mr. Hill is not satisfied with these illustrations, we will give him some direct answers. God gives a manifestation of his grace to those who make their reprobation sure by finally resisting his gracious Spirit; First, Because he will show himself as he is, "gracious and merciful," "true and long suffering toward all," so long as "the day of their visitation" lasts. Thus he bestows a talent upon all his slothful servants who bury it to the last, because he will display his equity and goodness,

although they will display their wickedness and sloth. Secondly, Because he is determined that if those servants will destroy themselves, their blood shall be upon their own heads, according to the well-known scripture: "O Israel, thou hast destroyed thyself. I would, — and ye would not." Thirdly, Because God will "judge the world in righteousness," and display his distributive justice in rendering to all according to "their works;" *deservedly* clothing his finally unfaithful servants with shame, and making the faithful walk with him in white, "because they are [evangelically] worthy." And, to sum up all in one, — because the two Gospel axioms are firm as the pillars of heaven and hell; and God will display their truth before men and angels and especially before Pharisees and Antinomians. Now, according to the first axiom, there is a Saviour, a measure of saving grace, and a day of initial salvation for all. And, according to the second axiom, there is free will in all, and a day of judgment, with a final salvation or damnation for all, according to their good or bad works, that is, according to their free agency; the good works of the righteous being the product of their free, avoidable co-operation with God's grace; and the bad works of the wicked springing from their free, avoidable rebellion against that grace.

Hence it appears, that the second article of the *Fictitious Creed* contains indeed a "shocking, not to say blasphemous" consequence, but that this consequence is nothing but a sprig of Mr. Hill's supposed "orthodoxy," absurdly grafted upon the supposed "heresy" which St. John and St. Paul maintain in these words: "He [Christ] was the true light which lighteth every man that cometh into the world. The grace of God which bringeth salvation has appeared unto all men, teaching [not forcing] us to deny ungodliness, &c, and to live soberly," &c, if we are obedient to its teachings.

THE FICTITIOUS CREED.

ARTICLE III.

"I believe it depends WHOLLY on the will of the creature whether he shall or shall not RECEIVE ANY benefit from Divine grace."

THE GENUINE CREED.

ARTICLE III.

We believe that the benefits of a temporary redemption, of a day of salvation, and of the "free gift" which "came upon all men" to the justification mentioned Romans 5:18: we believe, I say, these benefits, far from "depending wholly on the will of the creature," as to the RECEIVING of them, depend no more upon us than our sight and the light of the sun. All those blessings are at first as gratuitously and irresistibly bestowed upon us, for Christ's sake, in our present manner of existence, as the Divine image and favour were at first bestowed upon our first parents in paradise, with this only difference; before the fall their pararadisiacal grace came immediately from God our *Creator*, whereas, since the fall, our penitential grace comes immediately and irresistibly from God our *Redeemer*, — I say *irresistibly*, because God does not leave to our option whether we shall receive a talent of *redeeming* grace or not, any more than he left it to Adam's choice whether Adam should receive five talents of *creative* grace or not: although afterward he gives us leave to bury or improve our talent of *redeeming* grace, as he gave leave to Adam to bury or improve his five talents of *creative* grace. Our doctrine of the general redemption and free agency of mankind stands therefore upon the same Scriptural and rational ground, which bears up Mr. Hill's system of man's creation and moral agency in paradise; it being impossible to make any objection against the personal loss of redeeming grace in Judas, that may not be retorted against the personal loss of creative grace in Adam or Satan.

But, with respect to all the temporal and eternal benefits which God has promised by way of *reward* to his every "good and faithful servant," we believe that they depend upon the concurrence of two causes; the *first* of which is the free grace of God in Jesus Christ; and the *second*, the faithfulness of our assisted and rectified free will, which faithfulness is graciously crowned by God's remunerative justice and evangelical veracity. And, instead of blushing at this doctrine, as if it were "shocking," we glory in it, as being perfectly rational, strictly Scriptural, and equally distant from the two rocks against which Calvinian orthodoxy is dashed in pieces: I mean, the twin doctrines of wanton free grace and eternal free wrath, according to which, God, without any respect to the faith or unbelief, to the good or bad works of free agents, absolutely ordained for some of them the robe of Christ's imputed righteousness, and the unavoidable reward of eternal life by the mean of unavoidable faith; while he absolutely appointed for all the rest the robe of Adam's imputed unrighteousness, and the unavoidable punishment of eternal death by means of necessary, unavoidable unbelief.

THE FICTITIOUS CREED.

ARTICLE IV.

"Though the Scripture tells me that the carnal mind is enmity against God, yet I believe that there is something in the heart of every natural man that can nourish and cherish the grace of God; and that the sole reason why this grace is effectual in some and not in others, is entirely owing to themselves, and to their own faithfulness or unfaithfulness, and not to the distinguishing love and favour of God."

THE GENUINE CREED.

ARTICLE IV.

Though the Scriptures tell us "that the carnal mind is enmity against God," and that "the flesh lusteth against the Spirit," yet we believe, that, from the time God initially raised mankind from their fall, and promised them the celestial bruiser of the

Creeds and Scripture Scales

serpent's head, there is a *gracious* free agency in the heart of every man who has not yet sinned away his day of salvation: and that, by means of this *gracious* free agency, all men, during the "accepted time," can concur with, and work under the grace of God, according to the dispensation they belong to. Again: we believe that no child of Adam is a "natural man" in the Calvinian sense of the word, [i.e. absolutely destitute of all saving grace,] except he who has actually sinned away his day of grace. And when we consider a man as absolutely graceless, or as "a child of wrath" in the highest sense of the word, we consider him in fallen Adam, *before* God began to raise mankind by the promise of the woman's seed: or we must consider that man in his own person *after* he has done final despite to the Spirit of that grace which has more or less clearly appeared to all men under various dispensations.

Mr. Hill greatly mistakes, if the thinks, that, according to our doctrine, God's grace is "effectual in some, and not in others;" for we believe that it is effectual in *all*, though in a different manner. It has its *first* and *most desirable* effect on them that "cherish it'"through the above-mentioned gracious free agency. And it has its *second* and *less desirable* effect on those who finally reject the gracious counsel of God toward them: for it reproves their sins; it galls their consciences; it renders them inexcusable; it vindicates God's mercy; it clears his justice; it shows that the Judge of all the earth does no wrong; and it begins in this world the just punishment which righteous vengeance will complete in the next.

The grace of God, therefore, like the Gospel that testifies of it, is *a two- edged sword*: it is a savour of life to those who cherish it, and a savour of death to those who resist it. That some cherish it, by its assistance work righteousness to the last, and then receive the reward of the inheritance, is not "entirely owing to themselves and to their own faithfulness," as the *Fictitious Creed* asserts: nor is it "entirely owing to the love and favour of God." This happy event has two causes: the *first* is *free grace*, by the assistance of which the faith and good works of the righteous are begun, continued, and ended: the *second* is *free will* humbly working with free grace, as appears by the numerous scriptures balanced in the Scripture Scales. And that some, on the other hand, resist the grace of God, and are personally given up to a reprobate mind that they might be damned, is not at all owing to God's free wrath, as the scheme of Mr. Hill supposes: nor is it entirely owing to the unfaithfulness and obstinacy of impenitent sinners. This unhappy event has also two causes: the first is man's free will finally refusing to concur with free grace, in working out his own salvation; and the second is just wrath, revenging the despite done to God's free grace by such a final refusal.

With respect to "the distinguishing love and favour" of God our Judge, and his distinguished hatred and ill will, (on which our eternal rewards and punishments unavoidably turn, according to Mr. Hill's twin doctrines of finished salvation and finished damnation;) we dare not admit them into our holy religion. We give to "distinguishing favour" an important place in our creed, as appears from the first article of this; but that favour has nothing to do with God's judicial distribution of rewards or punishments, i.e. with God's appointing of us to eternal life or to eternal death. We believe that it is a most daring attempt of the Antinomians to place distinguishing favour and distinguishing displeasure upon the judicial throne of God, and in the judgment seat of Christ; no decrees proceeding from thence, but such as are dictated by impartial justice putting Christ's evangelical law in execution, and strictly judging, (i.e. justifying or condemning, rewarding or punishing) moral agents, according to their works. We should think ourselves guilty of propagating "a shocking, not to say blasphemous" doctrine, if we insinuated, that" distinguishing favour," and not unbribed justice, dictates God's sentence; God himself having enacted, "Cursed be he that perverteth judgment, &c, and all the people shall say, Amen," Deuteronomy 27:19. Nor need I tell Mr. Hill this, who has hinted that God is such a partial Judge; — yea, that carries partiality to such a height, as to say to a man who actually defiles a married woman, and treacherously plots the murder of her injured husband, "Thou art all fair, my love, my undefiled, there is no spot in thee: thou art a man after my own heart." If Mr. Hill has forgotten this anecdote, I refer him to the *Five Letters*, the sale of which he does not scruple to advertise again in his *Three Letters*, saying: "I now think it the way of duty to permit — the Five Letters to Mr. Fletcher, &c, to be again sold, in order that both friends and enemies may, if possible, be convinced that *I never retracted my sentiments*." Strange confidence of boasting! *O mores!* What have *morality and godliness* done to Mr. Hill, that he will put them to a perpetual blush, lest his *Venus* (for she no longer deserves the name of *Diana*) should redden one moment?

THE FICTITIOUS CREED.

ARTICLE V.

"I believe that God sincerely wishes for the salvation of many who never will be saved; consequently, that it is entirely owing to want of ability in God, that what he so earnestly willeth is not accomplished."

THE GENUINE CREED.

ARTICLE V.

We believe that God's attributes perfectly harmonize. Accordingly his *goodness* and *mercy* incline him to "wish for the salvation of" all men, upon gracious terms laid down by his *wisdom* and *veracity*. As a proof of the sincerity of his wish, he swears by himself, that his antecedent will or decree is not "that sinners should die; but that," by the help of his free grace and the submission of their free will, "they should turn and live." He does more still' he grants to all men a day of initial salvation, and "all that day long he stretches forth his hands" to them. He reproves them for their sins' he calls upon them in various ways to repent; and gives them power to do it according to one or another dispensation of his grace; requiring little of those to whom he gives little; and much of those to whom much is given. But it is his *subsequent* decree, dictated chiefly by his *holiness*, *justice*, and *sovereignty*, that, if free agents will none of his reproofs, and finally disregard the offers of his grace, "his Spirit shall not always strive with them." A day of calamity shall follow the day of their neglected salvation; and justice shall be glorified in their righteous destruction. This is the sad alternative which God has set before them, if, in opposition to his antecedent will, they (through their free agency) finally choose death, in finally choosing the way that leads to it.

This part of our doctrine may be summed up in three propositions. (1.) God's mercy *absolutely* wills the *initial* salvation of all men by Jesus Christ. (2.) God's goodness, holiness, and faithfulness, *absolutely* will the *eternal* salvation of all those who, by the concurrence of their assisted, unnecessitated free will, with his redeeming grace, are found penitent, obedient believers, at the end of their day of initial salvation. And, (3.) God's justice, sovereignty, and veracity, absolutely will the destruction of all that are found impenitent at the close of the day of their gracious visitation, or initial salvation. To see the truth of these three propositions, we need only consider them in the light of these two Gospel axioms, and compare them with these declarations of Moses and Jesus Christ: "I set life and death before you, [free agents, who enjoy a day of initial salvation:] choose life:" (I offer it you *first:* "choose life," I say;) "that you may live eternally. But if you choose death in the error of your ways," your rejected Saviour will complain, "How often would I have gathered you as a hen gathereth her brood under her wings, but ye would not: and now the things that made for your peace are hid from your eyes:" that is, you are given up to judicial blindness, and to all its fearful consequences.

Hence it is evident, that the damnation of those who obstinately live and die in their sins, and whom God was willing to save as free agents upon Gospel terms, argues no "want of ability in him" to save them eternally, if he would give up the day of judgment, and exert his *omnipotence* in opposition to his *wisdom, justice, holiness,* and *veracity;* or if he would destroy the most wonderful of all his works, which is the free will of moral agents. We never doubted his ability to unman man, and eternally to save all mankind, if he would absolutely do it; it being evident that the Almighty can overpower all his creatures if he should be bent upon it, and drive them from sin to necessitated holiness, and from hell to heaven, far more easily than a shepherd can drive his frighted sheep from the market to the slaughter house. Therefore, the supposition that, upon our principles, "God wants ability to save" whom he absolutely will save, is entirely groundless; every man being actually saved so far as God* absolutely wills: for, *first,* God *absolutely* wills that *all men* should be *unconditionally* saved with *initial* salvation; and *thus all men* are *unconditionally* saved: and, *secondly,* he *absolutely* wills that all men, who are obedient and faithful unto death, should *absolutely* be saved with an eternal salvation: and *thus* all men who are obedient and faithful unto death are *actually* saved. They shall never perish, neither shall any pluck them out

---

* The reader is desired to take particular notice of this observation, because it cuts up by the root Bradwarden's famous argument. "If you allow, (says he,) (1.) That God is able to do a thing, and, (2.) That he is [absolutely] willing to do a thing: then, (3.) I affirm, that the thing will not, cannot go unaccomplished: otherwise God must either lose his power, or change his mind. If the [absolute] will of God could be frustrated and vanquished, its defeat would arise from the created wills either of angels or of men. But could any created will whatever, &c, counteract and baffle the will of God, the will of the creature must be superior either in strength or in wisdom to the will of the Creator: which can by no means be allowed." We fully grant to Mr. Toplady that the argument is "extremely conclusive," provided the two words "absolutely" and "absolute" be taken into it; and therefore, we maintain, as well as he, that man is actually saved, so far as God absolutely wills.

of Christ's protecting hand. But what has this Scripture doctrine to do with Calvinism? With the necessary, eternal, finished salvation of ALL the disobedient sheep, who turn goats, foxes, lions, and serpents? Who, far from remembering Lot's wife, slily rob their neighbours of their ewe lambs, — their heart's blood, — their reputation!

To conclude: the most that Mr. Hill can justly say against our principles, is: (1.) That, according to the Gospel which we preach, *man* is a *free agent*, and God is *wise, holy, true,* and *just*, as well as *good, loving, patient,* and *merciful*: and, (2.) That one half of these attributes do not permit him to *necessitate* free agents; that is, to *make them absolutely* DO *or* FORBEAR those actions, by which they are to stand or fall *in judgment*. And let men of reason and religion say, if this doctrine be not more *rational* and *Scriptural* than the Calvinian doctrine of *finished salvation*, and of its inseparable counterpart, *finished damnation*.

THE FICTITIOUS CREED.

ARTICLE VI.

"I believe that the Redeemer not only shed his precious blood, but prayed for the salvation of many souls who are now in hell; consequently that his blood was shed in vain, and his prayer rejected of his Father, and that therefore he told a great untruth when he said, I know that thou hearest me always."

THE GENUINE CREED.

ARTICLE VI.

We believe that the Redeemer did not shed his precious blood or pray absolutely in vain for any man: seeing he obtained for all men, in their season, a *day of grace* and *initial salvation*, with a thousand spiritual and temporal blessings. Nor were his prayers for the eternal salvation of those who die impenitent rejected by his Father; for Christ never prayed that they should be eternally saved in impenitency. Before Mr. Hill can reasonably charge us with holding doctrines which imply that Christ told *a gross untruth* when he said, "I know that thou hearest me always," he must prove that Christ ever asked the eternal salvation of some men, whether they repented or not; or that he ever desired his Father to force *to the last* repentance, faith, and obedience, upon any man. If Mr. Hill cannot prove this, how can he make it appear that, according to our doctrines of grace, one of our Lord's prayers was ever rejected? We grant that Christ asked the forgiveness of his murderers, and of those who made sport with his sufferings; but he asked it upon Gospel terms, that is, *conditionally*. Nor was his prayer ineffectual; for it obtained for them time to repent, and uncommon helps so to do, with a peculiar readiness in God to pardon them upon their application for pardon: and if, after all, through the power of their free agency, they despised the pardon offered them in the Gospel, and repented not, they shall deservedly perish according to Christ's own declaration. He has acted toward them the part of a gracious Saviour: he never engaged himself to act that of a tyrant: I mean, he never sent either his good Spirit, or the evil spirit of Satan, to bind the wills of men with adamantine chains of necessitated righteousness, or of necessitated iniquity, that he might cast some into Abraham's bosom, and others into hell, as Nebuchadnezzar sent the strongest men in his army to bind Daniel's companions, and to cast them into the burning fiery furnace.

Once more: we believe that, with respect to the reward of the inheritance, and the doctrine of eternal salvation, Christ's atonement and intercession are like his Gospel. Now his Gospel is guarded by what one of Mr. Hill's seconds queerly calls "the valiant Sergeant IF," that is, the conditionality of the, promises and threatenings which relate to eternal salvation and eternal damnation; and this conditionality is the rampart of the old Gospel, and the demolition of the new; strongly guarding the ancient doctrines of free grace, free will, and just wrath, against the novel doctrines of overbearing grace, bound will, and free wrath.

I should not do justice to our cause, if I dismissed this article without retorting Mr. Hill's objection. I have shown how unreasonably we are accused of holding doctrines, which, by "unavoidable" consequence, represent Christ as "telling a gross untruth:" and now we desire Mr. Hill, or his seconds, to show how the Son of God could, consistently with truth, profess himself to be the "Saviour of men," the Saviour and "light of the world," and "the drawer of all men unto himself;" if most men have been from all eternity under the fearful curse of Calvinian reprobation, We ask, if the Redeemer would have "told a gross untruth," upon the supposition that Calvinism is true, had he called himself *the reprobator of men; the non- redeemer, the damner of the world, and the rejecter of all men from himself;* seeing that, according to the doctrines of grace, (so called,) the bulk of mankind were ever reprobated, *never* redeemed, *never* initially saved, and *never* drawn to Christ. We beseech candid Protestants to say, if the Bible do not clear up all the difficulties with which prejudiced divines have clogged the genuine doctrines of grace, when it testifies that our Redeemer and Saviour has procured a *general* temporary *redemption*, together with an initial salvation, for all men *universally*; and a *particular* eternal *redemption*, together with a finished salvation, for "them that obey him, and endure to the end." And we entreat the lovers of the whole truth as it is in Jesus to help us to bring about this scriptural plan, a reconciliation between those who contend for the doctrines of particular redemption and finished salvation; and those who maintain the doctrines of general redemption, and of "a day of salvation" for all mankind.

THE FICTITIOUS CREED.

ARTICLE VII.

"I believe that God, foreseeing some men's nature will improve the grace which is given them, and that they will repent, believe, and be very good, elects them unto salvation."

THE GENUINE CREED.

ARTICLE VII.

We believe that out of mere mercy, and rich free grace in Jesus Christ, without any respect to foreseen repentance, faith, or goodness, God places all men in a state of initial salvation; electing them to that state according to the mysterious counsel of his distinguishing love, which places some under the bright and direct beams of Gospel truth; while he suffers others to receive the external light of it only through that variety of clouds which we call Calvinism, Popery, Judaism, and Mohammedanism;* leaving most in Gentilism, that is, in the dispensation under which Cain, Abel, Abimelech, king of Gerar, and Melchisedec, king of Salem, formerly were.

2. We believe that God, for Christ's sake, peculiarly (although with different degrees of favour) accepts all those who, in all the above- mentioned religions, i.e. "in every nation, fear him and work righteousness." These, when considered as enduring to the end, are his elect, according to the election of remunerative justice. For these he is gone to "prepare the many mansions in his Father's house:" for these he designs the "reward of the inheritance that fadeth not away in heaven." And when he speaks of some men as belonging to this number, it is always with respect to his foreknowledge that they will freely persevere in the obedience of faith; it being the highest pitch of Antinomian dotage to suppose that God, the true, the wise, the holy, and righteous God, elects men to the reward of persevering obedience, without taking any notice of persevering obedience in his election.

To sum up all in a few lines: the doctrine of election has two branches: according to the *first* branch we are *chosen that we should be holy* and obedient, in proportion to the ordinary or extraordinary helps which Divine grace affords us under one or other of its dispensations. This election to holiness has nothing to do with prescience; it depends entirely on free grace and distinguishing favour. According to the second branch of the doctrine of election, we are chosen to receive the rewards of perfected holiness and of persevering obedience, in proportion both to the talents which free distinguishing grace has afforded us, and to the manner in which our assisted free will has improved those talents. This remunerative election depends on four things: (1.) On *free grace*, promising for Christ's sake the reward of the inheritance to the persevering obedience of faith. (2.) On *faithful free will*, securing that reward by the assistance of free grace, and by the free obedience of faith. (3.) On *Divine faithfulness*, keeping its Gospel promise for ever. And, (4.) On *distributive justice*,

---

* *Calvinism* is Christianity obscured by mists of Pharisaic election and reprobation, and by a cloud of stoical fatalism. *Popery* is Christianity under a cloud of Pharisaic bigotry, and under thick fogs of heathenish superstition. *Judaism* is Christianity under the veil of Moses. *Mohammedanism* is a jumble of Christianity, Judaism, Gentilism, and imposture. And *Gentilism* is the religion of Cain and Abel; or, if you please, of Shem, Ham, and Japheth, under a cloud of false and dark tradition. Some call it the *religion of nature.* I have no objection to the name, if they understand by it the religion of our *nature* in its present state of initial recovery, through Christ, from its *total* fall in Adam.

dispensing the reward according to the law of Christ, and according to every man's work. This election therefore has much to do with Divine prescience, as depending in part upon God's knowledge that "some men have improved, or will improve, the grace which is given them, repent, believe, and be good [if not 'very good'] and faithful servants unto the end."

Unprejudiced readers will easily see how much our doctrine of election is preferable to that of our opponents. Ours draws after it only a harmless reprobation from some peculiar favours, and a righteous reprobation from rewards of grace and glory obstinately despised, or wantonly forfeited; but the election of the Calvinists is clogged with the dreadful dogmas of an unscriptural and terrible reprobation, which might be compared to a well- known monster, *"Prima Leo, postrema Draco, media ipsa Chimera."* Its head is *free wrath*; its body, *unavoidable sin*; and its tail, *finished damnation*. In a word, our *election* recommends God's free, distinguishing grace, without pouring any contempt on the holiness of Christ's precepts, the sanction of his law, the veracity of his threatenings, and the conditionality of his promises. And our *reprobation* displays God's absolute sovereignty, without sullying his mercy, impeaching his veracity, or disgracing his justice. In a word, *our* election doctrinally guards the throne of sovereign grace, and *our* reprobation that of sovereign justice: but *Calvinian* election and reprobation doctrinally overthrow both those thrones: or if they are left standing, it is to allow free wrath to fill the throne of justice, and unchaste, bloody Diana to step into the throne of grace, whence she hints to Laodicean believers that they may with advantage commit adultery, murder, and incest; calling as many as take her horrid innuendoes, "My love, my undefiled," &c, and assuring them that they shall never perish, and that all things (the most grievous sins not excepted) shall work for their good.

THE FICTITIOUS CREED.

ARTICLE VIII.

"I believe that the love and favour of Him, with whom is no variableness nor shadow of turning, and whose gifts and callings are without repentance, may vary, change, and turn every hour, and every moment, according to the behaviour of the creature."

THE GENUINE CREED.

ARTICLE VIII.

We believe that God's works were all originally very good, and that God did love or approve of them all as very good in their places. We maintain that some of God's works, such as some angels, and our first parents, by free avoidable disobedience forfeited God's love or approbation. He approved or loved them while they continued righteous; and disapproved or hated them when the bad use which they made of their free will deserved his disapprobation or hatred. Again: we believe that God's *absolute gifts and callings are without repentance.* God never repented that he gave all mankind his paradisiacal favour in Adam, and yet all mankind forfeited it by the fall. God never repented that he called all his servants, and "gave to every one" of them his talents, as he thought fit; and yet, when the "wicked and slothful servant had buried" and forfeited his talent, God said, "Take the talent from him!"

Once more: we believe, that so certain as God is the gracious Creator and the righteous Judge of angels and men, the doctrines of Divine grace and Divine justice (or the two Gospel axioms) are perfectly reconcilable; and that, of consequence, God can justly curse mankind with temporal death, after having blessed them with paradisiacal life; and punish them in hell, after having blessed them a second time with initial salvation during their day of personal probation on earth. To deny this, is to deny that there are graves on earth, or torments in hell, for any of the children of men.

Nevertheless, we believe that there is no positive change in God. From eternity to eternity he is the same holy and faithful God; therefore he unchangeably "loves righteousness and hates iniquity." Apostasy in men or in angels does not imply any change in him; the change being only in the receptive disposition of his free willing creatures. If I make my eyes so sore that I cannot look with pleasure at the sun, or that its beams, which cheered me yesterday, give me pain to-day; this is no proof that the sun has changed its nature. The law that condemns a murderer, absolves me now; but if I stab my neighbour in ten minutes, the same law that now absolves me, will in ten minutes condemn me. Impossible! says Mr. Hill's scheme: "the law changes not." I grant it; but a free agent may change; and the law of liberty, which is but the transcript of God's eternal nature, is so ordered, that, without changing at all, it nevertheless treats all free agents according to their changes. The changes that God makes in the world do not change him; much less is he changed by the variations of free agents: such variations indeed lay rebels and penitents open to a new aspect from the Deity; but that aspect was in the Deity before they laid themselves open to it. Fire, Without changing its nature, melts wax and stiffens clay; now, if a rebel's heart absolutely hardens itself, so that it becomes like unyielding clay; or if a penitent's heart humbles itself, so that it becomes like yielding wax, God changes not any more than the fire, when he hardens the stiff rebel by resisting him, and melts the yielding penitent by giving him more grace.

To understand this better, we must remember that God's eternal nature is to "resist the proud, and give grace to the humble;" and that when free grace, (which has appeared to all men,) assists us, we are as free to choose *humility* and *life*, as we are to choose pride and death when we dally with temptation, or indulge the natural depravity of our own hearts. Hence it follows that the *judicious difference* which God makes when he alternately smiles and frowns, dispenses rewards and punishments, springs not from any alteration in his unchangeable nature, but from a change in the mutable will and behaviour of free agents; a change this, which arises from their will *freely resisting* Divine grace, if the alteration be for the worse; and from *their will* yielding *without necessity* to that grace, if the change be for the better. Nor are we any more ashamed to own man's free agency before a world of fatalists, than we are ashamed to say, "Verily there is a reward for the righteous: though hand join in hand, the wicked shall not be unpunished: doubtless there is a God that judgeth the earth, and will render to every man according to his works;" that is, according to his free will; works being our own works only so far as they spring from our own free will. And we think that the opposite doctrine is one of the most absurd errors that ever disgraced Christianity; and one of the most dangerous engines which were ever invented in Babel to sap the walls of Jerusalem; — a dreadful engine this, which, if it rested upon truth, would pour floods of disgrace on all the Divine perfections: would overset the tribunal of the Judge of all the earth; and would raise upon the tremendous ruins the throne of the doctrinal idol of the day: I mean the spurious doctrine of grace, which I have sometimes called the great Diana of the Calvinists, because, like the great Diana of the Ephesians, it may pass at once for LUNA, or *finished salvation* in heaven, and for HECATE, or *finished damnation* in hell.

THE FICTITIOUS CREED.

ARTICLE IX.

"I believe that the seed of the word by which God's children are born again, is a *corruptible* seed; and that so far from enduring *for ever*, (as that mistaken Apostle Peter rashly affirms,) it is frequently rooted out of the hearts of those in whom it is sown."

THE GENUINE CREED.

ARTICLE IX.

We believe that *the word* or *the truth* of God is the Divine seed by which sinners are born again when they receive it, that is, when they believe; and this spiritual seed (as that enlightened Apostle Peter justly affirms) "endures for ever;" — but not for Antinomian purposes; — not to say to fallen believers, in the very act of adultery or incest, "My love! my undefiled!" No: it "endures for ever," as a seed of reviving or terrifying truth' "it endures for ever" as a two-edged sword to defend the righteous, or to wound the wicked; to protect obedient believers, or to pierce disobedient and obstinate unbelievers; "it endures for ever" as a sweet "savour of life" to them that receive and keep it; and as a bitter "savour of death" to them that never receive it, and to them that finally cast it away, and never "bring forth fruit to perfection."

But although the seed of the word can never be lost with respect to both its effects, yet (as we have already observed) it is too frequently lost with regard to its more desirable effect: if Mr. Hill doubts of it, we refer him to the parable of the sower, where our Lord observes that the good seed was thus lost in three sorts of people out of four, merely, through the want of co-operation or concurrence on the part of free will, which he calls good or bad ground, soft or "stony ground," &c, according to the good or bad choice it makes, and according to the steadiness or fickleness of that choice. And if Mr. Hill exclaim against the obvious meaning of so well- known a portion of the Gospel, the world will easily see that, supposing his doctrine of grace deserves to be called chaste, when it prompts him to vindicate, as openly as he dares, the profitableness of adultery and incest to fallen believers; it by no means merits to be called devout, when it excites him to insinuate that our Lord preached a "shocking, not to say blasphemous doctrine."

THE FICTITIOUS CREED.

ARTICLE X.

"I believe that Christ does not always give unto his sheep eternal life; but that they often perish, and are by the power of Satan frequently plucked out of his hand."

THE GENUINE CREED.

ARTICLE X.

We believe that Christ's sheep, mentioned in John 10, are obedient, persevering believers; that is, as our Lord himself describes them, John 10:4, 5, 27, persons that "hear [i.e. obey] his voice," and "whom he knows," [i.e. approves;] persons that "know [i.e. approve] his voice;" that "know not [i.e. do not approve] the voice of strangers;" and "flee from a stranger," instead of following him: in a word, persons that actually "follow the good Shepherd" in some of his folds or pastures. In this description of a sheep, every verb is put in the *present* tense, to show us that the word *sheep* denotes a character, or persons actually possessed of such a character. So that the moment the character changes; the moment a man who once left all to follow Christ, leaves Christ to "follow a stranger," he has no more to do with the name and privileges of a sheep, than a *deserter* or a *rebel* has to do with the name and privileges of his majesty's *soldiers* or *subjects*.

According then to our doctrine, no "*sheep of Christ*," that is, no *actual follower* of the Redeemer, perishes. We think it is shocking to say, that any of them are plucked out of his hand. On the contrary, we frequently say, with St. Peter, "Who will harm you [much more, who will separate you from the love of Christ] if ye be followers of that which is good?" i.e. if you be sheep: and we insist upon the veracity of our Lord's promise, "He that endureth unto the end," in the character of a sheep, i.e. in the way of faith and obedience, "the same shall be [eternally] saved." And we maintain, that so long as a believer does not make shipwreck of the faith and of a good conscience; so long as he continues a sheep, a harmless follower of the Lamb of God, he can no more perish than God's everlasting throne can be overturned. But what has this doctrine of our Lord to do with Calvinism?

With regard to the sheep mentioned in Matthew 25:33, 34, whom our Lord calls "blessed of his Father," we believe that they represent the multitude of obedient, persevering believers, whom two apostles describe thus: "Blessed are they that do his [God's] commandments, that they may have right [or if Mr. Hill pleases, *privilege*] to the tree of life, and enter, &c, into the city," Revelation 22:14. "Blessed is the man that endureth temptation! for when he is tried, he shall receive the crown of life, which the Lord hath promised to them that love him." "And this is the love of God, that we keep his commandments," James 1:12; 1 John 5:3. For such *enduring, obedient* believers a kingdom of glory "is prepared from the foundation of the world:" and to it they are and shall be judicially elected; while the goats, i.e. unbelievers, or disobedient, fallen believers, are and shall be judicially reprobated from it. Hence it is, that when our Lord accounts for his judicial election of the obedient, (whom he parabolically calls sheep,) he does not say," Inherit the kingdom," &c; *for I absolutely finished your salvation*: but he says, "Inherit the kingdom, for ye gave me meat," &c; ye fed the hungry from a right motive; and what you did in that manner, I reward it as if you had done it to myself. In other terms, "Ye heard my voice, and followed me;" in hearing the whispers of my grace, and following the light of your dispensation; and now I own you as my eternally rewardable elect, my *sheep*, which have *followed* me without finally drawing back.

Again: when our Lord gives an account of the judicial reprobation of the finally disobedient, whom he parabolically calls *goats*, he does not say, "Depart, ye cursed, into everlasting fire, prepared for you from the foundation of the world;" for then I absolutely finished your eternal reprobation. No: this is the counterpart of the Gospel of the day. But he says, "Depart, &c; for ye gave me no meat," by feeding the hungry in your generation, &c: that is, ye did not believingly follow me in following your light and my precepts. Either you never began your course, or you drew back before you had finished it. Either you never voluntarily listed under my banner, or you deserted before you had "fought the good fight" out: either you never believed in me, the light of the world, and your light; or, instead of keeping the faith, you voluntarily, avoidably, unnecessarily, and resolutely made shipwreck of it, and of a good conscience: and therefore your damnation is of yourselves. You have *personally* forfeited your conditional election to the rewards of persevering obedience, and *personally* made your conditional reprobation from those rewards sure by your final disobedience.

From these evangelical descriptions of the *sheep* and the *goats*, mentioned in John 10, and Matthew 25, it appears to us indubitable: (1.) That these *sheep* [i.e. obedient, persevering believers] "shall never perish;" although they might have perished, if they had "brought upon themselves swift destruction by denying the Lord that bought them." (2.) That they shall be eternally saved, although they might have missed eternal salvation, if they had finally disregarded our Lord's declaration: "He that endureth unto the end, the same shall be [finally] saved." (3.) That the good Shepherd peculiarly laid down his life for the *eternal* redemption of obedient, persevering believers; and that these believers are sometimes eminently called God's *elect*, because they make their *conditional* calling to the rewards of perseverance sure, by actually persevering in the obedience of faith. (4.) That the peculiarity of the eternal redemption of Christ's persevering followers, far from being connected with the absolute reprobation of the rest of mankind, stands in perfect agreement with the doctrines of a *general, temporary redemption*, and a *general initial salvation*; and with the doctrines of a *gratuitous election* to the blessings of one or another dispensation of God's saving grace; and of a *conditional election* to the rewards of voluntary, unnecessitated obedience. (5.) That our opponents give the truth as it is in Jesus two desperate stabs, when they secure the *peculiar, eternal redemption* of finally disobedient believers, and comfort mourning backsliders in so unhappy a manner, as to overthrow the *general, temporary redemption* of all mankind, and to encourage or countenance the present disobedience of Laodicean believers. (6.) That the Calvinian doctrines of grace, which do this double mischief under such fair pretences are, of all the tares which the enemy sows, those which come nearest to the wheat, and of consequence those by which he can best feed his immoral goats, deceive simple souls, set Christ's moral sheep at perpetual variance, turn the fruitful field of the Church into a barren field of controversy, and make a Deistical world think that faith is enthusiastical fancy; that orthodoxy is immoral nonsense; and that revelation is nothing but an apple of discord. (7.) And, lastly, that the doctrines of grace which we maintain do equal justice to the Divine attributes; defend faith, without wounding obedience; oppose Pharisaism, without recommending Antinomianism; assert the truth of God's promises, without representing his most awful threatenings as words without meaning; reconcile the Scriptures, without wounding conscience and reason; exalt the gracious wonders of the day of atonement, without setting aside the righteous terrors of the great day of retribution; extol our heavenly Priest, without pouring contempt upon our Divine Prophet; and celebrate the honours of his cross, without turning his sceptre of righteousness into a Solifidian reed, his royal crown into a crown of thorns, and his *law of liberty* into a *rule of life*, by which his subjects can no more stand or fall in judgment, than an Englishman can stand or fall by the *rules of civility* followed at the French court.

To the best of my knowledge, reader, thou hast been led into the depth of our doctrines of grace. I have opened to thee the mysteries of the evangelical system, which Mr. Hill attacks as the heresy of *Arminians*. And now let *impartiality* hand thee up to the judgment seat: let reason and *revelation* hold out to thee their consentaneous light: pray that the "Spirit of truth" may help thine infirmities: turn *prejudice* out of the court; and let *candour* pronounce the sentence, and say, whether our principles or those of Mr. Hill "inevitably" draw after them "shocking, not to say blasphemous," consequences?

I shall close this answer to the creed which that gentleman has composed for Arminians, by an observation which is not entirely foreign to our controversy. In one of the Three Letters which introduce the *Fictitious Creed*, Mr. Hill says: "Controversy, I am persuaded, has not done me any good;" and he exhorts me to examine closely whether I cannot make the same confession. I own that it would have done me harm, if I had blindly contended for my opinions. Nay, if I had shut my eyes against the light of truth; if I had set the plainest scriptures aside, as if they were not worth my notice; if I had overlooked the strongest arguments of my opponents; if I had advanced groundless charges against them; if I had refused to do justice to their good meaning or piety: and, above all, if I had taken my leave of them by injuring their moral character, by publishing over and over again arguments which they had properly answered, without taking the least notice of their answers; if I had made a solemn promise not to read one of their books, though they should publish a thousand volumes; if, continuing to write against them, I had fixed upon them (as "unavoidable" consequences) absurd tenets, which have no more necessary connection with their principles than the doctrine of general redemption has with Calvinian reprobation; if I had done this, I say, controversy would have wounded my conscience or my reason; and, without adding any thing to my light, it would have immovably fixed me in my prejudices, and perhaps branded me before the world for an *Arminian bigot*. But, as matters are, I hope I may make the following acknowledgment without betraying the impertinence of proud boasting.

Although I have often been sorry that controversy should take up so much of the time, which I might with much satisfaction to myself have employed in devotional exercises; and although I have lamented, and do still lament my low attainments in the "meekness of wisdom," which should constantly guide the pen of every controversial writer; yet I rejoice that I have been enabled to persist in my resolution either to wipe off, or to share the reproach of those who have hazarded their reputation in defence of pure and undefiled religion: and, if I am not mistaken, my repeated attempts have been attended with these happy effects. In vindicating the moral doctrines of grace, I hope, that, as a man, I have learned to think more closely, and to investigate truth more ardently than I did before. There are rational powers in the dullest souls, which lie hid as sparks in a flint. Controversial opposition and exertion, like the stroke of the steel, have made me accidentally find out some of these latent sparks of reason for which I should never have thanked my Maker, if had never discovered them. I have frequently been thankful to find that my horse could travel in bad roads better than I expected; nor do I think that it is a piece of Pharisaism to say, I am thankful to find that my mind can travel with more ease than I thought she could through theological roads, rendered almost impassable by heaps, of doctrinal rubbish brought from all parts of Christendom, and by briers of contention which have kept growing for above a thousand years. To return: As a *divine*, I see more clearly the gaps and stiles at which mistaken good men have turned out of the narrow way of truth, to the right hand and to the left. As a *Protestant*, I hope I have much more esteem for the Scriptures in general, and in particular for those practical parts of them which the Calvinists had insensibly taught me to overlook or despise: and this increasing esteem is, I trust, accompanied with a deeper conviction of the truth of Christianity, and with a greater readiness to defend the Gospel against infidels, Pharisees, and Antinomians. As a *preacher*, I hope I can do more justice to a text, by reconciling it with seemingly contrary scriptures. As an *anti-Calvinist*, I have learned to do the Calvinists justice in granting that there is an *election of distinguishing grace* for God's peculiar people, and a *particular redemption* for all believers who are faithful unto death; and by that means, as a *controvertist*, I can more easily excuse pious Calvinists, who, through prejudice, mistake *that* Scriptural election for *their* Antinomian election; and who consider *that* particular redemption as the only redemption mentioned in the Scriptures. Nay, I can without scruple allow Mr. Hill, that his doctrines of *finished salvation* and *irresistible grace*, are TRUE with respect to all those who die in their infancy. As one who is called an *Arminian*, I have found out some flaws in Arminianism, and evidenced my impartiality in pointing them out, as well as the flaws of Calvinism. (See the preface.) As a *witness* for the truth of the Gospel, I hope I have learned to bear reproach from all sorts of people with more undaunted courage: and I humbly trust, that, were I called to seal with my blood the truth of the doctrines of grace and justice against the Pharisees and the Antinomians, I could (Divine grace supporting me to the last) do it more rationally, and of consequence with greater steadiness. Again: as a *follower of Christ*, I hope I have learned to disregard my dearest friends for my heavenly Prophet: or, to speak the language of our Lord, I hope I have learned to "forsake father, mother, and brothers, for Christ's sake and the Gospel's." As a *disputant*, I have learned that solid arguments and plain scriptures make no more impression upon bigotry than the charmer's voice does upon the deaf adder; and by that mean, I hope, I depend less upon the powers of reason, the letter of the Scripture, and the candour of professors, than I formerly did. As a *believer*, I have been brought to see and feel that the power of the Spirit of truth, which teaches men to be of one heart and of one mind, and makes them think and speak the same, is at a very low ebb in the religious world; and that the prayer Which I ought continually to offer is, O Lord, baptize Christians with the Spirit of truth, and the fire of love. Thy kingdom come! Bring thy Church out of the wilderness of error and sin into the kingdom "of righteousness, peace, and joy in the Holy Ghost." As a *member of the Church of England*, I have learned to be pleased with our holy mother for giving us floods of pure morality to wash away the few remaining Calvinian freckles still perceptible upon her face. As a *Christian*, I hope I have learned in some degree to exercise that charity which teaches us boldly to oppose a dangerous error without ceasing to honour and love its abettors, so far as they resemble our Lord; and teaches us to use an irony with St. Paul and Jesus Christ, not as an enemy uses a dagger, but as a surgeon uses a lancet or a caustic: and, lastly, as a *writer*, I have learned to feel the truth of Solomon's observation: "Of making many books there is no end, and much study is a weariness of the flesh; let us hear the conclusion of the whole matter: fear God and keep his commandments; for this is the whole duty of man," and the sum of the anti-Solifidian truth, which I endeavour to vindicate.

I do not say that I have learned any of these lessons as I should have done; but I hope I have learned so much of them as to say, that in these respects my controversial toil has not been altogether in vain in the Lord. And now, reader, let me entreat thee to pray, that if I am spared to vindicate more fully what appears to us the *Scriptural doctrine of grace*, I may be so helped by the Father of lights and the God of love, as to speak the *pure* truth in *perfect love*, and never more drop a needlessly severe expression. Some such have escaped me before I was aware. In endeavouring to render my style nervous, I have sometimes inadvertently rendered it provoking. Instead of saying that the doctrines of grace (so called) represented God as "absolutely graceless" toward myriads of "reprobated culprits;" I would now say, that, upon the principles of my opponents, God appears "devoid of grace" toward those whom he has absolutely" reprobated" from all eternity. The thought is the same, I grant; but the expressions are less grating and more decent. This propriety of language I labour after, as well as after more meekness of wisdom. The Lord help me and my antagonists to "keep our garments clean!" Controvertists ought to be clothed with an ardent, flaming love for truth, and a candid, humble regard for their neighbours. May no root of prejudice stain that flaming love! no malice rend our seamless garments! and, if they are ever "rolled in blood," may it be only in the blood of our common enemies, destructive error, and the man of sin!

AN EQUAL CHECK

TO

PHARISAISM AND ANTINOMIANISM:

PART I.

CONTAINING

I. An Historical Essay on the Danger of Parting Faith and Works.
II. Salvation by the Covenant of Grace, a Discourse preached in the Parish Church of Madeley, April 18, and May 9, 1773.
III. A Scriptural Essay on the astonishing Rewardableness of Works, according to the Covenant of Grace.
IV. An Essay on Truth; or a Rational Vindication of the Doctrine of Salvation by Faith, with a Dedicatory Epistle to the Right Hon. the Countess of Huntingdon.

BY THE AUTHOR OF THE

CHECKS TO ANTINOMIANISM.

The armour of righteousness on the right hand and on the left, 2 Corinthians 6:7.

PREFACE TO EQUAL CHECK.

----

1. THE first piece of this Check was designed for a preface to the discourse that follows it: but as it swelled far beyond my intention, I present it to the reader under the name of *An Historical Essay*; which makes way for the tracts that follow.

2. With respect to the discourse, I must mention what engages me to publish it. In 1771, I saw the propositions called *the Minutes.* — Their author invited me to "review the whole affair." I did so; and soon found that I had "leaned too much toward Calvinism," which, after mature consideration, appeared to me exactly to coincide with speculative Antinomianism; and the same year I publicly acknowledged my error in these words: —

"But whence springs this almost general Antinomianism of our congregations? Shall I conceal the sore because it festers in my own breast? Shall I be partial? No: in the name of Him, who is no respecter of persons, I will confess my sin, and that of many of my brethren, &c. Is not the Antinomianism of hearers fomented by that of preachers? Does it not become us to take the greatest part of the blame upon ourselves, according to the old adage, *Like priest, like people?* Is it surprising that some of us should have an Antinomian audience? Do *we* not make or keep it so? When did we preach such a practical sermon as that of our Lord on the mount? or write such close letters as the Epistles of St. John?" (*Second Check*, Letter III, Sec. III, par.2)*

When I had thus openly confessed that I was involved in the guilt of "many of my brethren," and that I had so leaned toward *speculative*, as not to have made a proper stand against *practical* Antinomianism; who could have thought that one of my most formidable opponents would have attempted to screen his mistakes behind some passages of a manuscript sermon, which I preached twelve years ago, and of which, by some means or other, he has got a copy?

I am very far, however, from recanting that old discourse. I still think the doctrine it contains excellent in the main, and very proper to be enforced, (though in a more guarded manner,) in a congregation of hearers violently prejudiced against the first Gospel axiom. Therefore, out of regard for the grand leading truth of Christianity, and in compliance with Mr. Hill's *earnest entreaty*, (Finishing Stroke, p. 45,)

---

* Volume 1, page 110

I send my sermon into the world, upon the following reasonable conditions: (1.) That I shall be allowed to publish it, as I preached it a year ago in my church; namely, with additions in brackets, [...] to make it at once a fuller check to Pharisaism, and a finishing check to Antinomianism. (2.) That the largest addition shall be in favour of free grace. (3.) That nobody shall accuse me of forgery, for thus adding my present light to that which I had formerly; and for thus bringing out of my little treasure of experience things new and old. (4.) That the press shall not groan with the charge of disingenuity, if I throw into notes some unguarded expressions, which I formerly used without scruple, and which my more enlightened conscience does not suffer me to use at present. (5.) That my opponent's call to print my sermon will procure me the pardon of the public for presenting them with a plain, blunt discourse, composed for an audience chiefly made up of colliers and rustics. And (lastly,) that, as I understand English a little better than I did twelve years ago, I shall be permitted to rectify a few French idioms, which I find in my old manuscript; and to connect my thoughts a little more like an Englishman, where I can do it without the least misrepresentation of the sense.

If these conditions appear unreasonable to those who will have heaven itself without any condition, I abolish the distinction between my old sermon and the additions that guard or strengthen it; and referring the reader to the title page, I publish my discourse on Romans 11:5, 6, as a guarded sermon delivered in my church on Sunday, April 18, &c, 1773, exactly eleven years after I had preached upon the same text a sermon useful upon the whole, but in some places unguarded, and deficient with respect to the variety of arguments and motives, by which the capital doctrines of *free grace* and *Gospel obedience* ought to be enforced.

3. With regard to the Scriptural Essay upon the rewardableness, of evangelical worthiness of works, I shall just observe that it attacks the grand mistake of the Solifidians, countenanced by three or four words of my old sermon. I pour a flood of scriptures upon it; and after receiving the fire of my objector, I return it in a variety of Scriptural and rational answers, about the solidity of which the public must decide.

4. The *Essay on Truth* will, I hope, reconcile judicious moralists to the doctrine of salvation *by faith*, and considerate Solifidians to the doctrine of salvation by the *works* of faith; reason and Scripture concurring to show the constant dependence of works upon faith; and the wonderful agreement of the doctrine of present salvation by TRUE *faith*, with the doctrine of eternal salvation by GOOD *works*.

I hope that I do not dissent, in my observations upon faith, either from our Church, or approved Gospel ministers. In their highest definition of that grace, they consider it only according to the fulness o! the Christian dispensation: but my subject has obliged me to consider it also according to the dispensations of John the Baptist, Moses, and Noah. Believers, under these inferior dispensations, have not always assurance; nor is the assurance they sometimes have so bright as that of adult Christians; Matthew 11:11. But undoubtedly assurance is inseparably connected with the faith of the Christian dispensation, which was not fully opened till Christ opened his glorious baptism on the day of pentecost, and till his spiritual kingdom was set up with power in the hearts of his people. Nobody therefore can truly believe, according to this dispensation, without being immediately conscious both of the forgiveness of sins, and of peace and joy in the Holy Ghost. This is a most important truth, derided indeed by fallen Churchmen, and denied by Laodicean Dissenters; but of late years gloriously revived by Mr. Wesley and the ministers connected with him. A truth this, which cannot be too strongly, and yet too warily insisted upon in our lukewarm and speculative age: and as I would not obscure it for the world, I particularly entreat the reader to mind the last *erratum*; without omitting the last but one, which guards the doctrine of initial salvation by absolute free grace.

I do not desire to provoke my able opponents; but I must own, I should be glad to reap the benefit of my Checks, either by finding an increase of religious sobriety and mutual forbearance among those who make a peculiar profession of faith in Christ; or by seeing my mistakes (if I am mistaken) brought to light, that I might no longer recommend them as Gospel truths. With this view only I humbly entreat my brethren and fathers in the Church to point out by Scripture or argument the doctrinal errors that may have crept into the *Equal Check*. But if, upon close examination, they should find that it holds forth the two Gospel axioms in due conjunction; and marks out the evangelical mean with strict impartiality; I hope the moderate and judicious, in the Calvinistic and anti- Calvinistic party, will so far unite upon this plan, as to keep on terms of reciprocal toleration and brotherly kindness together; rising with redoubled indignation, not one against another, but against those pests of the religious world, prejudice and bigotry, the genuine parents of implacable fanaticism, and bloody persecution.

MADELEY, *May* 21, 1774.

EQUAL CHECK.

PART FIRST.

AN HISTORICAL ESSAY,

Upon the importance and harmony of the two Gospel precepts, believe and obey; and upon the fatal consequences that flow from parting faith and works.

WHEN the Gospel is considered as opposed to the error of the Pharisees, and that of the Antinomians, it may be summed up in the two following propositions: (1.) In the day of conversion we are saved freely as sinners, (i.e. made freely partakers of the privileges that belong to our Gospel dispensation in the Church militant,) through the merits of Christ, and by the instrumentality of a living faith. (2.) In the day of judgment we shall be saved freely as saints, (i.e. made freely partakers of the privileges of our Gospel dispensation in the Church triumphant,) through the merits of Christ, and by the evidence of evangelical works. Whence it follows: (1.) That nothing can absolutely hinder our justification in a Gospel day but the want of true faith; and, (2.) That nothing will absolutely hinder our justification in the day of judgment but the want of good works. If I am not mistaken, all the evangelical doctrine of faith and works turns upon those propositions. They exactly answer to the grand directions of the Gospel. Wilt thou enter into Christ's sheepfold? *Believe.* Wilt thou stay there? *Believe and obey.* Wilt thou be numbered among his sheep in the great day? *Endure unto the end: continue in well doing,* that is, persevere in faith and obedience.

To believe then and obey, or, as Solomon expresses it, "to fear God and keep his commandments is the whole duty of man." Therefore, a professor of the faith without genuine obedience, and a pretender to obedience without genuine faith, equally miss their aim; while a friend to faith and works put in their proper place, a possessor of the faith which works by love, hits the Gospel mark, and so runs as to obtain the prize: for the same "true and faithful Witness" spoke the two following, and equally express declarations: — "He that believeth on the Son hath everlasting life; and he that believeth not the Son shall not see life; but the wrath of God abideth on him," John 3:36. And, "The hour is coming, in the which all that are in their graves shall come forth, they that have done good unto the resurrection of life; and they that have done evil unto the resurrection of condemnation," John 5:29.

See that sculler upon yonder river. The unwearied diligence and watchful skill with which he plies his two oars point out to us the work and wisdom of an experienced divine. What an even, gentle spring does the mutual effort of his oars give to his boat! Observe him: his right hand never rests but when the stream carries him too much to the left; he slacks not his left hand unless he is gone too much to the right; nor has he sooner recovered a just medium than he uses both oars again with mutual harmony. Suppose that for a constancy he employed but one, no matter which, what would be the consequence? He would only move in a circle; and if neither wind nor tide carried him along, after a hard day's work he would find himself in the very spot where he began his idle toil.

This illustration needs very little explaining: I shall just observe that the Antinomian is like a sculler, who uses only his right hand oar; and the Pharisee, like him who plies only the oar in his left hand. One makes an endless bustle about grace and faith, the other about charity and works; but both, after all, find themselves exactly in the same case, with this single difference, that one has turned from truth to the right, and the other to the left.

Not so the judicious, unbiassed preacher, who will safely enter the haven of eternal rest, for which he and his hearers are bound. He makes an equal use of the doctrine of faith, and that of works, if at any time he insist most upon faith, it is only when the stream carries his congregation upon the Pharisaical shallows on the left hand. And if he lay a preponderating stress upon works, it is only when he sees unwary souls sucked into the Antinomian whirlpool on the right hand. His skill consists in so avoiding one danger as not to run upon the other.

Nor ought this watchful wisdom to be confined to ministers; for though all are not called to direct congregations, yet all moral agents are, and always were, more or less, called to direct themselves, that is, to occupy till the Lord come, by making a proper use of their talents according to the parable, Matthew 25:15-31. God gave to angels and man "*remigium alarum*," the two oars, or, if you please, the equal wings of faith and obedience; charging them to use those grand powers according to their original wisdom and enlightened conscience. Or, to speak without metaphor, he created them in such a manner that they believed it their duty, interest, and glory, to obey him without reserve; and this faith was naturally productive of a universal, delightful, perfect obedience. Nor would they ever have been wanting in practice if they had not first wavered in principle. But when Lucifer had unaccountably persuaded himself, in part at least, either that obedience was mean, or that rebellion would be advantageous; and when the crafty tempter had made our first parents believe, in part, that if they ate of the forbidden fruit, far From dying, they should be as God himself: how possible, how easy was it for them to venture upon an act of rebellion! By rashly playing with the serpent, and sucking in the venom of his crafty insinuations, they soon gave their faith a wilful wound, and their obedience naturally died of it. But, alas! it did not die unrevenged; for no sooner had fainting faith given birth to a dead work, than she was destroyed by her spurious offspring. Thus faith and obedience, that couple more lovely than David and his friend, more inseparable than Saul and Jonathan, in their death were not divided. They even met with a common grave, the corrupt, atrocious breast of a rebellious angel, or of apostate man.

Creeds and Scripture Scales

Nor does St. James give us a less melancholy account of this fatal error. While faith slumbered, "lust conceived and brought forth sin, and sin finished, brought forth death," the death of faith, and consequently the moral death of angelic spirits and human souls, who equally live by faith* during their state of probation. So fell Lucifer from heaven, to rule and rage in the darkness of this world: so fell Adam from paradise, to toil and die in this vale of tears: so fell Judas from an apostolic throne, to hang himself, and go to his own place.

Nor can we rise but in a way parallel to that by which they fell. For as a *disbelief* of our CREATOR, productive of *bad works*, sunk our first parents; so a *faith* in our REDEEMER, productive of *good works*, must instrumentally raise their fallen posterity.

Should you ask which is most necessary to salvation, faith or works? I beg leave to propose a similar question: Which is most essential to breathing, inspiration or expiration? If you reply, that "the moment either is absolutely at an end, so is the other; and therefore both are equally important:" I return exactly the same answer. If humble faith receive the breath of spiritual life, obedient love gratefully returns it, and makes way for a fresh supply. When it does not, the Spirit is grieved: and if this want of co- operation is persisted in to the end of the day of salvation, the sin unto death is committed, the Spirit is quenched in his saving operation, the apostate dies the second death, and his corrupt soul is cast into the bottomless pit, as a putrid corpse into the noisome grave.

Again: if faith has the advantage over works by giving them birth, works have the advantage over faith by perfecting it. "Seest thou," says St. James, speaking of the father of the faithful, "how faith wrought with his works, and by works was faith made perfect?" And if St. Paul affirms that works without faith are dead, St. James maintains, "faith without works is dead also."

Once more: Christ is always the primary, original, properly meritorious cause of our justification and salvation. To dispute it is to renounce the faith, and to plead for antichrist. And yet to deny that, under this primary cause, there are secondary, subordinate, instrumental causes of our justification, and consequently of our salvation, is to set the Bible aside, and fly in the face of judicious Calvinists, who cannot help maintaining it, both from the pulpit and from the press.† Now, if in the

---

* Faith in God as a Creator, Lawgiver, and Judge, was not, less necessary to Lucifer and Adam, in order to their standing in a state of innocence, than faith in God as Redeemer, Sanctifier, and Rewarder of them that diligently seek him, is necessary to sinners in order to their recovery from a state of guilt; or to believers, in order to avoid relapses and final apostasy. Faith, therefore, so far as it implies an unshaken confidence in God and a firm adherence to his will, is as eternal as love and obedience. But when it is considered as "the substance of things hoped for, and the evidence of things not seen," which are essential properties of a believer's faith in this present state of things, it is evident that it will necessarily end in sight, as soon as the curtain of time is drawn up; and terminate in enjoyment, as soon as God's glory appears without a veil.

† The Rev. Mr. Madan does not scruple to call our faith "the instrumental *cause*" of our justification. (See his sermon on James 2:24, printed by Fuller, London, 1761, page 18.) And if we shall be justified in the day of judgment by our words, they shall undoubtedly be at least an evidencing *cause* of our final justification. Hence it is that the same judicious divine speaks (p. 30, 1. 4, &c,) of our being "justified in this three-fold sense of the word, meritoriously by Christ, instrumentally by faith, and declaratively by works, which are the fruits of faith." The

day of our conversion *faith* is the secondary, subordinate cause of our acceptance as *penitent sinners*; in the day of judgment works, even the works of faith, will be the secondary, subordinate cause of our acceptance *as persevering saints*. Let us therefore equally decry dead faith and dead works, equally recommend living faith and its important fruits.

Hitherto I have endeavoured to check the rapid progress of speculative Antinomianism that perpetually decries works, and centres in the following paragraph, which presents without disguise the doctrine of the absolute, unconditional perseverance of adulterous believers, and incestuous saints: —

Saving faith, being immortal, can not only subsist without the help of good works, but no aggravated crimes can give it a finishing stroke. A believer may in cool blood murder a man, after having seduced his wife, without exposing himself to the least real danger of forfeiting either his heavenly inheritance, or the Divine favour; because his *salvation*, which is *finished in the full extent of the word*, without any of his good works, cannot possibly be frustrated by any of his evil ones.

It will not be improper now to attempt a check to Pharisaism, which perpetually opposes faith, and whose destructive errors, collected in one position, may run thus: — If people perform external acts of worship toward God, and of charity toward their neighbour, their principles* are good enough: and should they be faulty, these good works will make ample amends for that deficiency. Upon this common plan of doctrine, if the filthy sepulchre is but whitewashed, and the noisome grave adorned with a flowery turf, it little matters what is within, whether it be a dead man's bones, a dead heart swelled with pride, or all manner of corruption.

---

reader will permit me to illustrate the essential difference there is between primary and secondary causes, by the manner in which David became Saul's son-in-law. The primary causes of this event were undoubtedly, on God's part, assisting power and wisdom; and on King Saul's part, a free promise of giving his daughter in marriage to the man who should kill Goliah. The secondary causes, according to the Rev. Mr. Madan's plan, may be divided into instrumental and declarative. The instrumental causes of David's honourable match were his faith, his sling, his stone, Goliah's sword, &c. And the declarative or evidencing causes were his works. He insists upon fighting the giant, he renounces carnal weapons, puts on the armour of God, runs to meet his adversary, slings a fortunate stone, brings his adversary down, flies upon him, and cuts off his head. By these works he was evidenced a person duly qualified to marry the princess; or, to keep to the Rev. Mr. Madan's expression, "by" these "works" he was "declaratively" judged a man fit to be rewarded with the hand of the princess. Now, is it not clear that his works, upon the evidence of which he received such a reward, had as important a part in his obtaining it, as the faith and sling, by whose instrumentality he wrought the works? And is it not strange that the Rev. Mr. Madan should be an orthodox divine, when he says that "we are declaratively justified by works," and that Mr. Wesley should be a dreadful heretic for saying that we are "saved, not by the merit of works, but by works as a condition;" or, in other terms, that we are finally justified, not by works as the primary, meritorious cause; but as a secondary, evidencing, declarative cause?

* The ingenious author of a new book, called "Essays on Public Worship, Patriotism," &c, does not scruple to send such an exhortation abroad into the world: — "Let us substitute honesty instead of faith. It is the only foundation of a moral character, and it ought to be the only test of our religion. It should not signify what, or how little a man believed, if he was honest. This would put Christianity upon the best footing." (See the Monthly Review for March, 1773.)

Creeds and Scripture Scales

It is hard to say who do Christianity most disservice, the Solifidians, who assert that works are nothing "before God;" or the Pharisees, who maintain that certain religious ceremonies, and external duties of morality, are the very soul of religion. O thou true believer, bear thy testimony against both their errors; and equally contend for the tree and the fruit, the faith of St. Paul and the works of St. James; remembering that if ever the gates of hell prevail against thee, it will be by making thee overvalue faith and despise good works, or overrate works, and slight "precious faith."

The world, I grant, is full of Gallios, easy or busy men, who seldom trouble themselves about faith or works, law or Gospel. Their latitudinarian principles perfectly agree with their loose conduct: and if their volatile minds are fixed, it is only by a steady adherence to such commandments as these: — "Be not righteous overmuch: get and spend: marry or be given in marriage: eat and drink: lie down to sleep, and rise up to play: care neither for heaven nor hell: mind all of earth, but the awful spot allotted thee for a grave," &c. However, while they punctually observe this decalogue, their conscience is sometimes awakened to a sense of corroding guilt, commonly called uneasiness, or low spirits: and if they cannot shake it off by new scenes of dissipation, new plunges into sensual gratifications, new schemes of hurrying business; if a religious concern fastens upon their breasts, the tempter deludes them, by making his false coin pass for the "gold tried in the fire:" if his dupes will have *faith*, he makes them take up with that of the *Antinomians*. If they are for *works*, he recommends to them those of the *self righteous*. And if some seem cut out to be brands in the Church — fiery, persecuting, implacable zealots — he gives them a degree in the university of Babel. *One is a bachelor* of the science of sophistry; another a *master* of the liberal art of calumny; and a third a *doctor* in human, or diabolical *divinity*. But if all these graduates have not as much faith as Simon Magus, or as many works as the conceited Pharisee, yet they may have as much zeal for the Church as the bigot, who set out from Jerusalem for Damascus in pursuit of heretics. They may sometimes pursue those who dissent from them, even "unto strange cities."

Has not the world always swarmed with those devotees, who, blindly following after faith without loving obedience, or after obedience without loving faith, have "made havoc of the Church," and driven myriads of worldly men to a settled contempt of godliness: while a few, by equally standing up for true faith and universal obedience, have alone kept up the honour of religion in the world? Take a general view of the Church, and you will see this observation confirmed by a variety of black, bright, and mixed characters.

The first man born of a woman is a striking picture of perverted mankind. He is at once a sullen Pharisee, and a gross Antinomian: he sacrifices to God, and murders his brother. Abel, the illustrious type of converted sinners, truly believes, and acceptably sacrifices. Faith and works shine in his life with equal lustre; and in his death we see what the godly may expect from the impious Church and the pious world. Protomartyr for the doctrine of this Check, he falls the first innocent victim to Pharisaical pride and Antinomian fury. "The sons of God" mix with "the daughters of men, learn their works," and "make shipwreck of the faith." Enoch nevertheless truly believes in God, and humbly walks with him: faith and works equally adorn his character. The world is soon full of misbelief, and the earth of violence. Noah, however, believes and works: he credits God's word, and builds the ark. This WORK "condemns the world, and he becomes heir of the righteousness which is by FAITH." Consider Abraham; see how he believes and works! God speaks, and he leaves his house, his estate, his friends, and native country. His faith works by love; he exposes his life to recover his neighbour's property; he readily gives up to Lot his right of choice to prevent a quarrel; he earnestly intercedes for Sodom; he charitably hopes the best of its wicked inhabitants; he gladly entertains strangers, humbly washes their feet, diligently instructs his household, and submissively offers up Isaac, his favourite son, the child of his old age, the hope of his family, his own heir, and that of God's promise. By these "works his faith is made perfect," and he deserves to be called the "father of the faithful."

Moses treads in his steps: he believes, quits Pharaoh's court, and suffers affliction with the people of God. Under his conduct the Israelites believe, obey, and cross the Red Sea with a high hand; but soon after they murmur, rebel, and provoke Divine vengeance. Thus the destruction, which they had avoided in Goshen through obedient faith, they meet in the wilderness, through "the works of unbelief." Nature is up in arms to punish their backslidings. The pestilence, the sword, earthquakes, fiery serpents, and fire from heaven, combine to destroy the ungrateful, Antinomian apostates.

In the days of Joshua, that eminent type of Christ, faith and works are happily reconciled; and while they walk hand in hand, Israel is invincible, the greatest difficulties are surmounted, and the land of promise is conquered, divided, and enjoyed.

Under the next judges faith and works seldom meet; but as often as they do, a deliverance is wrought in Israel. Working believers carry all before them: they "can do all things through the Lord strengthening them." They are little omnipotents. But if they suffer the Antinomian Delilah to cut off their locks, you may apply to them the awful words of David, (spoken to magistrates who forsake the way of righteousness,) "I have said, Ye are gods, and all of you are children of the Most High; but ye shall die like men, and fall like one of the princes;" like Zimri or Korah, Dathan or Abiram.

The character of Samuel, the last of the judges, is perfect. From the cradle to the grave he believes and works: he serves God and his generation. His sons, like those of Eli, halt in practice, and their faith is an abomination to God and man. David believes, works, and kills the blaspheming Philistine. He slides into Antinomian faith, wantonly seduces a married woman, and perfidiously kills an honest man. Solomon follows him in the narrow path of working faith, and in the broad way of speculative and practical Antinomianism. The works of the son correspond with those of the father. Happy for him, if the repentance of the idolatrous king equalled that of his adulterous parent!

In the days of Elijah the gates of hell seemed to have prevailed against the Church. Queen Jezebel had "cut off the prophets of the Lord," and appointed four hundred chaplains to his majesty King Ahab, who shared the dainties of the royal table, and therefore found it easy to demonstrate, that "pleading for Baal" was orthodoxy, and prosecuting honest Naboth as "a blasphemer of God and the king," was an instance of true loyalty. But then all were not lost: seven thousand men showed their faith by their works: they firmly believed in Jehovah, and steadily refused bowing the knee to Baal.

Creeds and Scripture Scales

In the days of Isaiah and Jeremiah, wickedness, persecution, and imaginary good works prevailed, under a show of zeal for the temple, and of regard for the people of God. But even then, also, there was a small remnant of believing and working souls, who set fire to the stubble of wickedness during the pious reign of Hezekiah and Josiah.

Follow the chosen nation to Babylon. They all profess the faith still: but how few believe and work! Some do, however: and by their "work of faith" and "patience of hope" they "quench the violence of fire," and" stop the mouths of lions." And what is more extraordinary still, they strike with astonishment a fierce tyrant, a Nebuchadnezzar; they fill with wonder a cowardly king, a Darius: and disarming the former of his rage, the latter of his fears, they sweetly force them both to confess the true God among their idolatrous courtiers, and throughout their immense dominions.

In the days of Herod the double delusion is at the height. John the Baptist boldly bears his testimony against it in the wilderness, and our Lord upon the mount, in the temple, and every where. But, alas! what is the consequence? By detecting the Antinomianism of the Pharisees, and the Pharisaism of Antinomians, he makes them desperate. The spirit of Cain rises with ten-fold fury against an innocence far superior to that of Abel. Pharisees and Herodians must absolutely glut their malice with his blood. He yields to their rage; and while he "puts away sin by the sacrifice of himself," he condescends to die a martyr for the right faith, and the true works: he seals as a dying priest the truth of the two Gospel axioms, which he had so often sealed as a living prophet, and continues to seal as an eternal Melchisedec.

The apostles, by precept and example, powerfully enforce their Lord's doctrine and practice. Their lives are true copies of their exhortations. Their deepest sermons are only exact descriptions of their behaviour. It is hard to say which excite men most to believe and obey, their seraphic discourses, or their angelic conduct. Their labours are crowned with general success. Judaism and heathenism are every where struck at, and fall under the thunder of their words of faith, and the shining power (might I not say the lightning?) of their works of love. Thus the world is "turned upside down" before faith and works; "the times of refreshing come from the presence of the Lord;" and earth, cursed as it is, becomes a paradise for obedient believers.

Hell trembles at the revolution; and before all is lost Satan hastens to "transform himself into an angel of light." In that favourable disguise he puts his usual stratagem in execution against the believing, working, and suffering Church. He instils speculative faith, pleads for relaxed manners, puts the badge of contempt upon the daily cross, and gets the immense body of the Gnostics and Laodiceans into his snare. Sad and sure is the consequence. The genuine works of faith are neglected: idle works of men's invention are substituted for those of God's commandments: and fallen Churches, through the smooth way of Antinomianism, return to the covert way of Pharisaism, or to the broad way of infidelity.

Such was the deplorable condition of the western Church when Luther appeared. True faith was dethroned by superstitious fancy: and all the works of the former were well nigh choked by the thorns that sprang from the latter. The zealous reformer, with his sharp scythe, justly cut them down through a considerable part of Germany. His terribly successful weapon, which had already done some execution in the Netherlands, France, and Italy, might have reached Rome itself, if the effects of his unguarded preaching had not dreadfully broke out around him in the north.

There the balance of the evangelical precepts was lost. Solifidians openly prevailed. Our Lord's sermon upon the mount, and St. James' Epistle, were either explained away, or wished out of the Bible. The amiable, *practicable law of Christ* was perpetually confounded with the terrible, impracticable *law of innocence*; and the avoidable penalties of the former were injudiciously represented as one with the dreadful curse of the latter, or with the abrogated ceremonies of the Mosaic dispensation. Then the law was publicly wedded to the devil, and poor Protestant Solifidians were taught to bid equal defiance to both.

The effects soon answered the cause. Lawless believers, known under the name of Anabaptists, arose in Germany. They fancied themselves the dear, the elect people of God; they were complete in Christ; their election was absolutely made sure; all things were theirs; and they went about in religious mobs to deliver people from *legal bondage*, and bring them into *Gospel liberty*, which, in their opinion, was a liberty to despise all laws, Divine and human, and to do every one what was right in his own eyes. Luther was shocked, and cried out: but the mischief was done, and the reformation disgraced. Nor did he perseveringly apply the proper remedy pointed out in the Minutes, "Salvation, not by the merit of works, but by the works of faith as a condition."

Nevertheless, he was wise enough to give up the root of the mischief in the Lutheran articles of religion, presented to the Emperor Charles the Fifth at Augsburg, whence they were called, *The Augsburg Confession*. In the twelfth of those articles, which treats of repentance, we find these remarkable words: "We teach, touching repentance, that those who have sinned after baptism may obtain the forgiveness of their sins *as often* as they are converted," &c. Again' "We condemn the Anabaptists, who say that those who have been once justified can no more lose the Holy Spirit."

This doctrine clearly opened, and frequently enforced, might have stopped the progress of Antinomianism. But, alas! Luther did not often insist upon it, and sometimes he seemed even to contradict it. In the meantime Calvin came up; and though I must do him the justice to acknowledge that he seldom went the length of modern Calvinists in speculative Antinomianism, yet he made the matter worse by advancing many unguarded propositions about absolute decrees, and the necessary final perseverance of backsliding believers.

This doctrine, which, together with its appendages, so nicely reconciles Baal and free grace; a *little*, or (if the backslider is so minded) a *good deal* of the world and heaven; this flesh-pleasing doctrine, which slily parts faith and works, while it decently unites Christ and Belial, could not but be acceptable to injudicious and carnal Protestants. And to make it pass with others, it was pompously decorated with the name of *the doctrine of grace*; and *free grace preachers*, as they call themselves, insinuated that St. James' doctrine of "faith being dead without works," was a doctrine of wrath, an uncomfortable, anti-christian doctrine, which none but "proud Justiciaries" and rank Papists could maintain. Time would fail to mention all the books that were indirectly written against it; or to relate all the abuse that was indirectly thrown upon these two propositions of St. Paul, "Whatsoever a man soweth, that shall he also reap," and, "If ye live after the flesh ye shall die."

Creeds and Scripture Scales

Let it suffice to observe, that by these means the hellish sower of Antinomian tares prevailed. Thousands of good men were carried away by the stream; and, what is more surprising still, not a few of the wise and learned, favoured, embraced, and defended the Antinomian delusion.

Thus what Luther's Solifidian zeal had begun, and what Calvin's predestinarian mistakes had carried on, was readily completed by the synod of Dort; and the Antinomianism of many Protestants was not less confirmed by that assembly of Calvinistic divines, than the Pharisaism of many Papists had been before by the council of Trent.

It is true, that as some good men in the Church of Rome have boldly withstood Pharisaical errors, and openly pleaded for salvation by grace through faith; so some good men in the Protestant Churches have also steadily resisted Antinomian delusions, and publicly defended the doctrine of salvation, not by the proper merit of works, but by the works of faith as a condition. But, alas! As the popes of Rome crushed or excommunicated the former almost as fast as they arose; so have petty Protestant popes blackened or silenced the latter. The true Quakers, from their first appearance, have made as firm a stand against the Antinomians, as the Valdenses against the Papists; and it is well known that the Antinomians, who went from England to America with many pious Puritans, whipped the Quakers, men and women, cut off their ears, made against them a law of banishment upon pain of death, and upon that tyrannical law hanged four of their preachers, three men and one woman,* in the last century for preaching up the Christian perfection of faith and obedience, and so disturbing the peace of the elect, who were "at ease in Sion," or rather in Babel.

I need not mention the title of heretic with which that learned and good man, Arminius, is to this day dignified, for having made a firm and noble stand against wanton free grace. The banishment or deprivation of Grotius, Episcopius, and other Dutch divines, is no secret. And it is well known that in England Mr. Baxter, Mr. Wesley, and Mr. Sellon, are to this day "an abhorrence to all *Antinomian* flesh."

I am sorry to say, that, all things considered, these good men have been treated with as much severity by Protestant Antinomians, as ever Luther, Melancthon, and Calvin were by Popish Pharisees. The Antinomian and Pharisaic spirit run as much into one, as the two arms of a river that embraces an island. If they divide for a time, it is only to meet again, and increase their mutual rapidity. I beg leave to speak my whole mind. It is equally clear from Scripture and reason that we must believe in order to be saved consistently with God's mercy; and that we must obey in order to be saved consistently with his holiness. These propositions are the immovable basis of the two Gospel axioms. Now if I reject either of them, it little matters which. If I blow my brains out, what signifies it whether I do it by clapping the mouth of a pistol to my right or to my left temple?

---

* Their names were William Leddra, Marmaduke Stephenson, William Robinson, and Mary Dyer. (See The History of the Quakers, by Sewell; and New-England Judged, by George Bishop.)

Error moves in a circle: extremes meet in one. A warm Popish Pharisee, and a zealous Protestant Antinomian, are nearer each other than they imagine. The one will tell you that by going to mass and confession he can get a fresh absolution from the priest for any sin that he shall commit. The other, whose mistake is still more pleasing to flesh and blood, assures you that he has already got an eternal absolution, so that "under every state and circumstance he can possibly be in, he is justified from all things, his sins are for ever and for ever cancelled."

But, if they differ a little in the idea of their imaginary privileges, they have the honour of agreeing in the main point. For, although the one makes a great noise about faith and free grace, and the other about works and true charity, they exactly meet in narrow grace and despairing uncharitableness. The Pharisee in Jerusalem asserts, that "out of the Jewish Church there can be no salvation," and his companions in self election heartily say, Amen! The Pharisee in Rome declares, that "there is no salvation out of the apostolic, Romish Church," and all the Catholic elect set their seal to the antichristian decree. And the Antinomian in London insinuates, (for he is ashamed to speak quite out in a Protestant country,) that there is no salvation out of the Calvinistic Predestinarian Church. Hence, if you oppose his principles in ever so rational and Scriptural a manner, he supposes that you are "quite dark," that all your holiness is "self made," and all your "righteousness a cobweb spun by a poor spider out of its own bowels." And if he allows you a chance for your salvation, it is only upon a supposition, that you may yet repent of your opposition to his errors, and turn Calvinist before you die. But might not an inquisitor be as charitable? Might he not hope that the poor heretic, whom he has condemned to the flames, may yet be saved, if he cordially kiss a crucifix, and say, "*Ave, Maria!*" at the stake?

And now, candid reader, look around, and see what these seemingly opposite errors have done for Christ's Church. Before the reformation Christendom was overspread with superstition and fanaticism; and since, with lukewarmness and infidelity. But let us descend to particulars.

What has Pharisaism done for the Church of Rome? It has publicly rent from her all the Protestant kingdoms, and secretly turned against her an innumerable multitude of Deists: for while bigots continue ridiculous bigots still; men of wit, headed by ingenious infidels, continually pour undeserved contempt upon Christianity, through the deserved wounds which they give to Popery. They represent Christ's rational and humane religion as one of the worst in the world, unjustly charging it with the persecuting spirit, and horrible massacres of those Catholics, so called, who, mangling the truth, and running away with one half of the body of Christian divinity, disgrace the whole by childish fooleries, and worse than barbarian uncharitableness.

And what does Pharisaism for the Protestant Churches? So far as it prevails, spreads it not around its fatal leaven, a general indifference about heart-felt religion? Turns it not the lively oracles of God into a dead letter, the sacraments into empty ceremonies, the means of grace into rattles, to quiet a guilty conscience with; the precious blood of Christ into a common thing, his hallowed cross into an inglorious tree, external devotion into a cloak for secret hypocrisy; and some acts of apparent benevolence into the rounds of a ladder, the bottom of which reaches hell, and behold spiritual fiends (all manner of diabolical tempers) are seen continually "ascending and descending on it?"

Does it not incline us to despise those who are eminently pious, as if they were out of their senses; to despair of those who are notoriously wicked, as if they were absolute reprobates: and to prefer a popular imitator of Barabbas to a meek follower of Jesus? Does it not prompt us to lay an undue stress upon trifles, and make an endless ado about some frivolous circumstance of external worship, while we "pass over judgment, mercy, and the love of God?" And by that means does it not confirm modern Herodians in their Antinomianism, and modern Sadducees in their infidelity? In a word, does it not render the stiff neck stiffer, the blind understanding blinder, the hard heart stouter, the proud spirit more rebellious, more indifferent about mercy, more averse to Gospel grace, more satanical, readier for all the curses of the law, and riper for all the woes of the Gospel?

But let us consider the other extreme. What has Calvinism done for Geneva? Alas! It has in a great degree shocked and driven it into Arianism, Socinianism, and infidelity. See the account lately given of it in the *French Encyclopedia*, article *Geneva*. "Many of the clergy of Geneva (says judicious Mr. D'Alembert) no longer believe the divinity of Jesus Christ, of which Calvin their leader was a zealous defender, and for which he had Servetus burned, &c. They believe that there are punishments in another world, but only for a limited time. Thus purgatory, which was one of the chief causes of the reformation, is now the only punishment which many Protestants admit after death. A new proof this that man is a being full of contradictions. To sum up all in one word, the religion of many pastors at Geneva is *perfect Socinianism.*"

What good has Calvinism done in England? Alas! very little. When a bow is bent beyond its proper degree of tension, does it not fly to pieces? When you violently pull a tree toward the west, if it recovers itself, does it not violently fly to the east? Has not this generally been the case with respect to all the truths of God, which have been forced out of their Scriptural place one way or another? Calvinism, in the days of Oliver Cromwell, was at the very same height of splendour at which Popery had attained in the days of King Henry the Eighth, and they share the same downfall. *Mole ruunt sua.* At the reformation, the first grand doctrine of Christianity, (*salvation by grace through faith,*) which had been forced out of its place, and almost broken by the Papists, flew back upon them with such violence that it shook the holy see, frightened the pope, and made some of the richest jewels fall from his triple crown. In like manner the second grand doctrine of Christianity, (*salvation, not by the proper merit of works, but by the works of faith as a condition,*) which had been served by the Antinomians just as the first Gospel axiom by the Papists, recovering itself out of their hands, flew back upon them with uncommon violence at King Charles' restoration; by an indirect blow shook two thousand Calvinistic ministers out of their pulpits; and getting far beyond its Scriptural place, began to bear hard upon, and even thrust out the grand doctrine of salvation by grace. Thus the absurdity and mischief of Antinomianism began to drive again the generality of English Protestants into Pharisaism, Arianism, Socinianism, or open infidelity; that is, into the state in which most of the learned are at Rome and Geneva.

I grant that near forty years ago some clergymen from the university of Oxford returned to the principles of the reformation, and zealously contended again for salvation by grace, and for universal obedience. By the Divine blessing upon their indefatigable endeavours, faith and works met again, and for some time walked undisturbed together. A little revolution then took place: practical Christianity revived, and leaning upon her fair daughters, truth and love, took a solemn walk through the kingdom, and gave a foretaste of heaven to all that cordially entertained her.

She might, by this time, have turned this favourite isle into a land flowing with spiritual milk and honey, if Apollyon, disguised in his angelic robes, had not played, and did not continue to play his old game. Nor does he do it in vain. By his insinuations men of a contrary turn rise against practical Christianity. Many of the devout call her *heresy*, and many of the gay name her *rank enthusiasm*. In the meantime she drops a tear of tender pity, prays for her mistaken persecutors, and quietly retires into the wilderness. Lean obedience is soon driven after her, to make more room for speculative faith, who is so highly fed with luscious food and wild honey that she is quite bloated, and full of humours. Nay, in some she is degenerated into an impatient, quarrelsome something, which calls itself *orthodoxy*, or *the truth*, and must be treated with the greatest respect; while charity, cold, sickly, and almost starved for want of work, is hardly used with common good manners.

In a word, Antinomian Christianity is come, and makes her public entry in the professing Church. A foolish virgin, who assumes the name of free grace, walks before her, and cries, "Bend the knee, bow the heart, and entertain the old, the pure, the only Gospel." An ugly black boy, called free wrath, bears her enormous train, and with wonderful art hides himself behind it. While thousands are taken with the smiles and cheerfulness of *wanton free grace*, (for that is the virgin's right name,) and for her sake welcome her painted mother, a grey-headed seer passes by, fixes his keen eyes upon the admired family, sees through their disguise, and warns his friends. This is highly resented, not only by all the lovers of the sprightly, alluring maid, but by some excellent people, who, in the simplicity of their hearts, mistake her for the celestial Virgin Astrea. Mr. H. and Mr. T., two of her champions, fall upon the aged monitor; and to the great entertainment of the Pharisaic and Antinomian world, who do the best to tread down his honour in the dust.

While they are thus employed, a rough countryman, who had taken the seer's warning, throws himself full in the way of Antinomian Christianity, and tries to stop her in her triumphal march. Wanton free grace is a little disconcerted at his rudeness, she reddens, and soon shows herself the true sister of free wrath. To be revenged of the clown, she charges him with — guess what — a rape? No: but with being great with "the scarlet whore," and concerned with the Romish "man of sin." If he is acquitted of these enormities, they say that she is determined to indict him for murder or "forgery;" and if that will not do, for highway robbery, or "execrable Swiss slander." The mountaineer, who "counts not his life dear," stands his ground, and in the scuffle discovers the black boy, lays fast hold of him, and notwithstanding the good words that he gives one moment, and the floods of invectives which he pours out the next, he drags him out to public view, and appeals to the Christian world. *Et adhuc sub judice lis est.*

But leaving England, the scene of the present controversy, I ask, What does Calvinism at this day for Scotland, where national honours are paid to it, and where for some ages it has passed for the pure Gospel? Alas! not much, if we may depend upon the observations of a gentleman of piety and fortune, who went last year with an eminent minister of Christ to inspect the state of spiritual Christianity in the north, and brought back this melancholy account: — "The decay of vital religion is yet more visible in Scotland than in England."

Should, by this time, some of my readers be ready to ask what Arminianism has done for Holland and England, I reply: If by *Arminianism* you mean the pure doctrine of Christ, especially the doctrine of our free justification through Christ, by the instrumentality of faith in the day of a sinner's conversion, and by the evidence of the works of faith afterward: if you mean, as I do, a system of evangelical truth, in which the two Gospel precepts, *believe* and *obey*, are duly balanced, and faith and works kept in their Scriptural place; I answer: That under Christ it has done all the good that has been done, not only in Holland and England, but in all Christendom.

Be not then mistaken: when ministers, leaning toward speculative Antinomianism, have done good, it has not been by preaching wanton free grace, and by shackling the free Gospel, but by powerfully enforcing "the truth as it is in Jesus;" by crying aloud, "Believe, thou lost sinner, and be saved by grace: obey, thou happy believer, and evidence thy salvation by works: and whosoever will, let him come and take of the water of life freely, for all things are now ready." So far as they have started aside from this guarded, and yet encouraging Gospel, they have pulled down with one hand what they built with the other; they have tried to make up the Pharisaic, by widening the Antinomian gap; they have departed from what we call Christianity, and what you are at full liberty to call *Arminianism, Baxterianism*, or *Wesleyanism*.

To return: I observed, just now, that Antinomianism drives us into Pharisaism, Socinianism, and infidelity: but might I not have added fatalism, the highest degree of fashionable infidelity? And after all, what is fatalism, in which the greatest infidels unanimously shelter themselves in our day? Is it not the beginning or the end of high Calvinism, whose emblematical representation may be a serpent forming a circle while it bites its tail, with this motto, *In sese volvitur error*, "After a large circuit error ends where it began?" If high Calvinism is the *head*, is not fatalism the *tail*?

For my part I shall not wonder if some of our high Predestinarians find themselves, before they are aware, even at Hobbes' or Voltaire's feet, humbly learning there the horrible lessons of fatalism. Nay, if I am not mistaken, they perfectly agree with the French philosopher in the capital point. One might think that they have converted him to their orthodoxy, or that he has perverted them to his infidelity. Candid reader, judge of it by the following extract of his lecture on destiny: —

"Homer (says he) is the first writer in whose works we find the notion of fate. It was then in vogue in his time. Nor was it adopted by the Pharisees till many years after: for these Pharisees themselves, who were the first men of letters among the Jews, were not very ancient, &c. But philosophers needed neither the help of Homer, nor that of the Pharisees, to persuade themselves that all things happen by immutable decrees, that *all is fixed, that all is necessary*." Now for the proof: "Bodies (adds he) tend to the centre; pear trees can never bear pine apples; a man cannot have above a certain number of teeth." And directly flying from teeth to ideas, he would have us infer, that we can no more arrange, combine, alter, or dismiss our ideas, than our grinders; and that an adulterer defiles his neighbour's bed as necessarily as a pear tree produces pears. He even adds, "If thou couldst alter the destiny of a fly, thou shouldst be more powerful than God himself." (See *Dictionaire Philosophique Portatif*, Londres, 1764, pp. 163, 164.)

This ingenious infidel is quite as *orthodox* (in the Calvinistic sense of the word) in his article on *liberty*: — "What does then your free will consist in, (says he,) if it is not in a power to do willingly what absolute necessity makes you choose?" Nay, he is so staunch a Predestinarian, so complete a fatalist, that he maintains no one can choose *even or odds* without an irresistible order of all-directing fate. And he concludes by affirming that all "liberty of indifference," that is, all power to do a thing, or to leave it undone at our option, without the necessitating agency of fate, "is arrant nonsense." (See the same book, page 243, &c.)

Thus the most subtle, self. righteous infidel in France, by going full east, and the most rigid, thorough-paced Antinomian in England, by going full west in the ways of error, meet at last face to face in the antipodes of truth. O may the shock caused by their unexpected encounter wake them both out of their fatal dreams, to call upon Him, who "takes the wise in their own craftiness," imparts true wisdom to the simple, and crowns the humble with grace and glory.

As high Calvinism on the left hand falls in with fatalism, so on the right hand it runs into the wildest notions of some deluded mystics, and ranting Perfectionists. Judicious reader, you will be convinced of it by the following propositions, advanced by Molinos* the Father of the mystics and Perfectionists, who are known abroad under the name of Quietists. These positions, among many others, were condemned by the pope as "rash, offensive to pious ears, erroneous, scandalous," &c. I extract them from the bull of his holiness, given at Rome, 1687, and published by the archbishop of Cambray at the end of his book called *Instruction Pastorale*, printed at Amsterdam, 1698. (See page 192, &c.)

"*Velle operari active est Deum offendere, qui vult esse solus agens*, &c. To be willing to be active and work, is to offend God, who will be the sole agent, &c. Our natural activity stands in the way of grace, and hinders the Divine operation and true perfection, *quia Deus vult operari in nobis sine nobis*, because God will work in us without us. The soul ought not to think upon rewards and punishments. We must leave to God the caring of all that concerns us, that he may do in us, without us, his Divine will. He that will be resigned to God's will, must not ask him any thing, because petitions savour of our own will, and therefore are imperfect," or, to speak in the Calvinistic way, sinful.

Again: "God, to humble and transform us, permits and wills that the devil should do violence to the bodies of some perfect souls, [i.e. established believers,] and should make them commit carnal actions against their will. God now sanctifies his saints by the ministry of devils, who, by causing in their flesh the above-mentioned violent impulses, makes them despise themselves the more, &c. St. Paul felt such violent impulses in his body: hence he wrote, 'The good that I would, I do not: and the evil which I would not, I do.' These violent impulses are the best means

---

* He was a pious, but injudicious clergyman of the Church of Rome, who, in some of his works, spoiled the doctrine of grace by Calvinistic refinements; and that of Christian perfection by Antinomian rant.

to humble the soul to nothing, and to bring it to true holiness and the Divine union: there is no other way, *et hæc est via facilior et tutior*, and this is the easier and the safer way. David, &c, suffered such violent impulses to external impure actions," &c.

Who does not see here some of the most absurd tenets or dangerous consequences of Calvinism? Man is a mere machine in the work of salvation. The body of holy Paul is sold under sin. David in Uriah's bed is complete and perfect in Christ. Actual adultery humbles believers, and is an excellent mean of sanctification, &c.

When we see Antinomianism thus defiling the sounder part of the Romish and Protestant Churches: when the god of this world avails himself of these "Antinomian dotages" to confirm myriads of stiff Pharisees in their self- righteous delusions; and when the bulk of men, shocked at the glaring errors of both, run for shelter to Deism and gross infidelity; who would not desire to see the doctrines of faith and works, grace and obedience, so stated and reconciled, that men of reason might no longer be offended at Christianity; nor men of religion one at another?

This is again attempted in the following discourse, the substance of which was committed to paper many years ago, to convince the Pharisees and Papists of my parish that there is no salvation by the faithless works of the law, but by a living faith in Jesus Christ. With shame I confess that I did not then see the need of guarding the doctrine of faith against the despisers of works. I was chiefly bent upon pulling up the tares of Pharisaism: those of Antinomianism were not yet sprung up in the field which I began to cultivate; or my want of experience hindered me from discerning them. But since, what a crop of them have I perceived and bewailed!

Alas! they have in a great degree ruined the success of my ministry. I have seen numbers of lazy seekers enjoying the dull pleasures of sloth on the couch of wilful unbelief, under pretence that God was to do all in them without them. I have seen some lie flat in the mire of sin, absurdly boasting that they could not fall; and others make the means of grace, means of idle gossiping or sly courtship. I have seen some turn their religious profession into a way of gratifying covetousness or indolence; and others their skill in Church music, their knowledge and their zeal into various nets to catch esteem, admiration, and praise. Some have I seen making yesterday's faith a reason to laugh at the cross to-day; and others drawing from their misapprehensions of the atonement arguments to be less importunate in secret prayer, and more conformable to this evil world, than once they were. Nay, I have seen some professing believers backward to do those works of mercy, which I have sometimes found persons, who made no professions of godliness, quite ready to perform. And O! tell it in Sion, that watchfulness may not be neglected by believers, that fearfulness may seize upon backsliders, and that trembling may break the bones of hypocrites and apostates; I have seen those who had equally shined by their gifts and graces strike the moral world with horror by the grossest Antinomianism; and disgrace the doctrine of salvation through faith by the deepest plunges into scandalous sin.

Candid reader, I need say no more to make thee sensible of the necessity of the additions and notes, by which I have strengthened and guarded my old discourse, that it might be an *EQUAL Check to Pharisaism and Antinomianism*, an equal prop to faith and works. If it afford thee any edification, give God the glory, and pray for the despised author. Ask, in the words of the good Bishop Hopkins, that I may so

"BELIEVE, so rest on the merits of Christ, as if I had never wrought any thing; and withal so would, as if I were only to be saved by my own merits." And O! ask it again and again, for I find it a *difficult thing to give to each of these its due in my practice*. It is the very depth and height of Christian perfection.

POSTSCRIPT.

MADELEY, Jan. 10, 1774.

ABOVE fifteen years ago I looked into Baxter's Aphorisms on Justification, and through prejudice or sloth I soon laid them down, as being too deep for me. But a few days since a friend having brought me Mr. Wesley's extract of them, I have read it with much satisfaction, and present my readers with a compendium of my discourse in the words of those two judicious and laborious divines.

"As there are two covenants, with their distinct conditions, so there is a two-fold righteousness, and both of them absolutely necessary to salvation. Our righteousness of the first covenant is not personal, or consisteth not in any actions performed by us; for we never personally satisfied the law, [of innocence,] but it is wholly without us in Christ. In this sense every Christian disclaimeth his own righteousness or his own works. Those only shall be in Christ legally righteous who believe and obey the Gospel, and so are in themselves evangelically righteous. Though Christ performed the conditions of the law [of innocence] and satisfied for our non- performance, yet we ourselves must perform the conditions of the Gospel. These two [last] propositions seem to me so clear, that I wonder any able divines should deny them. Methinks they should be articles of our creed, and a part of children's catechisms. To affirm that our evangelical or new-covenant righteousness is in Christ, and not in ourselves, or performed by Christ, and not by ourselves, is such a monstrous piece of Antinomian doctrine as no man, who knows the nature and difference of the covenants, can possibly entertain." (*Bax. Aphor. Prop.* 14-17.)

SALVATION BY THE COVENANT OF GRACE:

A DISCOURSE ON ROMANS 11:5, 6.

"Even so then, at this present time also, there is a remnant according to the election of grace: and if by grace, then it is no more of works, otherwise grace is no more grace: but if it be of works, then it is no more grace; otherwise work is no more work."

INTRODUCTION AND DIVISION.

THE apostle complains in the preceding chapter that Israel was blinded, and did not see the way of salvation' "I bear them record," says he, Romans 10:2, "that they have a zeal for God, but not according to knowledge; for being ignorant of God's righteousness," i.e. of God's way of saving sinners* merely through Jesus Christ; "and going about to establish their own righteousness," that is, endeavouring to save themselves by their own good works [so called, by works which, strictly speaking, deserve rather to be named Pharisaical than good;] "they have not submitted to the righteousness of God:" to that faith in Christ which makes sinners righteous before God: "for Christ," adds he, "is the end of the law for righteousness to every one that believeth," Romans 10:4: that is, [since the fall,] it is the very design of the [Adamic] law, [the law of innocence given to sinless Adam; yea, and of the Mosaic law, when it is considered as "written in stones," and decorated with shadows or types of good things to come,] to bring men to believe in Christ for justification and salvation; as he alone gives that pardon and life which the law [of innocence] shows the want of, [and which the Mosaic law, abstracted from Gospel promises, points unto,] but cannot possibly bestow.

The apostle, resuming the same subject in the chapter out of which the text is taken, comforts himself by considering, that although Israel in general were blinded, yet all were not lost. Old Simeon and Anna had "seen the salvation of God," and had "departed in peace." Nicodemus, a doctor in Israel, had received the doctrine of the new birth and salvation by faith. "Three thousand" Jews had been "pricked to the heart" by penitential sorrow, and "filled with peace and joy by believing" in Jesus Christ. And "even at this present time," says the apostle, "there is a remnant [of my countrymen saved,] according to the election of grace:" that is, there are some of them, who, [like Nathanael and Nicodemus,] casting away their dependence on their own righteousness, [and trusting only in Christ's merits,] are numbered among the elect, according to that gracious decree of [election in Christ, which] God [has so

---

* (1.) When I say that God saves sinners "merely" through Jesus Christ, I do not exclude our *faith*, the *instrumental cause* of our salvation; nor our *works* of faith, the *evidencing cause* of it, any more than I exclude Divine mercy. I only meant that Christ is the *primary, meritorious* cause of our justification; and that from him all secondary instrumental causes receive whatever influence they have toward our eternal salvation. Nor do I take away from the Redeemer's glory, when I affirm, with the Rev. Mr. Madan, that "we are justified instrumentally by faith, and declaratively by works;" or that faith is the instrumental, and works are the declarative cause of our complete justification. For as I speak of faith in Christ, "the light of men and the Saviour of the world;" and as I mean the works of that faith, I secure his mediatorial honours; such works being all wrought through his influence, perfumed with his merits, and accepted through his intercession. Christ is then all in all still; the primary and meritorious cause passing through all the secondary and instrumental causes, as light does through our windows and eyes; food through our mouths and stomachs; and vital blood through our arteries and veins.

N. B. The parts of this discourse, which are enclosed in brackets, [ ] are the additions that guard or strengthen the old sermon which my opponent calls for; and the parts contained between the two hands, ☞ are the passages which he has extracted from it, and published at the end of his *Finishing Stroke*.

clearly revealed,] in the covenant of grace, "He that believeth shall be saved," &c, Mark 16:16.*

From thence the apostle takes occasion to show, that pardon and salvation are not, in whole or in part, attained by [the covenant of] works, but merely by [the covenant of] grace. A remnant of those self-righteous Pharisees is saved, [not indeed by their self righteousness,] but by [the covenant of] grace, according to which we must equally part with our self righteousness and our sins. "And if by [the covenant of] grace," then "it is no more [by that] of works," whether of the ceremonial law [of Moses,] or of the moral law [of innocence perverted to Pharisaic purposes;] "else [the] grace [of Christ] is no longer grace" [bestowed upon a criminal:] the very nature of [Gospel grace†] is lost. "And if it be [by the covenant] of works, then it is no more [by Gospel] grace: else work is no longer [the] work" [of a sinless creature,] but the very nature of it is destroyed [according to the first covenant, which requires perfect conformity to the law in the work, and perfect innocence in the worker.]

As if the apostle had said, There is something so absolutely inconsistent between being saved by [the covenant of] grace, and being saved by [that of] works, that if you suppose either, you of necessity exclude the other: for what is given to

---

* (2.) My sentiment concerning election is thus expressed by a great Calvinist minister: "In the written word a decree of God is found, which shows who are the chosen and the saved people: 'He that believeth and is baptized shall be saved.' The chosen people therefore are a race of true believers, convinced by God's Spirit of their ruined estate, endowed with Divine faith, by which they seek to Christ for help; and seeking do obtain pardon, peace, and holiness." (*The Christian World Unmasked*, second edition, p. 186.) Judicious Christians will probably agree here with this pious divine, if he does not deny, (1.) That in the Divine decree of election the word "believeth" excludes from the election those who "have cast off their faith," or "have made shipwreck of the faith." And (2.) That the word "is baptized," implies "professing the faith in word and work;" or making and standing to the baptismal vow, which respects not only the believing the articles of the Christian faith, but also keeping God's holy will and commandments.

† (3.) I say Gospel grace, because it is that which the apostle means. It may with propriety be distinguished from the original grace which Adam had before the fall, and which Deists and Pharisees still suppose themselves possessed of. Some people imagine, that if our first parents had well acquitted themselves in the trial of their faithfulness, their reward would not have been of grace; they would (strictly speaking) have merited heaven. But this is a mistake. From the Creator to the creature, all blessings are, and must for ever be of grace, of mere grace. Gabriel himself enjoys heaven through free grace. Unless some gracious promise interposes, God may this instant put an end, without injustice, not only to his glory, but to his very existence. Should you ask what difference there is between original and Gospel grace; I answer, that original, Adamic grace naturally flowed from God, as Creator and Preserver, to innocent, happy creatures: but Gospel grace, that for which St. Paul so strenuously contends in my text, supernaturally flows from God, as Redeemer and Comforter, to guilty, wretched mankind: and here let us take notice of the opposition there is between Pharisaic and evangelical obedience, between the works of the law and the works of faith. The former are done with a proud conceit of the natural strength which man lost by the fall; and the latter with an humble dependence on Divine mercy through the Redeemer's merits, and on the supernatural power bestowed upon lost mankind for his sake. When St. Paul decries the works of the law, it is merely to recommend the works of faith: and yet, O the dreadful effects of confusion! In Babel people suppose that he pours equal contempt upon both.

works [upon the footing of the first covenant] is [improperly speaking] the payment of a debt [which God, by his gracious promise, contracted with innocent mankind without the interposition of a Mediator:] whereas [Gospel] grace implies [not only] a favour [strictly speaking] unmerited [by us; but also an atoning sacrifice on the Redeemer's part, and a damnable demerit on our own:] so that the same benefit cannot, in the very nature of things, be derived from both [covenants.]

Having thus opened the context, I proceed to a more particular illustration of the text; and that I may explain it as fully as the time allotted for this discourse will permit: —

First, I shall premise an account of the two covenants: the covenant of works, to which the Pharisees of old trusted, and [most of] the Roman Catholics, with too many false Protestants, still trust in our days: and the covenant of grace, by which alone a remnant was saved in St. Paul's time, and will be saved in all ages.

Secondly, I shall prove that the way of salvation by [obedient] faith only, or, which is the same thing, by the covenant of grace, is the only way that leads to life, according to the Scriptures, and the articles of our Church, to whose holy doctrine I shall publicly set my seal.

Thirdly, I shall endeavour to show the unreasonableness and injustice of those who accuse me of "preaching against good works," when I [decry Pharisaic works, and] preach salvation through the covenant of grace only.

Fourthly and lastly, after having informed you why [even] good works [truly so called] cannot* [properly] deserve salvation in whole or in part, I shall answer the old objection of [some ignorant] Papists [and Pharisaical Protestants.] "If good works cannot† [properly merit us heaven,] why should we do them? There is no need to trouble ourselves about any."

---

* (4.) I prefer "properly" to "absolutely," the word which I formerly used; because "absolutely" bears too hard upon the second Gospel axiom, and turns out of the Gospel the rewardable condecency, that our whole obedience, even according to Dr. Owen, hath unto eternal life, through God's gracious appointment.

† (5.) I say now "properly merit us heaven," and not "save us, get us heaven, or procure us heaven," expressions which occur a few times in my old sermon; because (taking the word "merit" in its full and proper sense,) the phrase "cannot merit us heaven," leaves room to defend the necessity of evangelical obedience, and of the works of faith, by which we shall be saved, not indeed as being the first and properly meritorious cause of our salvation, (for to ascribe to them that honour would be to injure free grace, and place them on the Mediator's throne,) but as being the secondary instrumental cause of our justification in the great day, and consequently of our eternal salvation.

Nor does the expression, "properly merit us heaven," clash with such scriptures as these: "When the wicked man turneth from his iniquity, he shall save his soul alive — save some with fear — save thy husband — save thy wife — we are saved by hope — work out your own salvation — he that converteth a sinner shall save a soul from death — thy faith hath saved thee — in doing this thou shalt save thyself, and them that hear thee." A preacher should do justice to every part of the Scripture: nor should he blunt one edge of the sword of the Spirit, under pretence of making the other sharper. This I inadvertently did sometimes in the year 1762. May God endue me with wisdom that I may not do it in 1774! I find it the nicest thing in practical, as well as in polemical divinity, so to defend the doctrine of God's free grace as not to wound that of man's faithful obedience, and *vice versa*. These two doctrines support the two Gospel axioms, and may be called the breasts of the Church. A child of God, instead of peevishly biting the one or the other, should suck them alternately; and a minister of Christ, instead of cutting off either, should carefully protect them both.

Should any one object, that if Calvinism is supported by the Rev. Mr. Berridge's distinction between *if* and *if*, (see the *Fifth Check*, second part,) the Gospel axioms, about which we make so much ado, have not a better foundation, since they depend upon a distinction between original merit and derived merit: I reply, that the distinction between legal *if* and evangelical *if* is unworthy of Christ, and not less contrary to Scripture, than to reason and morality. On the contrary, the distinction between original or proper merit, and derived or improper worthiness, far from being frivolous, is Scriptural, (see Vol. 1, *Fourth Check*, p. 236, &c,) solid, highly honourable to Christ, greatly conducive to morality, very rational, and lying within the reach of the meanest capacity.

This will appear from the following propositions, which contain the sum of our doctrine concerning merit. (1.) All proper worthiness, merit, or desert of any Divine reward is in Christ, the overflowing fountain of all original excellence. (2) If any of the living water of that rich spring is received by faith, and flows through the believer's heart and works, it forms improper worthiness, or derived merit; because, properly speaking, it is Christ's merit still. (3.) Original merit answers to the first Gospel axiom, and derived worthiness to the second. (4.) According to the first covenant, we can never merit a reward, because, of ourselves as sinners, we deserve nothing but hell; and that covenant makes no provision of merit for hell-deserving sinners. But (5.) According to the second covenant, by God's gracious appointment and merciful promise we can, improperly speaking, be worthy of heaven, through the blood of Christ sprinkled upon our hearts, and through his righteousness derived to us and to our works by faith. (6.) Hence it is that God will give some, namely, impenitent murderers, blood to drink, "for they are worthy," they properly deserve it; while others, namely, penitent believers, shall walk with Christ in white, "for they are worthy," they *improperly* merit it, Revelation 16:6, and 3:4.

An illustration, taken from a leaden pipe full of water, may show how it is possible that unworthy man should become worthy, through the righteousness which Christ supplies believers with. Strictly speaking, water does not belong to a pipe, any more than merit or worthiness to a believer; for a pipe is only a number of dry sheets of lead soldered together. But if that dry, leaden pipe really receive some of the water which a river supplies, I make myself ridiculous by asserting that the man who hints there is water in the pipe confounds the elements, seeks to dry up the river, and is guilty of a dreadful philosophical heresy.

However, if our prepossessed brethren feel an invincible aversion to our Lord's word [αξιος, meriting,] we are willing to become all things to them for his sake. If it may be a mean of restoring tranquillity to their minds, we cheerfully consent to use only the word of our translators "worthy;" and here I give full leave to my readers, whenever they meet the noun "merit," or the verb "to merit," in my Checks, to read "worthiness" instead of the one, and "to be worthy" instead of the other. It may indeed puzzle unbiassed persons to find a difference between those expressions; but no matter. If others will expose their prejudice, we ought not only to maintain the truth, but to show our condescension. The word merit is absolutely nothing to Mr. Wesley and me; but the doctrine of faithful obedience in Christ, and of the gracious rewards with which it shall be crowned for his sake, contains all our duty on earth, and draws after it all our bliss in heaven. Therefore, only grant us truly the second Gospel axiom: — grant us, that God has not appointed his creatures to endless punishments and heavenly rewards out of mere caprice: — grant us, that while the wicked shall properly and "legally deserve their own [and not Adam's] place in hell," the righteous shall improperly and "evangelically be worthy to obtain that world," where they "shall be equal to the angels," Luke 20:35: — grant us that man is in a state of probation, and shall be recompensed for, and" according to what he has done in the body, whether it be good or bad:" — in a word, grant us

----

PART FIRST.

I BEGIN by laying before you an account of the two [grand] covenants that God entered into with man. The first was made with Adam, when he was in a state of innocence in paradise. The condition of it, which is excessively hard [nay, absolutely impossible] to fallen man, was easy before the fall. It runs thus: — "Do this [thou sinless man] and live: the [innocent] man that does these things shall live by them," Romans 10:5: that is, "If thou [who art now a guiltless, holy, and perfect creature] yield a constant, universal, and perfect obedience to the moral law," now summed up in the ten commandments, "thou shalt be rewarded with glory in heaven. But if thou fail in any one particular, whether it be in thought, word, or deed, ' thou shalt surely die,' Genesis 2:17; for 'the soul that sinneth it shall die,' Ezekiel 18:4. 'The wages of sin is death,' Romans 6:23. And 'cursed is every one that continueth not in ALL things written in the book of the law to do them,'" Galatians 3:10.

Nor does this covenant make any allowance for deficiencies, or pass by one transgression, great or little, without pronouncing the threatened curse; [for it made no provision for repentance, neither did it offer sinners the help of a sacrificing priest, or interceding mediator.] Whether therefore the sin be murder and adultery, or only eating some forbidden fruit, its language is,* "Whosoever shall keep the whole law, and yet offend in one point, he is guilty of all," James 2:10: that is, all the curses denounced against those who break the covenant of works hang upon his guilty head, [and will fall upon him in a degree proportionable to the aggravations of his sin.]

This first covenant we have all broken in our first parents, for ["in Adam all die"] "by one man sin entered into the world, and death by sin; and so death passed upon all men, for that all have sinned," Romans 5:12. We are then all born [or conceived] in sin, Psalm 51:5, and consequently "we are by nature children of wrath," Ephesians 2:3. But this is not all. This root of original sin produces in every man many actual iniquities, whereby, as we imitate Adam's rebellion, so we make the guilt of it our own, and fasten the curse attending that guilt upon our own souls, Romans 7:24.

Therefore, while we remain in our natural state, [or, to speak more intelligibly, while we continue in sin, guilt, and total impenitency, we not only trample the covenant of grace under foot, but] we stand upon the [broken] covenant of works; and consequently lie under the dreadful curse which is already denounced

---

the capital doctrine of a day of retribution, in which "God shall judge the world in wisdom and righteousness," not in solemn folly or satanical hypocrisy, and we ask no more. This note is a key to all the doctrines which we maintain in the Minutes, and explain in the Checks.

* (6.) Whoever reads the Scriptures without prejudice will be of Mr. Burgess' mind concerning this awful text. (See Vol. 1, *Fourth Check*, p. 224.) It was evidently spoken with reference to Christ's law of liberty, as well as some of the passages quoted in the preceding paragraph; and if they guard even that law, how much more the law of innocence, which, though it cannot be holier in its precepts, is yet much more peremptory in its curses!

against every transgressor of the law, Galatians 3:10, [as well as against every despiser of the Gospel, Hebrews 10:27.]

Hence it is that "by the deeds of the law," i.e. by the [unsprinkled] good works commanded in the law [of innocence: or by the ceremonies prescribed in the law of Moses,] "shall no flesh living [no sinner] be justified: for as many as are of the works of the law [as it stands opposed to the Gospel; yea, as many also as rest, like the impenitent Pharisees, in the letter of the Mosaic law] are under the curse; the Scripture having concluded all under sin," [i.e. testified that all are sinners by conception and practice] and consequently under the curse [of the first covenant,] "that every mouth may be stopped, and all the world may become guilty [i.e. may humbly confess their fallen and lost estate] before God," [and gladly accept his offers of mercy in the second covenant,] Romans 3:19, 20.

In this deplorable state of guilt and danger, we [generally] remain careless and insensible, [when we have once taken to the way of vanity] ☞making what we call "the mercy of God" a pack horse [if I may use so coarse an expression] to carry us and our sins to heaven, upon the filthy rags* of our own [Pharisaic] righteousness.☜ Here we continue till Divine grace awakens us by the preaching of the Gospel, or by some other means, Ephesians 5:14. Being then roused to a serious consideration of our fallen state in Adam, and to a sensibility of the curse which we lie under, through our numerous breaches of [the second as well as of] the first covenant; after many fruitless attempts to remove that curse, by fulfilling the law [of innocence;] after many [faithless] endeavours to save ourselves by our own [anti-evangelical] works, and righteousness, ☞we despair at last of getting to heaven, by building a Babel with the "untempered mortar" of our own [fancied] sincerity, and the bricks of our wretched good works, [or rather of our splendid sins.]☜ And leaving the impassable road of the covenant of works, we begin to seek [as condemned criminals] the way which God's free mercy has opened for lost sinners in Jesus Christ, Acts 2:37; Philippians 3:6, &c.

This "new and living way," [for I may call it by the name which the apostle emphatically gives to the last dispensation of the Gospel,] Hebrews 10:19, 20, is the new covenant, the covenant of grace [in its various editions or dispensations. For, if the Christian edition is called new in opposition to the Jewish, all the editions together may well be.] called new, in opposition to the old covenant, the covenant of works [made with Adam before the fall.] It is also termed Gospel, that is, glad tidings, because [†with different degrees of evidence] it brings comfortable news of free salvation in Christ, to all that see they are undone in themselves.

---

* (7.) Here that expression is used in the Scriptural sense.

† (8.) This and the preceding clauses are added to guard the doctrine of the Gospel dispensations, of which I had but very confused views eleven years ago. (See Vol. 1, Third Check, p. 140.) Leaning then too much toward Calvinism, I fancied, at times at least, that the Gospel was confined within the narrow channel of its last dispensation; which was as absurd as if I had imagined that the swell of our rivers at high water is all the ocean. But turning to my Bible, and "reviewing the whole affair," I clearly see that the Jewish and Christian Gospel are not the everlasting Gospel, but only two of its brightest dispensations. Should the reader ask me what I mean by "the everlasting Gospel," when I consider it in its full latitude, I answer, that I mean with St. Paul, "The riches of God's goodness, forbearance, and long suffering,

Creeds and Scripture Scales

☞The second covenant, then, or the Gospel, is a dispensation of free grace and mercy [not only to little children, of whom is the kingdom of heaven, but also] to poor, lost, helpless sinners, who, seeing and feeling themselves condemned by the law [of innocence,] and utterly unable to obtain justification upon the terms of the first covenant, come to [a merciful God through] Jesus Christ [the light of men, according to the helps afforded them in the dispensations which they are under,] to seek in him [and from him those merits and] that righteousness which they have not in themselves. For the Son of God, being both God and man in one person; and by the invaluable sacrifice of himself upon the cross, having suffered the punishment due to all our breaches of the law [of works;] and by his most holy life having answered all the demands of the first covenant* "God can be just, and the justifier of him that

---

leading men to repentance" for Christ's sake, who in all ages is the "Saviour of the world." Yea, and the severe strokes of his gracious providence driving them to it. I dare not insinuate that Jonah, one of the most successful preachers in the world, was not a Gospel preacher, when he stirred up all the people of Nineveh to repentance by the fear of impending destruction; and that St. John the divine was a stranger to true divinity when he gave us the following account of the manner in which a celestial evangelist preached the everlasting Gospel: "I saw another angel having the everlasting Gospel to preach unto them that dwell on the earth, and to every nation, and kindred, and tongue, and people, [here is free grace!] saying, with a loud voice, Fear God, and give glory to him, for the hour of his judgment," as well as of his mercy, "is come: and worship him that made heaven and earth, and the sea, and the fountains of waters." Here is, if I am not mistaken, the Gospel according to which many shall come from the east, and from the west, and shall sit down at the heavenly feast with the father of the faithful, when the unloving Pharisees shall be thrust out notwithstanding their great ado about absolute election. This note will probably touch the apple of my reader's eye, if he be a rigid Predestinarian. But if he be offended, I entreat him to consider, whether his love does not bear some resemblance to the charity of those strong Predestinarians of old, those monopolizers of God's election, who despised poor "sinners of the Gentiles." How violent was their prejudice! They vastly admired our Lord's sermon at Nazareth, till he touched the sore that festered in their strait-laced breast. But no sooner did he insinuate that their election was not yet made sure, and that the poor Pagan widow of Serepta, and Naaman the Syrian were not absolute reprobates, than "they were filled with wrath, and rose up, and thrust him out of the city, and led him to the brow of the hill, that they might cast him down headlong" He had touched their great Diana, and therefore, to be sure, he had committed the unpardonable sin; he had spoken treason, heresy, blasphemy. (See Luke 4:28.)

* (9.) Although there were some very unguarded passages in my original sermon, yet what was unguarded in one place was in a great degree guarded in another. Thus even in this paragraph, which is the first that Mr. Hill produces in his extract, by saying that "Christ has answered all the demands of the FIRST covenant" for believers, I indirectly assert, that he has not answered the demands of the SECOND; and that, according to the Gospel, we must personally repent, believe, and obey, to be finally accepted: the covenant of grace insisting as much upon the works of faith, as the covenant of works did upon the works of the law of innocence, in order to our continuance and progress in the Divine favour. A doctrine this, which is the ground of the Minutes, the quintessence of the Checks, and the downfall of Antinomianism. It was only with respect to the covenant of works and to the law of innocence that I said in the next paragraph, transposed by Mr. Hill, "This obedience, when we are united to Christ by a Faith of the operation of God, is accepted instead of our own." How greatly then does he mistake me, when he supposes I asserted that the personal, Adamic, and (in one sense) anti-evangelical obedience of Christ, which sprang neither from Gospel faith nor from Gospel repentance, is

believes in Jesus," Romans 3:26. ℗ Therefore, If a sinner, whose mouth is stopped, and who has nothing to pay, pleads from the heart the atoning blood of Christ, [and supposing he never heard that precious name, if according to his light he implores Divine mercy, for the free exercise of which Christ's blood has made way,] not only God will not "deliver him to the tormentors," but will "frankly forgive him all," Luke 7:41, &c.

☞ Herein then consists the great difference between the first and the second covenant. Under the first, an absolute, unsinning, universal obedience in our own persons is required; and such obedience we [in our fallen state] can never perform. Under the second covenant, this obedience [to the law of innocence, payed by, and] in our surety Christ Jesus, when we are united to him by a faith of the operation of God, is accepted instead of our own. ℗ For [as our sins were transferred upon the Redeemer's guiltless head,] so his merits are brought home to our guilty souls by the powerful operation of Divine grace through faith; and being thus "complete in Christ,"* [*with regard to the fulfilling of the* FIRST *covenant*,] we can "rejoice in God, who has made him unto us wisdom, righteousness, sanctification, and redemption." [I say, *with regard to the fulfilling of the* FIRST *covenant*, to guard against the error of thousands,

---

accepted instead of the personal, penitential, evangelical obedience of believers! It is just here that the Calvinists turn aside from the truth to make void the law of Christ and follow Antinomian dotages. Because Christ has fulfilled the Adamic law of innocence for us, they fancy that he has also fulfilled his own evangelical law of Gospel obedience, according to which we must stand or fall, when "by our words we shall be justified, and by our words we shall be condemned."

* (10.) If I say that penitent believers are complete in Christ, with respect to the first covenant, I do not intimate that fallen believers, who "crucify the Son of God afresh," may even commit deliberate murder, and remain "complete in him," or (rather as the original means also) "filled with him." Far be the horrid insinuation from the pen and heart of a Christian. I readily grant that the true believers are not less dead to the Adamic law of innocence, than to the ceremonial law of Moses; and that with respect to it, they heartily say as David, "Enter not into judgment with thy servant, O Lord, for in thy sight shall no man living be justified." But mistake me not; I would not insinuate that they are lawless, or only under a rule of life, which they may break without endangering their salvation. No: they "are under the law of Christ, the law of liberty, the law of the Spirit of life, the royal law" of Gospel holiness; and according to this law they shall all be rewarded or punished in the day of judgment. Although this law admits of repentance after a fall, at least during the day of salvation; and although it does not condemn us for not obeying above our present measure of power; yet it does not make the least allowance for wilful sin, any more than the Adamic law; for St. James informs a believer that "if he offend in one point, he is guilty of all." And indeed our Lord's parable confirms this awful declaration. The favoured servant, who had the immense debt of "ten thousand talents forgiven him," sinned against Christ's law only in one point, namely, in refusing to have mercy on his fellow servant, as his Lord had had compassion upon him: and for that one offence he was delivered to the tormentors, as notoriously guilty of breaking the whole law of liberty and love. "If he who despised the law of Moses perished under two or three witnesses, of how much sorer punishment shall he be thought worthy, who" despises the law of Christ! This is the ground of the Epistle to the Hebrews. But who considers? Who believes that the Son of God will command even the unprofitable servant to be cut asunder? "When the Son of man cometh, shall he find faith upon earth?" Lord! help my unbelief.

who vainly imagine that Christ has fulfilled the terms of the second covenant for us, and talk of finished salvation, just as if our Lord had actually repented of our sins, believed in his own blood, and fulfilled his own evangelical law in our stead; a fatal error this, which makes Christians lawless, represents Christ as the minister of sin, and arms the Antinomian fiend with a dreadful axe to fell the trees of righteousness, and cut down the very pillars of the house of God.]

From what has been observed, it follows, that before any one can believe [to salvation] in the Gospel sense of the word, he must be "convinced of sin" by the Spirit of God, John 16:8. He must feel himself a guilty, lost, and helpless sinner, unable to recover the favour and image of God by his own strength and righteousness, Acts 2:37, 38.

This conviction and sense of guilt make the sinner "come travelling and heavy laden to Christ," earnestly claiming the rest which he offers to weary souls, Matthew 11:28. This rest the mourner seeks with the contrite publican in the constant use of all the means of grace; endeavouring to "bring forth fruit meet for repentance," till the same Spirit, that had convinced him of sin, and alarmed his drowsy conscience, "convinces him also of righteousness," John 16:8; that is, shows him the all sufficiency of the Saviour's [merits or] righteousness to swallow up his [former* sins and] unrighteousness; and the infinite value of Christ's meritorious death to atone for his [past†] unholy life; enabling him to "believe with the heart," and consequently to feel that he has an interest in the Redeemer's blood and righteousness; [or, that he is savingly interested in the merit of all that the Son of God suffered, did, and continues to do for us.]

This lively faith, this "faith‡ working by love," is "that which is imputed for righteousness," Romans 4:3, and that whereby a soul is born of God, [according to

---

* (11.) Without the words "former" and "past," the sentence leaned toward Antinomianism. It gave fallen believers room to conclude that their "future" or "present" unholy lives were unconditionally atoned for; contrary to St. Paul's guarded Gospel, "God hath sent forth Christ to be a propitiation, to declare his righteousness for the remission of sin's that are past." Here is no pleasing inuendo, that the present or future sins of Laodicean backsliders "are for ever and for ever cancelled."

† (12.) This is the very doctrine of the Minutes and of the Checks. Is it not astonishing that Mr. Hill should desire me to publish my sermon, as the "best confutation" of both!

‡ (13.) The judicious reader will easily perceive that the additions made to this, and some other paragraphs of my old sermon, are intended to guard the inferior dispensations of the Gospel. Are there not degrees of saving faith, inferior to the faith of the Christian Gospel? And are not those degrees of faith consistent with the most profound ignorance of the history of our Lord's sufferings, and consequently of any explicit knowledge of the atonement? Although mankind in general had some consciousness of guilt, and a confused idea of propitiatory sacrifices; and although all the Jewish sacrifices and prophecies pointed to the great atonement; yet how few, even among the pious Jews, seem to have had a clear belief that the Messiah would "put away sin by the sacrifice of himself!" How unreasonable is it then to confine the Gospel to the explicit knowledge of Christ's atoning sufferings, to which both the prophets and apostles were once such strangers! Does not St. Peter intimate that "the prophets searched" to little purpose, "what the Spirit signified, when it testified beforehand the sufferings of Christ;" since "it was revealed to them, that not unto themselves, but unto us, they did minister the things which are now reported" in the Christian Gospel? 1 Peter 1:11, 12. And how absurd is it to suppose that

the[*] Christian dispensation of the Gospel,] 1 John 5:1. By this faith the [Christian] believer being [strongly] united to Christ, as a member to the body, becomes entitled to [a much larger share in] the benefit of all that our Lord did and suffered; and in consequence of this [strong] vital union with him, who is the source of all goodness, he derives a [degree of] power, till then unknown, to do good works, truly so called; as a graft, which is [strongly] united to the stock that bears it, draws from it new sap, and power to bring forth fruit in [greater] abundance.

[O thou that professest the Christian faith, especially,] "show me thy faith by thy works," says an apostle: that is, show me that thou art grafted in Christ [according to the Christian dispensation] by serving God with all thy strength; by doing all the good thou canst to the souls and bodies of men with cheerfulness; by suffering wrong and contempt with meekness; by slighting earthly joys, mortifying fleshly lusts, having thy conversation in heaven, and panting every hour after a closer union with Christ, the life of all believers. If thou dost not bring forth these fruits, thou art not a Christian; thou art not "in Christ a new creature," 2 Corinthians 5:17. Thou mayest talk of faith, and suppose that thou believest; but give me leave to tell

---

nothing is Gospel but a doctrine, which the first preachers of the Christian Gospel knew little or nothing of, even while they preached the Gospel under our Lord's immediate direction? Did not John the Baptist exceed in evangelical knowledge "all that were born of women?" Were the apostles much inferior to him when they had been three years in Christ's school? Did not our Lord say to them. "Blessed are your eyes, for they see, and your ears, for they hear; for verily many prophets and righteous men have desired to see the things that ye see, and have not seen them; and to hear the things that ye hear, and have not heard them?" Again: did he not testify, that in general they had justifying faith, i.e. faith working by love? Did he not say, "Now are ye clean through the word which I have spoken unto you: the Father himself loveth you, because you have loved me, and believed that I came forth from God?" Nay, did he not send them two and two to preach, "The kingdom of heaven is at hand: repent and believe the Gospel?" And would he have sent them to preach a Gospel to which they were utter strangers? But were they not perfectly strangers to what passes now for the only Gospel? Had they the least idea that their Master's blood was to be shed for them, even after he had said, "This is my blood of the New Testament, which is shed for you and for many, for the remission of sins?" When he spoke to them of his sufferings, were not they so far from believing in the atonement which he was about to make, that they were offended at the very idea? Is not this evident from the words of Peter, their chief speaker, who "began to rebuke him, saying, Be it far from thee, Lord; this shall not happen unto thee?" i.e. we do not yet see the need of thy blood. Nay, when Christ had actually shed it, and the atoning work was finished, far from having the least notion about what is called "finished salvation," and "Gospel," in our day, did they not suppose that all their hopes were blasted, saying, "We trusted that it had been he who should have redeemed Israel?" Luke 24:21. Thus the very payment of their ransom made them despair of redemption; — so great was their ignorance of the doctrine of the atonement, notwithstanding their Gospel knowledge, which far exceeded that of most patriarchs and prophets! From these observations may I not conclude: (1.) That an explicit knowledge of Christ's passion and atonement is the prerogative of the Christian Gospel advancing toward perfection? And (2.) That those who make it essential to the everlasting Gospel most dreadfully curtail it, and indirectly doom to hell, not only all the righteous Jews, Turks, and heathens, who may now be alive; but also almost all the believers who died before our Lord's crucifixion, and some of. the disciples themselves after his resurrection?

[*] See previous footnote.

thee, that [unless thou art in the case of the eunuch, who searched the Scriptures even upon a journey; or of Cornelius, who sought the Lord in alms givings and prayer;] if thou believest at all, [I fear] it is with the drunkard's faith, the whoremonger's faith, the devil's faith, James 2:19. From such a faith may God deliver us, and give us, instead of this counterfeit, the faith once delivered unto the saints, the mystery of faith kept in a pure conscience!" Get it, O sinner, who bearest a Christian name, and Christ and heaven are thine: [but if thou] die without it, [whether it be by continuing in thy present sin and unbelief, or by "making shipwreck of thy faith,"] thou diest the second death; thou sinkest in the bottomless pit for evermore, Mark 16:16.

Having thus given you an account of both covenants, and laid before you the condition [or term] of each, namely, for the first a sinless, uninterrupted obedience to all the commands of the holy, spiritual, [and Adamic] law of God, performed by ourselves without the least [mediatorial assistance:] and for the second a lively faith in Christ, ["the light of the world," according to the Gospel dispensation we are under;] by which faith, the virtue of Christ's active and passive obedience to the law [of innocence] being imputed to us, and applied to our hearts, we are made "new creatures, born again," and "created in Christ Jesus unto good works," without which there can be no lively faith [under any of the Divine dispensations:] and having [by that important distinction of the two grand covenants] removed a great deal of rubbish out of the way, I hope it will not be difficult to prove, under the

SECOND HEAD,

That the way of salvation by such a lively faith only, or, which is the same, by the covenant of grace [alone,] is the one way that leads to life, according to the Bible and our articles of religion.

If you ask all the Pharisees, all the self-righteous heathens, Turks, Jews, and Papists in the world, which is the way of salvation? [with too many ignorant Protestants] they will answer, [without making the least mention of repentance and faith,] "Through doing good works, and leading a good life:" that is, "through the covenant of works;" flatly contrary to what I have proved in the first part of this discourse, namely, that "by the works of the law," by the first covenant, "shall no flesh living be justified," Galatians 2:16. Or if they have yet some sense of modesty, if they are not quite lost in pride, [supposing them Christians,] they will varnish over the blasphemy [which, I fear, is indirectly couched under their boasting speech,] with two or three words about God's mercy. "Why," say they, "it is to be hoped we shall all be saved by endeavouring to lead good lives, and do good works: and if that will not do, God's mercy in Christ will do the rest," which means neither more nor less than this: "We are still to be saved by the covenant of works, by putting on [sinful and guilty as we are] the robe of our own [Pharisaic, anti-evangelical, Christless] righteousness; and if it happen to be too short, or to have some holes, Christ [whom we are willing to make the *Omega*, but not the *Alpha*; the *last*, but not the *first*] will, in mercy, tear his spotless robe [of merits] to patch up and lengthen ours." [And this they say, it is to be feared, without the least degree of genuine repentance toward God, and heart-felt faith in our Lord Jesus Christ.] O how many dream of getting to heaven in this fool's coat, [this absurd dress of a Christian Pharisee!] How many, by thus blending the two covenants, which are as incompatible as fire and water, try to make for themselves a third covenant, that never existed but in their proud imagination! In a word, how many are there who say or think we must be saved partly by [the covenant of] works, and partly by [the covenant of] grace! giving the lie to God and my text! overturning at once the Gospel and Protestantism! No, no. If "a remnant is saved," it is by the covenant of grace; and if by grace, then it is no more [by the covenant] of works; otherwise grace is no more [Gospel] grace. But if it be [by the covenant] of works, then it is no more [Gospel] grace; otherwise work is no more work; [for the moment obedience is "the work of faith," it can no more be opposed to faith and Gospel grace, than the fruit of a tree can be opposed to the tree, and the sap by which it is produced.]

But "to the law and the testimony." Do the oracles of God, or the writings of our reformers, direct us for salvation to the covenant of works, or to a third covenant of [anti-evangelical*] works and [evangelical] grace patched up together? Do they not entirely and invariably point us to the covenant of grace alone?

Hear first the word of the Lord: "He that believeth on the Son [according to the light of the dispensation he is under] hath everlasting life. He that believeth not, shall not see life, but the wrath of God abideth on him," John 3:36. When the trembling jailer cries out, "What must I do to be saved?" Paul and Silas answer, "Believe in the Lord Jesus Christ, and thou shalt be saved," Acts 16:31. "God so loved the world," says St. John, "that he gave his only begotten Son, that whosoever believeth in him should not perish, but have everlasting life," John 3:16. "By grace," says St. Paul, "ye are [initially] saved through faith, and that not of yourselves, it is the gift of God: not by [the covenant of] works, [nor yet by the proper merit of any works,] lest any man should boast," [as the Pharisee; all who despise the way of faith, and put the instrumental causes in the room of the first and properly meritorious cause of our salvation, being no better than boasting Pharisees.] For "to him that worketh [without applying to the throne of grace, as a hell-deserving sinner] is the reward not reckoned of [evangelical] grace, but of [legal] debt. But to him that worketh not" [upon the footing of the first covenant;] to him who sees that he cannot [escape hell, much less] get heaven, by [setting] his good works, [if he has any, on the Redeemer's throne;] "but believeth [as a lost sinner,] on him that justifieth the ungodly; his faith is counted for righteousness:" he is saved by [obedient] *faith*, which is the *condition* of the covenant of grace, Romans 4:4.

Thus speak the Scriptures, and blessed be God! thus speak also our liturgy and articles.

In the absolution the priest declares that [in the day of conversion] "God pardoneth and absolveth," that is, sayeth, F not those [moralists] who [being ashamed

---

* (14.) I add the word anti-evangelical to point out the rise of the mistake of stone pious Protestants, who, being carried away by an injudicious zeal for the first Gospel axiom, and misled by the conciseness of the apostle's style, get upon the pinnacle of the Antinomian Babel, and thence decry all works in general; unhappily quoting St. Paul in confirmation of their error: although it is evident that the apostle never excluded from the Gospel plan of salvation by grace any works but the "works of unbelief," and sometimes pleaded for the "works of faith," and for the immense rewards with which they shall be crowned, in far stronger terms than St. James himself; denouncing "indignation and wrath, tribulation and anguish upon every soul of man that neglects them, or doth evil," Romans 2.

to repent, and scorning to believe the Gospel, endeavour to] lead a good life, to get a pardon [by their own merits,] E but "all those who truly repent, and unfeignedly believe in his holy Gospel;" that is, all those who, by "true repentance," renounce [together with their sins] all dependence upon the covenant of works; and by a "faith unfeigned" flee for refuge only to [God's mercy in Christ, which is so kindly offered to sinners in] the covenant of grace. Hence it is that, in the communion service, we are commanded to pray, that "by the merits and death of Christ, and through faith in his blood, we and all the whole Church may obtain remission of sins, and all other benefits of his passion."

This holy doctrine is most clearly maintained, and strongly established in the ninth, tenth, eleventh, twelfth, and thirteenth of our articles of religion. And upon these five pillars it will remain unshaken as long as the Church of England shall stand.

The ninth shows that since the fall of Adam "the corruption of our nature deserves God's wrath and damnation;" so that [being considered without the free gift that came upon all men in Christ unto justification of life, Romans 5:18,] we are, of ourselves, evil trees ready for the axe of death, and the fire of hell.

The tenth adds that we cannot consequently get grace and glory, that is, save ourselves by bearing good fruit, [through our original powers, according to the first covenant,] because an evil tree can only produce evil fruit: [and that "we have no power to, do works acceptable to God without the grace of God by Christ preventing us," according to the second covenant.]

The eleventh affirms that we are saved, that is, accepted of God, changed, and made good trees, trees of the Lord's planting, "only for the merit of our Lord Jesus Christ, by faith, and not for our own works and deservings;" F as we can do no good works before we are [at least] in a state of [initial] salvation. E "Make the tree good," says our Lord, "and its fruit shall be good." [In our infancy we are freely blessed with the seed of light from "Christ, the light of men;" and at the same time we are freely justified from the damning guilt of original corruption. As we grow up, and personally repent and "believe in the light" after a personal fall, we are again freely pardoned. Thus, so long at least as "the accepted time," and "the day of salvation" last,] God has first respect to our persons in Christ, and then to our sacrifices or works, [of faith,] Hebrews 11:4; Genesis 4:4, 5.

The twelfth declares that good works, works which necessarily follow free justification, do not serve "to put away [or atone for] sins;" but to declare the truth of our faith: "insomuch that by them a lively faith may be as evidently known as a tree discerned by the fruit." A tree is first planted, and then it brings forth fruit. ☞A believer is first saved, [i.e. freely made partaker of initial salvation,] and then he does good works. ☜ [A lively faith necessarily produces them, though a believer does not necessarily persevere in a lively faith.] If he do them not, his faith is dead; it is not [now a living and] saving faith; he is no [longer an obedient] believer; [but an Antinomian or an apostate, a Demas or a Judas.]

The thirteenth insists upon that point of doctrine which confounds the Pharisees in all ages, and lays our virtuous pride in the dust before God: namely, that [when we have sinned away the justification* of infants] ☞ "works done before [that] justification, [is restored,] before faith" alone has put us [again] into a state of [initial] salvation not only "do not fit us to receive grace, but have in themselves the nature of sin," [nay, the worst of sins, spiritual pride and Pharisaic hypocrisy,] and consequently deserve death, the wages of sin, so far [are they] from meriting grace and glory. ☜

This is agreeable to reason as well as to Scripture; for if, "of ourselves," as says our Church, [i.e. before any degree of grace is instilled into our infant hearts, or before God freely visits us again when we have personally fallen away from him,] "we cannot by our good works [so called] prepare ourselves to faith: if we are such crab trees as can bring forth no apples [Without the grace of God by Christ preventing us, that we may have a good will, and working with us when we have that good will," it is plain that] by producing as many crabs [i.e. as many works of unbelief] as [blaspheming] Paul before his conversion; and of as fine a colour and as large a size as those which the self-righteous Pharisee bore; we cannot change our own nature, nor force from ourselves the sweet fruit of one [truly] good work. "Many who have not the true faith," says our Church, "yet flourish in works of mercy. But they that shine in good works [so called] without faith, are like dead men, who have goodly and precious tombs:" or, to carry on the allegory of our reformers, the fine crabs which such people produce please the eye of the spectator, who thinks them good apples; but God, who sees their hearts, tastes in the deceitful fruit nothing but the sourness of a crab. Such crabs are the alms of whoremongers, the prayers of unjust persons, the public worship of swearers and drunkards, the tithes and fasts† of Pharisees, Isaiah 1:11, &c.

---

* (15.) Those who start at every expression they are not used to, will ask if our Church admits the justification of infants. I answer: Undoubtedly, since her clergy, by her direction, say over myriads of infants, "We yield thee hearty thanks, most merciful Father, that it has pleased thee to regenerate this infant with thy Holy Spirit, to receive him for thy own child," &c. And in her catechism she teaches all children to say, as soon as they can speak, "I heartily thank our heavenly Father that he hath called me to this state of salvation." If my objector urges that our Church puts those words only in the mouth of baptized children, I reply: True, because she instructs no others. But why does she admit to baptism all the children that are born within her pale? Does she not vindicate her practice in this respect, by an appeal to our Lord's kind command: "Let little children come unto me, and forbid them not, for of such is the kingdom of heaven?" This I had not considered, when I said, in my Appeal, that our Church returns thanks for the regeneration of baptized infants only [I should have said chiefly] upon a charitable supposition, &c. For it is evident that she does it also upon Christ's gracious declaration, Mark 10:13, &c, the precious Gospel of her office, upon which she comments in a manner most favourable to children; concluding her charge on the occasion by these words: — "Wherefore, we being thus persuaded of the good will of our heavenly Father toward this [unbaptized] infant, declared by his Son Jesus Christ, and nothing doubting." &c. These words I had not attended to when I wrote my Appeal. I take this first opportunity of acknowledging my mistake, which shall be rectified in the next edition.

† (16.) Here is a short enumeration of good works, so called, which I decry in this sermon. Had my opponent considered it, he would never have supposed that my discourse is "the best refutation" of what I have advanced in the Checks, in favour of the good works maintained by St. James and Mr. Wesley.

☞ Having thus shown you how self-righteous, unawakened sinners dream of salvation, either by the covenant of works or by a third imaginary covenant, in which two incompatible things [Pharisaical] works and [evangelical] grace, [antichristian] merits and mercy [in Christ] are jumbled together; and having proved by plain, unanswerable passages, and by the thirty-nine articles, that the Gospel and our Church show us salvation cannot be attained but under the second covenant, that is, by [obedient] faith only, and not by [the covenant of] works; I beg leave to recapitulate the whole in three articles, which contain the sum of the Gospel, and of the doctrine that I have constantly preached among you, and am determined to preach, God being my helper, till my tongue cleave to the roof of my mouth* [unless a flaw can be found] in any of them, by the word of God or the articles of our Church. ☜

Upon the proofs before advanced, I solemnly declare, and publicly affirm: 1. That there is no salvation to be attained by [the covenant of] works since the fall. The best man, having broken a hundred times the first covenant, deserves a hundred times damnation by his works, and can no more be saved from hell by his obedience to God's law [of innocence] than a thief can be saved from the gallows, by the civil law which condemns him to be hanged.

2. Respecting the primary and properly meritorious cause of our salvation, [from first to last,] "we are saved," as it is written in our eleventh article, "only for the merit of our Lord Jesus Christ by faith, and not for our works or deservings: and that [in the day of conversion] we are justified by faith only, is a most wholesome doctrine, and very full of comfort:" yea, the only doctrine that can melt down the hearts of sinners, and make them constantly zealous of all sorts of good works, [if it be not made to supersede justification of believers by the evidence of works, both in the day of trial and in the day of judgment. A doctrine this, which few Antinomians are daring enough directly to oppose.]

3. As all mankind are condemned by the covenant of works, "he that believeth not [in the light of his dispensation] being condemned already;" ☞ and as by the covenant of grace there is no salvation to be had but in Christ through faith: so there is no mixing these two covenants without renouncing Christ and his Gospel. He that stands with one foot upon the covenant of works, and with the other foot upon the covenant of grace; [he that talks of Divine mercy, while his heart continues as regardless of it as if he were sinless; he that ends his prayers by the name of Christ, while he remains unconcerned about his fallen state,] is in the most imminent danger of eternal ruin. ☜ He that says, "I will do first what I can to merit heaven — I will do my best — and Christ, I hope, will do the rest; and God, I trust, will have mercy

---

* (17.) The words enclosed in brackets are in my manuscript, and were written several years ago, when looking over my sermon I thought they savoured more of Christian modesty than those which Mr. Hill has in his copy: [and here I give a public challenge to any man living to find a flaw:] I challenge nobody now, but I promise that if any man living will be kind enough to show me my errors by plain Scripture and solid argument, he shall have my sincere thanks: for if I know my heart, pure and unmixed truth is the object of my desires and controversial pursuits.

upon me," is yet without God, and without Christ in the world; he knows neither the nature of God's law nor that of Christ's Gospel.

[This is, my dear hearers, the substance of the three articles which eleven years ago I publicly laid down in this church, as the ground of the doctrine which I had preached, and was determined still to preach among you. And I solemnly declare, that to this day I have not seen the least cause to reject any one of them as erroneous: though I must confess that I have found abundant reason particularly to guard the second against the daring attacks that Antinomians in principle, or in practice, make upon St. James' undefiled religion. To return:]

We are undoubtedly obliged to do what we can, and to use the means of grace at all [proper] times and in all [convenient] places; but to rest in those means [like the Pharisees;] to suppose that they will save us; and upon this supposition to be easy without the experience of [converting] grace in our hearts, is very absurd. It is a mistake as foolish as that of the man who supposes that his garden will be the most fruitful for pipes which convey no water; or that his body can be refreshed by empty cups.

The language of the penitent sinner is, "Lord, I pray, and hear [thy word!] I fast, and receive [the commemorative tokens of thy passion;] I give alms, and keep the Sabbath: but after all 'I am an unprofitable servant.' [I must 'work out my salvation with fear and trembling,' and yet] 'without thee I can do nothing,' I cannot change my heart; I cannot root up from my breast the desire of praise, the thirst of pleasure, and the hankering after gold, vanity, beauty, or sensual gratifications, which I continually feel; I cannot force my heart to repent, believe, and love: to be meek and lowly, calm and devout. Lord, deliver me from this body of death; Lord, save, or I perish."

Christ will have all the glory [worthy of him] or none. We must be* wholly saved by him, or lost for ever: [for although we must be "co- workers with him," by walking religiously in good works; and if we are not, we shall have our portion with the "workers of iniquity;" yet it is he that "worketh in us," as in moral agents, "both to will and to do of his good pleasure." It is he that appoints and blesses all the inferior means of our salvation; therefore all the glory properly and originally belongs to him alone.]

[All our pardons flow down to us in the streams of his precious blood. All our life, light, and power, are nothing but emanations from Him who is "the fountain of life, the Sun of righteousness, the wisdom and the power of God," and, in a word, "Jehovah our righteousness." All that gracious rewardableness of the works of faith, all that aptitude of our sprinkled obedience unto eternal life, all that being worthy which he himself condescends to speak of, Revelation 3:4, and Luke 20:35, spring not only from his gracious appointment, but from his overflowing merits. A comparison will illustrate my meaning.]

[You see the cheerful light that flows in upon us through those windows, and renders the glass as bright as this spring day. You know that this brightness *in* the glass is not *from* the glass, which was totally dark some hours ago; a fit emblem THEN

---

* (18.) See the first note upon the word MERELY. N. B. Here begins the greatest addition to my old sermon. It is in favour of free grace, and runs through fourteen paragraphs.

of "the works of darkness," the works of unbelief; such works being as much devoid of rewardableness, as those panes were of light at midnight. Let us not forget, then, that if our works are graciously rewarded, it is only when they are the works of faith, whose peculiar property it is freely to admit the merits of Christ, and the beams of the "Sun of righteousness;" just as it is the property of the transparent matter, which composes these windows, necessarily to admit the genial warmth and cheerful rays of the natural sun.]

[If I admire a poor widow, gladly casting her last mite into the treasury; or a martyr, generously giving his body to blood-thirsty executioners; it is only because their lively faith receives, and their pure charity reflects, the light of Him who, for our sake, became poor; and, for our sake, joyfully surrendered to his bloody murderers. But although this image of our Lord's meritorious holiness and sufferings does great honour to the saints who reflect it; yet the praise of it originally and properly belongs to him alone.]

[An illustration will make you sensible of it. You have seen a glass perfectly reflecting the beauty of a person placed over against it; you have admired the elegant proportion of features which composed her beauty: but did you ever see any man so void of good sense as to suppose that the beauty was originally in the glass which reflected it; or that the lovely appearance existed without depending on its original; or that it robbed the living beauty of her peculiar glory? And shall any, on the one hand, be so full of voluntary humility as to maintain that Christ is dishonoured by the derived worthiness of the works of faith, whose office it is to receive, embrace, and trust in the Redeemer's original and proper merit? Shall any, on the other hand, be so full of Pharisaic pride as to fancy that the distinguishing excellence of our good works, if we have any, springs from, or terminates in ourselves? No, my brethren. As rivers flow back to the sea, and lose themselves in that immense reservoir of waters, whence they had their origin; so let all the "rewardable condecency"* of our evangelical obedience flow back to, and lose itself in the boundless and bottomless ocean of our Lord's original and proper merits.]

He, he alone is worthy — properly worthy! Worthy, — supremely "worthy is the Lamb that was slain!" Let us then always say, with the humble men of old, "Our goods are nothing unto thee," our good works cannot possibly benefit thee. "What have we," great God, "that we have not received" from thy gracious hand? And shall we keep back part of thy incontestable property, and impiously wear the robes of praise? Far be the spiritual sacrilege from every pious breast! As "thine is all the kingdom and power; so thine be all the glory for ever and ever!"

[If, therefore, my brethren, we have the honour of "filling up that which is behind of the afflictions of Christ in our flesh, for his body's sake, which is the Church: if we are *even* offered upon the sacrifice of *each other's* faith;" let us dread as blasphemy the wild thought of completing, and perfecting our Lord's infinitely complete and perfect atonement. As God, who is infinite in himself, was not made

---

* (19.) I need not inform my judicious readers that I use the uncouth, barbarian expression of Dr. Owen, "rewardable condecency," to convey the meaning of our Lord, when he graciously speaks of our meriting or being worthy. If sick persons will not take a draught but out of a certain cup, made in the height of a queer fashion, we must please them for their good.

greater by the immense bulk of created worlds; nor brighter by the shining perfections of countless myriads of angels and suns: so the infinite value of that "one offering, by which Christ has for ever perfected [in atoning merits] them that are sanctified," is not augmented by the works of all the saints, and the blood of all the martyrs. And as the heat of the fire adds nothing to the nature of the fire, or the beams of the sun to the sun; so the righteousness of the saints does not increase that of Christ, nor adds their holiness any thing to his personal excellence.]

[Keep we then at that awful distance from the gulf which self-righteous Pharisees set between themselves and the Justifier of those who, like the contrite publican, are sensible of their ungodliness. With indignation rise we against the delusions of the Romanists, who countenance the absurd and impious doctrine of indulgences, by the worse than Pharisaic doctrine of their works of supererogation. Let us not only receive and defend in a Scriptural manner the important articles of our Church which I have already mentioned; but with undaunted courage before men, and with penitential contrition before God, let us stand to our fourteenth article, which teaches us, after our Lord, to say before the throne of inflexible justice, refulgent holiness, and dazzling glory, "We are unprofitable servants," even "when we have done all that is commanded us." In point of strict equivalence, our best works of faith, our holiest duties, cannot properly merit the least heavenly reward. But, O! may the humbling truth keep us for ever in the dust! in point of strict justice our every bad work properly deserves infernal torments.]

[Therefore, while we earnestly contend for practical, pure, undefiled religion, take we the greatest care not to obscure the genuine doctrines of grace. With meekness let us maintain, unto blood, the honour of our Saviour's merits, against the hypocritical sons of virtuous pride, who cast the destructive veil of unbelief over the invaluable sacrifice of his body. And in our little sphere let every one of us testify, with the beloved disciple, "God so loved the world, that he gave his only begotten Son, in whom he is well pleased" with us; and for whose sake he works in us to repent, believe, and obey; when we yield to the drawings of his grace, and concur with his Spirit in the work of our salvation.]

[Through that dear Redeemer, then, we receive all the favours which the Father of mercies bestows upon us. Are our hearts softened? It is through the influence of his preventing grace. Are our sins blotted out? It is through the sprinkling of his atoning blood. Are our souls renewed? It is by the communications of his powerful righteousness. Are we numbered among God's adopted children, and made partakers of his loving Spirit? It is through a faith that receives him as the "light of the world," and the "life of men."]

[The very graces which the Spirit works in us, and the fruits of holiness which those graces produce in our hearts and lives, are accepted only for Christ's sake. It is he who presents them to God, sprinkled with his precious blood, and perfumed with his meritorious intercession. Nor are the defects of our holiest things any other way atoned for than by the full, perfect, and sufficient sacrifice, oblation, and satisfaction which he made upon the cross for the sins of the whole world.]

[For Christ's sake God has annexed certain rewards of grace and glory to the works of faith which Christ's Spirit excites us to; and, I repeat it, for the sake of Christ only we receive the rewards promised to humble, evangelical, spinkled obedience. All Christian believers say, "Not we but the grace of God in Christ." So far as their tempers and actions have been good, they cry out, "Thou hast wrought all our works in us." They all shout, "Christ for us," and "Christ in us, the hope of glory." They all ascribe "salvation to the Lamb:" and while they "cast their crowns of righteousness" and glory at his feet, they join in the grand chorus of the Church: "To him that loved us, and washed us from our sins in his own blood, and hath made us kings and priests unto God and his Father, to him be glory and dominion for ever and ever." Thus all is Christ; nothing without, nothing beside him. In a word, he is to believers, as the apostle justly calls him, "ALL IN ALL."]

[Indeed, in maintaining the doctrine of free grace he cannot but go even farther than our mistaken brethren, who suppose themselves the only advocates for it. They must forgive me if I cannot be of their sentiment, when they insinuate that they shall absolutely and necessarily be saved: for as reason dictates that absolute necessity vanishes before free grace; so Christ charges his dearest elect to "fear God" as a righteous Judge, who "CAN cast body and soul into hell;" yea, who can do it *justly*. No gracious promise therefore is made them, whose fulfilment in heaven, as well as upon earth, is not all of grace as well as of truth, and all through the merits of Christ.]

[O ye precious merits of my Saviour, and thou free grace of my God! I, for one, shall want you as long as the sun or moon endureth. Nay, when those luminaries shall cease to shine, I shall wrap myself in you; my transported soul shall grasp you; my insatiate spirit shall plunge into your unfathomable depths; and while I shall run the never-ending circle of my blessed existence, my overflowing bliss shall spring from you; my grateful heart shall leap through your impulse; my exulting tongue shall shout your praise; and I shall strike my golden harp to your eternal honour.]

[Nay, this very day I publicly set my seal again to the important truths contained in the following scriptures:] "There is no other name [no other deserving person] under heaven, given to men whereby we may [properly] be saved" in whole or in part, but only the name [or person] of Jesus Christ. "He trod the wine press of God's wrath alone, and of the people there was none with him. He alone is a Saviour, and there is none beside him." ["If he that converts a sinner" is said to "save a soul from death," it is because he has the honour of being the Saviour's agent, and not because he is "the original cause" of any man's salvation.]

☞ Wo then to those who teach sinners the double way, the Pharisaic way, the* [self-righteous] way of salvation, partly by man's [anti-Christian] merits, [according to the first covenant,] and partly by the [proper] merits of Jesus Christ [according to the second.] "If we, or an angel from heaven," says St. Paul, "preach any other Gospel unto you than that which we have preached," namely, that "we are saved [i.e. pardoned, absolved, and sanctified] by grace, through faith, [which worketh by love,] and that not of ourselves, [not without an atoning priest and the Spirit helping our infirmities,] it is the gift of God — let him be accursed," Galatians 1:8. ☜

---

* (20.) Eleven years ago I said "the Popish way:" I drop the expression now as savouring of Protestant bigotry. Though the Papists lean in general to that extreme, yet many of them have known and taught the way of salvation by a faith that interests us in the Redeemer's merits. Many have discovered and attacked self righteousness in its most deceitful appearances. Many have lived and died in the most profound humility. I would no more be a bitter Protestant, damning all the Papists in a lump, than a bitter Papist, anathematizing all Protestants without exception.

The Works of John Fletcher

☞ He really denies his Saviour, and tears the seamless robe of Christ's righteousness, who patches it with the rags of his own [anti-evangelical, faithless] righteousness. [Or, to speak without metaphor, he denies our Lord's meritorious fulfilling of the law of innocence, he despises the Saviour's complete observance of the Adamic law of works, who, being forgetful of his aggravated guilt, and regardless of his palpable impotence, refuses to submit to the law of faith, and to embrace the covenant of grace with an ardour becoming a poor, self-condemned, lost, and undone sinner. Nay, I go farther still:] he takes away [or obstructs] all the efficacy of Christ's atoning blood, who pretends to mend it by adding thereto the filthy drops of his own [fancied] goodness, [in order to make a more complete satisfaction to Divine justice.]☜

"It is mere blasphemy against Divine mercy," says our Church, "and great derogation from the blood shedding of our Saviour, to suppose that our works can deserve, or purchase to us remission of sins," and consequently salvation. No: "it is bestowed on believers of the free grace and mercy of God, by the mediation of the blood of his Son Jesus Christ, without merit or deserving on their part," [although their final justification is not without the evangelical worthiness which their faith derives from that dear Redeemer.] (*Homily on Fasting.*)

To conclude: by the covenant of works man has all the glory of his own salvation. Faith [in a Redeemer] is made of no effect, Christ is entirely set aside, and works are placed in the Mediator's throne. According to the imaginary, mixed covenant of salvation by our own good works, [so called, or, to speak with propriety, by our own faithless, hypocritical works] mended, [as we think,] with [some unscriptural notions and expressions about] Christ's merits; man has the first share of the glory; Christ has only man's leavings: [the Redeemer is allowed to be the last, but not the first: the Omega, but not the Alpha: the two covenants are confounded;] works and faith, [or rather, faithless works and faith, graceless works and grace] contrary to my text, and indeed to common sense, come in together for a part of the honour [as if they were the primary, meritorious cause of our salvation; whereas the good works of faith themselves are at the best only the secondary, evidencing cause of our final salvation.¨]

---

* (21.) Should a prejudiced reader charge me with having mixed the two covenants in my Checks, in opposition to the doctrine of this discourse: should he say that I have taught the double way of works and faith, i.e. of faithless works and faith, I protest against the groundless assertion, and appeal to all my candid readers, whether I have not constantly pointed out the one Gospel way to heaven, the good old way of faith, which worketh by love. An unfeigned faith in Christ, according to the light of our dispensation, a faith shown by evangelical works, is the Scriptural condition of the covenant of grace, which I have all along, insisted upon; whereas anti-evangelical works, helped out by a reigned faith, are the imaginary condition of the mixt, fantastic covenant, against which I so justly bore my testimony eleven years ago, and against which I bear it now, fully designing so to do, "God being my helper, till my tongue cleave to the roof of my mouth." As some persons through the force of prejudice, and others through some natural defect in their understanding cannot see any difference between "the way of faith working by obedient love," which I point out in the Checks, and "the way of works helped out by feigned faith," which I decry in this discourse, I shall, by a plain illustration, endeavour to show them the amazing difference. A good king pities two condemned malefactors just turned off; and, at the prince's request, not only gets them cut down from the

But by the Gospel all is set in a most beautiful order and exquisite harmony. The merits and sufferings of Christ, the Redeemer of the world, are the only meritorious, [or, as says our Church, "original] cause" of our salvation. The glory is entirely ascribed to him; and he alone sits upon the throne as a Saviour; while proud man has his mouth stopped, or opens it only in the dust to extol redeeming love. — Faith, whose office it is continually to borrow the merits of Christ, and to receive the quickening power of his Spirit; ☞faith, I say, is the only instrumental cause of our free salvation, [in the day of conversion;] it receives Christ and salvation as the hand of a beggar receives an alms. ☜ And as for good works, [properly so called,] so far are they from being left out of the Gospel plan, that they have a MOST EMINENT place in it. ☞They are the DECLARATIVE CAUSE* of our free justification [both in the day of trial and in the day of judgment:] a constant, uniform course of all sorts of good works, with a holy and heavenly-minded conversation, being the only evidence of a lively and saving faith, [when it has time to show itself by external works.]

---

gallows, but after restoring them by proper assistance to a degree of strength, he sets them up in a genteel business, which they are to carry on under the constant direction of the prince. One of them, who is a publican, deeply conscious of his crimes, and wondering at the prince's condescension, does with docility and diligence whatsoever he is commanded, frequently complaining that he does so little, and expressing the greatest thankfulness, not only for his life, but for the health, light tools, and skill he works with. The other, who is a Pharisee, forgets that he has been reprieved from the gallows. He is full of self importance and ingratitude; he wonders at the publican for making so much ado about the king's mercy, and the prince's favour. He pertly tells you that he does his duty; and that if he has been guilty of some faults, he thanks God they were not of a capital nature. He perpetually boasts of his diligence, and though he does nothing, or only spoils his work, by doing it entirely against the prince's directions, he says, that he is determined to maintain himself by his own industry; and that if he do not find it possible to get his living without help, he will condescend to accept some assistance from the prince to make both ends meet; but it shall be as little as he can help; for he does not love to be under an obligation to any body, no, not to the king himself. Now who does not see, that while the king graciously rewards the humble diligence of the penitent publican, he may justly punish the proud Pharisee for his wretched hypocritical obedience?. And that, when Mr. Wesley and I have sometimes contended for the works of the publican, and sometimes decried those of the Pharisee, we have only done the work of evangelists, and declared with the prophets and apostles of old that "God resisteth the proud and giveth grace to the humble;" and that "he will give grace and glory, and no good thing shall he withhold from them that live a godly life?" If this be an error, I ask, Whereto does it differ from that frequent and awful declaration of our Lord, "Whosoever shall exalt himself shall be abased; and he that shall humble himself shall be exalted?"

* (22.) The word CAUSE, left out by my opponent in his quotation of this part of my old sermon, evidently shows that even formerly I did not so far lean to Antinomianism as not to assert the absolute necessity of good works, in order to the eternal salvation of adults. For if works are the secondary cause of our final justification, they can no more be dispensed with, in the great day, than faith in the day of conversion, an effect necessarily supposing its cause. If therefore I call the justification of adults free, it is not to exclude faith and works, its instrumental causes in the day of conversion and judgment; but to intimate that all along we are primarily justified by Christ's merits, and that we never have one single grain of original worthiness.

Thus, [to sum up all in one sentence,] Christ alone [properly] merits, faith alone [properly] apprehends, and good works alone [properly] evidence salvation. Yea, they are the fruit of salvation [begun:] ✍ for [all works meet for repentance spring from the free justification and initial salvation in which We are put in our infancy; and] "the love of God shed abroad in *a believer's* heart by the Holy Ghost given unto him," is salvation itself; this love being the tree on which all [the external] good works [of real Christians] grow, and making our gracious heaven below, as it will make our glorious heaven above.

PART THIRD.

[SINCE I give good works, as I have just observed, a most eminent place in the Gospel plan, even the place of the evidences that will, under Christ, cause our eternal salvation, I may well] proceed to show the injustice or unreasonableness of those who accuse me of preaching against good works. For "he exclaims against good works; he runs down good works," is an objection [which is still at times] urged against my ministry.

[Although I confess with sorrow that, some years ago, when I had more zeal than prudence, I dropped among you some unguarded expressions, and did not always clearly distinguish between the "good works," so called, of unhumbled Pharisees, and the genuine obedience of penitent believers; yet I should wrong the truth, and undervalue my character as your minister, if I did not observe that, as professed Antinomians have always loathed the doctrine of a believer's justification by works, so the Pharisaical world has always abhorred the doctrine of a sinner's justification by faith. Hence it is that] the above-mentioned aspersion with abundance of cruel mockings, and pitiful false reports, have been in all ages the lot of all those who have [steadily] preached the Gospel of Christ, that is, the glad news of free salvation through [obedient] faith in his blood.

"We preach Christ crucified," says St. Paul, "to the Jews a stumbling 'block, and to the Greeks foolishness; but to them that believe, Christ the power and wisdom of God," 1 Corinthians 1:23. It is plain from this and several other passages in the epistles, that the primitive Christians suffered much reproach on this account. St. Peter exhorts them thus: "Have your conversation honest among the Gentiles, that whereas they speak against you as evil doers, they may glorify God by your good works, which they shall behold; for it is his will, that with well-doing ye put to silence the ignorance of foolish men, and make them ashamed that falsely accuse your good conversation in Christ," 1 Peter 2:12, 15; and 3:16.

St. Paul had the same objection continually cast in his face.* "Do we then make void the law through faith?" says he in his own defence, Romans 3:31; that is,

---

* (23.) The Antinomians "by fair speeches deceive the hearts of the simple." Because St. Paul fully answers this objection, they make the injudicious believe that he was of their sentiment; though upon their plan of doctrine the objection which he states is absolutely unanswerable. They say, "We establish the law by preaching Christ, who has kept it for us; and by extolling his imputed righteousness, through which we are for ever complete in justifying obedience before

by preaching salvation through faith do we hinder people from doing the good works commanded in the law? "God forbid! yea, we establish the law:" i.e. our preaching is so far from superseding good words, that it [enforces them by the greatest variety of motives, and] puts our hearers into [the best, not to say] the only method of doing them: for it shows them how, being "sprinkled from an evil conscience," and having their "heart purified by faith," they shall naturally [i.e. spontaneously] produce all' sorts of good works, instead of bringing forth a few counterfeit ones.

The apostle answers the same objection, Romans 6:1. "Shall we then," who are saved by grace through faith, "continue in sin that grace may abound?" Shall we omit doing good works; shall we do evil works because salvation is not [by the covenant] of works, [but by that] of grace? "God forbid! How shall we, that are dead to sin, live any longer therein!" As if he had said, Is not the faith which we preach a "faith of the operation of God?" Is it not a powerful and active principle, that turns* the heart from all sin to all righteousness? Is it not a faith by which we are made new creatures, and "overcome the world?" 1 John 5:1, 4.

[When people "lie in darkness," doing "the works of darkness," which in the dark pass either for good works that Divine justice will reward, or for trifling offences that Divine mercy will overlook; then heart-felt repentance is totally neglected, and deep mourning for sin passes for despair. Few know what it is to "look on him whom they have pierced and mourn." Very few, if any, can experimentally say, "Being justified by faith, we have peace with God through our Lord Jesus Christ, by whom we have now received the atonement."]

[Suppose the lot of a minister, acquainted with the privileges of the Christian dispensation, is cast in a place where these Pharisaic and common delusions generally prevail: the first thing he has to do is undoubtedly to uncover and shake the false foundations on which his awakened hearers build their hope. He must show them that their partial, external, faithless obedience will never profit them. He must decry their imaginary good works, tear off their filthy rags of fancied righteousness, sweep away "their refuges of lies," and scourge their consciences with the curse of the law, till they see their nakedness, feel their guilt, and "receive the sentence of death in themselves." Then, and not till then, will they stand on a level with the poor contrite publican, and

---

God." Now although we humbly and thankfully acknowledge with them that our Lord has kept the Adamic law of innocence and made it honourable for us: yet we absolutely deny that he has kept the evangelical law of liberty for us. — Personal obedience to it is indispensably required of every man, and if a believer do not fulfil it for himself, St. Paul and St. James inform us that a sorer punishment and a more merciless judgment await his disobedience, than if he had never believed, Hebrews 10:29; James 2:13. Thus those holy apostles fully make up the gap of Antinomian free grace, which some of our Gospel ministers make it their business to widen.

* (24.) How could I have had the assurance of asking these questions, if I had believed, as my late opponent, that a man who actually commits the greatest crimes may actually have as true, justifying faith as Abraham ever had? I should expect that if such a faith did not, as I said eleven years ago, "turn the heart from all sin to all righteousness," it would at least turn it from deliberate adultery, murder, and incest.

Groan the sinner's only plea,
"God be merciful to me."]

[When a preacher is engaged in that important and thankful business, how natural is it for him, especially if he be yet young and inexperienced, or if he be heated by the opposition of obstinate Pharisees and bigoted Papists, to drop some unguarded expressions against good works; or at least not to make always a proper distinction between the Pharisaical works of unbelief, which Isaiah calls filthy rags, and the works of faith, which our Lord calls good and ornamental works? And how glad are his adversaries to have such a plausible pretence for throwing an odium upon him, by affirming that he explodes all sorts of works, even those for which our "reward will be great in heaven!"]

☞The devil fought against our reformers with such weapons. All the books that the Papists wrote against them rang with the charge of their turning good works out of Christianity.☜ Hear good Bishop Latimer, one of the best livers that ever were: — "You will say now, *Here is all faith, faith; but we hear nothing of good works:* for some carnal people make such carnal objections like themselves," &c. (*Sermon on Twelfth Day.*)

Of the same import is the following passage out of *the Homily on Fasting:*— "Thus much is said of good works, &c, to take away so much as may be from envious minds and slanderous tongues all JUST occasion of slanderous speaking, as though good works were rejected."

Thus St. Peter, St. Paul, and our reformers were accused of despising good works, because they exalted Christ, [and with a holy indignation trampled upon the works of unbelief, which are the foundation of all Pharisaic hopes,] and [so far as I have not, by unguarded expressions, given a just cause of offence to those who are glad of any occasion to decry the fundamental doctrine of salvation by faith,] I own that I rejoice to be counted worthy of suffering the same reproach with such a cloud of faithful witnesses. Nevertheless, as the Scriptures say that we must "not let the good that is in us be evil spoken of," I shall advance some arguments, which, by God's blessing, will either convince or shame my accusers.

You say, [and this I speak particularly to you that are fully set against the doctrine of salvation by faith,] you say, "that I preach against good works — that I run down good works," &c: but pray, do you know what good works are? I am afraid you do not, or else you would* [not accuse me so rashly.] Give me leave therefore to instruct you once in this point.

All divines agree that good works are of three sorts: (1.) Works of *piety* toward God. (2.) Works of *charity* toward our neighbour; and, (3.) Works of *self denial* toward ourselves.

---

* (25.) Instead of these words [not accuse me so rashly] I formerly wrote [be ashamed to accuse me so falsely.] I reject them now, because a minister of the Gospel should not only speak the truth, but endeavour to speak it in the most acceptable manner. It is enough to give offence when it cannot be avoided. We should not provoke the displeasure of our hearers without necessity.

Creeds and Scripture Scales

[To say nothing now of the good works of the heart, such as good thoughts, good tempers, and internal acts of repentance, faith, hope, and love;] in the first class, [of external good works,] which includes "works of piety," divines rank public prayer in the Church, family prayer in private houses, and [meditation and] private prayer in one's closet: singing psalms, hymns, and spiritual songs: reading the Bible and other good books: hearing the word preached or expounded: receiving the sacraments: keeping the Sabbath day and festivals holy: confessing Christ before a wicked world: and suffering the loss of one's estate, of one's good name, or life itself, for the Gospel's sake.

Now I appeal to every impartial hearer, yea, and to thy own conscience, O man, who accusest me of preaching against good works, whether I ever taught, directly or indirectly, that we ought not constantly to attend public worship in the house of God, as well as private worship in our own houses, and to perform secret worship in our closets: whether I ever spoke against singing psalms, hymns, and spiritual songs; or against reading the Bible and other good books: whether I ever so much as hinted that we ought not to endeavour so to despatch our worldly business, as to hear [if possible] the word preached or expounded both on Sundays and working days: whether I have intimated* that we can live in the neglect of God's ordinances, and break his Sabbaths, without bringing upon ourselves "swift destruction:" and, lastly, whether at any time I cried down suffering reproach for Christ, and parting with all things, even life itself, to follow him and his doctrine.

Nay, do not you know in your own breasts that my insisting upon these good works, and encouraging all I can to do them, is what makes me to be despised and rejected by many, and perhaps by yourself? How can you then, without wounding† [your own conscience,] accuse me of preaching against good works? Are you not rather the person who speaks against them? Are you not yourself one of these [loose moralists] who say, that "for their part they see no need of so many sermons, lectures, and sacraments in the Church; no need of so much singing, reading, praying, and godly conversation, in private houses: no need of such strictness in keeping the Sabbath day holy," &c.

If you are one of them, you add [I fear] detraction to infidelity, and bearing false testimony to open profaneness, [or Laodicean lukewarmness.] You decry good works yourself by your words, your practice, and your example; and when you have done, you lay the sin at my door; you say that I preach against them! O how will you reconcile this conduct, I shall not say to Christianity, but to good manners, good sense, or even to heathen honesty!

---

* (26.) My opponent has not only done this, but he has intimated that all believers may commit adultery, murder, and incest, not only without bringing upon themselves swift destruction, but with this additional advantage, that they shall infallibly "sing louder" in heaven for their deepest falls, which can never finally hurt them, because all their sins are unconditionally for ever and for ever forgiven. Had I ever insinuated such loose principles among my parishioners, I should have had a brazen forehead indeed to look them in the face while I made the above-mentioned appeal.

† (27.) Eleven years ago I said [common sense and common honesty.] I now discard the expression as needlessly offensive.

In the second class of good works, divines place works of [justice and] charity; and these are of two sorts: such as are done to the bodies, and such as are done to the souls of men. The former are, [for the most part,] enumerated by our Lord, Matthew 25. They consist in being true and just in all our dealings; in "providing things honest in the sight of all men," for us and ours; in paying our just debts as soon as possible; in protecting widows and fatherless children; in giving food to the hungry and drink to the thirsty; in entertaining strangers, easing the oppressed, clothing the naked, attending the sick, visiting the prisoners, [and burying the dead, from Scriptural and not Pharisaic motives.]

Now will any one, who scruples advancing an untruth, dare affirm, that I ever spoke a word against doing any one of these good works? Against doing them *at improper times, from bad motives, in a wrong manner, and to wrong ends,* I have often spoken; and so have all the preachers who do not "daub the wall with untempered mortar:" Christ first, Matthew 6:2; St. Paul next, 1 Corinthians 12:1, 2, 3; and our Church after them. (See the *Homily on Fasting.*) But I ask it again, Who ever heard me speak one word *against doing them?* On the contrary, have I not declared again and again that even "a cup of cold water, given in Christ's name, shall in no wise lose its reward" — should certainly be rewarded in eternal life? [And do not some of you know, that within these two years I have lost many of my religious friends, by making a stand for the evangelical worthiness of the works of faith?]

As for works of mercy done to the souls of men, such as [giving a Christian education to our children and apprentices,] comforting the afflicted, encouraging the dejected, strengthening the weak, exhorting the careless, succouring the tempted, instructing the ignorant, sympathizing with mourners, warning the stubborn, [detecting hypocrisy,] reproving sin, stopping immorality, rebuking profaneness, and helping each other in the narrow way; it is known to many that my name is cast out as evil by many Sabbath breakers, swearers, and drunkards, for endeavouring to walk in these good works myself, and to induce others to walk in them.

And yet you, [I still address myself to the inveterate enemies of salvation by faith,] you, who possibly ridicule all those good works, and dream of being saved without them; you, who do perhaps just the reverse of them, strengthening one another's hands in licentiousness and profaneness, in Sabbath breaking, sweating, or scoffing at every thing that looks like seriousness; you accuse me of despising or discountenancing good works! O tell it not in Gath, publish it not in Askelon, lest the very Philistines laugh at the glaring inconsistency of your words and conduct!

Good works of the third class relate to keeping under the flesh, and all its sinful appetites. The chief of these works are a moderate use of meat, drink, and sleep; self denial [in apparel, furniture, and equipage;] chastity [in all its branches; subduing our slothful, rebellious flesh, by] early rising, abstinence, fasting: and, in a word, "by taking up our daily cross," and following our abstemious, and yet laborious Lord.

[Permit me to do as St. Paul — "to speak as it were foolishly in this confidence of boasting."] Have I not enforced the necessity of these good works both publicly and from house to house? Have you not sometimes even gone away from this place of worship, secretly displeased at my insisting so much upon them; complaining, perhaps, "that I went too far, or that nobody could live up to what I preach;" and making a hundred such remarks, instead of meditating upon these words of our Lord, "With man indeed it is impossible, but with God all things are possible?" And yet you now complain that I do not preach up good works. Pray, my brethren, be consistent; keep to one point, and do not say and unsay. I can no more be too strict, and yet make too little of good works, than I can go east and west at the same time. Only think — and you will perceive that your very complaints justify me, that your sayings overturn one another, and that "your own mouths prove you perverse."

You will probably say, "Have we not heard you affirm, more than once, that nobody can be saved by his works: yea, that a man may go as constantly to church as the* Pharisee did to the temple, be as virtuous as he was, pay tithes exactly as he did, and be damned after all? Can you deny having preached this doctrine twenty times?"

Deny it! By no means. It is a doctrine for which, God being my helper, I am ready to go to the stake. It is the very doctrine that I have established in the former part of this discourse. How, then, can I deny it?

Here methinks a Pharisee replies in triumph: "Well, then, you plead guilty to the charge: you confess that you have preached twenty times against good works."

I deny the conclusion. Have you not understanding enough to see there is a vast difference between preaching† against the [proper] merit of good works, and preaching against good works themselves? Between saying that obedience to the king will never get us the crown of Great Britain, and affirming that we owe the king no obedience? In a word, between saying that good works will never procure us heaven, [as the primary, and, strictly speaking, meritorious cause of our salvation,] and declaring that we ought not to do good works? Surely your rational faculties are not so impaired but you may perceive those propositions are by no means of the same import.

If I say that eating will never make me immortal, that drinking will never turn me into an angel, and that doing my work will never take me to the third heaven, do I so much as hint that eating is useless, drinking Of no service, and doing my business unprofitable? O how does prejudice blind even men of reason and religion! How hardly does truth go down with us, when we do not love it! How gladly do we dress it up in a fool's coat, that we may have some pretence to despise and reject it!

If you would speak according to strict truth, my brethren, you would not say that I "preach against good works, that I run down good works," &c, which is a mistake, as! showed just now: but you would say, that I preach *against the [proper] merit of good works in point of salvation.* This is very true, so I do, and so I am determined to do, by God's grace, as long as I live. So did Christ and his apostles; so do our articles and homilies; and so the children of God have done in all ages. ☞Those of the Old Testament‡ [far from mentioning any proper merits of their own, cried out, "Now

---

* (30.) From this objection, it is evident that the works which I decried eleven years ago were those against which I now bear my testimony, namely Pharisaical works.

† (31.) It appears to me that my sermon, far from being "the best confutation of the Minutes," is consonant to that proposition, which has given such offence: *Not by the merit of works, but by works as a condition.*

‡ (32.) Instead of this addition, eleven years ago I said [owned that all their righteousnesses were as filthy rags, Isaiah 64:6.] For leaning then too much toward Calvinism, I supposed that

mine eye seeth thee, I abhor myself, and repent in dust and ashes," Job 43:5. "Wo is me, for I am undone, because I am" by nature, and have been by practice, "a man of unclean lips," Isaiah 6:5.] Those of the New prayed to "be found in Christ, not having their own [Pharisaic] righteousness which is of the law of works, but the [evangelical] righteousness which is by faith in Jesus Christ," Philippians 3:9. And those of our Church profess, that they "are not worthy to gather the crumbs under the Lord's table," and that they "do not come to it, trusting in their own righteousness," or good works, "but in God's manifold and great mercies through Jesus Christ;" so far are they from thinking that they [properly] merit salvation [either in whole or in part.] (See *Communion Service*.)

☞Yea, I declare it as, "upon the house-top," of all the false doctrines that ever came out of the pit of hell, none has done such execution for Satan in the Church of God [as the Pharisaic conceit that we have, or may have any proper, original merit.] Stealing, drunkenness, and adultery have slain their thousands: but this damnable error, which is the very root of unbelief, its ten thousands.☜ It blinded the Pharisees, and hardened the Jews against Christ.* It plunges into everlasting fire all nominal Christians," who have a form of godliness, but deny the power thereof."

Yea, strange as the assertion may seem to some, this [pernicious error] feeds immorality and secretly nourishes all manner of vice. The Scripture tells us, 1 Corinthians 6:9, that "neither fornicators, nor effeminate, neither thieves nor covetous, neither drunkards nor revilers, neither unrighteous nor extortioners, shall inherit the kingdom of God." Now, how comes it to pass that so many, who are guilty of one or another of these abominations, remain as easy as if they were guiltless? Why, this damnable notion, that the merit of their works will atone for the guilt of their sins, makes them think that they shall do well enough in the end. "I get drunk now and then," says one, "but I am honest." "I oppress or cheat my neighbour," says another, "but I go to church and sacrament." "I love money or diversions above all things," says a third, "but I bless God, I am neither a thief nor a drunkard." "I am passionate, and swear sometimes," says a fourth, "but my heart is good, and I never keep malice in my breast; beside, I'll repent and mend some time or other before I die." Now the sum of all those pleas amounts to this: "I do the devil's work, but I do good works too. I am guilty of one piece of wickedness, but not of all: and I hope that through the merit of the good which I do, and of the evil which I

---

the prophet in this passage spoke of the righteousness of faith: but since I have dared to read my Bible without prejudice, and to consult the context, I have found that text is spoken only of the hypocritical righteousness of the wicked; and in the Fourth Check, page 263 (Vol. I, pp. 259-260), I have tried to rescue it from the hands of the Antinomians, who had taught me to wrest it from its proper meaning.

* Here I leave out those words: "It [the Pharisaic conceit of merit] damned the foolish virgins and the man who had not on a wedding garment." And I do it because, upon second thoughts, it appears to me that the boldness of the foolish virgins, and the insolence of the men, who pressed to the marriage feast, without proper dress, exactly represent the vain confidence with which immoral Solifidians cry, "Lord! Lord! and make a shining profession in the robe of self-imputed righteousness; despising the evangelical robe of real righteousness and true holiness, and calling them cobwebs spun by spiders out of their own bowels.

have left undone hitherto, or purpose to leave undone by and by, Christ will have mercy upon me."

☞Thus all our [Pharisaic*] delays of conversion, and all our [self- righteous] remorseless going on in sin and wickedness, are founded upon the doctrine of [Pharisaic] merits. Well then may our Church call it "a devilish doctrine, which is mere blasphemy against God's mercy:" a doctrine which turns Christ out of his throne [by refusing him the honour of being the primary and the properly meritorious cause of our salvation.] A doctrine which [by crooked ways] leads first to [worldly mindedness or] licentiousness, as the conduct of many who cry up the [self-righteous] merit of good works [so called] too plainly shows; and next to Pharisaic morality and formality; and from both, except [a timely submission to] converting grace prevent it, into endless misery: for "no doubt," says Bishop Latimer, in his sermon on Twelfth Day, "he that departeth out of this world in that opinion [or, as he expresses it in the same paragraph, those who "think to be saved by the law," by the first covenant] shall never come to heaven."☜ For they set their hearts against Christ; and, like the Pharisees of old, not only mistake the words of unbelief for good works; but give them also the place of the primary, meritorious cause of eternal salvation; when, if they were the works of faith, they would only be a secondary evidencing cause of it. Now as such men cannot possibly do this, without the greatest degree of spiritual pride, impenitency, and unbelief, it is plain that, if they die confirmed in this grand antichristian error, they cannot be saved: for St. Paul informs us that pride is "the condemnation of the devil;" and our Lord declares that "except we repent we shall all perish," and that "he who believeth not shall be damned."

FOURTH PART.

[HAVING thus laid before you the destructive nature of self righteousness,] it is time to come to the last thing proposed, which was to show why good works cannot [properly speaking] deserve salvation in whole or in part; and to answer the old cavil, "If good works cannot save us,† why should we trouble ourselves about them?" [In doing the former I shall attempt to give Pharisaism a finishing stroke; and in doing the latter I shall endeavour to guard the Scriptural doctrine of grace against Antinomianism, which prevails almost as much among professed believers as Pharisaism does among professed moralists.]

---

* I had the word *Pharisaic* and *self righteous*, to come at Mr. Fulsome and his numerous fraternity, whom I now should be glad to convince of their remorseless going on in sin, and of their Antinomian delays of conversion.

† (33.) This is strictly true; nevertheless, we must grant that as cold water, when it is put over the fire in a proper vessel, imbibes the fiery heat, and boils without damping the fire; so our works of faith, when they are laid with proper humility on the golden altar of Christ's merits, are so impregnated with his diffusive worth as to acquire "a rewardable condecency unto eternal life." And this they do without mixing in the least with the primary or properly meritorious cause of our salvation; and consequently without obscuring the Redeemer's glory.

And first, that good works cannot [strictly speaking] merit salvation in part, much less altogether, I prove by the following arguments: —

1. We must be wholly saved by the covenant of works or by the covenant of grace; my text showing most clearly that a third covenant made up of [Christless] merits [according to the first,] and Divine mercy [according to the second,] is as imaginary a thing in divinity as a fifth element made up of fire and water would be in natural philosophy.*

2. There is less proportion between heavenly glory and our works, than between the sun and a mote that flies in the air: therefore to pretend that they will avail toward [purchasing, or properly meriting] heaven, [see the fifth note,] argues want of common sense, as well as want of humility.

3. God has wisely determined to save proud man in a way that excludes boasting. "God is just and the justifier of him that believes in Jesus. Where is boasting then?" says the apostle. "It is excluded," answers he. "By what covenant," does he ask? Is boasting excluded by the covenant of works? No, "but by the law of faith," by the covenant of grace, whose condition is [penitential, self-abasing, obedient] faith in Jesus Christ. "Therefore we conclude," says he, "that a man is justified by faith without the works of the law," Romans 3:27, 28. If our good works [properly speaking] deserve the least part of our salvation, we may justly boast that our own arm has got us that part of the victory; and we have reason to glory in ourselves, contrary to the Scriptures, which say that" every mouth must be stopped," that "boasting is excluded," and that "he who glories must glory in the Lord."

[If St. Paul glories in his sufferings and labours, it is not then without Christ before God, but with Christ before the Corinthians, and under peculiar circumstances. He never imagined that his works were meritorious according to the first covenant; much less did he imagine that they had one single grain of proper merit. He perfectly knew that if they were rewardable, it was not from any self excellence which he had put into them; but merely from God's gratuitous promise in the second covenant; from Christ's grace, by which they were wrought; from his atoning blood, in which they were washed; and from his proper merits with which they were perfumed.]

[To suppose that Adam himself, if he had continued upright, would have gloried in his righteousness as a Pharisee, is to suppose him deeply fallen. In paradise God was all in all; and as he is also all in all in heaven, we may easily conceive that with respect to self exaltation, the mouth of Gabriel is not less shut before the throne than that of Mary Magdalene. Therefore, if any out of hell Pharisaically glory in themselves, it is only those self- righteous sons of Lucifer and pride, to whom our Lord says still, "You are of your father the devil, whose works ye do," when "ye seek to kill me," and "glory in yourselves."]

4. Our evil works far overbalance our good works, both in quantity and quality. Let us first then pay a righteous God the debt [the immense debt of ten thousand talents that] we owe him, by dying the second death, which is the wages of our bad works; and then we may talk of buying heaven with our good works.

---

* That the works of faith save us by the covenant of grace [next to Christ and faith] will be proved in the *Scriptural Essay*.

5. Our best works have such a mixture of imperfection that they must be atoned for and made acceptable by Christ's blood; so far are they from atoning for the least sin* [and properly meriting our acceptance] before God [even according to the second covenant.]

6. If ever we did one truly good work, the merit[†] is not ours, but God's, who, by his free grace, "prevented, accompanied, and followed us" in the performance. For it is God, who "of his good pleasure worketh in us both to will and to do," Philippians 2:12. "Not I," says the apostle, after mentioning his good works, "but the grace of God in me," 1 Corinthians 15:10, compared with James 1:17.

7. We perpetually say at church, "Glory be to the Father," as Creator, "and to the Son," as Redeemer, "and to the Holy Ghost," as Sanctifier. Christ is then to have all the glory of our redemption: but if our good works come in for any share in the purchase of heaven, we must come in also for some share of the glory of our [redemption.‡] Thus Christ will no longer be the only Redeemer. We shall be co-redeemers with him, and consequently we shall have a share in the doxology; which is a blasphemous supposition.

8. Our Lord himself decides the question in those remarkable words,
☞ "When you have done all that is commanded you;" and where is the man that [according to the law of innocence§] has done, I shall not say all, but the one half of it? say, "We are unprofitable servants."☜ Now it is plain that unprofitable servants do not [properly] merit, in whole or in part, to sit down at their master's table, and be admitted as children to a share of his estate. Therefore, if God gives heaven to believers, it is entirely owing to his free mercy, through the merits of Jesus Christ, and not at all through the [proper] merits of our own works.

---

* (34.) Eleven years ago I said [and making us accepted.] I now reject the expression as unguarded, for it clashes with this proposition of St. Peter: "In every nation he that worketh righteousness is accepted of him." We should take care so to secure the foundation, as not to throw down the building.

† (35.) This is the very doctrine of evangelical rewardableness, or improper, derived merit, so honourable to Christ, so humbling to man, which I have maintained in the Vindication, (page 48, &c.) Therefore, if I am a merit monger and a heretic now, it is evident that I was so eleven years ago, when I wrote a, sermon, which, as my late opponent is pleased to say, (Finishing Stroke, p. 44,) "does me much credit, and plainly shows that I was once zealously attached to the doctrines of the Church of England."

‡ (36.) I substitute the word "redemption" for the word "salvation," that I formerly used; because English logic demands it. By the same reason I leave out in the end of the paragraph the words "Saviour," and "joint saviours," which I had illogically coupled with "Redeemer," and "co- redeemers." For although it is strictly true that no man can redeem his brother's soul or even ransom his body from the power of the grave; yet, according to the doctrine of secondary instrumental causes, it is absolutely false that no man can save his neighbour; for "in doing this," says St. Paul, "thou shalt both save thyself and them that hear thee," 1 Timothy 4:16

§ (37.) I say [the law of innocence] to defend the works of the law of faith, by the instrumentality of which we shall be justified or saved in the great day. For these works flowing from Christ's grace, and never aspiring at any higher place than that which is allotted them, viz. the place of justifying evidences, they can never detract from the Saviour's honour or his grace.

9. I shall close these observations by St. Paul's unanswerable argument: "If righteousness come by the law," if salvation come by [the covenant of works,] "then Christ died in vain," Galatians 2:21. Whence it follows, that if it come in part by the works of the law, part of Christ's sufferings were vain, a supposition which ends in the same blasphemy against the Mediator.

10. That man might deserve any thing of God upon the footing of proper worthiness, or merit of equivalence, God should stand in need of something, which it is in man's power to bestow: but this is absolutely impossible. For God, being self sufficient in his infinite fulness, is far above any want; and man, being a dependent creature, every moment supported by his Maker and Preserver, has nothing to which God has not a far greater right than man himself. This is what the apostle asserts where he says, "Who has given him first, and it shall be recompensed unto him again?" But much more in this remarkable passage: "Who maketh thee to differ from another?" If thou sayest, The number of my talents, and the proper use I have made of them: I ask again, Who gave thee those talents? And who superadded grace, wisdom, and an opportunity to improve them? Here we must all give glory to God, and say with St. James, "Every good gift is from above, and cometh down from the Father of lights."

Upon this consideration the apostle proceeds to check the Christian Pharisee thus' "What hast thou that thou didst not receive? Now if thou didst receive it, why dost thou glory as if thou hadst not received it?" Whence it follows that, though St. Paul himself glories in, and boasts of his disinterestedness, yea, solemnly declares, "No man shall stop me of this boasting," yet he did not glory in that virtue, "as if he had not received it." No, he gave the original glory of it to "Him of whom, through whom, and to whom are all things." The glory of bestowing original gifts upon us belongs then to God alone; and the original glory of the humility with which we receive, and of the faithfulness with which we use those gifts, belongs also to him alone; although in the very nature of things we have such a derived share of that glory as gives room to the reasonableness of Divine rewards. For why should one be rewarded more than another; yea, why should one be rewarded rather than punished, if derived faithfulness does not make him more rewardable?

Observe, however, that although by this derived faithfulness, one man makes himself to differ enough from another, for God to reward h im reasonably rather than another; yet no man can say to his Maker, without satanic arrogance, "I have made myself to differ from such a one, therefore I make a lawful demand upon thy justice: thus much I have done for thee; do as much for me again." For while God dispenses punishments according to the rules of strict justice, he bestows his rewards only according to the rules of moral aptitude and distributive equity, in consequence of Christ's proper merits, and of his own gracious promise; all men on earth and all angels in heaven being far less capable of properly deserving at God's hands, than all the mites and ants in England are of properly meriting any thing at the hands of the king.]

[Lastly, what slaves earn is not their own, but the masters to whom they belong; and what your horses get is your property, not theirs. Now, as God has a thousand times more right to us than masters to their slaves, and you to your horses; it follows that, supposing we were sinless and could properly earn any thing, our profit would be God's, not ours. So true it is that, from the creature to the Creator, the idea of proper merit is as contrary to justice as it is to decency.] As the preceding arguments [against the proper merit of works] will, I hope, abundantly satisfy all those [modern Pharisees] who have not entirely cast away the Christian revelation, I pass to the old objection of [some ignorant] Papists [and injudicious Protestants.] "If good works cannot [merit us heaven, (see fifth note,) or properly] save us, why should we trouble ourselves about them?" [And in answering it I shall guard the doctrine of obedience against the Antinomians.]

As this quibbling argument may puzzle the simple, and make the boasting Pharisees that use it triumph as if they had overturned the Protestant doctrine of salvation by faith, without [the] works [decried by St. Paul;] I beg leave to show its weakness by a comparison.

Suppose you said to me, "Your doing the work of a parish priest will never [merit] you an archbishopric;" and I answered with discontent, "If doing my office will never [merit] me the see of Canterbury, why should I do it at all? I need not trouble myself about preaching any more:" would you not ask me whether a clergyman has no reason to attend his flock but the wild and proud conceit that his labour must [deserve*] him a bishopric. And I ask, in my turn, Do you suppose that a Christian has no motive to do good works, but the wilder and prouder notion that his good works must [properly speaking] merit him heaven?. (See fifth note.)

If therefore t can show that he has the strongest motives and inducements to abound in good works, without the doctrine of [proper] merits; I hope you will drop your objection, You say, "If good works will never [properly merit us salvation,] why should we do them?" I answer, For six good reasons, each of which [in some degree†] overturns your objection.

1. ☞ We are to do good works to show our obedience to our heavenly Father.☜ As a child obeys his parents, not to purchase their estate, but because he is their child, [and does not choose to be disinherited:] so believers obey God, not to get to heaven for their wages, but because he is their Father, [and they would not provoke him to disinherit them.‡]

2. ☞ We are to abound in all good works, to be justified before men [now, and before the Judge of all the earth in the great day;] and to show that our faith is

---

* (38.) This illustration is not strictly just. If the king had millions of bishoprics to give, if he had promised to bestow one upon every diligent clergyman; solemnly declaring that all who neglect their charge should not only miss the ecclesiastical dignity annexed to diligence, but be put to a shameful death, as so many murderers of souls, the cases would then be exactly parallel. Beside, every clergyman is not a candidate for a bishopric, but every man is a candidate for heaven. Again: a clergyman may be as happy in his parsonage as a bishop in his palace; but if a man miss heaven he sinks into hell. These glaring truths I overlooked when I was a "late evangelical preacher."

† Formerly I said [entirely] but experience has taught me otherwise.

‡ (39.) This argument is weak without the additions. Our Lord informs us that when the father in the Gospel says to his fair-spoken child, Son, "go work to-day in my vineyard," he answers, "I go, sir," and goes not: and God himself says, "I have nourished and brought up children, but they have rebelled against me." We to the parents who have such children, and have no power to cut off an entail!

saving. St. James strongly insists upon this, James 2:18. ☜ "Show me thy faith without thy works," says he, "and I will show thee my faith by my works:" that is, thou sayest thou hast faith, [because thou wast once justified by faith;] but thou doest not the works of a believer; thou canst follow vanity, and conform to this evil world: thou canst swear or break the Sabbath; lie, cheat, or get drunk; rail at thy neighbour, or live in uncleanness; in a word, thou canst do one or another of the devil's works. Thy works therefore give thee the lie, and show that thy faith is [now like] the devil's faith; for if "faith without works be dead," how doubly dead must faith with bad works be!* [And how absurd is it to suppose that thou canst be instrumentally justified by a dead faith, or declaratively justified by bad works, either before men or in the sight of God!] But "I will show thee my faith by my works," adds the apostle: i.e. by constantly abstaining from all evil works, and steadily walking in all sorts of good works, I will make thee confess that I am really "in Christ a new creature," and that my faith is living and genuine.

3. Our Saviour told his disciples that they were to ☞ do good works, not to purchase heaven, but that others might be stirred up to serve God. You, then, that have found the way of salvation by Christ, "let your light so shine before men, that even they," who speak evil of the doctrine of faith, "seeing your good works, may† glorify your Father who is in heaven," ☜ Matthew 5:16.

4. ☞ We are to do good works out of gratitude and love to our dear Redeemer, who, having [conditionally] purchased heaven for us with his precious blood, ☜ asks the small return of our love and obedience. "If you love me," says he, "keep my commandments," John 14:15. [This motive is noble, and continues powerful so long as we keep our first love. But, alas! it has little force with regard to the myriads that rather fear than love God: and it has lost its force in all those "who have denied the faith," or "made shipwreck of it," or "cast off their first faith," and consequently their first love and their first gratitude. The multitude of these, in all ages, has been innumerable. I fear we might say of justified believers what our Lord did of the cleansed lepers: — "Were there not ten cleansed? But where are the nine?" Alas! like the apostates mentioned by St. Paul, they "are turned aside" after the flesh, after the world, "after fables," after Antinomian dotages, after "vain jangling, after Satan" himself, 1 Timothy 5:15.]

---

* (40.) If this single clause in my old sermon stand, so will the Minutes and the Checks. But the whole argument is a mere jest, if a man that wallows in adultery, murder, or incest, may have as true, justifying faith as David had when he killed Goliah.

† (41.) This argument is quite frivolous if my late opponent is right. "How has many a poor soul," says he, "who has been faithless through the fear of man, even blessed God for Peter's denial?" (*Five Letters*, second edition revised, p. 40.) Hence it appears, that denying Christ with oaths and curses will cause "many a poor soul to bless God," i.e. to "glorify our heavenly Father." Now if horrid crimes do this as well as good works, is it not absurd to enforce the practice of good works, by saying that they alone have that blessed effect?. But my opponent may easily get over this difficulty before those whose battles he fights. He needs only charge me with disingenuity for not quoting the third revised edition of his book, if he has published such a one.

5. We are to be careful to maintain good works, [not only that we may not lose our confidence in God, 1 John 3:19, &c, but also] that we may nourish and increase our faith or spiritual life: [or, to use the language of St. James, that faith may work with our works, and that by works our faith may be made perfect.] As a man [in health who is* threatened by no danger] does not walk that his walking may procure him life, [or save his life from destruction,] but that he may preserve his health, and [add to] his activity: so a believer does not walk in good works to get [an initial life of grace, or a primary title to an] eternal life [of glory,] but to keep up and increase the vigour of his faith, by which he has [already a title to, and the earnest of] eternal life. For as the best health without any exercise is soon destroyed, so the strongest faith without works will soon droop and die. Hence it is that St. Paul exhorts us to "hold faith and a good conscience, which some having put away," by refusing to walk in good works, "concerning faith have made shipwreck."]

6. ☞ We are not to do good works to obtain heaven by them, [as if they were the properly meritorious cause of our salvation.] This proud,† antichristian motive would poison the best doings of the greatest saints, if saints could thus trample on the blood of their Saviour: such a wild conceit being only the Pharisee's cleaner way to hell. But we are to do them because they shall be rewarded in heaven.‡☜ To understand this we must remember that, according to the Gospel and our liturgy, God "opens the kingdom of heaven to all believers:" [because true believers are always true workers; true faith always working by love to God's commandments. Next to Christ, then, to speak the language of some injudicious divines,] faith alone, when it works by love, takes us to heaven: [or rather, to avoid an apparent contradiction, faith and its works are the way to heaven.] But as there are stars of different magnitude in the material heaven, so also in the spiritual. Some who, like St. Paul, have eminently shined by "the works of faith, the patience of hope, and the labour of love," shall shine like the brightest stars, [or the sun:] and ☞ others, who, like the dying thief and infants, have had [little§ or] no time to show their faith

---

* (42.) Formerly I did not consider that as Noah walked into the ark, and Lot out of Sodom, to save their lives; so sinners are called to turn from their iniquity, and do that which is lawful and right to save their souls alive. Nor did I observe that saints are commanded to walk in good works lest the destroyer overtake them, and they become sons of perdition. However, in Babel such capital oversights did me "much credit."

† (43.) Here I leave out the word "selfish," as being ambiguous. It is not selfishness, but true wisdom and well-ordered self love, evangelically to "labour for the meat that endureth to everlasting life." Not to do it is the height of Laodicean stupidity, or Antinomian conceit.

‡ (44.) Here I leave out [although not with heaven,] for the reasons assigned in the Scriptural Essay.

§ (45.) Here Mr. H. triumphs in his Finishing Stroke, p. 50, last note, through my omission of those two words. But without having recourse to "magical power," or even to "Logica Helvetica" to reconcile my sermon with my Checks. I desire unprejudiced Calvinists to mention any one beside the dying thief that ever evidenced his faith by confessing Christ when his very apostles denied or forsook him; by openly praying to him when the multitude reviled him; by humbly pleading guilty before thousands; by publicly defending injured innocence; by boldly reproving blasphemy; by kindly admonishing his fellow malefactor; and by fully acknowledging Christ's kingly office, when he was crowned with thorns, and hanging on the [or holiness] by their works, shall enjoy a less degree of glorious bliss. But all shall ascribe the whole of their salvation only to the mercy of God, the merits of Christ, and the efficacy of his blood and Spirit, ☞ according to St. John's vision: "I beheld, and lo a great multitude of all nations, and kindreds, and people, and tongues, stood before the throne, with palms in their hands, clothed with robes that they had washed and made white in the blood of the Lamb: and" [while our Lord said to them by his gracious looks, according to the doctrine of secondary, instrumental causes, "Walk with me in white, for you are worthy, and inherit the kingdom prepared for you, for I was hungry and ye gave me meat," &c,] they cried [according to the doctrine of primary and properly meritorious causes] not "salvation to our endeavours and good works;" but "salvation to our God, who sitteth upon the throne, and unto the Lamb for ever and ever."

[Thus, by the rules of celestial courtesy, to which our Lord vouchsafes to submit in glory, while the saints justly draw a veil over their works of faith, to extol only their Saviour's merits, he kindly passes over his own blood and righteousness to make mention only of their works and obedience. They, setting their seal to the first Gospel axiom, shout with great truth, "Salvation to God and the Lamb:" and He, setting his seal to the second Gospel axiom, replies, with great condescension, Salvation "to them that are worthy! Eternal salvation to all that obey me," Revelation 3:4; Hebrews 5:9.]

[Therefore, notwithstanding the perpetual assaults of proud Pharisees, and of self-humbled Antinomians, the two Gospel axioms stand unshaken upon the two fundamental, inseparable doctrines of faith and works — of proper merit in Christ, and derived worthiness in his members. Penitent believers freely receive all from the God of grace and mercy, through Christ; and humble workers freely return all to the God of holiness and glory, through the same adorable Mediator. Thus God has all the honour of freely bestowing upon us a crown of righteousness, in a way of judicious mercy, and distributive justice; while we, through grace, have* all the honour of freely receiving it in a way of penitential faith and obedient gratitude. To him, therefore, one eternal Jehovah in Father, Son, and Holy Ghost, be ascribed all the merit, honour, praise, and dominion, worthy of a God, for ever and ever.]

---

cross. Did St. John, did Mary Magdalene, did even the Virgin Mary show their faith by such glorious works, under such unfavourable circumstances? O ye Solifidians, where is your attention?

* (46.) OBJECTIONS. "We have all the honour through grace! (says a friend of voluntary humility.) What honour can you possibly ascribe to man when you have already ascribed all honour to God? But one who begins his sermon by pleading for merit; may well conclude it by taking from God part of his honour, dominion, and praise."

ANSWER. I plead only for an interest in Christ's merits through faith and the works of faith. This interest I call derived worthiness, which would be as dishonourable to Christ, as it is honourable to believers. I confess, also, that I aspire at the honour of shouting in heaven, "Allelujah to God and the Lamb!" In the meantime I hope that I may pay an inferior honour to all men, ascribe derived dominion to the king, bestow deserved praise upon my pious opponents, and claim the honour of being their obedient servant in Christ, without robbing the Lamb of his peculiar worthiness, and God of his proper honour, and dominion, and praise.

APPENDIX.

I FLATTER myself that the preceding discourse shows, (1.) That it is very possible to preach free grace, without directly or indirectly preaching Calvinism and free wrath: and (2.) That those who charge Mr. Wesley and me with subverting the articles of our Church, which guard the doctrine of grace, do us great wrong. Should God spare me, I shall also bear my testimony to the truth of the doctrine of conditional predestination and election, maintained in the seventeenth article, to which I have not had an opportunity of setting my seal in this work.

As I have honestly laid my Helvetic bluntness and Antinomian mistakes before the public in my notes, I am not conscious of having misrepresented my old sermon in my enlarged discourse. Should, however, the keener eyes of my opponents discover any real mistake in my additions, &c, upon information, I shall be glad to acknowledge and rectify it. Two or three sentences I have left out, merely because they formed vain repetitions, without adding any thing to the sense. — But whenever I have, for conscience' sake, made any alteration that affects, or seems to affect the doctrine, I have informed the reader of it, and of my reason for it in a note; that he may judge whether I was right twelve years ago, or whether I am now: and where there is no such note at the bottom of the page, there is an addition in the context, directing to the fifth note, where the alteration is acknowledged and accounted for according to the reasonable condition which I have made in the preface.

I particularly recommend the perusal of that note, of the first, and of the twenty-first, to those who do not yet see their way through the straits of Pharisaism and Antinomianism, through which I have been obliged to steer my course in handling a text, which, of all others, seems at first sight best calculated to countenance the mistakes of my opponents.

Sharp-sighted readers will see by my sermon that nothing is more difficult than rightly to divide the word of God. The ways of truth and error lie close together, though they never coincide. When some preachers say that "the road to heaven passes very near the mouth of hell," they do not mean that the road to heaven and the road to hell are one and the same. If I assert that the way of truth runs parallel to the ditch of error, I by no means intend to confound them. Let error therefore come, in some things, ever so near to truth, yet it can no more be the truth, than a filthy ditch, that runs parallel to a good road, can be the road.

You wonder at the athletic strength of Milo, that brawny man, who stands like an anvil under the bruising fist of his antagonist. Through the flowery paths of youth and childhood trace him back to his cradle; and, if you please, consider him unborn: he is Milo still. Nay, view him just conceived or quickened, and though your naked eye scarcely discovers the *punctum saliens* by which he differs from a non-entity or a lifeless thing; yet even then the difference between him and a non-entity is not only real, but prodigious; for it is the vast difference between something and nothing, between life and no life. In like manner trace back truth to its first stamina; investigate it till you find its *punctum saliens*, its first difference from error; and even then you will see an essential, a capital difference between them, though your short-sighted or inattentive neighbour can perceive none.

It is often a thing little in appearance that turns the scale of truth; nevertheless, the difference between a scale turned or not turned is as real as a difference between a just and a false weight, between right and wrong. I make this observation, (1.) To show that although my opponents come very near me in some things, and I go very near them in others, yet the difference between us is as essential as the difference between light and darkness, truth and error. And (2.) To remind them and myself that we ought so much the more to exercise Christian forbearance toward each other, as we find it difficult, whenever we do not stand upon our guard, to do justice to every part of the truth, without seeming to dissent even from ourselves. However, our short sightedness and twilight knowledge do not alter the nature of things. The truth of the anti-Pharisaic and anti-Crispian Gospel is as immutable as its eternal Author; and whether I have marked out its boundaries with a tolerable degree of justness or not, I must say as the heathen poet: —

> *Est modus in rebus, sunt certi denique fines,*
> *Quos ultra citraque nequit consistere rectum.*[*]

---

[*] Truth is confined within her firm bounds; nay, there is a middle line equally distant from all extremes; on that line she stands, and to miss her, you need only step over it to the right hand or to the left.

A SCRIPTURAL ESSAY

ON THE

ASTONISHING REWARDABLENESS OF WORKS,

ACCORDING TO

THE COVENANT OF GRACE.

CONTAINING,

I. A variety of plain scriptures, which show that heaven itself is the gracious reward of the works of faith, and that believers may lose that reward by bad works.

II. An answer to the most plausible objections of the Solifidians against this doctrine.

III. Some reflections upon the unreasonableness of those who scorn to work with an eye to the reward, which God offers to excite us to obedience.

To the law and to the testimony, Isaiah 8:8.

A SCRIPTURAL ESSAY

ON THE ASTONISHING REWARDABLENESS OF WORKS, ACCORDING TO THE COVENANT OF GRACE.

PART FIRST.

HAVING particularly guarded, in the preceding discourse, the doctrine of salvation by the covenant of grace, and having endeavoured to secure the foundation of the Gospel against the unwearied attacks of the Pharisees, I shall now particularly guard the works of the covenant of grace, and by that mean I shall secure the superstructure against the perpetual assaults of the Antinomians; a part of my work this, which is so much the more important, as the use of a strong foundation is only to bear up a useful structure.

None but fools act without motive. To deprive a wise man of every motive to act, is to keep him in total inaction: and to rob him of some grand motive, is considerably to weaken his willingness to act, or his fervour in acting. The burning love of God is undoubtedly the most generous motive to obedience; but alas! thousands of good men, like Cornelius, are yet strangers to that powerful principle shed abroad in their hearts by the Holy Ghost. In thousands of weak believers love is not yet properly kindled; it is rather a smoking flax than a blazing fire: in thousands of Laodicean professors it is scarcely lukewarm; and in all apostates it is waxed cold. Therefore, in the sickly state of the Church militant, it is as absurd in preachers to urge no motive of good works but grateful love, as it would be in physicians to insist that a good stomach must be the only motive from which their patients ought to take either food or physic.

Our Lord, far from countenancing our doctrinal refinements in this respect, perpetually secures the practice of good works, by promising heaven to all that persevere in doing them; while he deters us from sin, by threatening destruction to all that persist in committing it; working thus alternately upon our hopes and fears, those powerful springs of action in the human breast.

The force of this double incentive to practical religion I greatly weakened, when, being carried away by the stream of Solifidianism, I rashly said in my old sermon, after some of our reformers, that "good works shall be rewarded in heaven and eternal life, although not with eternal life and heaven." An Antinomian error this, which I again publicly renounce, and against which I enter the following Scriptural protest.

If the oracles of God command us to work from an initial life of grace for an eternal life of glory, frequently annexing the promise of heavenly bliss to good works, and threatening all workers of iniquity with hell torments; it follows, that heaven will be the gracious reward of good works, and hell the just wages of bad ones.

I readily grant, however, that if we consider ourselves merely as sinners, in the light of the first Gospel axiom, and according to the covenant of works, which we have so frequently broken, heaven is merely the gift of God through our Lord Jesus Christ: for, according to that covenant, destruction is the wages of all who have committed sin. But if we be converted sinners, or obedient believers, and if we consider ourselves in the light of the second Gospel axiom, and according to the covenant of grace, every unprejudiced person, who believes the Bible, must allow that heaven is the gracious reward of our works of faith.

An illustration may help the reader to see the justness of this distinction. A charitable nobleman discharges the debts of ten insolvent prisoners, sets them up in great or little farms, according to their respective abilities, and laying down a thousand pounds before them, he says: — "I have already done much for you, but I will do more still. I freely give you this purse to encourage your industry. You shall share this gold among you, if you manage your farms according to my directions; but if you let your fields be overrun with thorns, you shall not only lose the bounty I design for the industrious, but forfeit all my preceding favours." Now, who does not see that the thousand pounds thus laid down are a free gift of the nobleman; that nevertheless, upon the performance of the condition or terms he has fixed, they become a gracious reward of industry; and that consequently the obtaining of this reward turns now entirely upon the works of industry performed by the farmers.

Just so eternal salvation is the free gift of God through Jesus Christ; and yet the obtaining of it (on the part of adults) turns entirely upon their works of faith; that is, upon their works as well as upon their faith. Hence the Scripture says indifferently, "He that believeth is not condemned;" and, "If thou doest well shalt thou not be accepted?" "All that believe are justified;" and, "He that worketh righteousness is accepted." Our Lord, speaking of a weeping penitent, says equally: "Her sins, which are many, are forgiven, for she loved much;" and, "Thy sins are forgiven; thy faith hath saved thee." As for St. Paul, though he always justly excludes the works of unbelief, and merely ceremonial works, yet he so joins faith, and the works of faith, as to show us they are equally necessary to eternal salvation. "There is no condemnation," says he, "to them that are in Christ by faith," (here is the Pharisee's portion,) "who walk not after the flesh, but after the Spirit." (Here is the Antinomian's portion.) Hence it appears, that living faith now and always works righteousness, and that the works of righteousness now* and always accompany faith, so long as it remains living.

"I know this is the doctrine," says the judicious Mr. Baxter, "that will have the loudest outcries raised against it, and will make some cry out, *Heresy, Popery,*

---

* I use the word now, to stop up the Antinomian gap which one of my opponents tries to keep open by insinuating, that though a true believer may commit adultery and murder now, yet he will always work righteousness before he die.

Socinianism! and what not? For my own part, the Searcher of hearts knoweth that not singularity, nor any good will to Popery, provoketh me to entertain it: but that I have earnestly sought the Lord's direction upon my knees before I durst adventure on it; and that I resisted the light of this conclusion as long as I was able." May this bright testimony make way for an illuminated cloud of prophets and apostles! and may the Sun of righteousness, rising behind it, so scatter the shades of error, that we may awake out of our Laodicean sleep, and Antinomian dreams, and see a glorious, unclouded Gospel day!

That, in subordination to Christ, our eternal salvation depends upon good works, i.e. upon the works of faith, will, I think, appear indubitable to them that believe the Bible, and candidly consider the following scriptures, in which heaven and eternal life in glory are suspended upon works, if they spring from a sincere belief in the light of our dispensation; I say, if they spring from true faith, it being absolutely impossible for a heathen, and much more for a Christian, to work righteousness without believing in some degree "that God is, and that he is the rewarder of them that diligently seek him," as well as the punisher of them that presumptuously sin against him. "For without faith it is impossible to please God;" all faithless works springing merely from superstition, like those of Baal's priests, or from hypocrisy, like those of the Pharisees. Having thus guarded again the doctrine of faith, I produce some of the many scriptures that directly or indirectly annex the above-mentioned reward to works: And,

1. *To consideration, conversion, and exercising ourselves to godliness.*— "Because he considereth, and turneth away from his transgressions, &c, he shall surely live, he shall not die. When the wicked man turneth away from his wickedness, &c, he shall save his soul alive. Wherefore turn yourselves and live ye. Exercise thyself unto godliness, for it is profitable unto all things; having the promise of the life that now is, and that which is to come."

2. *To doing the will of God.* — "He that does the will of my Father shall enter into the kingdom of heaven. He that does the will of God abideth for ever. Whosoever shall do the will of God, the same is my brother and sister, i.e. the same is an heir of God, and a joint heir with Christ."

3. *To confessing Christ, and calling upon the name of the Lord.*— "With the mouth confession is made to salvation. Whosoever, therefore, shall confess me before men, him will I confess also before my Father: but whosoever shall deny me before men, him will I also deny before my Father. Whosoever shall call upon the name of the Lord shall be saved."

4. *To self denial.* — "If thy hand offend thee, cut it off: it is better for thee to enter into life maimed, than having two hands to go to hell, &c. And if thine eye offend thee, pluck it out: it is better for thee to enter into the kingdom of God with one eye, than having two eyes to be cast into hell fire. There is no man that hath left house, or brethren, &c, for my sake and the Gospel's, but he shall receive a hundred fold now, and in the world to come eternal life. He that loseth his life for my sake shall find it, &c. He that hateth his life in this world, shall keep it unto life eternal." And our Lord supposes that by "gaining the world" a man may "lose his own soul:" for, according to the covenant of grace, even reprobates are not totally lost till they make themselves sons of perdition, like Judas, i.e. till they personally and absolutely

"lose their own souls" and heaven by their personal and obstinate pursuit of worldly things.

5. *To diligent labour and earnest endeavours.*— "O man of God, lay hold on eternal life, Work out your own salvation. Labour for the meat that endureth to everlasting life. Keep thy heart with all diligence, for out of it are the issues of life. In so doing thou shalt save thyself. Narrow is the gate that leads to life. Strive to enter in. The violent press into the kingdom of God, and take it by force."

6. *To keeping the commandments.*— "Blessed are they that do his commandments, &c, that they may enter through the gates 'into the city, i.e. into heaven. There shall in no wise enter into it any thing that worketh abomination. If thou wilt enter into life,[*] keep the commandments. Thou hast answered right; this do and thou shalt live. There is one Lawgiver, who is able to save and to destroy: [some of whose laws run thus:] Forgive, and ye shall be forgiven. Blessed are the merciful, for they shall obtain mercy. With what judgment ye judge, ye shall be judged. For he shall have judgment without mercy, that hath showed no mercy. Blessed are the peace makers, for they shall be called the children of God, [and, of course, the heirs of the kingdom.] The King shall say unto them, Come, ye blessed of my Father, inherit the kingdom prepared for you, for I was hungry and ye gave me meat, &c. Whatsoever ye do, do it heartily, as to the Lord, knowing that of the Lord ye shall receive the reward of the inheritance: but he that does wrong, shall receive for the wrong which he hath done, and there is no respect of persons. Be ye therefore followers of God as dear children, &c, for this ye know, that no whore-monger, &c, hath any inheritance in the kingdom of God. The works of the flesh are manifest, which are these, adultery, &c, of which I tell you [believers] that they who do such things shall not inherit the kingdom of God."

7. *To running, fighting, faithfully laying up treasure in heaven, and feeding the flock of God.*— "They who run in a race run all; but one receiveth the prize: so run that you may obtain. Now they are temperate in all things to obtain a corruptible crown; but we an incorruptible. I therefore so run, fight, and bring my body into subjection, [that I may obtain;] lest I myself should be cast away;" i.e. should not be approved of, should be rejected, and lose my incorruptible crown. "Fight the good fight of faith, lay hold on eternal life. Lay up treasure in heaven. Make yourselves friends with the mammon of unrighteousness, that when you fail on earth they may receive you into everlasting habitations. Charge them who are rich that they do good, that they be rich in good works, laying up in store for themselves a good foundation against the time to come, that they may lay hold on eternal life. Feed the flock of God, &c, being examples to the flock, and when the Chief Shepherd shall appear, ye shall receive the crown of glory that fadeth not away."

8. *To love and charity.*— "Though I have all faith, &c, and have no charity, I am nothing. She [the woman] shall be saved, &c, if they [womankind] continue in faith and charity. Whosoever hateth his brother hath not eternal life. He that loveth not his brother abideth in death. We know we have passed from death unto life, because we love the brethren. If any man love not the Lord Jesus, let him be anathema. The crown of life, which the Lord hath promised to them that love him."

---

[*] See the excellent comment of our Church upon these words of our Lord, Fourth Check.

Creeds and Scripture Scales

9. *To a godly walk.* — "There is no condemnation to them, &c, that walk not after the flesh. As many as walk according to this rule, mercy [be, or will be] on them. If we walk in the light [of good works, Matthew 5:15,] the blood of Christ cleanseth us from all sin. The Lord will give grace and glory, and no good thing will he withhold from them that walk uprightly. Many [fallen believers] walk, &c, enemies of the cross of Christ, whose end is destruction."

10. *To persevering watchfulness, faithfulness, prayer, &c.* — "He that endureth unto the end, the same shall be saved. Be faithful unto death, and I will give thee the crown of life. Blessed is the man that endureth temptation, for when he is tried he shall receive the crown of life. Because thou hast kept the word of my patience, I will also keep thee, &c. To him that overcometh will I grant to sit with me in my throne. To him that keepeth my words unto the end, &c, will I give the morning star. Take heed to yourselves, &c, watch and pray always, that ye may be counted worthy to escape, &c, and to stand before the Son of man." In a word,

11. *To patient continuance in mortifying the deeds of the body, and in well doing.* — "If ye live after the flesh, ye shall die; but if ye through the Spirit mortify the deeds of the body, ye shall live. For he that soweth to his flesh, shall of the flesh reap perdition; but he that soweth to the Spirit, shall of the Spirit reap life everlasting. And let us not be weary in well doing, for in due season we shall reap, [not if we faint or not, but] if we faint not. He that reapeth receiveth wages and gathereth fruit unto life eternal. Ye have your fruit unto holiness, and the end everlasting life." God, at the revelation of his righteous judgment "will render to every man according to his deeds: eternal life to them who, by patient continuance in well doing, seek for glory. Anguish upon every soul of man that does evil, &c, but glory to every man that worketh good, &c, for there is no respect of persons with God."

Is it not astonishing, that in sight of so many plain scriptures the Solifidians should still ridicule the passport of good works, and give it to the winds as a "paper kite?" However, if the preceding texts do not appear sufficient, I can send another volley of Gospel truths, to show that the initial salvation of believers themselves may be lost through bad works.

I know thy works, &c, so then, "because thou art lukewarm, I will spue thee out of my mouth." "What doth it profit, my brethren, though a man [τις any one, and two verses below, any one of you, James 2:14, 16,] say he hath faith, and hath not works," [now?] "Can faith save him, &c? Faith if it hath not works is dead, being alone." Grudge not one against another, brethren, lest ye be condemned." [In the original it is the same word which is rendered damned, Mark 16:16.] "If we suffer, we shall also reign with him. If we [believers] deny him, he will also deny us. Add to your faith virtue, &c, charity, &c. If ye do these things ye shall never fall, for so an entrance shall be ministered unto you abundantly into the everlasting kingdom of our Lord. It had been better for them that have escaped the pollutions of the world through the knowledge of our Saviour, [i.e. for believers,] not to have known the way of righteousness, than after they have known it to turn from the holy commandment delivered unto them. Every tree that bringeth not forth good fruit is cut down and cast into the fire. Every branch in me that beareth not fruit my Father taketh away. Abide in me, &c. If a man abide not in me [by keeping my commandments in faith] he is cast forth as a branch, and is withered; and [he shall share the fate of the branches that have really belonged to the natural vine, and now bear no more fruit] men gather them, and cast them into the fire, and they are burned." The fig tree in the Lord's moral vineyard is cut down for not bearing fruit. "Him that sinneth I will blot out of my book. Some, having put away a good conscience, concerning faith have made shipwreck. Such as turn back to their own wickedness, the Lord shall lead them forth with the evil doers. — Toward thee goodness, if [by continuing in obedience] thou continue in his goodness, otherwise thou shalt be cut off."

Again: "For the wickedness of their doings I will drive them out of my house, I will love them no more. Some are already turned aside after Satan, having damnation because they have cast off their first faith; the faith that works by love; the mystery of faith kept in a pure conscience; the faith unfeigned [that the apostle couples with] a good conscience;" the faith that is made perfect by works; the faith that cries, like Rachel, Give me children, give me good works, or else I die; — the faith that faints without obedience, and actually dies by bad works; the following scriptures abundantly proving that faith, and consequently the just who live by faith, may die by bad works.

"When a righteous man[*] doth turn from his righteousness and commit iniquity, &c, he shall die in his sin, and his righteousness which he has done shall not be remembered," Ezekiel 3:20. Again: "When the righteous, &c, does according to all the abominations that the wicked man does, shall he live? All his righteousness that he has done shall not be mentioned' in his trespass that he hath trespassed, and in his sin that he hath sinned, in them shall he die," Ezekiel 18:24. Once more: "The righteousness of the righteous shall not deliver him in the day of his transgression, &c. When I say to the righteous that he shall surely live;[†] if he trust to his righteousness, and commit iniquity, he shall die for it" Ezekiel 33:13.

It seems that God, foreseeing the Solifidians would be hard of belief, notwithstanding the great ado they make about faith, condescended to their infirmity, and kindly spoke the same thing over and over; for setting again the broad seal of

---

[*] That this is spoken of a truly righteous man, i.e. of a believer, appears from the following reasons: (1.) The righteous here mentioned is opposed to the wicked mentioned in the context. As surely then as the word wicked means there one really wicked, so does the word righteous mean here one truly righteous. (2.) The righteous man's turning from his righteousness is opposed to the wicked man's turning from his iniquity. If therefore the righteous man's righteousness is to be understood of feigned goodness, so the wicked man's iniquity must be understood of reigned iniquity. (3.) The crime of the righteous man here spoken of is turning from his righteousness: but if his righteousness were only a hypocritical righteousness, he would rather deserve to be commended for renouncing it; a wicked, sly Pharisee being more odious to God than a barefaced sinner, who has honesty enough not to put on the mask of religion, Rev. 3:15. (4.) Part of this apostate's punishment, will consist, in not having the righteousness that he has done remembered. But if his righteousness is a false righteousness, or mere hypocrisy, the Divine threatening proves a precious promise; for you cannot please a hypocrite better than by assuring him that his hypocrisy shall never be remembered. What a pity is it, that to defend our mistakes we should fix egregious nonsense and gross contradiction upon the only wise God!

[†] These words are another indubitable proof that the righteous here mentioned is a truly righteous person; as the holy and true God would never say to a wicked Pharisee, that he shall surely live.

heaven to the truth that chiefly guards the second Gospel axiom, he says for the fourth time, "When the righteous turneth from his righteousness and committeth iniquity, he shall even die thereby: but if the wicked turn from his wickedness, and do that which is lawful and right, he shall live thereby," Ezekiel 33:18, 19.

If Ezekiel be not allowed to be a competent judge, let Christ himself be heard' "Then his Lord said unto him, O thou wicked servant, I forgave thee all that debt, &c: shouldst not thou also have had compassion on thy fellow servant, even as I had pity on thee? And his Lord was wroth, and delivered him to the tormentors," Matthew 18:26, &c.

All the preceding scriptures are thus summed up by our Lord, Matthew 25:46, "These [the persons who have not finally done the works of faith] shall go into everlasting punishment; but the righteous [those who have done them to the end, at least from the time of their re-conversion, if they were backsliders] shall go into eternal life." This doctrine agrees perfectly with the conclusion of the sermon on the mount: "Whosoever heareth these sayings of mine, and doeth them, I will liken him to a wise man, who built his house upon a rock. And every one that heareth these sayings of mine, and doeth them not, shall be likened unto a foolish man, who built his house upon the sand." — Nay, this is Christ's explicit doctrine. No words can be plainer than these: "They that are in their graves shall hear his voice and come forth; they that have done good unto the resurrection of life; and they that have done evil unto the resurrection of condemnation," John 5:29. All creeds, therefore, like that of St. Athanasius, and all faith, must end in practice. This is a grand article of what might, with peculiar propriety, be called the catholic faith — the faith that is common to, and essential under all the dispensations of the everlasting Gospel, in all countries and ages: "the faith which, except a man believe faithfully," i.e. so as to work righteousness, like the good and faithful servant, "he cannot be saved."

PART SECOND.

As some difficulties probably rise in the reader's mind against the preceding doctrine, it may not be amiss to produce them in the form of objections, and to answer them more fully than I have yet done.

I. OBJECTION. "All the scriptures that you have produced, are nothing but descriptions of those who shall be saved or damned: you have therefore no ground to infer from such texts, that in the great day our works of faith shall be rewarded with an eternal life of glory, and our bad works punished with eternal death."

ANSWER. Of all the paradoxes advanced by mistaken divines, your assertion is perhaps the greatest. You have no more ground for it than I have for saying that England is a lawless kingdom, and that all the promises of rewards, and threatenings of punishments, stamped with the authority of the legislative power, are no legal sanctions. If I seriously maintained that the bestowing of public bounties upon the inventors of useful arts; that the discharge of some prisoners, and the condemnation of others, according to the statutes of the realm, are things which take place without any respect to law; that the acts of parliament are mere descriptions of persons, which the government rewards, acquits, or punishes without any respect to worthiness, innocence, or demerit; and that the judges absolve or condemn criminals merely out of free grace and free wrath; if I maintained a paradox so dishonourable to the government and so contrary to common sense, would you not be astonished! And if I gave the name of Papist to all that did not receive my error as Gospel, would you not recommend me to a dose of Dr. Monro's hellebore? And are they much wiser, who fix the foul blot upon the Divine government, and make the Protestants believe that the sanctions of the King of kings, and the judicial dictates of Him who judges the world in righteousness, are not laws and sentences, but representations and descriptions?

A comparison will show the frivolousness of your objection. There is, if I mistake not, a statute that condemns a highwayman to be hanged, and allows a reward of forty pounds to the person that takes him. A counsellor observes that this statute was undoubtedly made to deter people from going upon the highway, and to encourage the taking of robbers. "Not so," says a lawyer from Geneva; "though robbers are hanged according to law, yet the men that take them are not legally rewarded; the sum mentioned in the statute is given them of free, gratuitous, undeserved, unmerited, distinguishing grace." Nay, says the counsellor, if they do not deserve the forty pounds more than other people, that sum might as well be bestowed upon the highwaymen themselves as upon those who take them at the hazard of their life. "And so it might," says the Geneva lawyer; "for although poor, blind legalists make people believe that the promissory part of the law was made to excite people to exert themselves in the taking of robbers; yet we know better at Geneva; and I inform you that the clause you speak of is only a description of certain men, for whom the government designs the reward of forty pounds gratis." The admirers of Geneva logic clap their hands and cry out, "Well said! down with legality!" but an English jury smiles and cries, "Down with absurdity!" (See *Fourth Check*, Vol. 1, pg 269.)

II. OBJECTION. "You confound our title to, with our meetness for heaven, two things which we carefully distinguish. Our title to heaven, being solely what Christ has done and suffered for his people, has nothing to do with either our holiness or good works; but our meetness for heaven supposes holiness, if not good works. Therefore God's unconverted, sinful people, who have, in Christ, a complete title to heaven, by right of 'finished salvation,' shall all be made meet for heaven in the day of his power."

ANSWER 1. I understand you, and so does Mr. Fulsome. You insinuate that, till the day you speak of comes, unconverted sinners and backsliders may indulge themselves like the servant mentioned in the Gospel, who said, My master delayeth his coming, and began to drink with the drunken; but alas! instead of "a day of power," he saw a day of vengeance, and his "finished salvation," So called, ended in weeping, wailing, and gnashing of teeth.

2. Your distinction is contrary to the Scriptures, which represent all impenitent workers of iniquity as having a full title to hell according to both law and Gospel; so far are the oracles of God from supposing that some workers of iniquity have a full title to heaven, absolutely independent on the obedience of faith.

3. It is contrary to reason; for reason dictates that whosoever has a full title to a punishment, or to a reward, is fully meet for it. Where is the difference between saying that a murderer is fully meet for, or that he has a full title to the gallows? If a

palace richly furnished was bestowed upon the most righteous man in the kingdom, and you were the person, would it not be absurd to distinguish between your title to, and your meetness for that recompense? Or if the king, in consequence of a valuable consideration received from the prince, had promised a coronet to every swift runner in England, next to the prince's interposition and his majesty's promise, would not your running well be at once your title to, and meetness for that honour? And is not this the case with respect to the incorruptible crowns reserved in heaven for those who so run that they may obtain?

4. Your distinction draws after it the most horrid consequences: for if a full title to heaven may be separated from a meetness for the lowest place in heaven, it necessarily follows that Solomon had a full title to heaven when he worshipped Ashtaroth; and the incestuous Corinthian when he defiled his father's bed; in flat opposition to the dictates of every man's conscience, (if you except Mr. Fulsome and his fraternity.) It follows that St. Paul told a gross untruth when he said, "This ye know, that no idolater and no unclean person hath any inheritance in the kingdom of Christ and of God." In a word, it follows that believers "sanctified with the blood of the covenant, who draw back to perdition," (such as the apostates mentioned Hebrews 10:29,) may have no title to heaven in all their sanctifying faith; while some impenitent murderers, like David and Manasses, have a perfect title to it in all their crimes and unbelief.

5. This is not all. Our Lord's mark, "By their fruits ye shall know them," is absolutely wrong if you are right: for your distinction abolishes the grand characteristic of the children of God and those of the devil, which consists in not committing or committing iniquity, in doing or not doing righteousness, according to these plain words of St. John, "He that committeth sin is of the devil. In this the children, of God are manifest, and the children of the devil. Whosoever does not righteousness is not of God, neither he that loveth not [much less he that murders] his brother," 1 John 3:8, 10. Thus the Lord's sacred enclosure is broken down, his sheepfold becomes a fold for goats, a dog kennel, a swine stye. Nay, for what you know, all bloody adulterers may be "sheep in wolves' clothing;" while all "those that have escaped the pollution that is in the world" may only be "wolves in sheep's clothing;" it mattering not, with regard to the goodness of our title to heaven, whether "filthiness to Belial," or "holiness to the Lord" be written upon our foreheads. O sir, how much more dangerous is your scheme than that of the primitive Babel builders! They only brought on a confusion of the original language; but your doctrine confounds light and darkness, promises and threatenings, the heirs of heaven and those of hell, the seed of the woman and that of the serpent.

6. As to your intimation that holiness is secured by teaching that God's people shall absolutely be made willing to forsake their sins, and to become righteous in the day of God's power, that so they may have a meetness for, as well as a title to heaven; it drags after it this horrid consequence: the devil's people, "in the day of God's power," shall absolutely be made willing to forsake their righteousness, that they may have a meetness for, as well as a title to hell. A bitter reverse this of your "sweet Gospel!"

To conclude. If by your distinction you only want to insinuate that Christ is the grand and properly meritorious procurer of our salvation, from first to last, and that the works of faith are only a secondary, instrumental, evidencing cause of our final salvation, you mean just as I do. But if you give the world to understand that election to eternal glory is unconditional, or, which comes all to one, that no sin can invalidate our title to heaven; from the preceding observations it appears that you deceive the simple, make Christ the minister of sin, and inadvertently poison the Church with the rankest Antinomianism.

III. OBJECTION. "You call the works of Christ the primary and properly meritorious cause, and our works of faith the secondary and instrumental cause of our eternal salvation. But according to your doctrine, our works should be called the first cause, and Christ's work the second: for you make the final success of Christ's work to depend on our work, which is manifestly setting our performances above those of the Redeemer."

ANSWER 1. When a gardener affirms that he shall have no crop unless he dig and set his garden, does he manifestly set his work above that of the God of nature? And when we say that "we shall not reap final salvation, if we do not work out our salvation," do we exalt ourselves above the God of grace?

2. Whether our free agency turns the scale for life or death, to all eternity Christ shall have the honour of having died to bestow an initial life of grace even upon those who choose death in the error of their ways, and to have made them gracious and sincere offers of an eternal life of glory. In this sense then Christ's work cannot be rendered ineffectual; it being his absolute decree that the word of his grace shall be the savour of life to obedient free agents, and the savour of death to the disobedient. Therefore, if we will not have the eternal benefit of his Redeeming work, we cannot take from him the eternal honour of having shed his blood even for those who tread it under foot, and who "bring upon themselves swift destruction by denying the Lord that bought them."

3. Christ is not dishonoured by the doctrine that represents the effect of the greater wheel as being thus in part suspended upon the turning of the less. The light of the sun shines in vain for me if I shut my eyes. Life is a far nobler gift than food. I can give my starving neighbour bread, but I cannot give him life. Nevertheless, the higher wheel stops, if the inferior is quite at a stand: he must die if he has no nourishment. Thus, by God's appointment, the preservation of all the first born of the Israelites in Egypt depended upon the sprinkling of a lamb's blood; the life of all them that were bitten by the fiery serpents was suspended on a look toward the brazen serpent; and that of Rahab and her friends hung, if I may so speak, on a scarlet thread. Now, if God did not dishonour his wisdom when he made the life of so many people to depend upon those seemingly insignificant works; and if he continues to make the life of all mankind depend upon breathing; is it reasonable to say that he is dishonoured by his own doctrine, which suspends our eternal salvation upon the works of faith?

4. Your objection can be retorted. Most Calvinists grant that our justification in the day of conversion depends upon believing. Thus the Rev. Mr. Madan, in his sermon on James 2:24, (p. 18,) says, "Though the Lord Jesus has merited our justification before God, yet we are not actually justified, till he be received into the heart by faith, and rested on," &c. Therefore, in the day of conversion, that great minister being judge, our justification is suspended on the work which he calls "receiving Christ," or "resting on him." And how much more may our

eternal salvation be suspended on faith and works; i.e. on resting upon Christ and working righteousness!

5. This is not all. Both Mr. Madan and Mr. Hill call faith the instrumental CAUSE of our justification, and every body knows that the effect is always suspended on the CAUSE. Now, if so great an effect as a sinner's present justification may be suspended upon the single CAUSE of faith, why may not a believer's eternal justification be suspended upon the double CAUSE of faith and its works? In a word, why must Mr. Wesley be represented as heterodox for insinuating that believing and working instrumentally CAUSE our eternal justification; when Mr. Madan wears the badge of orthodoxy, although he insinuates that believing instrumentally CAUSES our justification?

If Mr. Madan say that he allows faith to be an instrumental CAUSE, on account of its being the gift of God by which we receive Christ; I answer, that we allow the work of faith to be an instrumental cause, because it springs from the Spirit of Christ, and constitutes our likeness to Christ, and our evangelical righteousness; a righteousness this which Christ came into the world to promote. "For God sending his Son, &c, condemned sin in the flesh, that the righteousness of the law might be fulfilled in us, who walk not after the flesh, but after the Spirit," i.e. who walk in good works. If it is asserted that there can be but one instrumental cause of our salvation, that is, faith; I appeal to reason, which dictates that Christian faith implies a variety of causes, such as preaching Christ, and hearing him preached: for faith comes by hearing, and hearing by the word of God. This argument, therefore, carries its own answer along with it.

6. To conclude: Mr. Madan, in the above-quoted sermon, (p. 16,) says with great truth: — "Christ and faith are not one and the same thing; how then can we reconcile the apostle with himself, when he says, in one place, we are justified by Christ; and in another, we are justified by faith? This can only be done by having recourse to the plain distinction which the Scriptures afford us .in considering Christ as the meritorious cause, and faith as the instrumental cause, or that by which the meritorious cause is applied unto us, so that we are benefited thereby." Now all our heresy consists in applying Mr. Madan's judicious reasoning to all the scriptures that guard the second Gospel axiom, thus: "How can we reconcile the apostle with himself, when he says in one place, 'We are saved by Christ,' and in other places, 'We are saved by faith, We are saved by hope. Work out your own salvation. Confession is made to salvation,' &c, for Christ and faith, Christ and hope, Christ and works, Christ and making confession, are not one and the same thing? This seeming inconsistency in St. Paul's doctrine vanishes by admitting a plain distinction, which the Scriptures afford us: that is, (1.) By considering Christ, from first to last, as the properly meritorious cause of our present and eternal salvation. (2.) By considering faith as the instrumental cause of our salvation from the guilt and pollution of sin on earth. And, (3.) By considering the works of faith not only as the evidencing cause of our justification in the great day, but also as an instrumental cause of our continuing in the life of faith; just as eating, drinking, breathing, and such works, that spring from natural life, are instrumental causes of our continuing in natural life." Thus faith, and its works, are two inferior causes, whereby the properly meritorious cause is so completely applied to obedient, persevering believers, that they are now, and for ever

shall be benefited by it. As I flatter myself that this six-fold answer satisfies the candid reader, I pass on to another plausible objection.

IV. OBJECTION. "Though you assert that from first to last the works and sufferings of Christ are the grand and properly meritorious cause of our salvation; yet, according to your scheme, man having a life of glory upon his choice, and heaven upon working out his salvation, the honour of free grace is not secured. For, after all, free will and human faithfulness, or unfaithfulness, turn the scale for eternal salvation or damnation."

ANSWER. 1. In the very nature of things we are free agents, or the wise and righteous God would act inconsistently with his wisdom and equity in dispensing rewards and punishments. If, through "the saving grace of God" which "has appeared to all men," we were not again endued with an awful power to "choose life," and to be faithful, it would be as injudicious to punish or recompense mankind as to whip a dead horse for not moving, condemn fire for burning, or grant water an eternal reward for its fluidity. 2. Were I ashamed of my moral free agency, I should be ashamed of the noble power that distinguishes me from the brute creation. I should be ashamed of the Old Testament, and of Moses, who says, "Behold, I call heaven and earth to record, that I have set before you life and death, blessing and cursing; therefore choose life." I should be ashamed of the New Testament, and of Christ, who complains, "You will not come unto me that you might have life," i.e. you will not use the power which my preventing grace has given you, that you might live here a life of faith and holiness, and be hereafter rewarded with a life of happiness and glory. In a word, I should give up the second Gospel axiom, and tacitly reproach my Maker, who says, "Why will ye die, O house of Israel? For I have no pleasure in the death of him that dieth; wherefore turn yourselves, and live ye."

3. To convince you that free agency, and a right use of it, are by no means inconsistent with Divine grace and genuine humility, I ask, Did not God endue our first parents with free will? Are not even some rigid Calvinists ashamed to deny it? If free will in man is a power dishonourable to God, did not our wise Creator mistake when he pronounced man "very good," at the very time man was a free willer? For how could man be very good if he had within him a power that necessarily militates against the honour of God, as the Calvinists insinuate free will does!

4. I go one step farther, and ask, Did God ever endue one child of Adam with power to avoid one sin? If you say no, you contradict the Scriptures, your own conscience, and the consciences of all mankind; you fix the blot of folly on all the judges who have judicially punished malefactors with death; and when you insinuate that the Lawgiver of the universe will send all workers of iniquity personally into hell for not "doing what is lawful and right to save their souls alive," or for not avoiding sin, when he never gave them the least power personally so to do, you pour almost as much contempt upon his perfections as if you hinted that he will one day raise all creeping insects, to judge them according to their steps, and to cast into a place of torment as many as did not move as swiftly as a race horse.

If you answer in the affirmative, and grant that God has graciously endued one child of Adam with power to avoid one sin, so far you hold free will as well as Moses and Jesus Christ. Now if God has bestowed free will upon one child of Adam with respect to the avoiding of one sin; why not upon two, with respect to the avoiding of two sins? Why not upon all, with respect to the avoiding of all the sins that are incompatible with the obedience of faith?

5. Again: as it would be absurd to say that God gave a power to avoid one sin only to one child of Adam; so it would be impious to suppose God gave him this power, that, in case he faithfully used it, he should necessarily boast of it. Pharisaic boasting is then by no means the necessary consequence of our moral liberty, or of a proper use of our free will. Thus it appears that your specious objection is founded upon a heap of paradoxes; and that to embrace free wrath lest we should not make enough of free grace, and to jump into fatalism lest we should be proud of our free will, is not less absurd than to prostrate ourselves before a traitor lest we should not honour the king, and to run to a house of ill fame lest we should be proud of our chastity.

6. Our doctrine secures the honour of free grace as well as Calvinism. You will be convinced of it if you consider the following articles of our creed with respect to free grace: — (1.) Before the fall, the free grace of our Creator gave us in Adam holiness, happiness, and a power to continue in both. (2.) Since the fall, the free grace of our Redeemer indulges us with a reprieve, an accepted time, a day of visitation and salvation; in a word, with a better covenant, and a "free gift that is come upon all men unto [initial] justification of life," Romans 5:18. (3.) That nothing may be wanted on God's part, the free grace of our Sanctifier excites us to make a proper use of the free gift, part of which is moral liberty. (4.) Thus even our free will to good is all of creating, redeeming, and sanctifying grace. Therefore, with regard to that glorious power, as well as to every other talent, we humbly ask, with St. Paul, "What hast thou, that thou hast not received?" (5.) This is not all: we are commanded to "account the long suffering of God [a degree of] salvation;" and so it is: for without forcing, or necessarily inclining our will, God's providential free grace disposes a thousand circumstances in such a manner as to second the calls of the everlasting Gospel. The gracious Preserver of men works daily a thousand wonders to keep us out of the grave, and out of hell. A thousand wheels have turned ten thousand times, in and out of the Church, to bring us the purest streams of Gospel truth. Countless breathings of the Spirit of grace add virtue to those streams; free grace therefore not only prevents, but also in numberless ways accompanies, follows, directs, encourages, and assists us in all the works of our salvation.

And yet, while God thus works in us, as the God of all grace, "both to will and to do of his good pleasure;" that is, while he thus gives us the faculty to will, and the power to do; and while he secretly, by his Spirit, and publicly, by his ministers and providences, excites us to make a proper use of that faculty and power; yet, as the God of wisdom, holiness, and justice, he leaves the act to our choice; thus treating us as rational creatures, whom he intends wisely to reward, or justly to punish, according to their works, and not according to his own.

Hence it appears that we go every step of the way with our Calvinist brethren while they exalt Christ and free grace in a rational and Scriptural manner; and that we refuse to follow them only when they set Christ at naught as a prophet, a lawgiver, a judge, and a king; under pretence of extolling him as a priest; or when they put wanton free grace and unrelenting free wrath in the place of the genuine free grace testified of in the Scriptures.

The Works of John Fletcher

V. OBJECTION. "One more difficulty remains: if I freely obey the Gospel and am saved; and if my neighbour freely disobeys it and is damned, what makes me to differ from him? Is it not my free obedience of faith?"

ANSWER. Undoubtedly. And his free disobedience makes him differ from you; or it would be very absurd judicially to acquit and reward you rather than him, according to your works. And it would be strange duplicity to condemn and punish him rather than you in a day of judgment, after the most solemn protestations that equity and impartiality shall dictate the Judge's sentence.

As to the difficulty arising from St. Paul's question, 1 Corinthians 4:7, "Who maketh thee to differ?" to what I have said about it in the preceding sermon, (p. 479,) I add: 1. According to the covenant of works "all fall short of the glory of God." And when any one asks, with respect to the law of innocence, "Who makes thee to differ?" the proper answer is, "There is no difference: every mouth must be stopped: all the world is guilty before God: enter not into judgment with thy servant, O Lord." But, according to the covenant of grace, he that freely believes and obeys in the strength of free grace, undoubtedly makes himself to differ from him that by obstinate disobedience "does despite to the Spirit of grace." If this point be given up, the Diana and the Apollo, or rather the Apollyon of the Antinomians (I mean wanton free grace, and merciless free wrath) are set up for ever. However,

2. If the question, "Who maketh thee to differ?" be asked with respect to the number of our talents, the proper answer is, "God's distinguishing grace alone maketh us to differ." And that this is the sense which the apostle had in view, is evident from the context. He had before reproved the Corinthians for "saying every one, I am of Paul, and I of Apollos," &c; and now he adds, "These things I have in a figure transferred to myself and to Apollos, that ye might learn in us not to think [of gifted, popular men, or of yourselves] above that which is written, that no one of you be puffed up for one against another: for who maketh thee to differ?" Why is thy person graceful? And why art thou naturally an eloquent man, like Apollos, while thy brother's speech is rude, and his bodily presence weak and contemptible like mine? But, —

3. If you ask, "Who maketh thee to differ?" with respect to the improvement or non-improvement of our gifts and graces: if you inquire whether God necessitates some to disbelieve that they may necessarily sin and be damned; while he necessitates others to believe that they may necessarily work righteousness and be saved: I utterly deny the last question, and in this sense St. Paul answers his own misapplied question thus: "Be not deceived: what a man [not what God] soweth, that shall he also reap;" perdition if he sow to the flesh, and eternal life if he sow to the Spirit. Nor am I either afraid or ashamed to second him, by saying, upon the walls of Jerusalem, that, in the last-mentioned sense, *We make ourselves to differ.* And Scripture, reason, conscience, the Divine perfections, and the trump of God, which will soon summon us to judgment, testify that this reply stands as firm as one half of the Bible, and the second Gospel axiom on which it is immovably founded.

Nay, there is not a promise or a threatening in the Bible that is not a proof of our Lawgiver's want of wisdom, or of our Judge's want of equity; if we are not graciously endued with a capacity to make ourselves differ from the obstinate violators of the law, and despisers of the Gospel, — that is, if we are not free agents. There is not an exhortation, a warning, nor an entreaty in the sacred pages, that is not a demonstration of the penman's folly, or of the freedom of our will. In a word, there is not a sinner justly punished in hell, nor a believer wisely rewarded in heaven, that does not indirectly say to all the world of rationals: "Though the God" of grace draws thee to obedience, yet it is with "the bands of a man." For, after all, he "leaves thee in the hand of thy counsel, to keep the commandments, and perform acceptable obedience if thou wilt. Before man is life and death, and whether him liketh shall be given him," Ecclus. 15:14, &c.

But, although your obedience of faith makes you to differ from your condemned neighbour, you have no reason to reject the first Gospel axiom, and to indulge a boasting* contrary to faith and free grace: for your Christian faith, which is the root of your obedience, is peculiarly the gift of God; whether you consider it as to its precious seed, ("the word nigh;") as to its glorious object, (Christ and the truth;) as to the means by which that object is revealed, (such as preaching and hearing;) as to the opportunities and faculties of using those means, (such as life, reason, &c,) or as to the Spirit of grace, whose assistance in this case is so important, that he is called "the Spirit of faith." And yet that Spirit does not act irresistibly; all believers unnecessarily and freely yielding to it, and all unbelievers unnecessarily and freely resisting it. So far only does the matter turn upon free will. Thus it appears, that although the act of faith is ours, we are so much indebted to free grace for it, that believers can no more boast of being their own saviours, because they daily believe and work in order to their final salvation, than they can boast of being their own preservers, because they daily breathe and eat in order to their continued preservation.

On the other hand, although your condemned neighbour's disobedience makes him differ from you, he has no reason to reject the second Gospel axiom, and to exculpate himself by charging Heaven with capricious partiality and horrid free wrath: because God, whose mercy is over all his works, and who is no respecter of persons, graciously bestowed a talent of free grace upon him as well as upon you, according to one or another of the Divine dispensations. For the royal master,

---

* There is a two-fold glorying: the one Pharisaic and contrary to faith: of this St. Paul speaks, where he says, "Boasting is excluded, &c, by the law of faith," Romans 3:27. The other evangelical and agreeable to faith, since it is a believer's holy triumph in God, resulting from the testimony of a good conscience. Concerning it the apostle says, "Let every man prove his own work, and then shall he have rejoicing [boasting] in himself alone, and not in another," Galatians 6:4. [The word in the original is καυχησις in one passage, and καυχημα in the other.] These seemingly contrary doctrines are highly consistent; their opposition answering to that of the Gospel axioms. The first axiom allows of no glorying but in Christ, who has alone fulfilled the law of works, or the terms of the first covenant: but the second axiom allows obedient believers an humble καυχημα, "glorying" or "rejoicing," upon their personally fulfilling the law of faith, or the gracious terms of the second covenant, 2 Corinthians 1:12. This rejoicing answers to what St. Paul calls the "witness of our own spirit," or "the testimony of a good conscience;" which, next to the witness of the word and Spirit concerning God's mercy and Christ's blood, is the ground of a Christian's confidence. "Beloved, if our heart condemn us not, then have we confidence toward God, &c, because we keep his commandments," 1 John 3:21, 22. And yet, astonishing! this blessed rejoicing, so strongly recommended by St. Paul and St. John, who, one would think, knew something of the Gospel, is now represented by some modern evangelists as the quintessence of Pharisaism.

mentioned in the Gospel, gave a pound to the servant that buried it, as well as to him that gained ten pounds by occupying till his lord came.

"But, upon that footing, what becomes of distinguishing grace?" If by "distinguishing grace" you mean Calvinistic partiality, I answer, it must undoubtedly sink, together with its inseparable partner, unconditional reprobation, into the pit of error, whence they ascended to fill the Church with contentions, and the world with infidels. But if you mean *Scriptural, distinguishing grace*, that is, the "manifold wisdom of God," which makes him proceed gradually, and admit a pleasing variety in the works of grace, as well as in the productions of nature; — if you mean his good pleasure to give the heathens one talent, the Jews two, the Papists three, the Protestants four; or if you mean the different methods which he uses to call sinners to repentance, such as his familiar expostulation with Cain: his wonderful warning of Lot's sons-in-law: his rousing King Saul by the voice of Samuel, and Saul of Tarsus by the voice of Christ: (Samuel and Christ coming, or seeming to come from the invisible world for that awful purpose:) his audibly inviting Judas and the rich ruler to follow him, promising the latter heavenly treasure if he would give his earthly possessions to the poor: his shocking, by preternatural earthquakes the consciences of the Philippian jailer and the two malefactors that suffered with him: his awakening Ananias, Sapphira, and thousands more by the wonders of the day of pentecost, when Lydia and others were called only in the common way: if you mean this by "distinguishing grace," we are agreed. For grace displayed in as distinguishing a manner as it was toward Capernaum, Chorazin, and Bethsaida, greatly illustrates our Lord's doctrine: "Of him to whom little is given, little shall be required; but much shall be required of them that have received much;" the equality of God's way not consisting in giving to all men a like number of talents, any more than making them all archangels; but in treating them all equally, according to the various editions of the everlasting Gospel, or law of liberty; and according to the good or bad uses they have made of their talents, whether they had few or many.

To return to your grand objection: you suppose (and this is probably the ground of your mistake) that when a deliverance, or a Divine favour, turns upon something which we may do, or leave undone, at our option, God is necessarily robbed of his glory. But a few queries will easily convince you of your mistake. When God had been merciful to Lot and his family, not looking back made all the difference between him and his wife; but does it follow that he claimed the honour of his narrow escape? Looking at the brazen type of Christ made some Israelites differ from others that died of the bite of the fiery serpents; but is this a sufficient reason to conclude that the healed men had not sense to distinguish between primary and secondary causes, and that they ascribed to their looks the glory due to God for graciously contriving the means of their cure? One of your neighbours has hanged, and another has poisoned himself; so that not hanging yourself, and taking wholesome food, has so far made the difference between you and them: but can you reasonably infer that you do not live by Divine bounty, and that I rob the Preserver of men of his glory, when I affirm that you shall surely die if you do not eat, or if you take poison?

Permit me to make you sensible of your mistake by one more illustration. An anti-Calvinist, who observes that God has suspended many of his blessings upon industry, diligently ploughs, sows, and weeds his field. A fatalist over the way, lest free grace should not have all the glory of his crop, does not turn* one clod, and expects seed to drop from the clouds into furrows made by an invisible plough on a certain day, which he calls "a day of God's power." When harvest comes, the one has a crop of wheat, and the other a crop of weeds. Now, although industry alone has made the difference between the two fields: who is most likely to give God the glory of a crop, the Solifidian farmer who reaps thistles? or the laborious husbandman who has joined works to his faith in Divine Providence, and joyfully brings his sheaves home, saying, as St. Paul, "By Divine bounty I have planted and Apollos has weeded, but God has given the increase, which is all in all?"

PART THIRD.

FLATTERING myself that the preceding answers have removed the reader's prejudices, or confirmed him in his attachment to genuine free grace, I shall conclude this Essay by some reflections upon the pride, or prejudices of those who scruple working with an eye to the rewards that God offers with a view to promote the obedience of faith.

"If heaven, (say such mistaken persons,) if the enjoyment of God in glory be the reward of obedience, and if you work with an eye to that reward, you act from self, the basest of all motives. Love, and not self interest, sets us, true believers, upon action. We work *from gratitude* and not for profit; *from life*† and not for life. To do good with an eye to a reward, though that reward should be a crown of life, is to act as a mercenary wretch, and not as a duteous child or a faithful servant."

---

* This is not spoken of pious Calvinists; for some of them are remarkably diligent in good works. They are Solifidians by halves; — in principle, but not in practice. Their works outshine their errors. I lay nothing to their charge, but inattention, prejudice, and glaring inconsistency. I compare them to diligent, good-natured druggists, who, among many excellent remedies, sell sometimes arsenic. They would not for the world take it themselves, or poison their neighbours; but yet they freely retail it, and in so doing they are inadvertently the cause of much mischief. Mr. Fulsome, for example, could tell which of our Gospel ministers taught him that good works are dung, and have nothing to do with eternal salvation. He could inform us who lulled him asleep in his sins with the syren songs of "unconditional election" and "finished salvation, in the full extent of the word;" that is, he could let us know who gave him his killing dose; and numbers of Deists could tell us that a bare taste or smell of Calvinism has made them loath the genuine doctrines of grace, just as tasting or smelling a tainted partridge has for ever turned some people's stomachs against partridge.

† The reader is desired to observe that we recommend working from life and gratitude, as well as our opponents. Life and thankfulness are two important springs of action, which we use as well as they. We maintain, that even those who "have a name to live, and are dead in trespasses and sins," cannot be saved without "strengthening the things that remain and are ready to die;" and that thankfulness for being out of hell, and for having a day of salvation through Christ, should be strongly recommended to the chief of sinners. But thankfulness and life are not *all* the springs necessary, in our imperfect state, to move all the wheels of obedience; and we dare no more exclude *the other* springs, because we have these two, than we dare cut off three of our fingers, because we have a little finger and a thumb.

The Works of John Fletcher

This specious error, zealously propagated by Molinos, Lady Guion; and her illustrious convert, Archbishop Fenelon, (though afterward renounced by him,) put a stop to a great revival of the power of godliness abroad in the last century; and it has already struck a fatal blow at the late revival in these kingdoms. I reverence and love many that contend for this sentiment; but my regard for the truth overbalancing my respect for them, I think it my duty to oppose their mistake, as a pernicious refinement of Satan transformed into an angel of light. I therefore attack it by the following arguments: —

1. This doctrine makes us "wise above what is written." We read that hunger and want of bread brought back the prodigal son. His father knew it, but instead of treating him as a hired servant, he entertained him as a beloved child.

2. It sets aside, at a stroke, a considerable part of the Bible, which consists in threatenings to deter evil workers, and in promises to encourage obedient believers: for if it be base to obey in order to obtain a promised reward, it is baser still to do it in order to avoid a threatened punishment. Thus the precious grace of faith, so far as it is exercised about Divine promises and threatenings, is indirectly made void.

3. It decries "godly fear," a grand spring of action, and preservative of holiness in all free agents that are in a state of probation; and by this mean it indirectly charges God with want of wisdom, for putting that spring in the breast of innocent man in paradise, and for perpetually working upon it in his word and by his Spirit, which St. Paul calls "the spirit of bondage unto fear;" because it helps us to believe the threatenings denounced against the workers of iniquity, and to fear lest ruin should overtake us if we continue in our sins.

If ever there was a visible Church without spot and wrinkle, it was when "the multitude of them that believed were of one heart and of one soul." The worldly mindedness of Ananias and Sapphira was the first blemish of the Christian, as Achan's covetousness had been of the Jewish Church on this side Jordan. God made an example of them, as he had done of Achan; and St. Luke observes upon it that "great fear came upon all the Church;" even such fear as kept them from "falling after the same example of unbelief." Now were all the primitive Christians mean-spirited people, because they were filled with great fear of being punished as the first backsliders had been, if they apostatized? Is it a reproach to righteous Noah, that "being moved with fear he prepared an ark for the saving of his house?" And did our Lord legalize the Gospel, when "he began to say to his disciples first of all, &c, I say unto you, my friends, be not afraid of them that kill the body, &c; but fear him, who, after he hath killed, hath power to cast into hell; yea, I say unto you, fear him?" Does this mean, "Be mercenary yea,! say unto you, be mercenary?"

4. HOPE has a particular, necessary reference to *promises* and *good things* to come. Excellent things are spoken of that grace. If St. Paul says, "Ye are saved through FAITH," he says also, "We are saved by HOPE." Hence St. Peter observes, that "exceeding great promises are given to us, that we might be partakers of the Divine nature:" and St. John declares, "Every man that hath this hope in him purifieth himself even as God is pure." Now hope never stirs, but in order to obtain good things in view: a motive this which our Gospel refiners represent as illiberal and base. Their scheme therefore directly tends to ridicule and suppress the capital, Christian grace, which faith guards on the left hand, and charity on the right.

5. Their error springs from a false conclusion. Because it is mean to relieve a beggar with an eye to a reward from him, they infer that it is mean to do a good work with an eye to a reward from God; not considering that a beggar promises nothing, and can give nothing valuable; whereas the Parent of good promises and can give "eternal life to them that obey him." Their inference is then just as absurd as the following argument' "I ought not to set my heart upon an earthly, inferior, transitory good; therefore I must not set it upon the chief, heavenly, permanent good. It is foolish to shoot at a wrong mark; therefore I must not shoot at the right: I must not aim at the very mark which God himself has set up for me ultimately to level all my actions at, next to his own glory, viz. the enjoyment of himself, the light of his countenance, the smiles of his open face, which make the heaven of heavens."

6. God says to Abraham, and in him to all believers, "I am thy exceeding great reward." Hence it follows, that the higher we rise in holiness and obedience, the nearer we shall be admitted to the eternal throne, and the fuller enjoyment we shall have of our God and Saviour, our reward and rewarder. Therefore, to overlook Divine rewards, is to overlook God himself, who is "our great reward;" and to slight "the life to come," of which "godliness has the promise."

7. The error I oppose can be put in a still stronger light. Not to strive to obtain our great reward in full, amounts to saying, "Lord, thou art beneath my aim and pursuits: I can do without thee, or without So much of thee. I will not bestir myself, and do one thing to obtain either the fruition, or a fuller enjoyment of thy adorable self." An illustration or two, short as they fall of the thing illustrated, may help us to see the great impropriety of such conduct. If the king offered to give all officers, who would distinguish themselves in the field, his hand to kiss, and a commission in his guards, that he might have them near his person; would not military gentlemen defeat the intention of this gracious offer, and betray a peculiar degree of indifference for his majesty, if in the day of battle they would not strike one blow the more on account of the royal promise?

Again: when David asked, What shall be done to him that killeth the giant? And when he was informed that Saul would give him his daughter in marriage; would the young shepherd have showed his regard for the princess, or respect for the monarch, if he had said, "I am above minding rewards: what I do, I do freely: I scorn acting from so base a motive as a desire to secure the hand of the princess, and the honour of being the king's son-in-law?" Could any thing have been ruder and more haughty than such a speech? And yet, O see what evangelical refinements have done for us! We, who are infinitely less before God than David was before King Saul; — we, worms of a day, are so blinded by prejudice, as to think it beneath us to mind the offers of the King of kings, or to strive for the rewards of the Lord of lords.

"Wo to him that striveth [in generosity] with his Maker! Let the potsherds strive thus with the potsherds of the earth: [but let not] the clay say to him that fashioneth it," "What doest thou when thou stirrest me up to good works by the promise of thy rewards? Surely, Lord, thou forgettest that the nobleness of my mind, and my doctrine of finished salvation, make me above running for a reward, though it should be for a life of glory, and thyself. Whatever I do at thy command, I am determined not to demean myself; I will do it as Araunah, like a king." What depths of Antinomian pride may be hid under the covering of our voluntary humility!

8. The Calvinists of the last century, in their lucid intervals, saw the absolute necessity of working for heaven and heavenly rewards. We have a good practical discourse of J. Bunyan upon these words, "So run that you may obtain." The burden of it is, "If you will have a heaven, you must run for it." Whence he calls his sermon, *"The heavenly footman;"* and Matthew Mead,* a staunch Calvinist, in his treatise on *The Good of Early Obedience*, (p. 429,) says, with great truth," Maintain a holy, filial fear of God. This is an excellent preservative against apostasy. 'By the fear of the Lord men depart from evil,' says Solomon, and he tells you, 'The fear of the Lord is the fountain of life, whereby men depart from the snares of death;' and backsliding from Christ is one of the great snares of death. Think much of the day of recompense, and of the glorious reward of perseverance in that day: 'Be thou faithful unto death, and I will give thee a crown of life.' It is not those that begin well, but those who end well, that receive the crown. It is not mercenary service to quicken ourselves to obedience by the hope of a recompense. *Omnis amor mercedis non est mercenarius, &c.* David said, 'I have hoped for thy salvation, and done thy commandments.' He encouraged himself to duty by the hope of glory, &c. Hope of that glorious recompense is of great service to quicken us to perseverance. And to the same end does the apostle urge it: 'Be unmovable, always abounding in the work of the Lord, forasmuch as ye know that your labour is not in vain in the Lord.'"

9. When voluntary humility has made us wise above what is written by the apostles and by our forefathers, it will make us look down with contempt from the top of our fancied orthodoxy, upon the motives by which the prophets took up their cross, to serve God and their generation. When St. Paul enumerates the works of Moses, he traces them back to their noble principle, faith working by a well ordered self love: (a love this which is inseparable from the love of God and man; the law of liberty binding us to love our neighbour *as ourselves*, and God *above ourselves*.) "He chose," says the apostle, "to suffer affliction with the people of God, rather than to enjoy the pleasures of sin," &c. But why? Because he was above looking at the prize? Just the reverse: Because "he had respect to the recompense of reward," Hebrews 11:26.

10. In the next chapter the apostle bids us to take Christ himself for our pattern in the very thing which our Gospel refiners call mercenary and base:

---

* As a proof of his being sound in the doctrines of Calvinistic grace and confusion, I present the reader with the following passage, taken from the same book, printed in London, 1683, (p. 307:) "A believer is under the law for conduct, but not for judgment, &c. It is the guide of his path, but not the judge of his state. The believer is bound to obey it, but not to stand or fall by it." That is, in plain English, he should obey it, but his disobedience will never bring him under condemnation, and hinder him to stand in judgment. "It is a rule of life, &c, and therefore it obliges believers as much as others, though upon other motives, &c: for they are not to expect life or favour from it, nor fear the death and rigour that comes by it. The law has no power to justify a believer, or condemn him, and therefore can be no rule to try his state by." In flat opposition to the general tenor of the Scriptures, thus summed up by St. John: "In this," namely, committing or not committing sin, "the children of God are manifest, and the children of the devil." What this author says is true, if it be understood of the Adamic law of innocence; but if it be extended to St. Paul's law of Christ; and to St. James' law of liberty, it is one of the dangerous tenets that support the chair of the Antinomian "man of sin."

"Looking to Jesus," says he, "who, for the joy that was set before him, endured the cross, despising the shame, and is set down at the right hand of the throne of God." The noble reward this, with which his mediatorial obedience was crowned, as appears from these words: "He became obedient unto death; wherefore God also hath highly exalted him." If the scheme of those who refine the ancient Gospel appears to me in a peculiarly unfavourable light, it is when I see them impose upon the injudicious admirers of unscriptural humility, and make the simple believe that they do God service when they indirectly represent Christ's obedience unto death as imperfect, and him as mercenary, actuated by a motive unworthy of a child of God. He says, "Every one that is perfect shall be as his master:" but we (such is our consistency!) loudly decry perfection, and yet pretend to a higher degree of it than our Lord and Master; for he was not above "enduring the cross [for the joy of] Sitting down at the right hand of the throne of God:" but we are so exquisitely perfect, that we will work *gratis*. It is mercenary, it is beneath us to work for glory!

11. I fear this contempt is by some indirectly poured upon the Lord of glory, to extol the spurious free grace which is sister to free wrath; and to persuade the simple that "works have nothing to do with our final justification and eternal salvation before God." A dogma this, which is as contrary to reason as it is to Scripture and morality; it being a monstrous imposition upon the credulity of Protestants to assert that works, which God himself will reward with final justification and eternal salvation, have nothing to do with that justification and that salvation before him: just as if the thing rewarded had nothing to do with its reward before the rewarder!

12. The most rigid Calvinists allow that St. Paul is truly evangelical: but which of the sacred writers ever spoke greater things of the rewardableness of works than he? What can be plainer, what stronger than these words, which I must quote till they are minded: "Whatsoever ye do, do it heartily, as to the Lord, &c, knowing [i.e. considering] that of the Lord ye shall receive the reward of the inheritance. But he that doth wrong, shall receive for the wrong which he hath done; for there is no respect of persons," Colossians 3:23, &c. Again: "Whatsoever a man soweth, that shall he also reap: for he that soweth to his flesh, shall of the flesh reap perdition; but he that soweth to the Spirit, shall of the Spirit reap everlasting life," Galatians 6. 7, 8.

From those scriptures it is evident that doing good or bad works is like sowing good or bad seed; and that going to heaven or hell is like gathering what we have sown. Now, as it is the *madness* of unbelievers to sow wickedness, and to expect a crop of happiness and glory; so it is the *wisdom* of believers to sow righteousness, expecting to "reap in due time if they faint not." Nor do we act reasonably, if we do not sow more or less with an eye to reaping: for if reaping be quite out of the question with Protestants, they may as wisely sow chaff on a fallow, as corn in a ploughed field. Hence I conclude that a believer may obey, and that, if he be judicious, he will obey, looking both to Jesus and to the rewards of obedience; and that the more we can fix the eye of his faith upon his "exceeding great reward, and his great recompense of reward," the more he will "abound in the work of faith, the patience of hope, and the labour of love."

13. St. Paul's conduct with respect to rewards was perfectly consistent with his doctrine. I have already observed, he wrote to the Corinthians, that he so "ran and so fought as to obtain an incorruptible crown;" and it is well known that in the

Olympic games, to which he alludes, all ran or fought with an eye to a prize, a reward, or a crown. But in his Epistle to the Philippians he goes still farther; for he represents his running for a crown of life, his pressing after rewards of grace and glory, as the whole of his business. His words are remarkable: "This one thing I do; forgetting those things which are behind, and reaching forth unto those things which are before, I press toward the mark for the prize of the high calling of God in Christ Jesus." And when he had just run his race out, he wrote to Timothy, "I have finished my course; henceforth there is laid up for me [as for a conqueror] a crown of righteousness, which the Lord, the righteous Judge, shall give me at that day" — the great day of retribution. As for St. John, when he was perfected in love, we find him as "mercenary" as St. Paul; for he writes to the elect lady, and to her believing children: "Look to yourselves, that we lose not those things which we have wrought, but that we receive a full reward."

14. When I read such scriptures; I wonder at those who are so wrapt up in the pernicious notion that we ought not to work* for a life of glory, as to overlook even the "crown of life," with which God will reward those who are "faithful unto death." And I am astonished at the remains of my own unbelief, which prevent my being always ravished with admiration at the thought of the rewards offered to fire my soul into seraphic obedience. An idle country fellow, who runs at the wakes for a wretched prize, labours harder in his sportive race than, I fear, I do yet in some of my prayers and sermons. A sportsman, for the pitiful honour of coming in at the death of a fox, toils more than most professors do in the pursuit of their corruptions. How ought confusion to cover our faces! Let those that refine the Gospel glory in their shame. Let each of them say, "I thank thee, O God, that I am not like a Papist, or like that Arminian, who looks at the rewards which thou hast promised. I deny myself, and take up my cross, without thinking of the joy and rewards set before me," &c. For my part, I desire to humble myself before God, for having so long overlooked the "exceeding great reward," and the "crown of life," promised to them that obey him: and my thoughts shall be expressed in such words as these: —

"Gracious Lord, if he that receiveth a prophet in the name of a prophet shall have a prophet's reward;' if 'our light affliction,' when it is patiently endured, 'worketh for us a far more exceeding and eternal weight of glory;' if thou hast said, 'Do good and lend, hoping for nothing again [from man,] and your reward shall be

---

* Truth is so great that it sometimes prevails over those that are prejudiced against it. I have observed that Dr. Crisp himself, in a happy moment, bore a noble testimony to undefiled religion. Take another instance of it. In the volume of the Rev. Mr. Whitefield's sermons, taken in short hand, and published by Gurney, (p. 119,) that great preacher says: "FIRST, We must work FOR spiritual life, AFTERWARD FROM it." And (pages 153, 154) he declares: "There are numbers of poor that are ready to perish; and if you drop something to them in love, God will take care to repay you when you come to judgment." I find but one fault with this doctrine. The first of those propositions does not guard free grace so well as Mr. Wesley's Minutes do. We should always intimate that there is no working FOR a life of glory, or FOR a MORE ABUNDANT LIFE of grace, but FROM an initial life of grace, FREELY given to us in Christ BEFORE any working of our own. This I mention, not to prejudice the reader against Mr. Whitefield, but to show that I am not so prejudiced in favour of works, as not to see when even a Whitefield, in an unguarded expression, leans toward them to the disparagement of free grace.

great, and ye shall be the children of the Highest:' if thou animatest those who are persecuted for righteousness' sake, by this promissory exhortation, 'Rejoice and be exceeding glad, for great is your reward in heaven:' nay, if a cup of cold water only, given in thy name, 'shall in no wise lose its reward;' and if the least of thy rewards is a smile of approbation; let me be ready to go round the world, shouldst thou call me to it, that I may obtain such a recompense.

"Since thou hast so closely connected holiness and happiness, my duty and thy favours, 'let no man beguile me of my reward in a voluntary humility,' nor suffer me to be ' carried about with every wind of doctrine by the sleight of men,' and 'cunning craftiness, whereby they lie in wait to deceive.' And 'whatsoever my hand findeth to do, help me to do it with all my might;' not only lest I lose my reward, but also lest I have not 'a full reward;' lest I lose a beam of the light of thy countenance, or a degree of that peculiar likeness and nearness to thee with which thou wilt recompense those who excel in virtue. So shall I equally avoid the delusion of the Pharisees, who expect heaven through their faithless works; and the error of Antinomians, who hope to enter into thy glory without the passport of the works of faith.

"And now, Lord, if thy servant has found favour in thy sight, permit him to urge another request; so far as thy wisdom, and the laws by which thy free grace works upon free agents will permit, incline the minds of Papists and Protestants to receive the truth as it is in Jesus. Let not especially this plain testimony, borne to the many great promises which thou hast made, and to the astonishing rewards which thou offerest them that work righteousness, be rejected by my Calvinist brethren. Keep them from fighting against thy goodness, and despising their own mercies, under pretence of fighting against 'Arminian errors,' and despising 'Pelagian Checks to the Gospel.' And make them sensible that it is absurd to decry in word the pope's pretensions to infallibility, if by an obstinate refusal to 'review the whole affair,' and to weigh their supposed orthodoxy in the balances of reason and revelation, they in fact pretend to be infallible themselves; and thus, instead of one Catholic pontiff, set up ten thousand Protestant popes.

"Thou knowest, Lord, that many of them love thee; and that, though they disgrace thy Gospel by their doctrinal peculiarities, they adorn it by their godly conversation. O endue them with more love to their remonstrant brethren! Give them and me that charity which 'behaveth not itself unseemly,' which 'rejoiceth not in' a favourite error, 'but rejoiceth in the truth,' even when it is advanced by our opponents. Thou seest, that if they decry true holiness and good works as 'dung and dross,' it is chiefly for fear thy glory should be obscured by our obedience. Error transformed into an angel of light has deceived them, and they think to do thee service by propagating the deception. O gracious God, pardon them this wrong. They 'do it ignorantly in unbelief;' therefore seal not up their mistake with the seal of thy wrath. Let them yet 'know the truth,' and let the truth enlarge their hearts, and 'make them free' from the notion that thou art not ' loving to every man' during 'the day of salvation,' and that there is neither mercy nor Saviour for the most of their neighbours, even during 'the accepted time.'

"Above all, Lord, if they cannot defend their mistakes, either by argument or by Scripture quoted according to the context, and the obvious tenor of thy sacred oracles, give them more wisdom than to expose any longer the Protestant religion, which they think to defend; and more piety than to make the men of the world abhor thy Gospel, and blaspheme thy name, as free thinkers are daily tempted to do, when they see that those who pretend to 'exalt thee' most, are of all Protestants the most ready to disarm thy Gospel of its sanctions; to turn thy judicial sentences into frivolous descriptions; to overlook the dictates of reason and good nature; and to make the press groan under illogical assertions, and personal abuse!

"Let thy servant speak once more: thou knowest, O Lord, that thy power being my helper, I would choose to die rather than wilfully to depreciate that grace, that free grace of thine which has so long kept me out of hell, and daily gives me sweet foretastes of heaven. And now, let not readers of a Pharisaic turn mistake what I have advanced in honour of the works of faith, and by that mean build themselves up in their self-righteous delusion, and destructive contempt of thy merits: help them to consider, that if our works are rewardable, it is because thy free grace makes them so; thy Father having mercifully accepted our persons for thy sake, thy Holy Spirit having gently helped our infirmities, thy precious blood having fully atoned for our sins and imperfections, thy incessant intercession still keeping the way to the throne of grace open for us, and our poor performances. Suffer not one of the sons of virtuous pride, into whose hands these sheets may fall, to forget that thou hast annexed 'the reward of the inheritance' to the assemblage of the works of faith, or to 'patient continuance in well doing,' and not to one or two splendid works of hypocrisy done just to serve a wordly turn, or to bribe a disturbed, clamorous conscience; and enable them so to feel the need of thy pardon for past transgression, and of thy power for future obedience, that, as the chased hart panteth after the water brooks, so their awakened souls may long after Christ, in whom the penitent find inexhaustible springs of righteousness and strength; and to whom, with thee and thy eternal Spirit, be for ever ascribed praise, honour, and glory, both in heaven and upon earth — *praise* for the wonders of general redemption, and for the innumerable displays of thy free grace unstained by free wrath — *honour* for bestowing the gracious reward of a heavenly salvation up. on all believers that make their election sure 'by patient continuance in well doing' — and *glory* for inflicting the just punishment of infernal damnation upon all that neglect so great salvation, and to the end of the accepted time dare thy vengeance by obstinate continuance in ill doing."

APPENDIX.

MADELEY, March 10, 1774.

YESTERDAY a friend lent me Mr. Baxter's *Confession of Faith*, printed in London, 1655. The third part of this valuable book extends through above one hundred and forty large pages, and the title of that long section runs thus: — "The Testimony of Reformed Divines, ascribing as much to Works as I; and many of them delivering the same Doctrine." He produces a hundred witnesses, some of whom are collective bodies, such as the assembly of divines, the compilers of the homilies of the Church of England, and even the synod of Dort. As the Antinomian spirit which flamed against Baxter's Works in the last century will probably sparkle against the preceding Essay, I beg leave to take shelter behind that great man, and a few of his numerous quotations. I shall cite only Baxter's page, to which I refer those who desire to see the original of his Latin quotations, together with the books, chapters, and pages of the various authors.

Page 322, he quotes the following words from Bishop Davenant: — "As no man receiveth that general justification which dischargeth from the guilt of all foregoing sins, but on the concurrence of repentance, faith, a purpose of a new life, and other actions of the same kind; so no man retaineth a state free from guilt in respect of following sins, but by means of the same actions of believing in God, calling on God, mortifying the flesh, daily repenting and sorrowing for sins daily committed. The reason why all these are required on our part is this; because these cannot be still absent, but their opposites will be present, which are contrary to the nature of a justified man. As therefore to the conservation of natural life it is necessarily required that a man carefully avoid fire, water, precipices, poisons, and other things destructive to the health of the body; so to the conserving of spiritual life, it is necessarily required that a man avoid incredulity, impenitency, and other things that are destructive and contrary to the salvation of souls; which cannot be avoided, unless the opposite and contrary actions be exercised. And these actions do not conserve the life of grace properly and of themselves, by touching the very effect of conservation; but improperly and by accident, by excluding and removing the cause of destruction."

Page 324, Baxter produces these words of the same pious bishop: — "We do therefore fight against, not the bare name of merit, in a harmless sense frequently used of old by the fathers, but the proud and false opinion of merit of condignity, brought lately by the Papists into the Church of God."

And again, (page 325,) "The works of the regenerate have an ordination to the rewards of this life and that to come: (1.) Because God hath freely promised (according to the good pleasure of his will) the rewards of this life and that to come, to the good works of the faithful and regenerate, 1 Timothy 4:8; Galatians 6:8; Matthew 20:8.

Page 328, he quotes the following passage from Dr. Twiss: — "It lieth on all the elect to seek salvation, not only by faith, but by works also, in that without doubt salvation is to be given by way of reward, whereby God will reward not only our faith, but also all our good works."

Pages 330 and 334, he quotes Melancthon thus: — "New obedience is necessary by necessity of order of the cause and effect; also by necessity of duty or command; also by necessity of retaining faith, and avoiding punishments, temporal and eternal. Cordatus stirreth up against me the city, and also the neighbour countries, and also the court itself, because, in explaining the controversy of justification, I said that new obedience is necessary to salvation."

Pages 360, 361, he quotes these words of Zanchius: — "Works are necessary, (1.) To justify our faith [*coram Deo*] before God, &c. (2.) They are necessary to the obtaining eternal life, &c. (3.) They are necessary to inherit justification as causes, &c. (4.) They are profitable to conserve the increase of faith; also to pro-merit of God, and obtain many good things, both spiritual and corporal, both in this life and in another." The words of Zanchius are, "*Opera utilia sunt, &c, ad multa bona tum spiritualia tum corporalia, tum in hac vita tum in alia a Deo promerenda et obtinenda.*" (Zanch. Tom. 8, p. 787, loc. de Just. Fidei.) How much more tenderly did Mr. Wesley speak of merit than the orthodox Zanchius, whom Mr. Toplady has lately rendered famous among us! I hope that if this gentleman ever open his favourite book to the above-quoted page, he will drop his prejudices, and confess that his dear Zanchius himself nobly contends for the Wesleyan "heresy."

Page 462, Baxter concludes his book by praying for those who had misrepresented him to the world, and obliged him to spend so much time in vindicating his doctrine. I most heartily join him in the last paragraph of his prayer, in which I beg the reader would join us both: "The Lord illuminate and send forth some messenger that may acquaint the Churches with that *true, middle, reconciling method of theological verities which must be the mean of healing our divisions.* Let men be raised of greater sufficiency for this work, and of such blessed accomplishments as shall be fit to cope with the power of prejudice; and let the fury of blind contradiction be so calmed that TRUTH may have opportunity to do its work."

AN ESSAY ON TRUTH;

BEING

A RATIONAL VINDICATION

OF THE

DOCTRINE OF SALVATION BY FAITH.

WITH

A DEDICATORY EPISTLE

TO THE

RIGHT HON. THE COUNTESS OF HUNTINGDON.

Without faith it is impossible to please God, Hebrews 11:6.
Whatsoever is not of faith is sin, Romans 14:23.
Faith, if it hath not works, is dead, being alone, James 1:17.
Good works spring out necessarily of a true and lively faith. (Twelfth Article.)
In Christ Jesus, &c, nothing availeth but faith, which worketh by love, Galatians 5:6

A DEDICATORY EPISTLE

TO THE

RIGHT HON. THE COUNTESS OF HUNTINGDON.

MY LADY, — Because I think it my duty to defend the works of faith against the triumphant errors of the Solifidians, some of your ladyship's friends conclude that I am an enemy to the doctrine of salvation by faith, and their conclusion amounts to such exclamations as these: "How could a lady, so zealous for God's glory and the Redeemer's grace, commit the superintendency of a seminary of pious learning to a man that opposes the fundamental doctrine of Protestantism! How could she put her sheep under the care of such a wolf in sheep's clothing!" This conclusion, my lady, has grieved me for your sake; and to remove the blot that it indirectly fixes upon you, as well as to balance my *Scriptural Essay on the Rewardableness of the Works of Faith*, I publish, and humbly dedicate to your ladyship, this piece of my *Equal Check to Pharisaism and Antinomianism*. May the kindness which enabled you to bear for years with the coarseness of my ministrations, incline you favourably to receive this little token of my unfeigned attachment to Protestanism, and of my lasting respect for your ladyship!

Your aversion to all that looks like controversy can never make you think that an Equal Check to the two grand delusions, which have crept into the Church, is needless in our days. I flatter myself, therefore, that though you may blame my performance, you will approve of my design. And indeed what true Christian can be absolutely neuter in this controversy? If God has a controversy with all Pharisees and Antinomians, have not all God's children a controversy with Pharisaism and Antinomianism? Have you not for one, my lady? Do you not check in private, what I attempt to check in public? Does not the religious world know that you abhor, attack, and pursue Pharisaism in its most artful disguises? And have I not frequently heard you express, in the strongest terms, your detestation of Antinomianism, and lament the number of sleeping professors whom that Delilah robs of their strength? Nor would you, I am persuaded, my lady, have countenanced the opposition which was made against the Minutes, if your commendable, though (as it appears to me) at that time too precipitate zeal against Pharisaism had not prevented your seeing that they contain the Scripture truths which are most fit to stop the rapid progress of Antinomianism.

However, if you still think, my lady, that I mistake with respect to the importance of those propositions; you know I am not mistaken when I declare before the world that a powerful, practical, actually saving faith is the only faith I ever heard your ladyship recommend as worthy to be contended for. And so long as you plead only for such a faith: so long as you abhor the winter faith that saves the Solifidians In their own conceit: while they commit adultery, murder, and incest, if they choose to carry Antinomianism to such a dreadful length; so long as you are afraid to maintain either directly or indirectly, that the evidence and comfort of justifying faith may indeed be suspended by sin; but that the righteousness of faith, and the justification which it instrumentally procures, can never be lost, no not by the most enormous and complicated crimes; whatever diversity there may be between your ladyship's sentiments and mine, it can never be fundamental. I preach salvation by a faith that actually works by obedient love: and your ladyship witnesses salvation by an actually operative faith. Nor can I, to this day, see any material difference between those phrases: for if I profess a faith that is actually operative, I cannot with propriety find fault with a faith that actually operates: I cannot with decency sacrifice its works to "Antinomian dotages."*

Permit me also to observe, that the grand questions debated between my opponents and me are not (as I fear your ladyship apprehends) whether Pharisaic merit shall eclipse the Redeemer's worthiness; or whether the doctrine of salvation by a lively faith shall be given up to mere moralists, I no more plead either for the one or for the other, than I do for placing the pretender upon the British throne, and for sacrificing the great charter to arbitrary power. No, my lady. What we contend about is: (1.) Whether Christ's law is not perfectly consistent with his blood. (2.) Whether we are to set him at naught as a Prophet, a King, and a Judge, under pretence of exalting him as a Priest, an Advocate, and a "Surety of the better covenant," that threatens fallen believers with a "sorer punishment" then that which was inflicted upon the despisers of the Mosaic covenant. (3.) Whether the evangelical worthiness, which a true believer really derives from Christ, is not absolutely necessary to salvation. (4.) Whether such a worthiness is not as consistent with Christ's original and paramount merit, as the light that shines in your apartment is consistent with the original and transcendent brightness of the sun. (5.) Whether that faith is living, which evidences itself by gross immoralities. (6.) Whether it is not rather the "dead faith" that St. James exclaims against. And (7.) Whether the Solifidians do not set up the "abomination of desolation in the holy place," when they directly or *indirectly*† teach that all believers may go any length in sin, without losing their heavenly thrones, or the Divine favour: that a man may have the justifying, saving, operative faith which your ladyship pleads for, while he adds idolatry to incontinence, murder to adultery, and curses to the repeated denial of Jesus Christ: that fallen believers, who have returned to their sins "as a sow that is washed does to her wallowing in the mire," stand immaculate before God in a robe of imputed righteousness, even while they "turn God's grace into lasciviousness, and commit all uncleanness with greediness:" that they shall all infallibly sing in heaven in consequence of their most grievous falls on earth; and that a kind of hypocritical, lying free grace is to be preached to all sinners, which necessarily shuts up most of them under the absolute free wrath of a God ever merciless toward the majority of mankind.

---

* The name which Flavel gives to Dr. Crisp's modish tenets

† Mr. Hill has done it "directly" in the fourth of the Five Letters which he has inscribed to me and all the Solifidians do it "indirectly."

Creeds and Scripture Scales

Now, my lady, as I am persuaded that you do not admire such an immoral and narrow Gospel: as I believe that if at any time it creeps into your chapels, it is without your approbation, under the mask of decency, and only by the means of the *specious phrases of free Gospel, electing, everlasting love, finished salvation, and free distinguishing grace,* which, according to the analogy of the modish faith, sweetly make way for the inseparable and bitter doctrines of a *confined Gospel of everlasting hate, reprobating unmercifulness, finished damnation, and free, distinguishing wrath;* and as I do your ladyship the justice to acknowledge, that your most earnest desire is to support what appears to you a free and holy Gospel, at the expense of your fortune, life, and character; I beg, my lady, you will also do me the justice to believe that if I oppose the Solifidian Gospel of the day, it is only because it appears to me a confined and unholy Gospel, calculated to foster the Antinomianism of Laodicean believers, and to render Christ's undefiled religion *contemptible* to the RATIONAL, and *execrable* to the MORAL world. If you grant me this request, I shall only trouble you with one more, which is, to believe that, notwithstanding the part I have taken in the present controversy, I remain, with my former respect and devotedness, my lady, your ladyship's most obliged and obedient servant in the Gospel,

J. FLETCHER

MADELEY, March 12, 1774.

AN ESSAY ON TRUTH, &c.

INTRODUCTION.

EXCEEDINGLY sorry should I be if the testimony which I have borne to the necessity of *good* works caused any of my readers to do the worst of *bad* works, that is, to neglect *believing*, and to depend upon some of the external, *faithless* performances which conceited Pharisees call "good works;" and by which they absurdly think to make amends for their sins, to purchase the Divine favour, to set aside God's mercy, and to supersede Christ's atoning blood. Therefore, lest some unwary souls, going from one extreme to the other, should so unfortunately avoid Antinomianism as to run upon the rocks which are rendered famous by the destruction of the Pharisees, I shall once more vindicate the fundamental anti-Pharisaic doctrine of salvation by faith: I say *once more*, because I have already done it in my guarded sermon. And to the scriptures, articles, and arguments produced in that piece, I shall now add rational and yet Scriptural observations, which, together with appeals to matter of fact, will, I hope, soften the prejudices of judicious moralists against the doctrine of faith, and reconcile considerate Solifidians to the doctrine of works. In order to
630
this, I design in general to prove that true faith is the only plant which can possibly bear good works; that it loses its operative nature, and dies, when it produces them not; and that it as much surpasses good works in importance, as the motion of the heart does all other bodily motions. Inquire we first into the nature and ground of saving faith.

SECTION I.

A plain definition of saving faith, how believing is the gift of God, and whether it is in our power to believe.

WHAT is faith? It is *believing heartily.* What is saving faith? I dare not say that it is "believing heartily, my sins are forgiven me for Christ's sake;" for if I live in sin, that belief is a destructive conceit, and not saving faith. Neither dare I say that "saving faith is only a sure trust and confidence that Christ loved me, and gave himself for me;"* for, if I did, I should damn almost all mankind for four thousand years. Such definitions of saving faith are, I fear, too narrow to be just, and too unguarded to keep out Solifidianism. A comparison may convince my readers of it. If they desired me to define man, and I said, "Man is a rational animal that lives in France in the year 1774;" would they not ask me whether I suppose all the rational animals that lived on this side the English channel in 1773 were brutes? And if you desired to know what I mean by saving faith, and I replied, It is a supernatural belief that Christ has actually atoned for my sins upon the cross: would you not ask me whether Abraham, the father of the faithful, who would have believed a lie if he had believed this, had only damning faith?

To avoid therefore such mistakes; to contradict no scriptures; to put no black mark of damnation upon any man, that in any nation "fears God and works righteousness;" to leave no room for Solifidianism; and to present the reader with a definition of faith adequate to "the everlasting Gospel," I would choose to say, that "justifying or saving faith is believing the saving truth with the heart unto internal, and [as we have opportunity] unto external righteousness, according to our light and dispensation." To St. Paul's words, Romans 10:10, I add the epithets internal and external, in order to exclude, according to 1 John 3:7, 8, the filthy imputation under which fallen believers may, if we credit the Antinomians, commit internal and external adultery, mental and bodily murder, without the least reasonable fear of endangering their faith, their interest in God's favour, and their inamissible title to a throne of glory.

But "how is faith the gift of God?" Some persons think that faith is as much out of our power as the lightning that shoots from a distant cloud; they suppose that God drives sinners to the fountain of Christ's blood as irresistibly as the infernal legion drove the herd of swine into the sea of Galilee; and that a man is as passive in the first act of faith, as Jonah was in the act of the fish, which cast him upon the shore. Hence the absurd plea of many who lay fast hold on the horns of the devil's altar, unbelief, and cry out, "We can no more believe than we can make a world."

I call this an *absurd* plea for several reasons: (1.) It supposes that when "God commands all men every where to repent and to believe the Gospel," he commands them to do what is as impossible to them as the making of a new world. (2.) It supposes that the terms of the covenant of grace are much harder than the terms of the covenant of works. For the old covenant required only perfect human obedience: but the new covenant requires of us the work of an almighty God, i.e. believing; a work this which, upon the scheme I oppose, is as impossible to us as the creation of a world, in which we can never have a hand. (3.) It supposes that the promise of salvation being suspended upon believing, a thing as impracticable to us as the making of a new world, we shall as infallibly be damned if God do not believe for us, as we should be if we were required to make a world on pain of damnation, and God would not make it in our place. (4.) It supposes that believing is a work which belongs

---

* When the Church of England and Mr. Wesley give us particular definitions of faith, it is plain that they consider it according to the Christian dispensation; the privileges of which must be principally insisted upon among Christians; and that our Church and Mr. Wesley guard faith against Antinomianism, is evident from their maintaining, as well as St. Paul, that by bad works we lose a good conscience, and "make shipwreck of the faith."

to God alone: for no man in his senses can doubt but creating a world, or its tantamount, believing, is a work which none but God can manage. (5.) It supposes that (if he, who *believeth not the Divine record, makes God a liar, and shall be damned,*) whenever unbelievers are called upon to believe, and God refuses them the power to do it, he as much forces them to make him a liar and to be damned, as the king would force me to give him the lie, and to be hanged, if he put me in circumstances where I could have no chance of avoiding that crime and punishment, but by submitting to the alternative of creating a world. (6.) It supposes that when Christ "marvelled at the unbelief of the Jews," he showed as little wisdom as I should were I to marvel at a man for not creating three worlds as quickly as a believer can say the three creeds. (7.) That when Christ reproved his disciples for their unbelief he acted more unreasonably than if he had rebuked them for not adding a new star to every constellation in heaven. (8.) That to exhort people to "continue in the faith," is to exhort them to something as difficult as to continue creating worlds. And, lastly, that when Christ fixes our damnation upon unbelief, see Mark 16:16, and John 3:18, he acts far more tyrannically than the king would do if he issued out a proclamation informing all his subjects that whosoever shall not, by such a time, raise a new island within the British seas, shall be infallibly put to the most painful and lingering death.

Having thus exposed the erroneous sense in which some people suppose that "faith is the gift of God," I beg leave to mention in what sense it appears to me to be so. Believing is the gift of God's grace, as cultivating the root of a rare flower given you, or raising a crop of corn in your field, is the gift of God's providence. Believing is the gift of the God of grace, as breathing, moving, and eating, are the gifts of the God of nature. He gives me lungs and air that I may breathe: he gives me life and muscles that I may move: he bestows upon me food, and a mouth, that I may eat: and when I have no stomach, he gives me common sense to see I must die, or force myself to take some nourishment or some medicine. But he neither breathes, moves, nor eats for me; nay, when I think proper, I can accelerate my breathing, motion, and eating; and if I please I may even fast, lie down, or hang myself, and by that mean put an end to my eating, moving, and breathing. Once more: faith is the gift of God to believers, as sight is to you. The Parent of good freely gives you the light of the sun, and organs proper to receive it: he places you in a world where that light visits you daily: he apprizes you that sight is conducive to your safety, pleasure, and profit; and every thing around you bids you use your eyes and see: nevertheless, you may not only drop your curtains, and extinguish your candle, but close your eyes also. This is exactly the case with regard to faith. Free grace removes (in part) the total blindness which Adam's fall brought upon us: free grace gently sends us some beams of truth, which is the light of the "Sun of righteousness;" it disposes the eyes of our understanding to see those beams; it excites us various ways to welcome them; it blesses us with many, perhaps with all the means of faith, such as opportunities to hear, read, inquire; and power to consider, assent, consent, resolve, and re-resolve to believe the truth. But, after all, believing is as much our own act as seeing. We may, nay, in general do suspend, or omit the act of faith; especially when that act is not yet become habitual, and when the glaring light that sometimes accompanies the revelation of the truth is abated. Nay, we may imitate Pharaoh, Judas, and all reprobates; we may do by the eye of our faith what some report that Democritus did by his bodily eyes. Being tired of seeing the follies of mankind, to rid himself of that disagreeable sight he put his eyes out. We may be so averse from "the light which enlightens every man that comes into the world;" we may so dread it because our works are evil, as to exemplify, like the Pharisees, such awful declarations as these: — "Their eyes have they closed, lest they should see, &c: wherefore God gave them up to a reprobate mind," and "they were blinded."

When St. Paul says that Christians "believe according to the working of God's mighty power, which he wrought in Christ when he raised him from the dead," he chiefly alludes to the resurrection of Christ, and the outpouring of the Holy Ghost; the former of these wonders being the great ground and object of the Christian faith, and the latter displaying the great privilege of the Christian dispensation. To suppose, therefore, that nobody savingly believes, who does not believe according to an actual, overwhelming display of God's almighty power, is as unscriptural as to maintain that God's people no longer believe, than he actually repeats the wonders of Easter day, and of the day of pentecost. Is it not clear that the apostle had no such notions when he wrote to the Corinthians? "I declare unto you the Gospel, which I preached unto you, which you have received; wherein ye stand; by which also ye are saved, if ye keep in memory [if ye hold fast, as the original means] what I preached unto you, unless ye have believed in vain. For I declared unto you, &c, that Christ died for our sins, that he was buried, and that he rose again, according to the Scriptures, &c, so we preach, and so ye believed." Again: how plain is the account that our Lord and his forerunner give us of faith and unbelief! "Verily we speak what we do know, and testify what we have seen, and ye receive not our witness. What he [Christ] hath seen and heard, that he testifieth, and no man [comparatively] receiveth his testimony; but he that hath received his testimony hath set to his seal that God is true."

Two things have chiefly given room to our mistakes respecting the strange impossibility of believing. The first is our confounding the truths which characterize the several Gospel dispensations. We see, for example, that a poor, besotted drunkard, an overreaching, greedy tradesman, a rich, skeptical epicure, and a proud, ambitious courtier, have no more taste for "the Gospel of Christ," than a horse and a mule have for the high-seasoned dishes that crown a royal table. An immense gulf is fixed between them and the Christian faith. In their present state they can no more believe "with their heart unto righteousness in Christ," than an unborn infant can become a man without passing through infancy and youth. But, although they cannot yet believe savingly in Christ, may they not believe in God according to the import of our Lord's words' "Ye believe IN GOD, believe also IN ME?" If the Pharisees could not believe in Christ, it was not because God never gave them a power equal to that which created the world; but because they were practical Atheists, who actually rejected the morning light of the Jewish dispensation, and by that mean absolutely unfitted themselves for the meridian light of the Christian dispensation. This is evident from our Lord's own words' "I know you, that ye have not the love of God [or a regard for God] in you. I come in my Father's name, and ye receive me not, [though ye might do it; for] if another shall come in his own name, him ye will receive. How can ye believe, who receive honour one of another? &c. There is one that accuseth you, even Moses, in whom ye trust. For had ye believed Moses, [and submitted to his dispensation,] ye would have believed me, [and submitted to] my Gospel. But if ye believe not his writings, how shall ye believe my words?"

Creeds and Scripture Scales

The second cause of our mistake about the impossibility of believing now, is, the confounding of faith with its fruits and rewards; which naturally leads us to think that we cannot believe, or that our faith is vain, till those rewards and fruits appear. But is not this being ingenious to make the worst of things? Had Abraham no faith in God's promise till Isaac was born? Was Sarah a damnable unbeliever till she felt the long-expected fruit of her womb stir there? Had the woman of Canaan no faith till our Lord granted her request, and cried out "O woman, great is thy faith, let it be done unto thee even as thou wilt?" Was the centurion an infidel till Christ "marvelled at his faith," and declared "he had not found such faith, no, not in Israel?" Was Peter faithless till his master said, "Blessed art thou, Simon Bar-jona," &c? Did the weeping penitent begin to believe only when Christ said to her, "Go in peace, thy faith hath saved thee?" And had the apostles no faith in "the promise of the Father," till their heads were actually crowned with celestial fire? Should we not distinguish between our sealing the truth of our dispensation with the seal of our faith, according to our present light and ability; and God's sealing the truth of our faith with the seal of his power, or actually rewarding us by the grant of some eminent and uncommon blessing? To believe is OUR part; to make "signs follow them that believe" is GOD'S part; and because we can no more do God's part than we can make a world, is it agreeable either to Scripture or reason to conclude that doing our part is equally difficult? Can you find one single instance in the Scriptures of a soul willing to believe, and absolutely unable to do it? From these two scriptures, "Lord, increase our faith; — Lord, I believe, help thou my unbelief," can you justly infer that the praying disciples and the distressed father had no power to believe? Do not their words evidence just the contrary? That we cannot believe any more than we can eat, without the help and power of God, is what we are all agreed upon; but does this in the least prove that the help and power, by which we believe, is as far out of the reach of willing souls as the help and power to make a world?

Such scriptures as these: "Unto you it is given to believe: a man can receive nothing, except it be given him from above: no man can come unto me except the Father draw him: every good gift [and of course that of faith] cometh from the Father of lights." Such scriptures, I say, secure indeed the honour of free grace, but do not destroy the power of free agency. To us that freely believe in a holy, righteous God, it is given freely to believe in a gracious, bleeding Saviour; because the sick alone "have need of a physician;" and none but those who believe in God can see the need of an advocate with him. But ought we from hence to conclude that our unbelieving neighbours are necessarily debarred from "believing in God?" When our Lord said to the unbelieving Jews, that they could not believe in him, did he not speak of a moral impotency — an impotency of their own making? I ask it again, If they obstinately resisted the light of their inferior dispensation; if they were none of Christ's Jewish sheep, how could they be his Christian sheep? If an obstinate boy sets himself against learning the letters, how can he ever learn to read? If a stubborn Jew stiffly opposes the law of Moses, how can he submit to the law of Christ? Is it not strange that some good people should leap into reprobation, rather than admit so obvious a solution of this little difficulty?

From the above-mentioned texts we have then no more reason to infer that God forces believers to believe, or that he believes for them, than to conclude that God constrains diligent tradesmen to get money, or gets it for them, because it is said,

"We are not sufficient to think any thing as of ourselves, but our sufficiency is of God — who gives us all things richly to enjoy. Remember the Lord thy God, for it is he that giveth thee power to get wealth."

From the whole I conclude, that so long as "the accepted time" and "the day of salvation" continue, all sinners, who have not yet finally hardened themselves, may day and night (through the help and power of the general light of Christ's "saving grace," mentioned John 1:9, and Titus 2:11,) receive some truth belonging to the everlasting Gospel; though it should be only this: "There is a God, who will call us to an account for our sins, and who spares us to break them off by repentance." And their cordial believing of this truth would make way for their receiving the higher truths that stand between them and the top of the mysterious ladder of truth. I grant it is impossible they should leap at once to the middle, much less to the highest round of the ladder: but if the foot of it is upon earth, in the very nature of things the lowest step is within their reach, and by laying hold on it they may go on "from faith to faith," till they stand firm even in the Christian faith, if distinguishing grace has elected them to hear the Christian Gospel. The most sudden conversions imply this gradual transition. As in the very nature of things, when "the Spirit of the Lord caught away Philip" from the eunuch, and transported him to Azotus, he made Philip's body rapidly measure all the distance between the wilderness of Gaza and Azotus: so, when he helped the Philippian jailer from the gates of hell to the gates of heaven in one night, he made him rapidly pass through the fear of God, the dread of his justice, and the pangs of penitential desires after salvation, before he entered into the joyous rest that remains for those that heartily believe in Christ. Nor is this quick, though gradual transition from midnight darkness to noon-day light an unintelligible mystery, since we are witnesses of a similar event every revolving day. The vegetable and the animal world help us likewise to understand the nature of sudden conversions. Every philosopher knows that a mushroom passes through almost as many stages of the vegetative life in six hours as an oak does in two hundred years: and those animalculæ, that frisk into life in the morning of a summer's day, propagate their species at noon, are old at four o'clock, and dead at six, measure the length of animal life as really as Methuselah did his millennium.

SECTION II.

Saving truth is the object of saving faith. What truth is, and what great things are spoken of it. Our salvation turns upon it.

IT appears by the preceding section that saving TRUTH is the ground and object of saving FAITH; but "what is TRUTH?" This is the awful question that Pilate once asked of Him who was best able to answer it. But alas! Pilate was in such haste through the lying fear of man, that he did not stay for an answer. May I venture to give one. TRUTH is spiritual *substance*, and a LIE spiritual *shadow*. TRUTH is spiritual *light*, and a LIE spiritual *darkness*. Truth is the root of all *virtue*, and a lie is the root of all *vice*.

Truth is the celestial tincture that makes spirits good, and a lie the infernal tincture that makes them evil. A lie is as nearly related to the devil, as infection to one that has the plague, or opacity to the earth; and truth is as nearly related to God as fragrancy to burning incense, and light to the unclouded sun.

According to this definition of truth and error, may we not give plain and Scriptural answers to some of the deepest questions in the world? What is God? The reverse of "the prince of darkness," and of the "father of lies:" he is "the Father of lights," and "the God of truth:" he "is light, and in him is no darkness at all." What is Christ? He is "the brightness of his Father's glory; a light — a great light to them that dwell in the shadow of death." He is "the truth; the true witness; the truth itself; Emmanuel, God with us, full of grace and truth." What is the Holy Ghost? "The Spirit of truth:" yea, says St. John, "the Spirit is truth," and "leads into all truth." What is Satan? "The spirit of error" that "abode not in the truth; in whom there is no truth," and who "deceives the nations which are in the four quarters of the earth."

Again: what is the Gospel? "The word of truth, the word of God the word of faith, the word of the kingdom, the word of life, and the word of salvation." What are Gospel ministers? Men that "bear witness to the truth;" that "rightly divide the word of truth;" that are "fellow helpers to the truth;" that "speak forth the words of truth;" and "are valiant for the truth upon the earth." What is the preaching of the Gospel? "The manifestation of the truth." What is it to believe the Gospel? It is to "receive the knowledge of the truth;" to "receive the love of the truth;" and to "obey the truth." What is it to mistake the Gospel? It is to "err from the truth;" to "turn after fables;" and to "give heed to seducing spirits, and doctrines of devils." What is the Church? "The pillar and ground of truth, against which the gates of hell shall not prevail." What is the first fruit of sincere repentance? "The acknowledging of the truth." What are believers? Persons that are "chosen to salvation through the [unnecessitated] belief of the truth;" that "are of the truth;" that "know the truth;" that have "the truth in their inward parts;" that have "a good report of the truth; in whom dwells the truth; who have been taught the truth as it is in Jesus; in whom is the truth of Christ; who have purified their souls by obeying the truth;" and "walk in the truth." What are unstable souls? People "ever learning, and never able to come to the knowledge of the truth," with whom "the truth of the Gospel does not continue," and who are wilfully "bewitched, that they should not obey the truth." What are obstinate unbelievers? "Men of corrupt minds, destitute of the truth; unreasonable men," that "resist the truth;" that "glory and lie against the truth:" that "walk in darkness, and do not the truth." What are apostates? Men that "sin wilfully after they have received the knowledge of the truth," and instead of repenting, "count the blood of the covenant, wherewith they were sanctified, an unholy thing." What are perfect men in Christ? Men that are "established in the present truth," i.e. in the truth revealed under the Christian dispensation, and that can do nothing against the truth, but for the truth.

If all turns thus upon TRUTH, and if truth is at once spiritual light, and the object of saving faith, it follows: (1.) That to walk in the truth, to walk in the light, and to walk by faith, are phrases of the same import. (2.) That to be converted is to be "turned from darkness to light," that is, from the practical belief of a lie to the practical "belief of the truth;" or, as St. Paul expresses it, "from the power of Satan unto God." And (3.) That the chief business of the tempter is to "take the word of truth out of our hearts, lest we should believe and be saved;" or, in other terms, to "blind our minds, lest the light of the glorious Gospel of Christ should shine unto us."

If Jesus Christ is the truth, the light, the life, and the Word, that "was in the beginning with God, and was God;" the Word "by which all things were made," and are preserved, if he is "the light that shineth in darkness," even when the darkness comprehendeth it not:" if "he is the true light which lighteth every man that cometh into the world," while the day of salvation lasts: if he is the archetype, the eternal, living pattern of all saving truth: if he is the essential, almighty Word, from whom revealed truth and the word of our salvation flow as constantly as light and heat from the sun: do we not slight him, and despise eternal life, when we slight the truth, and despise the Word? And may not the great things spoken of the Word confirm what has been said of the truth, and help us to answer the questions already proposed in a manner equally scriptural and conclusive?

Not forgetting that there is such a thing as "the word nigh, the word behind" us, the "still small voice," and "the word of that grace which has appeared unto all men, teaching them to deny worldly lusts, and to live soberly," &c, I ask, What are evangelists? Men who "bear record of the word of God," and "bear witness of the light, that all men may believe." "Sowers, that sow the word of the kingdom: holding forth the word of life." What are false apostles? Men that "corrupt the word of God," that "handle the word of God deceitfully," and "preach another Gospel; whose words eat as does a canker." — What are believers? People that "hear the word of God and keep it;" that are "begotten of God by the word of truth;" that "are born again by. the word of God;" that "hear the sayings of Christ, and do them; in whose hearts the word of Christ dwells richly; who receive it not as the word of men, but, as it is in truth, the word of God, which worketh effectually in them that believe" it. They are persons that "receive with meekness the ingrafted word, which is able to save their souls;" that have "tasted the good word of God," that "desire the sincere milk of the word, that they may grow thereby;" that "gladly receive the word; have God's word abiding in them;" are made "clean through the word which Christ speaks" by his ministers, his Scriptures, his Spirit, his works, or his rod; and "in whom the seed of that word produces" thirty fold, sixty fold, or a hundred fold, according to their light, faithfulness, and opportunity.

Again: what are unbelievers? Antinomian hypocrites "that hear the sayings of Christ, and do them not;" or Pharisaic "despisers that stumble at the word, speak against those things which are spoken by" God's messengers; "contradicting and blaspheming;" and who, by "putting the word of God from them, judge themselves unworthy of eternal life." What are martyrs? Witnesses of the truth; "slain for the word of God." And what are apostates? Persons in whom "the word is choked by the cares of this world, or the deceitfulness of riches;" who "fall away when persecution ariseth because of the word; by reason of whom the way of truth is evil spoken of;" and in whom the seed of the word "becometh unfruitful." Thus all turns still upon truth and the word of God.

SECTION III.

That according to reason and Scripture there is a saving, almighty power in truth and the word of God.

SHOULD the reader ask here how it is possible the word and the truth should be so nearly related to our Saviour, that to receive them is to receive him, and to reject them is to reject him and his salvation: I answer, that in the spiritual, as well as in the political and mercantile world, signs are necessary by which to convey our thoughts and resolutions. Hence the use of letters, notes, bonds, and charters; of revelations, traditions, Scriptures, and sacraments. Now an honest man's word is as good as his bond or pledge, and as true as his heart; his word or bond being nothing but his mind or determination fairly conveyed to others by the means of his tongue or of his hand. Therefore, in the very nature of things, to receive the word of Christ is to receive Christ, who "dwells in our hearts by faith;" whom believers "know now after the flesh no more:" who commissioned his favourite apostle to say, "He that abideth in the doctrine of Christ hath both the Father and the Son;" and who personally declares, "My mother and my brothers are these," that "hear the word of God and keep it."

As the legislative power has appointed that pure gold duly stamped, and bank notes properly drawn up, shall represent the value, and procure the possession of all the necessaries and conveniences of life, which can be bought with money; so our heavenly Lawgiver has fixed that the "word of truth" shall answer, in his spiritual kingdom, the end of gold and letters of exchange in the kingdoms of this world; and this spiritual gold, this "word tried to the uttermost," he offers to all that are "poor, and blind, and naked, that they may be rich in faith. I counsel thee to buy of me gold tried in the fire, that thou mayest be rich."

Again: as a will conveys an immense fortune; and a death warrant a capital punishment; so does the word of God convey "the unsearchable riches of Christ" to obedient believers, and the dreadful punishments of the damned to obstinate unbelievers. I readily grant that a bank note is not gold, that a will is not an estate, and that a death warrant is not the gallows. Nevertheless, so strong is the connection between those seemingly insignificant signs, and the important things which they signify, that none but fools will throw away their bank notes, or the wills of their friends as waste paper; none but madmen will sport with their death warrant as with a play bill. Now if the written word of men, who, through forgetfulness, fickleness, impotence, or unfaithfulness, often break their engagements, can nevertheless have such force; how excessively fool hardy are sinners that disregard the word of the King of kings, "who cannot lie!" the proclamations of the "God of truth, with whom no word is impossible!" the promises and threatenings, the will and testament of the Almighty, who says, "Heaven and earth shall pass away, but my word shall not pass away!"

Once more: although "no man knows the Father" immediately "but the Son," yet the Father may be mediately known by his works, his word, and his Son. For, leaving room for the liberty of moral agents and their works, God's works are always as his word. Hence we read: "God said, Let there be light, and there was light. Cursed be the ground for man's sake," and the ground was cursed. "For he spake, and it was done; he commanded, and it stood fast." As God's works are the express image of his word uttered without, — of his out-going word (if I may so speak;) so his out-going word is the express image of his immanent, essential word, which is his eternal mind, and which the Scriptures call indifferently, "the Word, the Wisdom, the Son of God," or "the express image of his Father's glory." Hence it appears that as the essential Word, Christ, is one with the Father; so the word of saving truth is one with the Son; and that David, Solomon, and St. Paul, spoke noble truths when they said, "Whoso despiseth the word shall be destroyed. By the word of thy lips I have kept me from the ways of the destroyer. The law, or word of the Lord, is an undefiled word: it is sure, and giveth wisdom to the simple; it is right, and rejoiceth the heart; it is pure, and giveth light; it is true, and righteous altogether; more to be desired than gold, yea, than much fine gold: better to me than thousands of gold and silver: sweeter also than honey, and the honey comb. It is a lamp unto my feet, and a light unto my path; by it is thy servant taught and made wise to salvation; and in keeping of it there is great reward, even the reward of the inheritance," a kingdom of grace here, and a kingdom of glory hereafter.

But let our Lord himself be heard, and he will join himself in mystic trinity to the word, and to the truth of God. He promiscuously uses the expressions truth and word, which make the burden of the last section. When he recommends his disciples to his Father, he says, "Sanctify them through thy truth, thy word is truth." Hence it appears that the truth and the word are terms of the same import; that the word of truth is a sanctifying emanation from God, and the ordinary vehicle of the Divine power; and that our Lord uttered a rational mystery when he said, "He that receiveth you [the witnesses of my truth and the sowers of my word] receiveth me; and he that receiveth me receiveth him that sent me." But "whosoever shall be ashamed of me and of my words, of him shall the Son of man be ashamed when he cometh in the glory of his Father." And imperfect believers he encouraged thus: "If ye continue in my word, &c, ye shall know the truth, and the truth shall make you free, &c. If the Son shall make you free, ye shall be free indeed." Important scriptures these, which show the connection of the truth with the Son of God! Blessed scriptures, which St. Paul sums up in the following words: "Say not in thy heart, Who shall ascend into heaven? (that is, to bring Christ down from above;) or, Who shall descend into the deep? (that is, to bring up Christ again from the dead.) But what saith the righteousness which is of faith? The word is nigh thee, even in thy mouth and in thy heart; that is, the word of faiths which we preach."

Nor is this doctrine of the apostle contrary to what he says on another occasion: "The kingdom of God is not in words but in power," i.e. true religion does not consist in fine talking, but in powerful believing and holy living. For what is more powerful than truth? "Truth is great, and will prevail:" truth is the strongest thing in the world: it overturns the thrones of tyrants, and supports God's everlasting throne.

Again: the word of man brings strange things to pass. Let but a general speak, and an army of Russians marches up through clouds of smoke, flames of fire, and volleys of iron balls, to form heaps of dead or dying bodies before the intrenchments of the Turks. An admiral gives the word of command, it may be only by hoisting a flag, and a fleet is under sail; artificial clouds and thunders are formed over the sea; the billows seem to be mingled with fire; and the king of terror flies from deck to deck in his most dreadful and bloody forms.

If such is the power of the word of a man, who is but a worm, how almighty must be the word of God! "By the word of the Lord were the heavens made," saith David: "The worlds were framed by the word of God," adds St. Paul, "and he upholdeth all things by the word of his power." That word no necessary agents can resist. It rolls the planets with as much ease as hurricanes whirl the dust. If free agents can resist his word of commands it is only because he permits it for their trial. But wo to them that resist it to the end of their day of probation: for they shall feel the resistless force of his word of punishment' "Depart from me, ye cursed, into everlasting fire." And who is the God that shall break the adamantine, infernal chains, which that dreadful word will rivet upon them?

We read in the Gospel that our Lord marvelled at the centurion's faith, as greater faith than he had found in Israel. But wherein consisted the peculiar greatness of that man's faith? Is it not evident, from the context, that it was in the noble and lively apprehension which he had of the force and energy of Christ's word? "Lord," said he, "I am a man under the authority [of my colonel and general, and yet] having soldiers under me,! say to one, Go, and he goeth; and to another, Come, and he cometh," &c. Now, Lord, if my word has such power, what cannot thine do? "Speak the word only, and my servant shall be healed."

Why is Abraham called "the father of the faithful?" Is it not because "judging Him faithful [and almighty] that had promised, against hope he believed in hope, that he should become the father of many nations; according to that which was spoken, So shall thy seed be?" Is it not because "he staggered not at the promise, [or word] of God through unbelief; but was strong in faith, giving glory to God, and being fully persuaded that what he had promised he was able to perform; and therefore it was imputed to him for righteousness? And shall not the like faith be imputed to us also, if we believe" the saving truth revealed, or the Divine record given under the present dispensation of the Gospel, viz. "that God raised up Jesus our Lord from the dead, who was delivered for our offences, and raised again for our justification?"

O! who can describe the needless perplexities of those wilful unbelievers that have the truth of their dispensation clearly brought to them, and yet, like Thomas, resolutely set themselves against it, saying, "I will not believe?" And who can enumerate the blessings which those childlike souls inherit, who, instead of quarrelling with, cordially embrace the word of God, and set to their seal that God is true? They seal God's truth, and God seals their hearts. "Their faith is imputed to them for righteousness; their faith saves them; it is done to them according to their faith; the God of hope fills them with all joy and peace in believing." Thus, "through faith, they [not only] subdue the kingdom [of darkness, but] inherit the [present] kingdom of God, righteousness, peace, and joy in the Holy Ghost, received by the hearing of faith." Well disposed reader, if thou doubtest the truth of those scriptures, try it by believing now what appears to thee to be the saving truth of thy dispensation: believe it with all thy present might, be it little or be it much; and if in a little time thou dost not find thyself more settled and free, more able to fight against sin, and to take up thy cross, let me bear the blame for ever.

Did the success of God's word depend only upon him, the truth would always operate in a saving manner. If men were not to "work out their own salvation" by freely repenting, believing, and obeying, with the power "to will and to do," which God gives them of his good pleasure, all mankind would repent, believe, and obey, as passively as clocks go, and as regularly as the sun rises. But we are moral agents; and works morally good depend as much upon the concurrence of God's free grace, and of our free obedience of faith, as the birth of the prince of Wales did upon the marriage of the king and queen. Hence we read: "To whom sware he that they should not enter into his rest, but to them that believed not? For the word preached did not profit them," not because the seed was bad, or because they had no power to receive it, but because "it was not mixed with faith in them that heard it. Wherefore," says the apostle, "to-day if you will hear his voice, harden not your hearts, &c. Take heed lest there be in any of you an evil heart of unbelief, &c, and exhort one another daily" to believe.

The genuine seed of the word is then always good, always full of Divine energy. If it does not spring up, or if, after it has sprung up, it does not "bring forth fruit to perfection," it is entirely the fault of the ground. "The words that I speak," says our Lord, though it should be only by the mouth of my servants, "they are spirit and they are life" to believing hearts. For "Christ gave himself for the Church, that he might sanctify and cleanse it with the washing of water by the word; if it continue in the faith, holding fast the faithful word, — the word of the truth of the Gospel, which is come in all the world, and bringeth forth fruit" since the day it is heard in faith; it being the grand office of the Spirit to make "the word of God," when it is mixed with faith on our part, "sharper than any two-edged sword, piercing even to the dividing asunder of soul and spirit," and "to the discerning [and destroying of the bad] thoughts and intents of the heart."

Nothing, therefore, can be more certain than the connection between the power of God and the truth of the Gospel. "Truth (says a divine of the last century) is that eternal word of the Father which, in the Son, by the Holy Ghost, is revealed to us, to be our guide back again to that bosom whence it and we first came: it is that Jacob's ladder, let down to us from heaven to earth, whereby his angels (his messengers) lead up from earth to heaven: it is that Rahab's scarlet thread, let down from the window of heaven to wind us up by. The apostle calls it a girdle, 'the girdle of truth,' a girdle, that by many several links ending where it began, returning whence it first proceeded, clasps itself again in the bosom of its author, God." According to this noble description of truth, is it not evident that all the righteous power which works in the spiritual world is the power of God and of truth? And therefore that our Lord answered like Divine wisdom "manifest in the flesh" when he asserted that "to believe on him is to work the work of God:" that "he who believeth hath everlasting life:" that "though he were dead, yet shall he live:" that "he that liveth and believeth on him [which implies a continuance of the action] shall never die:" that "rivers of living water [streams of comfort and power] shall flow out of his belly [i.e. spring from his inmost soul;] and that he shall do great works, the Gospel being the power of God to salvation to every one that believeth;" and "all things being possible to him that believeth," because his faith apprehends the word, truth, and power of the Almighty.

SECTION IV.

There are various sorts of truths. Idolatry and formality consist in putting inferior in the room of superior truths. Evangelical and moral, i.e. religious truths alone change the heart.

WHEN I said that living faith has saving truth for its object, I did not use the word "saving" without reason: for as every stone is not precious, so every truth is not saving. There are then various sorts of truths. "There is a sun," is a *physical* or *natural* truth. "Our ideas of the sun are mental pictures of the sun," is a *metaphysical* truth. "All the points of a circle are equally distant from the centre," is a *mathematical* truth. "No just conclusion can be drawn from false premises," is a *logical* truth. "Alexander conquered Persia," is a *historical* truth. "There is a God, and this God is to be worshipped according to the different manifestations of Father, Son, and Holy Ghost," are two *religious* truths, the first of which belongs to *natural,* and the second to *revealed religion.* "Every man is to love his neighbour as himself," is a moral truth. "A spiritual Jew is circumcised in heart, and a spiritual Christian is baptized with the Spirit," is an *evangelical* truth, typified by the outward signs of circumcision and of baptism.

When *natural* and inferior truths raise our minds to the God of *nature* and of *grace,* they answer their *spiritual* ends: but if they are put in the place of their archetypes and antitypes, "the truth of God is changed into a lie." Take some instances of it: "The invisible things of God," says St. Paul, "are understood by the things that are made," or visible; but who considers the profound truth couched under his words? Certainly not those heathens who worship the *material,* instead of the *immaterial* Sun: nor those Jews who are regardless of the circumcision of the heart, and rest satisfied with an external circumcision: nor those Papists who pay Divine honours to a bit of typical bread which their fancy has turned into the identical body of our Lord: nor yet those Protestants who, being unmindful of the baptism of the Spirit, exert themselves only in sprinkling infants with, or dipping adults in material water: for they all equally forget that the letter of natural and typical things alone profiteth little, or nothing comparatively; and that it killeth, when it is opposed to the Spirit, and made to supersede the invisible and heavenly archetypes, which visible and earthly things shadow out; or when it causes us to set aside the precious antitypes which typical things point unto.

Thus thousands of sinners, like the rich glutton in the Gospel, are spiritually, if not corporally, killed by meats and drinks, which should raise them to their invisible archetypes, the heavenly manna, and the wine of God's kingdom. Thus conjugal love, which should raise married persons to a more lively contemplation of the mystical union between the heavenly bridegroom and his faithful spouse, has a quite contrary effect upon numbers. Absurdly resting in the fading type, they think that "I have married a wife," is a sufficient reason to give Christ a bill of divorce, or to show him the greatest indifference. Thus also the Jews committed the deadly sins of idolatry and murder, through their regard for their brazen serpent and the temple; an extravagant regard this, which caused them to neglect, and at last to crucify Christ, the invaluable antitype of both the brazen serpent and of the temple.

The Works of John Fletcher

Hence it appears that the sin of formalists is not unlike that of idolaters. As God has blessed his Church with various forms of worship, and literal manifestations of his truth, that they might lead us to the power of godliness, and to the truth in the Spirit; so he has filled the natural world with a variety of creatures which bear some signatures of his own unseen excellences. But alas! if we are only formal and letter-learned professors, we absurdly set up our forms and the letter against the power and spiritual operations which they shadow out: and if we are idolaters, we "love and serve the creature more than the Creator," who has given us the outlines of his invisible glories in the visible creation, that in and through every thing we "might feel after him and find him." Thus formality and idolatry equally defeat God's gracious designs toward mankind, the one by opposing forms, and the other by opposing creatures to God.

To return: all sorts of truths, if they are kept in their proper places, may improve the understanding: but religious truths only have a direct tendency to improve the will, which is the spring of our tempers and actions. Therefore, "although I have all knowledge" but that which is productive of "charity, I am nothing:" the faith of God's elect being only the cordial, practical acknowledging of "the truth, which is after godliness" — of the saving" truth, as it is in Jesus."

A total inattention to every kind of truth makes a man brutish. An eager pursuit of natural, mathematical, logical, historical truths, &c, attended with a neglect of religious truths, tends to make a man an infidel: and this neglect, grown up into an obstinate, practical opposition to moral as well as to evangelical truths, turns him into "an enemy of all righteousness," and a persecutor.

But when candour, a degree of which we may have through the light that enlightens every man; when free agency, assisted by the Spirit of power, that accompanies the word of truth; when candour, I say, and free agency thus assisted, attend and submit to the religious truths revealed under our dispensation; then the Divine "seed falls into good ground;" Christ begins to be formed in our hearts; and, according to our dispensation, "we receive power to become sons of God: for we [even as many as 'receive with meekness the ingrafted word'] are all the children of God through faith in the light of the world, — through faith in Christ Jesus, who is the Saviour of all men, but especially of them that believe unto righteousness;" whether they do it with meridian light and intense fervour, as true Christians; with morning light and growing vigour, as pious Jews; or only with dawning light and timorous sincerity, as converted heathens.

Some sorts of truth, like some kinds of food, are richer than others. Infants in grace must be fed with the plainest truths, which the apostle calls milk; but stronger souls may feast upon what would give a surfeit to "babes in Christ:" "for every one that useth milk is unskilful in the word of righteousness. But strong meat belongeth to them that are of full age, even those who, by reason of use, have their spiritual senses exercised to discern both good and evil," truth and error, as quickly and as surely as our bodily senses distinguish sweet from bitter, and light from darkness. Truth is spiritual light: too much of it might dazzle the weak eyes of our understanding. A parabolical blind is of great service in such a case. When the apostles were yet carnal, our Lord said to them, "I have many things to say to you, but ye cannot bear them now:" no, not in parables. "Howbeit, when the Spirit of truth is come, he will guide you into all [evangelical] truth." A sure proof this that truth is the light, the food, the way of souls; and that the grand business of the Spirit is to "lead us into the truth," as we can bear it, and as we choose to walk in it.

SECTION V.

Truth cordially embraced by faith saves under every dispensation of Divine grace, though in different degrees. A short view of the truths that characterize the four grand dispensations of the everlasting Gospel.

I HAVE signified that faith is more or less operative, according to the quality of the truths which it embraces. This observation recommends itself to reason: for as some wines are more generous, and some remedies more powerful, so some truths are more reviving and sanctifying than others. But every evangelical truth, being a beam of the "Sun of righteousness risen" upon us "with healing in his wings," is of a saving nature. Thus I am saved from ATHEISM, by heartily believing there is a God who will judge the world; — from PHARISAISM, by firmly believing that I am a miserable sinner, and that "without Christ I can do nothing;" — from SADDUCEISM, by truly believing that "the Spirit itself helpeth my infirmities;" — from ANTINOMIANISM, by cordially believing that "God is not a respecter of persons, but a rewarder of them that diligently seek him," and a punisher of all that presumptuously break his commandments; — and from DESPAIR, by steadily believing that "God is love," that "he sent his only begotten Son into the world to save that which is lost," and that I "have an Advocate with the Father, Jesus Christ the righteous."

Hence it appears, (1.) That every religious truth, suitable to our present circumstances, (when it is kindly represented by free grace, and affectionately embraced by prevented free will,) instantly forms, according to its degree, the saving, operative faith that converts, transforms, and renews the soul. And, (2.) That this faith is more or less operative, according to the quality of the truth presented to us; according to the power with which the Spirit of grace impresses it upon our hearts; and according to the earnestness with which we receive, espouse, and welcome it to our inmost souls.

When God fixed "the bounds of the habitation of mankind," he placed some nations in warm climates and fruitful countries, where the juice of the grape is plentiful next to water. And to others he assigned a barren, rocky soil, covered with snow half the year; water is their cordial, nor have they any more idea of their want of wine than St. Peter had of his want of the blood of Christ, when he made the noble confession upon which the Christian Church is founded. "O," says a Predestinarian geographer, "the God of providence has absolutely reprobated those poor creatures." "Not so," replies an unprejudiced philosopher, "they may be as healthy and happy over their cup of cold water as some of our men of fortune are over the bottles of Claret and Madeira that load their festive tables. And some of those poor creatures, as you call them, may 'come from the east and from the west to drink' the wine of the kingdom of God 'with Abraham,' when 'the children of the kingdom shall be thrust out.'"

What I have said of water and wine may illustrate what the Scriptures say of the truths peculiar to the Gospel dispensation. God forbid that an antichristian zeal for the Christian Gospel should make me drive into the burning lake Christ's sheep which are "big with young:" I mean the sincere worshippers that wait, like pious Melchisedec, devout Lydia, and charitable Cornelius, for brighter displays of Gospel grace. For there are faithful souls that follow their light under every dispensation, concerning whom our Lord kindly said, "Other sheep I have which are not of this [Jewish] fold: them also I must bring [into marvellous light,] and there shall be one fold and one Shepherd." Those feeble sheep and tender lambs I must take into my bosom; and to give them their portion of meat in due season, I venture upon the following remark: —

If free will, prevented by free grace, ardently receives the truths of the Christian Gospel, Christian faith is conceived. If the heart fervently embraces the truths of the Jewish or Gentile Gospel, (those which are peculiar to the Christian Gospel remaining as yet veiled,) the faith of a Jew or of a heathen is begotten. Nevertheless, if this faith, let it be ever so assaulted by doubts, impregnates the soul with truth, and works by love, it is saving in its degree.

I say *in its degree*; for as there are in the earth various rich tinctures, some of which form diamonds, while others form only rubies, emeralds, or agates; so there are in the universal Church of Christ various tinctures of Gospel truth, which form various orders of spiritual jewels, as appears from such scriptures as these: — "They that feared the Lord spake often one to another; and they shall be mine, saith the Lord of hosts, in that day when I make up my jewels. For in every nation he that feareth God and worketh righteousness is accepted of him," according to the dispensation he is under, and the progress he has made in practical religion.

This Gospel, for example, "God hath made of one blood all nations of men, that they should seek the Lord [as the gracious Author of their being, and] love one another as brothers:" this everlasting Gospel, I say, has in all countries leavened the hearts of pious heathens with "sincerity and truth." This doctrine, "Messiah will come to point out clearly the way of salvation," added to the Gospel of the Gentiles, has tinctured with superior goodness the hearts of all believing Jews. This truth, "Messiah is come in the flesh," superadded to the Jewish Gospel, has enlarged the hearts of all the disciples of John, or the "babes in Christ." And these truths, "Christ died for my sins, and rose again for my justification; he is ascended up on high; he has received the gift of the Spirit for men, — for me. I believe on him by the power of that Spirit. He dwells in my heart by faith. He is in me the hope of glory. The promise of the Father is fulfilled; the kingdom of God, righteousness, peace, and joy in the Holy Ghost is come with power." These richer truths, I say, superadded to those which are essential to the inferior dispensations, tincture the hearts of all adult Christians, and make them more or less intimately one with Christ, according to the degree of their faith, and the influences of his Spirit.

The field of truth is as boundless as the Divine perfections; and the treasures it contains are as unsearchable as the riches of Christ. Here We may literally say, "Deep calleth unto deep — Canst thou by searching find out the Almighty to perfection? It is as high as heaven, what canst thou do? Deeper than hell, what canst thou known" These three capital truths only — "God is — God is love — God is mine in Christ" — are more than sufficient to replace my soul in paradise. I know but little of them; and yet, thanks be to God! I know enough to make me anticipate heavenly bliss. Nor is it the least part of my present happiness to rejoice that there is an eternity before me to unfold the wonders of truth, and to explore the "mystery of God. Now I see through a glass darkly, but then face to face. Now I know but in part, but then I shall know even as also I am known."

SECTION VI.

Saving faith is more particularly described by its rise and operations; and distinguished from the faith of trembling devils, immoral Antinomians, penitents sold under sin, and modish professors who believe without frame and feeling.

IF we assent to a religious truth merely because we cannot resist its evidence; — if we hate it, wanting to shake it off, wishing it were a lie, and fretting because we cannot make it so; we have the faith of devils: for "devils believe and tremble;" the force of the awful truths which they cannot deny giving them a foretaste of infernal torments. Of this sort, it seems, was the faith of Felix, when St. Paul reasoned before him of "justice, temperance, and judgment to come." This alarming doctrine, supported by the suffrage of conscience, and impressed by "the Spirit of truth," made the noble heathen "tremble;" but soon recovering himself, he fought against the truth that had laid hold on him unawares, and he kept it at arm's length, till he could shake it off as the apostle did the viper that fastened on his hand; or at least till he could run away from it, by plunging as desperately into a sea of sensual delights, as the devils in the swine did into the sea of Galilee.

The faith of immoral professors is not much better than the faith of Felix and Satan. They believe some glorious truths, but not with the heart to righteousness. Two or three comparisons may help us to understand this "mystery of iniquity." When a person visits you, you may either receive him with cold civility, as a stranger; or embrace him with warm affection as a bosom friend. From secret motives you may show a peculiar regard to a man whom you secretly despise or detest. He has a good voice, you love music, and he ministers to your amusement. Perhaps you want him to cloak the sin of his Bathsheba; perhaps you are a party man; he is a proper tool for you; and therefore you make much of him. But while your regard for him springs merely from such external circumstances, can it ever be personal and sincere? Equally ungenerous however is the regard that Gallio and Fulsome have for the truth. Gallio holds fast the doctrine of general redemption, because he fondly supposes that he has only to avoid robbery and murder to go to heaven: Fulsome extols "everlasting love," but it is because he thinks that it gives him the liberty of loving the world, without the least danger of losing God's eternal favour. He embraces "justification by faith alone;" but it is because he confounds the works of faith and the works of the law, and vainly hopes to be finally justified without either. He shouts, "Free grace for ever!" because it insures,, as he thinks, his eternal salvation, whatever length he may go in sin. He is a partial anatomist; he dissects the body of truth, throws away the vitals, and only preserves those parts which seem to countenance his immoral scheme. I question if an Indian warrior is more fond of the scalp of an Englishman, than Gallio is of the doctrine of "God's mercy," separated from God's holiness and justice; or Fulsome of the doctrine of "Christ's merits," torn away from the evangelical worthiness of sincere obedience.

Nay, a judicious Gnostic may admire and espouse a well connected system of religious truth, just as a virtuoso admires and purchases a good collection of shells. The virtuoso contends for the beauty and rarity of his marine toys with as much passionateness as if they were parts of himself: but they only lie upon cotton in his drawers, far enough from his breast. And the Gnostic disputes for the truths he has taken a fancy to with as much warmth as if they were incorporated with himself; but he contrives that they shall pass like flying clouds over his understanding, without descending in fruitful showers upon his heart.

Truth is the wholesome food of souls. Hence it is said, "The just shall live by his faith," by his receiving Christ in the word of truth, and by mystically feeding upon him, according to these deep words: "Except you eat my flesh, and drink my blood, ye have no life in you:" or, as St. John expresses it, "the truth is not in you." Now, as food must be inwardly taken, and properly digested, before it can nourish us; so must truth. If men, therefore, who "buy the truth" in theory, and "sell it" in practice, who "profess it in words, and deny it in works," have not power to take up their cross and to follow Christ; we ought no more on that account to conclude that the truth is inefficacious to our salvation, than to suppose that good food is improper for our nourishment, because men that spend their time in preparing it for others, in drawing up bills of fare, in placing dishes to the best advantage, and in inviting others to eat heartily, while they live upon trash themselves, have not strength to go through a hard day's work.

Again: from such scriptures as these: "I will heal their backslidings: heal my soul, for I have sinned against thee: God shall send forth his mercy and his truth: he sent his word and healed them," &c, it is evident that evangelical truth is, next to Christ, the medicine as well as the food of souls. Now, as it is absurd to suppose that speculating upon a medicine, instead of taking it, can conduce to the recovery of our bodily health, so it is unreasonable to fancy that bare speculations upon the doctrines of the Gospel can be productive of saving health; cordial believing having no less necessary a reference to truth, than real drinking to a potion. Hence appears the necessity of clearly distinguishing between saving faith and Antinomian fancy; between the faith by which a man affectionately believes with an humble heart unto righteousness; and its counterfeit, by which a man idly believes with a conceited mind to practical Antinomianism, whether he be a follower of Mr. Wesley or of Mr. Romaine.

The soaring faith of an immoral Antinomian is far inferior to the abortive faith of an imperfect penitent, and even to doubting. When truth and error present themselves to our minds together, (as they always do in every trial of faith,) so long as we remain in suspense between them, we continue in the uneasy state, between faith and unbelief, which we call "doubting." But when truth appears more beautiful than error to the eye of our understanding, without appearing good enough prevalently to engage our affections; we are in the uncomfortable state of the carnal penitent whom St. Paul describes in his own person, Rom 7. We approve the revealed will of God, and "delight in his law after the inward man." If the celestial rose were not beset with thorns, we would instantly gather it, If we had no bodily appetites to resist, no ignominious cross to take up, no false wisdom to part with, we would heartily believe and "work the work of God." But we cannot yet give up our bosom sin; carnal reason and the flesh prevail still against the spirit, though not without a struggle; unbelief and abortive faith (if I may use the expression) wrestling in our distracted breasts, as Esau and Jacob did in Rebecca's womb; and making us complain, "The good that I would do," if it cost me nothing, "I do not: but the evil I would not, that I do," because it gratifies my fallen nature. Thus with his mind, his rational powers, the carnal penitent "serves the law of God" by good, though ineffectual resolutions; but with his flesh, his carnal appetites, he "serves the law of sin" by bad, though lamented performances.

Here I beg leave to account for the famous confession of the princess, who cries out in Ovid,* *Video meliora, proboque, — deteriora sequor,* which may be thus paraphrased' "I stand between the rough, steep, ascending path of virtue, [*bonum honestum,*] and the plain, flowery, downward road of vice, [*bonum jucundum.*] Conscience says that the one is far more commendable; passion declares that the other is far more pleasing. I madly give the casting vote to hurrying passion; it decides that the pleasure of a present, certain gratification, be it ever so sinful, overbalances the fear of a future, uncertain punishment, be it ever so terrible: and notwithstanding the remonstrances of my conscience, I submit to the hazardous decision of my appetite; secretly hoping that God does not regard my crimes, or that a day of retribution is a chimera."

To return: faith does not struggle into birth without her co-eval child and constant partner, hope. When faith fails, despair groans, "O wretched man that I am, who shall deliver me?" But when faith revives, hope lifts up her head, and cries, "I thank God [there is deliverance] through Jesus Christ our Lord." Thus we go on falling and rising, dying and reviving, till we are quite tired of the sins which hinder us from welcoming the saving truth with a more cordial embrace; and when we do this, our faith is unfeigned; the Lord sets to it the broad seal of his power; it proves victorious; we enter into Gospel liberty, and instead of the old note, "Who shall deliver me?" we sing, under the Christian dispensation, "Christ hath delivered us from the curse of the law" of sin, as well as from the curse of the law of innocence and of the ceremonial law. "There is no condemnation to them that [believe and] walk not after the flesh, but after the Spirit."

The manner in which this deliverance is generally wrought, may be more particularly described thus: — Free grace, "at sundry times and in divers manners," speaks to our consciences, recommending "the word nigh, — the commandment" that is "everlasting life," the truth that contains the regenerating power of God. If it be "the day of provocation," we unnecessarily begin "to make excuse." We cannot come to the marriage feast. We are either too good, too bad, or too busy to entertain the truth; and we say as civilly as Felix, "Go thy way for this time, [when I shall be more fit, or] when I shall have a more convenient season, I will call for thee." Perhaps we perversely "harden our heart, contradicting, blaspheming," and saying as the Pharisees, "We will not have this [truth] to reign over us. Away with it!" But if it be the day of conversion, if our free willing soul "know the time of our visitation,"

---

* I see what is right and approve it, but do what is wrong.

humbly bowing at the word of the Lord, and saying, as the Virgin Mary, "Behold the handmaid of the Lord, let it be done unto me according to thy word;" I am a lost sinner, but "there is mercy with thee that thou mayest be feared:" then the seed of the kingdom, the word of God, "is received in an honest and good heart;" for nothing is wanting to render the heart initially good and honest, but the sincere submission of our free will, to that free grace which courts us, and says, "Behold! I stand at the door [of every heart] and knock. If any man hear my voice and open, I will come in and sup with him, and he with me." He shall "taste how good the Lord is," he shall "taste the good word of God and the powers [of truth, which are the powers] of the world to come." And so shall he rise superior to shadows and lies, which are the powers of this present evil world.

Thus opens the kingdom of God in the believing soul: thus is Christ the "truth and the life," formed in the heart by faith: thus grace begins to "reign through righteousness unto eternal life by Jesus Christ."

I call that faith "saving and operative," because so long as it lives, it saves; and so long as it saves, it "works righteousness," — it works by a righteous fear of the evil denounced against sin; by a righteous opposition to every known sin; by a righteous hope of the good promised to obedience; and by a righteous love of the truth that has produced it, and of the Father of lights, from whom that truth proceeds; it being scarcely possible to welcome heartily a beam of the sun for its brightness, without indirectly welcoming the sun itself. Therefore, when living faith ceases to "work," it dies away, as the heart that ceases to beat; it goes out, as a candle that ceases to shine.

"But, upon this footing, what becomes of the modish doctrine of a faith without frame and feeling?" If the ministers, who recommend such a faith, mean that we must set our heart as a seal to the Gospel truths adapted to our present state, and stamp them with all our might, not considering whether our *fallen* nature and *carnal* reason relish them, and steadily following the poet's direction,

"Tu ne cede malis; sed contra audentior ito,

Quam MALA te NATURA sinit:"

they maintain a truth, a great truth, which cannot be too much urged upon tempted, desponding, and despairing souls. But if they mean that we must believe ourselves unconditionally elected to glory, be the frame of our minds ever so carnal, and the feelings of our hearts ever so worldly, they destroy "the health of the daughter of God's people," with as rank poison as ever grew in spiritual Egypt. I am no judge of what passes in the breasts of those gentlemen; but, for my part, I never feel faith more strongly at work than when I wrestle not only with flesh and blood, but with the banded powers of darkness.

None but a dead man is quite destitute of frame and feeling. It is not a real flame that neither warms in winter nor shines in the dark. The moment a light is not in its degree able to triumph over darkness, and even to turn it into light, it ceases to be a true light. You may see in Windsor Castle a candle most exquisitely painted; it shines as steadfastly as Mr. Fulsome believes. Was the coloured canvass as loquacious as that Antinomian hero, it might say, "I shine without feeling, though not without a frame." But even then Mr. Fulsome's faith would have the pre-eminence; for if we credit him it shines without either frame or feeling. How absurd is Solifidianism? how dangerous! If any man can show me a true light, that actually emits no beams, I will repent of the ridicule I cast upon the dotages, which make way for a "justifying faith" that works by adultery and murder; an ill-smelling candle this, which burns in the breasts of apostates to the honour of him that kindled it at the fire of Tophet; an infernal candle, sending forth darkness instead of light, and so far benighting the good men who follow it, that they look upon it as the inextinguishable "candle of the Lord," and upon sincere obedience as a "jack o'lantern."

The preceding pages represent truth as the remedy and nourishment of our souls; and I have already observed, that as we cannot take food without the continual help of the God of nature, so we cannot receive the truth without the continual assistance of the God of grace; it being the first axiom of the Gospel, that all our sufficiency and ability to do any good are of God. Nevertheless, lest those who seek occasion against the truth, which they do not relish, should call the free grace I hold forth Pelagianism, I shall conclude this section by asserting, that if Christ were not "the Saviour of all men," and if we were entirely destitute of the gracious, evangelical "light that enlightens every man," and "helps our infirmities," we should be, with respect to saving truths, like people who either have no kind of food, or no appetite at all to their food; nay, like sick people that have an insurmountable aversion to a medicine and an irresistible longing for poison. But the saving "grace of God having appeared to all men," and having mercifully given us an evangelical capacity to receive the truth as it is revealed to us in the dispensation we are under, we may either put that truth from us, as the unbelieving Jews did, or welcome it, as Job and his friends, although not without difficulty: yea, such difficulty as forms the "trial of our faith," and makes it reasonable in God to bid us "choose life" rather than death, when truth and error, blessing and cursing, are set before us.

SECTION VII.

The operative belief of a the two roots that produce all our good and all our bad actions. An appeal to reason and matter of fact.

No plant can grow without its root, and no moral action can spring into existence without its principle. When we do not dissemble, our principle of action is our prevalent persuasion, our predominant belief; a cordial, practical belief of the truth and rejection of a lie being always the principle of a good action; and a cordial, practical belief of a lie and rejection of the truth being always the principle of a bad action.

That good works can have no origin but the belief of the truth will appear indubitable, if we trace them back to their sources. To fear, love, and obey God are undoubtedly good works; but can I do them without believing the truth, that is, without believing that God is, that he is to be feared, loved, and obeyed, and that it is my duty or privilege so to do? Again: that bad works can have no other origin but the belief of a lie will also appear evident if we follow them to their spring. To neglect and disobey God are certainly bad works; but can we do them without "believing a lie?" without being more or less persuaded that although it may not be our duty, yet, upon the whole, in our present circumstances, it will be for our advantage or credit to neglect God and to swim with the stream?

May not the preceding argument concerning the importance of faith be confirmed by appeals to reason, experience, and matter of fact? Did not Eve stand in paradise so long as she forbore eating of the forbidden fruit? Did she not forbear eating so long as she believed the truth, that is, so long as she believed she should die if she ate of that fruit? Would she have sinned if she had not first believed a lie, yea, swallowed down a cluster of lies? "That she should not die; the fruit was as good as it was fair; it was to be desired to make one wise; she should be as God," &c; were not these untruths, freely entertained in her heart, the causes of her committing the direful deed?

Why did Judas once forsake all to follow the indigent Jesus? Was it not because he believed it his real advantage so to do? And did he not so far believe the truth and show his faith by corresponding works? By and by the spirit of error suggested that he should be a loser by following and a gainer by betraying his Master. Was not this an infamous lie? When he had believed it, did not his heart become a nest for the old serpent, a throne for the father of lies? And did not our Lord speak the words of soberness and truth when he said to his disciples, "One of you hath a devil?"

Why did Peter deny his dear Lord? Undoubtedly because in that fatal hour he believed that the Jews were more able and ready to fall upon and destroy him than Christ was to save and defend him. And was not this believing an untruth? When he had completed his crime, why did he go out to weep, and not to hang himself, like Judas? Was it not because he admitted the truth again; believing that where sin had abounded grace might yet superabound; and that great as his crimes were, God's mercy and Christ's love were yet greater? Saving truths these which Judas could no longer believe, having "done [final] despite to the Spirit of truth, [who] leads, [not drags,] into the truth."

Why did David attack Goliath with undaunted courage? Was it not because he heartily believed that the Lord would not be insulted by that blaspheming monster, and would stand by any one that attacked him in the name of the God of Israel? A great truth this, through which he waxed valiant in fight, killed his gigantic adversary, and turned to flight the armies of the aliens. Why did he afterward stain his righteous soul with atrocious crimes? Was it not because he practically, and therefore most cordially, believed a horrid untruth; namely, that the company of his neighbour's ewe lamb was preferable to the delights afforded by the Lamb of God? Why did he afterward repent? Was it not because he received the truth again; heartily believing that he had committed dreadful sins, and that he must repent or perish?

Again: why are men "lovers of the world more than lovers of God?" Is it not because they really believe that the world can make them happier than God? If I say, "I believe that God is preferable to the world," and do not seek my chief happiness in him, do not I deceive myself and tell a gross untruth? And while St. James charges me to show my faith by my works, does not St. John show himself a rational divine when he protests that "the truth is not in me?" Once more: why did Saul of Tarsus "breathe threatenings and slaughter" against Christ's members? Was it not because he believed the grand lie of his day, that is, that Christ was an impostor? And why did he afterward breathe nothing but fervent love to Christians and unextinguishable zeal for Christ's glory? Was it not because his inmost soul was penetrated with the force of this almighty truth, "Christ is the true Messiah; he loved me and gave himself for me?"

From these and a thousand such observations upon the *conversion* of sinners and the *perversion* of saints, I draw the following consequences, which, I trust, will recommend themselves to the reason of every calm inquirer after truth.

1. To convert or pervert a man, you need only change his principle of action, his predominant practical belief of a damnable lie or of a saving truth. For if the spring be new, so undoubtedly will be the streams. If you have a new tree, you will infallibly have new fruit. If the rudder be truly turned, the ship will certainly take a new course.

2. Truth is the heavenly seed that produces living faith; and living faith is the heavenly root that produces good works. Truth and faith, therefore, are at the bottom of every good work. To suppose them absent from a good work is to suppose that a good work can be void of sincerity and truth, and of course void of goodness. And is not this supposing a glaring absurdity? On the other hand, a lie is the hellish seed that produces unbelief: and unbelief is the hellish root that produces bad works. A lie and unbelief are then at the bottom of every bad work. To suppose them absent from a bad work, is to suppose that a bad work can be wrought in faith and in truth, which is as impossible as to do a good work in malice and wickedness.

As the rise and fall of a good weather glass infallibly show the real, though as yet invisible alterations of the atmosphere; so our rising from sin and our falling into sin surely evidence the secret, and perhaps unnoticed changes that happen in our faith, for the better or for the worse. For the whole of our words and actions, taken into connection with our views and tempers, are the certain result of our present faith or unbelief, and consequently the best marks that we please or displease God, according to the last and capital proposition of the Minutes.

4. When there is "truth in the inward parts," there is faith also, it being as impossible to admit religious truths any other way but by faith, as it is to partake of the light any other way but by sight. Truth and faith tincture with goodness the most extraordinary actions. Thus Samuel cuts Agag in pieces before the Lord; St. Paul strikes Elymas with blindness; St. Peter strikes Ananias with sudden death; Phinehas runs Zimri and Cosbi through the body; Abraham offers Isaac in truth and faith; and "God counts these actions to them for righteousness to all generations for evermore." On the other hand, the actions that do not spring from truth and faith, be they ever so good in the eyes of men, are an abomination in the sight of God, who requires "truth in the inward parts." Thus King Saul offers a sacrifice; Judas pleads for the poor; the Pharisees make long prayers; Pilate washes his hands from the blood of Christ; and God reckons these works to them for sin to all generations for evermore.

5. Some actions, such as the commission of adultery and of murder, can never be tinctured by truth and faith, because they have for their principle triumphant impurity, gross injustice, and flagrant unbelief; and whenever such sins prevail in the soul, the contrary virtues, holiness, truth, and faith are gone; just as when racking pains and a putrid fever prevail in the body, ease and health are there no more. To suppose, therefore, that living faith lurked in David's heart during his grievous apostasy, is as absurd as to suppose that health lurks in a body infected by the plague,

and life in a corpse. "Ay, but David's faith, like that of Peter, was raised up again." True: and so was the body of Lazarus, that of our Lord, and that of the ruler's daughter: but is this a proof that Lazarus, Christ, and the damsel, did not undergo a real death? A concession, however, I cheerfully make to my objector; wishing that it may be a mean of reconciling him as much to the faith of St. James, as I am reconciled to that of St. Paul. If he grant me that Peter's and David's faith went out as really as a candle which is put under an extinguisher; I will grant him, that through the long suffering of God, who never seals the absolute reprobation of sinners so long as their day of visitation lasts, the extinct faith of those fallen saints was as an extinguished light, that continues to smoke, and can the sooner be lighted again. Their falls, great as they were, did not amount to complete obduracy and the sin against the Holy Ghost. — "He will not quench the smoking flax," was a promise in which they were still interested with all those who have not yet done final "despite to the Spirit of grace." Free grace, therefore, visited them again; and when she put her candle to their hearts, they again knew their day; they welcomed the light; the smoking flax once more caught the pure flame of truth; and living faith, with her luminous train, was rekindled in their breasts. Thus, by improving what remained of the accepted time, they escaped the fate of Judas, who so hardened himself, that his candle was put out in final darkness; they avoided the doom of the foolish virgins, who so procrastinated repentance, that their extinguished lamps were never lighted again. To return: —

6. As our pulses all over the body exactly answer to the beating of our heart; so our inward works, that is, our thoughts, desires, schemes, and tempers exactly answer to our faith or principle of action. I say "our inward works," because hypocrites can mimic all external works. How improperly then is St. Paul quoted against the works of faith! Does he not assure us himself that saving "faith worketh by love?" And is it not as absurd to oppose the works of faith to faith, as to oppose the pulses to the beating of the heart; no two things in the world being more strongly connected? However, as the heart always beats before the arteries, and as a cannon is always fired before the explosion can be heard, the ball felt, or the flame perceived; so faith always moves before it can set fear, hope, desire, or love in motion. And if godly fear, hope, desire, and love, which are our internal good works, always spring from faith; our external good works, such as publicly worshipping God, doing good to our neighbour, &c, from a right principle and in a right manner, always flow from faith also. For our external works are nothing but the effects of the works which we have already wrought in our hearts; just as the rapid motion of a ball OUT of the cannon is nothing but the effect of the motion that was communicated to it, while it was yet IN the cannon.

7. If every internal good work (suppose a sincere operative desire to love my enemy for God's sake) necessarily springs from a good principle, that is, from true faith; it follows, that, so long as I consistently continue in the same disposition, my principle of action is good, and I am (so far) a good man, according to the standard of one or another of the Gospel dispensations. On the other hand, if any one inward bad work (suppose a malicious desire to hurt my neighbour) springs from a bad principle, it follows also that, so long as I continue in that bad disposition, whatever degree of sanctity I may pretend to, my principle of action is bad, I am a wicked man of the Pharisaic or of the Antinomian order. To conclude: —

8. As by suppressing the beating of the heart you may stop all the pulses; so by suppressing the act of faith you may put a stop to all good works. On the other hand, as by cutting the main arteries you may put an end to the motion of the heart; so by suppressing the good motions caused by faith you may put an end to the life of faith, and destroy the new creature in Christ Jesus.

SECTION VIII.

The reasonableness of the doctrine of salvation by faith is farther evinced by a variety of arguments. How much we are indebted to the Solifidians for having firmly stood up in defence of faith. How dearly they have made us pay for that service, when they have so enforced our eleventh article, which guards salvation by faith, as to make void the twelfth, which guards morality: and why the overpowering splendour of truth is qualified by some shades.

SHOULD some readers still think that it is unreasonable to dwell first upon faith, and to insist more upon it than upon the other works and graces which adorn the life and character of a Christian; to remove their scruples, and to vindicate more fully the fundamental doctrine of salvation by faith, I present them with the following remarks: —

1. If true faith is the root that produces hope, charity, and sincere obedience, as the preceding section evinces, is it not reasonable principally to urge the necessity of believing aright? The end of all preaching is undoubtedly to plant the tree of evangelical obedience; and how can that tree be planted but by its root? Was a gardener ever charged with unreasonableness, for not setting a tree by the branches?

2. If faith working by love is the heart of true religion, should we not bestow our chief attention and care upon it? Suppose you were a physician, and attended a patient, who had an imposthume in his stomach and another on his hand; would you do honour to your skill, if overlooking the internal mischief you confined your attention to the external ulcer?

3. The most excellent gift of God to man, next to the invaluable gifts of his Son and Spirit, is that of saving truth. Nay, the Son of God, in his prophetic character, came only to display the truth. He was manifested in the flesh to be its herald among men. St. Paul tells us that "Christ witnessed a good confession before Pilate;" and St. John informs us that part of this confession ran thus: "To this end was I born, and for this cause came I into the world, that I should bear witness unto the truth." Now if "bearing witness to the truth" was a great "cause," and a peculiar "end" of our Lord's coming into the world; if the Spirit itself is called the "Spirit of truth," because his grand office is to reveal and seal the truth; if truth is no better than error to us, till we receive it by faith; and if the Scripture declares four times that "the just shall live by his faith," a declaration this which St. Paul confirms by his own experience, when he says, "I live by faith;" is it not evident that when we practically reject the doctrine of faith, we reject life, together with all the blessings which are "brought to light by the Gospel;" a Gospel disbelieved being undoubtedly a Gospel rejected?

4. Our feelings and conduct greatly depend upon our apprehensions of things. A false report that your son is dead reaches your ears; you believe it, and pangs of grief distract your breast. Soon after a true account of his being drowned is brought to you; you disbelieve it, and you remain unaffected. A diamond by moonlight glitters at your feet; you think it is only a glow worm, and this mistake prevents your stooping to pick it up. A glow worm shines at some distance; you fancy that it is a diamond, and you run to it with a degree of hope and joy proportionable to the degree of your vain confidence. The God of truth is an infinite, spiritual diamond, if I may use the expression; and yet so faint are our ideas of his excellence that we overlook him, and madly run after deceitful objects, the brightest of which are but glow worms to the "Father of lights." Nothing, therefore, but a firm "belief of the truth," stamping our souls with just apprehensions of things, and fixing in us a strong persuasion of their intrinsic worth or vanity, can rectify our judgment, and make us regulate our conduct according to the dictates of God's word, which are invariably one with the truth, and with the nature of things.

5. When St. Paul exhorts his converts to the pursuit of things "honest, just, pure, lovely," &c, he mentions first, with great propriety, "whatsoever things are true." For as soon as obedient faith allows truth to sit upon the throne, there is an end of mental anarchy: all things resume their proper ranks and places. Creatures, in a great degree, disappear before their Creator; earth before heaven; and time before eternity. Thus Satan's charm is broken, God begins to be to us what he is in himself, "all in all;" and when we see him such, if our faith be lively and practical, we treat him as such: we answer the end of our creation' truth prevails: "Satan falls as lightning from heaven:" man is man, and God is God.

6. If truth, next to God, is the most powerful thing in the world; if we can have no communion with God but by the medium of truth; if falsehood is the rankest poison in hell; and if we take a draught of this poison as often as we take in a capital religious error; can you reasonably explode the doctrine of salvation by faith, since the office of living faith is to expel the poison of destructive error, and to receive the reviving, healing, strengthening cordial of Gospel truth?

7. If an unfeigned faith in the truths which God reveals under one or another of his evangelical dispensations is the instrumental cause of all our good works, while a cordial consent to one or more of Satan's lies is the parent of all our bad actions; if these two springs move every wheel of righteousness and of iniquity in the world; is it not highly consistent with reason to mind them first? Would you not pity your watch maker if he so regarded the hand and dial plate of your watch as to forget the wheel work and spring? And can you approve the method of Honestus, who insists upon good works, without ever touching upon the principles of sincere obedience, and upon faith, which is the spring that sets all in motion?

8. Again: if Abraham, by "not staggering at the promise of God through unbelief, and by being strong in faith, gave glory to God," and "set to his seal that God is true;" if you cannot honour a superior more than by receiving his every word with respectful confidence, and moving at his every beck with obedient alacrity; and if faith thus honours God, why should you refuse it the first place among the graces which support and adorn the Church militant? Especially since the Lord declares that "the pure in heart shall see God," and that our "hearts are purified by faith;" and

since the Scriptures testify that "without holiness no man shall see the Lord," and that we "are sanctified through faith that is in him."

9. All fulness dwells in God; creatures, abstracted from the Divine plenitude, are mere emptiness. Rational creatures, in their most perfect state, are only moral vessels, filled with the grace of God, and reflecting the light of Divine truth. Now if we can be saved any other way than "by grace through [obedient] faith," that is, by freely receiving the grace and light of God, through the practical belief of the truth proposed to us; if we are in any degree saved by our proper merit through faithless works; we may indulge Pharisaic boasting. But God does not so give his glory to human worms; therefore such a boasting is excluded by the law of faith; and the apostle wisely observes that salvation "is of faith, that it may be by grace;" the justifying faith of sinners always implying a cordial acknowledgment of their sin and misery, and a hearty recourse to "the tender mercy of our God, whereby the day spring from on high hath visited us," more or less clearly, according to the dispensation we are under.*

10. The manner in which faith and its works "exclude boasting," may be illustrated by a comparison. A beggar lies dying at your door, you offer him a cordial, he takes it, revives, and works. A deserter is going to be shot, you bring him a pardon

---

* To establish the doctrine of the Gospel dispensations; to show that saving truth, in its various manifestations, is the object of saving faith; I need only prove, that a man, in order to his salvation, is bound to believe at one time what he was not bound to believe at another. Take one instance out of many. If St. Peter had died just after he had been pronounced, "blessed," for acknowledging that our Lord was "the Son of God," he could not have been cursed with a "Depart from me," &c. He would have been saved; and in that case he would have obtained salvation without believing one tittle about our Lord's resurrection, and might I not also say about his crucifixion? And, nevertheless, St. Paul, a few years after, justly represented that article as essential to the salvation of those to whom it is revealed! "IF thou shalt BELIEVE with thy heart that God HATH RAISED the Lord Jesus from the dead, thou shalt be saved," Romans 10:9. Few people, I think, can read the Acts of the Apostles without seeing, that the numerous conversions wrought by St. Peter's preaching were wrought by the force of this truth, "God has raised up that Jesus whom you have crucified." A victorious truth this, which would have been a gross untruth three months before the day of pentecost. Nay, what is at one time an article of saving faith, may at another time become an article of the most confirmed unbelief. Thus the expectation of the Messiah, which was a capital article of the faith of the ancient Israelites, is now the buttress of the Babel of modern Jews. The property of faith is then to make our hearts bow to the truth as it is manifested to us; it being evident that God never blamed the children of men for not believing what was never revealed to them.

MEMORANDUM. — In page 142 (Section 3 of current work), I have said that the genuine seed of the word is always good, always full of Divine energy." I desire the candid reader to read the following lines, as more particularly expressive of my meaning: —

The word is TRUTH: and truth, like the sun, is always efficacious where its light penetrates. But I would by no means insinuate that the truth may not, like the sun, shine more brightly and powerfully at one time than at another; the word of truth, however, always performs, though more or less sensibly, that whereunto God sends it; being always a "savour of life unto life to them that believe," or of "death unto death" to wilful unbelievers, according to the grand decree of conditional election and reprobation: "He that believeth, &c, shall be saved; and he that believeth not shall be damned."

from the king, if he will receive it with grateful humility; he does so, join his regiment, and fights with such courage that he is promoted. Now, in these cases, it is evident that Pharisaic* boasting is excluded. If the beggar live ever so long, and work ever so hard, — if the deserter fight ever so manfully, and be raised ever so high; yet they can never say that their doings have procured them the life which they enjoy; for, before they did such works, that life was graciously given, or restored to them, upon the easy terms of confidently taking a remedy, and humbly accepting a pardon offered: The application is easy. By our fallen nature we are "conceived in sin, and children of wrath:" God freely gives us the light of life in Jesus Christ; faith, without necessity, humbly receives it, and works by it; the believer therefore, can never be so unreasonable and ungrateful as to suppose that his working merited him "the light of life," by which he began to work righteousness. So long as he deserves the name of a believer, he knows, he feels, that his faith is, in the first place, a mere receiver. "What hast thou that thou hast not received?" roars like thunder in the ears of a lively faith, and like lightning strikes dead the Pharisaic boast.

11. I say that "faith is, in the first place, a mere receiver." This deserves attention. If we consider faith as a conduit pipe, which at one end receives the truth and power of God, and at the other end refunds those living streams to water the garden of the Lord; we may with propriety compare that mother grace to the pipe of a watering pot, which at the internal, unseen opening, receives the water that is in the pot; and at the external, visible perforations, returns it and forms artificial showers over the drooping plants. According to the doctrine of grace, maintained by the Solifidians, faith does nothing but receive the grace of God through Christ; and according to the doctrine of works, maintained by the moralists, faith is a mere bestower; but, according to the Gospel of Christ, which embraces and connects the two extremes of truth, faith is first an humble, passive receiver, and then a cheerful, active bestower: it receives grace and truth, and returns love and good works. In that respect, it resembles the heart which continually receives the blood from the veins, and returns it into the arteries. If the heart cease either to receive or to return the blood, (no matter which,) its motion and our animal life are soon at an end; and if faith cease either to receive grace, or to return good works, its motion and its life soon terminate in spiritual death, according to the doctrine of St. James. If the Solifidians and moralists candidly looked at faith in this rational and Scriptural light, they would soon embrace the whole Gospel, and one another. By considering faith as a receiver, according to the first Gospel axiom, Honestus would avoid the Pharisaic extreme; and by viewing it as a bestower, according to the second Gospel axiom, Zelotes would avoid the Antinomian delusion; and both would jointly recommend the humble, cheerful, consistent passiveness and activity of Bible believers.

12. "If we receive the witness of men," says St. John, "the witness of God is greater: for [under the Christian dispensation] this is the witness of God which he hath testified of his Son: he that believeth on the Son of God hath the testimony in himself; but he that believeth not God hath made him a liar, because he believed not

---

* There is an evangelical boasting which St. Paul recommends to others, and indulges himself. See note, p. 111.

the record that God gave of his Son." Upon these awful words I raise the following argument: —

If a state of absolute doubt is quite unnatural: if it is almost impossible to keep the balance of our judgment unturned for one hour, with respect to all saving truths and destructive lies: if the stream of life, which hurries us along, calls us every moment to action: if we continually do good or bad works: if good works certainly spring from saving faith, and bad works from destructive unbelief: if skeptics are only so in imagination, theory, and profession: if our daily conduct demonstrates whether our heart inclines most to the lies of Satan, or to the truths of God: and if the moment we practically reject God's truths, we embrace the lies of the god of this world, and by that mean take him for our god; — if, I say, this is the case, what reasonable man can be surprised to hear the mild Jesus say, "He that believeth not shall be damned?" Can there be a greater sin — a sin more productive of all iniquity, and more horrid, than to make the lying devil a god, and the true God a liar? Nevertheless, dreadful to say! this double crime is actually committed by all that live in wilful, practical unbelief; and the commission of it is indirectly recommended by all those who decry the doctrine of salvation by faith.

Lastly. If our first parents fell by believing the gross lies told them by the serpent, is God unreasonable to raise us, by making us believe the great truths peculiar to our dispensation, that the Divine leaven of sincerity and truth may counterwork and at last expel the satanic leaven of malice and wickedness? Who ever thought it absurd in a physician to proportion the remedy to the disease, the antidote to the poison? And why should even the incarnation of the Son of God appear a mean too wonderful for an end so important? Why should it be thought incredible that the Son of God, who, as our Creator, is far more nearly related to us than our natural parents, should have graciously stooped as low as the human nature to redeem us; when Satan wantonly stooped as low as the beastly nature to tempt us? On the contrary, is it not absurd to suppose that hellish, wanton malice has done more to destroy, than heavenly, creating love to save the children of men? For my part, the more I compare the genuine Gospel with the nature of things, the more I admire their harmony; wondering equally at the prejudices of those hasty professors who pour perpetual contempt upon reason, to keep their irrational opinions in countenance; and at the unreasonableness of those pretended votaries of reason, who suppose that the doctrine of salvation by faith is incompatible with good sense.

OBJECTION. "But," says an objector, "if unfeigned faith, or a cordial belief of the truth, instrumentally turns us 'from the power of Satan to God;' why have you published tracts against the Solifidians whose favourite doctrine is, 'Believe; he that believeth hath everlasting life?'"

ANSWER. By the preceding pages it is evident that we do not differ from the Solifidians when they preach salvation by faith in a rational and a Scriptural manner. So long at they do this, we wish them good luck in the name of the Lord. Nay, I publicly return them my sincere thanks for the bold stand they have made for faith, when the floods of Pharisaic ungodliness lifted up their voice against that mother grace, and threatened to destroy her with all her offspring. But, alas! how dear have they made us pay for that service, when they have asserted or insinuated that true faith is inamissible, that it can live in a heart totally depraved, that a man's faith can be good when his actions are bad, detestable, diabolical; in a word, that true Christians may go any length in sin, may plunge into adultery, murder, or incest, and even proceed to the open worship of devils, like Solomon, without losing their title to a throne of glory, and their justifying, sanctifying, saving faith!

This they have done in flat opposition to our Lord's doctrine: "A good tree bringeth not forth corrupt fruit; neither does a corrupt tree bring forth good fruit; for every tree is known by its own fruit," Luke 6:43. And this some of them seem determined to do, to the stumbling of the judicious, the deceiving of the simple, and the hardening of infidels; notwithstanding our twelfth article, which strongly guards the doctrine of faith against their Solifidian error. "Good works" says our Church in that truly anti- Calvinistic article, "do [at this present time] spring out necessarily of a true and lively faith, [and consequently bad works, of a false and dead faith;] insomuch that by them a lively [and by bad works a dead] faith may be as evidently known, as a tree is discerned by the fruit."

But, in the meantime, how do they evade the force of that article? Why, thus: David bears this year the fruit of adultery, hypocrisy, treachery, and murder, before all his kingdom: last year he bore the fruit of chastity, sincerity, truth, and brotherly love. However, according to the Crispian doctrines of grace, David must be a tree of righteousness now, as much as when he bore the fruits of righteousness. If this be not the case, Mr. Fulsome's Gospel will be false: now this must not be. That Gospel must stand. "But if it stand, our twelfth article falls to the ground." O! we can prop it by saying, that though a child of God, a tree of righteousness, may now produce adultery, &c, &c, &c, yet he will certainly produce good fruit again by and by. To this salvo I answer, that the article has only two grand designs; the one inseparably to connect a lively faith and good works, and the other to indicate the manner in which I may know whether I have a lively or a dead faith. Now, if I may have a lively faith while I commit adultery, &c, &c, &c, it evidently follows, (1.) That the necessary connection between a lively faith and good works is totally lost. (2.) That adultery and murder may denote a lively faith as well as purity and love. And, (3.) That our twelfth article has not even the worth of a nose of wax, and may be burned with St. James' Epistle, as an article "of straw." And yet these gentlemen are the persons that represent themselves as the only fair subscribers to our articles, and charge us with prevarication for taking the seventeenth article in connection with the sixth, the twelfth, the sixteenth, and the thirty-first, as well as with the latter part of that article itself, which demands that the election it speaks of be understood of conditional election!

To return. Should the reader object, that "if God had suspended our salvation upon our practical belief of the truth, he would have put so conspicuous a badge upon the saving truth peculiar to each dispensation that nobody could have mistaken it for error, enthusiasm, priestcraft, or nonsense:" I answer —

1. God, having decreed to prove the loyalty and moral sagacity of his rational creatures, could not but place them in circumstances in which they might have an opportunity of exerting themselves. If hares were chained at the doors of dog kennels, what sagacity could hounds manifest above mastiffs? And if the deepest truths always lay within the reach of the most besotted souls, what advantage would candid, diligent inquirers have over those who wrap their minds in the veil of prejudice, and stupidly compose themselves to sleep in the arms of ignorance and sloth?

2. God will reward us according to our works of faith; but if the truth were attended with an irresistible energy, if it shone always upon our minds as transcendently bright as the dazzling sun does sometimes upon our faces, would God display his wisdom in rewarding us for confessing it? Did he, did any man in his senses, ever offer to reward us for believing that a bright luminary rules the day, when its meridian glory overpowers our sight?

3. Pearls are found in the bottom of the sea. Gold and diamonds lie generally deep in the earth. We sink pits to a prodigious depth only to come at the black mineral which we burn. Thousands of men go as far as the East and West Indies to fill our canisters with tea and sugar. Our meanest tradesmen sip the dews of both hemispheres at a breakfast. And yet, it may be, with a dish of tea in our hand, and a gold ring on our finger, we gravely complain that saving truth lies a great way off, and that God is unjust in placing it in obscure mines, which cannot be worked without some trouble and industry.

4. But although nobody can be established in the truth without "labouring for the meat that endureth for everlasting life;" yet God's terms of salvation are not so hard as some prejudiced people conceive. Nor do I scruple to assert, that if we could read the hearts of all men, we would see, that, for a time, unbelievers take as much pains to exclude the light of truth as believers do to welcome it, and that wicked men work as intensely, though not as intentionally, to make their reprobation and damnation certain, as good men do "to make their calling and election sure:" for "the wicked is snared in the work of his own hands. The reward of his hands shall be given him. The wages of [his] sin is death; [and he frequently toils like a horse for his wages,] drawing iniquity with cords of vanity, [and] sin as with a cart rope," to hale himself and others into the burning lake.

From the preceding answers I conclude, that God, who makes the golden light of the sun and the silver light of the moon succeed each other, and who wisely tempers the blaze of a summer's day by the mildness of the starry night, with equal wisdom qualifies the blaze of the day of truth by the mild obscurity of a night of probation; not only that the flaming truth may be more delightful at its return, but also that there may be room left for a gentle trial of our faith, and for the reasonable rewardableness of our works of faith.

SECTION IX.

Inferences.

1. IF faith be so closely connected with truth, present salvation with faith, and eternal salvation with the works of faith, how injudicious are those gentlemen, who assert that principles are nothing, and that it little matters what doctrines we hold, provided our actions be good! Alas! if our leading principles be wrong, how can our actions be right? If we be men of no principles, or of bad principles, and do seemingly good actions, do we not do them from bad, Pharisaical motives? Even when such actions appear good to man, who judges according to appearance, are they not evil before the Searcher of hearts? Are they not detestable before the Examinator

of principles? Undoubtedly; hypocrisy being the most odious Sort of iniquity in the sight of Him who "requires truth in the inward parts."

2. If the effects of truth be so wonderful, and if the pure word of God be essentially one with truth, how fatal is the mistake of the laymen who slight the Gospel word! who listen to a sermon with less attention than they do to a play! and who read the Scriptures with less eagerness than they do the newspapers! And how culpable are those clergymen who preach the first sermon they set their hand upon, without examining whether it contain truth or error, or a mixture of both; at least, without considering whether it be adapted to the capacity and circumstances of their hearers!

3. Can we decry prejudice too much, if it unfit our souls for receiving the truth, as trash unfits our stomachs for receiving proper food? Should not a narrow, bigoted spirit, that collects itself like a hedge-hog in its own fancied orthodoxy, and bristles up assertions and invectives instead of arguments, be firmly opposed by every generous inquirer after truth? Can we deplore too much the case of those sanguine persons, who judge of the strength of their faith by the force of their prepossession; and who fancy that a hundred plain scriptures, and as many cogent arguments, have no weight, if they do not countenance their favourite sentiments and misunderstood feelings? And can we too warmly recommend a candid, sober, fearless turn of mind, which lays us open to information, and disposes us publicly to espouse the cause of truth, even when destruction threatens her, and her despised adherents?

4. "Charity rejoiceth in the truth;" and "though I speak with the tongues of angels," says St. Paul, "if I have not charity," that is, if I do not "rejoice in the truth," whether it makes for or against my prejudices, "I am become as sounding brass." Upon this footing what can we say of those warm moralists who, in their zeal for works, are ready to burn against the doctrine of faith? What of those rash Solifidians who, in their zeal for faith, are ready to lay down their lives against the doctrine of works? Alas! like St. Paul, in the days of his ignorance, they court and yet persecute the truth; they embrace and yet stab the Divine stranger. These false martyrs may give their body to be burned for one truth against another; but God will say to them, "Who required this at your hands?" and they themselves will say, "It profiteth us nothing."

5. If there be various forms in the school of truth, how unreasonable is it to say that none have any acquaintance with her, but such as are in one of the highest forms! And if the temple of truth has various divisions to which we advance, as we go on "from faith to faith," how cruel is it to consign over to damnation the sincere souls who have yet got no farther than the porch!

6. If there are as many sorts of religious truths as there are of nourishing food, how irrational is it to despise those truths which the apostle compares to milk, merely because they are not the truths which he calls "strong meat!" On the other hand, if we cannot yet receive those strong truths, how rash are we, if we represent them as chaff or poison! And what mischief is done in the Church of Christ by those who deal in palpable absurdities, and in errors demonstrated to be of a stupifying or intoxicating nature; especially if they retail such errors to an injudicious, credulous populace, under the name of "rich honey" and" Gospel marrow!"

7. If Divine truth is one through its various appearances, and if "the light of the righteous [who holds on his way] shines more and more unto the perfect day;"

what shall we say of those prejudiced men, who oppose the truth with all their might, merely because it does not come up to their false standard, or because it appears in a dress to which they are not accustomed? Did a Persian ever refuse to admire the *rising* sun, because it was not the *meridian* sun, or laugh at it as being an insignificant meteor, because it rose under a cloud? If Christ is not ashamed to call himself "the light" and "the truth," should we be ashamed to confess him in his lowest appearances? If Christ, exalted at the right hand of God, is one with Christ transfigured on the mount, — bleeding on Calvary, — lying in the manger, — confined, a helpless embryo, in the virgin's womb; may not the triumphant truth that shines like the sun in the heart of a "father in Christ," have some affinity with the spark that glows in the heart of an infant in grace under the dispensation of Noah? Ought we to give up the greatest part of our neighbours as men that "never had grace," when the Scripture expressly declares, that "the saving grace of God has appeared unto all men," and that Christ is "the light of the world that enlightens every man?" Let mystical Herods seek the young child's life; but thou, man of God, leap for joy, like the unborn Baptist, before the least and feeblest appearance of thy Lord. Instead of calling it "common grace," that thou mayest cut it off the next moment as "no grace," cherish it as saving grace in thy own breast, and in the hearts of all that are around thee.

8. If the most powerful displays of truth improve its feeblest appearances, without ever contradicting them, how mistaken are the men who impose upon us the immoral doctrines of the Antinomians, and the unevangelical doctrines of the Pharisees! When we have once admitted that "there is a holy God, who makes a difference between the just and the unjust," can we, without renouncing that truth, become Antinomians, and think that a man, who actually defiles his neighbour's wife, can be "a man after God's own heart?" And when we have been taught our second gracious lesson, namely, that "we are miserable sinners," can we, without renouncing this principle, suppose that we can be saved any other way than by the covenant of grace and mercy? Away, then, for ever away with Antinomian and Pharisaic delusions, which are built upon the ruins of these two capital truths, "God is holy," and "man is sinful!"

SECTION X.

An address to baptized heathens.

HERE I would take leave of my readers; but they have consciences as well as reason, and therefore I beg leave to address the former of those powers, as bluntly as I have done the latter; diversifying my expostulations according to the different cases of the persons, into whose hands Providence may direct these sheets.

1. If you do not make the bulk of my readers, I fear you make the bulk of the nation, O ye that regard pleasure, profit, and honour, more than justice, mercy, and the fear of God; ye that, far from embracing Divine truth at the hazard of your character, spread abroad scandalous untruths, to the ruin of other people's

reputations: ye who try to persuade yourselves, that religion is nothing but a monstrous compound of superstition, enthusiasm, and priestcraft: ye who can violate the laws of temperance or honesty without one painful remorse; breaking through promises, oaths, and matrimonial or sacramental engagements, as if there were no future state, no supreme Judge, no day of retribution, no Divine law enacting that "whosoever loveth or maketh a lie shall be cast into the lake of fire; that the wicked shall be turned into hell, with all the people that forget God:" ye are the persons that I beg leave to call baptized heathens. Baptismal water was applied to your bodies, as a figure of the grace which purifies believing souls. Ye received, and continue to bear, a Christian name, that binds upon you the strongest obligations you can possibly be under, to partake of Christ's holiness, and to lead a sober, Christian life: but how opposite is your conduct to that of Christ! Alas! conscientious heathens would disown you; and shall God own you? Shall the Searcher of hearts forgive your immorality, in consideration of your hypocrisy? Will you live and die with such a lie in your right hand and upon your forehead? God forbid! If you have not sold yourselves to the father of deceits for ever, pay yet some attention to natural, moral, and evangelical truths. They recommend themselves to your senses, your reason, and your conscience.

1. Regard natural truths. Earthly joys vanish like dreams. Life flies like an arrow. Your friends or neighbours are daily seized by sickness, and dragged into eternity. Death comes to terminate, your delusions, and set his black seal upon your false lips, your wanton eyes, your rapacious hands, your luxurious palates, your sinful, treacherous breasts. Ere long the king of terrors will screw you down in his hard couch, a coffin: he will convey you away in his black carriage, a hearse: he will confine you to his loathsome dungeon, a grave; and there he will keep you in chains of darkness and corruption, till the trump of God summon you to judgment.

2. And say not that the doctrine of a day of judgment is a fable. If you do, I appeal to moral truths. Is there not an essential difference between truth and falsehood, between mercy and cruelty, between honesty and villany? Have you, with all the pains you have taken about it, been able to erase from your breasts the law of truth and mercy, which the righteous God has deeply engraven there? Is there not something within you, that, bad as you are, forbids you to wish your father dead, that you may have his estate; and your wife poisoned, that you may marry the woman you love? If you say that these are only prejudices of education; I ask, How come these prejudices to be universal? Why are they the same, even where the methods of education are most contrary? Why do they reign in the very countries where there are neither magistrates nor priests; and where of course politics and priestcraft never bore the sway? If your consciences would condemn you for the above-mentioned crimes; how much more will God do it, who is the Author and Judge of your consciences? Does not your good sense tell you, that so sure as the wonderful machine of this world did not make, and does not preserve itself, there is a God who made and preserves it? And that this God is possessed of ten thousand times more truth, equity, impartiality, justice, and power, than all the righteous rulers in the world were ever endued with? And, to say nothing of the gracious checks and sad forebodings of your guilty consciences, does not your reason discover, that as certainly as this great God is possessed of infinite wisdom, power, and justice; and has

given us a moral law, he will call us to an account for our breaches of it; and that, as he does not in general do it in this world, he will infallibly do it in a future state?

3. If reason and conscience thus lead you to religion; regard religious truths. They are supported by so great a variety of well attested facts, by such clouds of righteous witnesses, by so many astonishing miracles and accomplished prophecies' they so perfectly agree with the glory of our Creator, the interests of mankind, the laws of our nature, and the native desire we have for immortality: they so exactly coincide with our present, as well as future happiness, that you cannot expose your unreasonableness more, and do yourselves greater injury, than by rejecting them.

What reasonable objection can you make to these Scriptural directions? "Cease to do evil. Learn to do good. Speak the truth in love. Return to the Lord. Call upon his name." Say, "Grant to us in this world the knowledge of thy truth, and in the world to come life everlasting." Confess yourselves sinners, great sinners: spread this melancholy truth before the throne of Divine mercy; — spread it with tears of undissembled repentance: "Except you repent, you shall all perish:" but if you "sow in tears, you shall reap in joy."

And suppose not that I want to drive you to despair. On the contrary, I declare that, dangerous as your case is, it is not absolutely desperate. The Gospel offers you a remedy. You have dealt with lying shadows, but you may yet embrace the eternal substance. You have wounded the truth; but Christ, from whom you have the name of Christian, — Christ, who says, "I am the truth," has been wounded for you. You have crucified revealed truth, and the Prince of life has been crucified in your place. I point you to his cross, and declare, in the name of unprejudiced reason, that few histories are supported by such a variety of indisputable evidences as the wonders that redeeming love wrought on Calvary for you.

Let not the scandalous falls of apostates, and the bad lives of hypocritical Christians, frighten you from the Gospel. Immoral and unloving men, high as their pretensions to faith may be, are no more Christians than you. Suffer not the disputes of professors to keep you in infidelity; for they prove the truth, and not the falsehood of Christianity; being expressly foretold, Acts 20:30; 1 Corinthians 11:19; Jude 1:4; 1 Timothy 4:1. Nor stupidly wonder that the serpent should most spitefully bruise the heel of the truth that most powerfully bruises his head. Above all, be candid; be inquisitive; apply to the "Father of lights" for direction; and his invisible hand will conduct you over every rock of offence, and lead you to the sure foundation, "the Rock of ages, the truth as it is in Jesus."

How near is that truth to you! It always embraces mercy, and mercy now embraces you. O! the length and breadth, the depth and height of redeeming mercy! It spares you to believe, to repent, to live. The arms of Divine patience still encircle your guilty souls, and bear up your mortal bodies above the terrors of the grave. Crying as your sins are, the cries of your Saviour's blood are yet heard above them. Provoking as your unbelief is, it has not yet provoked God to set upon you the seal of absolute reprobation. Unspotted holiness, glorious majesty, flaming power, thundering justice, weeping mercy, bleeding love; — all the Divine attributes join yet in a concert of grace and truth. You are the objects of it; and the burthen of their terrifying, melting accents is, "Turn ye, turn ye: why will ye die, O house of Israel?" Why should "iniquity be your ruin? Turn! for I have redeemed you. Turn! and the second death shall have no power over you." Turn! and you "shall have a crown of life."

Thus, my dear fellow sinners, and far more earnestly than I can describe, mercy and truth exert themselves in your behalf; waiting only for your consent, to diffuse their Divine perfumes through your convened souls. This is "the day of God's power" — your Gospel day. This is "a day of salvation," a day of spiritual jubilee, a day of "the year of release." Know it: improve it: break your bonds, claim your liberty: change your service: scorn to be the devil's drudges: become the servants of the Most High. Regard neither the husks nor the grunts of the swine: the heavenly feast is before you: the Father of the prodigal son runs to meet, to forgive, to welcome, to embrace you; and to raise your doubting hearts, he bids me impress these gracious promises upon your yielding breasts: "When the wicked man turneth away from his wickedness, and does that which is lawful and right, [and what is more lawful and right for sinners, than to repent, believe, and obey the Gospel?] he shall save his soul alive. Let the wicked forsake his way, and the unrighteous man his thoughts; and let him return unto the Lord, for he is merciful; and to our God, for he will abundantly pardon."

SECTION XI.

An address to Christianized Jews

AND ye, Christianized Jews, will you still be offended at our sincerely preaching free grace to all our fellow Gentiles? Will you still stop your ears and cry out, "The children of Abraham, the temple of the Lord are we?" Or, in other terms, we are the little flock necessarily contradistinguished from the immense herd of absolute reprobates. Will ye still assert,* *Reprobos ideo in hanc pravitatem addictos, quia justo et inscrutabili Dei judicio suscitati sunt ad gloriam ejus sua damnatione illustrandam:* "That the reprobates are devoted to wickedness, because, through the just and unsearchable judgment of God, they were raised up to illustrate his glory by their damnation?" Will ye still add* *Quos vero damnationi addicit, his justo quidem et irreprehensibili, sed incomprehensibili ejus judicio, vitæ aditum præcludi.* "That by God's just and irreprehensible, though incomprehensible judgment, the way to life is blocked up for those whom he has devoted to damnation?" Will ye never blush to intimate,* *Quos ergo Deus præterit, reprobat. Neque alia causa, nisi quod ab hæreditate, quam filiis suis prædestinat, illos vult excludere:* "Therefore those whom God passes by, he reprobates, for no other reason but this; he will exclude them from the inheritance which he predestinates for his sons?" Will ye still call "blind" all who think that God is sincerely loving to every man, without any exception, in the day of salvation? Will ye still monopolize "the light that enlightens every man who comes into the world?" Will ye still sound the bottomless abyss of Divine mercy with your short line, and judge of the Almighty's

---

* These three quotations are taken from Calvin's Institutes, Third Book, chap. 24, sec. 14; chap. 21, sec. 7; chap. 23, sec. 1.

enlarged heart by the narrowness of your own? O learn to know the God of love, the God of truth better. "He is not willing that any should perish, but that all should come to repentance. He commands all men every where to repent:" and he bids us "account his long suffering salvation; [assuring us that] the riches of his goodness, and forbearance, and long suffering lead to repentance [even those wretches who,] after their hardness and impenitent heart, treasure up unto themselves wrath against the day of wrath, and revelation of his righteous judgment."

If you will not credit God's *word*, pay at least some regard to his *oath*. "As I LIVE," says he, "I have no pleasure in the death of the wicked, but that he turn from his way and live." Just as if he had said, "By myself I swear that I have absolutely reprobated no man. If any perish, their destruction is of themselves, and not of merciless decrees rashly imputed to my sovereignty. Free agency in man, and not free wrath in me, sinks those who make their conditional rejection and reprobation sure by their *unnecessary* unbelief and *avoidable* impenitency. Far from delighting absolutely in the reprobation of any one sinner, I solemnly protest that I would offer violence to the liberty of the most obstinate, and force them all into heaven by the exertion of my omnipotence, if my truth as a lawgiver, my justice as a judge, my veracity as the inspirer of my prophets, my wisdom as a rewarder, and my equity as a punisher, did not absolutely forbid it."

Come then, my prepossessed brethren, show yourselves "the children of Abraham:" return to the God of your father, — the God by whom "ALL the families of the earth may be blessed in the seed" of Abraham. Think not that the Lord is only jealous of his supreme dominion; nor make him *graceless* and *merciless* toward countless myriads of reprobated infants, to extol the *grim sovereignty* which your imagination has set up.

> Set not at odds Heaven's jarring attributes;
> Nor, with one excellence, another wound.

Allow God to be "all over, consummate, absolute, full orb'd, in his whole round of rays complete." *Merciful* in the day of salvation, and just in the day of judgment, to every individual of the human race. What can you possibly object to a doctrine so rational, so Scriptural, so worthy of God!

If you complain that we make the way to heaven too broad, I ask, Ought we not to represent it as broad as the Scriptures make it? Do we make it wider than St. Peter did when truth and love made him divest himself of his Jewish prejudices, and cry out with pleasing amaze, "Of a truth I perceive that God is no respecter of persons; but in every nation he that feareth him and worketh righteousness is accepted of him?" Or do we make it narrower than St. Paul, when he wrote: "If ye live after the flesh, ye shall die: no adulterer, &c, hath any inheritance in the kingdom of God?"

For your own credit do not ask, "If all men may be saved through Christ, by following the light of the Gospel dispensation, which they are under, what advantage hath the Christian? and what profit is there of baptism and Christianity?" If you make such an objection, you "show yourselves to be Christianized Jews" indeed. The apostle has just said, "If the uncircumcision," i.e. if uncircumcised heathens (like Melchisedec or Job, Cornelius or the Canaanitish woman) "keep the righteousness of the law [according to their light,] shall not their uncircumcision be counted for circumcision?" That is, shall they not be saved as well as if they were circumcised Jews? St. Paul saw that the partial hearts of the Jews would take fright at his doctrine; and would start an objection, capable of demolishing, if possible, the impartiality of God, and the freeness of the everlasting Gospel. He therefore produces this formidable objection thus: — If the Gentiles may be saved by following their light, "what advantage hath the Jew? or what profit is there of circumcision?" Romans 3:1. The answer which he gives stops the mouths of all Jews, whether they live in London, Rome, or Jerusalem. "The Jews," says he, (and much more the Christians,) "have much advantage every way, chiefly because that unto them were committed the oracles of God." The heathens have only the light of God's works, the light of God's providence, the light of reason, the light of conscience, and the light of that saving grace which "has appeared to all men, teaching them to live soberly," &c, and reproving them when they do not. But the Jews, (to say nothing of the light of tradition, which is far brighter among them than among the heathens,) over and above this fivefold light, have the light of the Old Testament; and Christians the light of the New.

Come then, my prejudiced brethren, let St. Paul's answer satisfy you. Get from under your parched gourd of reprobation. "Let not your eye be evil because God is good;" nor fret, like Jonah, because the Father of mercies extends his compassion even to all the humbled heathens in the great city of Nineveh. "As the elect of God, put on bowels of mercy," and show yourselves the genuine children of Him who "is loving to every man, and whose mercy is over all his works." So shall your mistakes no longer straiten your minds, sour your tempers, and shut your hearts against your "non-elected" neighbours.

And supposing you are of the happy few, in whose souls the impartial grace of God overrules the ordinary consequences of your partial doctrines; — supposing you are "loving to every man," and have more bowels of mercy than the God whom you extol; — supposing you are true to all men, and surpass in sincerity the God whom you recommend, who calls "all men every where to repent," and all the day long stretches out his hands in token of his compassionate love to people, on whom he absolutely fixed his immortal hatred before the foundation of the world; — supposing, I say, you have the happiness of being so much better than your principles, so much holier than the god of your OPINIONS, [Note — I say not "the God of your SALVATION;"] yet, by renouncing those opinions, you will no longer countenance Antinomianism, deceive the simple, contradict yourselves, shock moralists, and render Christianity contemptible in the eyes of all that confound it with your doctrines of forcible grace to hundreds, and of forcible wrath to thousands.

Should you countenance your Jewish notions* by saying, "We are Christians: we have nothing to do with the heathens:" I answer: (1.) You have far too much to do with them, when, by the "doctrine of grace," which you so zealously inculcate, you

---

* Should the persons whom I now address say that I falsify my subscriptions to the eighteenth article of our Church, by asserting that even the heathens, who fear God and work righteousness by the general light of Christ's grace, are accepted through Christ's unknown merits; I refer them to the Vindication of Mr. Wesley's Minutes, Vol. 1, pages 171, 172, where that objection is answered.

indirectly send them, one and all, to the pit; unless they are brought under the Christian dispensation. (2.) You renounce the Church of England, if you disregard them: for on Good Friday (the day on which Christ "tasted death for every man,") she enjoins us to pray thus for them: "O merciful God, who hatest nothing that thou hast made, nor wouldest the death of a sinner, but RATHER that he should be converted and live, have mercy upon all Jews, Turks, infidels, and heretics." (3.) You indirectly sacrifice the feelings of humanity, and the honour of God's perfections, to your unscriptural doctrine of grace, when you embrace the horrid idea of the insured damnation of the heathens, for the injudicious pleasure of saying, "Why me! Why me!" and of teaching the "poor reprobated creatures," while they sink into the bottomless pit, to say, "Why me! Why me!" A dreadful *why me* this, which is not less offensive to God's justice, impartiality, goodness, and truth, than your *why me* is odious to his wisdom, equity, veracity, and holiness. (4.) If Cain was culpable for intimating that he had nothing to do with his brother, when he had just knocked him on the head, are they praiseworthy, who enjoy with peculiar delight, and recommend with uncommon glee, "doctrines of grace," so called, which absolutely the unavoidable damnation of perhaps, as many millions of their unborn fellow creatures, as Abel had hairs upon his head? And do they mend the matter, when, to vindicate their severe opinions, they calmly wipe their mouth, and say, "We have nothing to do with the heathens?" That is, in plain English, "our orthodoxy demands, that they should inevitably perish if they do not explicitly believe in Christ crucified, of whom they never heard: nor do we care what becomes of them. Let them sink, provided our doctrines of grace stand!"

O my dear brethren, my heart is enlarged toward you, though yours is straitened toward the heathens, and those who do not engross the light of "the Sun of righteousness." Suffer the word of expostulation one moment more. Do not you detest the character of a stiff Pharisee? I know you do, in the circumcised progeny. And why should you admire it in the baptized race? I am persuaded that you abhor the damnatory bull of those self- elected men of old, who, from the height of their conceited orthodoxy, looked down upon their neighbours and said, "This people who know not [what we call] the law are cursed." And will you exemplify their uncharitable positiveness by indirectly saying, "This people [these myriads of men] who know not [what we call] *the Gospel* are cursed?" Will ye become Christianized Pharisees, to contenance abandoned Antinomians. No: the spark of candour in your breast is stirred, and almost sets fire to your prejudices. You are staggered, you are ready to yield to the force of truth! Some of you would do it even now, if you were not afraid that *our* doctrine of free grace obscures the Christian dispensation, and encourages the pernicious delusion of antichristian moralists. To convince you that your fear is groundless, permit me to expostulate with them before you.

SECTION XII.

An address to antichristian moralists.

MORAL men, who ridicule the Christian faith; you suppose that your honesty counterbalances your sins, which, by a soft name, you call *foibles*; and for which you hope that God will never punish you with hell torments. I do not desire to make the worst of things. I wish you were as good as you fancy yourselves to be. I wish you may have been as exact in all the branches of your duty as you pretend. I would rejoice if the law of respectful obedience to your superiors, of courteous love to your equals, and of brotherly kindness to your inferiors, had always been fulfilled in your words and actions, in your looks and tempers. I am ready to congratulate you, if in all cases you have done to your fellow creatures exactly as you would be done to; and never plunged once into the gulf of intemperance. But permit me to ask, if you have *fellow creatures*, have you not a *Creator*? And if you have a Creator, do not reason and conscience command you to render him warm gratitude, cheerful praise, humble adoration, and constant obedience? But have you done this one year, one month, one day, one hour, in all your lives?

Although you are so ready to make us understand that you are not as other men, adulterers, unjust, uncharitable, hypocrites, &c, are you entirely satisfied with your own goodness? Nay, if you ever "looked into the perfect law of liberty," and searched your breasts with "the candle of the Lord," can you say, before the omniscient Searcher of hearts and spirits, that there is one of the commandments which you never broke in its spiritual meaning?

If, upon second thoughts, you cannot acquit yourselves; and if God's dignity as a Creator, his veracity as a Lawgiver, his wisdom as a Governor, his justice as a Judge, his holiness as a God, forbid him to hold the guilty guiltless; or to forgive them in a manner inconsistent with any one of his infinite perfections; are you wise to despise all Advocate with him, a Divine Prophet, an atoning Mediator? Is it prudent in you to run from the city of refuge, to which you should flee with unabated swiftness? Do you act a reasonable part when you take shelter under the dispensation of the heathens, from the blessings that pursue, and from the light that surrounds you, in this Christian land? If I may allude to the mysterious divisions of Solomon's temple — will ye obstinately remain in "the court of the Gentiles," when you are graciously invited to enter into "the holy place," with true Christians? Think ye, that because righteous heathens are saved without the explicit knowledge of Christ, *ye* may be saved upon *their* plan? If ye do, may the following remarks help you to see the unreasonableness of this conclusion!

1. Not to repeat the hints already given to baptized heathens, I ask, Is not a grain of sincere love to truth the very beginning of a true conversion? Is that man a sincere lover of light who runs away from the light of the sun and moon, under pretence that he has the light of a star? Do those people sincerely love money, who, when they are presented with gold and silver, throw it back to the face of their benefactor, because they have some brass? And is that moralist a sincere lover of truth, who contemptuously rejects the silver truths of the Jewish dispensation, and

the golden truths of the Christian Gospel, under pretence that he is an adept in "the religion of nature," and has what I beg leave to call, *the brass* of heathenism?

2. You talk much of "the religion of nature;" but should you not distinguish between the religion *natural* to man in his unfallen state, and that which is *natural* to him in his fallen condition? Is not the regimen which is natural to the healthy, *unnatural* and frequently *destructive* to the sick? If upright, innocent man, needed not a spiritual Physician, does it follow that depraved, guilty man can do without one? Does not heathenism allow the fall and degeneracy of man? Have not some of the wisest Pagans seen, though darkly, their need both of a Mediator, and of a propitiatory sacrifice? Do you think it prudent, so to depend upon your self righteousness, as to trample under foot the Jewish and Christian revelations, together with the discoveries of considerate heathens? Does your wisdom show itself to advantage, when it thus makes you sink below heathenism itself?

3. No adult heathen was ever saved without the repentance of the contrite publican. "I am a guilty, helpless sinner, totally undone, if the mercy of Him that made me do not extend itself to me. Great Author of my existence, pity, pardon, and save me for thy mercy's sake." Now, if you were brought to this genuine repentance, would you despise the light of revelation that recommends it, and leads on to farther attainments? Think ye, that those who sincerely rejoice in the dawn of day, will readily decry morning light? Is it not therefore much to be feared that Pharisaism and impenitency stand in your way to Christianity, more than a mistaken respect for reason and truth? Nay, does not reason bid you assent to well attested matters of fact? And are not the Jewish and Christian revelations so inseparably connected with notorious events, that it is less absurd to doubt the exploits of Alexander and Cesar, than to disbelieve the miracles of Moses and Jesus Christ?

4. The heathens, who were saved without the explicit knowledge of Christ, far from despising it as you do, implicitly desired it; and those that were blessed with a ray of it, rejoiced in it like Abraham. That precious knowledge is offered to you; and (shocking to say!) you reject it! you make sport with it! you pass jests upon it! you call it *imposture! enthusiasm!* O! how much more tolerable will it be for Pharisaic heathens; yea, for Chorazin and Bethsaida, in the day of judgment, than for you, if you die under so fatal an error! And how can ye flatter yourselves, that because righteous heathens, who have but one talent, shall be saved in the faithful improvement of it; you, who have five, shall be saved, though you bury four of them?

"O! but I, for one, improve the fifth: I am moral." God forbid I should discountenance morality! I value it next to piety: nay, true morality is the second branch of true piety. Nevertheless, this you must permit me to say: Your morality hath either pride, impenitency, and hypocrisy at the bottom; or humility, sincerity, and truth. If the former, your morality, like Jonah's gourd, has a worm at its root. When the sun of temptation shall shine warmly upon you, or when death shall lay his cold hand upon you, your morality will wither, and afford you neither safety nor comfort: but if it has sincerity and truth at the bottom; and if you are faithful, your little light will increase, the clouds raised by your prejudices will break, and you shall "see the glory of God shining in the face of Jesus Christ," because, like Saul of Tarsus, you do not oppose the truth maliciously, but "ignorantly in unbelief." And O! may these pages convey to you the accents of that "truth which shall make you free!" and may the gracious voice, which formerly thundered in the ears of the great Jewish moralist, the fierce opposer of the Christian Gospel: "Saul! Saul! why persecutest thou me?" May that voice, I say, whisper to each of you, "Honestus! Honestus! why neglectest thou me? *I am Jesus whom thou persecutest*: Jesus, who yet act in the Mediator's part between my righteous Father and thy self-righteous soul. *It is hard for thee to kick against the pricks* of my truth, and the stings of thy conscience. I am a Sun of righteousness and truth: wrap thyself in unbelief no more: let the beams of my grace penetrate thy prejudiced soul, and kindle redeeming love in thy frozen breast. Nor force me, by an obstinate and final denial of me before men, to fulfil upon thee the most terrible of all my threatenings, by denying thee also before my Father and his angels;' for, 'if ye [to whom my Gospel is fully preached] believe not that I am He, ye shall die in your sins.'"

SECTION XIII.

An address to a penitent mourner.

THOU deniest that loving Redeemer no longer, O thou poor, mourning penitent, who art ready to sink under the burden of thy sins, and longest to find rest for thy soul. The Lord, who pronounces thee *blessed*, says, "Comfort ye, comfort ye my *mourning* people. By whom shall I comfort thee?" O! that it were by me! O! that I were so happy as to administer one drop of Gospel cordial to thy fainting spirit! Though I am less than the least of my Lord's servants, he sends thee by me a Benjamin's portion: be not above accepting it. Thou hast humbly received the *wounding* truths of the Gospel; why shouldst thou obstinately reject the *healing ones?* Thou hast eaten the bitter herbs of repentance: yea, thou feedest upon them daily, and preferrest them to all the sweets of sin. Why then, O! why should thy heart rise against the flesh and blood of the true paschal Lamb? Why shouldst thou starve, when "all things are now ready?" Why shouldst thou not believe the whole truth as well as *one part* of it? Will "the word of God's grace" be more true ten years hence than it is now? Is not "Christ the same yesterday, to-day, and for ever?" If thy dull "believing in God has already saved thee from thy vain conversation and thy outward sins; how much more will a cheerful "believing in the Lord Jesus," save thee into Christian righteousness. peace, and joy in the Holy Ghost.

Do not "begin to make excuse," and say, "I must not believe the joyous truths of the Gospel till they are first powerfully applied to my soul." It is right, very right for thee, for all, never to rest short of such an application. But how art thou to wait for it? In the way of duty, or out of it? Surely in the way of duty. And is it not thy duty no longer to "make God a liar?" Is it not thy bounden duty, as it is thy glorious privilege, to "set thy seal," as thou canst, to the word of God's grace, as well as to the declaration of his justice? Does he not charge thee to "believe," though it should be "in hope against hope," the reviving "record which he has given of his Son?" Is not "this the record: — That God has given to us eternal life, and this life is in his Son: that to as many as receive him, that is, to as many as believe on his name, he gives power to become the sons of God: that God commendeth his love toward us, in that when we were yet sinners, Christ died for us [men and for our salvation:] that his blood [through faith on our part] cleanseth from all sin: that he was delivered for our offences, and rose again for our justification:" and that he even now "maketh intercession for us;" bearing us up in the arms of his mercy, that we sink not into hell, and "drawing to Him, who justifieth the ungodly, all men," that renounce their ungodliness as thou hast done, and believe in Jesus as I want thee to do?

If it is "a saying worthy of all men to be received, *that Jesus Christ came into the world to save even the chief of sinners,*" upon Gospel terms; he undoubtedly came to save me and thee. Do not thou then foolishly excommunicate thyself from redeeming love. Away with thy unchristian, discouraging notions about absolute reprobation, preterition, non-election, &c, &c. Doubt not but thou art *conditionally* elected, that is, "chosen in Christ" to eternal salvation; yea, peculiarly chosen of God *explicitly* to "believe in that Just One who gave himself a ransom for all," and "by this one oblation of himself once offered, made a full, perfect, and sufficient sacrifice, oblation, and satisfaction for the sins of *the whole world.*" Believe then thy election, and that of God. As certainly as Christ hung upon the cross, flesh of thy flesh, and bone of thy bone, thou art "chosen to *eternal* salvation THROUGH sanctification of the Spirit, and belief of the truth." Wilt thou then be powerfully saved here, and eternally saved hereafter? Only "make thy calling and election sure, through sanctification of the Spirit;" and make "sanctification of the Spirit sure, through belief of the truth."

Believe, as well as thou canst, this comfortable, this sanctifying truth, "God so loved the world, that he gave his only begotten Son, that WHOSOEVER believeth on him should not perish, but have everlasting life." Be not afraid to conclude, upon the Divine record, that God loves thee, that *Christ gave himself for thee,* and that the Holy Ghost will gloriously witness the Saviour's love to thy soul. And calmly, yet earnestly wait for a Divine token, and an abiding sense of this love upon thy heart.

But, I repeat it, wait in faith: wait, believing the truth: wait, doing thy work; and Christ will surely finish his own: he will "save thee to the uttermost," from sin and hell into holiness and heaven. Remember, that as he once bled for thee, so he now "worketh in thee both to will and to do." Up then and be doing. "Work out thy own salvation with fear and trembling." Thou canst never do God's part, and he will never do thine: do not expect it; nor let the song of "finished salvation" make thee conclude that thou hast nothing to do. Even John Bunyan, in his "Heavenly Footman," cries out to the slothful, "If thou wilt have heaven, thou must run for it." And if thou dost not believe him, believe the Christians of the Lock Chapel, and of the Tabernacle, who, when they do justice to the second Gospel axiom, agree to "complain of spiritual sloth," in the following well known hymn: —

> Our drowsy powers, why sleep ye so?
> Awake, each sluggish soul;
> Nothing has half *thy work to do,*
> Yet nothing's half so dull, &c.

The God of truth will warm thy heart in a rational manner, by *the truth,* which is the Divine cordial generally used by the Comforter for that purpose. Thou must therefore take that cordial first. If thou art "of little faith," there is no need that thou shouldst be of *little sense* also. Some absurdly refuse to believe the Gospel till they can feel it, (if I may so speak,) with their finger and thumb: so gross, so carnal are their ideas of truth! And others think it their duty just to look at, or to hear about the Gospel feast; supinely waiting till all its rich blessings are forcibly thrust into their hearts, or at least conveyed there, without any endeavour of their own. "When the truth shall be powerfully applied to my soul," says a modern Thomas, "I will believe, and not before." Avoid this common mistake. If thou wert invited to a feast, and one said, "You must not eat this rich food, unless it is first powerfully applied to your stomach;" wouldst thou not reply, that thou must first eat it, in order to such an application? Be as wise in spiritual things; and remember that the way of relishing the Gospel, and "feeling it to be the power of God unto salvation," is actually to believe it till we can, till "the Spirit of truth" makes us feel its efficacy.

"To eat or drink spiritually," and "to believe or receive the truth," are Gospel terms of the same import. Come, then, leave all thy excuses to those who have learned the lessons of "voluntary humility." If the king offered thee a present, would it not be impertinent to make him stretch out his hand for one hour, under pretence that thou art not yet worthy of his bounty? And thinkest thou that a similar conduct is not highly provoking to the King of kings? Does he not complain, "I called and ye refused: I stand at the door and knock: all the day long have I stretched my hands to a gainsaying and disobedient people?" Come, then, know thy distance: know thy place: know thy God: send thy absurd ceremoniousness back to Geneva: crucify thy guilty fears on Calvary; and make the best of thy way to Sion, "the mountain where God has made unto all people a feast of fat things, a feast of wines, of fat things full of marrow, of wines well refined."

"There is room," says the Lord: "Draw them with the bands of a man;" with arguments, threatenings, promises, expostulations, &c. — "Compel them to come in." There is balm enough in Gilead, bread enough in my house, love enough in my heart, blood enough in the fountain that my Son has opened for sin, grace enough in the river that flows from my throne, truth enough in the Gospel of my grace to heal, nourish, delight, transport a world of prodigal sons and daughters. And is there not enough for thee, who "fearest God?" For thee, to whom "the word of this *Christian*, this great salvation is sent?" Did not Christ himself break the bread of consolation for thee, when he said, "Take, eat, this is my body which is broken for you?" Did he not offer thee the cup of salvation, when he added, "This is the cup of the New Testament in my blood, shed for the remission of sins; drink ye *all* of it," and carry it into all nations — "preach it," offer it "to every creature?" I bring thee this bread; it "came down from heaven to give life to the world;" it was surely consecrated in Gethsemane, and broken on Calvary for thee, man, and for thee, woman, and for thy salvation. O! if the fragments of perishing barley bread were so to be gathered, that none of them might be lost, with what thankfulness shouldst thou receive the morsel which I set before thee! With what "hunger after righteousness" shouldst thou feast upon it! How shouldst thou try to relish every crumb, every particle of Gospel truth; of "the meat that endureth to everlasting life;" of "the word of the Lord that abideth for ever!"

Wonder at our Lord's condescension. Lest thou shouldest think that the word of his servants is insignificant, although it is the word of truth, he prays particularly "for them that shall believe on him through their words;" and he asks, "How is it that ye do not discern this time" of love? "Yea, and why even of yourselves judge ye not what is right," and makes for your peace? "O ye that have no money, come, buy, and eat, buy wine and milk: yea, eat and drink abundantly, O beloved, without money, and without price. Hearken diligently unto me: eat ye that which is good: let your soul delight itself in fatness," in the richest Gospel truths. "Whosoever will, let him come and take of the *bread and* water of life freely." Thus "the water and the blood, the Spirit and the word," sweetly agree to invite thee, to chide thy delays, to bid thee come and welcome to Christ, and to all the unsearchable riches of his grace.

If thou refusest this drop of Gospel cordial, this crumb of the bread of life; or if, after a faint attempt to take it, thou sinkest back into thy stupid unbelief, I beg leave to inquire into the reason. (1.) Is it "the hour and the power of darkness?" Is thy mind so confused, and thy heart so distracted, that in this moment thou canst neither consider, nor welcome the truth? In this case, wait groaning: if thou canst not wait "in hope, believing against hope," endeavour at least not to yield ,o despair. This storm will soon blow over: "the time of refreshing will come;" and the Lord, who permits thee to have fellowship with him in Gethsemane, will soon enable thee to triumph with him upon the mount.

Hast thou little or no appetite for the truth? In this case, I fear, thou still feedest upon husks and ashes, which spoil thy spiritual digestion; and I advise thee to exercise repentance; remembering "that to be carnally minded is death," and that the promise is not made to the slothful, but to them who, "through faith and patient continuance in well doing, seek for glory" — to them who, in taking up their cross and denying themselves, inherit the Gospel promises.

Hast thou made an absurd covenant with unbelief, as Thomas? Art thou determined not to credit God's record, unless he come down to thy terms? Dost thou still confound faith with its first fruits, and God's works with thine own? If this be thy case, how justly may the Lord suffer thee to go on moping, not only for a week, as the obstinate apostle did, but for years! And after all, when thou hast long dishonoured God, and tormented thyself by thy wilful unbelief, thou wilt be glad to do upon a death bed what I want thee to do now. Being then surrounded by threatening billows, driven from thy carnal moorings, and tossed into true wisdom, thou wilt, without ceremony, venture upon the merits and blood of thy Saviour, and strive to enter, by wrestling faith, and agonizing prayer, into "righteousness, peace, and joy in the Holy Ghost." Happy would it be for thee, in the meantime, if thou wert not wiser in thy own conceit than seven men that can render a reason; if thou wert not obstinately bent upon nursing thy curse; if thou didst confer with flesh and blood no more; and if, regarding the Gospel passport more than Solifidian embargoes, and the word of God more than the dispiriting speeches of faint-hearted spies, thou becamest one of the "BABES to whom it is our heavenly Father's good pleasure to give the kingdom;" one of "the VIOLENT who take it by force," — thou wouldst soon find that these two dispositions are as compatible as the two Gospel axioms; and "receiving the end of thy faith," thou wouldst soon, perhaps to-day, experience the astonishing force of truth, and taste the ravishing powers of the world to come.

SECTION XIV.

An address to Christian believers.

YE taste those powers, happy believers, who see that God is love, boundless, free, redeeming, pardoning, comforting, sanctifying love in Jesus Christ. The more you believe it, the more you feel it. Do then always "the work of faith," and you shall always "abound in the patience of hope, and in the labour of love." You have believed the truth, and it has made you free. "Rejoice then in the truth:" worship the God of truth: triumph in Christ, "the living truth;" and be daily baptized "with the Spirit of truth." Beware of enthusiasm. "Speak the words of soberness and truth." God is not the author of nonsense.

Sail with all possible care through the straits of Pharisaism and Antinomianism. Many, by deviating from the word, have almost "made shipwreck of the faith." While some rest in high Pharisaic forms, others catch at empty Solifidian shadows, or slide into the peculiarities of a censorious mysticism, harden themselves against "the gentleness of Christ," and oppose a part of the truth as it is in Jesus. Embrace ye the whole: be valiant for the whole: recommend the whole: but above all, bring forth the fruits of the whole.

Be steady: many who believed once as firmly as you do, that Christ was a sacrifice for sin, consider him now only as a martyr for the truth. And some who were fully persuaded that God is "loving to every man" while the day of salvation lasts, now can *bear*, yea, perhaps *delight* to hear it insinuated that he is graceless and merciless to myriads of his unborn creatures. Be not thus carried about by a blast of vain doctrine, in opposition to the full tide of Scripture and reason. "Honour all men, and give double honour" to those to whom it is due; but be not moved from your steadfastness either by names or numbers. To judge of truth by popularity is absurd. Warm, zealous men, who can draw the attention, and work upon the passions of the populace, will always be popular; but popularity, you know, is no proof that any man's principles are unexceptionable. Go not then by that deceitful rule. When truth is at stake, mind popular applause as little as a syren's song; and regard a Bonner's rack as little as a Nebuchadnezzar's dulcimer. Be cast into the furnace of persecution with two companions, rather than bow with thousands to the most shining, the most celebrated, and the richest image of error. If your two companions forsake you, O! do not forsake the truth. Turn not your back upon her when she wants you most. Run not away from her colours when the enemy pours in like a flood. If she be driven out of the professing Church, follow her to the wilderness, — and if need be, to the den of lions. There the God of Daniel will be with you; and from thence he will bring you out; for God will stand by the truth, and she will prevail at last. "Buy her" therefore at any rate; buy her, though you should give your last mite of wealth, and your last scrap of reputation for her: "and sell her not," though you should gain the whole world by the unhappy bargain.

"These things," O men of God, "have I written unto you concerning them that [by fair shows of spirituality and voluntary humility] seduce you" into Pharisaism or Antinomianism: "but the anointing, which you have received of God, abideth in you, [since you have not been seduced,] and it is truth, and is no lie, abide in it therefore. Err not from the truth. Walk in the truth. Do nothing against the truth, but for the truth: and, as you have purified your souls by obeying the truth, through the Spirit unto unfeigned love of the brethren," see that his love extend itself particularly to your opponents. "Love them, love one another with a pure heart fervently." You will often be obliged to part with peace in order to maintain truth; but you never need to part with love. Be you herein followers of Christ and St Paul. You know that the Pharisees, the Herodians, the Sadducees, and the devil himself would gladly have made peace with those two champions of the truth upon the scandalous terms of betraying and giving her up. But St. Paul had not so learned Christ, and our Lord scorned to deny himself the truth, and to worship the father of lies. See how calmly, how lovingly, how resolutely they fight this good, this bloody fight of faith! Volleys of invectives and calumnies have been already thrown out against them: and now, reproving their persecutors, and yet praying for them, they go and meet bonds and prisons, stocks and scourges, the provoking taunt and the cruel mocking, the bloody sword and the ignominious cross. And how many stand by them in their extremity? Have ye forgotten the amazing number? "They ALL forsook him and fled. All men forsook me: I pray God, it may not be laid to their charge." And, astonishing! Judas, Peter, and Demas, led the van. O Jesus, stand by our weakness, and we will stand by thy truth! Thou sayest, "Will ye also go away?" And "to whom should we go," gracious Lord? "Hast thou not the words of truth, the words of everlasting life? Art thou not the light of the world and the light of men?" Our light and our life? Could all the *ignes fatui* in the professing world; could even all "the stars" in thy Church supply the want of thy light to our souls? No, Lord: be then our sun and shield for ever. Visit the earth again, thou uncreated Sun of righteousness and truth: hasten thy second advent: thy kingdom come! Shine without a cloud! Scatter the last remains of error's night! Kindle our minds into pure truth! Our hearts into perfect love! Our tongues into ardent praise! Our lives into flaming obedience!

> Bold may we wax, exceeding bold,
> No more to error's ways conform;
> Nor shrink the hardest truths t' unfold,
> But more than meet the gathering storm.

> Adverse to earth's erroneous throng,
> May each now turn his fearless face;
> Stand as an iron pillar strong,
> And steadfast as a wall of brass.

> Give us thy might thou God of pow'r,
> Then let or men or fiends assail;
> Strong in thy strength, we'll stand, a tower
> Impregnable to earth or hell.

AN APPENDIX,

TO PREVENT OBJECTIONS.

To plead for error in *an Essay on Truth*, would be preposterous. If I have done it, it has been inadvertently; and I shall be thankful to any of my readers who will be at the trouble to set me right. But I once more beg forward disputants not to produce assertions and invectives, instead of arguments and well applied scriptures; and not to wire draw the controversy by still urging objections which I have already directly or indirectly answered, unless they show that such answers are insufficient; that my arguments are inconclusive; and the scriptures I quote misapplied. Two of those objections, however, deserve a more direct and full answer.

I. Should it be said, "I puzzle people, by asserting that there can be any other saving faith but *the Christian faith*; and any other object of saving faith but *Christ crucified:*" I reply, that though *Christ crucified* is the capital object of my faith, I dare not admit the contracted notions that the Solifidians have of faith; because, if I did, I should subscribe to the necessary damnation of three parts of my fellow sinners out of four; and reject Christ's word, under pretence of exalting his person. Take a few more instances of it.

Did not our Lord himself say to his disciples, "Have faith in God;" distinguishing *that faith* from faith in himself, as Mediator? John 17:3. Does not St. Paul declare that, as believing God was imputed to Abraham for righteousness, so it shall be imputed to us, "if we believe on him that raised up Jesus our Lord from the dead?" Do I "forge" the following scriptures: "The righteousness of God is revealed from faith to faith — according to the proportion of faith — according as God hath dealt the measure of faith: if I have told you of EARTHLY things, and ye believe not; how shall ye believe if I tell you of HEAVENLY things?" And can we read Hebrews xi, without seeing that the faith there described is more general than the faith which characterizes the Christian dispensation? By what art can we make it appear that Christ crucified was the object of the faith of those believers, of whom the apostle says, "By faith Noah, moved with fear, built an ark: by faith Isaac blessed Jacob and Esau [the supposed reprobate] concerning things to come: by faith Jacob blessed the sons of Joseph: by faith Joseph gave commandment concerning his bones: by faith the harlot Rahab perished not with them that believed not when she had received the spies?" If you insinuate, with respect to Rahab, that Joshua sent the spies, whom she entertained, and that they informed her that Joshua was a type of Christ crucified; will you not render your "orthodoxy" as ridiculous as if you rested it upon the frivolous difference there is between *if* and *if?* Mr. B. cannot show that the apostle ever distinguished between a Jewish IF, and a Christian IF; but I can quote chapter and verse, when I assert that he clearly distinguishes between Jewish and Christian *faith*. For, not to transcribe Hebrews viii and x, does he not say, Galatians 3:23, "Before faith [i.e. before *Christian* faith] came, we were kept under the law," i.e. under the Jewish dispensation, and the obscurer faith peculiar to it? Nor was this a damnable state; for St. Paul begins the next chapter by telling us that "the heir, as long as he is a child, differeth nothing from a servant, though he be LORD OF ALL; but is under tutors and governors till the time appointed of the father. Even so we, When we were children, [when we were under the Jewish dispensation,] were in bondage under the elements of this world: but when the fulness of time was come, God sent forth his Son, made of a woman, made under the law, to redeem them that were under the law, that we [children differing nothing from servants] might receive the adoption of sons," i.e. the privileges of sons that are of age, and are no longer under tutors and governors. "For after that [Christian] faith is come, we are no longer under a school master, for we are all the [emancipated] children of God by faith in Christ Jesus," Galatians 3:25, 26. Is it not evident, from the comparing of these passages, that the faith of Jews constituted them children of God, but such children as, in general, "differed nothing from servants," — such children as were in a state of nonage and bondage? Whereas Christian faith, (emphatically called *faith*,) by its superior privileges, introduces true Christians into "the glorious liberty of the *adult* sons of God." Before we can overthrow this doctrine, must we not, to use St. Peter's words, "wrest our beloved brother Paul's words, so as to overthrow the faith of some," yea, of all the Jews that lived "before faith came," i.e. before Christ brought believers from Mount Sinai to Mount Sion; from the earthly "Jerusalem, which is in bondage with her children, to the new Jerusalem, which is free, and is the mother of us all — that stand fast in the liberty wherewith Christ hath made us free, and are not entangled again with the yoke of bondage?"

The difference between the privileges of the Jewish, and those of the Christian faith and dispensation, is still more clearly described, 2 Corinthians 3. There the Christian dispensation (called the ministration of the Spirit, because the promise of the Spirit is its great privilege, see John 7:39,) is opposed to the Jewish dispensation, which the apostle calls "the ministration of condemnation," because it appointed no particular sacrifices for penitents guilty of adultery, idolatry, murder, blasphemy, &c, and absolutely doomed them to die. This severe dispensation, says St. Paul, "was glorious, though it is done away: much more that which remaineth [the Christian dispensation] exceedeth in glory." Again: "Moses put a *typical* veil over his face, that the children of Israel could not steadfastly look to the end, &c: but we [Christians] all, with open face beholding, as in a glass, the glory of the Lord, are changed into the same image from glory to glory." What a privilege! And how many nominal Christians live below it; yea, below the privileges of the very heathens!

This, however, is *the one faith* of true Christians, who "have the same spirit of faith." It is one in its great object, "God manifest in the flesh" — one in its great promise, the promise of the Father, or "the kingdom in the Holy Ghost" — *one* in its new commandment, brotherly, universal love, that "perfects believers in one," and makes them partakers of so great salvation. This is the faith which St. Paul calls "the faith of God's elect," i.e. the faith of Christians, who are "chosen [above Jewish believers] to see the glory of the Lord with open face," when Jewish believers see it only "darkly through a veil." This very faith he calls, immediately after, the faith "common" to all Christians, "to Titus, my own son after the common faith," Titus 1:1, 4. With an eye to this faith he likewise names Timothy, his "own son in the faith, — which is in Christ Jesus." A faith this, whereby Timothy, who was a Jewish believer from a child, was "made a partaker of Christ the great [i.e. the Christian] salvation:" — a faith which St. Peter calls "precious faith," and St. Jude, "most holy faith;" indirectly comparing it to "the most holy place" in the temple: — a faith which

Christ calls "my faith," Revelation 2:13, and "faith that is in me," Acts 26:18. A faith this, far superior to the faith of the noble Jewish believers in Berea, who so candidly searched the Scriptures, when they had heard St. Paul preach, — and very far exceeding the candid disposition of those sincere heathens at Corinth, concerning whom our Lord said to St. Paul* "I have much people in this city." If the reader divests himself of prejudices, I hope that, instead of calling the doctrine of the Gospel dispensations, and the degrees of faith belonging to them, a "novel chimera," he will embrace and receive it as a truth which leads to a thousand others.

II. Some of my opponents, who find it easier to pass a jest than to answer an argument, will probably think that to beat me and the doctrine of the dispensations out of the field of truth, they need only laugh at my "inventing" different sorts of faith "by the dozen."

To nip this witticism in the bud, I declare, once more, that I make no more difference between the faith of a righteous heathen, and the faith of a father in Christ, than I do between daybreak and meridian light. That the light of a sincere Jew is as much one with the light of a sincere Christian, as the light of the sun in a cold, cloudy day in March, is one with the light of the sun in a fine day in May. And, that the difference between the saving faith peculiar to the sincere disciples of Noah, Moses, John the Baptist, and Jesus Christ, consists in a variety of *degrees*, and not in a diversity of *species*; saving faith under all dispensations agreeing in the following essentials: (1.) It is begotten by the revelation of some saving truth, presented by free grace, impressed by the Spirit, and received by the believer's prevented free agency. (2.) It has the same original cause in all, that is, the mercy of God in Jesus Christ. (3.) It actually saves all, though in various degrees. (4.) Its sets all upon working righteousness; "some bearing fruit thirty, some sixty, and some a hundred fold." And (5.) Through Christ it will bring all that do not make shipwreck of it, to one or another of "the many mansions," which our Lord is gone to prepare in heaven for his believing, obedient people.

III. Should it be objected, that "the doctrine of this Essay confounds faith and works;" to what I have said on this head in the preceding Checks I add: (1.) There is an essential difference between the holy faith of Adam in a state of innocence, and the justifying, sanctifying faith of a penitent sinner: for Adam only stood and worked by faith in God as Creator; but we rise, stand, and work, *chiefly* by faith in God as Redeemer and Sanctifier. (2.) Adam worked upon the terms of the first covenant, which requires innocence and perfect obedience; and we work upon the terms of the second, which, for Christ's sake, admits the sincere obedience of penitential faith. Here is then no mixing of the covenants, no confounding of faith and works; but only a vindication of the works of faith, and defending the faith that works by love. (3.) St. Augustine, the favourite father of the Solifidians, wrote a

---

* I prefer this sense to that of the Calvinists, not only because unconditional election to eternal glory appears to me an unscriptural doctrine; but because the apostle having named the sins in which all wicked heathens lived, says to the Corinthians, not "such were you ALL" but "such were SOME of you;" intimating that others were of those righteous people, concerning whom our Lord speaks when he says, "Inquire who is worthy." Let it be observed, however, that we do not rest our doctrine of free grace upon this or upon any one scripture brought in by the by, and rather by way of illustration than of proof. We have passages in abundance that are full to the point.

treatise (*De Fide el Operibus*) *upon Faith and Works*, in the twenty-first chapter of which he has these words: "By believing in God with a right faith, by worshipping and knowing him, we are so far benefited, (*ut et bene vivendi ab illo sit nobis auxilium, etsi peccaverimus ab illo indulgentiam mereamur*) as to be assisted by him to live well, and to obtain of him [for I must not literally translate the heretical word mereamur] a pardon, if we have sinned." And, chap. 23, he adds: "*Inseparabilis est bona vita a fide quæ per dilectionem operatur; imo vero ea ipsa est bona vita:* a good life is inseparable from the faith that works by love; nay, that faith itself is a good life." Had I spoken so unguardedly, there would be just room for raising the objection which I prevent; but I have carefully distinguished between faith and works; representing faith as *the beating of the heart*, and works as *the pulses* caused thereby; and holding forth faith as *the root*, and works as *the fruit* of evangelical obedience.

IV. If some readers think that my views of truth are singular, I reply, that when I have reason and Scripture on my side, I am not afraid of singularity. However, as I should be glad to obviate even this objection, I shall present the reader with the sentiments of two of the most judicious divines of the last century, Mr. Flavel and Mr. Goodwin.

Mr. Flavel says, in his *Discourse on Mental Errors:* "Truth* is the proper object, the natural and pleasant food of the understanding. 'Doth not the ear' (that is, the understanding by the ear) 'try words, as the mouth tasteth meat?' The minds of all that are not wholly immersed in sensuality, spend their strength in the laborious search and pursuit of truth. Answerable to the sharpness of the mind's appetite, is the fine edge of pleasure and delight which it feels in the discovery and acquisition of truth. If Archimedes, upon the discovery of a mathematical truth, was so ravished that he cried out, Ευρηχα ευρηχα, *I have found it! I have found it!* What pleasure must the discovery of a Divine truth give to a sanctified soul! 'Thy words were found of me,' says Jeremiah, 'and I did eat them' and thy word was to me the joy and rejoicing of my heart.' Truth lies deep [*Veritas in puteo*] as the rich veins of gold do; if we will get the treasure, we must not only beg but dig also. We are not to take up with what lies uppermost, and next at hand upon the surface. 'Be ye transformed by the renewing of your mind that you may prove what is that good, acceptable, and perfect will of God.' It is a very great judgment of God to be given over to an erroneous mind: for the understanding being the leading faculty, as that guides, the other powers of the soul follow, as horses in a team follow the fore horse. Now how sad and dangerous a thing is this, for Satan to ride the fore horse, and guide that which is to guide the life of man! That is a dreadful, spiritual, judicial stroke of God, which we read of, Romans 1:26: 'Because they received not the love of the truth, God gave them up to strong delusions,' 2 Thessalonians 2:13. They are justly plagued with error that slight truth. Beside, what shame and trouble it must be to the zealous promoters of errors, not only to cast away their own time and strength, but also to ensnare and allure the souls of others into the same or worse mischief! For though God may save and recover you, those that have been misled by you may perish."

Mr. Goodwin thus confirms Mr. Flavel's noble testimony in the preface to his *Redemption Redeemed:* "Truth is for the understanding, and the understanding for

---

* I produce this as an extract, and not as a continued quotation.

truth: truth, especially in things of a supernatural concernment, the knowledge whereof faceth eternity, &c, being nothing else (interpretatively) but God himself prepared, of and by himself, for a beatifical union with the understanding, and from hence with the heart and affections of men. Error, in things of high import, can be nothing else than Satan, contriving and distilling himself into a notion, or impression likely to be admitted by the understanding, under the appearance, and in the name of truth, into union with itself, and by means hereof into union with the hearts of men. All error (of that kind I now speak of) being seated in the understanding, secretly and by degrees infuseth a proportionable malignity into the will and affections, and occasioneth unholy dispositions. Error is the great troubler of the world. It is that fountain of death that sendeth out all those streams of sin which overflow the earth. Why do men so universally walk in ways of oppression, deceit, drunkenness, uncleanness, envy, pride, &c, but because they judge such ways as these (all circumstances considered) more desirable to them than ways of a contrary import? And what is this but a most horrid error and mistake, the result of those lying apprehensions concerning God, wherewith men willingly suffer their minds to be corrupted even to spiritual putrefaction? Neither could the devil have touched Adam or Eve but by the mediation of some erroneous notions or other concerning God." And in his Dedicatory Epistle to the University of Cambridge he hath this fine thought, which I address to my readers: — "If you condemn, who will justify? Only God's eldest daughter, truth, has one mightier than you on her side, who will justify her in due time, though you should condemn her; and will raise her up from the dead the third day, in case you shall slay her."

V. "By granting that people, who are under dispensations inferior to Christianity in its state of perfection, may have a degree of saving faith, although they have not yet the luminous faith of Christian believers, you damp the exertion of seekers, and invite them to settle, as most dissenters do, in a lukewarm, Laodicean state, short of assurance and 'the kingdom of God,' which consists not only in, righteousness, but in peace and joy by the Holy Ghost.'"

If this objection could not be answered, I would burn my Essay; for I had much rather it should feed my fire, than the Laodicean spirit, which is already so predominant in the Church. But that this new difficulty is by no means unanswerable, will appear, I hope, by the following observations: —

1. Judicious Mr. Baxter, by a variety of strong arguments, shows, that to represent assurance, or the kingdom of God in the Holy Ghost, as essential to all true faith, and promiscuously to shut up, in a state of damnation, all those to whom that "kingdom is *not yet* come with power," is both cruel and unscriptural. (See the arguments in his *Confession of Faith*, from p. 189 to 214.)

2. Ought we to keep from those who sincerely seek the kingdom of God the comfort that the Gospel allows them? Are not "they that seek the Lord" commanded "to rejoice?" And how can they do it, if "the wrath of God abideth on them," as it certainly does on all absolute unbelievers? Did not our Lord and St. Peter speak in a more evangelical strain, when they said to sincere seekers, "Fear not, little flock; for it is your Father's good pleasure to give you the kingdom" of grace, as well as that of glory? "The promise [of the kingdom in the Holy Ghost] is unto you and to your children, and to as many as the Lord our God shall call" to believe explicitly in Jesus Christ.

Creeds and Scripture Scales

3. When Joshua urged the Israelites to cross Jordan, would he have done right if he had made them believe that they were still in Egypt, and had not yet taken one true step toward Canaan? Did he not encourage them to go up and to possess the good land by the very consideration which my objector supposes would have made them sit down in the wilderness? Nay, did not those who had already taken possession of the kingdoms of Og and Sihon, on the other side Jordan, cross that river first, and nobly lead the van, when their brethren went on from conquering to conquer? And why should not spiritual Israelites, who turn their back upon spiritual Egypt, and seek the kingdom of God, be led on "from faith to faith" in the same comfortable manner?

4. It is trifling to say, "Dead dissenters, and the formal Scotch clergy, preach up a faith, short of Christian assurance, and therefore such a faith is a dangerous chimera:" for if they preach it in an unguarded, or in a careless manner, to set aside and not to illustrate the doctrine of Christian faith, they do the devil's work, and not the work of evangelists: what wonder is it then that such preaching should lull their congregations asleep? Again: if we ought not to give up the doctrine of sincere obedience and good works, though our opponents cry out perpetually, "It is the doctrine of all the carnal clergy in the kingdom:" and if it be our duty to maintain the doctrine of the trinity, though Dr. Priestley and all the Unitarians say, with great truth, "It is the doctrine of the superstitious Papists;" how absurd is it to urge that our doctrine, concerning a faith inferior to the faith of assurance, is false, merely because the objector says that this part of our doctrine is held by all the *sleepy* dissenters? Might we not, at this rate, be also ashamed of the doctrine of the Divine unity, which the Socinians, the Jews, and even the Turks hold, as well as we?

5. Are there not many pious and judicious ministers in the Churches of England and Scotland, as well as among the dissenters, who dare not countenance the present revival of the power of godliness, chiefly because they hear us sometimes unguardedly assert that none have any faith but such as have the faith of assurance; and that the wrath of God actually abides on all those who have not that faith? If we warily allowed the faith of the inferior dispensations, which such divines clearly see in the Scriptures, and feel in themselves; would not their prejudices be softened, and their minds prepared to receive what we advance in defence of the faith of assurance?

6. If it be urged, that the Spirit of God witnesses to all sincere seekers of the kingdom in the Holy Ghost, that they are in a damnable state till they feel the pardoning "love of God shed abroad in their hearts by the Holy Ghost given unto them:" I demand proof; I deny the fact, and assert that the Divine Spirit can no more bear witness to an accepted, mourning Cornelius, *that he is not accepted in any sense*, than it can give testimony to a palpable contradiction. The truth is, our unbelieving fears and awakened hearts are very prone to surmise the worst, and we are very apt to take their surmisings for Divine impressions, even when we "bring forth fruits worthy of repentance." I doubt not but St. Paul himself, in his agony of penitential grief, when he spent three days and three nights in fasting and prayer, had many such gloomy despairing thoughts; but they were certainly lying thoughts, as well as those which David wisely checks in some of his Psalms. Who will dare to say that Ananias found the apostle in a damnable state, though he found him without a sense of sin forgiven, as appears from the direction which he gave him, "Arise, why tarriest thou? Wash away thy sins, calling upon [and consequently *believing in*] the name of the Lord."

7. My objector's argument is as much levelled at St. Paul's doctrine as at my Essay: "Men and brethren," &c, said he to his audience at Antioch, "whosoever among you FEARETH God, to you is the word of THIS SALVATION sent," Acts 13:26. But none of the pious hearers, whom he thus addressed, were unwise enough to reply, "Thou acknowledgest that we 'fear God:' and David says, 'Blessed is the man that feareth the Lord.' Now, if we fear him, and are blessed, we are already in a state of salvation, and therefore need not 'this salvation' which thou preachest. If we see our way by the candle of Moses, as thou intimatest, what need is there that 'the Sun of righteousness' should arise upon us with 'healing in his wings?'" I demand proof, therefore, that men who fear God in our day are more ready to draw pernicious inferences from the doctrine of the dispensations, than they were in St. Paul's time.

8. The objections which I answer may, with equal propriety, be urged against St. Peter's doctrine. Acts 2:5, and 10:7, we read of "DEVOUT men out of every nation under heaven," and of "a DEVOUT soldier that waited continually" on Cornelius, who himself "feared God, wrought righteousness, and was accepted — with all his house." By Acts 11:9, 14, it evidently appears, that though Cornelius was cleansed by God himself, yet he must "send for Peter," who was to "tell him words whereby he and all his house SHOULD BE SAVED, that is, should become partakers of *the great salvation* revealed by the Gospel of Jesus Christ. But although St. Peter began his discourse by acknowledging that his pious hearers "were accepted with God," none of the congregation said, "Well, if we *are accepted*, we are already in a state of salvation, and therefore we need not 'hear words whereby we shall be saved.'" On the contrary, they all "believed the word of this *fuller* salvation: for the Holy Ghost fell on all them that heard the word;" and St. Paul informs us that we "receive the Spirit by the hearing of faith:" compare Acts 10:44, with Galatians 3:2, and John 7:39. It is plain, from this account, that no preaching was ever attended with a more universal blessing, and that no discourse was ever so instrumental in conveying to all the power of the faith of assurance, than that very sermon which the apostle began by intimating that his hearers were already accepted, according to an inferior dispensation. Hence it is evident that the doctrine we maintain, if it be properly guarded, far from having a necessary tendency to lull people asleep, is admirably calculated to excite every penitent to faith, prayer, the improvement of their talents, and the perfecting of holiness.

9. May we not sufficiently guard the Christian dispensation, by constantly affirming, (1.) That all *Christian* believers "have *now* the witness in themselves." (2.) That those who have it not either never had Christian faith, which is emphatically called *faith* in the Gospel, see Acts 14:27, or that they know only "'the baptism of John:" or that, with the unsettled Galatians, they are actually "fallen from grace, that is, from the Christian dispensation; and now live "under the law," that is, in the darkness of the Jewish dispensation; supposing they are not quite departed from God by indulging known sin. (3.) That if they do not press after the faith of assurance, they are in the utmost danger of losing their talent of grace; like the young man whom Jesus loved, and who nevertheless went away sorrowful, when he was unwilling to give up all, and follow Jesus without reserve; or like those thousands of Israelites, "whom the Lord SAVED OUT OF the land of Egypt, and whom he afterward destroyed," when "they believed not" the word by which they were to be SAVED INTO the land of promise, Jude 1:5.

10. Not to mention all the arguments by which the zealous Puritans defended the doctrine of assurance in the last century, and those by which the Methodists prove its necessity in our days, is not the first argument used in my address to the antichristian moralists, p. 564, sufficient, if it be properly managed, to enforce the absolute necessity of rising to higher dispensations, when God calls us to it? If Queen Vashti lost her crown for refusing to come to the royal banquet, at "the king's commandment:" if those who "begged to be excused," when they were invited to the Gospel feast, were at last dreadfully punished: if St. Paul says to loitering believers, who are backward to go on to perfection, "How shall we escape if we neglect so great salvation, which at first began to be spoken by the Lord;" nay, if Christ himself threatens to "spue lukewarm," slothful Laodiceans "out of his mouth;" do we want even terrifying arguments to lash the consciences of those carnal professors who, hoping they are perfectly safe in their low attainments, despise higher dispensations, and "bury their talent" of grace, till it be "taken from them, and given to" those who best improve their own? To conclude.

11. You are afraid that the doctrine of this Essay will make "seekers rest in Laodicean lukewarmness;" but permit me to observe that the seekers you speak of are either forward hypocrites, or sincere penitents. If they are *forward hypocrites*, preaching to them the faith of assurance will never make them either humble or sincere. On the contrary, they will probably catch at an election, and then at an assurance of their own making; and so they will profess to have the faith for which you contend, when in fact they have only the name and notion of it. The religious world swarms with instances of this kind. If, on the other hand, the seekers for whom you seem concerned are sincere penitents; far from being hurt, they will be greatly benefited by our doctrine: for it will at once keep them from chilling, despairing fears, and from false, Crispian comforts; the two opposite extremes into which upright, unwary mourners are most apt to run. Thus our doctrine, instead of being dangerous to sincere seekers, will prove a Scriptural clue, in following which they will happily avoid the gloomy haunts of Pharisaic despair, and the enchanted ground of Antinomian presumption.

SECOND APPENDIX.

CONTAINING

1. Ten more arguments to prove that all men universally, in the day of their visitation, have some gracious power to believe some saving truth. And, 2. An answer to three more objections.

BEING conscious that I cannot be too careful and guarded in writing upon so important and delicate a subject as that of the preceding Essay, I once more take up the pen to explain, strengthen, and guard the doctrine that it contains.

I. I have said, (p. 131,) that "faith [considered in general] is believing heartily:" I add, "and sometimes it may signify a power to believe heartily." For, as God gives to all the heathens, in the day of their visitation, "a power to believe heartily that God is," &c, indulging them with gracious calls and opportunities to use that power; we may say that he gives them *the faith* of their dispensation. Nevertheless all the heathens have not *that faith:* for many obstinately bury their talent, till at last it is taken from them.

As this doctrine of faith entirely subverts the doctrine of finished damnation, which is so closely connected with the doctrines of absolute election and finished salvation; and as a Calvinist clergyman, who has seen part of this Essay, assures me that it shall be taken notice of; I beg leave to add the following arguments to those which I have produced, section first, to prove that faith is not the work of God in the sense of our adversaries, and that in the day of salvation, through "the free gift which is come upon all men," we have all some gracious power to believe *some* saving truth.

1. If faith be the work of God in the same sense in which the creation is his performance, when Christ "marvelled at the centurion's faith," he marvelled that God should be able to do what he pleases, or that a man should do what he can no more help doing, than he can hinder the world from existing' that is, he marvelled at what was not at all marvellous: and he might as well have wondered that a ton should outweigh an ounce.

2. When God invites "every creature" in "all the world" to believe, Mark 16:15, if he denies most of them power so to do, he insults over their wretched impotence, and acts a part which can hardly be reconciled with sincerity. What would the world think of the king, if he perpetually invited all the Irish poor over to England to partake of his royal charity, and took care that most of them should never meet with any vessels to bring them over, but such as would be sure to founder in the passage?

3. When our Lord endeavoured to shame the Pharisees for their unbelief, he said, "John came to you, &c, and ye believed him not, but the publicans and harlots believed him: and ye, when ye had seen it, repented not afterward, that ye might believe." But if faith is the work of God in the sense of our adversaries, was it any shame to the Pharisees that God would not do his own work? Had they any more

reason to blush at it, than we have to redden, because God does not give us wings and fins, as he does to birds and fishes?

4. To suppose that Christ assiduously preached the Gospel to the inhabitants of Capernaum, while all the time he withheld from them power to believe it, and that afterward he appointed them a more intolerable damnation for not believing: to suppose this, I say, is to cast the most horrible reflection upon the Lamb of God. But if it be allowed that those obstinate unbelievers will justly, be sent into a more dreadful hell for having buried to the end their talent of power to believe in their stronger light; is it not reasonable to suppose, that those who shall go to a less intolerable hell, will also be sent there for having finally refused to use their talent of power to believe in their weaker light?

5. Although Christ positively says that men shall be damned for their unbelief, John 3:18; Mark 16:16, yet some of our adversaries deny it, being deservedly ashamed of representing our Lord as damning myriads of men for not doing what is absolutely impossible. Hence they tell us that reprobates shall be damned only for their sins. But this unscriptural contrivance does not mend the matter; for I have shown, section seventh, that bad works, or sins, necessarily flow from unbelief. Now unbelief being nothing but the absence of faith, God, by absolutely withholding all saving faith, necessarily causes all unbelief; and unbelief, by necessarily causing all sin, necessarily causes also all damnation. For he that absolutely withholds all light, necessarily causes all darkness, and of course all the works of darkness. Thus "the doctrines of grace" (so called) that seem to rear their graceful head to heaven, end in the graceless, venomous tail of finished damnation. *"Desinet in piscem mulier formosa superne."*

6. The design of the Gospel, with regard to God, is evidently to extol his grace, and clear his justice. Now if an absolute decree of preterition or limited redemption hinders a vast majority of mankind from believing to salvation, both these ends of the Gospel are entirely defeated in all that perish: for God, by passing by the reprobated culprits, thousands of years before they were born, and by withholding every dram of saving grace from them, shows himself an absolutely graceless Creator to them all. Nor does this opinion less horribly impeach God's justice than his grace; for it represents him as judicially sentencing men to eternal torments, merely for the sin of a man whom most of them never heard of; or, which is all one, for the necessary, unavoidable, preordained consequences of that sin.

7. St. Paul, in his Epistle to the Romans, takes particular care to clear God's justice with respect to the condemnation of the wicked, "that every mouth may be stopped" — and (εις το ειναι) "that they may be without excuse," But the scheme which I oppose, instead of leaving men αναπολογητους *without excuse,* opens their mouths, and fills them with the best apology in the world: "Absolute necessity, and complete impossibility, caused by another before we were born." An apology this, which no candid person can ever object to.

8. Agreeable to St. Paul's doctrine, our Lord observes that the man, sentenced to be cast into outer darkness for "not having on a wedding garment, was speechless." But if the Crispian doctrines of grace be true, might not that man, with the greatest propriety, have said to the Master of the feast, while the executioners "bound him hand and foot," "To all eternity I shall impeach thy justice, O thou partial Judge: thou appointest me the hell of hypocrites, merely because "I have not

on a wedding garment," which thou hast from all eternity purposely kept from me, under the strong lock and key of thy irreversible decrees! Is this the manner in which thou "judgest the world in righteousness?"

9. The parable of the talents, and that of the pounds, decide the question. The wicked and slothful servants, whose destruction they inform us of, are not condemned because their master was "hard and austere;" but because the one had "buried his talent [of power] in the earth," and the other had hid his "pound [of grace] in a napkin" manufactured at Laodicea.

10. If salvation depends upon faith, and if God never gives reprobates power to "believe in the light that enlightens every man," and a sufficiency of means so to do; it follows that he never gives them any personal ability to escape damnation; but only to secure and increase their damnation; and thus he deals far more hardly with them than he did with devils. For Satan and his angels were all personally put in a state of initial salvation, and endued with a personal ability to do that on which their eternal salvation depended. To suppose, therefore, that a majority of the children of Adam, who are born sinful without any personal fault of their own, and who can say to the incarnate Son of God, Thou art flesh of our flesh, blood of our blood, and bone of our bone; — to suppose, I say, that a vast majority of these favoured creatures have far less favour shown them than Beelzebub himself had, is so graceless, so unevangelical doctrine, that one might be tempted to think it is ironically called *the doctrine of grace;* and to suspect that its defenders are styled "evangelical ministers" by way of burlesque.

From the preceding arguments I conclude, that when it is said in the Scriptures people could not believe, this is to be understood either of persons whose day of grace was over, and who of course were justly given up to a reprobate mind, as the men mentioned in Romans 1:21, 28, or of persons who, by not using their one talent of power to believe the obvious truths belonging to a lower dispensation, absolutely incapacitated themselves to believe the deep truths belonging to Christianity.

II. Although I flatter myself that the preceding arguments guard the doctrine of free grace against the attacks of those who indirectly contend for free wrath; I dare not yet conclude this appendix. Still fearful lest some difficulty unremoved should prejudice the candid reader against what appears to me to be the truth, I beg leave to intrude upon his patience, by answering three more plausible objections to the doctrine of this Essay.

OBJECTION VI. "If faith be the gift of the God of grace to us, as sight is the gift of the God of nature, according to your assertion, (p. 525;) does it not follow that as we may see when we will, so we may believe in Christ — believe the forgiveness of our sins; and by that means fill ourselves with "peace and joy in the Holy Ghost" when we have a mind? But is not this contrary to experience? Do not the best Christians remember a time when they could no more believe than they could make a world, though they prayed for faith with all the ardour they were capable of?"

ANSWER 1. You still seem to take it for granted that there is no true faith, but an explicit faith in Christ; and no explicit faith in Christ, but the faith of full assurance. But I hope that I have already proved the contrary in my answer to the fifth objection, (p. 183-4.) There are two extremes in the doctrine of faith which should be carefully avoided by every Christian: the one is that of the author of *Pietas*

Creeds and Scripture Scales

Oxoniensis, who thinks that an adulterous murderer may have true, saving faith in the height of his complicated crimes: and the other is that of those who assert there is no saving faith but that which actually cleanses us from all inbred sin, and opens a present heaven in our breasts. The middle path of truth lies exactly between those opposite mistakes, and that path I endeavour to point out.

As, on the one hand, it never came into my mind that an impenitent murderer can have even the saving faith of a heathen: so, on the other hand, it never entered my thoughts, that a penitent can believe with the faith of full assurance when he will: for this faith depends not only upon our general belief of the truth revealed to us, but also upon a peculiar* operation of God, or revelation of his powerful arm. It is

---

* Mr. Wesley exactly describes this faith in his sermon on Scriptural Christianity, of which you have here an extract: — "By this 'faith of the operation of God,' which was the very 'substance (or subsistence) of things hoped for,' the demonstrative' evidence of invisible things,' he, [the penitent 'pricked to the heart,' and expecting the promise of the Father,] instantly 'received the Spirit of adoption, whereby he [now] cried,, Abba, Father!' Now first it was that he could 'call Jesus Lord by the Holy Ghost, the Spirit itself bearing witness with his spirit, that he was a child of God.' Now it was that he could truly say, 'I live not, but Christ liveth in me,' &c. 'His soul magnified the Lord, and his spirit rejoiced in God his Saviour. He rejoiced in him with joy unspeakable, who had reconciled him to God, even the Father; in whom he had redemption through his blood, the forgiveness of sins.' He rejoiced in that 'witness of God's Spirit with his spirit, that he was a child of God;' and more abundantly 'in hope. of the glory of God,' &c. 'The love of God [was also] shed abroad in his heart by the Holy Ghost which was given to him. Because he was a son, God had sent forth the Spirit of his Son, crying, Abba, Father!' And that filial love of God was continually increased by the 'witness he had in himself' of God's pardoning love to him, &c, so that God was the desire of his eyes, and the joy of his heart; his portion in time and eternity, &c. He that thus loved God, could not but love his brother also, &c. This lover of God embraced all mankind for his sake, &c, not excepting the evil and unthankful, and least of all, his enemies, &c. These had a peculiar place both in his heart and his prayers. He loved them 'even as Christ loved us,' &c. By the same almighty love was he saved, both from passion and pride, from lust and vanity, from ambition and covetousness, and from every temper which was not in Christ, &c. He spake evil of no man; nor did an unkind word ever come out of his lips, &c. He daily grew in grace, increasing in strength, in the knowledge and love of God, &c. He visited and assisted them that were sick or in prison, &c. He 'gave all his goods to feed the poor.' He rejoiced to labour or to suffer for them; and whereinsoever he might profit another, there especially to 'deny himself.' Such was Christianity in its rise, [i.e. Christianity contradistinguished from the dispensation called the baptism of John.] Such was a Christian in ancient days, [i.e. a Christian contradistinguished from a disciple of John or of Christ, before the dispensation of the Holy Ghost took place.] Such was every one of those who, 'when they heard [the threatenings] of the chief priests and elders, lifted up their voice to God with one accord, and were all filled with the Holy Ghost.'"

I here set my seal to this Scriptural description of *Scriptural Christianity*, being fully persuaded of two things: (1.) That till a man be thus "born of the Spirit," he "cannot see the [Christian] kingdom of God:" he cannot be under that glorious dispensation of Divine grace which Christ and the apostles spake of when they preached, "Repent, and believe the Gospel, for the kingdom of heaven is at hand." (2.) That whosoever has not in his breast the above described kingdom, i.e. righteousness, peace, and joy in the Holy Ghost; and does not bring forth its excellent fruits in his life, either never was a spiritual Christian, or is fallen back from the "ministration of the Spirit" into the dispensation of the letter, or the base form of godliness, if not into open wickedness. See the next note.

always attended with a manifestation of "the Spirit of adoption witnessing with our spirits that we are the children of God." And such a manifestation God in general grants to none but them that groan deeply under "the spirit of bondage unto fear," as Paul did while he remained blind at Damascus; — or them that are peculiarly faithful to the grace of their inferior dispensation, and pray as earnestly for "power from on high," as the apostles did after our Lord's ascension.

Therefore, from my asserting (p. 136) that "so long, as the day of salvation continues, all sinners, who have not yet finally hardened themselves, may day and night [through the help and power of the general light of Christ's grace mentioned John 1:9, and Titus 2:11,] receive some truth belonging to the everlasting Gospel," which takes in the dispensation of the heathens; from my asserting this, I say, you have no reason to infer that I maintain any man may, day and night, believe the forgiveness of his sins, and the deep truths of the Gospel of Christ; especially since I mention immediately what truth it is which all may believe, if they improve their talent, namely, this' "There is a God, who will call us to an account for our sins, and who spares us to break them off by repentance."

2. It would be absurd to suppose that you can believe with the luminous faith of assurance, when God is casting your soul into the dark prison of your own guilt to bring down your Pharisaic looks, and make you feel the chains of your sins. But even then may you not believe that God is just, holy, and patient? May you not acknowledge that you deserve your spiritual imprisonment far more than Joseph's brethren deserved to be "put all together into ward three days" by their loving, forgiving brother? May you not believe that, although "heaviness may endure for a night," yet "joy cometh in the morning?" And when you have humbly groaned with David, "I am so fast in prison that I cannot get forth;" may you not pray in faith, "Bring my soul out of prison, that I may praise thy name. Let the bones which thou hast broken rejoice. Give me the garment of praise for the spirit of heaviness. Convince" me as powerfully "of righteousness," as thou hast "of sin:" and let thy Spirit, which now acts upon me as a "Spirit of bondage unto fear," begin to act as a "Spirit of adoption" and liberty — of "righteousness, peace, and joy?" May you not even add, "O God, I believe thy promise concerning the coming of the Comforter; 'help thou my unbelief,' and grant me such a faith as thou wilt vouchsafe to 'seal with that Holy Spirit of promise.' Thou shakest before me the rod of infernal vengeance: I deserve it a thousand times; but, O Father of mercies, O my Father, if for the sake of thine only begotten Son thou wilt yet permit such a wretch as I am to call thee Father, give me the Spirit of adoption; and witness to my spirit that I am a child of thine. But if thou wilt still hide thy face from me, never suffer me to entertain one dishonourable thought of thee; never let me think thee a Moloch. Though thy justice slay me, let me still trust in thee, and believe that for Christ's sake thy mercy will revive my soul?" Is it Scriptural to rank among absolute unbelievers a penitent who thus humbly and obediently waits for the faith of full assurance — the faith of Christianity in its state of perfection? If our Lord pronounces such mourners blessed, does it become us to pronounce them accursed? But I return to your objection.

3. The latter part of it confirms, instead of overturning my doctrine; it being evident that if the persons you speak of prayed with ardour for the faith of assurance, they had already some degree of faith: for praying is "calling upon the Lord," and St.

Paul speaks "the words of soberness," where he says, "How shall they call on him in whom they have not believed?"

4. I am so far from thinking our power to believe is absolute, that I have asserted, (p. 136,) it is impossible heartily to believe the truths which do not suit our present state. And (page 145, &c,) I have observed, that we savingly believe the "truth suitable to our present circumstances, when it is kindly presented by free grace, and affectionately embraced by prevented free will;" adding, that when we believe our "faith is more or less operative, not only according to the earnestness with which we welcome the truth to our inmost souls," but also "according to the power with which the Spirit of grace impresses it upon our hearts." Nay, I have ascribed so much to the power of the free grace by which saving faith is "instantly formed," as to insinuate that sometimes (as at St. Paul's conversion) this power for a while bears all down before it. This at least was my meaning, when I said, section first, "We may in general suspend the act of faith. especially when the glaring light [i.e. the luminous power] that some. times accompanies the revelation of truth is abated." Consider the force of the words, *in general* and *especially;* advert to the exception for which they make room; and you will see I allow that free grace, at times, acts with almost as much irresistibility, as some moderate Calvinists contend for.

5. With respect to my comparison between our power to believe, and our power to see, far from showing that all men may at any time believe the Gospel of Christ, it intimates, nay, it proves the very reverse. Can you see when you will, and what you will? Can you see in a dark night without a light? Can you see in a bright day, when a thick veil covers your face? Can you see if you place an opaque body full in your light? Can you see what is out of the reach of your eyes? Can you see the rising sun when you look full west, or the stars when you pore upon a dung hill? Can you see when you obstinately shut your eyes? Or when you have let a wicked man put them out, lest you should not live in idleness? Apply to faith these queries about sight; recollect the preceding observations: and you will perceive, (1.) That our power to believe is various ways circumscribed; it being impossible that he who has but one talent, perhaps unimproved, should carry on as extensive a trade as the man who diligently improves his five or ten talents. (2.) That nevertheless, supposing we have still a ray of the light of truth, and have not yet been given up to judicial blindness, or to final hardness, we may day and night [if we do not still bury our talent] believe, by the above-mentioned helps, some obvious truth belonging to the lowest dispensation of Divine grace, and begin to follow our Lord's direction, "While ye have the light, believe in the light, that ye may be the children of the light." And, (3.) That if we oppose this doctrine, we begin to follow our Calvinist brethren into Crispianity; and are just ready to bow at the shrine of the great Diana of the day, and to kiss her iron-clay feet, finished salvation and finished damnation.

OBJECTION VII. "Your doctrine concerning the school of faith, and its several forms; concerning the temple of faith, and its capital partitions, is entirely founded upon the doctrine of the dispensations of Divine grace; a doctrine this which many people will rank with what they call, *The novel chimeras of your Checks.*"

I hope that I have proved what I have advanced concerning the dispensations, by arguments founded upon Scripture, reason, and conscience. However, that the idea of novelty may not stand in the way of any of my readers, out of fifty authors, whom I may quote in support of this important doctrine, I shall produce two, a Calvinist and an anti- Calvinist; not doubting but their consentaneous testimony will sufficiently break the force of your objection. The first is the Rev. Mr. Green, late curate of Thurnscoe, in Yorkshire, and once an assistant to Mr. Whitefield. In his book, called *Grace and Truth Vindicated*, (page 116,) you will find the following just remarks: —

"It appears to me, from Scripture as well as experience, that there are divers dispensations, but the same Spirit: the kingdom of heaven consists of various degrees, and different mansions. This is true, whether by the kingdom of heaven we understand the outward professors of religion and the privileges, the inward kingdom of grace, or the kingdom of glory: [in all which senses the words in Scripture are frequently used.] As face answers to face in a glass, so do these respectively answer each other. Thus the outward privileges of religion from Adam to Moses were least; from Moses to Christ greater; and from Christ to the restitution of all things greatest. Again: to be a spiritual or enlightened heathen, as Socrates, Plato, or Cornelius before he heard Peter, is one degree or dispensation of grace. To be a spiritual or enlightened Jew, and with Peter and the other disciples before the day of pentecost to believe and acknowledge that Jesus is the Messiah, though not spiritually come, is a greater. But to be a spiritual Christian, to have Christ, the exalted God-man, revealed in us from heaven, and to be sealed with the Holy Spirit of promise unto the day of the redemption of this vile body, is the last and most perfect dispensation of grace, he that is feeble here shall be as David, and he that is strong, &c, shall be, &c, as the angel of the Lord, &c. For it may be observed, that every dispensation admits of a growth therein; and moreover, that each of them is in some sort and degree experienced by a spiritual Christian," &c.

My second witness is the Rev. Mr. J. Wesley, who, even in his first sermon on *salvation by faith*, preached near forty years ago, clearly distinguishes Christian faith, properly so called, or faith in Christ glorified, not only from the faith of a heathen, but also from the faith of initial Christianity, that is, "the faith which the apostles had while our Lord was upon earth."

"And first," says he, "it [the faith that saves us into the great salvation described in the second part of the sermon] is not barely the faith of a heathen. Now God requires of a heathen to believe 'that God is, that he is a rewarder of them that diligently seek him, &c, by glorifying him as God,' &c, and by a careful practice of moral virtue, &c. A Greek or Roman therefore, yea, a Scythian or Indian, was without excuse if he did not believe thus much: the being and attributes of God, a future state of reward and punishment, &c. For this is barely the faith of a heathen." Soon after he adds: — "And herein does it [this faith in Christ glorified] differ from that faith which the apostles themselves had while our Lord was upon earth, that it acknowledges the necessity and merit of his death, and the power of his resurrection."

The doctrine of Christian perfection is entirely founded on the privileges of the Christian dispensation in its fulness: privileges these which far exceed those of the Jewish economy and the baptism of John. Accordingly Mr. Wesley in his sermons on Christian perfection makes the following just and Scriptural distinction between those dispensations: — "It may be granted, (1.) That David, in the general course of his life, was one of the holiest men among the Jews. And, (2.) That the holiest men among the Jews did sometimes commit sin. But if you would hence infer that all Christians do, and must commit sin, as long as they live; this consequence we utterly deny. It will never follow from those premises. Those who argue thus seem never to have considered that declaration of our Lord, Matthew 11:11, 'Verily I say unto you, among them that are born of women, there hath not arisen a greater than John the Baptist. Notwithstanding, he that is least in the kingdom of heaven is greater than he.' I fear indeed there are some who have imagined the kingdom of heaven here to mean the kingdom of glory: as if the Son of God had just discovered to us that the least glorified saint in heaven is greater than any man upon earth. To mention this is sufficient to refute it. There can, therefore, no doubt be made, but the kingdom of heaven here (as in the following verse, where it is said to be taken by force) or the kingdom of God, as St. Luke expresses it, is that kingdom of God on earth, whereunto all true believers in Christ, all real Christians belong. In these words then our Lord declares two things: (1.) That before his coming in the flesh, among all the children of men, there had not been one greater than John the Baptist: whence it evidently follows that neither Abraham, David, nor any Jew, was greater than John. (2.) That he who is least in the kingdom of God (in that kingdom which he came to set up on earth, and which the violent now began to take by force) is greater than he. Not *a greater prophet* (as some have interpreted the word) for this is palpably false in fact: but greater in the grace of God, and the knowledge of our Lord Jesus Christ. Therefore we cannot measure the privileges of real Christians by those formerly given to the Jews. 'Their ministration,' or dispensation, we allow 'was glorious;' but ours 'exceeds in glory.' So that whosoever would bring down the Christian dispensation to the Jewish standard, doth 'greatly err, neither knowing the Scriptures, nor the power of God.'" From these excellent quotations, therefore, it appears that you do me an honour altogether undeserved, if you suppose that I first set forth the doctrine of the dispensations.

OBJECTION VIII. "I cannot help thinking, that the doctrine of a faith proper to all those dispensations is above the capacity of plain Christians, and should never be mentioned, lest it should puzzle, instead of edifying the Church."

If your fears be well grounded, even the apostles' creed is above the capacity of plain Christians; for that creed, the simplest of all those which the primitive Church has handed down to us, evidently distinguishes three degrees of faith: (1.) Faith "in God the Father Almighty, who made heaven and earth," which is the faith of the heathens. (2.) Faith in the Messiah, or "in Jesus Christ, his only begotten Son, our Lord," which is the faith of pious Jews, of John's disciples, and of imperfect Christians, who, like the apostles before the day of pentecost, are yet strangers to the* great outpouring of

---

* I beg the reader will not mistake me. When I say that pious Jews and our Lord's disciples, before the day of pentecost, were strangers to the great outpouring of the Spirit, I do not mean that they were strangers to his directing, sanctifying, and enlivening influences, according to their dispensation. For David had prayed, "Take not thy Holy Spirit from me:" John the Baptist had been visited by his exhilarating power, even in his mother's womb: our Lord had "breathed upon his disciples, saying, Receive ye the Holy Ghost," and had imparted him to them as a "Spirit of grace and supplication," to help them to wait in faith and unceasing prayer, "till they were endued with power from on high.' Beside, they had called him Lord in truth; and no man can do this, but by "the Spirit of faith," which "helps our unbelief" and infirmities under all the Divine dispensations. Nevertheless, they were not fully baptized. The Comforter that visited them did not properly dwell in them. Although they had already wrought miracles

the Spirit: and (3.) Faith "in the Holy Ghost;" faith of the operation of God, by which Christians complete in Christ believe "according to the working of God's almighty power," and are "filled with righteousness, peace, and joy in [thus] believing."

And here honesty obliges me to lay before the public an objection which I have had for some time against the appendages of the Athanasian creed. I admire the Scriptural manner in which it sets forth the Divine unity in trinity, and the Divine trinity in unity: but I can no longer indiscriminately use its damnatory clauses. It abruptly takes us to the very top of the Christian dispensation, considered in a doctrinal light. This dispensation it calls *the catholic faith:* and, without mentioning the faith of the inferior dispensations, as our other creeds do, it makes us declare that, "except every one keep that faith [the faith of the highest dispensation] whole and undefiled — he cannot be saved; without doubt he shall perish everlastingly." This

---

by his power, "the promise of the Father was not yet fulfilled to them." They had not yet been "made perfect in one," by the assimilating power of the heavenly fire. They would have been puzzled by such questions as these: — "Have ye received the Holy Ghost since ye believed?" Acts 19:2. "Is he fallen upon you?" Acts 10:44. "Is the love of God shed abroad in your heart by the Holy Ghost given unto you?" Romans 5:5. Is the "fountain springing up into everlasting life" opened in your breast? John 6:14. "After that ye believed, were ye sealed with that Holy Spirit of promise?" Ephesians 1:18. That Spirit which forms those "rivers of living water that flow out of the belly," the inmost soul of believers? That Spirit which "was not given [before] Christ was glorified?" John 7:39. That Comforter which it is more expedient for us to receive, than even to have Christ's bodily presence and constant instructions? John 16:7. If these and the like questions would have perplexed the apostles, before Christ had opened his spiritual baptism, and set up his kingdom with power in their hearts, we ought not to be surprised that professors, who "know only the baptism of John," should ingenuously confess they "never heard there was a Holy Ghost [to be received] since they believed," Acts 19:2. Nor should we wonder if devout Jews and easy Laodiceans should even mock and say, "You would have us to be 'filled with new wine;' but we are 'rich, and increased with goods, and have need of nothing.' The water of our old cisterns is preferable to the new wine of your enthusiastic doctrine, and our baptismal ponds to your baptismal flames."

This, however, was not Mr. Whitefield's language when he admitted an adult person to baptism; (and he knowingly admitted none but believers.) He knew then how to pray for the promise of the Father, and how to point the disciple of John to the perfection of Christ's dispensation. As a proof of it, take part of the truly Christian hymn which he sung on that occasion: —

> Anoint with holy fire,
>   Baptize with purging flames
> This soul, and with thy grace inspire
>   In ceaseless, living streams.
>
> Thy heavenly unction give,
>   Thy promise, Lord, fulfil;
> Give power, [that is, faith] thy Spirit to receive,
>   And strength to do thy will.

This good old Gospel is far more clearly set forth in Mr. Wesley's sermon. called "Scriptural Christianity," and in his "Hymns for Whitsunday," which I earnestly recommend, as pointing out the "one thing needful" for all carnal professors.

dreadful denunciation is true with regard to proud, ungodly infidels, who, in the midst of all the means of Christian faith, obstinately, maliciously, and finally set their hearts against the doctrine of the Father, Son, and Holy Ghost; equally despising the Son's atonement and the Spirit's inspiration. But I will no more invade Christ's tribunal, and pronounce that the fearful punishment of damnation shall, "without doubt," be inflicted upon "every" Unitarian, Arian, Jew, Turk, and heathen, "that fears God and works righteousness," though he does not hold the faith of the Athanasian creed whole. For if you except the last article, thousands, yea millions, are never called to hold it at all; and therefore shall never perish for not holding it whole. See the notes, pages 451 and 551. At all hazards then, I hope, I shall never use again those damnatory clauses, without taking the liberty of guarding them agreeably to the doctrine of the dispensations. And if Zelotes presses me with my subscriptions, I reply beforehand, that the same Church which required me to subscribe to St. Athanasius' creed, enjoins me also to believe this clause of St. Peter's creed: "In every nation he that feareth God, and worketh righteousness, is accepted of him." And if those two creeds are irreconcilable, I think it more reasonable that Athanasius should bow to Peter, warmed by the Spirit of love; than that Peter should bow to Athanasius, heated by controversial opposition.

To return: that the distinction of the three degrees of saving faith, omitted in the Athanasian creed, but expressed in the apostles' creed, and in the Nicene creed; that this distinction, I say, is neither chimerical nor enthusiastical, may be proved by a variety of arguments, two or three of which, I hope, will not intrude too long upon the reader's patience.

1. The first is taken from the doctrine expressly laid down in the New Testament. To what I have said on this head, p. 179, &c, I add here what Christ said to his disciples, "Ye believe in God, believe also in me." Here the most prejudiced may see that faith in the Father is clearly contradistinguished from faith in the Son. As for faith in the Holy Ghost, see in what manner our blessed Lord sowed the seed of it in the hearts of his disciples. "When the Comforter is come, whom I will send unto you from the Father, even the Spirit of truth, he shall testify of me. It is expedient for you that I go away: for if I go not away, the Comforter will not come unto you; but if I depart, I will send him unto you. Behold I send the promise of my Father unto you: but tarry ye in the city of Jerusalem, until ye be endued with power from on high." Nor was this great promise made to the apostles alone; for "in the last day, that great day of the feast, Jesus stood and cried, saying, If any man [not if an apostle] thirst, let him come to me and drink. He that believeth on me, as the Scripture hath said, out of his belly shall flow rivers of living water. But this he spake of the Spirit, which they that believed on him should receive: for the Holy Ghost was not yet given; [his dispensation, which is the highest of all, was not yet opened;] because that Jesus was not yet glorified." And the opening of this dispensation in our hearts requires, on our part, not only faith in Christ, but a peculiar faith in the promise of the Father; a promise this, which has the Holy Ghost for its great object.

2. My second argument is taken from the experiences of those who, by the Holy Ghost, were made partakers of Christ glorified, either on the day of pentecost, or after it; and could feelingly confess Christ dying for us, and Christ living "in us, the hope of glory." Acts 2:5, we read of "devout men out of every nation under heaven," who were come to worship at Jerusalem. But how could they have been devout men

if they had not believed in God? What could have brought them from the ends of the earth to keep a feast to the Lord, if they had been mere Atheists? And yet it is evident, that through prejudice many of them rejected our Lord; putting him to open shame and a bloody death. But when Peter preached Christ on the day of pentecost, they at first believed on him with a true, though not with a luminous faith. This appears from the anguish which they felt upon being charged with having "slain the Prince of life." No man in his senses can be "pricked to the heart" merely for having had a hand in the just punishment of an impostor and a blasphemer, who "makes himself equal with God." If therefore keen remorse pierced the hearts of those penitent Jews, it is evident that they looked no more upon Christ as an impostor, but already believed in him as the true Messiah.

No sooner had they thus passed from faith in the Father to an explicit faith in the Son, but they cried out, "What shall we do?" And Peter directed them to make, by baptism, an open, solemn profession of their faith in Christ, and to believe the great promise concerning the Holy Ghost. "The promise is unto you," said he. "Be baptized every one of you, in the name of Jesus Christ, for the remission of sins; and ye [every one of you] shall receive the gift of the Holy Ghost." And upon their "gladly receiving the word," that is, upon their heartily believing the gladdening promise relating to pardon and to the Comforter; and no doubt upon their fervently praying that it might be fulfilled in them, "they were all filled with the Spirit," all their hearts overflowed with "righteousness, peace, and joy in the Holy Ghost."

St. Peter, speaking, Acts 11, of a similar outpouring of the Spirit, says: "The Holy Ghost fell on them [Gentiles] as on us [Jews] at the beginning. Then remembered I the word of the Lord, how that he said, John indeed baptized with water, [them that entered his dispensation,] but ye shall be baptized with the Holy Ghost," when you shall enter the full dispensation of my Spirit: "God," adds Peter, "gave them the like gift as he did unto us, who believed on the Lord Jesus Christ." And when "the apostles heard these things, they glorified God;" not indeed by shouting, "Then hath God given the Gentiles power to speak Arabic:" but by saying, "Then hath God also to the Gentiles granted repentance unto life," according to the fulness of the Christian dispensation.

That this dispensation of the Holy Ghost, this coming of Christ's spiritual kingdom with power, is attended with an uncommon degree of sanctifying grace, is acknowledged by all; and that the gift of tongues, &c, which at first, on some occasions and in some persons, accompanied the baptism of the Spirit, for a sign to bigoted Jews, or to stupid heathens; — that such a gift, I say, was a temporary appendage, and by no means an essential part of Christ's spiritual baptism, is evident from the merely spiritual effect which the receiving of the Holy Ghost had upon the penitent Jews, who, being "born of water and the Spirit," pressed after the apostles into the kingdom on the day of pentecost.

"Even in the infancy of the Church," says an eminent divine, "God divided those [miraculous] gifts with a sparing hand. 'Were all [even then] prophets? Were all workers of miracles? Had all the gifts of healing? Did all speak with tongues?' No, in no wise. Perhaps not one in a thousand. Probably none but the teachers of the Church, and only some of them. It was therefore for a more excellent purpose than this that they, the brethren and apostles, 'were all filled with the Holy Ghost.' It was to give them [what none can deny to be essential to all Christians in all ages] 'the mind which was in Christ,' those holy 'fruits of the Spirit,' which whosoever hath not, is none of his; to fill them with 'love, joy, peace, long suffering, gentleness, goodness.'"

It is very remarkable, that although three thousand converts "received the gift of the Holy Ghost" on the memorable day in which Christ opened the dispensation of his Spirit, no mention is made of so much as one of them working a single miracle, or speaking with one new tongue. But the greatest and most beneficial of miracles was wrought upon them all: for "all that believed," says St. Luke, "were together; continuing daily with one accord in the temple, breaking bread from house to house, eating their meat with gladness and singleness of heart, praising God and having favour with all the people," by their humble, affectionate, angelical behaviour. Or, as the same historian expresses it, Acts 4:32, "The multitude of them that believed" — spoke Greek and Latin! No: but "were of one heart and of one soul; neither said any of them that aught of the things which he possessed was his own; but they had all things common;" having been made perfect in one, agreeably to our Lord's deep prayer, recorded by St. John: "Neither pray I for these [my disciples] alone, but for them also who shall believe on me through their word, that they may be one; I in them, [by my Spirit,] and thou in me, that they may be made perfect in one."

3. To this argument, taken from the experiences of the primitive Christians, I may add, that the doctrine of the dispensations is indirectly taught by our Church even to children, in her Catechism, where she instructs them to say, "By the articles of my belief I learn, *first*, to believe in God the Father, who made me, &c. *Secondly*, in God the Son, who redeemed me, &c. And, *thirdly*, in God the Holy Ghost who sanctifieth me." For these three distinctions are expressive of the three grand degrees of the faith, "whereby we inherit all the promises of God," and "are made partakers of the Divine nature." They are not descriptive of faith in three gods, but of the capital manifestations of the triune God, in whose name we are baptized; and of the three great dispensations of the everlasting Gospel, namely, that of the heathens, that of the Jews, and that of spiritual Christians; the dispensation of Abraham being only a link between heathenism and Judaism; and the dispensation of John the Baptist or of Christianity begun, being only a transition between Judaism and Christianity perfected.

Our Church Catechism brings to my remembrance the office of confirmation. It was, it seems, originally intended to lead young believers to the fulness of the Christian dispensation, agreeably to what we read, Acts 8:12, &c. Peter and John went from Jerusalem to Samaria to lay their hands on the believers who had not yet been baptized with the Holy Ghost, and to "pray that they might receive him: for as yet he was fallen upon none of them, only they were baptized by Philip in the name of the Lord Jesus. When the Son of man cometh, shall he find faith upon the earth?" I fear but little of the faith peculiar to his full dispensation. Most professors seem satisfied with John's baptism or Philip's baptism. The Lord raise us apostolic pastors to pray in the demonstration of the Spirit and of power. "Strengthen thy servants, O Lord, with the Holy Ghost, the Comforter; and daily increase in them thy manifold gifts of grace; the spirit of wisdom and understanding; the spirit of counsel and ghostly strength; the spirit of knowledge and true godliness; and fill them with the spirit of thy holy fear now and for ever." (*Order of confirmation*.) Can it be said that those in whom that prayer is not now answered live under the dispensation of Christianity perfected? Are they either established Christians or spiritual Churchmen? How long shall the mystery of iniquity prevail? How long shall a Pharisaic, Deistical world destroy the faith of the Son, under colour of contending for faith in the Father? And how long shall a world of Antinomian, Solifidian professors destroy faith in the Holy Ghost, under pretence of recommending faith in the Son? O Lord, exert thy power. "Pour out thy Spirit upon all flesh," and give wisdom to all thy ministers to divide the word of truth aright, and to feed thy people according to their states and thy dispensations!

If these answers give my objector no satisfaction, and he still think it his duty to attack my Essay, I beg leave to address him in the words of a judicious divine of the last century: — "I shall not need, I presume, to desire you, that in your answer you will not rise up in your might against the weaker, looser, or less considerate passages or expressions, (of which kind you may very possibly meet more than enow,) but that you will rather bend the strength of your reply against the strength of what you shall oppose. You well know that a field may be won, though many soldiers of the conquering side should full in the battle; and that a tree may flourish and retain both its beauty and firmness of standing in the earth, though many of the smaller twigs and lesser branches should prove dry, and so be easily broken off. So may a mountain remain unmoved, yea, unmovable, though many handfuls of the lighter and looser earth about the sides of it should be taken up, and scattered into the air like dust. In like manner the body of a discourse may stand entire in its solidity, weight, and strength, though many particular expressions, sayings, and reasonings therein, that are more remote from the centre, should be detected either of inconsiderateness, weakness, or untruth."

ZELOTES AND HONESTUS RECONCILED:

OR,

THE SECOND PART

OF

AN EQUAL CHECK

TO

PHARISAISM AND ANTINOMIANISM:

BEING THE FIRST PART

OF THE

SCRIPTURE SCALES

O WEIGH THE GOLD OF GOSPEL TRUTH, TO BALANCE A MULTITUDE OF OPPOSITE SCRIPTURES, TO PROVE THE GOSPEL MARRIAGE OF FREE GRACE AND FREE WILL, AND RESTORE PRIMITIVE HARMONY TO THE GOSPEL OF THE DAY.

WITH A PREFACE,

CONTAINING SOME STRICTURES UPON THE THREE LETTERS OF RICHARD HILL, ESQ., WHICH HAVE BEEN LATELY PUBLISHED.

BY A LOVER OF THE WHOLE TRUTH AS IT IS IN JESUS.

How is the most fine gold changed! Take heed that ye be not deceived; for many shall come in my name, saying, "I am Christ," *doctrinal*: "I am Christ," *moral*: but, "to the law, and to the testimony; if they speak not according to this word, it is because there is no light in them, [or at least because] their wine is mixed with water, and their silver is [partly] become dross." — Bible.
Si non est Dei gratia, quomodo salvat mundum? Si non est liberum arbitrium, quomodo judicat munduni? — Aug.

ADVERTISEMENT.

IT is the author's desire that the following pages should be considered as written for all those whom they exactly suit. And in order to this, he informs the reader that, in general,

ZELOTES represents any zealous Solifidian, who, through prejudice, looks upon the doctrine of *free will* as heretical.

HONESTUS — -any zealous moralist, who, through prejudice also, looks upon the doctrine of *free grace* as enthusiastical.

LORENZO — -any man of sense, yet unsettled in his religious principles.

CANDIDUS — -any unprejudiced inquirer after truth, who hates bigotry, and would be glad to see the differences among Protestants settled upon rational and Scriptural terms.

A SOLIFIDIAN is one who maintains that we are completely and eternally saved [*solâ fide*] by sole faith — by faith alone; and who does it in so unscriptural a manner as to make good works unnecessary to eternal salvation; representing the law of Christ as a mere rule of life; and calling all those who consider that law as a rule of judgment, *legalists, Pharisees, or heretics*.

A PREFATORY EPISTLE,

HUMBLY ADDRESSED TO THE TRUE PROTESTANTS

IN GREAT BRITAIN AND IRELAND.

Containing some remarks upon the distinguishing character of true Protestants, and upon the contrary disposition — True Protestants are chosen judges of the doctrines advanced in this book — A sketch of the author's plan — Observations upon the manner in which it is executed — General directions to the reader — True Protestants are encouraged to protest against religious absurdities, and unscriptural impositions — The author enters a double protest against the ANTINOMIAN and PHARISAIC gospels of the day, and continues to express his love and esteem for the good men, who, through the force of prejudice, espouse and defend those partial gospels.

BRETHREN AND FATHERS, — Ye know how hard the Romanists fought for their errors at the time of the reformation. They pleaded that antiquity, synods, councils, fathers, canons, tradition, and the Church were on their side: and they so obscured the truth by urging Scripture metaphors, and by quoting unguarded passages from the writings of the fathers, that thousands of simple people knew not which of the contending parties had the truth on its side. The great question debated in those days was, whether *the host,* that is, the bread consecrated by the priest in the Lord's Supper, was to be worshipped as *the identical body of our Lord.* The Romanists produced Christ's own words: "Take and eat, THIS is my body — this is my blood — drink of it. Except you eat my flesh, and drink my blood, ye have no life in you." The reformers answered, "That those expressions being *figurative,* it was *absurd* to take them in a *literal* sense;" and they proved their assertion by appeals to *reason* and to the *Scriptures,* where the consecrated bread is plainly called *bread.* The Romanists replied, "that in matters of faith we must set aside *reason:*" and some of them actually decried it as the greatest enemy to faith; while others continued to produce crude quotations from all the injudicious, inconsistent, overdoing fathers. The reformers seeing that at this rate there would be no end to the controversy, *protested* three things in general: (1.) That right reason has an important place in matters of faith. (2.) That all matters of faith may and must be decided by Scripture understood reasonably, and consistently with the context. And, (3.) That antiquity and fathers, traditions and councils, canons and the Church, lose their authority when they depart from sober reason and plain

Scripture. These three *protests* are the very ground of our religion, when it is contradistinguished from popery. They who stand to them deserve, in my humble opinion, the title of *true Protestants;* they are, at least, the only persons to whom this epistle is inscribed.

If the preceding account be just, *true* Protestants are all *candid.* Christian candour being nothing but a readiness to hear right *reason* and plain *Scripture.* Sincerely desirous to "prove all things, to hold fast that which is good, and to approve things which are excellent," Protestants are then never afraid to bring their creed to a reasonable and Scriptural test. And conscious that the mines of natural and revealed religion are not yet exhausted, they think, with the apostle, that if any man supposes he has learned all that he should know, "he is vainly puffed up in his fleshly mind, and knows nothing yet as he ought to know."

Hence it is, that of all the tempers which true Protestants abhor, none seems to them more detestable than that of those Gnostics, — those pretenders to superior illumination, who, under the common pretence of *orthodoxy* or *infallibility*, shut their eyes against the light, think plain Scripture beneath their notice, enter their protests against reason, steel their breasts against conviction, and are so rooted in blind obstinacy, that they had rather hug error in an *old* fantastic dress, than embrace the pure truth, *newly* emerging from under the streams of prejudice. Impetuous streams these, which "the dragon casts out of his mouth, that he may cause *the celestial virgin* to be carried away by the flood," Revelation 12:15. Alas! how many professors are there, who, like St. Stephen's opponents, judges, and executioners, are neither able to resist, nor willing to admit the truth; who make their defence by "stopping their ears, and crying out, The temple of the Lord, the temple of the Lord are we!" who thrust the supposed heretic out of their sanhedrim; who, from the press, the pulpit, or the dictator's chair, send forth volleys of hard insinuations or soft assertions, in hope that they will pass for solid arguments; and who, when they have no more stones or snow balls to throw at the supposed Philistine, prudently avoid drawing "the sword of the Spirit," retire behind the walls of their fancied orthodoxy, raise a rampart of slanderous contempt against the truth that besieges them, and obstinately refuse either candidly to give up, or manfully to contend for the unscriptural tenets which they would impose upon others as pure Gospel.

Whether some of my opponents, good men as they are, have not inclined a little to the error of those sons of prejudice, I leave the candid reader to decide. They have neither answered, nor yielded to the arguments of my Checks. They are shut up in their own city. Strong and high are thy walls, O mystical Jericho! Thy battlements reach unto the clouds; but truth, the spiritual ark of God, is stronger, and shall prevail. The bearing of it patiently around thy ramparts, and the blowing of rams' horns in the name of the Lord, will yet shake the very foundation of thy towers. O that I had the honour of successfully mixing my feeble voice with the blasts of the champions who encompass the devoted city! O that the irresistible shout, "Reason and Scripture, Christ and the truth" were universal! If this were the case, how soon would Jericho and Babylon, Antinomianism and Pharisaism, fall together!

Those two antichristian fortresses are equally attacked in the following pages: and to you, true Protestants, I submit the inspection of the attack. Direct me where I am wrong, assist me where I am right, nor refuse to support my feebleness by your ardent prayers; for, next to the Captain of our salvation, I look to you for help and comfort.

My opponents and I equally pretend to Protestantism; and who shall judge between us? Shall it be the men of the world? No: for St. Paul says, "I speak to your shame. Is it so, that there is not a WISE MAN among you? No, not one that shall be able to judge among his brethren?" There are *wise men* in our despised camp, *able to judge* between us, and ye are the men, honoured brethren; for ye are all willing to hear reason, and ready to weigh Scripture. Therefore, on my part, I sincerely choose you as judges of the present dispute.

And that you may not look upon this office as unworthy of your acceptance, permit me to tell you, that our controversy is one of the most important which was ever set on foot. To convince you of it. I need only remind you, that the grand inquiry, *What shall I do to be saved?* is entirely suspended on this greater question, *Have I any thing* to do *to be eternally saved?* A question this which admits of three answers: (1.) That of the *mere Solifidian,* who says, "If we are *elect,* we have nothing to do in order to eternal salvation, unless it be to believe that Christ has done all for us, and then to sing *finished salvation;* and if we are not elect, whether we do nothing, little or much, eternal ruin is our *inevitable* portion." (2.) That of the *mere moralist,* who is as great a stranger to the doctrine of *free grace* as to that of free wrath; and tells you "that there is no free, initial salvation for us; and that we must work ourselves into a state of initial salvation by dint of care, diligence, and faithfulness." And (3.) That of the *reconciler,* whom I consider as a rational Bible Christian, and who asserts: (1.) That Christ has done the part of a sacrificing priest and teaching prophet upon earth, and does still that of aft interceding and royal priest in heaven, whence he sends his Holy Spirit to act as an enlightener, sanctifier, comforter, and helper in our hearts. (2.) That "the free gift of initial salvation," and of one or more talents of saving grace, "is come upon all" through the God-man Christ who "is the Saviour of all men, especially of them that believe." And (3.) That our free will, assisted by that saving grace imparted to us in the free gift, is enabled to work with God in a subordinate manner: so that we may freely (*without necessity*) do the part of penitent, obedient, and persevering believers, according to the Gospel dispensation we are under.

This is the plan of this work, in which I equally fight *pro aris et focis,* for faith and works, for gratuitous mercy and impartial justice; reconciling all along Christ our *Saviour* with Christ our *Judge,* heated Augustine with Pelagius, free grace with free will; Divine goodness with human obedience, the faithfulness of God's promises with the veracity of his threatenings, FIRST with SECOND causes, the original merits of Christ with the derived worthiness of his members, and God's foreknowledge with our free agency.

The plan, I think, is generous; standing at the utmost distance from the extremes of bigots. It is deep and extensive; taking in the most interesting subjects about which professors generally divide, such as the origin of evil, liberty, and necessity, the law of Moses and the Gospel of Christ, general and particular redemption, the apostasy and perseverance of the saints, the election and reprobation maintained by St. Paul, &c. I entirely rest the cause upon Protestant ground, that is, upon *reason* and *Scripture.* Nevertheless, to show our antagonists that we are not afraid to meet them upon any ground, I prove, by sufficient testimonies from the fathers and the reformers, that the most eminent divines, in the primitive Church and our own, have passed the straits that I point out; especially when they weighed the heavy anchor of prejudice, had a good gale of Divine wisdom, and steered by the Christian mariner's compass, *the word of God*, more than by the *false lights* hung out by party men.

If I have in any degree succeeded in the execution of this *reconciling* plan, I hope that my well meant attempt will provoke abler pens to exert themselves; and will excite more respectable divines to strike heavier blows, and to repeat them, till they have given the finishing stroke to divisions, which harden the world against Christianity, which have torn the bosom of the Church for above twelve hundred years, and which have hurt or destroyed myriads of her injudicious children; driving some into Pharisaic obedience, others into Antinomian immorality, and not a few into open infidelity or fierce uncharitableness.

If a tradesman be allowed to recommend his goods, when he does it in a manner consistent with modesty and truth, shall I be accused of self conceit if I make some commendatory remarks upon the following papers? I venture to do it in the fear of God. And,

1. They are plain. I deal in *plain reason* and *plain Scripture;* and when the depth of my subject obliges me to produce arguments that require close attention, I endeavour so to manage them, that they do not rise above the reach of mechanics, nor sink beneath the attention of divines.

2. I have been charged with widening the breaches, which the demon of bigotry has made among religious people; but, if I have done it, I take the Searcher of hearts to witness, that it has been with such a design as made our Lord *bring fire upon the earth,* — the fire of truth, to burn the stubble of error, and to rekindle the flame of love. However, if I have, in years past, made a wound *rashly,* (of which I am not yet conscious,) in this book I bind it up, and bring the *healing,* though (to proud or relaxed flesh) *painful* balsam. This book is entirely written upon a *pacific* plan. If I sometimes give the contending parties a keen reproof, in obedience to the apostolic precept, "Rebuke them sharply," it is only to make them ashamed of their contentious bigotry, that I may bring them to reason the sooner. And if prejudiced readers will infer from thence that I am a bad man, and that my pen distils gall, I forgive their hasty conclusion: I once more send them back to the good men of old, who have reproved far *less* errors with far *greater* severity than I allow myself to use: and I ask, if persons, impatient of control, do not always put wrong constructions upon the just reproofs which they are determined to disregard?

3. I hope that, notwithstanding the outcry raised against my former Checks, they have been of some service to such readers as are not steeled against argument and Scripture; but I flatter myself that, through God's blessing, this tract will be more useful: I prefer it, at least, far before the others, because it has far more of GOD'S word, far less of *mine;* the Scriptures having so large a place in the following sheets, that you will find whole sections filled with balanced passages, to which, for brevity's sake, I have added nothing but a few illustrations in brackets [ ]

4. My method, so far as I know, is new. I have seen several Concordances made of Scripture *words,* but have not yet met with one of Scripture *doctrines* upon the delicate subjects handled in this book. And I flatter myself that, as whatever throws light upon the Bible has always met with approbation from true Protestants, you will not despise this attempt to make the seeming contradictions of that precious book

vanish away, by demonstrating that they are only wise oppositions, not less important in the world of grace, than the distinction of man and wife is in the world of nature.

5. I hope that you will see, in the following pages, many passages placed in such a light, as to have their force heightened, and their obscurity removed by the opposition of the scriptures with which they are balanced; the passages which belong to the doctrine of FREE GRACE, illustrating those which belong to the doctrine of FREE WILL, and *vice versa*, just as the lights and shades of a picture help to set off each other. I therefore earnestly entreat all my readers, especially those who read much and think little, to take time, and not to proceed to a new pair of scriptures till they have found out the balance of the last pair which they have reviewed. If they deny me this request, my trouble will be lost with respect to them; and, through their hurry, my Scales will degenerate into a dull collection of texts; the very life and spirit of my performance consisting in the harmonious opposition of the scriptures, which prove my capital doctrine, that is, the Gospel marriage of free grace and free will. And that the reader may find out, with ease, in every couple of texts, the *hands* by which they are joined, and see (if I may carry the allegory so far) the *ring*, by which their marriage is ascertained, and their gender known, I have generally put in DIFFERENT CHARACTERS the words on which the *opposition* or *connection* of the paired texts chiefly depends; hoping to help the reader's mind by giving his eyes a silent call, and by meeting his attention half way. If he exerts his powers, and

> "Si callida verbum
> Rediderit junctura novum,"*

he will, through God's grace, profit by his labour and mine. But I repeat it, he must find out the delicate *connection*, and harmonious *opposition* of the paired scriptures which I produce, or my Scales will be of as little service to him as a pair of scale bottoms *without a beam* would be to a banker, who wants to weigh a thousand guineas.

6. As I make my appeal to true Protestants, I lay a particular stress upon the Scriptures. And *there* I find a doctrine which, for a long succession of ages, has been partly buried in the rubbish of popery and Calvinism: I mean the doctrine of the various *dispensations* of Divine grace toward the children of men; or of the various *talents* of saving grace which the Father of lights gives to heathens, Jews, and Christians. To the obscurity in which this doctrine has been kept, we may chiefly impute the self-electing narrowness, and the wide-reprobating partiality of the Romish and Calvinian Churches. I make a constant use of this important doctrine. It is it chiefly which distinguishes this tract from most polemical writings upon the same subject. It is my key and my sword. With it I open the mysteries of election and reprobation; and with it I attempt to cut *the Gordian* (should I not say the *Calvinian and Pelagian?*) *knot*. How far I have succeeded is yours to decide.

If these general observations, O ye true Protestants, make you cast a favourable look upon my Scales; and if, after a close trial, you find that they contain the *reconciling truth*, and the ONE complete Gospel of Christ, rent by Zelotes and Honestus to make the TWO partial gospels of the day; let me entreat you to show

---

* If a delicate connection renders the word new to him.

what you are, by boldly standing up for reason and Scripture, that is, for true Protestantism. Equally enter your protest against the Antinomian innovations of Zelotes, and the Pharisaic mistakes of Honestus. These two champions have indeed their thousands, and tens of thousands at their feet; and they may unite their adverse forces to oppose you, as Jews and Gentiles did to oppose the Prince of Peace. But resist them with "the armour of righteousness on the right hand and on the left," and you will in time make them friends to each other and to yourselves; I say *in time*, because when peaceful men rush between fierce combatants in order to part them, they at first get nothing but blows. The confusion for a time increases; and idle spectators, who have not love and courage enough to rush into the danger, and to stop the mischief, say that the peace makers only add fuel to the fire of discord. Thus are the courageous sons of peace "hated of all men" but of true Protestants, for treading in the steps of the Divine Reconciler, whom the two rivals, Herod and Pilate, agreed to set at naught — whom Jews and Gentiles concurred to crucify, inveterate enemies as they were to each other! He died, the loving Reconciler — he died! but by his death "he slew the enmity — broke down the middle wall of partition — of twain made one new man; so making peace" between Herod and Pilate, between Jews and Gentiles. And so will you, honoured brethren, between Zelotes and Honestus, between the Calvinists and the Pelagians, between the Solifidians and the moralists; if you lovingly and steadily try to reconcile them. You may indeed be "numbered among transgressors" for attempting it. Your reputation may even die between that of the fool and of the knave — that of the enthusiast and of the felon: but be not afraid. Truth and the Crucified are on your side. God will raise you secret friends. A Joseph, a Nicodemus, will take down "the hand writing that is against you." A Mary and a Salome will embalm your name; and if it be buried in oblivion and reproach, yet it will rise again the third day.

If God is for you, fear not then what man can say of you, or even do to you. Smile at Antinomian preterition: triumph in Pharisaic reprobation: and when you are reviled for truth's sake, like blunt, resolute, loving Stephen, kneel down, and pray that the sin of your mistaken opposers may not be laid to their charge. O for the Protestant spirit which animated confessors of old, carried martyrs singing to the stake, and there helped them to clap their hands in the flames kindled by the implacable abettors of error! O for a Shadrach's resolution! The rich, glittering image towers toward heaven, and vies with the meridian sun. Nebuchadnezzar, the monarch of the kings of the earth, points at the burning fiery furnace. The princes, governors, captains, judges, counsellors, sheriffs, and rulers of provinces, in all their dazzling magnificence, increase the glory of his terror. The sound of the cornet, flute harp, sackbut, psaltery, dulcimer, and all kinds of music, recommends the pompous delusion: the enthusiastic multitudes are fired into universal applause. In Nebuchadnezzar's sense of the word, they are all *orthodox;* they all believe *the Gospel of the day,* "Great is the Diana of the Babylonians." "All people, nations, and languages, fall down" before her. But the day is not lost: Shadrach has not yet bowed the knee to Baal: nor have his two friends yet deserted him. "What! three!" Yes, three only. Nor are they unequally matched; one Shadrach against *all people!* One Meshach against *all nations!* One Abednego against *all languages!* One Luther, one Protestant against all the world! O ye iron pillars of truth — ye true Protestants of the day, my exulting soul meets you in the plain of Dura. Next to Him who witnessed *alone* a good confession before Pontius Pilate, of you I learn to *protest* against triumphant error. Truth and a furnace for us! The truth — the whole truth as it is in Jesus, and a burning fiery furnace for true Protestants!

And shall we forget thee, O thou "man greatly beloved," — thou pattern of undaunted Protestants? Shall we silently pass over thy bold protest against the foolish, absolute, irreversible *decree* of the day? No, Daniel: we come to pay our tribute of admiration to thy blessed memory, and to learn of thee also a lesson of true Protestantism. Consider him, my brethren. His sworn enemies watch him from the surrounding palaces: but he believes in "the Lion of the tribe of Judah," and his fearless soul has already vanquished their common lions. He opens his window, he looks toward desolate Jerusalem, with bended knees he presents his daily supplication for her prosperity, with uplifted hands he enters his *Jewish* protest against the *Persian* statute; and, animated by his example, I enter my *Christian* protest against the *Calvinian* decree.

"If Daniel, in sight of the lions, durst testify his contempt of an absurd and cruel decree, wantonly imposed upon his king; by which decree the king hindered his subjects from offering any true prayer for a month, under pretence of asserting his own *absolute sovereignty;* shall I be ashamed to enter my *protest* against a worse decree, absurdly imposed upon the Almighty on the very same absurd pretence? A decree which hinders 'the Saviour of the world' from 'praying for the world?' A decree which Calvin himself had the candour to call *horrible decretum?* O how much better is it to impose upon an earthly king a decree restraining the Persians from praying aright *for thirty days*, than to impose upon the King of kings a decree hindering the majority of men, in all countries and ages, from praying once aright during *their whole lives?* And if Darius stained his goodness by enacting that those who disobeyed his UN-FORCIBLE decree should be cast into the den of lions, and devoured in a moment; how do they stain God's goodness, who teach us, as openly as they dare, that he will cast into the den of devils, and cause to be devoured by flames unquenchable, all those whom his FORCIBLE decree binds either not to pray at all, or to offer up only hypocritical prayers! I PROTEST against *doctrines of grace*, which cannot stand without such *doctrines of wrath*. I PROTEST against an exalting of Christ, which so horribly debases God. I PROTEST against a new-fangled Gospel, which holds forth a robe of *finished salvation*, lined with such irreversible and *finished damnation*."

Again: "If Moses had courage enough in a heathen country, and in the midst of his enemies, to enter his protest against the oppressive decree by which Pharaoh required of the Israelites their usual tale of bricks, when he refused them fuel to burn them with: shall I be afraid, in this PROTESTANT kingdom, and in the midst of my friends, to bear also my testimony against the error of Honestus? An error this, which consists in asserting that our gracious God has decreed that we shall work out our own salvation without having *first* life and strength to work imparted to us in a state of *initial* salvation? Without being first *helped* by his free grace to do whatever he requires of us in order to our *eternal* salvation? Shall such a supposed decree as this be countenanced by a silence that gives consent? No: I must, I do also enter my *protest* against it, as being contrary to Divine goodness, derogatory to Christ's merits, subversive of the penitent's hope, destructive of the believer's joy, unscriptural, irrational. And agreeably to our tenth article, I PROTEST: (1.) In opposition to Pharisaic pride, *that we have no power to do good works, pleasant and acceptable to God, without the grace of God preventing us that we may have a good will, and working with us when we hate that good will.* And (2.) In opposition to Pharisaic bigotry, I PROTEST, upon the proofs which follow, that *God's saving grace has appeared in different degrees to all men;* PREVENTING [not FORCING] *them, that they may have a good will, and* WORKING WITH [Note, our Church does not say, DOING ALL FOR] *them when they have that good will.* And I hope, that when my Protestant brethren shall be acquainted with the merits of the cause, they will equally approve of my anti-Solifidian and of my anti-Pharisaic protest."

But shall a blind zeal for truth carry me beyond the bounds of love? Shall I hate Zelotes and Honestus, because I think it my duty to bear my *full* testimony against their errors? God forbid! I have entered two protests as a *divine*, and now permit me, my Protestant brethren, to enter a third as *a plain Christian*. Before the Searcher of hearts I once more protest, that I make a great difference between the persons of good men, and their opinions, be these ever so pernicious. The God who loves me, — the God whom I love, — the God of love and truth teaches me to give error no quarter, and to confirm my love toward the good men who propagate it; not knowing what they do, or believing that they do God service. And I humbly hope that their good intentions will, in some degree, excuse the mischief done by their bad tenets. But, in the meantime, mischief, unspeakable mischief is done, and the spreading plague must be stopped. If in trying to do it as soon and as effectually as possible, I press hard upon Zelotes and Honestus, and without ceremony drive them to a corner, I protest, it is only to disarm them, that I may make them submit to Christ's easy yoke of evangelical moderation and brotherly kindness.

A polemical writer ought to be a champion for the truth; and a champion for the truth who draws only a wooden sword, or is afraid lovingly to use a steel one, should, I think, be hissed out of the field of controversy, as well as the disputant who goes to Billingsgate for dust, mud, and a dirty knife, and the wretch who purposely misses his opponent's arguments that he may basely stab his character. I beg, therefore, that the reader would not impute to a "bad spirit," the keenness which I indulge for conscience' sake; assuring him that, severe as I am sometimes upon the errors of my antagonists, I not only love, but also truly esteem them: Zelotes, on account of his zeal for Christ; Honestus, on account of his attachment to sincere obedience; and both, on account of their genuine, though mistaken piety.

Do not think, however, that I would purchase their friendship by giving up one of my scales, that is one half of the Bible. Far be the mean compliance from a true Protestant. I hope that I shall cease to breathe, before I cease to enter protests against Antinomian faith and Pharisaic works, and against the mistakes of good men, who, for want of Scripture scales, *honestly* weigh the truth in a *false* balance, by which they are deceived first, and with which they afterward *inadvertently* deceive others.

But, although I would no more yield to their bare assertions or inconclusive arguments, than to hard names or soft speeches, I hope, my honoured brethren, that they and you will always find me open to, and thankful for, every reproof, admonition, and direction which is properly supported by the two pillars of Protestantism — sound reason* and plain Scripture: for, if I may depend upon the

---

* By "sound reason" I mean *the light of the world, — the true light which enlightens every man that comes into the world.*

settled sentiments of my mind, and the warm feelings of my heart, I am determined, as well as you, to live and die a *consistent Bible Christian.* And so long as I shall continue in that resolution, I hope you will permit me to claim the honour of ranking with you, and of subscribing myself, brethren and fathers, your affectionate brother, and obedient son in the WHOLE Gospel of Christ,

A TRUE PROTESTANT.

POSTSCRIPT.

CONTAINING SOME STRICTURES UPON A NEW PUBLICATION OF RICHARD HILL, ESQ.

SOME time after I had sent this epistle to the press, one of my neighbours favoured me with the sight of a pamphlet, which had been hawked about my parish by the newsman. It is entitled, *Three Letters written by Richard Hill, Esq., to the Rev. John Fletcher, &c.* It is a second *Finishing Stroke,* in which that gentleman gives his "reasons for declining any farther controversy relative to Mr. Wesley's principles." He quits the field; but it is like a brave Parthian. He not only shoots his own arrows as he retires, but borrows those of two persons whom he calls "a very eminent minister in the Church of England," and "a lay gentleman of great learning and abilities." As I see neither argument nor Scripture in the performances of these two new auxiliaries, I shall take no notice of their ingrafted productions.

With respect to Mr. Hill's arguments, they are the same which he advanced in his *Finishing Stroke:* nor need we wonder at his not scrupling to produce them over again, just as if they had been overlooked by his opponent; for, in the first page of his book, he says, "I have not read a single page, which treats on the subject, since I wrote my *Finishing Stroke.*" But, if Mr. Hill has not read my answer to that piece, some of our readers have; and they will remember that the crambe repetita — I mean his supposition that St. Paul and St. John held Dr. Crisp's doctrinal peculiarities, is answered in part first of the Fifth Check, [toward the close of the first volume.] As for his common plea taken from the objection, Who hath resisted his will? it is answered in this book.

As Mr. Hill's arguments are the same, so are also his personal charges. After passing some compliments upon me as an "able defender" of Mr. Wesley's principles, he continues to represent me as "prostituting noble endowments to the advancing of a party." He affirms, but still without shadow of proof, that he has "detected many misrepresentations of facts throughout my publications." He accuses me of using "unbecoming artifices, much declamation, chicanery, and evasion;" and says, "Upon these accounts I really cannot, with any degree of satisfaction, &c, read the works of one who, I am in continual suspicion, is endeavouring to mislead me by false glosses and pious frauds." If I were permitted to put this argument in plain English, it would run thus: — I bespatter my opponent's character, therefore his arguments are dangerous and not worth my notice. I do not find it easy to overthrow one of the many scriptures which he has produced against Antinomianism, but I can set them all aside at a finishing stroke; for I can say, "The shocking misrepresentations and calumnies you have been guilty of, will for the future prevent me from looking into any of your books if you should write a thousand volumes. So here the controversy must end." (*Finishing Stroke*, p. 40.) When Mr. Hill had explained himself so clearly about his reason for *declining the controversy*, is it not surprising that he should suffer his bookseller to get sixpence for a new pamphlet, "setting forth Mr. Hill's reasons for declining any farther controversy relative to Mr. Wesley's principles?" i.e. to Mr. Wesley's *anti- Solifidian* doctrine, of which I profess myself the vindicator.

But another author vindicates those principles also. It is Mr. Olivers, whom Mr. Hill calls "one Thomas Oliver, alias Olivers." This author was twenty five years ago a mechanic, and like "one" Peter, "*alias*" Simon, a fisherman, and "one" Saul, "*alias*" Paul, a tent maker, has had the honour of being promoted to the dignity of a preacher of the Gospel; and his talents as a writer, a logician, a poet, and a composer of sacred music, are known to those who have looked into his publications. Mr. Hill informs the public why he takes as little notice of this able opponent's arguments as he does of mine; and the "reason" he "sets forth" is worthy of the cause which he defends. *En argumentum palmarium!* "I shall not," says he, "take the least notice of him, or read a line of his composition, any more than if I was travelling on the road, I would stop to lash, or even order my footman to lash, every impertinent little quadruped in a village, that should come out and bark at me; but would willingly let the contemptible animal have the satisfaction of thinking he had driven me out of sight." How lordly is this speech! How surprising in the mouth of a good man, who says to the carpenter, *My Lord and my God!* When the author of "Goliah Slain" dropped it from his victorious pen, had he forgotten, the *voluntary humility* for which *his* doctrines of grace are so conspicuous? Or did he come off in triumph from *the slaughter of the gigantic Philistine?* O ye English Protestants, shall such *lordly* arguments as these make you submit to Geneva *sovereignty?* Will you be "lashed," by such *stately* logic as this, to the foot of the great image, upon whose back you see *absolute preterition* written in such large characters? Will you suffer reason and Scripture to be whipped out of the field of controversy in this *despotic* manner? Shall such *imperial* cords as these bind you to the horns of an altar, where myriads of men are intentionally slain before they are born, and around which injudicious worshippers so sing their unscriptural songs about *finished salvation*, as to drown the dismal cries of *insured destruction* and *finished damnation*.

Mr. Hill's performance is closed by "a shocking, not to say blasphemous confession of faith," in ten articles, which he supposes "must inevitably be adopted, if not in express words, yet in substance, by every Arminian whatsoever," especially by Mr. Wesley, Mr. Sellon, and myself. As we desire to let true Protestants see the depth of our doctrine, that they may side with us, if we are right, or point out our errors, if we are wrong, I publish that creed, (see the close of vol. i,) frankly adopting what is agreeable to our principles, and returning to Mr. Hill the errors which his inattention makes him consider as necessary consequences of our doctrines of grace.

With respect to the three letters, which that gentleman has published to set forth his *reasons for declining the controversy* with me, what are they to the purpose? Does not the first of them bear date "July 31, 1773?" Now I beg any unprejudiced person to decide if a private letter, written on July 31, 1773, can contain a reasonable overture for DECLINING THE CONTROVERSY, when the *Finishing Stroke*, which was given me publicly, and bears date January 1, 1773, contains (page 40) this explicit and

Creeds and Scripture Scales

final declining of it: "So *here* the *controversy must end*, at least it *shall end for me*. You may misquote and misrepresent whomsoever and whatsoever you please, and you may do it with impunity; I assure you, I shall give *myself no trouble* to detect you." The controversy, therefore, was "declined" in January, on the above-mentioned *bitter* reason. Mr. Hill cannot then *reasonably* pretend to have offered to decline it in July, six or seven months after this, from *sweet* reasons of brotherly kindness, and love for peace. "But in July Mr. Hill *wrote to his bookseller to sell no more of any of* his *pamphlets which relate to the Minutes*." True: but this was not *declining the controversy;* and here is the proof. Mr. Hill still professes *"declining any farther controversy about the Minutes,"* and yet in this his last publication, (page 11,) he advertises the sale of all the books which he has written against them, from the *Paris Conversation* to the *Finishing Stroke.* Therefore, Mr. Hill himself being judge, *declining the controversy,* and *stopping the sale of* his *books,* are different things.

Concerning the three letters I shall only add, that I could wish Mr. Hill had published my answers to them, that his readers might have seen I have not been less ready to return his private civilities, than to ward off his public strokes. In one of them in particular, I offered to send him my answer to his *Finishing Stroke* before it went to press, that he might let me know if in any thing I had misunderstood or misrepresented him; promising to alter my manuscript upon any just animadversion that he might make upon it; because, after his Finishing Stroke, he could not make a public reply without breaking his word. And it is to this proposal that he replies thus in his second letter: "As you intend to introduce my worthless name into your next publication, I must beg to decline the obliging offer you make of my perusing your manuscript."

With respect to that gentleman's character, this after clap does not alter my thoughts of it. I cannot but still love and honour him on *many — very many* accounts. Though his warm attachment to what *he* calls "the doctrines of grace," and what *we* call "the doctrines of *limited grace* and *free wrath*," robs him, from time to time, of part of the moderation, patience, and meekness of wisdom, which adorn the complete Christian character; I cannot but consider him as a very valuable person. I do not doubt but when the paroxysm of his Calvinistic zeal shall be over, he will be as great an ornament to the Church of England in the capacity of a gentleman, as he is to civil society in the capacity of a magistrate. And justice, as well as love, obliges me to say, that, in the meantime, he is in several respects a pattern for all gentlemen of fortune; few equalling him in devoting a large fortune to the relief of the poor, and their leisure hours to the support of what they esteem the truth. Happy would it be for him, and for the peace of the Church, if, to all his good qualities, he always added "the ornament of a meek and quiet spirit;" and if he so far suspected his orthodoxy, as to condescend to weigh himself in the *Scripture Scales.*

EQUAL CHECK,

PART SECOND.

BEING THE FIRST PART OF

THE SCRIPTURE SCALES.

SECTION I.

The cause of the misunderstandings of pious Protestants — The contrary mistakes of Zelotes and Honestus, who are invited to try their doctrines by the Scripture Scales — The manner of using them, and the need of them in our days.

FIRST and second causes, leading and subordinate motives, may perfectly agree together. The hinder wheels of a chariot need not be taken off because they are not the fore wheels. It would be absurd to pull down the left wing of a palace, merely because it is opposed to the right. And a man makes himself ridiculous who destroys one of his scales because it accidentally outweighs the other: for both scales may recover their equilibrium, and answer the best of purposes.

Such, if I mistake not, is the necessary distinction, and such the nice union, that subsist between those two opposite and yet harmonizing, exploded and yet capital doctrines of the Gospel, which we call *free grace* and *free will*. To demonstrate that their due conjunction in our hearts forms the spiritual marriage of *faith*, and gives birth to all good works, I have ventured upon the construction of "the Scales," which the reader will find in these pages. If their composition is human, their materials are Divine; for they consist of plain scriptures, chiefly placed under two heads of doctrine, which, for their justness and importance, may be called the weights of the sanctuary. (1.) *Our salvation is of God.* (2.) *Our damnation is of ourselves.* The *first* of these propositions is inseparably connected with the doctrine of *free grace;* nor can the *second* stand but upon the doctrine of *free will:* two doctrines these which the moralists and the Solifidians have hitherto thought incompatible; and about which some of them have contended with the utmost acrimony of temper and language.

Even men of piety have rashly entered the lists, some against free grace, others against free will; warmly opposing what they should have mutually defended. The cause of their misunderstanding is very singular. They are good men upon the whole, therefore they can never oppose truth *as truth:* and as they are not destitute of charity, they cannot quarrel merely for quarreling's sake. Whence then springs their continual contest? Is it not from gross partiality, excessive jealousy, wilful inattention, and glaring prejudice? They will not look Gospel truth full in the face: they are determined to stand on either side of her, and by that means seldom see above the half of her beauty.

But all the Protestants are not so partial: for while the Solifidians gaze upon the *side face* of Christianity on the *right* hand, and the moralists on the *left;* her unprejudiced lovers, humbly sitting at her feet, and beholding her in full, admire the exquisite proportion of *all* her features; an advantage this which the opposite rivals can never have in their present unfavourable position. Therefore, while a mere moralist considers as "enthusiastic rant," the doctrine of free grace extolled by the Solifidians; and while a bound- willer brands as "dreadful heresy," the doctrine of free will espoused by the moralists; an unprejudiced Christian equally embraces the pretended "enthusiasm" of the one, and the imaginary "heresy" of the other; being persuaded, that the different sentiments of those partial contenders for free grace and free will are only the opposite truths which form the *complete* beauty of genuine Protestantism.

This contrary mistake of the moralists, and of the Solifidians, is attended with the most fatal consequences; for, as they receive only one part of the truth, they think to do God service by attacking the other, which they rashly take for a dangerous error; and, so far as the influence of their contrary misconception reaches, the whole truth is destroyed. Primitive Christianity, in their busy hands, seems to be in as much danger of losing her capital doctrines, as the elderly man in the fable was of losing his hair between his two wives: one was young, and could not bear his partly silvered locks; the other, who was old, wanted him to be altogether as gray as herself. Both accordingly fell to work; and in a little time the young wife had so plucked out his white hairs, and the old woman his black ones, that he remained absolutely bald.

Will you see their ridiculous conduct exemplified in the religious world? Consider *Honestus*, the sedate moralist; and *Zelotes*, the warm Solifidian. HONESTUS, who values the ten commandments far above the three creeds, seldom dwells upon Christ's redeeming love and atoning blood. Out of the church he rarely mentions the inspiration of God's Spirit, or the comforts of the Holy Ghost; and it is well if he does not think that our addresses to the Mediator are remains of Papistical idolatry. He piques himself much upon his honesty; and hoping that his *free will*, best endeavours, and good works, are almost sufficient to save him, he leaves the doctrine of a sinner's justification by faith to Zelotes and Paul. ZELOTES flies to the other extreme. His creed is all; and, so far as decency permits, he insinuates that believers may break the first and second commandment with Solomon, the third with Peter, the fifth with Absalom, the sixth and seventh with David, the eighth with Onesimus, and the two last with Ananias and Sapphira; in short, that they may go any length in sin without endangering in the least their title to a crown of glory. He thinks that the contrary doctrine is rank popery. Some of his favourite topics are: (1.) *God's unconditional election of some to finished salvation;* an election this which necessarily includes *God's unconditional appointment of the rest of mankind to finished damnation!* (2.) *An unchangeable fondness of God, and a partial atonement of Christ, for a comparatively small number of the children of men;* a fondness and an atonement these, which include also *an unchangeable wrath against, and an absolute reprobation of all the world beside.* And, (3.) *A zealous decrying of free will and sincere obedience,* under the specious pretence of exalting

Creeds and Scripture Scales

Christ and free grace. As for the *justification of a* BELIEVER *by works and not by faith only*, he leaves it to Honestus, Bellarmine, and St. James.

If the sum of Christ's religion is, *Cordially believe, and sincerely obey;* and if Honestus makes almost nothing of *saving faith*, while Zelotes makes next to nothing of *sincere obedience*, is it not evident that between them both genuine Protestantism is almost destroyed? If I may compare Christianity to the woman that St. John saw in one of his visions; how barbarously is she used by those two partial lovers! Both pretend to have the greatest regard for her: both have publicly espoused her: both perhaps equally recommend her from the pulpit: but, alas! both, though without any bad design, use her with the greatest unkindness; for while Honestus divests her of her peculiar *doctrines and mysteries*, Zelotes robs her of her peculiar precepts and sanctions. Thus the one (if I may carry the allegory so far) puts out her right, and the other her left eye: the one stabs her in the right side, and the other in the left: and this they do upon a supposition that as soon as all their dreadful operations shall be performed, Christianity will shine in the perfection of her native beauty.

While the heavenly woman, mutilated by those partial lovers, lies thus bleeding and deformed in the midst of spiritual Egypt, LORENZO casts his eyes upon her; and starting back at the sight, he wisely protests that he cannot embrace so deformed a religion: and it is well if, in this critical moment, a painted Jezebel, who courts his affections, does not ensnare his unwary soul. She calls herself *Natural Religion*, but her right name is *Skepticism* in infancy, *Infidelity* in youth, *Fatalism* in ripe years, and *Abaddon* in old age. Guilty, thrice guilty will Honestus and Zelotes prove, if they continue to drive the hesitating youth into the arms of that syren, by continuing to render Christianity monstrous in his eyes!

O mistaken men of God, before you have caused Lorenzo's ruin, be persuaded to review your doctrine; nor refuse to weigh it in the balance of the sanctuary. If fine gold loses nothing in the fiercest fire, what can your sentiments lose in my Scripture Scales? Let *cheats* dread to have their weights tried by the royal standard; but do not *you* start from the trial. I acknowledge your honesty beforehand. If your weights should prove false, your reputation is safe. My readers will do you justice; they will perceive that, far from having had any intention to deceive others, you yourselves have been the dupes of your own prejudice; thus will your mistakes be found out to your profit, and not to your shame.

The error of Honestus and that of Zelotes being opposite, so must be their method of using the Scripture Scales. Honestus, who inclines to the neglect of Christ, and to the contempt of free grace, must weigh himself against the scriptures which follow No. I, and batter down Pharisaic dotages; that is, he must read those scriptures over with attention, asking his conscience if he honestly insists upon them as the *primary* truths of Christianity; and if he may not rank with modern Pharisees, so far as he opposes or despises those scriptures. On the other hand, Zelotes, who leans to the disregard of sincere obedience, good works, and free will, must weigh himself against No. II, under which he will find the scriptures that oppose the Antinomian delusion, confessing that, so far as he sets them aside, he clips away the *secondary* truths of the Gospel, mangles Bible Christianity, and strengthens the hands of immoral gospellers and flagitious Antinomians.

If Zelotes and Honestus will not weigh their doctrine in the Scripture Scales, *Candidus* will do it for them. Prejudice has not yet captivated him, nor is he unacquainted with Church history. He believes that the pope himself is not infallible. He knows all that glitters as Gospel, is not Gospel gold. He remembers, that for several hundred years the worship of a consecrated wafer was esteemed a capital part of "orthodoxy" all England over; and he has observed, that the cautions of my motto are particularly given with respect to those who say, *I am Christ,* that is, "I represent him as his Gospel minister, his faithful ambassador; I thank God that I am not like that Methodist ranter, or that dreadful heretic." In a word, Candidus is modest enough not to think any part of Scripture beneath his notice; and he is not such a bigot as to suppose it a crime to *compare spiritual things with spiritual;* and to make the candle of truth burn brighter, by snuffing away the black excrescence of error.

To you, therefore, Candidus, I particularly dedicate my Scripture Scales. Despise them not at a time when the Gospel gold, the coin current in the Church, is far lighter in proportion than the material gold was last year in these kingdoms; — at a time when the Antinomians have so filed away the arms of the King of kings, that it is hard to distinguish whether they are quartered with *a dove, a goose, or a hawk; a lamb, a lion, or a goat;* — at a time when the Solifidians have so clipped the royal motto, that many, instead of "holiness," inadvertently read "filthiness unto the Lord;" — at a time when, on the other hand, Pharisaic moralists make it their business so to deface the head of the King of saints on the Gospel coin, that you might take it for the head of Seneca, or that of M. Antonine; — at a time when dealers in orthodoxy publicly present you with one half of the golden truth, which they want to pass for the whole, — at a time when some openly assert, that dung is gold — that impure doctrines are the pure Gospel; and that gold is "dung" — that good works are "dross;" — at such a time, I say, stand upon your guard, Candidus. Beware of men; beware of me; nor use my Scales till you have tried them by the Old and New Testament, those balances of the sanctuary, which you have at home. But if, upon close examination, you find that they differ chiefly in cheapness, size, and conveniency, adopt the invention; and when you are going to read a religious book, or to hear a sermon, imitate the prudent trader, who goes to receive money; take your scales, and use them according to the following directions: —

1. Keep them even. Let not the strings of your entangled affections for this or that preacher, or your attachment to one or another party, give a hasty preponderance to either scale. Fairly suspend your judgment, till it honestly turn by the full weight of truth and evidence. Consider that *the Lord is a God of knowledge, by whom actions are weighed;* and call upon him for impartiality; remembering that *with what measure ye mete, it shall be measured to you again.*

2. Please to observe, that preaching the doctrines which follow No. I. does not prove that a minister is an *Antinomian,* any more than preaching the doctrines which follow No. II, proves that he is a *Pharisee;* but preaching them in such a manner as directly or indirectly attacks, opposes, or explains away the doctrines in the other scale; in open defiance of one half of the scriptures, which represent free grace and holy free will as the *flux* and *reflux* of Divine grace, by which alone the city of God flourishes, and through which only her commerce with heaven can be profitably carried on. If, therefore, you hear a man say, "I was by nature a child of wrath, and *by practice* the chief of sinners: not by works of righteousness which I have done, but by grace I am saved," &c, set him not down for a son of voluntary humility. And if he cries out, "I have lived in all good conscience unto this day, — touching the

righteousness which is in the law, I am blameless: be followers of me: work out your own salvation: in so doing you shall save yourself," &c, do not rank him with the barefaced sons of pride: but look into both scales; and if you find that he honestly uses ALL the weights of the sanctuary; and does the two Gospel axioms justice, as St. Paul, acknowledge him *a workman who needeth not to be ashamed, rightly dividing the word of truth.*

3. Consider times, persons, places, circumstances, and subjects; nor imitate the unreasonable scrupulosity of the man who will make no more allowance for the fair wear of a good old guinea, than for the felonious diminishing of the coin that was delivered last week at the mint. Do not *make a man an offender for a word*, or a phrase; no, not for such unscriptural phrases as "the *imputed* righteousness of Christ," and "*sinless*" perfection." Nor forget, that, although error is never to be propagated, yet all the branches of truth can never be displayed at once; and grant a man time to unfold his sentiments before you accuse him of countenancing Pharisaic or Antinomian dotages: otherwise you might charge St. Paul with Solifidianism, and Christ himself with Pharisaical errors.

4. Above all, remember that, although you have all orthodoxy and all faith, you are nothing without humility and love: therefore, when you weigh a preacher's doctrine, throw into his scale two or three grains of *the charity that is not puffed up, thinketh no evil, and hopeth all things* consistently with Scripture and reason. If you neglect this caution, you will slide into the severity of a lordly inquisitor; or at least into the implicit faith of a tame Papist: and the moment this is the case, throwing one scale away, and casting all your weights into the other, you will become a blind follower of the first warm preacher that shall hit your fancy, work upon your passions, foment your prejudices, tickle your itching ears, or encourage your party spirit; whether he be Honestus or Gallio, Elymas or Zelotes.

SECTION II.

Containing some general observations upon God's free grace and our personal free will, which are represented as the original causes of salvation and damnation.

CICERO, heathen as he was, asserted "that there is no great," and consequently no good "man," (*sine aliquo afflatu divino,*)" without some influence from the Deity." This influence our Church calls *inspiration*: ("Cleanse the thoughts of our hearts by the inspiration of thy Holy Spirit:") and St. Paul calls it *grace*, giving that name sometimes to the *fountain* of Divine goodness, and sometimes to the innumerable *streams* which flow from that eternal fountain. A man must then be darker than a thoughtful heathen, and as blind as an Atheist, if he absolutely denies the existence of Divine *grace*. And, on the other hand, if we deny that there is in man *a power to will* or *to choose*, the words *I will, I choose, I will not, I refuse*, which are in every body's mouth, will prove us perverse. Now, if there is such a thing as *grace* in God, and *will* or *power of choosing* in man; both that grace and that will are free. The nature of the thing, and the well known meaning of the words, imply as much; a bounty, which we are *obliged* to bestow, hardly deserving the name of grace or favour; and a choice, to which we are *forced*, — a choice, which is not accompanied with an *alternative*, — deserving the name of *necessity* or *compulsion* better than that of *will, choice, or liberty*.

Again: are not *God's grace* and *man's will* perpetually mentioned, or alluded to by the sacred writers? Nay, does not Honestus himself sometimes indirectly set his seal to the doctrine of free grace, when he implores Divine mercy at the foot of the throne of grace? And warmly as Zelotes exclaims against the doctrine of free will, does he not frequently grant that there is such a thing as choice, liberty, or free will, in the world? And if there be, is not this *choice, liberty,* or *free will,* the reverse of *necessity,* as well as of *unwillingness?* If I freely choose to blow my brains out, is it not evident that I have a liberty not to commit that crime, as well as a *willingness* to do it? Would not Zelotes expose his good sense by seriously asserting that if he were in prison, a willingness to continue there would make him free; unless, together with that *willingness,* he had *a power* to go out if he pleased? And is it right in him to impose the doctrine of necessity upon the simple, by playing upon the double meaning of the word *free?* I beg leave to explain this a little more.

According to the full meaning of the word *free,* can it be said with any propriety that Judas went *freely* to hell, if he never had power to go to heaven? Or that David went *freely* to heaven, if he was always hindered by an *absolute, irresistible* decree from going to hell? And, alluding to mechanical freedom, I ask, Was the motion of those scales ever free, which never were as free to ascend as to descend? Does not experience convince us, that, when one scale is kept from freely descending, the opposite scale is by the same means kept from ascending freely? Is it not evident, from the same rational principles, that no sinner can freely "choose death in the error of his ways," who has not power to "choose life;" a free choice of death necessarily implying a free refusal of life, and a free choice of life necessarily supposing a free refusal of death, in a state of temptation and probation? And is not this doctrine perfectly agreeable to such scriptures as these: "He shall know to refuse the evil and choose the good. *Choose* whom you will serve. Because ye *refused,* &c, and *did not choose* the fear of the Lord, &c; therefore shall they eat the fruit of *their own way,* and be filled with *their own devices?"*

Upon the preceding observations, seconded by the arguments which shall follow; — upon the consent of all judicious and good men, who, sooner or later, grant that there are such things as God's grace and man's unnecessitated choice; and consequently such things as free grace and free will in the moral world; — upon the repeated testimonies of the most pious Christians of all denominations, who agree that we ought to "give God the glory" of our salvation, and to *keep to ourselves the blame* of our damnation; and upon almost numberless declarations of the Scriptures, I rest these two propositions, which, if I mistake not, deserve the name of GOSPEL AXIOMS: (1.) Our salvation is ORIGINALLY of God's FREE GRACE. (2.) Our damnation is ORIGINALLY of our own FREE WILL.

HONESTUS, who believes in general that the Bible is true, cannot decently oppose the first axiom; for according to the Scriptures, God's free grace gave Christ freely *for* us, and *to* us: *for* us, that he might "be a propitiation for the sins of the whole world:" and *to* us, that by "the light which enlightens every man that comes into the world," the strong propensity to evil which we had contracted by the fall of Adam might be counterbalanced; and that, by "the saving grace of God, which has appeared to all men," we might, while the day of salvation lasts, be blessed with a gentle bias to good, to counteract our native bias to evil; and be excited by internal helps, external calls, and gracious opportunities, to resist our evil inclinations, to follow the bias of Divine grace, and to "work out our own salvation with fear and trembling," in due subordination to the Saviour and his grace.

Nor can ZELOTES, who professes a peculiar regard for God's glory, reject the second Gospel axiom with any decency: for if our own free will makes us freely and unnecessarily "neglect so great salvation" as Christ *initially* imparts to us, and offers *eternally* to bestow upon us on the gracious terms of the Gospel; is it not ridiculous to exculpate us, by charging either God or Adam, or both together, with our damnation? And do we not cast the most horrible reflection upon "the Judge of all the earth, and the Father of mercies," if we suppose that he "has appointed a day to judge the world in righteousness," and sentence to the gnawings of a worm that dieth not, and to the preyings of a fire that is not quenched, numberless myriads of his poor creatures, merely for *wanting* a faith which he determined they should never have; or for doing what they could no more help to do, than a pound can help weighing sixteen ounces?

Impartially read any one book in the Bible, and you will find that it establishes the truth of the two following propositions: —

I.

God hath *freely* done great things *for* man; and the still greater things which he *freely* does for believers, and the mercy with which he daily crowns them, justly entitle him to all the honour of their salvation; so far as that honour is worthy of the PRIMITIVE Parent of good, and FIRST CAUSE of all our blessings

II.

He *wisely* looks for some return *from* man; and the little things which obstinate unbelievers refuse to do, and which God's preventing grace gives them ability to perform, justly entitle them to all the shame of their damnation. Therefore, although their *temporal* misery is originally from Adam, yet their *eternal* ruin is originally from themselves.

The first of these propositions extols God's *mercy*, and the *second* clears his *justice;* while both together display his *truth* and *holiness.* According to the doctrine of free grace, Christ is a compassionate Saviour; according to that of free will, he is a righteous Judge. By the first his rewards are gracious; by the second his punishments are just. By the first the mouths of the blessed in heaven are opened to sing deserved hallelujahs to God and the Lamb; and by the second the mouths of the damned in hell are kept from uttering *deserved** blasphemies against God and his Christ.

---

* I do not mean that any blasphemy against God *is deserved;* but that, according to all our ideas of justice, this would be the case, if the doctrine of free will were false. For supposing men and angels are not endued with free agency, is it not evident that they are mere instruments in the hand of a superior, irresistible Agent, who works wickedness in and by them, agreeable to this unguarded proposition of Elisha Coles: "*All things* were present with God from eternity; and his decree *the cause* of their *after existence?*" And does not reason cry aloud, that such an almighty Agent is more culpable than his overpowered, or passive tools? Can Zelotes himself say that a highwayman does not deserve hanging more than the pistol which he fires, and the horse

According to the first, God remains the genuine Parent of good; and according to the second, devils and apostate men are still the genuine authors of evil. If you explode the first of those propositions, you admit Pharisaic dotages and self-exalting pride; if you reject the second; you set up Antinomian delusions, and voluntary humility: but if you receive them both, you avoid the contrary mistakes of Honestus and Zelotes, and consistently hold the Scriptural doctrines of faith and works, — free grace and free will, — Divine mercy and Divine justice, — a sinner's impotence and a saint's faithfulness.

Read the Scriptures in the light which beams forth from those two capital truths; and that precious book will in some places appear to you almost new. You will at least see a beautiful agreement between a variety of texts that are irreconcilable upon the narrow, partial schemes of the Pharisees and of the Antinomians. Permit me to give you a specimen of it by presenting you with my *Scales;* that is, by placing in one point of view a number of opposite truths which make one beautiful whole, according to the doctrine of the two Gospel axioms. And may the Father of lights so bless the *primary* truths to Honestus, that he may receive the doctrine of free grace; and the *secondary* ones to Zelotes, that he may espouse the doctrine of free will! So shall those inveterate contenders be happily reconciled to moderation, to the whole Gospel, and to one another.

SECTION III.

Containing, (1.) The golden beam of the Scripture Scales. (2.) The chains by which they are suspended. And, (3.) A rational account of the origin of evil.

SCRIPTURAL PRINCIPLES,
MAKING THE BEAM OF THE SCRIPTURAL SCALES.

I.
There is a God, that is, a wise, good, and *just Governor* of his creatures.

It was a design highly worthy of a wise Creator to place mankind in a

II.
There are men, that is, rational creatures, capable of being *morally governed.*

Our wise Creator has actually executed that design. To have done

which he rides when he commits murder? What an immense field does the doctrine of *bound will* open in hell for the most execrable blasphemies! The Lord forgive its supporters, for they know not what they do! The Gospel leaves even heathen unbelievers *without excuse,* Romans 1:20; but the modern "doctrines of grace" furnish all sorts of infidels with the best excuses in the world. "God's predestination caused Adam's sin and his own; and God's decree kept Christ from dying for, and his Spirit from sincerely striving with them." As these necessary consequences of Calvinism encourage "Mr. Fulsome" to sin here; so (if his doctrines of grace were true) they would comfort him in hell hereafter.

state of earthly bliss, and to put their loyalty to the trial, that he might graciously reward the obedient, and justly punish the rebellious.

The Lord is LOVING to every man, and his *mercy* is over all his works, Psalm 145:9.

Grace superabounded, when God, in the midst of wrath remembering mercy, promised a SAVIOUR to Adam personally, and to us seminally, Romans 5:20; Genesis 3:15.

Not as the offence, so also is the *free gift*. For if through the offence of one many be dead; much more the grace of God and the gift by grace, which is by Jesus Christ, hath abounded unto MANY, Romans 5:15.

By man came the *resurrection* of the dead — for in Christ shall all be made alive.

By the *obedience* of one shall many be made *righteous*, Romans 5:19.

That *grace* might reign, through righteousness, unto eternal *life* by Jesus Christ our Lord, Romans 5:21.

Therefore, &c, by the *righteousness* of one, the *free gift* came upon all men to justification of life, Romans 5:21.

The Lord is long suffering to us-ward, not willing that *any* should perish, but that *all* should come to repentance, 2 Peter 3:9.

Hence it follows, that,

1. God's *free grace gave Christ* to atone for man, and initially gives the Spirit of grace to sanctify man.

To guard the doctrine of grace, Divine justice appointed that a certain sin, called "a doing despite to the Spirit of grace," and "a sinning against the Holy Ghost," or a wilful persisting in disobedient unbelief to the end of the day of salvation, should be emphatically *the sin unto* eternal *death*;

otherwise would have been inconsistent with his *distributive justice,* an attribute as *essential* to him as goodness, knowledge, or power.

The Lord is RIGHTEOUS to every man, and his *justice* is over all his works.

Sin abounded, when the first man personally fell by the wrong use of his free will, and caused us to FALL in him seminally, Romans 5:20; Genesis 3:6.

Death reigned from Adam. By one man sin entered into the world, and death by sin; and so death passed upon ALL MEN, for that ALL have sinned, Romans 5:12, 14.

By man came *death* — for in Adam all die, 1 Corinthians 15:21, 22.

By one man's *disobedience* many were made *sinners*, Romans 5:19.

As *sin* hath reigned [through righteousness] unto *death*, [by Adam,] Romans 5:21.

Even so, by the *offence* of one, *judgment* came upon all men to condemnation. (Ibid.)

Why will ye die, O house of Israel? For I have no pleasure in the death of him that dieth; wherefore *turn* yourselves, and live ye, Ezekiel 18:31, 32.

Hence it follows, that,

2. Man's *free will*, helped by the Spirit of grace, *may receive Christ* implicitly as "the light of men," or explicitly as "the Saviour of the world."

Some men commit that sin. For some men "tread under foot the Son of God, count the blood of the covenant, wherewith they were sanctified, an unholy thing, do despite to the Spirit of grace, — and draw back unto *perdition*," Hebrews 10:29, 39. "Falling from their own steadfastness, and that those who commit it, should be *the sons of perdition*: see Matthew 12:32; Mark 3:29; Luke 12:10; 1 John 5:16; John 17:12.

and even denying the Lord that bought them, they bring upon themselves swift *destruction*, (2 Peter 2:1,) and *perish* in the gainsaying of Core," Jude 1:11.

THREE PAIR OF GOSPEL AXIOMS,

Which may be considered as GOLDEN CHAINS, *by which the Scripture Scales hang on their beam.*

I.

I. Every obedient believer's *salvation* is originally of God's free grace.

II. God's free grace is always the first cause of what is good.

III. When God's *free grace* has begun to work moral GOOD, man may faithfully follow him by believing, ceasing to do evil, and working righteousness, according to his light and talent.

Thus is God the WISE *rewarder* of them that diligently seek him, according to these words of the apostle: — "God, at the revelation of his *righteous* judgment, will render to every man according to his deeds; eternal life to them who by patient continuance in well doing seek for glory. Seeing it is a *righteous* thing with God to *recompense* rest to them who are troubled" for his sake, to give them "a crown of righteousness" as a *righteous* Judge, and to make them "walk with Christ in white, because they are *worthy*," (in a gracious and evangelical sense.

II.

I. Every unbeliever's *damnation* is originally of his own personal free will.

II. Man's free will is always the f irst cause of what is evil.

III. When man's *free will* has begun to work moral EVIL, God may justly follow him by withdrawing his slighted grace, revealing his deserved wrath, and working natural evil.

Thus is God the RIGHTEOUS *punisher* of them that obstinately neglect him, according to such scriptures as these: "Shall not the Judge of all the earth do right? Ye say, *The way of the Lord is not equal*: hear now, O ye house of Israel, Is not my way equal? I will judge you every one after his way. Is God unrighteous, who taketh vengeance? God forbid! How then shall God judge the world? Thou art *righteous*, O Lord, &c, because thou hast *judged* thus. Thou hast given them blood to drink, for they are *worthy*," (in a strict and legal sense.)

Hence it appears, that God's design in the three grand economies of man's creation, redemption, and sanctification, is to display the riches of his FREE GRACE AND DISTRIBUTIVE JUSTICE, by showing himself the bounteous *Author of every good gift*, and by *graciously* rewarding the worthy: while he *justly* punishes the unworthy according to their works, agreeably to these awful words of Christ and his prophets: "For judgment I am come into this world. The Lord hath made all things for himself; yea, even the [men who to the last will remain] wicked, for the day of evil. Because he hath appointed a day in which he will judge the world in righteousness;" and to all the wicked that day will be *evil, and terrible:* "For behold, the day cometh," says the Lord, "that shall burn as an oven; and all that do wickedly shall be as stubble; and the day that cometh shall burn them up, says the Lord of hosts. But the righteous shall rejoice when he seeth the vengeance: so that a man shall say, *Verily there is a* REWARD *for the righteous! Doubtless there is a God that* JUDGETH THE EARTH!"

Upon this rational and Scriptural plan, may we not solve a difficulty that has perplexed all the philosophers in the world? "How can you," say they, "reasonably account for the *origin of evil,* without bearing hard upon God's infinite goodness, power, or knowledge? How can you make appear, not only that a good God *could* create a world, where evil now exists in ten thousand forms; but also, that it was highly expedient he should create such a world rather than any other?"

ANSWER. — When it pleased God to create a world, his wisdom obliged him to create upon the plan that was most worthy of him. Such a plan was undoubtedly that which agreed best with all the Divine perfections taken together. Wisdom and power absolutely required that it should be a world of rational, as well as of irrational creatures; of free, as well as of necessary agents; such a world displaying far better what St. Paul calls ωολυποικιλος σοφια, "the multifarious, variegated wisdom of God," as well as his infinite power in making, ruling, and overruling various orders of beings.

It could not be. expected that myriads of free agents, who necessarily fell short of absolute perfection, would *all* behave alike. Here God's goodness demanded that those who behaved well should be rewarded; his sovereignty insisted that those who behaved ill should be punished; and his distributive justice and equity required that those who made the best use of their talents should be entitled to the highest rewards; while those who abused Divine favours most should have the severest punishments; mercy reserving to itself the right of raising rewards and of alleviating punishments, in a way suited to the honour of all the other Divine attributes.

This being granted, (and I do not see how any man of reason and piety can deny it,) it evidently follows, (1.) That a world, in which various orders of free, as well as of necessary agents are admitted, is most perfect. (2.) That this world, having been formed upon such a wise plan, was the most perfect that could possibly be created. (3.) That, in the very nature of things, evil *may*, although there is no necessity it *should*, enter into such a world; else it could not be a world of free agents who are candidates for rewards offered by distributive justice. (4.) That the blemishes and disorders of the natural world are only penal consequences of the disobedience of free agents. And (5.) That, from such penal disorders we may indeed conclude that man has abused free will, but not that God deals in free wrath. Only admit, therefore, the free will of rationals, and you cannot but fall in love with our Creator's plan; dark and horrid as it appears when it is viewed through the smoked glass of the fatalist, the Manichee, or the rigid Predestinarian.

SECTION IV.

Containing, (1.) An observation upon the terms of the covenants; and, (2.) A balanced specimen of the anti-Pharisaic Gospel, displaying Christ's glory in the first scale; and of the anti-Solifidian Gospel, setting forth the glory of evangelical obedience in the second scale.

To reconcile the opposite parts of the Scriptures, let us remember that God has made two covenants with man; *the covenant of justice,* and *the covenant of grace.* The first requires uninterrupted obedience to the law of paradisiacal innocence. The second enjoins repentance, faith, and humble obedience to all those Gospel precepts, which form what David calls *the law of the Lord;* St. Paul, *the law of Christ;* St. James, *the law of liberty;* and what our Lord calls *my sayings, — my commandments, &c.*

Being conceived in sin since the fall, and having all our powers enfeebled, we cannot personally keep the first covenant: therefore as the first Adam broke it for us, Christ, "the second Adam, the Lord from heaven," graciously came to make the law of innocence honourable, by keeping it for us, and to give us "power" to keep his own "law of liberty," that is, to repent, believe, and obey for ourselves. Therefore, with respect to the law of the first covenant, Christ alone is, and must be, our foundation, our righteousness, our way, our door, our glory, and all our salvation.

But with respect to the second covenant, the case is very different: for this covenant, and its law of liberty, requiring of us personal repentance and its fruits, — personal faith and its works, — all which together make up evangelical obedience, or "the obedience of faith;" it is evident, that, according to the requirements of the covenant of grace, our "obedience of faith" is (in due subordination to Christ) our righteousness, our narrow way, our strait gate, our glory, and our salvation: just as a farmer's care, labour, and industry are, in due subordination to the blessings of Divine Providence, the causes of his plentiful crops.

If you do not lose sight of this distinction; — if you consider that our salvation or damnation have each *two causes,* the second of which never operates but in subordination to the first; — if you observe, that the FIRST cause of our eternal salvation is God's *free grace* in making, and *faithfulness* in keeping through Christ his Gospel promises to all sinners, who freely submit to the terms of the Gospel; and that consequently the SECOND cause of that salvation is our own prevented *free will,* submitting to the obedience of faith, through the helps that Christ affords us; — if, on the other hand, you take notice, that the FIRST cause of our eternal damnation is always our own *free will,* doing despite to the Spirit of grace; and that the SECOND cause of it is God's *justice* in denouncing, and his faithfulness in executing, by Christ, his awful threatenings against all that persist in unbelief to the end of their day of initial salvation, generally called "the day of grace;" — if you consider these things, I say, you will see, that all the scriptures which compose my Scales, and some hundreds more, which I omit for brevity's sake, agree as perfectly as the different parts of a good piece of music.

We now and then find, it is true, a *solo* in the Bible; I mean a passage that displays *only* the powerful voice of free grace, or of free will. Hence Zelotes and Honestus conclude that there is no harmony, but in the single part of the truth which they admire; supposing that the accents of free grace and free will, justly mixed together, form an enthusiastical or heretical noise, and not an evangelical, Divine concert. Thus much by way of introduction.

FIRST SCALE.

Scriptures that display the glory of CHRIST, the importance of *primary causes*, the excellence of *original merit*, and the power of *free grace*.

Jesus saith unto him, I am the way, &c; no man cometh to the Father, but by me. I am the door; by me if any man enter in he shall be saved, John 14:6; 10:9.

Other foundation can no man lay, than that is laid, which is *Jesus Christ.* I lay in Sion a chief corner stone, &c. He that believeth on him shall not be confounded, 1 Corinthians 3:11; 2 Peter 2:6.

God forbid that I should *glory.* save in the cross of CHRIST. He that glorieth, let him glory in the Lord, Galatians 6:14; 1 Corinthians 1:31.

My soul shall be *joyful* in MY GOD, for he hath clothed me with the garments of salvation, Isaiah 61:10. My spirit hath *rejoiced* in God my Saviour, Luke 1:47.

Put ye on *the Lord Jesus Christ.* He hath covered me with the robe of righteousness, as a bride adorneth herself with her jewels, Romans 13:14; Isaiah 61:10.

Christ is made unto us of God righteousness, 1 Corinthians 1:30.

Neither is there salvation in any other; for there is none other name [or person] under heaven whereby we must be *saved,* Acts 4:12.

Christ was once offered to bear the sins of many, Hebrews 9:28.

Behold the Lamb of God that *taketh away* the sin of the world, John 1:29.

SECOND SCALE.

Scriptures that display the glory of OBEDIENCE, the importance of *secondary causes*, the excellence of *derived worthiness*, and the power of *free will*.

Christ, in his sermon upon the mount, strongly recommends the obedience of faith, as the strait gate, and the narrow way, which lead unto life, Matthew 7:13.

Not laying again the foundation of *repentance.* Charge the rich that they do good, &c, laying up in store for themselves a good foundation against the time to come, Hebrews 6:1; 1 Timothy 6:17.

Let every man prove his own work, and then shall he have καυχημα, *glorying* in HIMSELF alone, and not in another, Galatians 6:4. [*It is the same word in the original.*]

This is our *rejoicing*, the testimony of *our conscience*, that in simplicity and GODLY SINCERITY, &c, we have had our conversation in the world, and to youward, 2 Corinthians 1:12.

I caused the widow's heart to sing for joy. I put on *righteousness* and it covered me; my judgment was a robe and a diadem. I was eyes to the blind, &c, Job 29:14, 15.

The righteousness of the righteous shall be upon him, and the wickedness of the wicked shall be upon him, Ezekiel 18:20.

Take heed to thyself and to thy doctrine, &c, for in *doing* this thou shalt both *save* thyself and them that hear thee, 1 Timothy 4:16.

Let every man prove his own work, for every man shall bear his own burden, Galatians 4:4, 5.

Put away the evil of your doings from before mine eyes, Isaiah 1:16.

Look unto *me*, Isaiah 45:22.

Consider the High Priest of our profession, *Jesus Christ*, Hebrews 3:1.

Jesus was made a surety of a better testament, Hebrews 7:22. [Note: it is not said that *Jesus is the surety of disobedient believers; but of that testament which cuts off the entail of their heavenly inheritance.* See Ephesians 5:5.]

Who his own self *bare our sins* in his own body on the tree.

God has made him [Christ] to be sin *for us*, who knew no sin, that we might be made the righteousness of God in him, 2 Corinthians 5:21.

By *his knowledge* shall my righteous servant [Christ] justify many, Isaiah 53:11.

Preach the GOSPEL to every creature — and *forgiveness* of sins in [my] name, Mark xvi; Luke 24:47.

Saul *preached* CHRIST in the synagogues; we preach not ourselves, but CHRIST JESUS the Lord, Acts 9:20; 2 Corinthians 4:5.

We preach Christ crucified, unto the Jews a stumbling block, and unto the Greeks foolishness; but unto them that are called [and obey the call] Christ the power of God, and the wisdom of God. For I determined not to know any thing among you [Corinthians] save Jesus Christ, and him crucified, 1 Corinthians 1:23, 24; 2:2.

Preaching *peace* by *Jesus Christ*, he is Lord of all — the Prince of Peace, Acts 10:36; Isaiah 9:6.

He that *hath the Son* hath life; and he that hath not the Son of God, *hath not life*, 1 John 5:12.

He that *acknowledgeth* the Son, hath the Father also, 1 John 2:23.

Christ is our *life*, Colossians 3:4.

Look to *yourselves*, John 8.

Consider *thyself* — let us consider *one another*, Galatians 6:1; Hebrews 10:24.

The Lord is our Judge, the Lord is our Lawgiver, the Lord is our King; he will save us; [consistently with those glorious titles,] Isaiah 33:22.

That we being *dead to sin* should live unto righteousness, 1 Peter 2:24.

Be not deceived: God is not mocked: for *whatsoever* a man *soweth, that* shall he also *reap.* For he that soweth to his flesh, shall, &c, reap destruction, Galatians 6:7, 8.

He judged the cause of the poor and needy, then it was well with him. Was not this *to know me?* saith the Lord, Jeremiah 12:16.

Teaching them to *observe all things* whatsoever I have *commanded* you, Matthew 28:20.

As he *reasoned* of righteousness, [or JUSTICE,] TEMPERANCE, and the JUDGMENT to come, Felix trembled, Acts 24:25.

And yet when the apostle exhorts these very Corinthians to relieve the poor, he uses a variety of motives beside that of Christ's cross. Other churches had abundantly given. He had boasted of their forwardness. Their charity would make others praise God, and pray for them. He that soweth bountifully shall reap bountifully, &c, 2 Corinthians 8:2; 9:3, 6, 12, 14.

There is no *peace* to the wicked; he that will love *life*, &c, let him *do good,* seek *peace*, and pursue it, Isaiah 57:21; Psalm 34:14.

Beloved, &c, he that *doeth good* is of God: he that doeth evil *hath not seen* God, 3 John 1:11.

Whosoever *transgresseth* hath not God, 2 John 1:9.

To be spiritually minded is *life*,

JESUS CHRIST, who is *our hope*, 1 Timothy 1:1.

I have laid help upon one that is mighty. Without me ye can do *nothing*, Psalm 89:19; John 15:5.

Neither is he that planteth *any thing*, [comparatively,] &c, but God that giveth the increase, 1 Corinthians 3:7.

Yet not I [*alone*, not I *first*,] but the *grace* of God which was with me, 1 Corinthians 15:10.

Call *no man* your *father* upon earth; for one is your Father, who is in heaven, Matthew 23:9.

Christ is made unto us of God *wisdom*, 1 Corinthians 1:30.

God *only wise*, Jude 1:25.

Why callest thou me *good?* There is none *good* but one, that is GOD, Matthew 9:17.

THOU ART WORTHY, O Lord, to receive glory and honour, Revelation 4:11.

I am the light of the world, John 8:12.

If God be for us, *who* can be against us? *Who* is he that condemneth? It is Christ that died, yea, rather that is risen again, who is even at the right hand of God, who also maketh intercession for us, Romans 8:31, 34.

If any man sin, we have an *Advocate* with the Father, JESUS CHRIST the righteous, 1 John 2:1.

CHRIST ever liveth to make *intercession* for them that come unto God by him, Hebrews 7:25.

The Son of man hath power on earth

Romans 8:6.

What is *our hope?* &c. Are not even YE [Thessalonians?] 1 Thessalonians 2:19.

I [Paul] can do *all things* through Christ, who strengtheneth me, Philippians 4:13.

We are *labourers* together *with God*. As a wise master builder I have laid the foundation, 1 Corinthians 3:9, 10.

I [Paul] *laboured* more abundantly than they all [the apostles,] 1 Corinthians 15:10.

Ye have not many *fathers*, for in Christ Jesus I *have begotten* you through the Gospel, 1 Corinthians 4:15.

Whoso keepeth the law is a *wise son*, Proverbs 28:7.

Five virgins were *wise*, Matthew 25:2.

A *good* MAN, out of the *good* treasure of the heart, [an honest and *good* heart] bringeth forth *good* things, Matthew 12:35; Luke 8:15.

They shall walk with me in white, for [or rather οτι *because*] THEY ARE WORTHY, Revelation 3:4.

Ye are the light of the world, Matthew 5:14.

Hearken unto me, ye men of understanding: far be it from God that he should do wickedness. &c. For the *work* of a man shall he render unto him, and cause every man to find according to *his ways*. Yea, surely God will not do wickedly, neither will the Almighty pervert judgment, Job 34:10, 11, 12.

If ANY MAN see his brother sin, &c, *he shall ask*, and he [God] will *give him life* for them that sin not unto death, 1 John 5:16.

I will that *intercessions* be made for all men. The effectual fervent prayer of A RIGHTEOUS MAN availeth much, 1 Timothy 2:1; James 5:16.

Whosoever *sins ye remit*, they are

to *forgive sins,* Mark 2:10.

CHRIST, by whom we have now received the *atonement,* Romans 5:11.

There is *one* Mediator between God and men, the man CHRIST JESUS, 1 Timothy 2:5.

O God, shine on thy sanctuary, for *the Lord's sake.* For my name's sake will I defer mine anger, Dan. 9:17; Isaiah 48:9.

The Son of man is come to — &c, SAVE that which was *lost,* Luke 19:10.

Christ is ALL and in all, — it pleased the Father that IN HIM should all fulness dwell — and ye are complete IN HIM, Colossians 3:11; 1:19; 2:10. To him that hath *loved* us, and *washed* us from our sins in his own blood, and hath *made us* kings and priests, &c, to him be glory and dominion for ever and ever, Revelation 1:5, 6.

remitted to them, John 20:23.

PHINEHAS was zealous for God, and made an *atonement* for the children of Israel, Num. 25:13.

MOSES his chosen stood before him in the breach to *turn away* his wrath, lest he should destroy them, Psalm 106:23.

I will not do it [i.e. I will not rain fire and brimstone from the Lord upon Sodom] for *ten righteous' sake,* Genesis 18:32.

He became the author of eternal SALVATION to all them that *obey* him, Hebrews 5:9.

Is Christ the minister of *sin?* God forbid! By their FRUITS ye shall know them. We *labour* that we may be *accepted* of him, for we must all appear before the judgment seat of Christ, that every one may receive the things *done* in his body, according to that he hath done, whether it be good or bad, Galatians 2:17; Matthew 7:20; 2 Corinthians 5:9, 10.

Is it not evident from the balance of these, and the like scriptures that Honestus and Zelotes are both under a capital, though contrary mistake? and that to do the Gospel justice, we must Scripturally join together what they rashly put asunder?

SECTION V.
Setting forth the glory of faith and the honour of works.

FIRST SCALE.

Whosoever *believeth* on him [Christ] shall not be ashamed, Romans 10:11.

This is the work of GOD, that ye *believe* on him whom he hath sent, John 6:29.

Abraham *believed* God, &c, and he was called the *friend* of God, James 2:23.

To him that worketh not, but *believeth,* &c, his faith is counted for

SECOND SCALE.

Then shall I not be ashamed, when *I have respect unto all thy commandments,* Psalm 119:6.

What does the Lord require of thee, but *to do justly, to love mercy, and to walk humbly* with thy God, Micah 6:8.

Ye are my *friends,* If ye do whatsoever I command you, John 15:14.

Faith, *if it hath not works,* is dead, being alone, James 2:17.

righteousness, Romans 4:5.

If ye believe not that I am he, *ye shall die* in your sins, John 8:24.

Only believe: [I particularly require a strong exertion of thy faith at this time,] Luke 8:50.

He that *believeth* on him that sent me, hath everlasting life, and shall not come into condemnation; but is passed from death unto life, John 5:24.

Thy *faith* hath SAVED thee, Luke 7:50.

Through *faith* they wrought righteousness, obtained promises, &c, Hebrews 11:33.

With the heart man *believeth to righteousness*, Romans 10:10.

Received ye the Spirit by the *works* of the law, or by the hearing of *faith?* Galatians 3:2.

Through his name, whosoever *believeth* on him shall receive remission of sins, Acts 10:43.

If Abraham were *justified* by WORKS, he hath whereof to glory, Romans 4:2.

Without FAITH it is impossible to please God, Hebrews 11:6.

They that are of *faith* are blessed with faithful Abraham, Galatians 3:9.

To them that are *unbelieving* is NOTHING PURE, Titus 1:15.

Believe in the Lord, &c, so shall you be established, 2 Chronicles 20:20.

To the praise of the glory of his *grace*, &c, he hath made us accepted in the beloved, Ephesians 1:6.

I *live* by FAITH in the Son of God, who loved me, and gave himself for me, Galatians 2:20.

For me to *live* is CHRIST, Philippians 1:21.

THIS [Christ] is the true God, and *eternal life*, 1 John 5:20.

Brethren, &c, *if ye live* after the flesh, *ye shall die*, Romans 8:13.

The *devils* believe, [therefore *faith* is not sufficient without its *works*,] James 2:19.

With *the merciful* thou [O God] wilt show thyself merciful: and with the froward thou wilt show thyself unsavoury, 2 Samuel 22:26, 27.

We are SAVED by *hope*, Romans 8:24.

Remembering, &c, your *labour of love* — let *patience* have her perfect work, 1 Thessalonians 1:3; James 1:4.

And with *the mouth, confession is made* to salvation. (Ibid.)

I know thy *works*, that thou art neither cold nor hot, &c, so then, &c, I will spue thee out of my mouth, Revelation 3:15, 16.

Forgive, and ye shall be forgiven. If we *confess* our sins, he is faithful and just to forgive us, Luke 6:37; 1 John 1:9.

Was not Abraham our father *justified* by WORKS? James 2:21.

O vain man, faith without WORKS is dead, James 2:20.

If ye were Abraham's children, ye would do the *works* of Abraham, John 8:39.

Give alms, &c, and behold ALL THINGS are CLEAN unto you, Luke 11:41.

If thou *doest* well, shalt not thou be *accepted?* Genesis 4:7.

In every nation he that feareth God and *worketh* righteousness, is accepted with him, Acts 10:35.

If ye, through the Spirit, MORTIFY the deeds of the body, ye shall *live*, Romans 8:13.

KEEP my commandments and *live*, Proverbs 4:4.

His [my Father's] COMMANDMENT is *life everlasting*, John 12:50.

Though I have *all knowledge*, &c, and

This is eternal life, *to know* thee, &c, and Jesus Christ, John 17:3.

He that *believeth* on the Son hath everlasting life, John 3:36.

Israel, which followed after the law of righteousness, hath not attained to the law of righteousness. Wherefore? Because they sought it not by *faith*, but as it were by the works of the law [opposed to Christ;] for they stumbled at that stumbling stone, Romans 9:31, 32.

Abraham *believed* God, and it was *imputed* [or counted] to him for righteousness, Romans 4:3.

Trust [i.e. believe] ye in the Lord for ever; for in the Lord Jehovah is everlasting strength, Isaiah 26:4.

He that *believeth* on him is not condemned, but he that *believeth not* is condemned already, John 3:18.

Be it known unto you that through this man is preached unto you the forgiveness of sins; and by him all that *believe* are JUSTIFIED, Acts 13:38, 39.

We have *believed* in Jesus Christ, that we might be JUSTIFIED [as sinners] by the *faith* of Christ, Galatians 2:16.

have not *charity*, I am nothing, 1 Corinthians 13:2.

And he that [απειθει] *disobeyeth* the Son, shall not see life. (*Ibid.*)

If any man among you, &c, *bridleth* not his tongue, &c, this man's religion is vain. Pure religion and undefiled before God is this: to *visit* the fatherless and widows in their affliction, and to *keep* himself unspotted from the world, James 1:26, 27.

Phinehas *executed* judgment, and that was *counted* [or imputed] unto him for righteousness for evermore, Psalm 106:30, 31.

If I *regard* iniquity in my heart, the Lord will not hear me. If our heart condemn us not, then have we *confidence* toward God, Psalm 66:18; 1 John 3:21.

He that *humbleth* himself shall be exalted, and every one that *exalteth himself* shall be abased, Luke 14:11.

The *doers of* the law [of faith] shall be JUSTIFIED, — in the day when God shall judge the secrets of men, &c, according to my Gospel, Romans 2:13, 16.

In the day of judgment — by thy *words* thou shalt be JUSTIFIED, and by thy *words* thou shalt be condemned, Matthew 12:36, 37.

The balance of the preceding scriptures shows that FAITH, and the works of faith, are equally necessary to the salvation of adults. *Faith*, for their justification as *sinners*, in the day of CONVERSION; and the *works* of faith, for their justification as *believers*, both in the day of TRIAL and of JUDGMENT. Hence it follows, that when Zelotes preaches *mere Solifidianism*, and when Honestus enforces *mere morality*, they both grossly mangle Bible Christianity, which every real Protestant is bound to defend against all Antinomian and Pharisaic innovators.

SECTION VI.

Our translation makes St. Paul speak unguardedly, where it says that "the law is not made for a righteous man" — The absurdity of making believers afraid of the decalogue — The moral law of Christ, and the moral law of Moses are one and the same — The moral law is rescued from under the feet of the Antinomians — Christians are not less under the moral law to Christ as a rule of judgment, than the Jews were under it to Moses — The Sinai covenant is proved to be an edition of the covenant of grace — The most judicious Calvinists maintain this doctrine — Wherein consists the difference between the Jewish and the Christian dispensation. As the latter is most glorious in its promises, so it is most terrible in its threatenings — Two capital objections are answered.

WHEN justice has used her *scales*, she is sometimes obliged to wield her *sword*. In imitation of her, I lay by my Scales to rescue a capital scripture, which, I fear, our translators have inadvertently delivered into the hands of the Antinomians.

1 Timothy 1:8, 9, the apostle is represented as saying, "We know that the law is good, if a man use it lawfully; knowing this, that *the law is not made for a* RIGHTEOUS MAN." "Now," say some Antinomians, "all believers, being complete in Christ's imputed righteousness, are and shall for ever be perfectly righteous in him; therefore 'the law is not made for them:' they can no more be *condemned* for breaking the moral, than for transgressing the ceremonial law." A horrible inference this, which, I fear, is countenanced by these words of our translation: "The law is not made for the righteous." Is this strictly true? Were not angels and our first parents *righteous*, when God "made for them" the (then) easy yoke of the law of innocence? And is not the law "made for" the absolution of "the righteous," as well as for the condemnation of the wicked? Happily St. Paul does not speak the unguarded words, which we impute to him; for he says, δικαιω νομος ου κειται, literally, "The law *lieth not at*, or is *not levelled against* a righteous man, but against the lawless and disobedient," that is, against those who break it. This literal sense perfectly agrees with the apostle's doctrine, where he says," Rulers are not a terror to good works, but to the evil. Wilt thou then not be afraid of the power? Do that which is good, and thou shalt have [absolution and] *praise* of the same."

This mistake of our translators seems to be countenanced by Galatians 5:23. "Against such [the righteous] there is no law." Just as if the apostle had said εστι νομό ουδεί, whereas his words are κατα των τοιαυτων ουκ εστι νομό, literally, "The law is not against such!" Whence it appears (1.) That believers are under the law of Christ, not only as a rule of life, but also as a rule of judgment. (2.) That when they "bear one another's burdens and so fulfil that law," it is "not against them," it does not condemn them. (3.) That as there is no medium between the condemnation and the absolution of the law; the moment the law does not *condemn* a believer, it *acquits* him. And (4.) That consequently every penitent, obedient believer is actually justified by the law of Christ, agreeably to Romans 2:12, and Matthew 12:37: for, says the apostle, "the law is not AGAINST such," plainly intimating that it is FOR them.

It had been well for us if some of our divines had been satisfied with insinuating, that we need not keep the commandments to obtain eternal salvation through Jesus Christ: but some of them even endeavour to make us as much afraid of the decalogue, as of a battery of cannon. With such design it is that pious J. Bunyan says, in one of his unguarded moments, "Have a care of these great guns, the ten commandments;" just as if it were as desperate an attempt to look into the law of God, in order to one's salvation, as to look into the mouths of ten loaded pieces of cannon, in order to one's preservation. What liberty is here taken with the Gospel! Christ says, "If thou wilt enter into life, keep the commandments;" the obedience of faith being "the narrow way," that through him "leads to life." "No," say some of our Gospel ministers, "sincere obedience is a jack o'lantern: and what you recommend as a way to life, is a tenfold way to death." O ye that fear God, do not so rashly contradict our Lord. Who among you regard yet his sayings? Who stand to their baptismal vow? Who will not only "believe all the articles of the Christian faith," but also "keep God's holy will and commandments, and walk in the same all the days of their life?" Let no Solifidian make you afraid of the commandments. Methinks I see the bleeding "Captain of our salvation" lifting up the standard of the cross, and giving thus the word of command' 'Dread not my precepts. 'If you love me, keep my commandments. Blessed are they,' who 'keep God's commandments, that they may enter into the city by the gate,' and 'lay hold on eternal life.'" If this is the language of inspiration, far from dreading "the ten great guns," love them next to the wounds of Jesus. Stand behind the cross; ply there the heavenly ordnance, and you shall be invincible: yea, one of you shall chase a thousand. It is the command broken in unbelief, and not the command kept in faith, that slays: for that very ordnance which is loaded with a fearful curse, levelled "unto the third or fourth generation of them that hate God," is loaded with mere "mercy to a thousand generations of them that love him and keep his commandments."

Zelotes probably wonders at the *legality* of the preceding lines, and is ready to exclaim against my "blindness," for not seeing that Moses' moral law, delivered on Mount Sinai, is a mere covenant of works, diametrically opposed to the covenant of grace. As his opinion is one of the strongest ramparts of Antinomianism, I beg leave to erect a battery against it. If I am so happy as to demolish it, I shall not only be able to recover the decalogue — the "ten great guns," but a considerable part of the Old Testament, such as most of the lessons which our Church has selected out of Deuteronomy and Ezekiel, and which the Solifidians consider as Jewish trumpery, akin to the Arminian heresy; merely because they contain powerful incentives to sincere, evangelical obedience, according to the doctrine of the second Gospel axiom.

I humbly conceive then: (1.) That the moral law delivered to Moses on Mount Sinai was a particular edition of that gracious and holy law which St. James calls "the law of liberty," St. Paul "the law of Christ." (2.) That our Lord solemnly adopted the *moral* part of the decalogue, in his sermon upon the mount, where he rescued the *moral* precepts from the false glosses of the scribes; representing those precepts as the evangelical law, according to which we must live, if ever "our righteousness exceeds that of the Pharisees;" and by which we must be "justified in the day of judgment," (agreeable to his own doctrine, Matthew 12:37,) if ever we escape the curse which will fall on the ungodly. And (3.) That although we are not bound to obey the decalogue, as delivered to Moses literally written in stone, (in which St. Paul observes that it is "done away," 2 Corinthians 3:7, 11,) yet we are obliged to obey it, so far as it is a transcript of the moral law, that eternally binds all rational agents, and so far as Christ has made it his own by spiritualizing and enforcing its moral precepts on the mount; — I say its *moral* precepts, because the fourth commandment, which is rather of the ceremonial than of the moral kind, does not bind us so strictly as the others do. Hence it is that St. Paul says, "Let no man judge you in respect of the Sabbath days," Colossians 2:16, and even finds fault with the Galatians for "observing days," with a Jewish scrupulosity.

That the moral law of Sinai was a peculiar edition of God's evangelical law adapted to the Jewish commonwealth, and not an edition of the Adamic law of innocence, I prove by the following arguments: —

1. Romans 10:5, St. Paul produces Moses as describing the righteousness which is of the law of Sinai: "That the man who does these things *shall live* by them." And Romans 8:13, he himself describes the righteousness which is of "the law of liberty" thus: "If ye live after the flesh ye shall die; but if ye, through the Spirit, mortify the deeds of the body, ye shall live." Now are not those people excessively prejudiced, who deny either that in both these descriptions the promise, *shall live*, is the same; or that it is suspended on sincere obedience? And therefore is it not evident that St. Paul never blamed the Jews for seeking salvation by an humble obedience to the moral precepts of the Mosaic covenant, in due subordination to faith in the Divine mercy and in the promised Messiah; but only for opposing their *opus operatum*, their formal, partial, ceremonious, Pharisaic obedience, to that very faith which should have animated all their works?

2. The truth of this observation will appear in a still stronger light, if you consider, that when the evangelical apostle asks, "What says the righteousness of *faith?*" he answers almost in the very words in which the legal prophet asserts the practicableness of his own *law*. For St. Paul writes, "The *word* is nigh thee, in thy mouth, and in thy heart; that is, the *word* of *faith* which we preach," Romans 10:8. And Moses says, Deuteronomy 30:11, "The word is very nigh unto thee, even in thy mouth, and in thy heart, that thou mayest *do* it;" which undoubtedly implies a *believing* of that word, in order to the *doing* of it; agreeably to the doctrine of our Church, which asks, in her catechism, "What dost thou learn in the commandments?" and answers, "I learn my duty toward God, &c, which is to *believe* in him," &c. Thus we see, that as the Mosaic law was not without *Gospel* and *faith*, so the Christian Gospel is not without *law* and *obedience;* and consequently that those divines who represent Moses as promiscuously cursing, and Christ as indiscriminately blessing all the people under their respective dispensations, are greatly mistaken.

3. Whatever liberty the apostle takes with the superannuated ceremonies of the Jews, which he sometimes calls "carnal ordinances," and sometimes "beggarly elements," it is remarkable that he never speaks disrespectfully of the *moral* law, and that he exactly treads in the steps of Moses' evangelical legality: for if Moses comes down from Mount Sinai, saying, "Honour thy father and mother," &c, St. Paul writes from Mount Sion, "Honour thy father and mother, (which is the first commandment of the second table with promise,) that it may be well with thee," Ephesians 6:2, 3. As for Christ, we have already seen, that when he informs us how *well it will be with us* if we keep his commandments, he says, "This do, and thou shalt live;" i.e. thou shalt "inherit eternal life" in glory.

4. As Christ freely conversed with Moses on the mount, so St. Paul is freely conversant with Moses' legality in his most evangelical epistles. Take another instance of it. "Thou shalt love thy neighbour as thyself," says the Jewish lawgiver, Leviticus 19:28. "Love one another," says the Christian apostle, "for he that loveth another hath fulfilled the law, for, &c, love is the fulfilling of the law," Romans 13:8, 10. And that he spoke this of the moral law of Sinai, as adopted by Christ, is evident from his quoting in the 9th verse the very words of that law, "Thou shalt not kill, thou shalt not commit adultery, thou shalt not steal, thou shalt not bear false witness, thou shalt not covet, and — any other commandment," &c.

5. St. James forms a threefold cord, with Moses and St. Paul, to draw us out of the ditch of Antinomianism, into which pious divines have inadvertently led us. "If you fulfil the royal law," says he, "ye do well; but if ye have respect to persons, ye commit sin, &c. So speak ye, and so do, as they that shall be judged by the law of liberty," James 2:8, 9, 13. "True," says Zelotes; "but that law of liberty is the free Gospel preached by Dr. Crisp." Not so; for St. James immediately produces part of that very law of liberty, by which fallen believers, "that have showed no mercy, will have judgment without mercy:" and he does it in the very words of Moses and St. Paul, "Do not commit adultery, do not kill," James 2:11. Any one who can set aside the testimony which those apostles bear in favour of the moral law of Moses, may, by the same art, press the most glaring truths of the Bible into the service of any new-fangled dotages.

6. Because the Mosaic dispensation, considered with respect to its superannuated types and ceremonies, is an *old* covenant with regard to the Christian dispensation, Zelotes rashly concludes that Moses' moral law is the covenant of unsprinkled works, and of perfect innocence, which God made with Adam in paradise. Hence he constantly opposes the ten commandments of God to the Gospel of Christ, although he has no more ground for doing it, than for constantly opposing Romans 2, to Romans 8; Galatians 6, to Galatians 2; and Matthew 25, to John 10. Setting therefore aside the ceremonial and civil laws of Moses, the difference between him and St. Paul consists principally in two particulars: (1.) The books of Moses are chiefly historical; and the epistles of St. Paul chiefly doctrinal. (2.) The great prophet chiefly insists upon *obedience*, the *fruit* of faith; and the great apostle chiefly insists upon *faith*, the *root* of obedience. Hence it appears, that those eminent servants of God cannot be opposed to each other with any more propriety, than Mr. B. has opposed a Jewish *if* to a Christian *if*.

7. The Sinai covenant does not then differ from the Christian dispensation *essentially*, as darkness and light, but only in degree, as the morning light and the blaze of noon. Judaism deals in types and veiled truths; Christianity in antitypes and naked truths. Judaism sets forth the second Gospel axiom, without destroying the first; and Christianity holds out the first, without obscuring the second The Jews waited for the first coming of Christ "to put away sin by the sacrifice of himself:" and the Christians look for his "appearing a second time without sin," i.e. without that humiliation and those sufferings which constituted him "a sacrifice for sin." I see, therefore, no more reason to believe that Mount Sinai flames only with Divine wrath, than to think that Mount Sion burns only with Divine love; for if a beast was to be thrust through with a dart for rushing upon Mount Sinai; Ananias and Sapphira were thrust through with a word for rushing upon Mount Sion. And if I read that Moses himself "trembled

exceedingly" at the Divine vengeance displayed in Arabia, I read also that "great fear came upon all the Church," on account of the judgment inflicted upon the first backsliders in the good land of Canaan. In a word, as Christ is "the Lion of the tribe of Judah," as well as "the Lamb of God;" so Moses was "the meekest man upon earth," as well as the *severest* of all the prophets.

8. To prove that the decalogue is a Gospel "law of liberty," and not the Adamic law of innocence, one would think it is enough to observe that the law of innocence was given *without* a mediator, whereas the law of Sinai was given *by* one. For St. Paul informs us, that "it was ordained by angels in the hand of a mediator," Moses, a mighty intercessor, and a most illustrious type of Christ, to whom he pointed the Israelites. This makes the apostle propose a question, which contains the knot of the difficulty raised by the Antinomians: "Is the law then against the promises of God?" Is the Sinai covenant against the Gospel of Christ? And he answers it by crying out, "God forbid!" Nay, as a "school master" it "brings us to Christ" that we may be "justified by faith" as sinners; and afterward it makes us keep close to him for power to obey it, that we may be justified by works as believers; "for," says he in another place, "the *doers* of the *law*, [and none but they,] shall be justified, &c, in the day when God shall judge the secrets of men by Jesus Christ according to my *Gospel.*" A plain proof this, that the moral law, with all its sanctions and precepts, is a capital part of the Christian, as well as of the Jewish dispensation.

9. Again: the Adamic moral law was given without a sacrificing priest: but not so the Mosaic moral law. For while Moses was ready to act his part as an interceding prophet; Aaron was ready to second him by offering up typical incense and propitiatory sacrifices; and God graciously invested him with power to give a sacerdotal blessing to penitent transgressors; appointing him the representative of Christ, whom St. Paul calls "the high priest of *our* dispensation."

Once more: the preface of the decalogue is altogether evangelical; and the second commandment speaks of "punishing" only "unto the third generation," while it mentions "showing mercy unto a thousand generations," which, if I mistake not, intimates that the decalogue breathes *mercy* as well as *justice;* and therefore that it is an edition of Christ's evangelical, and not of Adam's anti-evangelical law.

These observations make me wonder that pious divines should set aside the moral part of Moses' law as being the impracticable law of innocence. But when I reflect that Aaron himself helped to set up the golden calf, and that Moses in a fit of intemperate zeal for God, dashed the material tables of his own law to pieces, I no more wonder that pious Solifidians should help the practical Antinomians to set up their great Diana; and that warm men should break the Almighty's laws to the diminutive, insignificant pieces which they are pleased to call "rules of life."

And let nobody say that these arguments are only "novel chimeras;" for the most judicious Calvinists have been of this sentiment. Flavel, after mentioning several, such as Bolton, Charnock, and Burgess, adds, "Mr. Greenhill on Ezekiel 16, gives us demonstration from that context, that since it (the Mosaic law) was a marriage covenant, as it appears to be, verse 8, it cannot possibly be a distinct covenant from the covenant of grace. The incomparable Turretine" (one of Calvin's most famous successors at Geneva) "learnedly and judiciously states this controversy, and both positively asserts, and by many arguments fully proves, that the Sinai law cannot be a pure covenant of works, or a covenant specifically distinct from the covenant of grace." (See *Flavel's Works*, folio edition p. 423.)

The same candid author helps me to some of the following supernumerary arguments: (1.) Nothing can be more unreasonable than to suppose that God brought his chosen people out of the Egyptian bondage, to put them under the more intolerable bondage of the law of innocence. (2.) If God had done this, instead of bettering their condition, he would have made it worse: nay, he would have brought them from the *blessing* to the *curse:* for in Egypt they were nationally under the covenant made with Abraham: a gracious covenant this, into which they were all admitted by the sacrament of circumcision. Nor could they be put under the Adamic covenant of works, without being first cut off from the covenant of grace made with Adam after the fall, renewed with all mankind in Noah, and peculiarly confirmed to the Jews in their ancestors, Abraham, Isaac, and Jacob; it being evident that no man can be at the same time under two covenants absolutely different. Nay, (3.) If the law given to the Israelites upon Mount Sinai was not an evangelical law; if it was the law of paradisiacal innocence; God treated his peculiar people with greater severity than he did the Egyptians, who were all under the gracious dispensation which St. Peter describes in these words: "In every nation he that feareth God and worketh righteousness is accepted of him." (4.) If, because St. Paul decries the obsolete ceremonies of Moses' law, it follows that the moral law delivered to Moses was not a Gospel law, it will also follow that the covenant of circumcision made with Abraham was not a Gospel covenant: for the apostle expressly decries circumcision, the great external work of that covenant. But as Abraham's covenant was undoubtedly a Gospel covenant, although circumcision is now abolished; so was Moses' law a Gospel law, although the ceremonial part is now abrogated. Lastly' St. Paul, Romans 9:4, placed "the giving of the law" among the greatest *privileges* of the Jews, but if by the law he meant the Adamic covenant, he should have called it the greatest *curse* which could be entailed upon a fallen creature: for what can be more terrible than for a whole nation of sinners to be put under a law that absolutely curses its violaters, and admits of neither repentance nor pardon?

Flavel, in the page which I have already quoted, makes the following just observation: "The law is considered two ways in Scripture. (1.) Largely, for the whole[*] Mosaical economy, comprehensive of the ceremonial as well as moral precepts; and that law is of faith, as the learned Turretine has proved by four Scripture arguments. (i.) Because it contained Christ, the object of faith. (ii.) Because it impelled men to seek Christ by faith. (iii.) Because it required that God should be worshipped, which cannot rightly be without faith. And (iv.) because Paul describes the righteousness of faith in those very words whereby Moses had declared the precepts of the law. Again: (2.) The law in Scripture is taken strictly for the moral law only, considered abstractedly from the promises of grace. These are two different senses and acceptations of the law.

---

[*] Thus when St. John says the law came by Moses, but grace and truth came by Jesus Christ, he does not mean that the law of Moses is a *graceless* and *lying* law: he only declares, that whereas the Jewish dispensation, which is frequently called the law, came by Moses, with all its shadowy types, the Christian dispensation, which is frequently called grace, came by Jesus Christ, in whom the shadows of the ceremonial law have their truth and reality.

Creeds and Scripture Scales

Apply this excellent distinction of the refinements, with which the doctrine of the law has been perplexed, and you will easily answer the objections of those who, availing themselves of St. Paul's laconic style, lay their own farrago at his door. For instance, when he says, "As many as are of the works of the law are under the curse, for it is written, Cursed is every one that continueth not in all things, &c," he means, (to use Flavel's words,) the law "considered abstractedly from the promises of grace;" for, in that case, the law immediately becomes the Adamic covenant of works, which knows nothing of justification by faith in a *merciful* God, through an *atoning Mediator;* and, in this point of view, the apostle says with great truth, "The law is not of faith, but the man that doth these things shall live in them," without being under any obligation to a Saviour. From the curse of this Adamic, merciless law, as well as from the curse of the ceremonial burthensome law of Moses, "Christ has delivered us;" but he never intended to deliver us from the curse of his own "royal law," without our personal, sincere, penitential, and faithful obedience to it; for he says himself, "Why call ye me Lord! and do not the things which I say?" "Those mine enemies," who put honour upon my cross, while they pour contempt upon my crown, — "those mine enemies" who would not that I should reign over them, bring hither and slay them before me.

From the preceding arguments I conclude that what St. James calls "the royal law," and the "law of liberty," and what St. Paul calls "the law of Christ," is nothing but the moral law of Moses, which Christ adopted, and explained in his sermon upon the mount; a law this, which is held forth to public view duly connected with the apostles' creed in our Churches, to indicate that Solifidianism is the abomination of desolation, and that the commandments ought no more to be separated from the articles of our faith in our pulpits and hearts, than they are in our chancels and Bibles.

And that we shall stand or fall by the moral part of the decalogue in the great day is evident, not only from the tenor of the New Testament, but even from St. Paul's express declarations to those very Galatians to whom he says, "Christ has delivered us from the curse of the law:" for he charges them to "fulfil the law of Christ;" adding, "God is not mocked; whatsoever a man soweth, that shall he also reap: for he that soweth to his flesh, shall of the flesh reap destruction. I have told you, that they who do such things [adultery, fornication, uncleanness, murders, drunkenness, and such like] shall not inherit the kingdom of God. But the fruit of the Spirit is love, &c, goodness, temperance; against such [as bear this fruit] there is no law:" or rather, *the law is not against them:* for, as the apostle observes to the Corinthians, "We are not" Antinomians — "We are not without law to God, but under the law to Christ."

Among the many objections which Zelotes will raise against this doctrine, two deserve a particular answer: —

"I. If the Mosaic dispensation is an edition of the everlasting Gospel, why does St. Paul decry it when he writes to the Galatians and Corinthians? And why does he say to the Hebrews, 'Now hath Christ obtained a more excellent ministry, by how much also he is the Mediator of a better covenant, which was established upon better promises,' &c, Hebrews 8:6, &c. For of these two dispensations the apostle evidently speaks in that chapter, under the name of an *old* and a *new* covenant."

1. Although Christ is the one procurer of grace under all the Gospel dispensations, yet his own peculiar dispensation has the advantage of the superannuated dispensation of Moses on many accounts, chiefly these: Christ is the Son, and Moses was the *servant* of God: Christ is a *sinless, eternal* priest, "after the" royal "order of Melchisedec;" and Aaron was a *sinful, transitory, Levitical* high priest: Christ is a *living*, spiritual temple: and Moses' tabernacle was a *lifeless*, material building: Christ writes the decalogue *internally*, upon the table of the believer's heart; and Moses brings it written *externally*, upon tables of stone: Christ by "one offering for ever perfected them that are sanctified;" but the Mosaic sacrifices were daily renewed: Christ shed his own precious blood, the blood of "the Lamb, of God;" but Aaron shed only the vile blood of bulls and common lambs: Christ's dispensation remaineth, but that of Moses "is done away," 2 Corinthians 3:11: Christ's dispensation is "the ministration of *the Spirit;*" but that of Moses is "the ministration of *the letter,* — of condemnation, — of death," not only because it eventually killed the carnal Jews, who absurdly opposed the *letter* of their dispensation to the *spirit* of it; but also because Moses condemned to instant death blasphemers, adulterers, and rebels; destroying them with volleys of stones, earthquakes, fire from heaven, waters of jealousy, &c. All these strange executions were acts of severity, which our mild Redeemer not only never did himself, but never permitted his apostles to do while he was upon earth; kindly delaying the execution of his woes, and chiefly delighting to proclaim peace to penitent rebels. Hence it is that St. Paul says, "If the" Mosaic "ministration," [which, in the preceding respect, was comparatively a "ministration of *righteous* condemnation,] be glory, much more does the ministration of" Christ [which, in the sense above mentioned, is comparatively a ministration of righteous mercy] "exceed in glory!" 2 Corinthians 3:9.

2. With regard to the *better promises*, on which the apostle founds his doctrine of the superior excellence of the Christian over the Jewish dispensation, they are chiefly these: (1.) "The Lord whom ye seek, even the Messenger of the *better* covenant, shall suddenly come to his temple." (2.) "To you that fear my name shall the Sun of righteousness arise with healing in his wings." (3.) "I will be merciful to your unrighteousness, and your sins I will remember no more: giving *you* the knowledge of salvation by the remission of sins;" a privilege this which is enjoyed by all *Christian* believers. (4.) "All shall know me from the least to the greatest' they shall all be taught of God; for I will pour out of my Spirit upon all flesh, and my servants and my handmaids shall prophesy, i.e. speak the wonderful works of God." This blessing, which under the Jewish dispensation was the prerogative of prophets and prophetesses only, is common to all true Christians. The four evangelists and St. Peter, our Lord and his forerunner, agree to name it "the baptism of the Holy Ghost." St. Peter calls it "the Spirit of promise." Christ terms it also "power from on high, and the promise of the Father." The fulfilment of this great promise is the peculiar glory of Christianity in its state of perfection, as appears from John 7:39, and 1 Peterer 1:12; and it is chiefly on account of it that the Christian dispensation is said to be founded on *better promises;* but to infer from it that the Jewish dispensation was founded on *a curse*, is a palpable mistake.

3. Therefore, all that you can make of Hebrews 8:2 Corinthians 3, and Galatians 4:1, is, (1.) That the Jewish dispensation puts a heavy yoke of ceremonies upon those who are under it, and by that means "gendereth to *bondage,*" whereas the

Gospel of Christ begets glorious *liberty;* not only by breaking the yoke of Mosaic rites, but also by revealing more clearly, and sealing more powerfully, the glorious promise of the Spirit. And, (2.) That the "Gospel of Moses," if I may use that expression after St. Paul, Hebrews 4:2, was good in its time and place, and was founded upon *good promises;* but that the Gospel of Christ is better, and is established upon *better promises,* the latter dispensations illustrating, improving, and ripening the former; and altogether forming the various steps by which the mystery of God hastens to its glorious accomplishment.

"II. If the Mosaic dispensation is so nearly allied to the Gospel of Christ, why does the apostle, Hebrews 12:18-21, give us so dreadful a description of Mount Sinai? And why does he add, ' o terrible was the sight [of that mount burning with fire] that Moses said, I exceedingly fear and quake?'"

ANSWER. The apostle in that chapter exalts, with great reason, Mount Sion above Mount Sinai; or the *Christian* above the *Jewish* dispensation; and herein we endeavour to tread in his steps. But the argument taken from the dreadful burning of Mount Sinai, &c, does by no means prove that the Sinai covenant was essentially different from the covenant of grace. Weigh with impartiality the following observations, and they will, I hope, remove your prejudices, as they have done mine: —

1. If the dispensation of Moses is famous for the past terrors of Mount Sinai; so is that of Christ for the *future* terrors of the day of judgment. "His voice," says the apostle, "then shook the earth; but now he hath promised, saying, Yet once more I shake not the earth only, but also heaven. *We too look for* the shout of the archangel, *and the blast of the* trump of God;" and are persuaded, that the flames which ascended from Mount Sinai to the midst of heaven were only typical of those flames that shall crown the Christian dispensation, when our "Lord shall be revealed in flaming fire, to take *a more dreadful* vengeance on them that obey not the Gospel," than ever Moses did on those who disobeyed his dispensation. "Seeing then that all these things shall be dissolved, what manner of persons ought ye to be in all holy conversation; looking for and hasting unto the day of God, wherein the heavens being on fire shall be dissolved, and the elements shall melt with fervent heat!" How inconsiderable do the Mosaic terrors of a *burning bush* and a *flaming hill* appear, when they. are compared with the Christian terrors of *melting elements,* and of *a world,* whose inveterate curse is pursued from the circumference to the centre, by a pervading fire; and devoured by rapidly spreading flames!

2. How erroneous must the preaching of Zelotes appear to those who believe *all* the Scriptures! "I do not preach to you *duties* and sincere *obedience,* like Mr. Legality on Mount Sinai; but *privileges* and *faith,* like St. Paul on Mount Sion." How unscriptural, I had almost said how deceitful is this modish effeminate divinity! Does not the very apostle, who is supposed to patronize it most, speak directly against it, where he says, "We labour that we may be accepted of Him, (the Lord;) for we must all appear before the judgment seat of Christ, &c. Knowing therefore the *terror of the Lord* [in that great day of retribution,] we persuade men?" Nay, does not he conclude his dreadful description of Mount Sinai, and its terrors, by threatening Christian believers, who "are come to Mount Sion," with more dreadful displays of Divine justice than Arabia ever beheld, if they do not obey "Him that speaks from heaven?" Hebrews 12:25. And does he not sum up his doctrine, with respect to Mount Sinai

and Mount Sion, in these awful words? "Wherefore, we receiving [by faith] a kingdom which cannot be moved, let us have grace, whereby we may serve God acceptably, with reverence and GODLY FEAR: for OUR God" is not the God of the Antinomians, but "A CONSUMING FIRE:" i.e. the God who delivered the moral law upon Mount Sinai in the midst of devouring flames, and gave a fuller edition of it in his sermon upon the mount, solemnly adopting that law into his own peculiar dispensation, as "the law of liberty," or his own evangelical law — this very "God is a consuming fire." He will come in the great day, "revealed in flaming fire, to consume the man of sin by the breath of his mouth, and to take vengeance on all that obey not the Gospel," whether they despise its gracious offers, or trample under foot its righteous precepts. If Zelotes would attentively read Hebrews 12:14- 29, and compare that awful passage with Hebrews 2:2, 3, he would see that this is the apostle's anti-Solifidian doctrine: but, alas, while *the great* Pharisaic *whore* forbids some Papists to read the Bible, will the *great* Antinomian *Diana* permit some Protestants to mind it?

Should not the preceding observations have the desired effect upon the reader, I appeal to witnesses. Moses is the first. He comes down from Mount Sinai with an angelic appearance. Beams of glory dart from his seraphic face. His looks bespeak the man that had conversed forty days with the God of glory, and was saturated with Divine mercy and love. But I forget that Christianized Jews *will* see *no* glory in Moses, and have a veil of prejudice ready to cast over his radiant face: I therefore point at a more illustrious witness: it is the Lord Jesus. "Behold! he cometh with ten thousand of his saints," says St. Jude, "to execute judgment upon all;" and particularly upon those that "sin wilfully after they have received the knowledge of the truth. There remaineth no more sacrifice for *their* sins," says my third witness, "but a fearful looking for of judgment and fiery indignation, which shall devour the adversaries. He that despised Moses' law died without mercy; of how much sorer punishment shall he be thought worthy, who hath" despised the Christian dispensation, and "done despite to the Spirit of grace? For we know him that hath said, Vengeance belongeth unto me — the Lord shall judge HIS people. It is a fearful thing to fall into the hands of the living God," Hebrews 10:26-31.

Thus speaks the champion of free grace. Such is the account which he gives of Christ's severity toward those who despise his dispensation, — a severity this, which will display itself by the infliction of a punishment *much sorer* than that inflicted on the rebels destroyed by Moses. And are we not come to the height of inattention, if we can read such terrible declarations as these, and maintain that nothing but vinegar and gall flows from Mount Sinai, and nothing but milk and honey from Mount Sion? How long shall we have "eyes that do not see, and hearts that do not understand?" Lord, rend the veil of our prejudices. Let us see "the truth as it is in" Moses, that we may more clearly see "the truth as it is in Jesus."

The balance of the preceding arguments shows that the *Mosaic* and the *Christian* covenants equally set before us *blessing* and *cursing;* and that, according to both those dispensations, the obedience of *faith* shall be crowned with gracious rewards; while disobedience, the sure fruit of *unbelief,* shall be punished with the threatened curse. I throw this conclusion into my Scales, and weigh it before my readers, thus: —

BLESSINGS OF THE MOSAIC COVENANT, *Being the words of Moses.*

I.

Moses said, Consecrate yourselves to-day to the Lord, &c, that he may bestow upon you a *blessing* this day, Exodus 32:29. Behold, I set before you this day a *blessing*, &c, if ye obey the commandments of the Lord. And it shall come to pass, that thou shalt put the *blessing* upon Mount Gerizim, &c, Deuteronomy 11:20, 29. And it shall come to pass, if thou shalt hearken diligently, &c, that the Lord thy God will *bless* thee. All these *blessings* shall overtake thee, &c. *Blessed* shalt thou be in the city and *blessed* in the field, &c. *Blessed* shalt thou be when thou comest in, and *blessed* when thou goest out, &c. The Lord shall command the *blessing* upon thee, &c. The Lord shall establish thee a holy people to himself, if thou shalt walk in his ways. And, &c, he shall open to thee his good treasure, Deuteronomy 28:1-12.

This is the *blessing* wherewith Moses, the man of God, *blessed* the children of Israel. And he said, The Lord came from Sinai, &c, with ten thousands of saints, from his right hand went a fiery law; yea, he loved the people. Let *Reuben live,* and not die. And of Levi he said, Let thy *Thummim* and thy *Urim* [thy *perfections* and thy *lights*] be with thy holy one. And of Napthali he said, O *Napthali, satisfied with favour,* and *full with the blessing* of the Lord, possess thou the west. *Happy* art thou, O Israel; who is like unto thee, *O people saved by the Lord,* the shield of thy help? Thine enemies shall be found liars, and thou shalt tread upon their high places, Deuteronomy 33:1 to 29.

The Lord passed by before Moses,

CURSES OF THE CHRISTIAN DISPENSATION, *Being the words of Christ.*

II.

Jesus began to upbraid the cities, wherein most of his mighty works were done, because they repented not. Wo unto thee, Chorazin: — wo unto thee, Bethsaida: — I say unto you, It shall be *more tolerable* for Tyre and Sidon, at the day of judgment, than for you. And thou Capernaum, which art exalted unto heaven, shalt be brought down to *hell*, &c. I say unto you, It shall be *more tolerable* for the land of Sodom in the day of judgment, than for thee, Matthew 11:20, 25. I tell you, Nay; but except ye repent, ye shall *all likewise perish. Cut it down,* [the barren fig tree:] why cumbereth it the ground? Let it alone this year also; — if it bear fruit, well; and if not, then, after that, *thou shalt cut it down,* Luke 13:5, 9.

The Lord of that [once *blessed* but now *backsliding*] servant will come in a day when he looketh not for him, and will cut *him asunder,* and will appoint him his portion with the unbelievers. And that servant, who knew his Lord's will, and prepared not himself, neither *did* according to his will, shall be beaten with *many stripes,* Luke 12:46. Wo unto you, hypocrites: — ye shall receive the *greater damnation:* — ye make a proselyte twofold more a child of hell than yourselves. Wo unto you, ye blind guides — ye fools, and blind — ye pay tithe of mint, and have omitted judgment, mercy, and faith, &c. Fill ye up then the measure of your fathers; ye serpents, ye generation of vipers, how can ye escape *the damnation of hell?* Matthew 23:13.

Wo to that man by whom the

and proclaimed, The Lord, the Lord God, *merciful* and *gracious, long suffering* and *abundant in goodness* and truth, *keeping mercy for thousands, forgiving* iniquity, transgression, and sin, &c. And Moses made haste, &c, and said, If now I have found grace in thy sight, O Lord, &c, *pardon our iniquity*, and our sin, and take us for *thine inheritance*. And he (the Lord) said, I make a (or the)*covenant*, Exodus 34:6-10.

offence cometh; wherefore if thy hand or thy foot offend thee, cut them off. It is better to enter into life maimed, rather than be cast into *everlasting fire*, Matthew 18:7, 8. Wo unto you that are rich,&c. Wo unto you that are full, &c.Wo unto you that laugh now, &c.Wo unto you, when all men shall speak well of you, Luke 6:24. *Depart* from me, ye *cursed*, into *everlasting fire*, prepared for the devil — for I was hungry, and ye gave me no meat, &c, Matthew 25:42.

I flatter myself, that if Zelotes and Honestus candidly weigh the preceding arguments and scriptures, they will reap from thence a double advantage: (1.) They will no more tread the honour of Christ's moral law in the dust — no more rob it of its chief glory, that of being *a strict rule of judgment*. (2.) Honestus will be again benefited by a consider. able part of the New Testament; and Zelotes by a considerable part of the law and the prophets, which (as our Lord himself informs us) "hang on" those very "commandments" that the Antinomians divest of their sanction, and the Pharisees of their *spirituality*.

SECTION VII.

The doctrine of the preceding section is weighed in the Scripture Scales — According to Christ's Gospel, keeping the moral law in faith is a SUBORDINATE *way to eternal life, and some Protestants are grossly mistaken when they make believers afraid sincerely to observe the commandments, in order to obtain through Christ a more abundant life of grace here, and an eternal life of glory hereafter.*

IF I have spent so much time in attempting to remove the difficulties with which the doctrine of the law is clogged, it has not been without reason; for the success of my Checks in a great degree depends upon clearing up this part of my subject. If I fail here, Pharisaism will not be checked, and gross Antinomianism will still pass for the pure Gospel; fundamental errors about the law being the muddy springs whence the broken cisterns, both of the Pharisees and of the Antinomians, have their constant supplies. Honestus will have an anti-evangelical, Christless law, or at least a law without spirituality and strictness; the law he frames to himself being an insignificant twig, and not the Spirit's two-edged piercing sword. And Zelotes contrives a Gospel without law; or, if he admits of a law for Christ's subjects, it is such a one as has only the shadow of a law — "*a rule of life*," as he calls it, and NOT *a rule of judgment*. That at first sight Honestus may perceive the spirituality of the law, and the need of *Christ's Gospel;* and that Zelotes may discover the need of *Christ's law*, and see its awful impartiality, I beg leave to recapitulate the contents of the last section; presenting them to the reader, in my Scales, as the just weights of the sanctuary exactly balancing each other.

WEIGHTS OF FAITH AND FREE GRACE. I.	WEIGHTS OF WORKS AND FREE WILL. II.
When the Philippian jailer cried out, Sirs, what must I do to be saved? Paul and Silas said, [according to the first Gospel axiom,] BELIEVE in the Lord Jesus Christ, and thou shalt be saved, Acts 16:31.	*When the young ruler, and the pious lawyer, asked our Lord* What shall I do to inherit eternal life? *He answered them,* [according to the second axiom,] If thou wilt enter into life, KEEP THE COMMANDMENTS. This *do*, and thou shalt *live,* Matthew 19:17; Luke 18:19; 10:28.

Here Zelotes, as if he were determined to set aside the left Gospel scale, cries out, "There is no entering into life by *doing* and *keeping the commandments.* The young ruler and the lawyer were both as great legalists as yourself, and Christ answered them according to their error; the wise man having observed, that we must sometimes 'answer a fool according to his folly.'" I understand you, Zelotes; you suppose that one Pharisaic fiend had driven the poisoned nail of legality into their breasts, and that Christ was so officious as to clinch it for him. "Not so," replies Zelotes, "but I think Christ's answer was ironical, like that of the Prophet Micaiah, who said one thing to King Ahab, and meant another." What! Zelotes, two men, at different times and in the most solemn manner, propose to our Lord the most important question in the world. He shows a particular regard for them; and returns them similar answers. When one of them had described the way of obedience, an evangelist observes, that "Jesus saw he had answered *discreetly,* Mark 12:34. St. Luke informs us that Christ commended him and said, "Thou hast answered *right,*" Luke 10:28; and yet you intimate, that not only our Lord's answers, but his commendations were ironical. In what an unfavourable light do you put our Saviour's kindness to poor sinners, who prostrate themselves at his feet, and there ask the way to heaven! If "cursed is he that maketh the blind to wander out of their *earthly* way;" how can you, upon your principles, exculpate our Lord for doing this with respect to the blind seekers, who inquire the way that leads to eternal life and *heaven?*

But this is not all. It is evident, that although from the taunting tone of Micaiah's voice, Ahab directly understood that the answer given him was ironical; yet, lest there should be deception in the case, the prophet dropped the mask of irony, and told the king the naked truth before they parted. Not so Jesus Christ, if Solifidianism is the Gospel: for although neither the ruler nor the lawyer suspected that his direction and approbation were ironical, he let them both depart without giving them, or his disciples who were present, the least hint that he was sending them upon a fool's errand. Therefore, if setting sinners upon *keeping the commandments* in faith to go to heaven be only showing them the clearer way to hell, as Zelotes sometimes intimates, nobody ever pointed sinners more clearly to hell than our blessed Lord. This mistake of Zelotes is so much the more glaring, as the passages which he supposes to be ironical agree perfectly with the sermon on the mount, and with Matthew 25; two awful portions of the Gospel, which I am glad the Solifidians have not yet set aside as evangelical ironies.

Once more: if our Lord's direction was *not* true with regard to the covenant of grace, it was *absolutely false* with respect to the covenant of works; for as the ruler and the lawyer had undoubtedly broken the Adamic law of perfect innocence, they never could obtain life by keeping *that* law, should they have done it to the highest perfection for the time to come. Therefore, which way soever Zelotes turns himself, upon *his* scheme our Lord spoke either a *deceitful irony,* or a *flat untruth:* — I resume the Scales.

I.

I am the Lord* *thy God,* who brought thee out of the house of bondage.

The righteousness of *faith* speaketh on this wise: — Say not in thine heart, Who shall ascend into heaven? &c, or, Who shall descend into the deep? &c. But what saith it? *The word is nigh thee,* Romans 10:5, &c.

Christ hath *redeemed* us from the curse of *the law,* being made a curse for us, Galatians 3:13.

If they that are of the [*anti- evangelical*] law be heirs, *faith* is made void, and the *promise* of none effect, Romans 4:14.

I do not frustrate the *grace* of God: for if *righteousness* came by the [anti-evangelical] *law;* [or if it came *originally* by any] law; then CHRIST is dead in vain, Galatians 2:21.

I, through the law, am dead to the *law.* Ye are not under the law. Now we are delivered from the law, [both as a cumbrous burden of carnal commandments; as a heavy load of typical ceremonies; and as an anti-evangelical, Christless covenant of

II.

Thou shalt have no other *god before me, &c,* [to the end of the decalogue.]

This *commandment,* which I command thee this day, is not, &c, far off. It is not in heaven, that thou shouldst say, Who shall go up for us to heaven? &c. Neither is it beyond the sea, that thou shouldst say, Who shall go over the sea for us? &c. But *the word is very nigh unto thee,* Deuteronomy 30:11, &c.

So *speak* ye, and so *do,* as they that shall be *judged* by *the law* of liberty, James 2:12.

If ye *fulfil* the royal law, &c, "Thou shalt love thy neighbour as thyself," ye *do well*: for he shall have *judgment* without mercy, that *hath showed* no mercy, James 2:8, 13.

God sending his own Son, &c, for sin, condemned sin in the flesh, that the *righteousness of the law* might be fulfilled in [or by] *us who walk* not after the flesh, &c, Romans 8:3, 4.

Do we make void the *law* through faith? God forbid: yea, we establish the law. Whosoever shall keep the *whole* law, and yet offend in *one* point, he is guilty of *all,* James 2:10. Think not that I am come to destroy the law, &c. Verily I say unto you, &c, one jot or

---

* Here observe, that God prefaces the decalogue by evangelically giving himself to the Jews as *their* God — a gracious God, who had already "*saved*" them out of the land of Egypt," Jude 1:5, and who had a peculiar right to their *faith* and grateful evangelical *obedience.*

works,] Galatians 2:19; Romans 6:14; 7:6.

CHRIST is the end of the law for *righteousness* to every one that *believeth*, Romans 10:4.

O foolish Galatians, who hath bewitched you, that you should not obey the truth, before whose eyes CHRIST has been evidently set forth, crucified among you, &c? Received ye the Spirit by the works of the law, or by the *hearing of faith?* Galatians 3:1, 2.

Stand fast in the liberty wherewith CHRIST hath *made us free*, and be not entangled again with the yoke of bondage; [i.e. with the curse of a Christless law, or with the galling yoke of Mosaic rites,] Galatians 5:1.

If there had been a law given, which could have given life, verily *righteousness* should have been by the law, Galatians 3:21. [Note. *No law of works can justify a sinner: he must be justified by grace, or not at all. If he is not crushed into an atom for his native sinfulness, or sent instantly to hell for his first sin; or if he has an opportunity to repent and turn, all is of grace, and springs from* "the free gift," which "is come upon all men unto justification of life," Romans 5:11.]

tittle shall *in no wise* pass from the [moral] law till all be fulfilled. Whosoever therefore *shall break one* of these *least* commandments, &c, shall be called the* least in the kingdom of heaven, Matthew 5:17.

Ye are *his servants* whom ye *obey;* whether of sin unto death, or of *obedience* unto *righteousness*, Romans 6:16.

We are not without law to God, but *under the law* to Christ, 1 Corinthians 9:21. Let brotherly love continue. He that *loveth* another hath *fulfilled the law*. Love is the *fulfilling of the law*. Fulfil the law of Christ, Hebrews 13:1; Romans 13:10; Galatians 6:2.

Why call ye me *Lord, Lord*, and *do not do* the things which I say? Those mine enemies, who would not that I should reign over them, [or who would not receive and keep my law,] bring hither and slay them before me, Luke 6:46; 19:27.

Awake to *righteousness*, and *sin not*, 1 Corinthians 15:34. Except *your righteousness* shall exceed the righteousness of the scribes, &c, ye shall *in no case* enter into the kingdom of heaven, Matthew 5:20. As it is written, He hath dispersed abroad; he hath given to the poor. *His righteousness* remaineth for ever. Now he that ministereth seed to the sower, multiply your seed sown, and increase the fruits of *your righteousness*, 2 Corinthians 9:9, 10. And it shall be† *our righteousness*, if

---

* Thus apostates (by breaking *one* of the ten commandments, and not repenting according to the privilege, which "the law of liberty" allows in the day of salvation) are *last*, though they were once *first*. I say apostates; because our Lord, St. Paul, and St. James, evidently speak of believers, i.e. of persons already in the kingdom of heaven, or in the Christian dispensation.

† The reader will be glad to see what *judicious* Calvinists make of this passage. Diodati, one of Calvin's most famous successors, comments thus upon it: "God, out of his fatherly benignity and clemency, shall accept from us, his children, this endeavour and study to keep his law, instead of a perfect righteousness, &c. All this discourse ought to be referred to the new obedience, &c, which is the plainer, because most of these statutes were *concessions, remedies,* and *expiations* for sin." (DIOD. in loc.) Mr. Henry is exactly of the same sentiment. "Could we

By the works of the law [when it is opposed to Christ, or abstracted from the promise] shall no flesh living be *justified* [at any time,] Galatians 2:16.

When you have *done all* that is commanded you, say, We are *unprofitable servants*, Luke 17:10.

we observe to do all these commandments, Deuteronomy 6:25.

In the day of judgment — by thy words thou shalt be *justified*. The doers of the law [of liberty — the law connected with the Gospel promises] shall be *justified*, Matthew 12:37; Romans 2:10.

Cast the *unprofitable servant* into outer darkness; there shall be weeping and gnashing of teeth, Matthew 25:30.

If I am not mistaken, the balance of these scriptures shows, that, although we are not under the moral law without Christ, yet we are *under it to Christ,* both as a rule of *life* and a rule of *judgment:* or, to speak more plainly, although we shall not be judged by the law of innocence, i.e. the moral law abstracted from Gospel promises, yet we shall be judged by the "law of liberty," i.e. the moral law connected with the promise of the Gospel: an evangelical law this, under which the merciful God for Christ's sake put mankind in our first parents, when he graciously promised them "the seed of the woman," the atoning Mediator, the royal "Priest, after the order of Melchisedec."

SECTION VIII.

Showing what is God's work, and what is our own; how Christ saves us, and how we work out our own salvation

FIRST SCALE.
Containing the weights of FREE GRACE.

SECOND SCALE.
Containing the weights of FREE WILL.

The hour is coming and now is, when the *dead* shall hear the voice of the Son of God; and they that *hear shall live,* John 5:25.

I *am come,* that they might have LIFE, and that they might have it more abundantly, John 10:10.

You hath he *quickened,* who were dead

Awake, thou that sleepest, *arise* from the *dead*, and Christ *shall give* thee light, Ephesians 5:14.

Except *ye eat* the flesh of the Son of man, &c, ye have no LIFE in you, John 6:53.

Ye *will not* come unto me, that ye

---

perfectly fulfil but that one command of loving God with all our heart, &c, and could we say we had never done otherwise, that would be so our righteousness as to entitle us to the benefits of the covenant of *innocency*, &c. But *that* we cannot pretend to; therefore our *sincere obedience* shall be accepted through a Mediator, to denominate us (as Noah was) '*righteous* before God.'" (HENRY *in loc.*)

in trespasses and sins, Ephesians 2:1.

You being *dead* in your sins, &c, hath he quickened together With him, Colossians 2:13.

Except a man be *born again*, he cannot see the kingdom of God, John 3:3.

The wind bloweth *where it listeth*, &c, so is every one that is *born of the Spirit*, John 3:8.

Being born again, not of corruptible *seed*, but, &c, *by* the word* of God; and this is the word, which by the Gospel is *preached* unto you, 1 Peter 1:23, 25. *Of his own will* begat he us *with the word* of truth, James 1:18.

Christ our *passover* is *sacrificed* for us, 1

might have *life*, John 5:40.

Thou hast a name that thou livest, and *art dead*, &c. *Strengthen* the things that remain, and are *ready to die*, Revelation 3:1, 2.

Every one that *loveth* — every one that *does* righteousness, is *born of God*, 1 John 4:7; 2:29.

Humble yourselves under the mighty hand of God, that he may *exalt* you. For God resisteth the proud and giveth grace to the humble, 1 Peter 5:6, 5.

Wherefore, &c, *lay apart* all filthiness, &c, and receive, f8 &c, the ingrafted word, James 1:19, 21. Whosoever *believeth*, &c, is born of God [according to his dispensation,] 1 John 5:1. As many as *received* him, *to them* [of his own gracious will] gave he power to *become the sons* of God, even to them that *believe* on his name, John 1:12. For ye are all the children of God *by faith* in Christ Jesus. Faith cometh by *hearing* [which is our work,] Galatians 3:26; Romans 10:17. They [the Bereans] *received* the word with all readiness of mind, and *searched* the Scriptures daily, whether those things were so; therefore many of them *believed*: [i.e. received," the ingrafted word," and by that means were "born again" according to the Christian dispensation;] Acts 17:11, 12.

Purge out the old leaven [of wickedness]

---

* How mistaken were the divines that composed the synod of Dort, when speaking of regeneration, they said, without any distinction, (*Illam Deus in nobis sine nobis operatur,*) "God works it in us, without us!" Just as if God believed in us without us! Just as if we received the word without our receiving of it! Just as if the sower and the sun produced corn without the field that bears it! What led them into this mistake was, no doubt, a commendable desire to maintain the honour of free grace. However, if by regeneration they meant the first communication of that fructifying, "saving grace, *which* has appeared to all men" — the first visit, or the first implanting of "that light of life, which enlightens every man that cometh into the world," they spoke a precious truth: for God bestows this *free gift* upon us, absolutely "without us!" Nor could we ever do what he requires of us in the scale of *free will*, if he had not first given us a talent of grace, and if he did not continually help us to use it aright when we have a good will.

Corinthians 6:7.

The blood of Christ *cleanseth* us from all sin, 1 John 1:7.

By one offering *he hath perfected* for ever [in atoning merits] them that are sanctified, Hebrews 10:14.

He by himself purged our sins. Of the people there was *none* with him, Hebrews 1:3; Isaiah 63:3. [Here the incommunicable glory of making a proper atonement for sin is secured to our Lord.]

He *put away sin* by the sacrifice of himself, Hebrews 9:26.

Ye are *sanctified*, &c, in the name of the Lord Jesus, and by the Spirit of our God, 1 Corinthians 6:11.

Surely one shall say, *In* [or *through*] the Lord have I *righteousness* and strength, Isaiah 45:24.

I will make mention of *thy righteousness*, even of thine only, &c. My mouth shall show forth *thy righteousness, and thy salvation* all the day, Psalm 71:15, 16.

My righteousness is near, my salvation is gone forth, Isaiah 51:5.

I bring near *my righteousness*, it shall not be far off; and *my salvation* shall not tarry, Isaiah 46:13.

God sent his Son *Jesus* to *bless you*, in *turning*, &c, *you* from your iniquities, Acts 3:26.

Him [Christ] hath God exalted to *give repentance* to Israel, and *forgiveness of sins*, Acts 5:31.

Be it known unto you, that through this man [Christ] is preached unto you *the forgiveness of sins*, Acts 31:38.

Not by *works of righteousness* which we have done; but of his mercy he saved us, Titus 3:5.

that ye may be a new lump. (*Ibid.*)

Cleanse your hands, ye sinners; and *purify* your hearts, ye double minded, James 4:8.

Let *us go on unto perfection*. This one thing I *do*, &c. I *press* toward the mark, Hebrews 6:1; Philippians 3:13.

Ye have purified your souls in *obeying* the truth. Verily I have *cleansed my heart* in vain, and *washed my hands* in innocency. [The word in vain refers only to a temptation of David when he "saw the prosperity of the wicked,"] 1 Peter 1:22; Psalm 73:13.

Put away the evil of your doing from before mine eyes, Isaiah 1:16.

If a man *purge himself* from these, he shall be a vessel unto honour, *sanctified*, and meet for the Master's use, 2 Timothy 2:21.

In every nation he that *worketh righteousness* is accepted of Him, Acts 10:35.

Then [*when* thou dealest thy bread to the hungry, bringest the poor to thy house, &c,] *then* shall *thy righteousness* go before thee, and the glory of the Lord shall be thy rereward, Isaiah 58:8.

Whosoever *does not righteousness* is not of God, 1 John 3:10.

The Lord rewarded me [David] according to *my righteousness*, according to *the cleanness of my hands*, 2 Samuel 22:21.

I *thought* on my ways, and *turned my feet* unto thy testimonies. I *made haste, and delayed not to keep* thy commandments, Psalm 119:59, 60.

Repent ye, therefore, and *be converted, that* your sins may be *blotted out*, Acts 3:19.

Arise: why tarriest thou? *Wash away thy sins;* calling upon the name of the Lord, Acts 22:16.

Except *your righteousness* exceed the righteousness of the scribes, ye shall *in no case* enter into the kingdom of

And this is the name whereby he shall be called the Lord *our righteousness,* Jeremiah 23:6.

Them that have obtained like precious faith with us, through *the righteousness of God* and our Saviour Jesus Christ, 2 Peter 1:1.

CHRIST is made unto us of God, &c, *righteousness,* 1 Corinthians 1:30.

Even for mine own sake *will I do it,* Isaiah 48:11.

No man can say that Jesus is the Lord, but *by the Holy Ghost* — the Spirit of faith, 1 Corinthians 12:3; 2 Corinthians 4:13.

I will put my *Spirit* within you, Ezekiel 36:27. I will pour out of my Spirit upon all flesh, Acts 2:17.

Hear me, O Lord, that this people may know, &c, that *thou hast turned their heart* back again, 1 Kings 18:37.

A *new heart* will *I give* you, &c. I will take away the stony heart, &c, and I will give you a heart of flesh, Ezekiel 36:26.

The *preparation* of the heart in man is from the Lord. Thou wilt *prepare* their heart, [the heart of the humble,] Proverbs 16:1; Psalm 10:17.

The Lord will *give grace* and glory, Psalm 84:11.

Exceeding great and precious *promises are given* us; that by these you might be partakers of the Divine nature, 2 Peter 1:4.

Come, for all things are now *ready,* Luke 14:17.

The Lord will wait to be gracious, Isaiah 30:18.

Be not dismayed, for I am *thy God;* I will *strengthen* thee, Isaiah 41:10.

Yea, *I will uphold* thee with the *right hand* of my righteousness, Isa. 41:10.

heaven, Matthew 5:20.

He that *does righteousness is* righteous, even as he [Christ] is righteous, 1 John 3:7.

Though Noah, Daniel, and Job were in it [the place about to be destroyed] they should *deliver* but *their own souls by their righteousness,* Ezekiel 14:14.

The *righteousness of* the RIGHTEOUS shall be upon him, Ezekiel 18:20.

I will for this *be inquired of,* &c, to *do* it for them, Ezekiel 36:37.

Your heavenly Father will give his Holy Spirit to them that ask him — to them that obey him, Luke 11:13; Acts 10:32.

Repent and be baptized, &c, [or stand to your baptismal vow,] and ye shall receive the gift of *the Holy Ghost,* Acts 2:38.

Take with you words, and turn to the Lord. *Turn ye* even to me with all *your* heart, Hosea 14:2; Joel 2:12.

Harden not your heart: *rend your heart: make you a new heart,* for why will ye die? Psalm 95:8; Joel 2:13; Ezekiel 18:31.

Nevertheless, there are good things found in thee, in that, &c, *thou hast prepared thine heart* to seek God, 2 Chronicles 19:3.

No good thing will he withhold from them that *walk* uprightly. (*Ib.*)

Having therefore *these promises,* let us *cleanse ourselves* from all filthiness of the flesh and spirit, 2 Corinthians 7:1.

The Lamb's wife hath *made herself ready.* Be ye also *ready,* Revelation 19:7; Matthew 24:44.

Wait on the Lord, &c: wait, I say, on the Lord, Psalm 27:14.

David *encouraged himself in his God,* 1 Samuel 30:6. They that *wait* on the Lord shall renew *their strength,* Isaiah 40:31.

Cursed is the man that *maketh flesh his arm,* Jeremiah 17:5. *Cast* thy burden

I will sprinkle clean water upon you, and ye shall be clean: from all your filthiness, and from all your idols will I *cleanse* you, Ezekiel 36:25.

I the Lord do *keep* it [the spiritual vineyard] lest any hurt it. I will keep it night and day, Isaiah 27:3.

I will *give them* a heart of flesh, that they may walk in my statutes, Ezekiel 11:20.

David my servant shall be king over them; and, &c, they shall *walk* in my judgments, Ezekiel 37:24.

For we are his workmanship, *created in Christ Jesus* unto the good works which God [by his word of command, by providential occurrences, and by secret intimations of his will, ωροητοιμασε] hath before prepared, that we should *walk in them*, Ephesians 2:10.

God hath *saved* us, and called us with a holy CALLING; not according to our works, but according to his own purpose and grace, which was given us in Christ before the world began, 2 Timothy 1:9

I will give them a heart to *know* me, that I am the Lord, Jeremiah 24:7.

I will *put my fear* in their hearts, Jeremiah 32:40.

upon the Lord, and he will sustain thee, Psalm 55:22.

Wash ye, make you clean, Isaiah 1:16. O Jerusalem, *wash thy heart* from wickedness, that thou mayest be saved, Jeremiah 4:14.

Keep thyself pure, 1 Timothy 5:22. Keep thy heart with all diligence, for out of it are the issues of life, Proverbs 4:23.

What does the Lord require of *thee* but, &c, to *walk* humbly with thy God? Micah 6:8. And Enoch[*] *set himself to walk* with God, Genesis 5:24.

He that saith he abideth in him, [God manifested in the flesh,] *ought himself also so to walk*, even as he walked, 1 John 2:6.

And as many as *walk* according to this rule, peace be on them and mercy, Galatians 6:16. That they might *set their hope* in God, &c, and not be as their fathers, a *stubborn* generation, &c, that *set not their heart* aright, &c, and *refused to walk* in his law. But as for me, I *will walk* in mine integrity, Psalm 78:7, 10; 26:11.

The grace of God; that bringeth *salvation*, hath appeared unto all men, teaching us that *we should live* soberly, &c. Give *diligence* to make your CALLING sure. How shall *we* escape if we neglect so great salvation? Titus 2:11, 12; 2 Peter 1:10; Hebrews 2:3.

Then shall we *know, if we follow on* to know the Lord, Hosea 6:3.

They shall not find me, &c, for that they did not *choose the fear of the Lord*, Proverbs 1:29.

---

[*] The word in the original is in the conjugation *Hithpahel*, which signifies *to cause one's self* to do a thing. Our translation does not do it justice. Nor can Zelotes reasonably object to the meaning of the word used by Moses, unless he can prove that Enoch had no hand, and no foot, in his *walking with God;* and that God dragged him as if he had been a passive cart, or a recoiling cannon. However, I readily grant that Enoch did not *set himself to walk* with God without the help of that "*saving grace*, which has appeared to all men," and which so many "receive in vain."

The Lord thy God will *circumcise* thine heart, Deuteronomy 30:6.

I will put my law in their inward parts, and write it in their hearts, Jeremiah 31:33.

We *love* him, *because* he first loved us, 1 John 4:19.

By *grace* ye are SAVED, through *faith;* and that not of yourselves, it is the *gift* of God, Ephesians 2:8. It is of faith, that it might be by grace, Romans 4:16.

Not *for thy righteousness*, &c, dost thou go and *possess their land*, Deuteronomy 9:5.

Not of *works*, lest any man should boast, Ephesians 2:9.

Thou hast hid those things from the *wise and prudent*, [in their own eyes,] and revealed them unto *babes*, Luke 10:21.

Circumcise therefore the foreskin of *your* heart, Deuteronomy 10:16.

Let every man *be swift to hear*, &c. *Receive with meekness* the ingrafted *word*, which is able to *save* your souls, James 1:19, 21. Thy word *have I hid* in my heart, Psalm 119:11.

The Father *loveth* you, *because ye* have believed, John 16:27.

Believe, &c, and thou shalt be SAVED, Acts 16:31. Receive not the grace of God *in vain*, 2 Corinthians 6:1. *Looking diligently* lest any man fail of [or be wanting to] the *grace* of God, Hebrews 12:15.

Inherit the kingdom, &c, for I was hungry, and ye *gave me meat*, &c, Matthew 25:34.

Charge them, &c, to *do good*, &c, that they may lay hold on eternal life, 1 Timothy 6:17, &c.

Who is *wise*, and he shall understand these things? *prudent*, and he shall know them? Hosea 14:9. None of the *wicked* shall understand, but the wise shall understand, Daniel 12:10.

If I am not mistaken, the balance of the preceding scriptures shows that Pharisaism and Antinomianism are equally unscriptural; the harmonious opposition of those passages evincing, (1.) That *our* free will is *subordinately* a worker with *God's* free grace in every thing but a *proper atonement* for sin, and *the first implanting* of the light which enlightens every man that comes into the world: such an *atonement* having been fully completed by *Christ's blood*, and such an *implanting* being entirely performed by *his Spirit*. (2.) That Honestus is most dreadfully mistaken, when he makes next to nothing of free grace and her works. (3.) That Zelotes obtrudes a most dangerous paradox upon the simple, when he preaches *finished salvation* in the Crispian sense of the word. And (4.) That St. Paul speaks as the oracles of God, when he says, "God worketh in you, &c, therefore work ye out your own salvation."

SECTION IX.

Displaying the most wonderful work of free grace, the general redemption of the lost world of the ungodly by Jesus Christ: and the most astonishing work of free will, the obstinate neglect of that redemption, by those who do despite to the Spirit of grace.

HONESTUS has such high thoughts of his uprightness and good works, that he sometimes doubts if he is a lost sinner by nature, and if the virtue of Christ's blood is absolutely necessary to his justification. And the mind of Zelotes is so full of absolute election and reprobating partiality, that he thinks the sacrifice of Christ was confined to the little part of mankind which he calls "the Church, the pleasant children, Israel, Jacob, Ephraim, God's people, the elect, the little flock," &c. Those happy souls, if you believe him, are loved with an everlasting love, and all the rest of mankind are hated with an everlasting hate. Christ never bled, never died for these. God purposely let them fall in the first Adam, and absolutely denied them all interest in Christ the second Adam, that they might necessarily be wicked and infallibly be damned, "to illustrate his glory by their destruction."

To rectify those mistakes; to show Honestus that *all* men, without exception, are *so wicked* by nature as to stand in need of Christ's atoning blood; and to convince Zelotes that Christ was *so good* as to shed it for *all* men, without exception; I throw into my Scales some of the weights stamped with *general* redemption: I say *some*, because others have already been produced in the third section.

HOW ALL men are *temporally* redeemed by Christ's *blood*.

Why some men are not *eternally* redeemed by Christ's *Spirit*.

THE WEIGHTS OF FREE GRACE.
NOTE. General redemption by price and free grace *cannot* fail, because it is entirely the work of CHRIST, who does all things well.

THE WEIGHTS OF FREE WILL.
NOTE. General redemption by power and free will can and *does* fail, because many refuse to the last, subordinately "to work out their own salvation."

We see Jesus, who was made a little lower than the angels [i.e. was made man] for the suffering of death, &c, that he, *by the grace of God*, should taste death for every man, Hebrew 2:9.

As I *live*, saith the Lord God, I have no pleasure in the death of the wicked; but that the *wicked turn* from his way and live; — *turn ye, turn ye*, from your evil ways; for why *will ye die*, O house of Israel? Ezekiel 18:23; 33:11.

When we were yet without strength, Christ *died for the ungodly*, Romans 5:6. The Son of man is come *to save that which is lost*, Luke 19:10. Behold the Lamb of God, that taketh away the sin of *the world*, John 1:29. God so loved the world, that he gave his only begotten Son, &c, that the world

And now, &c, judge, I pray you, between me and my vineyard. *What could* have been done *more* to my vineyard, that I have not done in it? Wherefore, when I looked that it *should bring forth* grapes, *brought it forth wild* grapes? And now I will, &c, lay it waste, &c, I will also command the through him might be saved [upon Gospel terms,] John 3:16, 17. This is indeed the Christ, the Saviour of the world, John 4:42. We have seen and do testify, that the Father sent the Son to be the Saviour of the world, 1 John 4:14. Behold, I bring you good tidings of great joy, which shall be to all people; for unto you is born, &c, a Saviour, who is Christ the Lord, Luke 2:10, 11.

Christ is our peace, who hath made *both* [Jews and Gentiles] one, &c, that he might [on his part] reconcile both unto God by the cross, Ephesians 2:14, 16. [Now Jews and Gentiles are equivalent to *the world*.] God was in Christ reconciling *the world* unto himself, not imputing their trespasses unto them, [when they believe,] 2 Corinthians 5:10.

It pleased the *Father*, &c, having *made peace* by the blood of his cross, by him to reconcile *all things* unto himself, by him, I say, whether they be *things in earth*, or things in heaven. And you, &c, hath he reconciled, &c, *through death*, to present you holy, &c, *if ye* continue in the faith, &c, and be not moved away from the hope of the Gospel, &c, which is *preached to every creature* that is under heaven, Colossians 1:19, 23.

We trust in the living God, Who is the *Saviour of all men*, especially of those that believe: [because such obediently submit to the terms of eternal salvation; for initial salvation depends on no terms on our part,] 1 Timothy 4:10.

The *philanthropy* [or] kindness of God our Saviour toward man appeared, Titus 3:4. The bread of God giveth life unto the world: the bread that I will give for *the life of the world*, John 6:33, 51.

clouds that they rain no rain upon it. For *the vineyard of the Lord* is the house of Israel, and the men of Judah are his *pleasant plant;* and he *looked for* judgment, but behold oppression; for righteousness, but behold a cry, Isaiah 5:3, 7. They have *turned* unto me *the back*, and not the face; though I taught them, rising early, Jeremiah 32:33.

And now, *because* ye have *done all these works*, saith the Lord, and I spake unto you, rising up early, and speaking, but *ye heard not;* and I called you, but *ye answered not;* therefore, &c, I will cast you out of my sight, &c; *therefore* pray not for this people, &c, for I *will not hear thee*, Jeremiah 7:13, 15, 16.

Wilt thou not from this time cry unto me, *my Father*, &c? Hast thou Seen that which backsliding Israel hath done? &c. And I said, after she had done all these things, *Turn thou* unto me; [return unto me, for I have redeemed thee, Isaiah 44:72,] but *she returned not*. And, &c, when for *all the causes* whereby backsliding Israel committed adultery, I had *put her away*, and given her *a bill of divorce*, yet her treacherous sister Judah feared not, but went and played the harlot also, Jeremiah 3:4-8.

If thou wilt receive my words, &c, so that thou *incline thine ear* to wisdom, and *apply thine heart* to understanding, &c, *then* shalt thou understand the fear of the Lord; and *find* the knowledge of God, Proverbs 2:1, &c.

As the girdle cleaveth to the loins of a man, *so have I caused to cleave to me* the *whole* house of Israel, saith the Lord; that they might be *unto me for a people*, &c. but *they would not* hear. Therefore &c, I will not pity, nor spare, nor have

Jesus said, I am the light of the world. I came, &c, *to save the world*, John 8:12; 12:47. That the world may *believe* thou hast sent me, John 17:21. This is a faithful saying, and worthy of all acceptation, [or, *of all men* to be received] that Christ came into the world to save* sinners, of whom I am chief, 1 Timothy 1:15.

I exhort, that first of all supplications, &c, and giving of thanks be made for *all men*, &c, for *this is good and acceptable*, [not in the sight of Zelotes,] but in the sight of *God our Saviour,* who will have all men to be saved, and come to the knowledge of the truth. For there is, &c, one Mediator between God and men, the man Christ, who gave himself *a ransom for* all, &c. I will, therefore, that men pray every where, &c, without doubting, 1 Timothy 2:1, &c.

Mine eyes have seen [Christ] thy salvation, which thou hast prepared before the face of all people, a light to lighten the Gentiles, and the glory of thy people Israel, [i.e. the Jews,] Luke ii, &c. It is a light thing that thou shouldst be my servant, to raise up the tribes of Jacob, [i.e. the Jews,] &c. I will also give thee for a light to the Gentiles, that thou mayest be my *salvation unto the end of the earth,* Isaiah 49:6. God, &c, preached before the Gospel to Abraham, saying, In thee, [i.e. thy seed, which is Christ] shall *all nations* [yea] all families of the earth be

mercy, but *destroy* them, Jeremiah 13:11, 12, 14.

This is the condemnation, that *light is come into the world,* and men loved darkness rather than light, *because* their deeds were evil. For every one that [*actually*] *does evil*, hateth the light, neither cometh to the light, lest his deeds should be reproved. But he that *does truth*, cometh to the light, John 3:19, &c.

Jeshurun, [i.e. the righteous,] waxed fat and kicked, &c. He forsook God, &c, and lightly esteemed the rock of his salvation, &c. They sacrificed to devils, &c. And, when the Lord saw it, he abhorred them, *because* of the provoking of his sons and daughters. And he said, I will hide my face from them, &c, for a fire is kindled in mine anger, and shall burn to the lowest hell, &c. I will spend mine arrows upon them, Deuteronomy 32:15, 23.

Because I have called, and *ye refused*, I have stretched out my hand, and *no man regarded;* but ye have *set at naught* all my counsel, and *would none* of my reproof; I also will mock when your destruction cometh as a whirlwind. Then shall they call upon me, but I will not answer, &c; for that they hated knowledge, and *did not choose* the fear of the Lord, &c, Proverbs 1:24, &c. If ye *walk* contrary to me, &c, I will bring seven times *more* plagues upon you, &c. And if ye *will not* be reformed by these things, I will punish you *yet* seven times, &c. And if ye *will not* for all this

* If Christ came to save sinners, yea, the *chief* of sinners, did his goodness, impartiality, equity, truth, and holiness, permit him *unconditionally* to reprobate any sinner *less* than the *chief?* And if he came to save sinners, the *chief* not excepted, why does Zelotes except all that die in unbelief? If they do not believe, and do their part as redeemed souls, is it right to infer that Christ did not die for them and do his part as the Redeemer or Saviour of *all* men? Especially since the Scriptures testify that eternal salvation is suspended on our *works* of faith; and that the reprobates perish, because they "deny in *works* the Lord that bought them?"

blessed, Galatians 3:8, 16; Genesis 12:3.

In him [the Word made flesh] was life, and the life was the light *of men;* and the light shineth [even] in the darkness, &c, [that] comprehended it not. John came for a witness, to bear witness of the light, that all men through it [δι αυτου φῶος] might believe, &c. That was the true light which lighteth *every man* that cometh into *the world,* John 1:4, &c

hearken to me, &c, I will cast down your carcasses upon the carcasses of your idols, &c, and my soul shall *abhor* you, Leviticus 26:21-30.

Every branch in me that beareth not fruit [during the day of salvation] he taketh away, &c, and it is *withered,* and men gather them, and cast them into the fire and they are burned, John 15:2-6. Ye shall bow down to the slaughter, *because* when I called ye did *not answer,* Isaiah 65:12.

From the preceding scriptures it appears, that as in a vine some branches are nearer the root than others; so among mankind some men have a stronger and more immediate union with Christ than others; but, so long as their *day of salvation* lasts, all men have some interest in him; there being as many ways of being in Christ, as there are dispensations of Gospel grace. That infants are interested in him, seems evident from Romans 5:18, and Mark 10:14: and that Cornelius, for example, was in Christ as a *just heathen,* before he was in him as a *Jewish proselyte,* much more before he was in him as a *Christian believer,* is not less evident from Matthew 25:29; Psalm 50:23; Luke 16:10, 11. But when the expression, *being in Christ,* is taken in its most confined sense, as it is in some of the epistles, it means a being so fully acquainted with, and so intimately united to Christ, as to enjoy the privileges peculiar to the Christian dispensation, like Cornelius, when he had believed the Gospel of Christ, and was baptized with the Holy Ghost. To say that he was in every respect *without Christ* before, is to strike a blow at the root: it is to suppose that a man can be accepted *out of* the Beloved, work righteousness *without* Christ's assistance, and "bring forth fruits meet for repentance," in a *total separation* from the vine. Thus it is, however, that the Solifidianism of Zelotes meets with the Pharisaism of Honestus.

I.

All men should honour the Son [by believing on him,] John 5:28. I will draw all men to me, John 12:32. The free gift came upon all men, Romans 5:18. The saving grace of God hath appeared unto all men, Titus 2:11. God giveth to all men liberally, and upbraideth not, James 1:5. The Lord is good to all [or loving to every man] and his tender mercies are over *all his works,* Psalm 145:9. If one died for all, then were all dead. He died for all, that

II.

I have purged thee [I have done the part of a Saviour] and thou wast not purged: [thou hast not done the part of a penitent sinner,] Ezekiel 24:13. Behold, I stand at the door and knock; if *any man hear* my voice, and open the door [by the obedience of faith] I will come in to him, and will sup with him, and he with me, Revelation 3:20.

they which live, should, &c, live to him who died for them, 2 Corinthians 5:14, 15.

He is despised and rejected of *men*, &c. We [men] esteemed him not, &c. Surely he was wounded for our transgressions, &c, and with his stripes we are [*initially*, and his seed, persevering believers, *completely*] healed. *All we* [men] like sheep have *gone astray: we have turned every one to his own way,* and the Lord hath laid on him the iniquity of us all, &c. He poured out his soul unto death, &c; he bore the sin [רבים] of the* multitudes, and made intercession for the transgressors, Isaiah 53:3-6, 12. If *any man* sin, we have *an Advocate* with the Father, Jesus Christ the righteous: and he *is the propitiation* for our sins; and not for ours *only*, but *also* for the sins of the whole world, 1 John 2:1, 2.

Of a truth I perceive that God *is no respecter* of persons, Acts 10:34. If ye have respect to persons, ye commit sin, James 2:9. It is written, *Be ye holy,* for I am holy. And if ye call on the Father, who, *without respect of persons, judgeth according to every man's work,* pass the time of your sojourning here in fear; forasmuch as ye know that ye were redeemed, &c, with the precious blood of Christ, 1 Peter 1:17, 18. [How different is this Gospel from the Gospel of the day] And *if to elect* and *to reprobate is to judge* that myriads of unborn people shall be eternally loved or hated *without any respect to their tempers and actions,* what can we say of doctrines, which fix upon God the spot that Solomon describes in the following words?] It is not good to have *respect of persons in judgment.* He that says to the wicked, Thou art righteous, [or he that says to what is not, *Thou art wicked, and I unconditionally appoint thee for eternal destruction,*] him shall the people curse: nations shall abhor him, Proverbs 24:23, 24.

GENERAL REDEMPTION *and* FREE GRACE *are the gracious spring whence flow the general, sincere, and rational missions, Gospel calls, commands, exhortations, and expostulations which follow.*

God hath reconciled us to himself by Jesus Christ, 2 Corinthians 5:18.

Him [Christ] God hath exalted to *give repentance to Israel* — [and] to the Gentiles, [i.e. to all mankind, who are made up of Jews and Gentiles,] Acts

Through the LIBERTY OF OUR WILL *we may* IMPROVE *or* NEGLECT *so great redemption; we may make, or refuse to make our sincere election and rational calling sure; as appears from the following scriptures:* —

We pray you, in Christ's stead, *be ye reconciled* to God, 2 Corinthians 5:20.

And they all, with one consent, began to *make excuse,* &c. I have married a wife, and therefore I *cannot* come, &c. Then the master of the

---

* The first signification of the Hebrew word רב (B R) is a *multitude;* and as Isaiah uses it in the plural number, I hope Zelotes will not think that I take an undue liberty, when I render it the multitudes: namely, the multitudes of "transgressors" mentioned in the same verse; or the multitudes of men that "have turned every one to his own ways." See verses 3, 6.

5:31; 11:18. [Hence it is that] God now commandeth *all men every where* to repent; because he will judge the world in righteousness, Acts 17:30, 31.

Thou [Paul] shalt be his [Christ's] witness unto *all men*. To make all men see what is the fellowship of the mystery [of redeeming and sanctifying love,] Acts 22:15; Ephesians 3:9.

Look unto me, and be ye *saved, all the ends of the earth*, Isaiah 45:22. Come unto me, all ye that travel [with sin] and are heavy laden [with troubles] and I will give you rest, Matthew 11:28.
Jesus spake unto them, saying, All power is given unto me in heaven, and *in earth*, go ye therefore and teach [proselyte] *all nations*, baptizing *them* in the name of the Father, and of the Son, and of the Holy Ghost. [A sure proof this that the Son has redeemed all nations, and purchased for them the influences of the Holy Ghost; Matthew 28:18, 19.]
Go into *all the world*, and preach the Gospel to every creature, &c, and they went forth preaching every where, Mark 16:15, 20. *Whosoever will*, let him take of the water of life *freely*, Revelation 22:17. The Lord is *not willing* that any should perish, but that *all* should come to repentance, 2 Peter 3:9.
Come now [ye rulers of Sodom, ye people of Gomorrah] and *let us reason together*, saith the Lord. Though your sins be as scarlet, they shall be as white as snow, &c. Ye shall eat *the good* of the land, Isaiah 1:10, 18, 19.
Ho, *every one* that thirsteth [for life and happiness] come ye to the waters, and he that *hath no money;* come ye, buy wine and milk, without money and

house being angry said, &c, None of those men, who were *bidden* [or *called*, and refused to make their calling and election sure] shall taste of my supper, Luke 17:18.
How *long, ye simple ones*, will ye love simplicity? and *the scorners* delight in scorning? and *fools* hate knowledge? *Turn you* at my reproof: behold, I will pour out my Spirit unto you, Proverbs 1:22, 23.
I am the Lord thy God, &c, *open* thy mouth wide, and *I will fill* it. But *my people would not* hearken to my voice, and *Israel would none of me*, Psalm 81:10, 11.
I call heaven and earth to record this day *against you*, that I have set before you life and death, blessing and cursing: therefore *choose life*, that thou mayest live, Deuteronomy 30:19. Mary hath *chosen* the good part, Luke 10:42. *Choose* you this day whom ye will serve, &c, but as for me, and my house, [we have made our choice] *we will serve* the Lord, Joshua 24:15.
He that *rejecteth me*, &c, hath one that *judgeth* him. The word [of the Gospel] that I have spoken, the same shall judge him in the last day, John 12:48. We *will not* have this man to reign over us. Those, &c, who *would not* that I should reign over them, slay them before me, Luke 19:14, 27.

If ye be willing and obedient, &c. But *if ye refuse* and rebel, *ye shall be devoured* with the sword; for the mouth of the Lord hath spoken it, verses 19, 20.

Thus spake the Lord of hosts, &c. But *they refused* to hearken, and *pulled away the shoulder* and *stopped their ears*, that they should not hear. Yea, *they* without price. *Incline** your ear, hear, and your *soul shall live;* and *I will make* an everlasting covenant with you, even the sure mercies of David, &c. *Seek* ye the Lord while *he may be found;* and *call* upon him while he is near. Let *the wicked forsake* his way, &c, and *return* unto the Lord, for he will *abundantly pardon*, Isaiah 55:1-7.

Wisdom standeth in the top of high places: she crieth at the gates, at the entry of the city, &c, Unto you, O *men*, I call, and my voice is to *the sons of men*, &c. Hear, for I will speak excellent things, &c. Receive my instruction, rather than choice gold, &c. Take *my yoke* upon you, and learn of me; for I am meek and lowly in heart, and ye shall *find rest* unto your souls; for my yoke is easy, and my burden is light, Proverbs 8:2, &c; Matthew 11:29, 30.

All the people [of bloody devoted Jerusalem] ran together unto them [Peter and John:] and when Peter saw it, he answered, Ye [all the people] are the children of the covenant, which God made, saying to Abraham, "And in thy seed shall *all the kindreds of the earth* be blessed." Unto you [all the people] first [as being Jews] God, &c, sent his Son Jesus to *bless you* [all the people] by turning away *every one of you* from his iniquities, Acts 3:9, 11, 12, 25, 26.

To whom [the Gentiles] I send thee to open *their* eyes, and to turn them from darkness to light, and from the

made their hearts as an adamant stone, *lest* they should hear the law, and the words which the Lord of hosts hath sent *in his Spirit*, &c. *Therefore* it is come to pass, that as he cried, and *they would not hear;* so they cried, and *I would not hear*, saith the Lord of hosts, Zechariah 7:8, 13.

I also will *choose* their delusions, &c, *because* when *I called*, none did answer; when I spake, they *did not hear;* but they *did evil* before mine eyes, and *chose* that in which I delighted not, Isaiah 66:4.

The Jews were *filled with envy*, and spake against those things which were spoken by Paul; contradicting and blaspheming. Then Paul waxed bold, and said, It was *necessary* that the word of God [the Gospel of Christ] should first have been spoken to *you:* but, seeing *ye put it from you, and judge yourselves unworthy of eternal life*, lo, we turn to the Gentiles: for so hath the Lord commanded, Acts 13:45, 46. [Query. How could it be necessary "that the Gospel should first be spoken to those Jews," if God had eternally fixed, that there should be no Gospel, — no Saviour, for them?]

Them that *perish because they received not* the love of the truth, that they might be saved. And *for this cause* God shall send them strong delusions, &c, that

---

* Zelotes represents the "sure mercies of David," and "the everlasting covenant," as absolutely unconditional. But I appeal to Candidus: does not this passage mention four requisites on our part? Inclining our ear: hearing: seeking the Lord: and forsaking our wicked way? And do not we accordingly find, Acts 13:34, that many of those to whom St. Paul offered those "sure mercies," missed them by "contradicting," instead of "inclining their ear?"

power of Satan unto God; *that they may* receive forgiveness of sins, and an inheritance among them who are sanctified by faith that is in me, Acts 26:17, 18.

Behold, NOW is the *accepted time!* behold, NOW is the *day of salvation,* 2 Corinthians 6:2. Wherefore, beloved, account that the *long suffering* of the Lord is salvation; even as our beloved brother Paul also hath written to you [in the next passage,] 2 Peter 3:9, 15. Despisest thou the *riches of God's goodness,* and forbearance, and long suffering; not knowing that the goodness of God leadeth thee to repentance, and of consequence to eternal salvation? Romans 2:4.

they all might be damned, who believed not the truth, but *had pleasure* in unrighteousness, 2 Thessalonians 2:10, &c.

O Jerusalem, &c, how often *would* I have gathered together thy children [among whom were the chief priests, scribes, and Pharisees] as a hen doth gather her brood under her wings, and *ye would not?* Luke 13:34. Thus saith the Lord of hosts, Behold, I will bring upon this city, &c, all the evil that I have pronounced against it; *because they have hardened their necks that they might not hear* my words, Jeremiah 19:15. The Lord is our God, and we are the people of his pasture and the sheep of his hand. To-day, if *ye will* hear his voice, *harden not* your hearts as in the provocation, &c, when your fathers saw my works. Forty years long I was grieved with that generation, and said, It is a people that *do err* in their hearts, &c. — To whom I sware in *my wrath,* that they *should not* enter into my rest, Psalm 45:7, &c

This is one of the "clouds of *Scripture* witnesses," which we produce in favour of redeeming free grace and electing free will. To some people this cloud appears so big with evidence, and so luminous, that they think Honestus and Zelotes, with all the admirers of Socinus and Calvin, can never raise dust enough to involve it in darkness, at least before those who have not yet permitted prejudice to put out both their eyes. It is worth notice, that Honestus has not one Scripture to prove that any man can be saved without the Redeemer's atonement. On the contrary, we read that there is salvation "in no other;" that there is "no other name," or person, "whereby we must be saved;" and that "no man cometh to the Father but by him — the light of the world, and the light of men." And it is remarkable, that although the peculiar gospel of Zelotes is founded upon the doctrine of a partial atonement, there is not in all the Bible one passage that represents "the world" as being made up of the elect only; not one text which asserts that Christ made an atonement for one part of the world exclusively of the other; no, nor one word which, being candidly understood according to the context, cuts off either man, woman, or child from the benefit of Christ's redemption; at least so long as the day of grace and initial salvation lasteth. Nay, the very reverse is directly or indirectly asserted: for our Lord threatened his very apostles with a hell, "where the worm dieth not, and the fire is not quenched," if they did not "pluck out the offending eye." St. Peter speaks of those who "bring swift destruction upon themselves by denying the Lord that bought them." And St. Paul mentions "destruction *of a* brother for whom Christ died;" yea, and the "much sorer punishment *of him* who had trodden under foot the Son of God, had counted the blood of the covenant, wherewith he was sanctified, [and consequently redeemed,] an unholy thing, and had done despite to the Spirit of grace," by which Spirit he and other apostates "were once enlightened, and had tasted the heavenly gift — the good word of God, and the powers of the world to come," Hebrews 10:29; 6:4.

Hence it appears, that of all the unscriptural doctrines which prejudiced divines have imposed upon the simple, none is more directly contrary to Scripture than the doctrine of Christ's particular atonement. — An Arian can produce, "My Father is greater than I;" and a Papist, "This is my body," in support of their error; but a Calvinist cannot produce one word that excludes even Cain and Judas from the temporary interest in Christ's atonement, whereby they had "the day of initial salvation," which they once enjoyed and abused.

The tide of Scripture evidence in favour of *general* redemption is so strong, that at times it carries away both St. Augustine and Calvin, notwithstanding their particular resistance. The former says, *Ægrotat humanum genus, non morbis corporis, sed peccatis. Jacet toto orbe terrarum ab oriente usque ad occidentem grandis ægrotus. Ad sanandum grandem ægrotum descendit omnipotens Medicus.* (AUG. *De Verbis Domini, Sermon* 59.) "MANKIND is sick, not with bodily diseases, but with sins. The HUGE PATIENT lies ALL THE WORLD over, stretched from east to west. To heal the huge patient, the omnipotent Physician descends from heaven." As for Calvin, in a happy moment, he does not scruple to say: *Se* TOTI MUNDO *propitium ostendit, cum sine exceptione omnes ad Christi fidem vocat, quæ nihil aliud est quam ingressus in vitam.* (CAL. *in Job,* 3:15, 16.) "God shows himself propitious to ALL THE WORLD, when he, *without exception,* invites ALL MEN to believe in Christ; faith being the entrance into life." Agreeable to this, when he comments upon these words of St. Paul, "There is one Mediator between God and men, the man Christ," he says with great truth: *Cum itaque* COMMUNE *mortis suæ beneficium* OMNIBUS *esse velit, injuriam illi faciunt, qui opinione sua quempiam arcent a spe salutis.* (CALV. in 1 Timothy 2:5.) "Since therefore Christ is willing that the *benefit of his death* should be COMMON TO ALL MEN; they do him an injury, who, by their opinion, debar any one from the hope of salvation." If, Calvin himself being judge, "they do Christ an injury, who by their opinion debar ANY ONE from the hope of salvation," how great, how multiplied an injury does Zelotes do to the Redeemer, by his opinion of particular redemption; an opinion this, which effectually debars all the unredeemed from the least well grounded hope of ever escaping the damnation of hell, be their endeavours after salvation ever so strong and ever so many.

As I set my seal with fuller confidence to the doctrine of our Lord's Divine carriage upon the cross, when I hear the centurion who headed his executioners cry out, "Truly this was the Son of God:" so I embrace the doctrine of general redemption with a fuller persuasion of its truth, when I hear Calvin himself say, "Forasmuch as the upshot of a happy life consists in the knowledge of God, lest the door of happiness should be shut against *any man,* God has not only implanted in the minds of men, that which we call THE SEED OF RELIGION; but he has likewise so manifested himself in all the fabric of the world, and presents himself daily to them in so plain a manner, that they cannot open their eyes, but they must needs discover him." His own words are: *Quia ultimus beatæ vitæ finis in Dei cognitione positus est, ne cui præclusus esset ad felicitatem aditus, non solum hominum mentibus indidit illud, quod dicimus*

RELIGIONIS SEMEN; *sed ita se patefecit in toto mundi opificio, ac se quotidie palam offert, ut aperire oculos nequeant quin eum aspicere cogantur. (Inst. lib.* i, *cap.* 5, sec. 1.) Happy would it have been for us, if Calvin the Calvinist had been of one mind with Calvin the reformer. Had this been the case, he would never have encouraged those who are called by his name to despise "THE SEED OF RELIGION which God has implanted in the minds of men, lest the door of happiness should be shut against *any one.*" Nor would he inconsistently have taught his admirers to do Christ, and desponding souls, that very "injury," against which he justly bears his testimony in one of the preceding quotations.

Although Zelotes has a peculiar veneration for Austin and Calvin, yet when they speak of redemption as the oracles of God, he begs leave to dissent from them both.

To maintain, therefore, even against them, his favourite doctrine of absolute election and preterition, he advances some objections, three or four of which deserve our attention, not so much indeed on account of their weight, as on account of the great stress which he lays upon them.

OBJECTION FIRST. "You assert," says he, "that the doctrine of general redemption is Scriptural, and that no man is absolutely reprobated: but I can produce a text strong enough to convince you of your error. If the majority of mankind were not unconditionally reprobated, our Lord would at least have prayed for them: but this he expressly refused to do in these words, "I pray for them [my disciples:] *I pray not for the world,*" John 17:9. Here *the world* is evidently *excluded* from all interest in our Lord's praying breath; and how much more from all interest in his atoning blood?"

ANSWER. I have already touched upon this objection, (Third Check, vol. first.) To what I have said there, I now add the following fuller reply: — Our Lord never excluded "the world" from all share in his intercession. When he said, "I pray for them, I pray not for the world;" it is just as if he had said, "The blessing which I now ask for my believing disciples, I do not ask 'for the world;' not because I have absolutely reprobated the world, but because the world is not in a capacity of receiving this peculiar blessing." Therefore; to take occasion from that expression to traduce Christ as a reprobating respecter of persons, is as ungenerous as to affirm that the master of a grammar school is a partial, capricious man, who pays no attention to the greatest part of his scholars, because, when he made critical remarks upon Homer, he once said, "My lecture is for the Greek class, and not the Latin."

That this is the easy, natural sense of our Lord's words, will appear by the following observations. (1.) Does he not just after (verse 11) mention the favour which he did not ask for the world? "Holy Father, keep, through thy name, those whom thou hast given me, [by the decree of faith,] that they may be one as we are." (2.) Would it not have been absurd in Christ to pray the Father to *keep* "a world" of unbelievers, and to make them *one?* (3.) Though our Lord prayed at first for his disciples alone, did he not, before he concluded his prayer, (verse 2,) pray for future believers? And then giving the utmost latitude to his charitable wishes, did he not pray (verse 21) "that the world *might believe*" — and (verse 23) "that the world *might know that God had sent him?*" (4.) Was not this praying that the world might be made partakers of the very blessing which his disciples *then* enjoyed: witness these words, (ver. 24, 25,) "O righteous Father, the world has not known thee: but I have known thee, and these [believers] have known that thou hast sent me?" (5.) "The world hateth me," said our Lord. Now if he "never prayed for *the world*," how could he be said to have loved and prayed for *his enemies?* How badly will Zelotes be off, if he stands only in the imputed righteousness of a man, who would never pray for the bulk of his enemies or neighbours? But this is not all; for (6.) If our Lord "never prayed for the world," he acted the part of those wicked Pharisees who "laid upon other people's shoulders heavy burthens which they *took care* not to touch with one of their fingers;" for he said to his followers, "Pray for them who despitefully use you and persecute you," [that is, pray for *the world*,] Matthew 5:44. But if we believe Zelotes, "he said and did not:" like some implacable preachers who recommend a forgiving temper, he gave good precepts and set a bad example.

I ask Candidus' pardon for detaining him so long about so frivolous an argument: but as it is that which Zelotes most frequently produces in favour of *particular* redemption, and the *absolute* reprobation of the world, I thought it my duty to expose his well meant mistake, and to wipe off the blot which his opinion (not he) fixes upon our Lord's character; — an opinion this, which represents Christ's prayer, "Father, forgive them," to be all of a piece with Judas' kiss. For, if Christ prayed with his lips, that his worldly murderers might be forgiven, while in his *heart* he absolutely excluded them from all interest in his intercession, and in the blood, by which alone they could be forgiven; might he not as well have said, My praying lips salute, but my reprobating heart betrays you: hail reprobates and be damned?

OBJECTION SECOND. "All your *carnal reasonings* and logical subtleties can never overthrow the plain word of God. The Scriptures cannot be broken, and they expressly mention particular redemption. Revelation 5:8, 9, we read that 'four-and-twenty elders having harps, sung a new song, saying, &c, Thou hast redeemed us to God by thy blood, out of every kindred, and tongue, and people, and nation.' Again, Revelation 14:1, &c, we read of one hundred and forty-four thousand 'harpers that stood with the Lamb on Mount Sion, having his Father's name written in their foreheads, &c, singing as it were a new song which no man could learn but the one hundred and forty-four thousand who were redeemed from the earth, &c; these were redeemed from among men.' Now if all men were redeemed, would not St. John speak nonsense if he said that the elect were redeemed from among men? But as he positively says so, it follows that the generality of men are passed by, or left in a reprobate state absolutely unredeemed."

ANSWER. There is a redemption by power distinct from, though connected with our redemption by price. *That* redemption is in many things particular; consisting chiefly in the actual bestowing of the temporal, spiritual, or eternal deliverances and blessings which the atoning blood has peculiarly merited for *believers;* "Christ being the Saviour of all men, but especially of them that believe." Various degrees of *that* redemption are pointed out in the following scriptures, as well as in the passages which you quote out of the book of Revelation. "The angel who redeemed me from all evil, bless the lads. The Lord hath redeemed you from the hand of Pharaoh. When these things begin to come to pass, then look up, for your redemption draweth nigh. Ye are sealed, &c, until the redemption of the purchased possession. We ourselves groan, waiting for the redemption of our body." When therefore some eminent saints sing, "Thou hast redeemed us to God by thy blood [sprinkled upon our consciences through faith] out of every kindred," &c, it is not because Christ shed more blood upon the cross for them than for other people; but because, through the faithful improvement of the *five talents*, which sovereign, distinguishing grace had entrusted them with, they excelled in virtue, and "overcame the accuser of the brethren by the blood of the Lamb," more gloriously than the generality of their fellow believers do.

One or two arguments will, I hope, convince the reader that Zelotes has no right to press into the service of free wrath the texts produced in his objection; as he certainly does, when he applies them to a particular redemption by price. (1.) God promised to Abraham, that "all the nations, *yea*, all the kindreds of the earth should be blessed in his seed, *that is*, in Christ, the propitiation for the sins of the whole world." And our Lord commands, accordingly, that his redeeming work be preached to "every creature among all nations:" but if there be no redemption but that of those *elders* and *saints* mentioned Revelation 5:8, 9, and said to be "redeemed to God, out of every kindred, and tongue, and people, and nation, *it follows, that* every kindred, and tongue, and people, and nation," is left unredeemed in flat contradiction to God's promise, as well as to the general tenor of the Scriptures. (2.) The number of the *saved* is greater than that of the *redeemed*. For St. John, Revelation 7:9, describes the saved as "a great multitude which no man could number." But the persons "redeemed from the earth and redeemed from among men," are said to be just one hundred and forty-four thousand: whence it follows, either that an "innumerable multitude" of men will sing "salvation to the Lamb," without having been redeemed; or that one hundred and forty-four thousand souls are "a multitude which no man can number;" and that as the number of these "redeemed from the earth and from among men," is already *completed*, all the rest of mankind are consigned over to inevitable, finished damnation. Thus, according to the objection which I answer, Zelotes himself is passed by, as well as "every kindred, and tongue, and people, and nation." O ye kindreds and tongues, ye people and nations, — ye English and Welsh, ye Scotch and Irish, awake to your native good sense; nor dignify any longer with the name of "doctrines of *grace*," inconsistent tenets imported from Geneva, — barbarous tenets that rob you nationally of the inestimable jewel of redemption, and leave you nationally in the lurch with Cain and Judas — with wretches whose reprobation (if we believe Zelotes) was absolutely insured before your happy islands emerged out of the sea, and the sea out of the chaos.

OBJECTION THIRD, But we are pressed with rational, as well as Scriptural arguments. To show that Christ, who was lavish of his tears over justly reprobated Jerusalem, was so sparing of his blood, that he would not shed one drop of it for the world, and for the reprobated nations therein, much less for the arch reprobate, Judas: to show this, I say, Zelotes asks, "How could Christ redeem Judas? Was not Judas' soul actually in hell, beyond the reach of redemption, when Christ bled upon the cross?"

ANSWER. The fallacy of this argument will be sufficiently pointed out by retorting it thus: — "How could Christ redeem David? Was not David's soul actually in heaven, beyond the need of redemption, when Christ bled upon the ignominious tree?" The truth is, from the foundation of the world Christ intentionally shed his blood, to procure a temporary salvation for all men, and an "eternal salvation for them that obey him, and work out their salvation with fear and trembling." With respect to David and Judas, "in the day of their visitation," through Christ's intended sacrifice, they had both an "accepted time;" and, while the one by penitential faith secured *eternal* salvation, the other by obstinate unbelief totally fell from *initial* salvation, and by his own sin "went to his own," and not to Adam's "place."

OBJECTION FORTH. As to the difficulty which Zelotes raises from a supposed "defect in Divine wisdom, if Christ offered for *all* a sacrifice which he foresaw *many* would not be benefited by:" I once more observe that all men universally are benefited by the sacrifice of the Lamb of God. For *all* men enjoy a day of *initial* and temporary salvation, in consequence of Christ's mediation: and if *many* do not improve their redemption so as to be *eternally* benefited thereby, their madness is no more a reflection upon God's wisdom, than the folly of those angels who did not improve their creation. Again: this objection, taken from Divine wisdom, and levelled at our doctrine, is so much the more extraordinary, as, upon the plan of particular redemption, Divine *wisdom* (to say nothing of Divine veracity, impartiality, and mercy) receives an eternal blot. For how can "God judge the world *in wisdom* according to the Gospel?" Romans 2:16. How can he wisely upbraid men with their impenitency, and condemn them because "they have not believed in the name of his only begotten Son," John 3:18, if there never was *for them* a Gospel to embrace, repentance to exercise, and an only begotten Son of God to believe in?

And now, reader, sum up the evidence arising from the scriptures balanced, the arguments proposed, and the objections answered in this section; and say whether the doctrines of bound will and curtailed redemption, or, which is all one, the doctrines of necessary sin, and absolute, personal, yea, national reprobation, can, with any propriety, be called either *sweet* "doctrines of *grace*," or *Scriptural* doctrines of *wisdom*.

SECTION X.

The doctrine of free grace is farther maintained against Honestus; and that of free will and just wrath against Zelotes.

The scale of FREE GRACE and JUST wrath in God.

Resistible FREE GRACE is the spring of all our graces and mercies.

The Father, as Creator, gives to the Son, as Redeemer, the souls that yield to his *paternal* drawings; and they who resist those drawings, *cannot* come to the Son for rest and liberty.

IT is GOD, who *worketh* in you both to *will* and to *do* of his good pleasure. [That is, God, as Creator, has wrought in you the power to will and to do what is right: God, as Redeemer, has restored you that noble power which

The scale of FREE WILL in man, without FREE wrath in God.

Perverse FREE WILL is the spring of all our sins and curses.

The Son, as Redeemer, brings to the Father, for the promise of the Holy Ghost, the souls that yield to his *filial* drawings; and they who resist those drawings, *cannot* come to the Father for the Spirit of adoption.

WHEREFORE *work out your own salvation* with fear and trembling. Arise and *be doing*, and the Lord be with you, 1 Chronicles 22:16. *Do* all things without disputing, &c, *that* I may rejoice, that I have not run *in vain*, was lost by the fall: and God, as Sanctifier, excites and helps you to make a proper use of it. Therefore "grieve him not:" for, as it is his good pleasure to help you now, so, if you "do despite to the Spirit of his grace," it may be his good pleasure "to give you up to a reprobate mind," and to "swear in his anger that his Spirit shall strive with you" no more. That this is the apostle's meaning, appears from his own words to those very Philippians, in the opposite scale.] Philippians 2:13.

Thy people [shall, or will be] *willing* in the day of thy power: or, as we have it in the reading Psalms, *In the day of thy power shall the people offer free will offerings,* Psalm 110:3.

God hath exalted him [Christ] *to give*

neither laboured in vain. I follow after, *if that* I may apprehend that for which I am apprehended of Christ. This one thing I *do,* &c, I *press* toward the mark, &c. *Be followers* of me, for many *walk* — enemies of the cross of Christ, whose end is *destruction.* Those things, which ye have seen in me, do: and the God of peace *shall* be with you, Philippians 2:12, &c; 3:12, &c; 4:9, &c.

I am not [personally] sent but to the lost *sheep* of the house of Israel. But *my people,* &c, would none of me, Matthew 15:24; Psalm 81:11. He came to his own, and his own received him not, John 1:11. The power of the Lord was present to heal them, but the Pharisees murmured. They *rejected* the counsel of God against themselves, Luke 5:17, 30; 7:30. If I by the finger [i.e. the power] of God cast out devils, no doubt the kingdom of God [the day of God's power] is come upon you, Luke 11:15, &c. He did not many mighty works [i.e. he did not mightily exert his power] there, because of their unbelief. He could do there no mighty work, [consistently with his wise plan,] and he marvelled because of their unbelief, [which was the source of their unwillingness,] Matthew 13:58; Mark 6:5, 6. Now the things which belong unto thy peace, &c, are hid from thine eyes, because thou knewest not the day of [my power, and of] thy visitation, Luke 19:42, &c. How *often would* I have gathered thy children, as a hen does gather her brood under her wings, and ye would not, Luke 13:34. [Any one of those scriptures shows, that free grace does not *necessitate* free will; and all of them together make a good measure, running over into Zelotes' bosom.]

God is willing that *all* should come to

repentance, Acts 5:31. God peradventure [i.e. if they are not judicially given up to a reprobate mind, and they do not obstinately harden themselves] will give them [that oppose themselves] repentance to the acknowledging of the truth, 2 Timothy 2:25.

Every good *gift,* &c, is from above, and cometh down from the Father of lights, James 1:17. *Faith* is the gift of God, Ephesians 2:8. They rehearsed how God had opened the door of faith [in Christ] to the Gentiles, Acts 14:27. To you it is *given,* on the behalf of Christ, to believe in him, Philippians 1:29.

When the Gentiles heard this they were glad, and as many as were [τεταγμενοι] *disposed** *for,* [our

repentance, 2 Peter 3:9. God's goodness leadeth thee to repentance, Romans 2:4. And the rest of men, which were not killed by these plagues, yet repented not, Revelation 9:20. Then began he to upbraid the cities, &c, because they repented not, Matthew 9:20. I gave her space to repent, and she repented not, Revelation 2:21.

Faith cometh by *hearing* [the work of man,] Romans 10:17. Lord, I *believe,* [not *thou believest for me,*] *help* thou my unbelief, Mark 9:24. He upbraided them with their unbelief, Mark 14:14. *How* is it ye have no faith? Mark 4:40. How can *you* believe, *who receive* honour one of another? John 5:44. The publicans believed, &c. And ye, when ye had seen it, repented not afterward, *that ye might believe,* Matthew 21:30. Thomas said, I will not believe, John 20:25. Having damnation, because they have cast off their first faith, 1 Timothy 5:12.

These (the Jews of Berea) were more noble [or *candid*] than those of Thessalonica, in that they *received* the

---

* The Rev. Mr. Madan, in his "Scriptural Comment upon the Thirty-nine Articles," second edition, p. 71, says, "This method of construction is attended with the disadvantage of giving the Greek language a sense which it disowns, and therefore to be rejected;" and in support of this assertion, and of Calvinism, he quotes Mr. Leigh's "Critica Sacra." But I think, most unfortunately, since in the very next page we have it under Mr. Leigh's, and of course under Mr. Madan's own hand, that the learned scholiast "Syrus renders it [the controverted word] 'dispositi,' [DISPOSED,] for he knew not that the heretics of our day would dream of understanding τεταγμενοι, &c, to signify INWARDLY DISPOSED." Now as "the remonstrants" are immediately after by name represented as "the heretics of our day," I beg leave to vindicate their heresy: though I fear it must be at the expense of Mr. Madan's and Mr. Leigh's "orthodoxy."

First, then, take notice, reader, that these gentlemen grant us all we contend for, when they grant that the word which our translators render "ordained," means also "disposed, placed, ordered," or "ranged, as soldiers that keep their ranks in the field of battle," which is the ordinary meaning of the expression in the classics. Now, according to Mr. Madan's scheme, the "disposition" of the persons that believed was merely "extrinsic, outward." They had no hand in the matter, God "disposed" them by his necessitating grace, as Bezaleel "disposed" the twelve precious stones which adorned Aaron's breastplate. But, according to our supposed "heresy," the free will of those candid Gentiles (in subordination to free grace) had a hand in "disposing them to take the kingdom of heaven by violence." They were like willing soldiers, who obey the orders of their general, and "range" or "dispose" themselves to storm a fortified town.

(2.) But, says Mr. Madan, "the Greek language disowns this sense." To this assertion I oppose all the Greek lexicons I am acquainted with, and (for the sake of my English readers) I produce Johnson's English dictionary, who, under the word "tactics," which comes from the controverted word "tatto," informs us that "tactics" is "the art of 'ranging' men in the field of battle;" and every body knows that before men can be ranged in the field, two things are absolutely necessary; an authoritative, directing skill in the general, and an active, obedient submission in the soldiers. This was exactly the case with the Gentiles mentioned in the text; before they could be "disposed for eternal life," two things were absolutely requisite; the helpful teaching of God's free grace, and the submissive yielding of their own free will, touched by that grace which the "indisposed (at least at that time) received in vain."

(3.) It is remarkable that the word τεταγμενό occurs but in one other place in the New Testament, Romans 13:1. "The powers that are, are τεταγμενοι, ordained or placed." And I grant that there it signifies a Divine, "extrinsic" appointment only. But why? Truly because the apostle immediately adds, υπο τε δεου, "They are ordained or placed OF GOD." Now, if the word τεταγμενό alone necessarily signified "ordained, disposed, or placed OF GOD," as Mr. Madan's scheme requires; the apostle would have given himself a needless trouble in adding the words, "OF GOD," when he wrote to the Romans; and as St. Luke adds them not in our text, it is a proof that he leaves us at liberty to think, according to the doctrine of the Gospel axioms, that the Gentiles, who believed, were "disposed" to it by the concurrence of free grace and free will — of GOD and THEMSELVES. God "worked," to use St. Paul's words, and they "worked out."

(4.) A similar scripture will throw light upon our text. Romans 9:22, we read that" God endureth with much long suffering the vessels of wrath κατηρτισμενα FITTED for destruction." The word "fitted," in the original, is exactly in the same voice and tense as the word "ordained" or "disposed" in the text. Now if Mr. Madan's observation about "the Greek language" be just, and if the Gentiles who believed were entirely "disposed OF GOD to eternal life," so these "vessels of wrath" were entirely "fitted OF GOD for destruction." But if he, and every good man, shudders at the horrid idea of worshipping a God who absolutely "fits" his own creatures "for destruction:" — if the words κατηρτισμενα εις απωλειαν mean not only "inwardly fitted," but SELF FITTED rather than GOD FITTED "for destruction," why should νοτ τεταγμενοι εις ζωην αιωνοιν mean SELF DISPOSED as well as GOD DISPOSED "for eternal life?"

(5.) St. Luke, who wrote the Acts, is the best explainer of the meaning of his own expression. Accordingly, Luke 2:51, we find that he applies to Christ a word answering to, and compounded of that of our text. He was, says he, (υποτασσομενος) "subject or subjected to his parents." Now I appeal to my readers, and ask whether the remonstrants deserve the name of "dreaming heretics" for believing, (1.) That our Lord's subjection to his parents was not merely "outward" and passive, as that of an undutiful child who is subject to his superiors, when, rod in hand, they have forced him to submit. And (2.) That it was "inward" and active, or, to speak plainer, that "he subjected himself" of his own free will to his parents.

(6.) St. Paul informs us that the "veil of Moses is yet upon the heart of the Jews, when they read" the Old Testament; and one would be tempted to think that Calvin's veil is yet upon the eyes of his admirers, when they read the New Testament. What else could have hindered such learned men as Mr. Leigh and Mr. Madan from taking notice, that when the sacred writers use the passive voice, they do it frequently in a sense which answers to the Hebrew voice "hithpahel," which means "to cause oneself to do a thing." I beg leave to produce some instances. 1 Corinthians 14:32, "The spirits of the prophets υποτασσεται are subject [that is, subject themselves] to the prophets." Romans 10:3, "Ουχ υπεταγησαν, They have not been subjected, or, (as our translators, Calvinists as they were, have not scrupled to render it,) They have not submitted themselves to the righteousness of God." Acts 2:40, "σωθητε, Be ye saved, or save yourselves." Ephesians 5:22, "Wives, υποτασσεσθε, be subject or submit yourselves to your own husbands." 1 Peter 5:6, "ταπεινωθητε, Be humble, or humble yourselves." James 4:7, "υποταγητε, Be ye submissive," or, as we have it in our Bibles, "submit yourselves to God," &c, &c. I hope these examples will convince my readers, that, if our translators had shown themselves "heretics," and men unacquainted with "the Greek language," supposing they had rendered our text, "As many as (through grace) had disposed themselves, or were (inwardly) disposed for eternal life, believed," they can hardly pass for orthodox or good Grecians now, since they have so often been guilty of the pretended error, which Mr. Leigh supposes peculiar to the "dreaming heretics of our day."

(7.) All the Scriptures show that man and free will have their part to do in the work of salvation, as well as Christ and free grace. If this is denied, I appeal to the multitude of passages which fill my second Scale; and I ask, Is it not strange, that a doctrine, supported by a variety of scriptures, should be called "heresy" by men that, "as real Protestants," profess to admit the Scriptures as the rule of their faith. I shall conclude this note by an appeal to the context.

(8.) St. Paul having called the Jews to believe in Christ, bids them "beware," Acts 13:40, lest they should be found among the despisers that perish in their unbelief. Now how absurd would this caution have been, if a forcible decree of absolute election or reprobation had irreversibly ordained them to eternal life, or to eternal death! Would the apostle have betrayed more folly if he had bid them "beware" lest the sun should rise or set at its appointed time? Again, verse 46, we are informed that these unbelievers "judged themselves unworthy of eternal life," and "put the word" of God's grace "from them." But if Mr. Madan's scheme were Scriptural, would not the historian have said, that God, from the foundation of the world, had absolutely "judged them unworthy of eternal life," and therefore had never "put" or sent to "them" the word of his grace? Once more: we are told, verse 45, that indulged envy, which the Jews were filled with, made them "speak against those things which were spoken by Paul, that is, made them disbelieve, and show their unbelief. Now is it not highly reasonable to understand the words of the text thus, according to that part of the context: "As many as" did not obstinately harbour envy, prejudice, love of honour, or worldly mindedness: — "As many as" did not "put the word from them, and judge themselves unworthy of eternal life, believed?" Nay, might we not properly explain the text thus, according to the doctrine of the talents, and the progressive dispensations of Divine grace, so frequently mentioned in the Scriptures: "As many as believed in God, believed also" in Christ, whom Paul particularly preached at that time; — as many as were humble and teachable, received the ingrafted word:" for "God resisteth the proud, but giveth grace to the humble. His secret is with them that fear him, and he will show them his covenant."

(9.) But what need is there of appealing to the context? Does not the text answer for itself, while Mr. Madan's sense of it affords a sufficient antidote to all who dislike absurd consequences, and are afraid of traducing the Holy One of Israel? Let reason decide. If "as many as [were in Antioch] were [Calvinistically] ordained to eternal life," believed under that sermon of St. Paul, (for almost the whole city came together to hear the word of God,) it follows, that all who believed not "then," were eternally shut up in unbelief; that all the elect believed at once; that they who do not believe at one time shall never believe at another; and that when Paul returned to Antioch, few souls, if any, could be converted by his ministry; God having at once taken "as many as were ordained to eternal life," and left all the rest to the devil. But,

(10.) The most dreadful consequence is yet behind. If they that believed did it merely because they "were absolutely ordained of God to eternal life," it follows, by a parity of reason, that those who disbelieved, did it merely because they were absolutely ordained of God to

Creeds and Scripture Scales

translators say *ordained to*] eternal life believed, Acts 13:48.

He *that hath* an ear to hear, let him hear what the Spirit saith. Revelation 2:7.

Can the Ethiopian change his skin, and the leopard his spots? *then* may ye also *do good* [without my gracious help] that are accustomed to do evil, Jeremiah 13:23.

Neither *knoweth* any man the Father, save, &c, he to whomsoever the Son *will reveal* him; [and he will reveal him unto babes, as appears from the context,] Matthew 11:25, 27. Flesh and blood hath not revealed this unto thee, [that Jesus is the Christ, &c,] but *my Father*, Matthew 16:17.

word with all readiness of mind and *searched* the Scriptures daily, whether those things were so: therefore many of them believed, Acts 17:11, 12.

They have ears to hear, and hear not; for they are a rebellious house, Ezekiel 12:2.

[It is very remarkable that the Lord, to show his readiness to help those obstinate offenders, says, just after] O Jerusalem, *wilt thou not* be made clean? *When* shall it once be?

God resisteth the proud, but *giveth grace* to the humble; [i.e. to babes,] &c. Submit therefore yourselves to God, &c, humble yourselves in the sight of the Lord, and he shall lift you up, James 4:6, &c. If any man will do his will, he *shall know* of the doctrine, whether it be of God, John 7:17. The secret of the Lord is with them that fear him, Psalm 25:14.

To understand aright some passages in St. John's Gospel, we must remember that, wherever the Gospel of Christ is preached, the Father particularly draws to the Son as Redeemer, those that believe in him as Creator. And this he does, sometimes by cords of love, sometimes by cords of fear, and always by cords of conviction and humiliation. They that yield to these drawings become "babes, poor in spirit," and members of "the little flock" of humble souls, "to whom it is the Father's good pleasure to give the kingdom. For he giveth grace to the HUMBLE; — yea "he giveth grace and glory, and no good thing will he withhold from them that" follow his drawings, and "lead a godly life."

Those convinced, humbled souls, conscious of their lost estate, and inquiring the way to heaven, as honest Cornelius, and the trembling jailer — those souls, I say, the Father in a particular manner gives to the Son, as being prepared for him, and just ready to enter into his dispensation. "They believe in God, they *must* also believe in Christ;" and the part of the Gospel that eminently suits them, is that which Paul preached to the penitent jailer; and Peter to the devout centurion.

The Jews about Capernaum showed great readiness to follow Jesus: but it was out of curiosity, and not out of hunger after righteousness. Their hearts went more after loaves and fishes, than after grace and glory. In a word, they continued to be grossly unfaithful to their light, under the dispensation of the Father, or of God as Creator. Hence it is, that our Lord said to them, "Labour not for the meat which

eternal death: God having bound them by the help of Adam in everlasting chains of unbelief and sin. Thus, while proud, wicked, stubborn unbelievers are entirely exculpated, the God of all mercies is indirectly charged with free wrath, and finished damnation.

perisheth, but for that which endureth to everlasting life." Mind your souls as well as your bodies: be no more practical Atheists. To vindicate themselves they pretended to have a great desire to serve God. "What shall we do," said they, "that we may work the works of God?" "This is the work of God," replied our Lord: "this is the thing which God" peculiarly requires of those who are under His dispensation, — " that ye believe on him whom he hath sent," — i.e. that ye submit to MY dispensation. Here the Jews began to cavil and say, "What sign showest thou, that we may believe thee?" Our Lord, to give them to understand that they were not so ready to believe upon proper evidence as they professed to be, said to them, "Ye have seen me" and my miracles, "and yet ye believe not." Then comes the verse, on which Zelotes founds his doctrine of absolute grace to the elect, and of absolute wrath to all the rest of mankind: "All that the Father [particularly] giveth me," because they are particularly convinced that they want a mediator between God and them; and because they are obedient to his drawings, and to the light of their dispensation; — all these, says our Lord, "shall or will come unto me," and I will be as ready to receive them, as the Father is to draw them to me, for "him that cometh to me, I will in no wise cast out:" I will admit him to the privileges of my dispensation; and, if he be faithful, I will even introduce him into the dispensation of the Holy Ghost, — into the kingdom, that does not consist in meat and drink, nor yet in bare penitential righteousness, but also in "peace and joy *in the Holy Ghost.*" "And this is the Father's will, that, of all whom he has given me," that I may bless them with the blessings of my dispensation, "I should lose nothing" by my *negligence* as *a Saviour,* or as *a Shepherd:* although some will lose themselves by their own perverseness and wilful apostasy. That this is our Lord's meaning, is evident from his own doctrine about his disciples being "the salt of the earth," and about some "losing their savour," and "losing their own soul." But above all, this appears from his express declaration concerning one of his apostles. This being premised, I balance the favourite text of Zelotes thus: —

I.

All that the *Father giveth me* [by the decree of faith, according to the order of the dispensations] shall [or will] come to me; and him that cometh unto me I will in no wise cast out. [If he be lost it will not be by my losing him, but by his *losing his own soul.* It will not be by my *casting him out,* but by his casting himself out. Witness the young man, who thought our Lord's terms too hard; and "went away sorrowful:" witness again Judas, who "went out," and of his own accord "drew back unto perdition."] John 6:37.

II.

I have manifested thy name [O Father] to the men whom thou *hast given me* out of the world. Thine they were [they belonged to thy dispensation, they believed in thee] and thou *gavest them me,* [they entered my dispensation, and believed in me.] Those that thou gavest me, I have kept [according to the rules of my dispensation] and none of them is lost BUT [he that has destroyed himself, Judas,] the son of perdition, that *the Scripture might be fulfilled,* John 17:6, 12.

Inquire we now what scriptures were fulfilled by the perdition of Judas. They are either *general* or *particular:* (1.) The general are such as these: "The turning away of the simple shall slay them," Proverbs 1:32. "When the righteous man turneth from his righteousness, [and who can be a 'righteous man' without true faith?] he shall die in his sin." Again: "When I say to the righteous," that "he shall surely live, if he trust to his righteousness, and commit iniquity, he shall die for it," Ezekiel 3:20; 33:13. (2.) The *particular* scriptures fulfilled by the destruction of Judas are these: Psalm 41:9, "Mine own familiar friend in whom I trusted, who did eat of my bread, hath lifted up his heel against me." These words are expressly applied to Judas by our Lord himself, John 12:18, and they demonstrate that Judas was not always a cursed hypocrite, unless Zelotes can make appear that our Lord reposed his *trust* in a hypocrite; whom he had chosen for his "own familiar friend." Again: "Let his days be few, and let another take his office, or his bishopric." These words are quoted from Psalm 109, and particularly applied to Judas by St. Peter, Acts 1:20. Now, to know whether Judas' perdition was absolute, flowing from the unconditional reprobation of God, and not from Judas' foreseen backsliding, we need only compare the two Psalms where his sin and perdition are described. The one informs us, that before he lifted up his heel against Christ, he was *Christ's own familiar friend,* and so sincere that the Searcher of hearts trusted in him: and the other Psalm describes the cause of Judas' personal reprobation thus: "Let his days be few, and let another take his office," &c, "because that [though he once knew how to tread in the steps of the merciful Lord, who honoured him with a share in his familiar friendship, yet] he remembered not to show mercy, but persecuted the poor, that he might even slay the broken in heart. As he loved cursing, so let it come unto him: as he delighted not in blessing, so let it be far from him: as he clothed himself with cursing like as with a garment, so let it come into his bowels like water," Psalm 109:8, 16, &c. Hence it is evident, that if Judas was lost agreeably to the Scriptural prediction of his *perdition;* and if that very prophecy informs us that "his days were few, because he remembered not to show mercy, &c," we horribly wrong God when we suppose that this means, because God never remembered to show any mercy to Judas, because God was a graceless God to Iscariot thousands of years before the infant culprit drew his first breath. Brethren and fathers, as many as are yet concerned for our Creator's honour, and our Saviour's reputation, resolutely bear your testimony with David and the Holy Ghost, against this doctrine; so shall Zelotes blush to charge still the Father of mercies with the absolute reprobation of Judas, not only in opposition to all good nature, truth, and equity; but against as plain a declaration of God, as any that can be found in all the Scriptures. "Let his days be few, and let another take his office, &c, because he remembered not to show mercy, but persecuted the poor, that he might [betray innocent blood, and] even slay the broken in heart."*

---

* To say that God stood in need of Judas' wickedness to deliver his Son to the Jews, is not less absurd than impious. "God has no need of the sinful man." Any boy that had once heard our Lord preach in the temple, and seen him go to the garden of Gethsemane, might have given as proper an information to the high priest, and been as proper a guide to the mob, as Judas: especially as Christ was not less determined to deliver himself, than the Jews were to apprehend him. With regard to the notion that Judas was a wicked man — an absolute unbeliever — a cursed hypocrite when our Lord gave him a place in his familiar friendship, and raised him to the dignity of an apostle, it is both unscriptural and scandalous. (1.) *Unscriptural:* for the Scripture informs us, that when the Lord immediately proceeds to an election of that nature, "he looketh on the heart," 1 Samuel 16:7. Again: when the eleven apostles prayed that God would overrule the lot which they were about to cast for a proper person to succeed Judas,

To conclude: if God has taken such particular care to clear himself from the charge of absolutely appointing Judas to be a "son of perdition!" Nay, if CHRIST himself asserts that the FATHER *gave him* Judas, as well as the other apostles: — and if the HOLY GHOST declares, by the, mouth of David, that Judas was once *Christ's familiar friend,* and as such honoured with his *trust* and confidence; is it not evident, that the doctrine of free wrath, and of any man's (even Judas') absolute,

---

they said, "Thou, Lord, who knowest the hearts of all men, show which of these two thou hast chosen, that he might take part of the ministry, from which Judas by transgression fell," Acts 1:24. Now as Judas *fell by transgression,* he was undoubtedly *raised by righteousness,* unless Zelotes can make appear, that he rose the same way he fell; and, that as he fell by a bribe, so he gave some of our Lord's friends a bribe, to get himself nominated to one of the twelve apostolic bishoprics: but even then, how does this agree with our Lord's "knowing the heart," and choosing accordingly? (2.) This notion is *scandalous:* it sets Christ in the most contemptible light. How will he condemn, in the great day, men of power in the Church, who for by-ends commit the care of souls to the most wicked of men? How will he even find fault with them, if he did set them the example himself, in passing by all the *honest* and good men in Judea, to go and set the apostolic mitre upon the head of a *thief* — of a "wolf in sheep's clothing?" In the name of wisdom I ask, Could Christ do this, and yet remain the "*good* Shepherd?" How different is the account that St. Paul gives us of his own election to the apostleship. "The glorious Gospel of God was committed to my charge," says he; "and I thank Christ, who hath enabled me, for that he counted me faithful, putting me into the ministry," 1 Timothy 1:11, 12. Now, if we represent Christ as putting Paul into the ministry because he counted him faithful, and Judas because he counted him *unfaithful* — a thief — a traitor — a cursed hypocrite, do we not make Christ a Proteus? Are his ways equal? Has he not two weights? God, I grant, sets sometimes a wicked king over a wicked people, but it is according to the ordinary course of human affairs, and in his anger; to chastise a sinful nation with a royal rod. But what had the unformed Christian Church done to deserve being scourged with the rod of apostolic wickedness? And what course of human affairs obliged our Lord to fix upon a wicked man in a new election to a new dignity — and, what is most striking, in an election to which he proceeded without the interposition of any free agent but himself?

O Zelotes, mistake me not: if I plead the cause of Judas' sincerity, when he "left all to follow Christ," and when our Lord passed by thousands, immediately to choose him for his "own familiar friend in whom he trusted;" — for a preacher of his Gospel, and an apostle of his Church; I do not do it so much for Judas' sake, as for the honour of Christ, and the comfort of his timorous, doubting followers. Alas: if Christ could show distinguishing favour and familiar friendship to a man, on whom he had absolutely set his black seal of unconditional reprobation — to a man whom, from the beginning of the world, he had without any provocation marked out for a goat, and for unavoidable damnation; if he could converse, eat, drink, travel, lodge, and pray for years with a man to whom he bore from everlasting, and will bear to all eternity, a settled ill will, an immortal hatred, where is sincerity? where is the Lamb without blemish? the Lamb of God in whose mouth no guile was ever found? If Christ be such a *sly damner* of one of his twelve apostles as the "doctrines of grace" (so called) represent him to be, who can trust him? What professor — what Gospel minister can assure himself that Christ has not chosen and called him for purposes as sinister as those for which it is supposed that Judas was chosen, and called to be Christ's *familiar friend?* Nay, if Christ, barely on account of Adam's sin, left Judas in the lurch, and even *betrayed* him into a deeper hell by a *mock* call, may he not have done the same by Zelotes, by me, and by all the professors in the world? O ye "doctrines of grace," if you are as sweet as honey, in the mouth of Zelotes, as soon as I have eaten you, my belly is bitter; poison corrodes my vitals; I must either part with you, my reason, or my peace.

unconditional reprobation is as gross an imposition upon Bible Christians, as it is a foul blot upon all the Divine perfections?

I.

Ye *believe* not, *because* ye are not of my sheep, as I said unto you, [John 8:37. He that is of God, heareth God's words: ye therefore hear them not, because you are not of God — i.e. *because ye are not godly, whatever ye pretend.*] My sheep [those that really belong to my dispensation, and compose my little flock] my sheep, I say, *hear my voice,* [they mind, understand, approve, embrace my doctrine,] and they follow me [in the narrow way of faith and obedience:] and [in that way] I give unto them eternal life, and [in that way] they shall never perish, neither shall any pluck them out of my hand. [For who shall harm them if they be followers of that which is good? 1 Peter 3:13.] My Father who gave them me, [who agreed, that where my dispensation is opened, those who truly believe on him as Creator, should be peculiarly given me as head of the Christian Church, to make them Christian priests and kings unto him:] my Father, I say, who gave them me, is greater than all, and none shall pluck them [that thus hear my voice and follow me] out of my Father's hand: for I and my Father are one [in *nature, power,* and *faithfulness,* to show that "the way of the Lord is strength to the upright; but destruction shall be to the workers of iniquity," Proverbs 10:29.] John 10:2, 26, &c.

No man can come unto me except the Father draw him, [and he be faithful to the Father's attraction:] every man, therefore, that hath *heard and learned of* [that is, submitted to] *the Father* [and to his drawings] cometh unto me. There are some of you that

II.

He that *believeth not* is condemned already, *because* he hath not believed, &c. And this is the [ground of unbelief and] *condemnation,* that light is come into the world, and men loved darkness rather than light, *because* their deeds were evil. For every one that [buries his talent of light, and] *doeth evil,* hateth the light, neither cometh to the light, *lest* his deeds should be reproved. But he that doth truth [he that occupies till I come with more light] cometh to the light, that his deeds may be made manifest, that they are wrought in God, John 3:18, &c. [All that our Lord meant, then, when he said to the Pharisees, "Ye believe not, *because* ye are not of my sheep," is explained in such scriptures as these.] He that is *faithful* in that which is *least,* is faithful also in *much,* Luke 16:10. How can ye believe, who *receive* honour one of another, and seek not the honour that cometh from God? [Had you been faithful to the light of conscience, you would have believed Moses; and] had ye believed Moses, ye would have believed me: but if ye believe not his writings, how shall ye believe my words? John 5:44, &c. [If ye believe not in God, how shall ye believe in me? If you dishonour my Father, how can you honour me?]

[FIRST PROPOSITION: *The Father draws all to himself, and gives to the Son all those who yield to his drawings. Witness the following scriptures.*] All the day long I have stretched forth my hand to [draw] *a disobedient people,* Romans 10:21. Despisest thou the riches of God's believe not, &c. Therefore said I unto you, that *no man can come unto me, except it be given him of my Father,* John 6:44, 45, 64, 65.

The meaning is, that *no man can believe in the Son, who has not first a degree of true faith in the Father.* "Ye believe in God, believe also in me," says Christ. "All must honour the Son, as they honour the Father." All, therefore, that do not "learn of," that is, submit to, and honour the Father, cannot come to the Son and pay him homage. He that obstinately refuses to take the first step in the faith, cannot take the second. To show, therefore, that Zelotes cannot with propriety ground the doctrine of free wrath upon John 6, any more than upon John 10, I need only prove the three propositions contained in the opposite Scale.

forbearance, *not considering* that his goodness *leadeth* [that is, gently draweth] thee to repentance, [and of consequence to faith in a Mediator between God and man?] Romans 2:4. Of those whom *thou hast given me none* is lost [hitherto] but [one, Judas, who is already so completely lost, that I may now call him] a son of perdition, John 17:12.

SECOND PROPOSITION. *The Son likewise,* "who is the light that enlightens every man, draws all to himself," and *then brings to the Father those who yield to his attraction,* "that they may receive the adoption of sons." Witness the following scriptures: — "And I, if I be lifted up from the earth, will draw all men unto me, John 12:32. Come unto me, all ye that labour [and are restless] and I will give you rest." If you come to me, I will plainly reveal to you the Father: I will enable you by my peaceful Spirit to call him ABBA, FATHER, with delightful assurance: [for] no man knoweth the Father but the Son, and he, to whomsoever the Son will reveal him [by the Holy Ghost,] Matthew 11:27, 28.

THIRD PROPOSITION. *These drawings of the Father, and of the Son, are not irresistible,* as appears from the following scriptures: "Because I have stretched out my hands, and no man [comparatively] regarded [my drawings,] I will mock when your destruction cometh as a whirlwind, Proverbs 1:24, 27. These things I say unto you [obstinate Pharisees,] that you might be [drawn unto me, and] saved, &c, and [notwithstanding my drawings] ye will not come unto me, that ye might have life," John 5:34, 40.

The preceding propositions are founded upon the *proportion of faith,* upon the relations of Father, Son, and Holy Ghost, and upon the doctrine of the dispensations explained in the Essay on Truth.

Creeds and Scripture Scales

Should Zelotes compare these propositions, he will see that if the Father does not particularly give all men to the Son, that they may receive the peculiar blessings of the Christian dispensation; and if the Son does not explicitly reveal the Father to all men by the Spirit of adoption, or the baptism of the Holy Ghost; it is not out of free, reprobating wrath; but merely for the two following reasons: (1.) As in the political world all men are not called to be princes and kings; so in the religious world all are not blessed with five talents; all are not called to believe explicitly in the Son and in the Holy Ghost, or to be "made kings and priests to God" in the Christian Church. (2.) Of the many that are called to this honour, few (comparatively) are obedient to the heavenly calling; and, therefore, "few are chosen" to "receive the crown of *Christian* righteousness:" or, as our Lord expresses it, few "are counted worthy to stand before the Son of man" among them that have been *faithful* to their five talents. But, as all men have one talent till they have buried it, and God has judicially taken it from them: as all men are at least under the dispensation of the Father, as a gracious and faithful Creator: as Christ, "the light that lighteth every man that cometh into the world," draws all men implicitly to this merciful Creator; while the Spirit, as "the saving grace which has appeared unto all men, *implicitly* teaches them to deny ungodliness," and to live soberly, righteously, and piously in this present world: as this is the case, I say, what can we think of the absolute election or reprobation of individuals, which insures saving grace and heaven to some, while (through the denial of *every degree* of saving grace) it secures damning sin and everlasting burnings to others?

If it be asked, how it has happened that so many divines have embraced these tenets? I reply, It has been chiefly owing to their inattention to the doctrine of the dispensations. Being altogether taken up with the *particular* dispensations of the Son and of the Holy Ghost, they overlooked, as Peter *once* did, the *general* dispensation of the Father, which is the basis of all the superior economies of Divine grace. They paid no manner of attention to the noble testimony, which that apostle bore when, parting with his last scrap of Jewish bigotry, he said: "Of a truth, I perceive that God is no respecter of persons: but in every nation he that feareth him, and worketh righteousness, is accepted of him." As if he had said, Though distinguishing grace should never give two talents to a heathen that fears God and works righteousness; though he should never explicitly hear of the Son, and of the Holy Ghost; yet shall he enter, as a faithful servant, into the joy of his merciful Lord, when many "children of the kingdom shall be thrust out:" for it is revealed upon earth, and of consequence it is decreed in heaven, that they who are chosen and called to partake of the Divine *peace*, which is essential to the peculiar dispensations of the Son, and of the unspeakable *joy*, which is essential to the peculiar dispensation of the Holy Ghost, shall be reprobated, or "thrust out," if they do not "make their *high* calling and election sure:" while they that were only chosen and called to the *righteousness* essential to the general dispensation of the Father, shall "receive the reward of the inheritance," if they do but "walk worthy of their *inferior* election and calling."

Methinks that Zelotes, instead of producing solid arguments in favour of his doctrines, complains that I bring certain strange things to his ears; and that the distinction between the *Christian* dispensation, and the *other* economies of grace, by which I have solved his Calvinistic difficulties, has absolutely no foundation in the Scripture. That I may convince him of his mistake in this respect, to what I have said on this subject in the *Essay on Truth*, I add the following proof of my dealing in old truths, and not in "novel chimeras." St. Paul, 1 Corinthians 9:17, declares that "the *dispensation* of the Gospel of Christ [which in its fulness takes in the ministration of the Spirit] was committed unto him." Ephesians 1:10, he calls this dispensation "*the dispensation* of the *fulness of times,* in which God gathers in one all things in Christ." Chap. 3:2, &c, after mentioning "the dispensation of the grace of God given him," as an apostle of Christ, he calls it "preaching among the Gentiles the unsearchable riches of Christ," and the "making all men see what is the fellowship of the *mystery,* which had been *hid* in God from the beginning of the world." Colossians 1:25, &c, speaking of the Christian Church, in opposition to the Jewish, he says, "Whereof I am made a minister according to the dispensation of God, which is given to me for you, &c, even the mystery which hath been hid from ages, but *now* is made manifest to his *saints:*" and he informs them that this mystery, now revealed, was "Christ in them, the hope of glory." Again, what he calls here the mystery hidden *before,* but *now* made manifest to Christians, he calls in another place "the new testament, — the ministration of righteousness, — where the Spirit of the Lord is" — and where "there is liberty," even the glorious liberty of the children of God; observing, that although the Mosaic dispensation or "ministration" was "glorious," yet that of Christ exceeds in glory," 2 Corinthians 3:6, &c.

To deny the doctrine of the *dispensations* is to deny that God made various covenants with the children of men since the fall: it is at least to confound all those covenants with which the various Gospel dispensations stand or fall. And to do so is not to divide the word of God aright, but to make a doctrinal *farrago,* and increase the confusion that reigns in mystical Babel. From the preceding quotations out of St. Paul's Epistles, it follows, therefore, either that there was no Gospel in the world, before the Gospel which was "hid from ages," and "made manifest" in St. Paul's days "to God's saints," when this mystery, "Christ in them the hope of glory," was revealed to them by the Holy Ghost: or, (which to me appears an indubitable truth,) that the evangelical dispensation of Adam and Noah was bright; that of Abraham and Moses brighter; that of initial Christianity, or of John the Baptist, explicitly setting forth "the Lamb of God that taketh away the sins of the world," brighter still; and that of perfect Christianity, (or of Christ revealed in us by the power of the Holy Ghost,) the brightest of all.

SECTION XI.

A rational and Scriptural view of St. Paul's meaning in the ninth chapter of the Epistle to the Romans — Some of the deepest passages of that chapter are thrown into the Scripture Scales, and by being weighed with parallel texts, appear to have nothing to do with free wrath and Calvinistic reprobation.

IF Zelotes find himself pressed by the weights of my second Scale, he will probably try to screen *his* "doctrines of grace," by retreating with them behind the ninth chapter of the Epistle to the Romans. But I am beforehand with him: and appealing to that chapter, I beg leave to show that the passages in it, which at first sight seem to favour the doctrine of free wrath, are subversive of it, when they are candidly explained according to the context, and the rest of the scriptures. Five couple of leading propositions open the section.

I.

II.

I. To *deny* that God out of mere distinguishing grace, may and does grant Church blessings, or the blessings of the *covenant of peculiarity*, to some men, making them *comparatively vessels to honour;* and making of consequence other men *comparatively vessels to dishonour*, or vessels *less* honourable: to deny this, I say, is to oppose the doctrine of the dispensations, and to rob God of a *gracious* sovereignty, which he justly claims.

To *insinuate* that God, out of mere distinguishing *wrath*, fixes the curse of absolute rejection upon a number of unborn men, for whom he never had any mercy, and whom he designs to call into being only to show that he can make and break *vessels of wrath* — to insinuate this, I say, is to attribute to God *a tyrannical* sovereignty, which he justly abhors.

II. God is too *gracious* unconditionally to reprobate, i.e. ordain to eternal death, any of his creatures.

God is too *holy* and too *just* not to reprobate his obstinately rebellious creatures.

III. In the day of initial salvation, they who through grace believe in their light, are *conditionally vessels of mercy, or God's elect*, according to one or another dispensation of his grace.

In the day of initial salvation, they who unnecessarily do despite to the Spirit of grace and disbelieve, are *conditionally vessels of wrath*, that "fit themselves for destruction."

IV. God *justly* gives up to *final* blindness of mind, and complete hardness of heart, them that *resolutely shut* their eyes, and harden their hearts to the end of their day of initial salvation.

Perverse free will in us, and not *free wrath* in God, or *necessity* from Adam, is the cause of our avoidable unbelief: and our personal avoidable unbelief is the cause of our complete personal reprobation, both at the end of the day of grace, and in the day of judgment.

V. There can be no sovereign, distinguishing *free grace* in a good God; because *goodness* can bestow free, undeserved gifts.

There can never be sovereign, distinguishing free wrath in a just God; because *justice* cannot inflict free, undeserved punishments.

Reason and conscience should alone, one would think, convince us that St. Paul, in Romans 9, does not plead for a fight in God so to hate any of his unformed creatures as to intend, make, and fit them for destruction, merely to show his absolute sovereignty and irresistible power. The apostle knew too well the God of *love*, to represent him as a mighty potter, who takes an unaccountable pleasure to form rational vessels, and to endue them with keen sensibility, only to have the glory of absolutely filling them, by the help of Adam, with sin and wickedness on earth, and then with fire and brimstone in hell. This is the conceit of the consistent admirers of unconditional election and rejection, who build it chiefly upon Romans 9. Should you ask, why they fix so dreadful a meaning on that portion of Scripture; I answer, that through inattention and prejudice, they overlook the two keys which the apostle gives us to open his meaning, one of which we find in the three first, and the other in the three last verses of that perverted chapter.

In the three first verses St. Paul expresses the "continual sorrow," which he "had in his heart," for the obstinacy of his countrymen, the Jews, who so depended upon their national prerogatives, as Jews; their Church privileges, as children of Abraham; and their Pharisaic righteousness of the law, as observers of the Mosaic ceremonies, that they detested the doctrine of salvation by faith in Jesus Christ. Now, if the apostle had believed that God, by a wise decree of preterition, had irreversibly ordained them to eternal death "to illustrate his glory by their damnation," as Calvin says; how ridiculous would it have been in him to sorrow night and day about the execution of God's wise design! If God, from the beginning of the world, had absolutely determined to make the unbelieving Jews personally and absolutely vessels of wrath, to the praise of the glory of his sovereign free wrath; how wicked would it have been in St. Paul to begin the next chapter by saying, "My heart's desire and prayer to God for *unbelieving* Israel — *for the obstinate Jews,* is that they might be saved!" Would he not rather have meekly submitted to the will of God, and said, like Eli, "It is the Lord: let him do what seemeth him good?" Did it become him — nay, was it not next to rebellion in him, so passionately to set his heart against a decree made (as we are told) on purpose to display the absoluteness of Divine sovereignty? And would not the Jews have retorted his own words! "Who art thou, O vain man, that repliest against God" by wishing night and day the salvation of "vessels of wrath:" of men whom he hath absolutely set apart for destruction?

"But if the apostle did not intend to establish the absolute, personal preterition of the rejected Jews and their fellow reprobates, what could he mean by that mysterious chapter?" I reply: He meant in general to vindicate God's conduct in casting off the Jews, and adopting the Gentiles. This deserves some explanation. When St. Paul insinuated to the Jews that they were rejected as a Church and people, and that the uncircumcised Gentiles (even as many as believed on Jesus of Nazareth) were now the chosen nation, "the peculiar people," and Church of God, his countrymen were greatly offended: and yet, as "the apostle of the Gentiles," to "provoke the Jews to jealousy," he was obliged peculiarly to enforce this doctrine among them. They generally gave him audience till he touched upon it. But when he "waxed bold," and told them plainly that Christ had bid him "depart from Jerusalem," as from an accursed city; and had "sent him far thence unto the Gentiles," they could contain themselves no longer; and "lifting up their voices, they said, Away with such a fellow from the earth," Acts 13:46; 22:21.*

* It is remarkable that Jewish rage first broke out against our Lord, when he touched their great Diana — the doctrine of their absolute election. You think, said he, to be saved, merely because you are Abraham's children, and God's chosen, peculiar people. "But I tell you of a truth," God is not so partial to Israel as you suppose. "Many widows were in Israel in the days of Elias, but to none of them was Elias sent, but to a *Zidonian* [heathen] widow. And many lepers were in Israel in the days Elisha, yet none of them was cleansed save Naaman the *Syrian,*" Luke 4:25, &c. The Jews never forgave our Lord that levelling saying. If he narrowly escaped their fury at Nazareth, it was only to meet it increased sevenfold in the *holy city.* So

Creeds and Scripture Scales

When St. Paul wrote to Rome, the metropolis of the *Gentile* world, where there were a great many *Jews*, the Holy Ghost directed him to clear up the question concerning the general election of the Gentiles, and the general rejection of the Jews. And this he did, both for the comfort of the humble, Gentile believers, and for the humiliation of his proud, self-elected countrymen; that being provoked to jealousy, they, or at least some of them, might with the Gentiles make their personal calling and election sure by believing in Christ. As the Jews were generally incensed against him, and he had a most disagreeable truth to write, he dips his pen in the oil of brotherly love, and begins the chapter by a most awful protestation of his tender attachment to them, and sorrowful concern for their salvation, hoping that this would soften them, and reconcile their prejudiced minds. But if he had represented them as absolute reprobates, and vessels of wrath *irreversibly* ordained of God to destruction, he would absurdly have defeated his own design, and exasperated them more than ever against his doctrine and his person. To suppose that he told them with one breath, he wished to be accursed from Christ for them, and with the next breath insinuated that God had absolutely accursed them with unconditional, personal reprobation, is a notion so excessively big with absurdity, that at times Zelotes himself can scarcely swallow it down. Who indeed can believe that St. Paul made himself so ridiculous as to weep tears of the most ardent love over the free wrath of his reprobating Creator? Who can imagine that the pious apostle painted out "the God of all grace," as a God full of immortal hatred to most of his countrymen: while he represented himself as a person continually racked with the tenderest feelings of a matchless affection for them all; thus impiously raising his own reputation, as a *benevolent man,* upon the ruins of the reputation of his *malevolent God?*

Come we now to the middle part of the chapter. St. Paul, having prepared the Jews for the disagreeable message which he was about to deliver, begins to attack their Pharisaic prejudices concerning their absolute right, as children of Abraham, to be God's Church and people, exclusively of the rest of the world whom they looked upon as reprobated dogs of the Gentiles. To drive the unbelieving Jews out of this sheltering place, he indirectly advances two doctrines: (1.) That God, as the Creator and supreme Benefactor of men, may do what he pleases with his peculiar favours; and that as he had now as indubitable a right freely to give five talents of Church privileges to the Gentiles, as he had once to bestow three talents of Church privileges upon the Jews. And, (2.) That God had as much right to set the seal of his wrath upon them, as upon Pharaoh himself, if they continued to imitate the inflexibleness of that proud unbeliever; inexorable unbelief being the sin that fits men for destruction, and pulls down the *wrath* of God upon the children of disobedience.

The first of those doctrines he proves by a reasonable appeal to conscience: (1.) Concerning the absurdity of replying against God, i.e. against a being of infinite wisdom, goodness, justice, and power. And (2.) Concerning a right which a potter has of the same "lump of clay" to make one vessel for* *honourable*, and another for

---

fierce and implacable are the tempers to which some professors work up themselves, by drinking into unscriptural notions of election!

* I have lived these fifteen years in a part of England where a multitude of potters make all manner of iron and earthen vessels. Some of these mechanics are by no means conspicuous for good sense, and others are at times besotted through excessive drinking; but I never yet saw or

comparatively *dishonourable* uses. The argument carries conviction along with it. Were utensils capable of thought, the *basin*, in which our Lord washed his disciples' feet, (a comparatively dishonourable use,)could never reasonably complain that the potter had not made it the *cup* in which Christ consecrated the sacramental wine. By a parity of reason, the king's soldiers and servants cannot justly be dissatisfied because he has not made them all generals and prime ministers. And what reason had the Jews to complain, that God put the Gentiles on a level with, or even above them? May he not, without being arraigned at the bar of slothful servants, who have buried their talents, give a peculiar, extraordinary blessing when he pleases, and to whom he pleases? "Shall the thing formed say to him that formed it, Why hast thou made me thus?" Shall the foot say, Why am I not the head? and the knee, Why am I not the shoulder? Or, to allude to the parable of the labourers, "if God chooses to hire the Gentiles, and send them into his favourite vineyard, blessing them with Church privileges as he did the Jews; shall the eye of the Jews "be evil because God is good" to these newly hired labourers? "May he not do what he pleases with his own?"

To this rational argument St. Paul adds another (*ad hominem*) peculiarly adapted to the Jews, who supposed it a kind of sacrilege to deny that, as children of Abraham, they were absolutely "the chosen nation," and "the temple of the Lord." To convince them that God was not so partial to the posterity of Abraham, Isaac, and Jacob, as they imagined, the apostle reminds them that God had excluded the first born of those favoured patriarchs from the peculiar blessings which by birthright belonged to them: doing it sometimes on account of the sin of those first born, and sometimes previously to any personal demerit of theirs, that he might show that his purpose, according to election to peculiar privileges and Church prerogatives, does "not stand of works, but of him that" chooseth, and "calleth" of his sovereign, distinguishing grace. St. Paul confirms this part of his doctrine by the instance of Ishmael and Isaac, who were both sons of Abraham: God having preferred Isaac to Ishmael, because Isaac was the child of his own promise, and of Abraham's faith by Sarah, a free woman, who was a type of grace and the Gospel of Christ: whereas Ishmael was only the child of Abraham's natural strength by Agar, an Egyptian bondswoman, who was a type of nature and the Mosaic dispensation.

With peculiar wisdom the apostle dwells upon the still more striking instance of Isaac's sons, Esau and Jacob, who had not only the same godly father, but the same free and pious mother; the younger of whom was nevertheless preferred to the elder without any apparent reason. He leaves the Jews to think how much more this might be the case, when there is an apparent cause, as in the case of Reuben, Simeon, and Levi, Jacob's three eldest sons, who, through incest, treachery, and

---

heard of one so excessively foolish as to make, even in a drunken fit, a vessel on purpose to break it, to show that he had power over the work of his own hands. Such, however, is the folly that Zelotes' scheme imputes to God. Nay, if a potter makes vessels on purpose to break them, he is only a fool; but if he could make sensible vessels like dogs, and formed them on purpose to roast them alive, and that he might show his sovereign power, would you not execrate his *cruelty* as much as you would pity his *madness?* But, what would you think of the man if he made five or ten such vessels for absolute destruction, while he made *one* for absolute salvation, and then assumed the title of *gracious* and *merciful* potter, and called his potting schemes "schemes of grace?"

murder, forfeited the blessing of the first born; a blessing this which by that forfeiture devolved on Judah, Jacob's fourth son, whose tribe became the first and most powerful of all the tribes of Israel, and had of consequence the honour of producing the Messiah, "the Lion of the tribe of Judah." St. Paul's argument is masterly, and runs thus: — If God has again and again excluded some of Abraham's posterity from the blessing of the peculiar covenant, which he made with that patriarch concerning the "promised seed:" — if he said, "In Isaac," Jacob, and Judah, "shall thy seed [the Messiah] be called," and not in Ishmael, Esau, and Reuben, the first born sons of Abraham, Isaac, and Jacob; how absurd is it in the Jews to suppose that merely because they are descended from Abraham, Isaac, and Jacob, they shall absolutely share the blessings of the Messiah's kingdom? If God excluded from the birthright Ishmael the scoffer, Esau the seller of his birthright, and Reuben the defiler of Bilhah, his father's wife; why might not Israel (his son called out of Egypt) his first born among nations, forfeit his birthright through unbelief? And why should not the Gentile world, God's prodigal son, inherit the blessing of the first born, if they submitted to the obedience of faith, and with the younger son in the parable, returned from "the far country" to their father's house; while the elder son insolently quarreled with God, reproached his brother, absolutely refused to come in, and thus made his calling void, and his reprobation sure?

The apostle's argument is like a two-edged sword. With one edge he cuts down the bigotry of the Jews, by the above-mentioned appeals to the history of their forefathers; and with the other edge he strikes at their unbelief, by an appeal to the destruction of Pharaoh; insinuating that God as Maker, Preserver, and Governor of men, has an undoubted right to fix the *gracious* or *righteous* terms, on which he will *finally* bestow salvation; or inflict damnation on his rational creatures.

With the greatest propriety St. Paul brings in Pharaoh, to illustrate the odious nature, fatal consequences, and dreadful punishment of unbelief. No example was better known, or could be more striking to the Jews. They had been taught from their infancy, with how "much long suffering" God had "endured" that notorious unbeliever; "raising him up," supporting him, and bearing with his insolence day after day, even after he had fitted himself for destruction. They had been informed, that the Lord had often reprieved that *father of the faithless*, that, in case he again and again hardened himself, (as Omniscience saw he would do,) he might be again and again scourged, till the madness of his infidelity should drive him into the very jaws of destruction; God having on purpose spared him, yea,* "raised him up" after every plague, that if he refused to yield, he might be made a more conspicuous monument of Divine vengeance, and be more gloriously overthrown by matchless power. So should "God's name," i.e. his adorable perfections, and righteous proceedings, "be

---

* Is it not strange that Zelotes should infer, from this expression, that God had *originally* "raised up," that is, created Pharaoh, on purpose to damn him? Is it not evident that Pharaoh justly looked upon every plague as a death? Witness his own words, "Intreat the Lord your God that he may take away from me this death only," Exodus 10:17. And if every plague was a death to Pharaoh, was not every removal of a plague a kind of resurrection, *a raising him up*, together with his kingdom, from a state of destruction, according to these words of the Egyptians, "Knowest thou not yet that Egypt is destroyed?" How reasonable and Scriptural is this sense! How dreadful, I had almost said, how diabolical is that of Zelotes!

declared throughout all the earth." And so should unbelief appear to all the world in its own odious and infernal colours.

St. Paul having thus indirectly, and with his usual prudence and brevity, given a double stab to the bigotry of the unbelieving Jews, who fancied themselves unconditionally elected, and whom he had represented as conditionally reprobated; lest they should mistake his meaning as Zelotes does, he concludes the chapter thus: "What shall we say then?" What is the inference which I draw from the preceding arguments? One which is obvious, namely, this: "That the Gentiles, [typified by Jacob the younger brother,] who followed not *professedly* after righteousness, have attained to righteousness, even the Christian righteousness which is of faith. But Israel," or the Jews, who professedly "followed after the law of *Mosaic* righteousness, [as the sportsman Esau did after his game,] have not attained to the law of *Mosaic or Christian* righteousness:" they are neither justified as Jews, nor sanctified as Christians. "True; and the reason is, because God had absolutely passed them by from all eternity, that he might in time make them vessels of wrath fitted for destruction." So insinuates Zelotes. But happily for the honour of the Gospel, St. Paul declares just the reverse. "Wherefore," says he, did not the reprobated Jews attain to righteousness? To open the eyes of Zelotes, if any thing will, he answers his own question thus: "Because they sought it not *by faith*, but as it were by the *external* works of the *Mosaic* law" opposed to Christian faith. "For they stumbled at that stumbling stone," Christ, who is "a rock of offence" to unbelievers, and "the rock of ages" to believers. "As it is written, Behold I lay in Zion a rock," that some shall, through their obstinate unbelief, make "a rock of offence." And others, through their humble faith, a rocky foundation, according to the decrees of conditional reprobation and election: "He that believeth not shall be damned, — and whosoever believeth on him shall not be ashamed," Romans 9:1-33; Mark 16:16.

That Zelotes should mistake the apostle's meaning when it is so clearly fixed in the latter part of the chapter is unaccountable: but that he should support by it his peculiar notion of absolute reprobation is really astonishing. The unbelieving Jews are undoubtedly the persons whom the apostle had first in view when he asserted God's right of appointing that obstinate unbelievers shall be "vessels of wrath." But hear what he said of those REPROBATED JEWS to the ELECTED Gentiles, in the very next chapter but one. "I speak to you Gentiles, &c, if *by any means* I may provoke to emulation them that are my flesh [the Jews] and might *save* some of them. If some of the branches [the unbelieving Jews] be broken off, &c, *because of unbelief* they were broken off, and thou [believing Gentile] standest *by faith*. Be not high minded but fear. For if God spared not the natural branches, take heed lest he also spare not thee, &c. Continue in his goodness, *otherwise thou also* shalt be *cut off*," and treated as a vessel of wrath "And they also, *if they abide not still in unbelief*, shall be grafted in," and treated as vessels of mercy, Romans 11:13, &c.

But what need is there of going to Romans 11 to show the inconsistency of the Calvinistic doctrines of free grace in Christ and free wrath in Adam? Of everlasting love to some and everlasting hate to others? Does not Romans ix itself afford us another powerful antidote? If the elect were from eternity God's *beloved* people, while the non-elect were the devil's people, *hated* of their Maker: and if God's love and hatred are equally unchangeable, whether free agents change from holiness to sin, or from sin to holiness; what shall we make of these words? "I will call them *my people* which *were not* my people; and her beloved which was not beloved. And where it was said unto them, Ye are not my people: there [upon their believing] shall they be called the children of God," Romans 9:25, 26. What a golden key is here to open our doctrine of *conditional* election, and to shut Zelotes' doctrine of *absolute* reprobation!

Having thus given a *general* view of what appears to me from conscience, reason, Scripture, and the context, to be St. Paul's meaning in that deep chapter; I present the reader with a *particular* and Scriptural explanation of some passages in it which do not puzzle Honestus a little, and by which Zelotes supports the doctrines of bound will and free wrath with some plausibility.

I.

It is not [primarily] of him that *willeth,* [in God's way,] nor is it [at all] of him that willeth [in opposition to God's will, as the self-righteous Jews did,] Romans 9:16.

It is not [primarily] of him that *runneth,* but* of God that showeth *mercy,* Romans 9:16.

[Ελεησω] [will have mercy on whom I will [or rather ελεω *I should*] *have mercy,* Romans 9:15.

[Οικτειρησω] I will have compassion on whom I will [or rather οικτειρω *I should*] have compassion, Romans 9:15.

II.

Ye *will not* come to me that you might have life, John 5:40. Whosoever will, let him come, Revelation 22:17. I have set before you life and death, &c, *choose,* Deuteronomy 30:19. I *would,* &c, and ye *would not,* Luke 13:34.

I went, &c, lest by any means I should *run* or had *run in vain,* Galatians 2:2. So run that [through mercy] you may obtain, 1 Corinthians 9:24.

Whoso forsaketh his sin shall *have mercy,* Proverbs 28:13. Let the wicked forsake his way, and, &c, the Lord will have mercy upon him, Isaiah 55:7. He shall have judgment without mercy, that hath showed no mercy, James 2:13. All the paths of the Lord are mercy to such as keep his covenant, Psalm 25:10.

As the heaven is high above the earth; so great is his *mercy toward them that fear him,* Psalm 103:11. The things that belong unto thy peace are hid from thine eyes, &c, *because thou knewest*

---

* In familiar and Scripture language the effect is frequently ascribed to the *chief* cause; while, for brevity's sake, *inferior* causes or agents are passed over in silence. Thus David says, "Except the Lord build the house, their labour is but vain that build it." St. Paul says, "I laboured, yet *not* I, but the grace of God." And we say, "Admiral Hawke has beat the French fleet." Would it not be absurd in Zelotes to strain these expressions so as to make absolutely nothing of the mason's work in the building of a house; of the apostle's preaching in the conversion of those Gentiles; and of the bravery of the officers and sailors in the victory got over the French by the English admiral? It is nevertheless upon such frivolous conclusions as these that Zelotes generally rests the enormous weight of *his* peculiar doctrines.

not the time of thy visitation, Luke 19:44. How is it that ye do not discern this time, yea, and why even of yourselves judge ye not what is right? Luke 12:56, 57. Hear, O heavens, &c, I have nourished children, and they have rebelled against me. The ox knoweth his owner, &c, but Israel doth not know, my people doth not consider. It is a people *of no understanding; therefore* he that formed them will show them *no favour,* Isaiah 1:3; 27:11. And God said to Solomon, *Because* thou hast asked for thyself understanding, &c, lo, I have given thee a wise and understanding heart, 1 Kings 3:11, 12. Because he considereth, &c, he shall not die, — he shall surely live, Ezekiel 18:28. [Who can help seeing through this cloud of scriptures, that "God has mercy on whom he should have mercy," according to his Divine attributes; extending initial mercy to all, according to his long suffering and impartiality; and showing eternal mercy, according to his holiness and truth, to them that use and improve their talent of understanding, so as to love him and keep his commandments?]

I.

The children being not yet born, neither having done any good or evil, that the purpose of God according to election might stand not of works, but of him that calleth [i.e. that God might show, he may and will choose some of Abraham's posterity to some peculiar privileges which he does not confer upon others: and likewise to teach us that grace and the new man mystically typified by Jacob, shall have the reward of the inheritance, — a reward this, which fallen nature and the old man, mystically typified by Esau, shall never receive: to teach us this] it was said to

II.

Thus saith the Lord, — Did I plainly appear to the house of thy father, &c, and did I *choose* him out of all the tribes of Israel to be my priest, &c. Why *kick ye* at my sacrifice? *Wherefore* the Lord God saith, *I said indeed* that thy house should walk before me for ever. *But now* the Lord saith, Be it far from me; for them that honour me I will honour; and they that despise me shall be lightly esteemed, 1 Samuel 2:27, &c. Again: the Lord said to Samuel, [I have not chosen,] I have refused him [Eliab] for the Lord seeth not as man seeth: the Lord *looketh at the heart* [and

Rebecca, The elder shall serve the younger [in his posterity* though not in his person:] that is, the younger shall have the blessing of the first born. And it was accordingly conferred upon Jacob in these words, *Be lord over thy brethren,* Genesis 27:20. To conclude, therefore, from Jacob's superior blessing, that Esau was absolutely cursed and reprobated of God, is as absurd as to suppose that Manasseh, Joseph's eldest son, was also an absolute reprobate, because Ephraim, his younger brother, had Jacob's chief

chooseth in consequence: accordingly, when] "Jesse made seven of his sons to pass before the Lord, Samuel said, *The Lord hath not chosen these,* 1 Samuel 16:7, 10. The Lord hath sought him a man after his own heart, [David,] because thou [Saul] hast not kept that which the Lord commanded thee. Once more: the Lord has rent the kingdom of Israel from thee this day, and hath given it to a neighbour of thine that is better than thou," 1 Samuel 13:14; 15:28.

The kingdom of Israel was an

---

* Mr. Henry says with great truth, "All this choosing" of Jacob and refusing of Esau "was typical, and intended to shadow forth some other election and rejection." And although he was a Calvinist, he does, in many respects, justice to St. Paul's meaning. "This difference," says he, "that was put between Jacob and Esau, he [the apostle] farther illustrates by a quotation from Malachi 1:2, where it is said, not of Jacob and Esau the persons, but the Edomites and Israelites their posterity: 'Jacob have I loved and Esau have I hated.' The people of Israel were taken into the covenant of peculiarity, had the land of Canaan given them, were blessed with the more signal appearances of God for them in special protection, supplies, and deliverances, while the Edomites were rejected, [from the covenant of peculiarity,] had no temple, altars, priests, prophets; no such particular care of them, &c. Others understand it of the election and rejection of particular persons; some loved and others hated from eternity. But the apostle speaks of Jacob and Esau, not in their own persons, but as ancestors: Jacob the people and Esau the people: nor doth God damn any, or decree so to do, merely because he will do it, without any reason taken from their own deserts, &c. The choosing of Jacob the younger was to intimate that the Jews, though the natural seed of Abraham, and the first born of the Church, should be laid aside: and the Gentiles, who were as the younger brother, should be taken in in their stead, and have the birthright and blessing." He concludes his comment upon the whole chapter by these words, which exactly answer to the double key I have given to the reader: "Upon the whole matter the unbelieving Jews have no reason to quarrel with God for rejecting them: they had a *fair* offer of righteousness and life, and salvation, made upon Gospel terms, which they did not like, and *would not* come up to; and therefore if they perish they may thank themselves. Their blood is upon their own heads."

What precedes is pure truth, and strongly confirms my doctrine. But what follows is pure Calvinism, and shows the inconsistency of the most judicious writers in that scheme. "Were the Jews hardened? It was because it was his own (God's) pleasure to deny them softening grace, &c. Two sorts of vessels God forms out of the great lump of fallen mankind: (1.) 'Vessels of wrath:' vessels filled with wrath, as a vessel of wine is a vessel filled with wine, 'full of the fury of the Lord,' &c. (2.) 'Vessels of mercy,' filled with mercy." And again: "he (the apostle) answers by resolving all into the *Divine sovereignty.* We are the thing formed, and he is the former, and it does not become us to challenge or arraign his wisdom in ordering and disposing of us into this or that shape or figure." That is, in plain English, free wrath, or, to speak smoothly as a Calvinist, Divine sovereignty may order and dispose us into the shape of vessels of wrath before we have done either good or evil. How could Mr. Henry thus contradict himself, and write for and against truth? Why, he was a *moderate Calvinist: as moderate,* he wrote glorious truths; and, as a *Calvinist,* horrid insinuations.

blessing: for the old patriarch refusing to put his right hand upon the head of Manasseh, said, "*Truly his younger brother shall be greater than he*," Genesis 48:19. But would Zelotes himself infer from such words that Manasseh was personally appointed from all eternity to disbelieve and be damned, and Ephraim to believe and be saved; that the purpose of God according to absolute reprobation and election might stand "not of works* but of him that *capriciously and irresistibly* calleth" some to finished salvation in Christ, and others to finished damnation in Adam? That God abhors such a proceeding is evident from the scriptures which fill my left scale, and in particular from the opposite texts.

unpromised gift to Saul and to David, and yet God's election to and reprobation from that dignity were according to dispositions and works. How much more may this be said of God's election to or reprobation from a crown of glory! a crown this, which God hath promised by way of reward to them that love him; refusing it by way of punishment to them that hate him; whom he clothes in hell with shame and with a vengeful curse, according to their works and his own declaration which follows: — "Yet saith the [Predestinarian] house of Israel, *The way of the Lord is not equal.* O house of Israel, are not my ways equal? Are not your ways unequal? Therefore I will judge you every one according to his ways. Repent and turn, &c, so iniquity shall not be your ruin," Ezekiel 18:29, &c. "I will do unto them according to their way; and according to their deserts [*secundum merita*] will I judge them, and they shall know that I am the Lord," Ezekiel 7:27. To these scriptures you may add all the multitude of texts where God declares that he will judge, i.e. justify or condemn, reward or punish, finally elect or finally reprobate men *for, by, according to,* or *because of* their works.

---

* This phrase: "That the purpose of God according to election might stand *not of works* but of him that calleth," is to be understood merely of those blessings which *distinguishing* grace bestows upon some men and not upon others, and which do not necessarily affect their eternal salvation or their eternal damnation. In this sense it was that God, for the above-mentioned reasons, preferred Jacob to Esau. In this sense he still prefers a Jew to a Hottentot, and a Christian to a Jew; giving a Christian the Old and New Testament, while the Jew has only the Old, and the Hottentot has neither. Far from denying the reality of this sovereign, distinguishing grace, which is independent on all works, and flows entirely from the superabounding kindness of "him that calleth," I have particularly maintained it, vol. i, p. 505. This is St. Paul's edifying meaning, to which I have not the least objection. But when Zelotes stretches the phrase so far as to make it mean that God *ordains* people to *eternal life* or *eternal death*, "not of works but of him that" without reason forcibly "calleth some to believe and be saved," leaving others *necessarily* to disbelieve and be damned: when Zelotes does this, I say, my reason and conscience are equally frighted, and I beg leave to dissent from him for the reasons mentioned in this section.

It is written, *Jacob have I loved, but Esau have I hated*, Romans 9:13.

God is *love*. God is *loving to every man*, and his tender mercies [in the accepted time] are over *all* his works. Yet the children of thy people say, *The way of the Lord is not equal:* but as for them, their way is not equal, &c, 1 John 4:8. Psalm 145, in the common prayers, Ezekiel 33:17.

Zelotes. who catches at whatever seems to countenance his doctrine of free wrath, thinks that this scripture demonstrates the electing and reprobating partiality, on which his favourite doctrines are founded. To see his mistake, we need only consider, that in the Scripture language a love of *preference* is emphatically called *love;* and an *inferior* degree of love is comparatively called *hatred*. Pious Jacob was not such a churlish man as positively to hate any body, much less Leah — his cousin and his wife: nevertheless, we read, "The Lord saw that Leah was hated: the Lord hath heard that I was hated: now, therefore, my husband will love me:" i.e. Jacob will prefer me to Rachel, his barren wife, Genesis 29:31, 32. Again: Moses makes a law concerning "a man that hath two wives, one beloved and another hated," without intimating that it is wrong in the husband to hate, that is, to be *less fond of* one of his wives than of the other, Deuteronomy 21:15. Once more: our Lord was not the chaplain of the old murderer, that he should command us positively to hate our fathers, mothers, and wives: for he, who thus "hateth another, is a murderer." Nevertheless, he not only says, "He that hateth his life [that invaluable gift of God] shall keep it unto life eternal; and he that loveth his life shall lose it:" but he declares, "If any man hate not his father, and mother, and wife, and children, and brethren, and sisters, he cannot be my disciple," Luke 14:26. Now, Christ evidently means, that whosoever does not *love* his father, &c, and his own life *less* than him, cannot be his sincere disciple. By a similar idiom it is said, "Esau have I hated:" an expression this, which no more means that God had absolutely rejected Esau, and appointed him to the pit of destruction, than Christ meant that we should absolutely throw away our lives, reject our fathers, wives, and children, and abandon them to destruction.

II.

*Whom *he will* he *hardeneth*, Romans 9:18.

That is, God judicially gives up to a reprobate mind *whom he will*, not

I.

The god of this world [not the Almighty] hath, [by their own free consent] blinded the minds of them that *believe not*. Now is the day of salvation.

* The reader is desired to take notice, that in this and the following paragraphs, where I produce scriptures expressive of God's just wrath, I have shifted the numbers that mark to which axiom the passage belongs. And this I have done: (1.) Because there is *no free* wrath in God. (2.) Because, when there is wrath in him, man's perverseness is the just cause of it. And (3.) Because in point of *evil*, man has the wretched diabolical honour of being *first cause;* and therefore, No. I. is his shameful prerogative, according to the principles laid down Sec. III.

according to Calvinistic caprice, but according to the rectitude of his own nature: and according to this rectitude displayed in the Gospel, *he will* give up all those who, by obstinately hardening their hearts to the last, turn *the day of* salvation into a day of final provocation, see Psalm 95:8, &c.

He hath blinded their eyes, and hardened their hearts, that they *should not see* with their eyes, nor *understand* with their heart, and be converted, and I should heal them, John 12:40.

That is, he hath judicially given them up to their own blindness and hardness. They had said so long, *We will not see,* that he said at last in his just anger, *They shall not see;* determined to withdraw the abused, forfeited light of his grace; and so they were blinded.

The Lord [in the above-mentioned sense] *hardened* Pharaoh's heart, [for his unparalleled cruelty to Israel,] Exodus 1:10, 22; 7:13. See the next note.

Despisest thou the riches of God's goodness, forbearance, and long suffering? not knowing that the goodness of God *leadeth thee* to repentance? But after thy hardness, and impenitent heart, treasurest up *unto thyself* wrath, 2 Corinthians 4:4; 6:2; Romans 2:4, 5.

In them is fulfilled the prophecy of Esaias, who says, By hearing ye shall hear, and shall not understand; and, seeing, ye shall see, and shall not perceive. For this people's heart *is waxed gross* [through their obstinately resisting the light;] and their ears are dull of hearing, and *their eyes they have closed,* lest at any time *they should see* with their eyes, and hear with their ears, and should understand with their heart, and should be converted, and I should heal them, Matthew 13:14, 15.

Pharaoh hardened his heart, and hearkened not, Exodus 8:15. Zedekiah *stiffened* his neck, and *hardened* his heart from turning unto the Lord, 2 Chronicles 36:13. *Take heed* lest any of you be hardened through the deceitfulness of sin, Hebrews 3:18. Happy is the man that feareth alway; but he that hardeneth his heart [as Pharaoh did] shall fall into mischief, [God will give him up,] Proverbs 28:14. They are without excuse: because, when they knew God, they glorified him not as God, &c. Wherefore God also gave them up to uncleanness, &c. For this cause God gave them up to vile affections, &c. And even as *they did not like* to retain God in their knowledge, God gave them over to a reprobate mind, Romans 1:20, 28.

II.

Thou wilt say then unto me, Why does he yet find fault? For who hath resisted his will? Romans 9:19.

I.

Shall not the Judge of all the earth do right? Genesis 18:25. That thou mightest be justified in thy saying, and clear when thou art judged, Psalm 51:4. Com. Prayer.

Who but Zelotes could justify an imaginary being that should, by the channel of irresistible decrees, pour sin and wrath into vessels made on purpose to hold both; and should call himself the God of love, the Holy One of Israel, and a God of judgment? Nay, who would not detest a king, who should absolutely contrive the contracted wickedness and crimes of his subjects, that he might justly sentence them to eternal torments, to show his sovereignty and power?

The rigid Calvinists triumph greatly in this objection started by St. Paul. They suppose that it can be reasonably levelled at no doctrine but their own, which teaches, that God by *irresistible* decrees has unconditionally ordained some men to eternal life, and others to eternal death; and therefore their doctrine is that of the apostle. To show the absurdity of this conclusion, I need only remind the reader once more, that in this chapter St. Paul establishes two doctrines: (1.) That God may admit whom he will into *the covenant of peculiarity*, out of pure, distinguishing, sovereign grace: and (2.) That he had an absolute right of *hardening whom he will* upon Gospel terms, i.e. of taking the talent of *softening grace from all that imitate the obstinate unbelief of Pharaoh; such inflexible unbelievers being the only people whom God will harden or give up to a reprobate mind. Now in both those respects the objection proposed is pertinent, as the apostle's answers plainly show. With regard to the first doctrine, that is, the doctrine of that *distinguishing* grace, which puts more honour upon one vessel than upon another; calling Abraham to be the Lord's "pleasant vessel," while Lot or Moab is only his "wash pot;" the apostle answers: "Nay, but, O man, who art thou who repliest against God? shall the thing formed say to him that formed it, Why hast thou made me thus?" Why am I a "wash pot," and not a "pleasant vessel?" "Hath not the potter power over the clay," &c. Beside, is it not a blessing to be comparatively a "vessel to dishonour?" Had not Ishmael and Esau a blessing, though it was inferior to that of Isaac and Jacob? Is not a wash pot as good in its place as a drinking cup? Is not a righteous Gentile — a Melchisedec, or a Job, &c, as acceptable to God, according to his dispensation, as a devout Jew and a sincere Christian according to theirs? With respect to the second doctrine, that of hardening obstinate unbelievers, and "making his *wrathful* power known" upon them: after tacitly granting, that it is impossible to resist God's absolute will, the apostle intimates in his laconic, and yet comprehensive way of writing, that God has a right to find fault with, and display his

---

* Mr. Henry comments thus upon these words, "I will harden his heart," that is, "*withdraw softening grace*," which God undoubtedly did upon just provocation. Whence it follows that, inconsistent Calvinists being judges, Pharaoh himself had once softening grace; it being impossible for God to *withdraw* from Pharaoh's heart what *never was there*. Query. Was this softening grace, which God withdrew from Pharaoh, of the reprobating or of the electing kind?

wrathful power upon hardened sinners, because "he hardens" none, but such as have personally made themselves "vessels of wrath," and "fitted *themselves* for destruction" by doing despite to the Spirit of his grace, instead of improving their day of initial salvation: and he insinuates, that even then, God, instead of presently dealing with them according to their deserts, "endures them with much long suffering," which, according to St. Peter's doctrine, is to be accounted a degree of salvation. Therefore in both senses the objection is pertinently proposed, and justly answered by the apostle, without the help of sovereign free wrath, and Calvinistic reprobation.

I.

Hath not the *potter* power over the *clay*, of the same lump to make one vessel unto honour, and another unto dishonour? Romans 9:21.

I have observed again and again that the apostle with his two-edged sword defends two doctrines: (1.) The right which God, our sovereign benefactor, has to give five talents, or one talent to whom he pleases, that is, to admit some people to the covenant of peculiarity, while he leaves others under a more general dispensation of grace and favour. Thus a Jew was once a vessel to honour, a person honoured far above a Gentile, and a Gentile, in comparison to a Jew, might be called "a vessel to dishonour." Moab, to use again the psalmist's expression, was once only God's "wash pot," Psalm 60:8, while Israel was his "pleasant vessel." But now the case is altered: the Jews are nationally become the "vessel wherein there is no pleasure," and the Gentiles are the "pleasant vessel." And where is the injustice of this proceeding? If a potter may make of the same lump of clay what vessel he pleases, some for the dining room, and others for the meanest apartment, all good and rueful in their respective places; why should not God have the same liberty? Why should he not, if he chooses it, place some moral vessels above others, and raise the Gentiles to the honour of being his peculiar

II.

The vessel that he [the potter] made of *clay*, *was marred* in the hand of the potter; so he made it again into another vessel, as seemed good to the potter, &c. O house of Israel, cannot I do with you as this potter, says the Lord, &c. At what instant I shall speak concerning a nation, &c, to destroy [for its wickedness:] if that nation, against whom I have pronounced, turn from their evil, *I will repent* of the evil that I thought to do unto them. And at what instant I shall speak concerning a nation, &c, to build it, *if it do evil* in my sight, that it *obey not* my voice, then I *will repent* of the good wherewith I said I would benefit them, Jeremiah 18:4.

When St. Paul wrote Romans 9:21, he had probably an eye to the preceding passage of Jeremiah, which is alone sufficient to rectify the mistakes of Zelotes; there being scarce a stronger text to prove that God's decrees respecting our salvation and destruction are conditional. Never did "Sergeant IF" guard the genuine doctrines of grace more valiantly, or give Calvinism a more desperate thrust than he does in the potter's house by the pen of Jeremiah. However, lest that prophet's testimony should not appear sufficiently weighty to Zelotes, I strengthen it by an express declaration of God himself: —

"Have I any pleasure at all that the wicked should die, saith the Lord; and people? An unspeakable honour this, which was before granted to the Jews only.

not that he should return from his ways and live? Yet ye say, *The way of the Lord is not equal* [in point of election to eternal life, and appointment to eternal death.] Hear now, O house of Israel, Is not my way equal? When a righteous man turneth away from his righteousness, &c, for his iniquity shall he die. Again: when a wicked man turneth from his wickedness, &c, he shall save his soul alive, Ezekiel 18:23, &c

The apostle's second doctrine respects "vessels of mercy and vessels of wrath," which in the present case must be carefully distinguished from the "vessels to honour," or to nobler uses, and "the vessels to dishonour," or to less noble uses: and, if I mistake not, this distinction is one of those things which, as St. Peter observes, are "hard to be understood in Paul's epistles." The importance of it appears from this consideration: God may, as a *just and gracious* sovereign, absolutely make a moral vessel for a more or less honourable use, as he pleases; such a preference of one vessel to another being no more inconsistent with Divine goodness, than the king's appointing one of his subjects lord of the bed chamber, and another only groom of the stable, is inconsistent with royal good nature. But this is not the case with respect to "vessels of mercy" and "vessels of wrath." If you insinuate, with Zelotes, that an absolute God, to show his absolute love and wrath, absolutely made some men to fill them *unconditionally* and *eternally* with love and mercy, and others to fill them unconditionally and eternally with hatred and wrath, by way of reward and punishment, you "change the truth of God into a lie," and serve the great Diana of the Calvinists more than the righteous Judge of all the earth. Whatever Zelotes may think of it, God never made an adult vessel of eternal mercy that did not *first* submit to the obedience of faith; nor did he ever absolutely look upon any man as a vessel of wrath, that had not by personal, obstinate unbelief *first fitted himself for destruction*. Considering then the comparison of the potter as referring in a secondary sense to the "vessels of mercy," and to the "vessels of wrath," it conveys the following rational and Scriptural ideas: — May not God, as the righteous maker of moral vessels, fill with mercy or with wrath whom he will, according to his essential wisdom and rectitude? May he not shed abroad his pardoning mercy and love m the heart of a believing Gentile, as well as in the breast of a believing Jew? And may he not give up to a reprobate mind, yea, fill with the sense of his just wrath a stubborn Jew, a Caiaphas, as well as a refractory Gentile, a Pharaoh? Have not Jews and Gentiles a common original? And may not the Author of their common existence, as their impartial lawgiver, determine to save or damn individuals, upon the gracious and equitable terms of the Gospel dispensations? Is he bound absolutely to give all the blessings of the Messiah's kingdom to Abraham's posterity, and absolutely to reprobate the rest of the world? Has a Jew more right to "reply against God" than a Gentile? When God propounds his terms of salvation, does it become any man to "say to him that formed him, Why hast thou made me thus" subject to thy government? Why must I submit to thy terms? If God without injustice could appoint that Christ should descend from Isaac, and not from Ishmael; if, before Esau and Jacob had done any good or evil, he could fix that the blood of Jacob, and not that of Esau, should run in his Son's veins; though Esau was Isaac's child as well as Jacob: how much more may he, without breaking the promise made to Abraham, Isaac, and Jacob, fix that the free-willing believer, whether Jew or Gentile, shall be a "vessel of mercy prepared for glory," chiefly by free grace; and that the free-willing unbeliever shall be a "vessel of wrath, fitted," chiefly by free will, "for just destruction?" Is not this doctrine agreeable to our Lord's expostulation, With "the light of life. which lightens every man, you will not come unto me that you might have life — more abundant life — yea, life evermore?" Does it not perfectly tally with the great, irrespective decrees of conditional election and reprobation, "He that believeth, and is baptized," that is, he that shows his faith by correspondent works, when his Lord comes to reckon with him, "shall be saved: and he that believeth not," though he were baptized, "shall be damned?" And is it not astonishing, that when St. Paul's meaning in Romans 9, can be so easily opened by the *silver* and *golden* key, which God himself has sent us from heaven, I mean *reason* and *Scripture*, so many pious divines should go to Geneva, and humbly borrow Calvin's *wooden* and *iron* key, I mean his election and reprobation? Two keys these, which are in as great repute among injudicious Protestants, as the keys of his holiness are among simple Papists. Nor do I see what great difference there is between the Romish and the Geneva keys: if the former open and shut a fool's paradise, or a knave's purgatory, do not the latter shut us all up in finished salvation or finished damnation?

Zelotes indeed does not often use the power of the keys; *one* key does generally for him. He is at times so ashamed of the *iron* key, which is black and heavy; and so pleased with the *wooden* key, which is light and finely gilt; that instead of holding them out fairly and jointly as St. Peter's pictures do the keys of hell and heaven, he makes the shining key alone glitter in the sight of his charmed hearers. Now and then, however, when he is driven to a corner by a judicious opponent, he pulls out his iron key, and holding it forth in triumph, he asks, "Who has resisted his will?" To these wrested words of St. Paul he probably adds two or three perverted scriptures —

Which I beg leave to weigh next in my Scales.

Shall [natural evil] be in the city, and the Lord hath not done it [for the punishment of the ungodly, and for the greater good of the godly?] Amos 3:6.	They have [done moral evil]—they have built the high places of Baal to burn their sons with fire, &c, which I commanded not, nor spake it, neither came it into my mind—neither came it into my heart, Jeremiah 19:5; 7:31. The sceptre of thy kingdom is a right sceptre: thou lovest righteousness and hatest wickedness, Psalm 45:6. Abhor that which is evil, Romans 12:9. Thus saith the Lord, I will bring [natural] evil upon this city, &c, because they have hardened their necks, that they might not hear my words, Jeremiah 19:15. Therefore, when David says, that "the

Creeds and Scripture Scales

Lord does whatsoever pleaseth him," he does not speak of either man's sin or duty, but only of God's *own* work, which HE absolutely intends to perform. (1.) Not of man's *sin:* for "God is not a God that hath pleasure in wickedness," Psalm 5:4. Nor (2.) Of man's *duty:* for though a master may do his servant's work, yet he can never do his servant's *duty.* It can never be a master's *duty* to obey his own commands: the servant must do it himself, or his duty (as *duty*) must remain for ever undone.

II.

There are certain men, &c, who* were before of old ordained to this condemnation, &c, [namely, the condemnation of] the angels who kept not their first estate, but left their own habitation, [whom] he [God] hath reserved in everlasting chains unto the judgment of the great day, Jude 1:4, 6.

I.

Ungodly men, turning the grace of our God into lasciviousness, and denying, &c, our Lord Jesus Christ, [as lawgiver, judge, and king,] &c. These be they who separate themselves [from their self-denying brethren] sensual, not having the Spirit [i.e. having quenched the Spirit]—walking after their own lusts; and their mouth speaketh great swelling words [whereby they creep in unawares into rich widows' houses; seducing the fattest of the flock, and] having men's persons in admiration because of advantage,

---

* The words παλαι προγεγραμμενοι rendered "before of old ordained," literally mean "formerly forewritten, foretypified, or foredescribed." The condemnation of these backsliders, or apostates, was of old forewritten by David, Psalm 125:5; and by Ezekiel 18:24. Their lusts were of old foretypified by those of Sodom; their apostasy by that of the fallen angels; and their perdition by that of the Israelites, whom the Lord "saved out of the land of Egypt," and "afterward destroyed" for their unbelief; three typical descriptions these, which St. Jude himself immediately produces, verses 5, 6, 7; together with Enoch's prophecy of the Lord's coming "to convince them of all their ungodly deeds and hard speeches," verses 15, 17. Is it not strange then that Zelotes should build his notions of absolute reprobation upon a little mistake of our translators, which is contrary both to the Greek and to the context? "Beloved," says St. Jude, verse 17, "remember ye the words [ωρωειρημενων, 'forespoken,' answering to Greek προγεγραμμενοι, 'forewritten,' and not 'foreappointed,'] which were spoken before of the apostles of our Lord Jesus Christ." For the apostles, no doubt, often enlarged upon these words of their Master: "Because iniquity shall abound the love of many shall wax cold [and they will fall away;] but he that shall endure unto the end, the same shall be saved."]

To them that are disobedient, &c, he is a rock of offence, even to them who stumble at the word, being disobedient, whereunto also they were appointed: [or rather] whereunto [namely, to be disobedient] they* have even disposed [or settled] themselves, 1 Peter 2:7, 8.

verses 4, 16, 19.

Ye will not come to me that ye might have life, John v, 40. Ye put the word of God from you, and judge yourselves unworthy of eternal life, Acts 13:46.

---

* A beautiful face may have some freckles. Our translation is good, but it has its blemishes; nor is it one of the least to represent God as appointing men to be disobedient. To vindicate all the Divine perfections, which such a doctrine in-jutes, of the two meanings that the word fairly bears in the original, I need only choose that which is not repugnant to reason and Scripture. If charity, which "thinketh no evil and hopeth all things" consistently with reason, — if charity, I say, obliges us to put the best construction upon the words of our neighbour, how much more should decency oblige us to do it with respect to the word of God? When a modest person drops a word, that bears either a chaste or an unchaste meaning, is it not cruel absolutely to fix an "unchaste" meaning upon it? To show that St. Peter's words bear the meaning which I fix to them, I need only prove two things. (1.) That the original word ετεθησαν, which is translated "appointed," means also "settled" or "disposed." And (2.) That a passive word in the Greek tongue frequently bears the meaning of the Hebrew voice called "hithpahel," which signifies the making oneself to do a thing, or the being caused by oneself to do it: a voice this, which in some degree answers to the middle voice of the Greeks, some tenses of which equally bear an active or a passive sense. To prove the first point, I appeal only to two texts, where the word τιθημι, undoubtedly bears the meaning which I contend for. Luke 21:14, θεσθε "SETTLE it in your hearts;" and Luke 9:62, ευθετος "fit," or more literally "well DISPOSED for the kingdom of God." And to prove my second proposition, (beside what I have already said upon that head, in my note upon Mr. Madan's mistake, p. 77,) I present the critical reader with indubitable instances of it, even in our translation. Jude, verse 10, φθειρονται, they are corrupted, or, "they corrupt THEMSELVES." 2 Corinthians 11:13, Greek μετασχηματιζομενοι, being transformed, or, "transforming themselves." Acts 18:6, αυτουν αντιτασσομενων, literally, they being opposed, or, as we have it in our Bibles, "when they opposed themselves." John 20:14, εστραφη, she (Mary) was turned, or "she turned herself." Matthew 16:23, Jesus στραφεις, being turned, or, "turning himself." Matthew 27:3, Judas μεταμεληθεις, having been penitent, or, "having repented himself," &c, &c. In such cases as these the sacred writers use indifferently the active and passive voice, because man acts, and is acted upon: he is worked upon, and he works. Thus we read Acts 3:19, επιστρεψατε, "convert," namely, yourselves, "actively;" though our translators render it passively, "be converted:" and Luke 22:32, our Lord, speaking to Peter, does not say, επιστραφεις, "when thou art converted," passively; but actively, επιστρεψας, "when thou hast converted," namely, "thyself." Now, if in so many cases our translators have justly rendered passive words, by words expressing "a being acted upon by ourselves," I desire Zelotes to show, by any one good argument, taken from criticism, Scripture, reason, conscience, or decency, that we must render the word of our text "they were appointed," namely, by God, "to be disobedient," when the word ετεθησαν may with as much propriety as in all the preceding eases, be rendered they disposed, set, or "settled themselves unto disobedience." What has the Holy One of Israel done to us, that we should dishonour him by charging our disobedience upon "his appointment?" Are we so fond of the doctrines of grace, finished salvation, and finished damnation, that, in order to maintain the latter, we must represent God as appointing, out of

sovereign, distinguishing free wrath, the disobedience of the reprobates, that by securing the "means" — their unbelief and sin, he may also secure the "end" — their everlasting burnings?

Zelotes makes too much of some figurative expressions in the sacred writings. He forgets, that what is said of God, must always be understood in such a manner as becomes God. If it would be absurd to take literally what the Scriptures say of God's "plucking his right hand out of his bosom;" of "his awakening as one out of sleep;" of "his riding upon the heavens;" of his "smelling a sweet savour from a burnt offering;" of his "lending an ear," &c, is it not much more absurd to take the three following texts in a literal sense? (1.) 2 Samuel 16:10, "The Lord said unto him, [Shimei,] Curse David." Is it not evident that David's meaning in these words is only this? "The Lord, by bringing me to the deplorable circumstances in which I now find myself, has justly given an opportunity to Shimei to insult me with impunity, and to upbraid me publicly with my crimes. This opportunity I call 'a bidding,' to humble myself under the hand of God, who lashes my guilty soul by this afflictive providence; but I would not insinuate that God literally said to Shimei, 'Curse David,' any more than I would affirm that he said to me, Murder Uriah." (2.) God is represented, 2 Samuel 12:11, as saying to David, "I will take thy wives before thine eyes, and give them to thy neighbour, and he shall lie with them in the sight of this sun, for thou didst it secretly, but I will do it before all Israel." And accordingly God took the bridle of his restraining power out of Absalom's heart, who had already murdered his own brother, and was, it seems, by that time a vessel of wrath self fitted for destruction. The Divine restraint being thus removed, the corrupted youth rushes upon the "outward" commission of those crimes which he had perhaps a hundred times committed in "intention," and from which the Lord had hitherto kept him, out of regard for his pious father — a regard this, which David had now forfeited by his atrocious crimes. The meaning of the whole passage seems then to be this: "Thou shalt be treated as thou hast served Uriah. Thy wild son Absalom has already robbed thee of thy crown, and defiled thy wives in his ambitious, libidinous heart. When thou wast a good man — a man after my own heart, I hindered him from going such lengths in wickedness, but now I will hinder him no more: he shall be thy scourge; thou sinnedst secretly against Uriah, but I will stand in the way of thy wicked son no longer, and he shall retaliate before the sun." This implies only a passive permission, and a providential opportunity to commit a crime "outwardly," nor could wicked men ever proceed to the "external execution" of their designs without such opportunities. (3.) By a like figure of speech we read, Psalm 105:25, that "God turned the heart of the Egyptians to hate his people, and to deal subtilly with his servants." But how did he do this? Was it by doing the devil's work? by infusing hatred into the hearts of the Egyptians? No: it was merely by blessing and multiplying the Israelites, as the preceding words demonstrate: "He increased his people greatly, and made them stronger than their enemies." Hence it was that fear, envy, jealousy, and hatred, were naturally stirred up in the breasts of the Egyptians. I repeat it; not to explain such scriptures in the manner becoming the God of holiness is far more detestable than to assert, that "the Ancient of Days" literally wears a robe, and his own white hair, because Daniel, after having seen an emblematic vision of his majesty and purity, said, "His garment was white as snow, and the hair of his head was like the pure wool." For every body must allow, that it is far less indecent "literally" to hold forth God as a venerable Jacob, than to represent him "literally" as a mischievous, sin-infusing Belial. (4.) With regard to Jeremiah 20:7, "O Lord, thou hast deceived me, and I was deceived," Mr. Sellon justly observes: (1.) That the Hebrew word here translated "deceive," signifies also to "entice" or "persuade," as the margin shows. And (2.) That the context requires the last sense; the prophet expressing his natural backwardness to preach, and saying, "O Lord, thou hast persuaded me" to do it, "and I was persuaded." It is a pity, that when a word has two meanings, the one honourable, and the other injurious to God, the worst should once be preferred to the better. If Zelotes take these hints, he will no more avail himself of some figurative expressions, and of some mistakes of our

The Works of John Fletcher

I shall close the preceding scriptures by some arguments which show the absurdity of supposing that there can be any free wrath in a just and good God. (1.) When Adam, with all his posterity in his loins, came forth out of the hands of his Maker, he was pronounced *very good*, as being "made in the likeness of God," and "after the image of him," who is a perfect compound of every possible perfection. God spake those words *in* time; but if we believe Zelotes, the supposed decree of absolute, personal rejection, was made *before* time; God having fixed, from all eternity, that Esau should be absolutely hated. Now, as Esau stood in and with Adam, before he fell in and with him; and as God could not but consider him as standing and righteous, before he considered him fallen and sinful; it necessarily follows, either that Calvinism is a system of false doctrine; or, that the God of love, holiness, and equity, once hated his righteous creature, once reprobated the innocent, and said by his decree, "Cain, Esau, Saul and Judas are *very good*, for they are seminal parts of Adam my son, whom I pronounce very good, Genesis 1:31. But I actually hate those parts of my unsullied workmanship: without any actual cause, I detest mine own perfect image. Yea, I turn my eyes from their present complete goodness, that I may hate them for their future pre-ordained iniquity." Suppose the God of love had transformed himself into the evil principle of the Manichees, what could he have done worse than thus to hate with immortal hatred, and absolutely to reprobate his innocent, his pure, his spotless offspring, at the very time in which he pronounced it *very good?* If Zelotes shudders at his own doctrine, and finds himself obliged to grant, that so long, at least, as Adam stood, Cain, Esau, Saul, and Judas stood with him, and in him were actually loved, conditionally chosen, and wonderfully blessed of God in paradise; it follows that the doctrine of God's everlasting hate, and of the eternal, absolute rejection of those whom Zelotes considers as the four great reprobates, is founded on the grossest contradiction imaginable.

2. But Zelotes possibly complains that I am unfair, because I point out the deformity of his "doctrine of grace," without saying one word of its beauty. "Why do you not," says he, "speak of God's absolute everlasting love to Jacob, as well as of his absolute, everlasting hate to Esau, Pharaoh, and Judas? Is it right to make always the worst of things?" Indeed, Zelotes, if I am not mistaken, your absolute election is full as subversive of Christ's Gospel, as your absolute reprobation. The Scripture informs us, that when Adam fell he lost the favour, as well as the image of God; and that he became "a vessel of wrath" from head to foot: but if everlasting, changeless love still embraced innumerable parts of his seed, his fall was by no means so grievous and universal as the Scriptures represent it: for "a multitude, which no man can number," ever stood, and shall ever stand on the Rock of ages: a rock this which, if we believe Zelotes, is made of unchangeable, absolute, sovereign, everlasting love for the elect, and of unchangeable, absolute, sovereign, everlasting wrath for the reprobates.

3. But this is only part of the mischief that necessarily flows from the fictitious doctrines of grace. They make the cup of trembling, which our Lord drank

---

translators, to represent God as the author of sin and the deceiver of men. When wicked men have long resisted the truth, God may indeed, and frequently does, judicially "give them up to believe a destructive lie;" but he is no more the author of the lie, than he is Beelzebub, "the father of lies."

in Gethsemane, and the sacrifice which he offered on Calvary, in a great degree insignificant. Christ's office as high priest was to sprinkle the burning throne with his precious blood, and to "turn away wrath" by the sacrifice of himself: but if there never was either a burning throne, or any wrath flaming against the elect; if unchangeable love ever embraced them, how greatly is the oblation of Christ's blood depreciated? Might he not almost have saved himself the trouble of coming down from heaven to "turn away a wrath" which never flamed against the elect, and which shall never cease to flame against the reprobates?

4. From God's preaching the Gospel to our first parents it appears that they were of the number of the elect, and Zelotes himself is of opinion that they belonged to the little flock. If this was the case, according to the doctrine of free, sovereign, unchangeable, everlasting love to the elect, it necessarily follows, that Adam himself was never a child of wrath. Nor does it require more faith to believe that our first parents were God's pleasant children, when they sated themselves with forbidden fruit, than to believe that David and Bathsheba were persons after God's own heart, when they defiled Uriah's bed. Hence it follows that the doctrine of God's everlasting love, in the Crispian sense of the word, is absolutely false, or that Adam himself was a child of changeless, *everlasting love*, when he made his wife, the serpent, and his own belly, his trinity under the fatal tree: while Cain was a child of *everlasting wrath*, when God said of him, in his father's loins, that he was *very good*. Thus we still find ourselves at the shrine of the great Diana of the Calvinists, singing the new song of salvation and damnation finished from everlasting to everlasting, according to the doctrine laid down by the Westminster divines in their catechism: "God from all eternity did, by the most wise and holy counsel of his own will, freely and unchangeably ordain whatever comes to pass."

5. This leads me to a third argument. If God from all eternity did "unchangeably ordain" all events, and, in particular, that the man Christ should absolutely die to save a certain, fixed number of men, who (by the by) never were children of wrath, and therefore never were in the least danger of perishing: if he unalterably appointed that the devil should tempt, and absolutely prevail over a certain fixed number of men who were children of wrath, before temptation and sin made them so: if this is the case, I say, how idle was Christ's redeeming work! How foolish the tempter's restless labour! How absurd Zelotes' preaching! How full of inconsistency his law messages of wrath to the elect, and his Gospel messages of free grace to the reprobates! And how true the doctrine, which has lately appeared in print, and sums up the Crispian gospel in these sentences: — Ye, elect, shall be saved do what ye will; and ye, reprobates, shall be damned, do what ye can; for in the day of his power the Almighty will make you all absolutely willing to go to the place which he has unconditionally ordained you for, be it heaven or hell; God, if we believe the Westminster divines, in their catechism, "having unchangeably foreordained whatever comes to pass in time, especially concerning angels and men." An unscriptural doctrine this, which charges all sin and damnation upon God, and perfectly agrees with the doctrine of the consistent Calvinists, I mean the doctrine of finished salvation and finished damnation, thus summed up by Bishop Burnet in his exposition of the seventeenth article: "They think, &c, that he," God, "decreed Adam's sin, the lapse of his posterity, and Christ's death, together with the salvation and damnation of such men as should be most for his own glory: that to those that

were to be saved he decreed to give such efficacious assistances as should certainly put them in the way of salvation; and to those whom he rejected, he decreed to give such assistances and means only as should render them inexcusable." Just as if those people could ever be inexcusable who only do what their almighty Creator has "unchangeably foreordained!"

SECTION XII.

Directions to understand the Scripture doctrine of election and reprobation — What election and reprobation are UNCONDITIONAL, *and what* CONDITIONAL — *There is an unconditional election of sovereign, distinguishing grace, and a conditional election of impartial, rewarding goodness — The difficulties which attend the doctrines of election and reprobation are solved by means of the Gospel dispensations; and those doctrines are illustrated by the parable of the talents — A Scriptural view of our election in Christ.*

WHEN good men, like Zelotes and Honestus, warmly contend about a doctrine; charging one another with heresy in their controversial heats, each has certainly *a part* of the truth on his side. Would you have *the whole*, Candidus? Only act the part of an attentive moderator between them: embrace their extremes at once, and you will embrace truth in her seamless garment, — the complete "truth as it is in Jesus." This is demonstrable by their opposite sentiments about the doctrine of election. Zelotes will hear only of an *unconditional*, and Honestus only of a *conditional* election: but the word of God is for both; and our wisdom consists in neither separating nor confounding what the Holy Ghost has joined, and yet distinguished.

To understand the Scripture doctrine of election, take the following directions: 1. God is a God of *truth*. His righteous ways are as far above our hypocritical ways, as heaven is above hell: every calling, therefore, implies an election on his part. Who can believe that God ever demeans his majestic veracity so far as to *call* people, whom he does *not choose* should obey his call? Who can think that the Most High plays boyish tricks? And if he chooses that those whom he calls should come, a sincere election has undoubtedly preceded his calling. Nor are the well-known words of our Lord, Matthew 22:44, "Many are called, but few are chosen," at all contrary to this assertion: for the context evidently shows that the meaning of this compendious elliptic saying is, "Many are called" to faith and holiness, "but few are chosen" to the *rewards* of faith and holiness. "Many are called" to be God's servants, and to receive his talents, "but few," comparatively, "are chosen" to enjoy the blessing of "good and faithful" servants. "Many are called *to* run *the race* but few are chosen *to* receive *the prize*." Not because God has absolutely reprobated any, in the Calvinian sense of the words, but because few are willing to "deny themselves;" few care to "labour;" few are faithful, few "so run that *they* may obtain;" few "make *their initial* calling and election sure" *to the end;* and of the many that are called to *enter* into the kingdom of God, few *strive* so to do; and therefore few "shall be able," see Luke 13:24.

Creeds and Scripture Scales

2. According to the dispensation of "the saving grace of God, which hath appeared to *all* men;" so long as the "day of salvation" lasts, *all* men are sincerely called, and therefore sincerely chosen to believe in their light, to fear God, and to work righteousness. This general election and calling may be illustrated by the general benevolence of a good king toward all his subjects. Whether they are peasants or courtiers, he elects them all to loyalty, that is, he *chooses* that they should all be loyal; and in consequence of this choice, by his royal statutes, he *calls* them all to be so. But when a rebellion breaks out, many do not "make their calling and election sure;" that is, many join the rebels, and in so doing forfeit their titles, estates, and lives. However, as many as oppose the rebels become hereby peculiarly entitled to the privileges of loyal subjects, which are greater or less according to their rank, and according to the boroughs or cities of which they have the freedom. Upon this general plan, as many of Adam's sons as, in any one part of the earth, make God's general calling and election sure, by actually fearing God, &c, are *rewardable elect,* according to the FATHER'S dispensation: that is, God actually approves of them, considered as obedient persons, and he designs eternally to reward their sincere obedience, if they "continue faithful unto death," Colossians 1:23; Revelation 2:10.

3. *Distinguishing,* or particular grace, chooses, and, of consequence, calls some men to believe explicitly in the Messiah to come, or in the Messiah already come; and as many as sincerely do so, are rewardable elect according to the SON'S dispensation, when it is distinguished from that of the SPIRIT, as in John 7:38, 89; for in general Christ's dispensation takes in that of the Holy Ghost, especially since "Christ is glorified," and when he is "known after the flesh no more." Compare John 16:7, with 2 Corinthians 5:16.

4. A still higher degree of distinguishing grace elects, and of consequence calls, believers in Christ to take by force the kingdom which consists in "righteousness, peace, and joy in the Holy Ghost;" and as many as make this calling and election sure, are God's rewardable elect, according to the dispensation of the Holy Ghost.

5. All true worshippers belong to one or another of these three classes of elect. The first class is made up of *devout heathens,* who worship in the court of the Gentiles. The second class is formed of *devout Jews,* or of such *babes in Christ* as are yet comparatively carnal, like John's disciples, or those of our Lord before the day of pentecost. These worship in the holy place. And the third class is composed of those holy souls who, by being fully possessed of Christ's Spirit, deserve to be called Christians in the full sense of the word. These (which, in our Laodicean days, I fear, are a little flock indeed) are all *perfected in one,* and, having "entered within the veil," worship now "in the holy of holies."

6. In order to eternal salvation, those three classes of elect must not only "make their calling and election sure," by continuing to-day in the faith of their dispensation; but also by going on "from faith to faith;" by rising from one dispensation to another, if they are called to it; and, above all, by "patiently continuing in well doing," or by "being faithful unto death;" none but such "having the promise of a crown of life that fadeth not away."

7. *Distinguishing* grace not only chooses some persons to see the felicity of God's chosen in the two great covenants of peculiarity, called the law of Moses, and the Gospel of Christ; but it *elects* them also to peculiar dignities, or uncommon

services in those dispensations. Thus Moses was elected to be the great prophet and lawgiver of the Jews: Aaron to be the first high priest of the Jewish dispensation: Saul, David, and Solomon, to be the three first kings of God's chosen nation. Thus again the seventy were chosen above the multitude of the other disciples, the twelve above the seventy; Peter, James, and John, above the twelve; and St. Paul, it seems, above Peter, James, and John. The following scriptures refer to this kind of extraordinary choice — to this election of *peculiar* grace: — "Moses his chosen stood in the gap. The man's rod whom I shall choose shall blossom. The man whom the Lord shall choose, he shall be holy," that is, he shall be set apart for the priesthood. "He chose David his servant, and took him from the sheep fold. Before I formed thee," Jeremiah, "in the belly, I knew thee; and before thou camest forth out of the womb, I sanctified thee," or, I set thee apart, "and I ordained thee a prophet unto the nations." Of his disciples he chose twelve apostles. "He," Paul, "is a chosen vessel unto me, to bear my name before the Gentiles." Agreeably to the doctrine of these peculiar elections to singular services, it is even said of Cyrus, a heathen king, by whose means the Jews were to be delivered from the Babylonish captivity: "Cyrus is my shepherd, and shall" or will "perform all my pleasure, saying to Jerusalem, Thou shalt be built, and to the temple, Thy foundation shall be laid, &c. For Jacob my servant's sake, and Israel mine elect, I have even called thee by thy name, though thou hast not known me." Once more: David, speaking of God's choosing the tribe of Judah before all the other tribes, says: "Moreover he refused the tabernacle of Joseph, and" reprobated, or "chose not the tribe of Ephraim, but chose" or elected "the tribe of Judah, the Mount Sion, which he" peculiarly "loved." But what have all those civil or ecclesiastical elections of persons and places to do with our election to a crown of glory? Will Zelotes affirm that Saul and Jehu are certainly in heaven, because they were as remarkably chosen to the crown as David himself? And though St. Paul knew that he was "a chosen vessel, *set apart* from his mother's womb" for great services in the Church, does he not inform us that he "so ran as to obtain the crown;" and that he "kept his body under lest, after he had preached to," *and* saved "others, he himself should become a castaway — a reprobate?"

8. Do not forget that frequently the word *chosen*, or *elect*, means *principal, choice, having a peculiar degree of superiority, or excellence.* This is evident from the following texts: "The wrath of God smote down the *chosen* of Israel," Psalm 78:31. "I lay in Sion a chief corner stone, *elect*, and precious," 1 Peter 2:6. "The elder to the elect lady," 2 John 1. And it would be the height of Calvinian orthodoxy to suppose that the prophet's words, "Thy *choicest*," or, as the original properly means, "thy *elect* valleys shall be full of chariots," are to be understood of Calvinian election. To render Zelotes less confident in that election, one would think it sufficient to throw into the Scripture Scales, and weigh before him, the following passages, which are literally translated from the original: —

I.	II.
For Israel, mine *elect*, I have called thee, Isaiah 14:4.	He [Kish] had a son whose name was Saul, an *elect*, 1 Samuel 9:2.
	Query. Is Saul also among the *elect* as well as among the *prophets*?

The *election* hath obtained it, Romans 11:7.

I have made a covenant with my *chosen* [or *elect*.] I have exalted one chosen out of the people. Mine *elect* shall inherit it, Psalm 89:3, 19; Isaiah 65:9.

The children of thy *elect* sister greet thee, 2 John 1:13.

His *elect*, whom he hath *chosen*, Mark 13:20.

I endure all things for the *elect's* sake, 2 Timothy 2:10. O ye children of Jacob, his *chosen* ones, 1 Chronicles 16:13.

I charge thee before the* *elect* angels, 1 Timothy 5:21. And shall not God avenge his own elect? Luke 18:7.

Set on a pot: fill it with the bones of *the election*, Ezekiel 24:4.

She committed her whoredoms with the *elect* of Assyria, Ezekiel 23:7. The tongue of the just is as *chosen* silver. Receive knowledge rather than *elect* gold, Proverbs 10:20; 8:10.

They shall cut down thine *elect* cedars, Jeremiah 12:7.

He [Jacob] *chose* all the *elect* of Israel, 2 Samuel 10:9.

Moab is spoiled, his *elect* young men are gone down to the slaughter, Jeremiah 48:15. His [Pharaoh's] *elect* captains also are drowned, Exodus 15:4.

Amaziah gathered Judah together, &c, and found them three hundred thousand *elect*, able to go forth to war, 2 Chronicles 25:5.

I grant that our translators, in some of the preceding passages, have used the word *choice*, and not the word *elect*. They say, for example, "choice cedars," and not "elect cedars;" but if they were afraid to make us suspect the dignity of Calvinian election, I am not. And as the original is on my side, the candid reader will not expect such scrupulousness of me, who wish to act the part of a reconciler, and not that of a Calvinist.

9. God's choosing and calling us to "come up higher" on the ladder of the dispensations of his grace, is called election and vocation. Thus the doctrine which St. Paul insists much upon in his Epistles to the Romans and Ephesians, is, that now Jews and Gentiles are equally *elected* and *called* to the privileges of the *Christian* dispensation. Nor does St. Peter dissent from him in this respect. Once indeed he took it for granted that the Gentiles were all reprobates; see Acts 10. But when he was divested of his Jewish prejudices, and wrote to the believers who were "scattered throughout Pontus," &c, he said "the Church that is at Babylon, *elected* together with you, saluteth you," 1 Peter 5:13. Just as if he had said, Think not that the election to the obedience of faith in Christ is confined to Judea, Pontus, or Galatia. No: God calls both Jews and Gentiles, even in Babylon, to believe in his Son. And as a proof

---

* If the expression "elect angel" is taken in a *vague* sense, which is most probable, it means *holy, beloved angels*, who are elected to the rewards of faithful obedience. If it be taken in a *particular* sense, it means those angels who, like Gabriel, are selected from the multitude of the heavenly host, and sent forth to minister for them who shall be heirs of salvation, and especially to guard such eminent preachers as Timothy and St. Paul were. In either sense, therefore, the words *elect angels*, which Zelotes greedily catches at to prop up his scheme, have nothing to do with Calvinian election. That the word *elect* sometimes means *darling or beloved*, will appear evident to those who compare the following passages: "Behold mine *elect*, in whom my soul delighteth," Isaiah 42:1. "This is my *beloved* Son, in whom I am well pleased," Matthew 3:17.

that this calling and election are sincere, with pleasure I inform you that several have already believed, and formed themselves into a Christian Church, which saluteth you, not only as being elected with you to hear the Christian Gospel; but as making their "election to so great salvation sure" through actual belief of "the truth as it is in Jesus." Therefore I do not scruple, in every sense of the word, to say that they are "elected together with you, and you may boldly consider them already as *holy* brethren, *partakers* of the heavenly calling." A glorious proof this that Christ has broken down the middle wall of partition between Jews and Gentiles; Babylon, in this respect, being as much elected as Jerusalem. But more of this in the next section.

10. To conclude: of all the directions which can be given to clear up the doctrine of election with respect to our eternal concerns, none appears to me so important as the following. Carefully distinguish between our election to run the race of faith and holiness, according to one or other of the Divine dispensations; and between our election to receive *the prize* — a crown of glory. St. Paul, speaking to Christians of the *first* of these elections, says, "God has chosen us that we should be holy." And our Lord, describing the *second* election, says, "Many are called, but few chosen. Well done, good and faithful servant, enter thou into the joy of thy Lord." The former of these elections is always *unconditional;* but the latter is always suspended upon the reasonable *condition* of persevering in the obedience of faith.

To show the propriety and importance of the preceding directions, I need only apply them to the parable of the talents, which displays every branch of the doctrine of election. "The kingdom of heaven," says Christ [if it be considered with respect to God's gracious and righteous dispensations toward the various classes of his moral vessels or servants] "is as a man who called, [and, of consequence, first freely chose] his own servants."

Observe here that every man is *unconditionally* chosen and called to serve God in his universal temple. Some may be compared to earthen vessels, made, chosen, and called to be useful in the court of the Gentiles, like humble Gibeonites: some to *silver* vessels, made, chosen, and called to be useful in the holy place, like pious Jews: and others to *golden*, i.e. most precious and honourable vessels, made, chosen, and called to be useful in the holiest of all, like true Christians. Hence it appears that God has assigned to all his moral vessels their proper place and use in his great temple, the universe. If they are unprofitable and unfit for the Master's use, it is not because he makes them so; but because they received a bad taint from their parents upon the wheel of generation, and afterward refuse to purge themselves by means of the talent of light, grace, and power, which is bestowed upon them as the seed of regeneration, according to their respective dispensations.

The difference that sovereign grace makes between God's servants, or, if you please, between his moral vessels, is evidently asserted by St. Paul, 2 Timothy 2:19, &c. "The Lord," says he, "knoweth them that are his:" that is, he approves the godly, the vessels of mercy, the clean vessels under every dispensation. "Let then every one that nameth the name of Christ," and who is, of consequence, under the strictest of all the dispensations, "depart from iniquity: for in a great house there are not only vessels of gold and silver, but also of wood and of earth; and some to honour,* and some to dishonour. If a man purge himself from these" [that are to dishonour] whether he be a vessel of gold, silver, wood, or earth, "he shall," according to his dispensation, "be a vessel unto honour, sanctified and meet for the Master's use, and prepared unto every good work;" though it should be only the work of a Gibeonite, hewing wood and drawing water. And if a Christianized Saul seeks to slay these spiritual Gibeonites in his zeal for the children of Israel, God himself will plead their cause: for he honours, in every dispensation, vessels that are clean and sanctified, according to his own decree, "Them that honour me, I will *peculiarly* honour, and they that despise me shall be lightly esteemed." That is, although those that honour me should be only fit to be compared to wooden or earthen vessels, like the devout soldiers of Cornelius, I will honour them with a place in my heavenly house. And were those that despise me compared to silver vessels, like the sons of Eli; or to a golden vessel, like Judas; if repentance do not interpose, they shall be broken with a rod of iron like vessels of wrath; and after "sleeping in the dust, they shall awake to the everlasting contempt" due to their sins; it being written among the decrees of Heaven, "If any man defile" the vessel, or "temple of God, him shall God destroy." Such will be the fearful end of those, who, by their wilful *unbelief*, make themselves positively unclean vessels. "For to them that are *unbelieving* is nothing pure, but even their mind and conscience are defiled." And these vessels of just wrath and positive dishonour must be carefully distinguished from those whom God comparatively makes vessels of dishonour, by giving them fewer talents than he does to his upper servants.

Return we now to the parable of the talents and to the several *classes* of servants, which St. Paul compares to several classes of vessels, in God's great house below. "To one of them" says our Lord, (to the Christian, I suppose,) according to the election of most particular, distinguishing grace, "he gave five talents." To another, suppose the Jew, still according to the election of particular grace, "he gave two talents." "And to another," suppose the heathen, according to the decree of general grace, "he gave one talent." Hence it appears that God reprobates no man absolutely, and is no Calvinistical respecter of persons; for, adds our Lord in the parable, "he gave to every one according to his several ability," or circumstances, Matthew 25:15. This first distribution of grace and privileges is previous to all works, and to it belong (as I have shown by parallel scriptures) those words of the apostle, "The children being not yet born, neither having *done any good or evil*, that the purpose of God according to" sovereign, distinguishing election to certain remarkable favours, "might stand, not of works, but of him that calleth, it was said, The elder shall serve the younger — Jacob have I loved, and Esau have I hated," i.e. I have preferred Jacob to Esau, in point of family honour; and the Israelites to the Edomites with respect to the covenant of peculiarity. And with as much propriety it might be said, in

---

* St. Paul having guarded the doctrine of sovereign, distinguishing grace, by the different matter, earth, wood, silver, &c, of which the vessels are formed: and not making any distinction between "vessels of dishonour" and "vessels of wrath," as he does in Romans 9, it necessarily follows, according to the doctrine of rewarding grace, that the expression "vessels to honour," and "vessels to dishonour," should not be taken *here* in a comparative sense, as in Romans 9; but in a positive sense; and then they answer to "vessels *sanctified*," and to "vessels *not purged*," expressions which occur in the context, and fix the apostle's meaning.

point of super-angelical dignity, Michael the archangel have I loved, and Gabriel the angel have I hated: i.e. I have reprobated the latter from a degree of dignity and favour to which I have elected the former.

Thus far the parable illustrates the doctrine of sovereign free grace, and of an *unconditional election* to receive and use different measures of grace; and thus far I walk hand in hand with Zelotes, because thus far he speaks as the oracles of God, except when he hints at his doctrine of absolute reprobation: for at such times he makes it his business to insinuate that there are some men to whom God never gave so much as one talent of saving grace, in flat opposition to that clause of the parable, "he gave to *every one*" one or two true talents at least: I say true, because whatever dreadful hints Zelotes may throw out to the contrary, I dare not allow the thought that the *true* God deals in *false* coin; or that, because he is the God of all grace, he deals also in damning grace: — damning grace I call it; for in the very nature of things, all grace bestowed upon an absolute reprobate — upon a man hated of God with an everlasting hate, and given up from his mother's womb unavoidably to sin and be damned: all grace, I say, flowing from such a reprobating God to such a reprobated man is no better than a serpent, whose head is Calvin's absolute reprobation and its tail Zelotes' finished damnation.

Zelotes, I fear, objects to the sovereign, free, distinguishing grace which I contend for, chiefly because it has no connection with the bound will, and distinguishing free wrath which characterize his opinions. Accordingly he soon takes his leave of me and the parable of the talents, the middle part of which illustrates what he calls my heresy, that is, the doctrine of free will. (1.) The doctrine of obedient free will, which our Lord secures thus: — "Then he that had received five talents went and traded with the same, and made them other five talents," &c. And, (2.) The doctrine of perverse free will, which Christ lays down in these words: — "But he that had received one talent went and digged in the earth, and hid his Lord's money." Here Christ, for brevity's sake, points out unfaithful free will in the lowest dispensation *only:* sloth and unfaithfulness being by no means necessary consequences of the least number of talents. For while some Christians bury their five, and some Jews their two talents, some heathens so improve their one talent as to verify our Lord's doctrine, "The last shall be first."

The third part of the parable illustrates the doctrine of *rewarding* grace, or of conditional election to, and reprobation from the rewards with which Divine grace crowns human faithfulness. I call this election and this reprobation conditional, because they are entirely suspended upon the good or bad use which our faithful, or unfaithful free will makes of the talent or talents bestowed upon us by free grace; as appears by the rest of the parable: "After a long time the Lord of those servants cometh, and reckoneth with them," proceeding first to the election of *rewarding* grace. "He that had received five talents came and brought other five talents, saying, Lord, thou deliveredst unto me five talents: behold, I have gained beside them five talents more." Here you see in an exemplifying glass the doctrine which Zelotes abhors, and which St. John recommends thus: "Beloved, if our heart condemn us not, then have we confidence toward God. Herein is our love made perfect, that we may have boldness in the day of judgment," 1 John 3:21; 4:17. His Lord [instead of driving him to hell as a poor, blind, unawakened creature, who never knew himself; or as a proud, self-righteous Pharisee, who was never convinced of sin] said unto him, "Well done, thou good and faithful servant, [thou vessel of mercy,] thou hast been faithful over a few things, enter thou into the joy of thy Lord" through my merciful Gospel charter, and the passport of thy sincere, blood-besprinkled obedience.

The servant, who through free grace and faithfulness had gained two talents, beside the two which distinguishing grace had given him, came next; and when he had been elected into the joy of his Lord in the same gracious manner, the trial of the faithless heathen came on. His plea would almost make one think that Zelotes had instilled into him his hard doctrine of reprobation. He is not ashamed to preach it to Christ himself. "Lord," says he, "I knew thee, that thou art a hard man," who didst contrive my reprobation from the beginning of the world, and gavest me only one talent of common grace, twenty of which would not amount to one dram of saving grace. "I knew thee," I say, "that thou art an austere" master, "reaping," or wanting to reap where thou hast not sowed the seed of effectual grace; "and gathering," or wanting to gather "where thou hast not strewed" one grain of true grace; "and I was afraid, and went and hid thy talent," thy ineffectual, false, common grace "in the earth. Lo, there thou hast that is thine. His Lord answered and said unto him, Thou wicked and slothful servant, &c, thou oughtest to have put my money to the exchangers," who sometimes exchange to such advantage for the poor, that their "little one becomes a thousand." Hadst thou made this proper use of my "common grace," as thou callest it, "at my coming I should have received mine own with usury. Take therefore the talent from him, and give it to him that hath ten talents: for every one that hath" to purpose, "shall have abundance: but from him that hath not" to purpose, "shall be taken away even that which he hath" — his unimproved, hidden talent: "and cast ye the unprofitable servant into outer darkness;" i.e. into hell: "there shall be weeping and gnashing of teeth," Matthew 25:15, 31. Hence it appears that a man may be freely *elected* to receive *one, two,* or *five* talents — freely chosen to trade with them, and afterward be justly *reprobated*, or cast away into outer darkness for not improving his talent, that is, for not "making his calling and election sure."

Zelotes, indeed, as if he were conscious that the parable of the talents overthrows all his doctrinal peculiarities, endeavours to explain it away by saying that it does not represent God's conduct toward his people with respect to grace and salvation, but only with regard to parts and natural gifts. To this I answer, (1.) The Scriptures no where mention a day of account, in which God will reward and punish his servants according to their natural parts, exclusively of their moral actions. — (2.) The servants had all the same master. Luke 19:13, they are all represented as receiving "one pound" each, to "occupy," or trade till their master came. He that did not improve his pound, or talent, is called "wicked" on that account. Now the non-improvement of a natural talent, suppose for poetry or husbandry, can never constitute a man "wicked;" nothing can do this but the non-improvement of a talent of grace. (3.) We have as much reason to affirm that the oil of the virgins, mentioned in the beginning of the chapter, and the good works of the godly, mentioned at the end of it, were "not of a gracious nature," as to assert it of the improvement of the pound, which constituted some of the servants "good and faithful." (4.) It is absurd to suppose that Christ will ever take some men into his joy, and will command others to be cast into outer darkness, for improving or not improving the natural talent of speaking, writing, or singing in a masterly manner. (5.) The description of the day of judgment, that closes the chapter, is a key to the two preceding parables. On the one hand the door is shut against the *foolish virgins* merely for their apostasy — for having burned out all their oil of faith working by love, so that their "lamps went out." The *slothful servant* is cast into outer darkness merely for not improving his talent of opportunity and power to believe, and to work righteousness according to the light of his dispensation. And the *goats* are sent into hell merely for not having done the works of faith. On the other hand, (considering salvation according to its second causes,) the *wise virgins* go in with the bridegroom, because their lamps are not gone out, and they have oil in their vessels; the *faithful servants* enter into the joy of the Lord, because they have improved their talents; and the *sheep* go into life eternal, because they have done the works of faith. The three parts of that plain chapter make a threefold cord, which, I apprehend, Zelotes cannot break, without breaking all the rules of morality, criticism, and common sense.

I shall close my parabolic illustration of the Scripture doctrine of unconditional and conditional election, by presenting Zelotes and Honestus with a short view of our *election in Christ;* that is, of our election to receive freely, and to use faithfully, the five talents of the Christian dispensation, that we may reap all the benefits annexed to "making that high calling and election sure."

I.

Blessed be the God and Father of our Lord Jesus Christ, who hath blessed us with all spiritual blessings in heavenly things *in* [the person and dispensation of] *Christ:* according as he hath* *chosen* us [to believe] in him, before the foundation of the world: that [in making our high calling and election sure] we should be holy and without blame before him in love, Ephesians 1:3, 4.

[If Zelotes be offended at my insinuating that St. Paul's phrase *"in*

II.

Hearken, my beloved brethren, hath not God *chosen* the poor of this world? [Yes, but *not absolutely,* for Zelotes knows that all the poor are not elected in his way: and St. James insinuates that their election to "the kingdom of heaven" is suspended on faith and love; for he adds that] God hath chosen the poor, *rich in faith*, and [of consequence] heirs of the kingdom, which he hath promised to them that love him, [i.e. to them that are rich in the "faith which works by love,"]

---

* This passage will be explained in the next section. In the meantime I desire the reader to take notice that the election of which St. Paul writes is not of the Antinomian kind; I mean, it is not Calvinian election, which insures eternal salvation to all fallen believers. That the apostle was an utter stranger to such a doctrine, appears from his own words to those *elect* Ephesians: "Putting away lying, speak truth: let him that stole steal no more: be not drunk: let not fornication or uncleanness be once named among you, &c, for this ye know, that no unclean person, &c, hath any inheritance in the kingdom of Christ. Let no man deceive you with vain words, for because of these things the wrath of God cometh upon the children of disobedience," that is, upon the disobedient children, who, by their bad works, lose their inheritance in the kingdom of God. Is it not surprising, that when St. Paul has thus warned the Ephesians against Antinomian deceptions, he should be represented as deceiving those very Ephesians first, by teaching them a doctrine which implies that no crimes, be they ever so atrocious, can deprive fallen believers of their "inheritance in the kingdom of Christ?"

Christ" is sometimes an ellipsis — a short way of speaking which conveys the idea of our Lord's Gospel and dispensation; I appeal to the reader's candour, and to the meaning of the following texts: — "Babes in Christ. Urbane, our helper in Christ. The Churches of Judea, which were in Christ. Baptized into Christ. The Mosaic veil is done away in Christ. In Christ Jesus circumcision availeth nothing," &c. Again: when St. Paul tells us that "his bonds in Christ are manifest in all the palace," does he not mean the chain with which he was personally bound, as a preacher of the Christian faith? And would not Zelotes make himself ridiculous, if he asserted that St. Paul's "bonds in Christ" were those with which he was bound in *the person of Christ* in the garden of Gethsemane?]

There is a remnant [of Jews, who believe] according to the election of grace [who, through sanctification of the Spirit to obedience, and sprinkling of the blood of Jesus Christ, make their calling and election sure according to the Christian dispensation, 1 Peter 1:2.] *The election* [those Jews who make their election to the blessings of the Christian dispensation sure by faith in Christ] hath obtained it [righteousness] and the rest were blinded: [that is, the unbelieving Jews have not obtained righteousness, because they sought it not by faith, but by blindly opposing their Pharisaic works of the law to Christ and the humble obedience of faith,] Romans 11:5, 7; 9:32.

James 2:5. Know this also, that the Lord hath chosen to himself [i.e. to his rewards of grace and glory, not this or that man out of mere caprice, but] the man that is godly: [that is] the man after his own heart. (*Com. Prayers*, Psalm 4:3; 1 Samuel 13:14,) God hath from the beginning chosen you to salvation [yea, out of mere distinguishing grace, he has chosen you to partake of the great salvation of Christians; not indeed absolutely, but] through sanctification of the Spirit, and belief of the truth, [as it is in Jesus — the truth as it is revealed under the Christian dispensation,] 2 Thessalonians 2:13.

Many are *called* [to repentance, yea, many are "chosen, that they should be holy," Ephesians 1:4,] but few are chosen [to receive the reward of perfected holiness — the reward of the inheritance,] Matthew 20:16. Wherefore, brethren, give diligence to make your calling and election SURE: for if ye do these things, ye shall never fall, 2 Peter 1:10. Put on, therefore, as the elect of God, bowels of mercies. For he shall have judgment without mercy, that hath showed no mercy, Colossians 3:12 James 2:13.

If I am not mistaken, the balance of the preceding scriptures shows that Honestus and Zelotes are equally in the wrong: Honestus, for not rejoicing in free grace, in the election of grace, and in God's power, love, and faithfulness, which are engaged to keep believers while they keep in the way of duty: and Zelotes, for corrupting the genuine doctrines of grace by his doctrines of Calvinian election, necessity, and unconditional reprobation from eternal life.

SECTION XIII.

A view of St. Paul's doctrine of election, laid down in Ephesians 1 — That election consists in God's choosing, from the beginning of the world, that the Gentiles should NOW share, through faith, the blessings of the Gospel of Christ, together with the believing Jews, who BEFORE were alone the chosen nation and peculiar people of God — It is an election from the obscure dispensation of the heathens to the luminous dispensation of the Christians; and not an election from a state of absolute ruin, to a state of finished salvation — It is as absurd to maintain Calvinian election from Ephesians i, as to support Calvinian reprobation by Romans ix — What we are to understand by the "book of life," and by the "names" written therein from the foundation of the world — A conclusion to the first part of this work.

WHEN Zelotes is made ashamed of what Calvin calls "*the horrible decree,*" he seems to give it up; — I have nothing to do with reprobation, says he, my business is with election. Thus he is no sooner beaten out of Romans 9, than he retires behind Ephesians 1, where he thinks he can make a more honourable defence. It may not be amiss, therefore, to follow him there also, and to show him that he entirely mistakes the "predestination," "purpose," and "election," mentioned in that chapter.

The design of the apostle in his Epistle to the Ephesians is twofold. In the three first chapters he extols their gracious election, their free vocation, and the unspeakable privileges of both; and in the three last, he exhorts them to walk worthy of their election and calling; warning them against Antinomian deceivers; and threatening them with the loss of their heavenly inheritance if they followed their filthy tenets and immoral example. This epistle therefore is a compendium of the New Testament: the former part contains a strong check to Pharisaism, or the doctrine of self-righteous boasters; and the latter part a severe check to Antinomianism, or to the doctrine and deeds of the Nicolaitans; see Ephesians 5:5, 6; Revelation 2:6, 15, 20.

To be a little more explicit: in the three first chapters St. Paul endeavours to impress the hearts of the Ephesians with a deep sense of God's free grace in Christ Jesus, whereby he had compassionately called, and of consequence mercifully elected them, ignorant and miserable sinners of the Gentiles as they were, to partake of all the blessings of the Christian dispensation. The apostle tries to inflame them with grateful love to Christ, for setting them on a level with his "peculiar people, the Jews, to whom pertained the adoption, and the glory, and the covenants, and the giving of the law, and the service of God, and the [explicit] promises; whose were the fathers, and of whom Christ came, as concerning the flesh."

To prove that this is St. Paul's design, I produce his own words, with short illustrations in brackets: "Remember, [says he,] that ye were in time past GENTILES in the flesh, called uncircumcision by the circumcision [&c, abhorred by the circumcised Jews, because you were uncircumcised heathens. Remember] that at that time ye were without [the knowledge of] Christ [not having so much as heard of the Messiah,] being aliens from the commonwealth of Israel, [hating the Jews, and hated of them,] strangers to the covenants of promise [which God had made with Abraham, Isaac, and Jacob,] having no [covenant] hope, and without [a covenant] God in the world. But now in Christ Jesus [who has sent us into all the world to preach the Gospel to every creature.] Ye [Gentiles,] who were sometimes afar off, are made nigh by the blood of Christ: for he is our peace, who hath made BOTH [Jews and Gentiles] one, and hath broken down the middle wall of partition between US, &c, that he might reconcile both [Jews and Gentiles] to God, &c, by the cross; having slain the enmity thereby: and came and preached peace to you [Gentiles] who were afar off, and to them that were nigh, [that is, to the Jews.] For through him we BOTH [Jews and Gentiles] have an access by one Spirit unto the Father. Now therefore ye [Gentiles] are no more strangers and foreigners, but fellow citizens with the [Jewish] saints, and of the household [or peculiar people] of God: and are built upon the foundation of the [Christian] apostles, and [Jewish] prophets; Jesus Christ himself being the chief corner stone [which unites the Jews and Gentiles who believe, as a corner stone joins the two walls which meet upon it, &c.] In whom you also [Gentiles of Ephesus] are builded together [with us believing Jews] for a habitation of God through the Spirit," Ephesians 2:11, &c.

The apostle explains his meaning still more clearly in the next chapter. "For this cause," [namely, that you might be quickened together with us (see Ephesians 2:5, 6, in the original,) unto Christ, that you might be raised up together, and placed together with us in heavenly privileges in or by Jesus Christ.] "For this cause, I Paul am the prisoner of Christ for you Gentiles; if ye have heard of the DISPENSATION of the grace of God, which is given me to YOU WARD: how he made known to me [once a Jewish bigot] the mystery, &c, that the Gentiles should be fellow heirs, and of the same body, and partakers of the promise of Christ by the Gospel, whereof I am made a minister, &c, that I should preach among the Gentiles [as Peter does among the Jews] the unsearchable riches of Christ, &c. Wherefore I desire that ye faint not at my tribulations for you [Gentiles] which is your glory," Ephesians 3:1-13.

The two preceding paragraphs are two keys, which St. Paul gives to open his meaning with, and to make us understand "God's eternal purpose, which he purposed in Christ Jesus our Lord, of gathering all things in Christ," by calling the Gentiles to be partakers of the Gospel of Christ, as well as the Jews: a "mystery" *this,* which had been hid in God from the beginning of the world, Ephesians 3:9; God having then purposed to take the Gentiles into the covenant of peculiarity: although, for particular reasons, he did it only in St. Paul's days, and chiefly by his instrumentality. What pity is it then that Zelotes should cast the veil of his prejudices over so glaring a truth; and should avail himself of the apostle's laconic style, and of our inattention to impose Calvin's predestination upon us! Does not the context demonstrate that St. Paul speaks *only* of God's predestinating and electing THE GENTILES IN GENERAL (and among them the Ephesians)to share the prerogatives of the Christian dispensation? Is it not evident, that as the unbelieving Jews boasted much of their being saved by the work of circumcision, through Abraham, St. Paul keeps the believing Gentiles humble, by reminding them that "by grace they were saved — [that is, made partakers of the great salvation of Christians] through faith: and that not of themselves, [nor of their forefathers,] it was the gift of God, not of works," not of circumcision or Mosaic ceremonies, "lest any *of them* should boast" like the Jews, who, by their fatal glorying in Abraham and in themselves, had hardened their hearts against Christ's Gospel, and brought God's curse upon their Church and nation? In a word, is it not clear that St. Paul no more speaks of God's having predestinated this Englishman, or that man of Ephesus to be absolutely saved; and this Scotch woman, or that Ephesian widow to be absolutely damned, than he has absolutely predestinated Honestus to be mufti, and Zelotes to be pope?

This being premised, I present the reader with what appears to me to be the genuine sense of the chapter, upon which Zelotes founds his doctrine of an absolute, particular, and personal election of some men to eternal life and glory. "Blessed be the God and Father of our Lord Jesus Christ, who hath blessed us," Jews and Gentiles, who do not put the word of his grace from us, and reject his gracious counsel against ourselves "with all spiritual blessings and heavenly" things "in Christ: according as he hath chosen us," Jews and Gentiles, "in *him* before the foundation of the world, that we," Jews and Gentiles, "should be holy, and without blame before him in love," as all Christians ought to be: "having predestinated us," Jews and Gentiles, "unto the adoption of children by Jesus Christ to himself, according to the good pleasure of his will, — by which he hath made both" Jews and Gentiles "ONE, and hath broken down the middle wall of partition between us; making in himself of twain," i.e. Jews and Gentiles, "one new man," i.e. one new ecclesiastical body, which is at unity in itself, though it be composed of Jews and Gentiles, who were before supposed to be absolutely irreconcilable, Ephesians 3:14. And this he hath done "to the praise of the glory of his grace, wherein he hath made us," Jews and Gentiles, equally accepted in the Beloved; in whom we," Jews and Gentiles," have redemption through his blood, the forgiveness of sins, according to the riches of his grace: wherein he hath abounded to us," Jews and Gentiles, "in all wisdom and prudence; having made known unto us," Jews and Gentiles, "the mystery of his will, according to his good pleasure, which he hath purposed in himself: that in the dispensation of the fulness of times," i.e. under his last dispensation, which is the Christian, "he might gather together in one all things in Christ, both which are in heaven," i.e. angels and glorified saints, "and which are on earth," i.e. Jews and Gentiles, "even in Him," who is the head of all: "in whom also we," Jews and Gentiles, "have obtained," through faith, "a common inheritance, being" equally "predestinated" to share the blessings of the Christian dispensation, "according to the purpose of Him who worketh all things after the counsel of his own" gracious "will: that we," Jews, "who FIRST trusted in Christ," (for the FIRST Gospel offer was always made to the Jews, and the FIRST Christian Church was entirely composed of Jews, compare Acts 2:5, with Acts 3:26, and Acts 13:46,) — "that we," Jews, I say, "should be to the praise of his glory, who first trusted in Christ; in whom ye," Gentiles, "also trusted, after that ye heard the word of truth, the Gospel of your salvation; in whom also, πιστευσαντες, having believed, YE were sealed" as well as WE "with that Holy Spirit of promise, which is the earnest of our" common "inheritance, &c. Wherefore I also, after I heard of your faith in the Lord Jesus, &c, cease not to give thanks for you, making mention of you in my prayers; that, &c, ye may know what is the hope of his calling" of you Gentiles, "and what the riches of the glory of his inheritance in the saints:" i.e. in them that "obey the heavenly calling," whether they be Jews or Gentiles, Ephesians 1:3-18.

This easy exposition is likewise confirmed by the beginning of the next chapter. "And you, Gentiles, "who were dead in trespasses and sins, wherein in time past ye walked according to, &c, the spirit that now worketh in the children of disobedience, among whom we all," Jews and Gentiles, "had our conversation in time past," &c, see Romans 1:2. "You," I say, and us, "God, who is rich in mercy" toward all, "for his great love wherewith he loved us," Jews and Gentiles, "hath quickened us together with Christ. By grace ye are saved" through faith as well as we: that is, ye are saved by the free grace of God in Christ, as the *first cause;* and by your believing the Gospel of Christ, which is GRACE AND TRUTH, John 1:17, as the second cause. "For, through him, WE BOTH," Jews and Gentiles, "have access by one Spirit unto the Father," Ephesians 2:1-5, 18.

If Zelotes doubts yet whether the apostle treats in this epistle of the predestination and election of the Gentiles, to partake of the blessings of Christianity, together with the Jews; let him consider what the commentators of his own party have candidly said of the design of the epistle; and his good sense will soon make him see the scope of the parts which I have produced.

I appeal first to Diodati, one of Calvin's successors, who opens his exposition by these words: "The summary of it [the Epistle to the Ephesians] is that he [the apostle] gives God thanks for the infinite benefit of eternal salvation and redemption in Christ, communicated out of mere grace and election through faith in the Gospel, to the apostle first, and his companions of the Jewish nation; then afterward to the Ephesians, who were Gentiles, &c, by the ministry of St. Paul appointed by God to preach to the Gentiles the mystery of their calling in grace, which was before unknown to the world." Burkitt says the same firing in fewer words: "This excellent epistle Divinely sets forth, &c, the marvellous dispensation of God to the Gentiles in revealing Christ to THEM." Mr. Henry touches thus upon the truth which I endeavour to clear up: "In the former part [of the epistle] he [St. Paul] represents the great privilege of the Ephesians, who, being in time past idolatrous HEATHENS, were now converted [and of consequence chosen and called] to Christianity, and received into covenant with God." And again: "This epistle has much of common concernment to all Christians; especially to all who, having been Gentiles, &c, were converted to Christianity." See one more flash of truth breaking out of a Calvinistic cloud. Pool, speaking of the mystery which God had made known to Paul by revelation, raises this objection after Estius: "But the mystery of the calling [and consequently of the election] of the Gentiles, of which it is evident the apostle speaks, was not unknown to the prophets," &c. Why then does he say that *it was not made known?* and Pool answers, That the prophets knew not explicitly, *"quod Gentiles pares essent Judæis quoad consortium gratiæ Dei,"* — "that the Gentiles should be put on a level with the Jews, with respect to a COMMON INTEREST in God's grace." (*Syn. Crit. on Ephesians* 3:5.)

If Zelotes do not regard the preceding testimonies, let him at least believe St. Paul himself, who, explicitly speaking of the calling and election of the Gentiles, which he names "the mystery of Christ," mentions his having "wrote *about it* afore in few words; whereby (adds he) when ye read, ye may understand my knowledge in *that* mystery," Ephesians 3:3. Hence it is evident, that the apostle, in the preceding part of the epistle, treats of God's electing the Gentiles to the prerogatives of Christianity: an election this by which they are admitted to share in privileges, which the apostles themselves, for a considerable time after the day of pentecost, durst not offer to any but their own countrymen, as appears by Acts 10, 11; — in privileges, which multitudes of Jewish converts would never allow the believing Gentiles to enjoy;

tormenting them with Judaism, and saying, "Except ye be circumcised," i.e. except ye turn Jews as well as Christians, "ye cannot be saved." Compare Acts 15, with the Epistle to the Galatians. But what has this election from Gentilism to Christianity — this "abolishing the enmity" between Jews and Gentiles, "even the law of commandments, contained in *Mosaic* ordinances, for to make of twain one new man," to make of Jews and Gentiles "one new chosen nation, and peculiar people," called Christians; — what has such an election, I say, to do with the election maintained by Zelotes? Who does not see that the *general* election of all the Gentiles from the obscure dispensation of the heathens, to the luminous dispensation of the Christians, (as the sound of the Gospel trump shall gradually reach them,) is the very reverse of Zelotes' *particular* election? an election by which (if we believe him] God only tithes (if I may so speak) the damned world of the Gentiles; absolutely setting apart for himself a dozen people, if so many, in an English village; half a dozen, it may be, in a Scotch district; and a less number, perhaps, in an Irish hamlet; Calvinistically passing by the rest of their neighbours; that is, absolutely giving them up to necessary sin and unavoidable damnation: binding them fast with the chain of Adam's unatoned sin; and, to make sure work, sealing them with the seal of his free wrath, even before the fall of Adam: for if we may credit Zelotes, this world was made AFTER the decree by which God *secured* the commission of Adam's sin, and the damnation of his reprobate posterity.

From the preceding observations I draw the following inference:-

Seldom did the perverter of truth play a bolder and more artful game than when he transformed himself into an angel of light, and produced Romans 9, and Ephesians 1, as demonstrations of the truth of Calvinian reprobation and election. St. Paul maintains, in Romans 9, that the Jews, as a circumcised nation, are rejected from the covenant of *peculiarity;* that God has an indubitable right to extend to whom he pleases the *peculiar* mercy which he before confined to the circumcised race; and that he now, according to the ancient purpose of his grace, extends that mercy to the Gentiles, i.e. to all other nations, among which, of consequence, the Gospel of Christ gradually spreads. Therefore, insinuates Zelotes, God has absolutely given over to necessary sin and certain damnation (it may be) the best half of the English, Scotch, and Irish. These poor reprobates, if we believe his doctrines of grace, were unconditionally cast away, not only from their mother's womb, but also from the time that He, who "tasted death for every man," forbade all his wounds to pour forth one single drop of blood for them. Nay, they were from all eternity intentionally made to be *necessarily* "vessels of wrath" to all eternity. But in the name of wisdom I ask, what has Zelotes' conclusion to do with St. Paul's premises? Has the one any more agreement with the other, than kindness with cruelty, Christ with Moloch, and sense with nonsense? Again: —

In Ephesians 1, the apostle "makes known" to the Ephesians "the mystery of God's will, who purposed in himself, predestinated, *or resolved,* before the foundation of the world, that, in the dispensation of the fulness of times, he would gather together in one all things in Christ," and call the Gentiles, as well as the Jews, to partake of the "unsearchable riches of Christ" by faith. But Zelotes, instead of gladdening the hearts of his countrymen by the Gospel news of this *extensive* grace, and general election of the Gentiles, takes occasion from it to confine redemption, to preach narrow grace, and to insinuate the personal Calvinistic election of some of his neighbours. Suppose Peter Penitent, Martha Forward, and Matthew Fulsome: an election this which is inseparable from the personal, absolute, eternal reprobation of his other neighbours: suppose John Endeavour, Thomas Doubter, George Honest, and James Worker, to say nothing of Miss Wanton, Mr. Cheat, Sarah Cannibal, and Samuel Hottentot. For it is evident that if none of Zelotes next neighbours are in "the book of life" but the three first mentioned; if those three can never be put out of the book, sin they ever so grievously; and not one of the others can possibly be put in, live they ever so righteously — it is evident, I say, upon this footing, that the salvation of some of Zelotes' neighbours, and the damnation of all the rest, are absolutely necessary; or, to speak his own language, absolutely "finished." Thus the gracious election of the Gentiles, which filled St. Paul's soul with transports of grateful joy, and would be a perpetual spring of consolation to *us*, European Gentiles, if it were preached in a Scriptural manner: — this gracious election, I say, becomes, by Zelotes' mistake, the source of all the presumptuous comforts which flow from Calvin's luscious, Antinomian election; and of all the tormenting fears which arise from his severe, Pharisaic reprobation.

Having just mentioned "the book of life," so triumphantly produced by Zelotes, it may not be amiss to hear what he and his antagonist Honestus think about it. Throw we then their *partial* sentiments into the Scripture Scales, and by balancing them according to the method of the sanctuary, let us see the meaning of that mysterious expression.

I.

Help, &c, my fellow labourers, whose *names* are written in *the book of life*, Philippians 4:3. All that dwell on the earth, whose names are not written in the book of life of the Lamb, shall worship him [the beast,] Revelation 17:8. Whose names were not written in the book of life *from the foundation of the world*, Revelation 17:8. Whosoever worketh abomination, &c, shall in no wise enter into it, [the city of God,] but they which are written in the Lamb's book of life, Revelation 16:27. And whosoever was not found written in the Lamb's book of life, was cast into the lake of fire, Revelation 20:15. At that time thy people shall be delivered, every one that shall be found written in the book, Daniel 12:1.

II.

Another book was opened, which is the book of life: and the dead were *judged* out of those things which were written in the books *according to their works*, Revelation 20:12. If thou wilt not forgive, blot me, I pray thee, out of thy book which thou hast written [from the foundation of the world.] And the Lord said to Moses, *Whosoever hath sinned* against me, *him will I blot* out of my book, [a sure proof this that he was before in the book,] Ezekiel 32:32, 33. Let them [persecutors] be blotted out of the book* of life, Psalm 69:28. They that feared the Lord spake often one to another, and the Lord heard it, and a book of remembrance was written before him, for them that feared the Lord: and they shall be

---

* I take the liberty to say "the book of *life*," and not "the book of *the living*," because our translators themselves, Genesis 2:7, have rendered the very same word "the breath of *life*," and not "the breath of *the living*."

mine, saith the Lord of hosts, in that day when I make up my jewels, Malachi 3:16. I will not blot out his name [the name of him that overcometh] out of the book of life, Revelation 3:5. If any man shall take away from the words of, &c, this prophecy, God shall take away his part out of the book of life, Revelation 22:19.

The balance of these scriptures evidently shows: (1.) That from the foundation of the world, God decreed to reward the righteous with eternal life. (2.) That, to show us the *certainty* of this decree, the sacred writers, by a striking, oriental metaphor, represent it as "written in a book," which they call "the book of life." (3.) That to carry on the allegory, the names of the *righteous* are said to be written in that book, and the names of the *wicked* not to be found in it; while the names of apostates are said to be "blotted out of it." (4.) That the NAMES written in this metaphorical "book of life" (if I may use the expression) are to be understood of *natures, properties,* and *characters;* in the sense in which Isaiah says of Christ, "His NAME shall be called Wonderful, Counsellor, *and* Prince of Peace;" or, in the sense in which God proclaimed his name to Moses; calling himself merciful, gracious, and long suffering. Whence it follows, that the "names written in the book of life from the foundation of the world are not Matthew Fulsome, Sarah Forward, or William Fanciful; but True Penitent, Obedient Believer, Good Servant, or "Faithful unto Death." And lastly, that it is as absurd to take this metaphor of the "book of life" literally, as to suppose that all David's *hairs* shall be glorified, and his *tears* literally bottled up in heaven, because it is said, "The very hairs of your head are numbered. All my members were written in thy book. Put thou my tears into thy bottle; are they not written in thy book?"

If Zelotes and Honestus condescend to weigh the preceding observations, their prejudices will, I hope, gradually subside; and while the one sends back to Geneva the *false*, intoxicating election recommended by Calvin, the other will bring us over from Ephesus the *true*, comfortable election maintained by St. Paul. That in the meantime we may all be thankful for our evangelical calling, improve our Gospel privileges, make our Scriptural election sure, and, as the apostle writes to the Ephesians, "walk worthy of the vocation wherewith we are called," is the ardent wish of my soul, which I cannot express in words more proper than those which I have just used in "receiving a child into the congregation of Christ's flock, and incorporating him into God's holy Church: — Heavenly Father, we give thee humble thanks, that thou hast vouchsafed to *call* us [and of consequence to choose us first] to the knowledge of thy grace and faith in thee. Increase this knowledge, and confirm this faith in us evermore; that we may receive the fulness of thy grace, live the rest of our life according to this beginning, continue Christ's faithful soldiers to our lives' end, and ever remain in the number of God's faithful and elect children, through Jesus Christ our Lord." (*Office of Baptism.*)

This truly Christian prayer shall conclude this section, and the first part of the Scripture Scales. Zelotes and Honestus have at this time given one another as much truth as they can well stand under. In a few days their strength will be recovered; they will meet again to fight it out, each from his scale: and when they shall have spent all their ammunition, they will, I hope, shake hands and be friends. But if they should be obstinate, and still jostle, instead of embracing each other, we will charge the peace. "When we are for a *Scriptural* peace, if they still prepare themselves for battle," we will bind them with all the cords we can borrow from reason, revelation, and experience. And if they then will not be quiet and agree, by a new kind of a metamorphose we will change them into *scales;* we will tie them to the solid *beam* of truth, and expose them in booksellers' shops, where they shall hang in logical chains, an eye-sore to bigots, — a terror to doctrinal clippers, who openly diminish the coin of the Church, — a comfort to those who are persecuted for truth and righteousness' sake, an encouragement to those who, like their Master, equally hate the doctrine of the Nicolaitans, and that of the Pharisees, — a new CHECK to those who spoil all by overdoing, — and a contrivance useful, I hope to novices, and to unwary professors, who, through an excess of simplicity, or for want of *scales* frequently take of masters in Israel a bare half shekel for "the full shekel of the sanctuary."

ZELOTES AND HONESTUS RECONCILED;

OR,

THE THIRD PART

OF

AN EQUAL CHECK

TO

PHARISAISM AND ANTINOMIANISM:

BEING THE SECOND PART

OF THE

SCRIPTURE SCALES

TO WEIGH THE GOLD OF GOSPEL TRUTH, TO BALANCE A MULTITUDE OF OPPOSITE
SCRIPTURES, TO PROVE THE GOSPEL MARRIAGE OF FREE GRACE AND FREE WILL, AND
RESTORE PRIMITIVE HARMONY TO THE GOSPEL OF THE DAY.

Si non est Dei gratito, quomodo salvat mundum? Si non est liberum arbitrium, quomod judicat mundum? — Aug.

PREFACE

TO THE THIRD PART OF AN EQUAL CHECK.

The reconciler invites the contending parties to end the controversy; and in order to this he beseeches them not to involve the question in clouds of evasive cavils or personal reflections; but to come to the point, and break, if they can, either the one or the other of his Scripture Scales; and if they cannot, to admit them both, and by that means to give glory to and the truth, and be reconciled to all the Gospel, and to one another.

BEING fully persuaded that Christianity suffers greatly by the opposite mistakes of the mere Solifidians and of the mere moralists, we embrace the truths and reject the errors which are maintained by these contrary parties. For by equally admitting the doctrines of grace and the doctrines of justice; — by equally contending for faith and for morality, we adopt what is truly excellent in each system; we reconcile Zelotes and Honestus; we bear our testimony against their contentious partiality; and, to the best of our knowledge, we maintain *the whole truth* as it is in Jesus. If we are mistaken, we shall be thankful to those who will set us right. Plain scriptures, close arguments, and friendly expostulations are the weapons we choose. We humbly hope that the unprejudiced reader will find no other in these pages: and to engage our opponents to use such only, we present to them the following petition: —

For the sake of candour, of truth, of peace, — for the reader's sake; and above all, for the sake of Christ, and the honour of Christianity; — whoever ye are that shall next enter the lists against us, do not wire-draw the controversy by uncharitably attacking our persons, and absurdly judging our spirits, instead of weighing our arguments and considering the scriptures which we produce. Nor pass over fifty solid reasons, and a hundred plain passages, to cavil about non-essentials, and to lay the stress of your answer upon mistakes which do not affect the strength of the cause, and which we are ready to correct as soon as they shall be pointed out.

Keep close to the question: do not divert the reader's mind by starting from the point in hand upon the most frivolous occasions; nor raise dust to obscure what is to be cleared up. An example will illustrate my meaning: Mr. Sellon, in vindicating the Church of England from the charge of Calvinism, observes, that her catechism is quite anti-Calvinistic, and that we ought to judge of her doctrine by her own catechism, and not by Ponet's Calvinian catechism, which poor young King Edward was prevailed upon to recommend some time after the establishment of our Church. Mr. Toplady, in his *Historic Proof,* instead of considering the question, which is, Whether it is not fitter to gather the doctrine of our Church from her own anti-Calvinian catechism than from Ponet's Calvinian catechism; Mr. Toplady, I say, in his answer to Mr. Sellon, fastens upon the phrase *poor young King Edward*, and works it to such a degree, that he raises from it clouds of shining dust and pillars of black smoke; filling, if I remember right, a whole section with the praises of King Edward, and with reflections upon Mr. Sellon. And, in his bright cloud of praise, and dark cloud of dispraise, the question is so entirely lost, that I doubt if one in a hundred of his readers has the least idea of it after reading two or three of the many pages which he has written on this head. By such means as these it is that he has made a ten or twelve shilling book, in which the Church of England is condemned to wear the badge of the Church of Geneva. And the Calvinists conclude Mr. Toplady has proved that she is bound to wear it; for they have paid dear for the *proof.*

That very gentleman, if fame is to be credited, has some thoughts of attacking the Checks. If he favour me with just remarks upon my mistakes (for I have probably made more than one; though I hope none of a capital nature) he shall have my sincere thanks: but if he involve the question in clouds of personal reflections and of idle digressions, he will only give me an opportunity of initiating the public more and more into the mysteries of *Logica Genevensis*. I therefore intreat him, if he think me worthy of his notice, to remember that the capital questions — the questions on which the fall of the Calvinian, or of the anti-Calvinian doctrines of grace turn, are not whether I am a fool and a knave; and whether I have made some mistakes in attacking Antinomianism; but whether those mistakes affect the truth of the anti-Solifidian and anti-Pharisaic Gospel which we defend: whether the two Gospel axioms are not equally true: whether our second Scale is not as Scriptural as the first: whether the doctrines of justice and obedience are not as important in their places as the doctrines of grace and mercy: whether the plan of reconciliation laid down in section iv, and the marriage of free grace and free will, described in section xi, are not truly evangelical: whether God can judge the world in righteousness and wisdom, if man be not a free, unnecessitated agent: whether the justification of *obedient believers*, by the WORKS OF FAITH, is not as Scriptural as the justification of sinners by FAITH itself: whether the eternal salvation of adults is not of remunerative justice as well as of free grace: whether *that* salvation does not secondarily depend on the evangelical, derived worthiness of obedient, persevering believers; as it primarily depends on the original and proper merits of our atoning and interceding Redeemer: whether man is in a state of probation; or, if you please, whether the Calvinian doctrines of finished salvation and finished damnation are true: whether there is not a day of initial salvation for all mankind, according to various dispensations of Divine grace: whether Christ did not taste death for every man, and purchase a day of initial redemption and salvation for all sinners, and a day of eternal redemption and salvation for all persevering believers: whether all the sins of real apostates, or foully fallen believers, shall so work for their good, that none of them shall ever be damned for any crime he shall commit: whether they shall all sing louder in heaven for their greatest falls on earth: whether our absolute, personal reprobation from eternal life is of God's free wrath through the decreed, necessary sin of Adam; or of God's just wrath through our own obstinate, avoidable perseverance in sin: whether our doctrines of non-necessitating grace and of just wrath do not exalt all the Divine perfections; and whether the Calvinian doctrines of necessitating grace and free wrath do not pour contempt upon all the attributes of God, his sovereignty not excepted.

Creeds and Scripture Scales

These are the important questions which I have principally debated with the Hon. and Rev. Mr. Shirley, Richard Hill, Esq., the Rev. Mr. Hill, the Rev. Mr. Berridge, and the Rev. Mr. Toplady. Some less essential collateral questions I have touched upon, such as, Whether Judas was an absolutely graceless hypocrite, when our Lord raised him to apostolic honours: whether some of the most judicious Calvinists have not, at times, done justice to the doctrine of free will and co-operation,* &c. These, and the like questions, I call *collateral*, because they are only occasionally brought in; and because the walls which defend our doctrines of grace stand firm without them. We hope, therefore, that if Mr. Toplady, and the other divines who defend the ramparts of mystical Geneva, should ever attack the Checks, they will direct their main batteries against our towers, and not against some insignificant part of the scaffolding, which we could entirely take down, without endangering our Jerusalem in the least. Should they refuse to grant our reasonable request; should they take up the pen to perplex, and not to solve the question; to blacken our character, and not to illustrate the obscure parts of the truth; they must give us leave to look upon their controversial attempt as an evasive show of defence, contrived to keep a defenceless, tottering error upon its legs, before an injudicious, bigoted populace.

If you will do us and the public justice, come to close quarters, and put an end to the controversy by candidly receiving our Scripture Scales, or by plainly showing that they are false. Our doctrine entirely depends upon the two Gospel axioms, and their necessary consequences, which now hang out to public view in our Gospel balances. Nothing therefore can be more easy than to point out our error, if our system be erroneous. But if our Scales be just, if our doctrines of grace and justice — of free grace and free will be true; it is evident that the Solifidians and the moralists are both in the wrong, and that we are, upon the whole, in the right. I say *upon the whole*, because insignificant mistakes can no more affect the strength of our cause, than a cracked slate or a broken pane can affect the solidity of a palace, which is firmly built upon a rock.

Therefore if you are an admirer of Zelotes, and a Solifidian opposer of free will, of the law of liberty, and of the remunerative justification of a believer by the works of faith, raise no dust; candidly give up Antinomianism; break the two pillars on which it stands, — necessitating free grace and forcible free wrath; or prove, if you

---

* The Rev. Mr. Whitefield, in his answer to the bishop of London's Pastoral Letter, says, "*That prayer is not the single work of the Spirit, without any cooperation of our own,* I readily confess. Who ever affirmed that *there was no cooperation of our own minds,* together with the impulse of the Spirit of God?" Now, that many rest short of salvation, merely by not co-operating with the Spirit's impulse, is evident, if we may credit these words of the reverend author: "There is a great difference between good desires and good habits. Many have the one who never attain to the other. Many (through the Spirit's impulse) have good desires to subdue sin; and yet resting (through want of co-operation) in those good desires, sin has always the dominion over them." (*Whitefield's Works*, vol. iv, pages 7, 11.) Mr. Whitefield grants, in these two passages, all that I contend for in these pages respecting the doctrine of our concurrence or co-operation with the Spirit of free grace, that is, respecting our doctrine of free will; and yet his warmest admirers will probably be my warmest opposers. But why? Because I aim at (what Mr. Whitefield sometimes overlooked) consistency.

can, that our second Scale, which is directly contrary to your doctrines of grace, is irrational, and that we have forged or misquoted the passages which compose it. But if you are a follower of Honestus, and a neglecter of free grace and salvation by faith in Jesus Christ, be a candid and honest disputant. Come at once to the grand question; and terminate the controversy, either by receiving our first Scale, which is directly contrary to your scheme of doctrine; or by proving that this Scale is directly contrary to reason and Scripture, and that we have misquoted or mistaken most of the passages which enter into its composition. I say *most*, though I could say *all;* for if only two passages, properly taken in connection with the context, the avowed doctrine of a sacred writer, and the general drift of the Scriptures; — if only two such passages, I say, fairly and truly support each section of our Scripture Scales, they hang firmly, and can no more, upon the whole, be invalidated than the Scripture itself, which, as our Lord informs us, "cannot be broken," John 10:35.

I take the Searcher of hearts, and my judicious, unprejudiced readers to witness, that through the whole of this controversy, far from concealing the most plausible objections, or avoiding the strongest arguments which are, or may be advanced against our reconciling doctrine, I have carefully searched them out, and endeavoured to encounter them as openly as David did Goliah. Had our opponents followed this method, I doubt not but the controversy would have ended long ago in the destruction of our prejudices, and in the rectifying of our mistakes. O, if we preferred the unspeakable pleasure of finding out the truth to the pitiful honour of pleasing a party, or of vindicating our own mistakes, how soon would the useful fan of Scriptural, logical, and brotherly controversy "purge the floor" of the Church! How soon would the light of truth and the flame of love "burn the chaff" of error and the thorns of prejudice "with fire unquenchable!" May the past triumphs of bigotry suffice! and instead of sacrificing any more to that detestable idol, may we all henceforth do whatever lies in us to hasten a general reconciliation, that we may all share together in the choicest blessings which God can bestow upon his peculiar people; — the Spirit of pure, evangelical truth, and of fervent, brotherly love.

MADELEY, March 30, 1775.

AN EXPLANATION

OF

SOME TERMS USED IN THESE SHEETS.

THE word *Solifidian* is defined, and the characters of Zelotes, Honestus, and Lorenzo, are drawn in the advertisement prefixed to the first part of this work. It is proper to explain here a few more words or characters.

PHARISAISM is the religion of a *Pharisee*.

A PHARISEE is a loose or strict professor of natural or revealed religion, who so depends upon the system of religion which he has adopted, or upon his attachment to the school or Church he belongs to; (whether it be the school of Plato, Confucius, or Socinus; whether it be the Church of Jerusalem, Rome, England, or Scotland;) who lays such a stress on his religious or moral duties, and has so good an opinion of his present harmlessness and obedience, or of his future reformation and good works, as to overlook his natural impotence and guilt, and to be insensible of the need and happiness of "being justified freely [as a sinner] by God's grace through the redemption that is in Jesus Christ," Romans 3:24. You may know him: (1.) By his contempt of, or coldness for the Redeemer and his free grace. (2.) By the antichristian confidence which he reposes in his best endeavours, and in the self-righteous exertions of his own free will. Or, (3.) By the jests he passes upon, or the indifference he betrays for the convincing, comforting, assisting, and sanctifying influences of God's Holy Spirit.

ANTINOMIANISM is the religion of an Antinomian.

AN ANTINOMIAN is a professor of Christianity, who is *antinomos*, against the law of Christ, as well as against the law of Moses. He allows Christ's law to be a rule of life, but not a rule of judgment for believers, and thus he destroys that law at a stroke, as a law; it being evident that a rule by the personal observance or non-observance of which Christ's subjects can never be acquitted or condemned, is not a law for them. Hence he asserts that Christians shall no more be justified before God by their personal obedience to the law of Christ, than by their personal obedience to the ceremonial law of Moses. Nay, he believes that the best Christians perpetually break Christ's law; that nobody ever kept it but Christ himself; and that we shall be justified or condemned before God, in the great day, not as we shall personally be found to have finally kept or finally broken Christ's law, but as God shall be found to have, before the foundation of the world, arbitrarily laid, or not laid to our account, the merit of Christ's keeping his own law. Thus he hopes to stand in the great day, merely by what he calls "Christ's imputed righteousness;" excluding with abhorrence, from our final justification, the evangelical worthiness of our own personal, sincere obedience of repentance and faith; — a precious obedience this, which he calls "dung, dross, and filthy rags:" just as if it were the insincere obedience of self-righteous pride, and Pharisaic hypocrisy. Nevertheless, though he thus excludes the evangelical, derived worthiness of the works of faith from our eternal justification and salvation, he does good works, if he is in other respects a good man. Nay, in this case, he piques himself on doing them; thinking he is peculiarly obliged to make people believe that, immoral as his sentiments are, they draw after them the greatest benevolence and the strictest morality. But Fulsome shows the contrary.

FULSOME represents a consistent Antinomian — that is, one who is such in practice as well as in theory. He warmly espouses Zelotes' doctrine of finished salvation; believing that, before the foundation of the world, we were all Calvinistically, i.e. personally ordained to eternal life in Christ, or eternal death in Adam, without the least respect to our own works, that is, to our own tempers and conduct. Hence he draws this just inference: "If Christ never died for me, and I am Calvinistically reprobated, my best endeavours to be finally justified, and eternally saved, will never alter the decree of reprobation, which was made against me from all eternity. On the other hand, if I am Calvinistically elected, and if Christ absolutely secured, yea, finished my eternal salvation on the cross, no sins can ever blot my name out of the book of life. God, in the day of his almighty power, will irresistibly convert or reconvert my soul; and then the greater my crimes shall have been, the more they will set off Divine mercy and power in forgiving and turning such a sinner as me: and I shall only sing in heaven louder than less sinners will have cause to do." Thus reasons Fulsome; and, like a wise man, he is determined, *if he be an absolute* REPROBATE, to have what pleasure he can before God pulls him down to hell in the day of his power; or, *if he be an absolute* ELECT, he thinks it reasonable comfortably to wait for "the day of God's power," in which day he shall be irresistibly turned, and absolutely fitted to sing louder in heaven the praises of Calvinistically distinguishing love: — a love this, which (if the Antinomian Gospel of the day be true) eternally, justifies the chief of sinners, without any personal or inherent worthiness.

INITIAL SALVATION is a phrase which sometimes occurs in these sheets. The plain reader is desired to understand by it, *salvation begun*, or, an inferior state of acceptance and present salvation. In this state sinners are actually saved from hell, admitted to a degree of favour, and graciously entrusted with one or more talents of grace, that is, of means, power, and ability "to work out their own [eternal] salvation," in due subordination to God, who, consistently with our liberty, "works in us both to will and to do," according to the dispensation of the heathens, Jews, or Christians, "of his good pleasure."

By the ELECTION OF GRACE, understand the free, and merely gratuitous choice which God (as a wise and sovereign benefactor) arbitrarily makes of this, that, or the other man, to bestow upon him one, two, or five talents of free grace.

Opposed to this election, you have an ABSOLUTE REPROBATION which does not draw damnation after it, but only rejection from a superior number of talents. In this sense God reprobated Enoch and David; Enoch with respect to the peculiar blessings of Judaism; and David with regard to the still more peculiar blessings of Christianity. But although neither of them had a share in the election of God's most peculiar grace; that is, although neither was chosen and called to the blessings of

Creeds and Scripture Scales

Christianity, their lot was never cast with those imaginary "poor creatures," whom Calvin and his followers affirm to have been from all eternity reprobated with a reprobation which infallibly draws eternal damnation after it. For Enoch and David made their election to the rewards of their dispensations sure by the timely and voluntary obedience of faith. And so might all those who obstinately bury their talent or talents to the last.

By FUTURE CONTINGENCIES, understand those things which will or will not be done; as the free, unnecessitated will of man shall choose to do them or not.

By SEMINAL EXISTENCE, understand the existence that we had in Adam's loins before Eve had conceived; or the kind of being which the prince of Wales had in the loins of the king before the queen came to England.

EQUAL CHECK,

PART THIRD.

BEING THE SECOND PART OF

THE SCRIPTURE SCALES.

SECTION I.

Containing the Scripture doctrine of the perseverance of the saints.

I PROMISED the reader that Zelotes and Honestus should soon meet again, to fight their last battle; and, that I may be as good as my word, I bring them a second time upon the stage of controversy. I have no pleasure in seeing them contend with each other; but I hope that when they shall have shot all their arrows, and spent all their strength, they will quietly sit down and listen to terms of reconciliation. They have had already many engagements; but they seem determined that this shall be the sharpest. Their challenge is about the doctrine of perseverance. Zelotes asserts that the perseverance of believers depends entirely upon God's almighty grace, which nothing can frustrate; and that, of consequence, no believer can finally fall. Honestus, on the other hand, maintains that continuing in the faith depends *chiefly*, if not *entirely* upon the believer's free will; and that of consequence final perseverance is *partly*, if not *altogether* as uncertain as the fluctuations of the human heart. The reconciling truth lies between those two extremes, as appears from the following propositions, in which I sum up the Scripture doctrine of perseverance: —

I.

God makes us glorious promises to encourage us to persevere.

God on his part gives us his *gracious* help.

Free grace always *does* its part.

Final perseverance depends, *first*, on the final, *gracious* concurrence of free grace with free will.

As free grace has in all things the pre-eminence over free will, we must lay much more stress upon God's faithfulness than upon *our own*. The spouse *comes* out of the wilderness,

II.

Those promises are neither compulsory nor absolute.

We must on our part *faithfully* use the help of God.

Free will *does not* always do its part.

Final perseverance depends, *secondly*, on the final, *faithful* concurrence of free will with free grace.

But to infer from thence that the spouse is to be *carried* by her Beloved every step of the way, is unscriptural. He gently *draws* her, and she runs. He gives her his arm, and she leans. But leaning upon her Beloved, and not upon herself.

The believer stands upon two legs, (if I may so speak,) God's faithfulness and his own. The one is always sound, nor can he rest too much upon it, if he does but *walk straight*, as a wise Christian; and does not foolishly *hop* as an Antinomian, who goes only upon his right leg; or as a Pharisee, who moves entirely upon the left.

When Gospel ministers speak of *our faithfulness*, they chiefly mean, (1.) Our faithfulness in *repenting*, that is, in renouncing our sins and Pharisaic righteousness; and in improving the talent of light, which shows us our natural depravity, daily imperfections, total helplessness, and constant need of an humble recourse to, and dependence on Divine grace. And, (2.) Our faithfulness in *believing* (even in hope against hope) God's redeeming love to sinners in Christ; in humbly apprehending, as returning prodigals, the gratuitous forgiveness of sins through the blood of the Lamb; in cheerfully claiming, as impotent creatures, the help that is laid on the Saviour for us; and in constantly coming at his word, to "take of the water of life freely." And so far as Zelotes recommends this evangelical disposition of mind, without opening a back door to Antinomianism, by covertly pleading for sin, and dealing about his imaginary decrees of forcible grace and sovereign wrath, he cannot be too highly commended.

If Zelotes will do justice to the doctrine of perseverance, he must speak of the obedience of faith, that is, of genuine, sincere obedience, as the oracles of God do. He must not blush to display the glorious rewards with

far from *dragging* her by main force, he bids her *remember Lot's wife*.

The believer's left leg, (I mean *his own* faithfulness,) is subject to many humours, sores, and bad accidents; especially when he does not use it at all, or when he lays too much stress upon it, to save his other leg. If it is broken, he is already fallen; and if he is out of hell, he must lean as much as he can upon his right leg, till the left begins to heal, and he can again run the way of God's commandments.

To aim *chiefly* at being faithful in external works, means of grace, and forms of godliness, is the high road to Pharisaism, and insincere obedience. I grant that he who is *humbly* faithful in little things, is faithful also in much; and that he who slothfully neglects little helps, will soon fall into great sins: but the professors of Christianity cannot be too frequently told that if they are not *first* faithful in maintaining true poverty of spirit, deep self humiliation before God, and high thoughts of Christ's blood and righteousness; they will soon slide into Laodicean Pharisaism; and, Jehu like, they will make more of their own partial, external, selfish faithfulness, than of Divine grace, and the Spirit's power: — a most dangerous and common error this, into which the followers of Honestus are very prone to run, and so far as he leads them into it, or encourages them in it, he deserves to be highly blamed; and Zelotes, *in this respect*, hath undoubtedly the advantage over him.

Would Honestus kindly meet Zelotes half way, he must speak of free grace, and of Christ's obedience unto death, as the Scriptures do. He must glory in displaying Divine faithfulness, and placing it in the most conspicuous and which God hath promised to crown it. He must boldly declare, that for want of it "the wrath of God cometh upon the children of disobedience" — upon fallen believers, "who have no inheritance in the kingdom of Christ and of God," Ephesians 5:5. In a word, instead of emasculating "Serjeant IF, who valiantly guards the doctrine of perseverance," he should show him all the respect that Christ himself does in the Gospel.

engaging light. He must not be ashamed to point out the great rewards of the faith which inherits promises, gives glory to God, and out of weakness makes us strong to take up our cross, and to run the race of obedience. In a word, he must teach his willing hearers to depend every day more and more upon Christ; and to lay as much stress upon his promises, as they ever did upon his threatenings

To sum all up in two propositions: —

I.

The infallible perseverance of *obedient* believers is a most sweet and evangelical doctrine, which cannot be pressed with too much earnestness and constancy upon sincere Christians, for their comfort, encouragement, and establishment.

II.

The infallible perseverance of *disobedient* believers is a most dangerous and unscriptural doctrine; and this cannot be pressed with too much assiduity and tenderness upon Antinomian professors, for their reawakening and sanctification.

To see the truth of these propositions, we need only throw with candour, into the Scripture Scales, the weights which Zelotes and Honestus unmercifully throw at each other; taking particular care not to break, as they do, the golden beam of evangelical harmony, by means of which the opposite scales and weights exactly balance each other.

I.

The weights of free grace thrown by Zelotes.

The Lord shall *establish* thee a *holy* people to himself, as he hath *sworn* unto thee, Deuteronomy 28:9.

Know therefore the Lord thy God; he is God, the faithful God, who keepeth *covenant*, Deuteronomy 7:9.

He hath made with me an *everlasting covenant*, ordered in all things and sure: for this is all my salvation and all my desire, 2 Samuel 23:5.

II.

The weights of free will thrown by Honestus.

If thou shalt *keep* the commandments of the Lord thy God, and *walk* in *his* ways. (Ibid.)

But they, &c, have transgressed the *covenant. They continued not in my covenant,* and I regarded them not, Hosea 6:7; Hebrews 8:9.

They have broken *the everlasting covenant:* therefore hath the curse devoured the earth, Isaiah 24:5. *They kept* not the covenant *of God, and refused* to walk in his law, &c, so a fire was kindled in Jacob, and anger also came up against Israel; because they believed not in God, and trusted not in his salvation, &c. The wrath of God came upon them, &c, and smote down the chosen of Israel, Psalm 78:10, 21, 22,

31.

Hence it appears, that part of the "everlasting covenant ordered in all things and SURE," is that those who break it presumptuously, and do not repent (as David did) before it be too late, shall SURELY be smitten down and destroyed.

I.

With him [the Father of lights] is *no variableness,* neither shadow of turning, James 1:17. I am the Lord, I *change not:* [I still bear with sinners during the day of their visitation;] therefore ye sons of Jacob are not consumed, Malachi 3:6.

[Observe here, that although God's essence, and the principles of his conduct toward man *never change;* yet, as "he loves righteousness and hates iniquity," and as he is the rewarder of the righteous and the punisher of the wicked, he must show himself pleased or displeased, a rewarder or a punisher, as moral agents turn from sin to righteousness, or from righteousness to sin. Without this kind of change, *ad extra,* he could not be holy and just; — he could not be the Judge of all the earth; — he could not be God.]

The *gifts* and *calling* of God are without *repentance,* Rom, 11:29. [The apostle evidently speaks these words of God's gifts to, and calling of the Jewish nation. The Lord is so far from *repenting* (properly speaking) of his having once called the Jews to the Mosaic covenant of peculiarity, that he

II.

The angel of *his* presence *saved* them: in his love and pity he remembered them. But they rebelled and vexed his Holy Spirit; therefore he was turned to be their enemy, Isaiah 63:9, 10. The Lord God of Israel saith, I said indeed that thy house and the house of thy father should walk before me *for ever;* but *now* be it far from me; for, &c, they that despise me shall be lightly esteemed, 1 Samuel 2:30. And the word of the Lord came to Jonah, saying, Preach unto Nineveh the preaching that I *bid thee.* And Jonah cried and said, Yet forty days and Nineveh shall be overthrown. So the people of Nineveh believed God, &c. For the king sat in ashes, and caused it to be proclaimed, &c. Cry mightily to God, yea, let every one *turn* from his evil way, &c. Who can tell, if God will *turn* and repent, that we perish not. And God saw their *works,* that they turned from their evil way, and God *repented* of the evil which *he had said* that he would do unto them, and *he did it not,* Jonah 3:1, &c. [From the preceding remarkable passages it is evident that, except in a few cases, the promises and the threatenings of God, so long as the day of grace and trial lasts, are conditional: and that, even when they wear the most *absolute* aspect, the condition is generally implied.]

I *gave* her time to repent and she repented not, Revelation 2:21. Because I have *called* and ye refused, &c, I also will mock — when your destruction cometh as a whirlwind, Proverbs 1:24, &c. The Lord [to speak figuratively and after the manner of men] *repented* that he had made Saul king over Israel, 1 is ready nationally to re-admit them to his peculiar favour, when they shall *nationally* repent, embrace the Gospel of Christ, and so make their sincere calling to the Christian covenant sure by believing. But does this prove that God forces repentance upon every Jew, and that when the Jews will nationally repent, God will absolutely and irresistibly work out their salvation for them? If Zelotes thinks so, I desire him to look into the scale of Honestus.

We (who hold fast the profession of our faith without wavering) are not of them who draw back unto perdition; but of them that believe to the saving of the soul, Hebrews 10:39. We believe that *through the grace* of our Lord Jesus Christ *we shall be saved*, Acts 15:11.

If his [David's] children *forsake* my law, &c, then will I visit their transgression with the rod, &c; nevertheless, my loving kindness will I not *utterly* take from *him*, [David, by utterly casting off his posterity] nor suffer my truth to fail, [as it would do if I appointed that the Messiah should

Samuel 15:35, [that is, when Saul proved unfaithful, the Lord rejected him in as positive a manner as a king would reject a minister, or break a general, when he repents of his having raised them to offices, of which they *now* show themselves absolutely unworthy.]

If that, which ye have heard from the beginning, shall remain in you, 1 John 2:24. If ye continue in the faith, Colossians 1:23. If ye continue in his goodness, Romans 11:22. If ye do these things, 2 Peter 1:10. If we hold fast the confidence firm unto the end, Hebrews 3:6. For he that shall endure *unto the end*, the same shall be saved, Matthew 24:18. [Should Zelotes endeavour to set aside these, and the like scriptures, by saying that each contains a Christian IF and not a Jewish IF, that is, *a description*, and not *a condition;* I refer him to the Equal Check, p. 104, where that trifling objection is answered.]

And thou Solomon, my son, know thou the God of thy father, and serve him with a perfect heart, and a willing mind: for the Lord searcheth all hearts, and understandeth all the imaginations of the thoughts: if thou seek him, he will* be found of thee; but *if thou forsake him*, he will *cast thee off for ever.* Take

---

* When Isaiah saith, "*I was found of them that sought me not*," &c, Romans 10:23, he does not contradict his own exhortation, to "seek the Lord while he may be found." That noble testimony to the doctrine of grace does not militate against the doctrine of liberty: but it proves, (1.) That free grace is always beforehand with free will: and (2.) That as God freely called the Jews to the Mosaic covenant of peculiarity; so he gratuitously calls the Gentiles to the Christian covenant of peculiarity; neither Jews nor Gentiles having previously sought that inestimable favour. But when God has so far revealed himself either to Jew or Gentile, as to say, "Seek ye my face," we to him who does not answer in truth and in time, "Thy face, Lord, will I seek."

come of another family,] Psalm 89:30, &c.

Thus saith the Lord, &c, O Israel, fear not; for I have redeemed thee: I have called thee by thy name, thou art mine. When thou passest through the waters, I will be with *thee;* and through the rivers, they shall not overflow thee; when thou walkest through the fire, thou shalt not be burnt, &c, Isaiah 43:1, 2.

All the promises of God in him [Christ] are *Yea,* and in him *Amen,* 2 Corinthians 1:20. [And so are all the menaces, for he is "the faithful Witness," and "the Mediator of the new covenant," which has its threatenings, as well as its promises; as appears from the opposite words spoken by Christ himself.]

God willing more abundantly to show to the heirs of promise [i.e. to obedient believers] the immutability of his counsel, confirmed it by an *oath;* that by two *immutable things* [the word and oath of the Lord] in which it was *impossible* for God to lie, we might have a strong consolation, who have fled for refuge to lay hold upon the hope set before us, Hebrews 6:17, 18.

And thou shalt call his name JESUS, for he shall *save his people* from their sins, Matthew 1:21.

I will take you to me for a people, and be to you *a God,* Exodus 6:7.

heed now, &c, 1 Chronicles 28:9.

And the Spirit of God came upon Azariah, and he went out to meet Asa, and said unto him, Hear ye me, Asa, and all Judah; the Lord is with you *while* *ye* be with him; and *if ye* seek him, he will be found of you; but if ye forsake him, he will forsake you, 2 Chronicles 15:1, 2.

Remember whence thou *art fallen,* repent, and do thy first works, or else I will *remove* thy candlestick. I will fight with the sword of my mouth against them that hold the doctrine of the Nicolaitans. I will kill her children with death. I will spue thee out of my mouth. [Awful threatenings these, which had their public and national, as well as private and personal accomplishment,] Revelation 2:5, 15, 16, 23; 3:16.

As truly as I live, saith the Lord, &c, your carcasses shall fall in this wilderness; and all that, &c, have murmured against me, *doubtless ye shall* *not* come into the land, concerning which *I sware to make you* dwell therein, save Caleb and Joshua, &c. Ye shall bear your iniquities, &c, and ye shall know *my breach of promise,* Numbers 14:28-34.

My mother and my brethren [that is, my people] are these, who hear the word of God, and keep it, Matthew 12:50. I will destroy [my backsliding] people, since they return not, Jeremiah 15:7.

But if thine heart *turn away,* so that thou wilt not hear, &c, I denounce unto you this day, that ye shall *surely* *perish,* Deuteronomy 30:17, 18. Indeed, the hand of the Lord was against them [when they disobeyed] to destroy them, &c, until they were consumed, Deuteronomy 2:15. Now all these things, &c, are written for our admonition, 1 Corinthians 10:11.

The Lord thy God hath chosen thee to be a special people unto himself. He brought forth his people with joy, and his chosen with gladness, Deuteronomy 14:2; Psalm 105:43.

My [faithful] people shall *never be ashamed,* Joel 2:27.

The work of righteousness shall be *peace,* quietness, and assurance *for ever,* and my people shall dwell in a peaceable habitation, and in sure dwellings, and in quiet resting places, Isaiah 32:17, 18.

The eternal God is thy refuge; and underneath are the everlasting arms, &c. Israel shall dwell in safety alone, &c. Happy art thou, O Israel! Who is like unto thee, O people *saved by the Lord,* the shield of thy help? Deuteronomy 33:27, &c.

The Lord will *pity* his people, Joel 2:18.

Hath God [absolutely] cast away his people [the Jews?] God forbid! God has not cast away his people, whom he foreknew [as believing. The Jews being as welcome to believe in Christ as the Gentiles,] Romans 11:1, 2.

Zion said, The Lord hath forsaken me, and my Lord hath forgotten me. Can a woman forget her sucking child, that she should not have compassion on the son of her womb? Yea, they may forget, yet will I not forget thee, Isaiah 49:14, 15.

Jesus having loved his own [disciples] he *loved them unto the end* [of his stay in this world, except him that was once "his own familiar friend, in whom he

And the Lord spake to Moses, saying, Get you up from among this congregation [this *special, chosen people*] that I may consume them in a moment, Num. 16:45.

Thou [my unfaithful people] hadst a whore's forehead: thou refusedst to be ashamed, Jeremiah 3:3.

Every one of the house of Israel, *that separateth himself* from me, saith the Lord, I will *cut him off* from the midst of my people, Ezekiel 14:7. There is no peace to the *wicked,* Isaiah 57:21.

That the house of Israel may *go no more* astray from me, &c, but that they *may be* my people, Ezekiel 14:11. Obey my voice, and ye shall be my people, Jeremiah 7:23. Wo unto them [Israel and Ephraim] for they have fled from me; *destruction unto them,* because they have transgressed against me. They return not to the Most High, Hosea 7:13, 16.

The Lord shall *judge* his people, Hebrews 10:30. *Judgment* must begin at the house of God, 1 Peter 4:17.

Ye are a chosen [choice] generation, &c, which in time past *were not* a people, but *are now* the people of God; which had not obtained mercy, but now have obtained mercy [by believing,] 1 Peter 2:9, 10.

Therefore, the children of Israel could not stand before their enemies, &c, because they were accursed; neither will I be with you *any more* [said the Lord] *except* ye destroy the accursed thing from among you, Joshua 7:12.

I will call her beloved, who was not beloved. Jesus loved him, [the young ruler, who went away sorrowing.] I will *love them no more,* Romans 9:24; Mark trusted," Judas, whom our Lord himself excepts, John 17:12;] John 13:1. I have loved thee with *an everlasting love,* [or with the love with which I loved thee of old, when I brought thee out of Egypt,] therefore, with loving kindness have I drawn thee, Jeremiah 31:3. [Compare the word *everlasting* in the original, with these words, "When Israel was a child, then I loved him, and called my son out of Egypt," Hosea 11:1.]

Truly God is good to Israel, Psalm 73:1. This God is our God *for ever and ever;* he will be our guide even unto death, Psalm 48:24.

Who shall lay any thing to the charge of God's elect? [them that "are in Christ, who walk not after the flesh, but after the Spirit."] It is God that justifieth; who is he that condemneth *them?* Romans 8:1, 33, 34.

All things are yours [ye Corinthians] and *ye are Christ's* and Christ is God's. Of him are ye in Christ Jesus, 1 Corinthians 3:21; 1:30.

To them that are sanctified by God the Father, and *preserved in Jesus Christ,* and called [to enjoy the blessings of his Gospel,] Jude 1:1.

If we believe not, yet *he abideth faithful;* he cannot deny himself, 2 Timothy 2:13. [Therefore]

Except *the Lord keep* the city, the watchman waketh but in vain, Psalm 127:1.

He [the Lord] led him [Jacob] about, &c, he kept him as the apple of his eye. As an eagle fluttereth over her young, taketh them, beareth them on her wings; so the Lord alone did lead him, Deuteronomy 32:10-12.

Holy Father, *keep through thy own name*

10:21; Hosea 9:15.

Even to such as are of a clean heart. (*Ibid.*) Depart from evil, *do good,* and dwell *for evermore.* Bind mercy and truth about thy neck, &c, so shalt thou find favour, &c, in the sight of God and man, Psalm 38:27; Proverbs 3:3, 4.

[No righteous judge will:] for to be spiritually minded is life and peace; but to be carnally minded is death, verse 6. Whosoever hath sinned against me, said the Lord, *him* will I blot out of my book, Exodus 32:33.

Examine yourselves [ye Corinthians] whether ye be in the faith, &c. Know ye not, &c, that Christ is in you, except *ye be reprobates?* 2 Corinthians 13:5.

To them, who by patient *continuance in well doing,* seek for glory, honour, and immortality, [God will render] eternal life, Romans 2:7.

If we deny him, he will also *deny us:* [for he abideth faithful to his threatenings, as well as to his promises,] ver. 12.

I say unto all, *Watch.* Watch thou *in all things.* He that is begotten of God *keepeth himself,* Mark 13:37; 2 Timothy 4:5; 1 John 5:18.

There was no strange god with him [Jacob.] But, &c, they forsook God, &c, sacrificed to devils, &c, and when the Lord saw it, he abhorred them; [and said] I will spend mine arrows upon them, verses 12, 15, 17, 19, 23.

Keep yourselves in the love of God.

those whom thou hast given me, [that I may impart unto them the peculiar blessings of my dispensation,] John 17:11.

You who are *kept* by the power of God unto salvation, ready to be revealed in the last time, 1 Peter 1:5.

I am persuaded that neither death nor life, &c, nor angels, &c, nor any other creature [Note: he does not say, *Nor any iniquity*] *shall be able to separate us* from the love of God, which is in Christ Jesus our Lord, Romans 8:38.

I know whom I have believed, and I am persuaded that he is able to keep that which I have committed unto him against that day, 2 Timothy 1:12.

In all these things we are more than conquerors, *through him* that loved us, Romans 8:37.

Moreover, whom he did predestinate [that is, appoint to be conformed to the image of his Son, according to the Christian dispensation] them he also called [to believe in Christ;] and whom he *thus* called [to believe in Christ, when they made their calling sure by actually believing,] them he also justified; and whom he justified [*as sinners* by FAITH, and as believers by THE WORKS of faith] them he also glorified, Romans 8:30. By one offering he hath perfected for ever [in atoning

Little children, keep yourselves from idols. Fathers, &c, love not the world, &c. If any [of you] love the world, the love of the Father is not in him. [He is fallen from God in spirit,] Jude 1:21; 1 John 5:21; 2:15.

Through faith [on your part.] (*Ibid.*) Holding faith, and a good conscience, which some having put away, concerning FAITH, *have made shipwreck,* 1 Timothy 1:19.

Your iniquities have separated between you and your God, Isaiah 59:2. I so run (for an incorruptible crown) not as uncertainly: so fight I, not as one that beateth the air: but I keep my body under, &c, *lest* that by any means I myself should be a castaway, or *a reprobate,* 1 Corinthians 9:26, 27.

There is no respect of persons with God. Thou partakest of the root of the olive tree, &c, some of the branches are broken off, &c, Boast not of thyself against them, &c. *By unbelief they were broken off,* and thou standest by faith, &c, fear, &c, lest he also spare not thee, Romans 2:11; 11:17, &c. Give all diligence to add to your faith virtue, &c, for *if ye do* these things, ye shall *never* fall, 2 Peter 1:5, 10.

I *have kept* the faith; — for I have kept the ways of the Lord, and have not wickedly departed from my God, 2 Timothy 4:7; Psalm 18:21.

Many are called [to believe] but few are chosen [to the rewards of faith,] Matthew 22:14. O thou wicked servant, I forgave thee all that debt [that is, I justified thee,] because thou desiredst me, &c, shouldst thou not also have had compassion on thy fellow servant, even as I *had pity* on thee? And his Lord was wroth, and delivered him to the tormentors, Matthew 18:32, &c. He that despised Moses' law, died without mercy, &c, of how *much sorer punishment* shall he be thought worthy, who hath merits] them that are sanctified, Hebrews 10:14. [Here we have a brief account of the method in which God brings *obedient, persevering believers* to glory. But what has this to do with Zelotes' personal and unconditional predestination to eternal life, or to eternal death? To show therefore that the sense which he gives to these passages is erroneous, I need only prove that all those who are called are not justified; and that all those who are justified, and sanctified, are not glorified; but only those who make their calling, election, justification, sanctification, and glorification *sure* by the obedience of faith unto the end. And I prove it by the opposite scriptures.]

counted the blood of the covenant, wherewith *he was sanctified*, an unholy thing! Hebrews 10:29. Ye [believers] shall be hated of all men, &c, but he [of you] that endureth *to the end*, shall be [eternally] *saved*, Matthew 10:22. (For God) will render eternal life to them, who by *patient continuance* in well doing seek for glory, Romans 2:7.

Can any unprejudiced person read the preceding passages without seeing, (1.) That, according to the Scriptures, and the Gospel axioms, our perseverance is suspended on two grand causes, the *first* of which is merciful free grace, and the *second* faithful free will. (2.) That those two causes must finally act in conjunction. And (3.) That when free grace hath enabled free will to concur, and to work out its own salvation, if free will obstinately refuse to do it till the night comes when no man can work, free grace gives up free will to its own perverseness; and then perseverance fails, and final apostasy takes place.

SECTION II.

The important doctrine of perseverance is farther weighed in the Scripture Scales.

THE scriptures produced in the preceding section might convince an impartial reader that Zelotes and Honestus are both in the wrong with respect to the doctrine of perseverance: and that a Bible Christian holds together the doctrines which they keep asunder. But considering that prejudice is not easily convinced; and fearing lest Zelotes and Honestus should both think they have won the day, the one against free will, and the other against free grace, merely because they can quote, behind each other's back, some passages which I have not yet balanced, and which each will think matchless; I shall give them leave to fight it out before Candidus, reminding him that Zelotes produces No. I. against free will; that Honestus produces No. II. against free grace; and that I produce *both numbers* to show that our free will must concur with God's free grace, in order to our persevering in the faith and in the obedience of faith.

I.

A vineyard of red wine. I the Lord *do keep it:* I will water it every moment: lest any hurt it, I will keep it night and day, Isaiah 27:2, 3.

The Lord God of Israel saith, that he hateth *putting away,* Malachi 2. 16. (And yet he allows it *for the cause of fornication,* Matthew 5:32.)

The righteous shall *never be moved,* Proverbs 10:30.

The mountains shall depart, &c, but my kindness shall *not depart* from thee, neither shall the covenant of my peace be *removed,* saith the Lord, Isaiah 54:10.

They that trust in the Lord shall be as Mount Zion, which *cannot be removed, but abideth for ever.* As the mountains are round about Jerusalem, so the Lord is round about his people, from henceforth, even for ever, Psalm 125:1, 2.

II.

I had planted thee a noble vine, wholly a right seed. How then art thou turned into the degenerate plant of a strange vine unto me? &c. Thou saidst, &c, I have loved strangers, and after them I will go, Jeremiah 2:21, 25. What could have been done more to my vineyard, that I have not done in it? Wherefore, when I looked that it should bring forth grapes, brought it forth wild grapes? And now I will tell you what I will do to my vineyard, &c; I will *lay it waste,* &c, and command the clouds that they rain no rain upon it, Isaiah 5:4, 5, 6.

Backsliding Israel, &c, hath played the harlot. And I said, &c, Turn thou unto me: but she returned not; and her treacherous sister Judah saw it. And I saw, when, for — adultery, I had *put her away,* and given her a bill of divorcement; yet her treacherous sister Judah feared not, Jeremiah 3:6, 7, 8.

I marvel that ye are *so soon removed* from him that called you.

Unto the wicked, God saith, What hast thou to do to declare my statutes, or that thou shouldst take my covenant in thy mouth? Psalm 50:16. O Israel, *if* thou wilt put away thy abominations out of my sight, thou shalt *not remove,* Jeremiah 4:1. Jerusalem hath grievously sinned; *therefore she is removed,* Lamentations 1:8. My God will cast them away, because they did not hearken unto him, Hosea 9:17.

Lord, who shall *abide* in thy tabernacle? He that *walketh* uprightly, and *worketh* righteousness, &c. He that *does* these things shall never be moved, Psalm 15:1, 2, 5 Abide in me, and I [will abide] in you, John 15:4. He that dwelleth in the secret place of the Most High, [thou, Lord, art my hiding place, Psalm 32:7,] shall abide under the shadow of the Almighty, Psalm 91:1.

He that does the will of God abideth for ever, 1 John 2:17. Draw out thy soul to the hungry, &c, and the Lord shall guide thee continually, and, &c, thou shalt be like a spring of water, whose waters fail not, Isaiah 58:10, 11.

The Lord will speak *peace* unto his people, and to his saints, Psalm 85:8. Peace shall be upon Israel, Psalm 125:5. *For* Christ is our peace, Ephesians 2:14.

Be diligent, that you may be found of him in *peace*. If the house be worthy, let your peace come upon it. As many as walk according to this rule, [i.e. as become new creatures,] peace be on them, and mercy, 2 Peter 3:14; Matthew 10:13; Galatians 6:15, 16.

O continue thy loving kindness unto them that know thee.

And thy righteousness to the upright in heart, Psalm 36:10. He [the apostate] flattereth himself in his own eyes, &c, he hath left off to be wise, and to do good, &c. He setteth himself in a way that is not good, he abhorreth not evil, &c. There are the workers of iniquity fallen, &c, and shall not be able to rise, verses 2, 3, 4, 12. Whoso continueth in the perfect law of liberty, he being a doer of the work, this man shall be blessed, James 1:25. They went out from us, but [in general] they were not of us [that continue in the perfect law of liberty.] For had they been of us [that are still doers of the work] they would no doubt have continued with us: [the Gnostics, or Antinomians, would not have been able to draw so many over to their pernicious ways, or tenets, 2 Peter 2, &c.] But they went out [they joined the Antinomians] that they might be made manifest, that they were not all of us, [i.e. that in general their heart had departed from the Lord, and from us; they of late being of us, more by profession than by possession of the faith which works by obedient love,] 1 John 2:19.

St. John says *they were not all of us,* to leave room for some exceptions. For as we are persuaded that many, who have gone over to the Solifidians in our days, are still of us that are *doers of the work,* so St. John did not doubt but some, who had been seduced by the primitive Antinomians, see verse 26, continued to obey the perfect law of liberty, which the Nicolaitans taught them to decry. May we, after his example, be always ready to make a proper distinction between the Solifidians that are *of us,* and those that are *not of us!* That is, between those who still keep Christ's commandments, and those who break them with as little ceremony as they break a ceremonious "rule of life," or burdensome *rule* of civility.

Let them that suffer according to the will of God, commit the *keeping of their souls to God,* &c, as unto a faithful Creator, 1 Peter 4:19.

In well doing. (*Ibid.*) Say ye to the righteous, that it shall be *well with them,* for they shall eat the fruit of *their doings,* Isaiah 3:10.

I will betroth thee unto me for ever, &c. I will even betroth thee unto me in *faithfulness.* The Lord is faithful who shall establish you, and *keep you* from evil. To him that is able to keep you from falling, and to present you faultless before the presence of his glory with exceeding joy, Hosea 2:19, 20; 2 Thessalonians 3:3; Jude 1:24.

If ye have not been *faithful* in the unrighteous mammon, (that which is least,) who will commit unto you the true riches? Luke 16:11. He made his own people to go forth like sheep, and guided them like a flock. And he led them on safely, so that they feared not, &c. Yet they *kept not* his testimonies; but turned back and dealt unfaithfully, &c. When God heard this, he, &c, greatly abhorred Israel: so that he forsook the tabernacle, &c, which he had placed among men, &c, Psalm 78:52, &c.

The earth which beareth thorns, is rejected; and, &c, its end is to be burned. But, beloved, we are persuaded better things of you, and things which accompany salvation, though we thus speak, Hebrews 6:8, 9.

For, &c, ye have ministered to the saints, and do minister: [so that, in the judgment of charity, which "hopeth all things," especially where there are favourable appearances, it is right in me to hope the best of you, nor will I suspect you, till you give me cause so to do. However, remember that] if we sin wilfully, &c, there remaineth [for us] a fearful looking for of judgment and fiery indignation, which shall devour the adversaries [that is, apostates,] Hebrews 6:10; 10:26, 27.

I am confident of this very thing,

It is meet for me to think this of you

that he who has begun a good work in you, will perform it until the day of Jesus Christ, Philippians 1:6.

The Lord is my rock, and my fortress, and my deliverer; my God, my strength, in whom I will trust, my buckler, and the horn of my salvation, and my high tower, Psalm 17:2.

I will put my Spirit within you, and cause you [so far as is consistent with your moral agency] to walk in my statutes, and ye shall (or *will*) keep my judgments and do them, Ezekiel 36:27.

Israel shall be saved in the Lord with an everlasting salvation, Isaiah 45:17.

O Lord, save me, and I shall be saved, for thou art my praise, Jeremiah 17:14. Salvation is of the Lord, Jonah 2:9.

The foundation of God standeth sure, having this seal, *The Lord knoweth them that are his,* 2 Timothy 2:19.

Thou wilt perform the truth to Jacob, and the mercy to Abraham, which thou hast sworn to our fathers from the days of old. *To perform* the mercy

all, because I have you in my heart [and charity *hopeth all things*] inasmuch as in my bonds, &c, ye are partakers of my grace, — ye have *always obeyed,* Philippians 1:7; 2:12. [Thus spake the apostle to those who *continued to obey.* But to his disobedient converts he wrote in a different strain:] O foolish Galatians, who hath bewitched you, that you should not obey the truth? Have ye suffered so many things in vain? I desire now to change my voice, for I stand in doubt of you, Galatians 3:1, 4; 4:20.

My defence is of God, who saveth the upright in heart, Psalm 7:10. Do good, O Lord, to those that are good and *upright* in their hearts: as for such as *turn aside* unto their crooked ways, the Lord shall lead them forth with the workers of iniquity, Psalm 125:4, 5.

Thus saith the Lord God, I will yet for this be inquired of by the house of Israel, to do it for them, Ezekiel 36:37. Ye stiffnecked, &c, ye do always resist the Holy Ghost, as your fathers did, Acts 7:51.

How shall we escape, if we neglect so great salvation? Hebrews 2:3. Remember Lot's wife, Luke 17:32.

Thy faith hath saved thee, Luke 7:50. Ye are saved, if ye keep [in memory and practice] what I have preached unto you, 1 Corinthians 15:2.

And let every one that nameth the name of Christ, depart from iniquity. (*Ibid.*) Now if any man have not the Spirit of God, *he is none of his,* Romans 8:9. His peculiar people (being) a holy nation, zealous of good works, 1 Peter 2:9; Titus 2:14. Be zealous, therefore, and repent; (or) I will spue thee out of my mouth, Revelation 3:19, 16.

I will perform the oath which 1 sware unto Abraham thy father, &c, *because that Abraham obeyed my voice, and kept my charge,* my commandments, my

The Works of John Fletcher

promised to our fathers, and to remember his holy *covenant* and *the oath* which he sware to our father Abraham, Micah 7:20; Luke 1:72.

Surely goodness and mercy shall follow me all the days of my life, Psalm 23:6.

A thousand shall fall at thy side, and ten thousand at thy right hand: but it shall not come nigh thee, Psalm 91:7.

My sheep [obedient believers] hear my voice, and I know [approve] them, and they follow me: and *I give* unto them eternal life, and they shall *never perish,* neither shall any *pluck them* out of my Father's hand, John 10:27, &c.

statutes, and my laws, Genesis 26:3, 5. Thus says the Lord God of Israel, *Cursed be the man that obeyeth not* the words of this covenant, which I commanded your fathers, (in the day that I brought them forth from the iron furnace,) saying, Obey my voice and do them, so shall ye be my people, and I will be your God; that *I may perform the oath which I have sworn* to your fathers, Jeremiah 11:3, 4, 5.

If thou continue in his goodness. Holding faith and a good conscience, which some having put away, concerning faith, have made shipwreck, Romans 11:22; 1 Timothy 1:18, 19.

Because thou hast made the Most High thy habitation. Because he hath set his love upon me, therefore will I deliver him, verses 9, 14.

The Lord preserveth *the faithful,* &c. Be of good courage, and he shall strengthen your heart, all ye that hope in the Lord, Psalm 31:23, 24. If ye will fear the Lord, and obey his voice, and not rebel against his commandment, then shall ye continue following the Lord your God. But if ye will not obey, &c, then shall the hand of the Lord be against you. Only serve him in truth, with all your heart: for consider how great things he has done for you. But if ye shall still do wickedly, ye shall be consumed, 1 Samuel 12:14, 15, 24, 25. [Lest Samuel's testimony should be rejected as unevangelical, I produce that of Christ himself; hoping that Zelotes will allow our Lord to understand his own Gospel.] Bear much fruit, so shall ye be my disciples. As the Father hath loved me, so have I loved you: *continue* in my love. *If ye keep* my commandments, ye shall *abide* in my love; even as I have kept my Father's commandments, and abide in his love, John 15:8, &c. Every branch in me that beareth not fruit, he taketh away — and they are burned, John 15:2, 6.

There shall arise false christs, and shall show great signs, insomuch that (if it were possible) they shall deceive πλανησαι [lead into error] the very elect, Matthew 24:24.

They shall deceive many. Take heed that no man deceive you, ver. 4, 5. They, (that cause divisions,) by good words deceive the hearts of the simple, Romans 16:18. [Query: are all *the simple believers* whom party men deceive, *very reprobates?*] I have espoused you to Christ, &c. But I fear, lest by any means, as the serpent beguiled Eve, so your minds should be corrupted, 2 Corinthians 11:2, 3. They have been deceived, (or have erred) from the faith (απεπλανηθησαν, the very word used by our Lord, and strengthened by a preposition,) 1 Timothy 6:10. [When Zelotes supposes that the clause (if it were possible) necessarily implies *an impossibility*, does he not make himself ridiculous before those who know the Scriptures? That expression, *if it were possible*, is used only on four other occasions; and in each of them it notes *great difficulty*, but by no means *an impossibility*. Take only two instances: "If it were possible, ye would have plucked out your own eyes, and have given them to me," Galatians 4:15. "Paul hasted to be at Jerusalem on the day of pentecost, if it were possible for him," Acts 20:16. Now is it not evident, either that Paul wanted common sense, if he hasted to do what could not absolutely be done; or that the expression, *if it were possible*, implies no impossibility? And is not this a proof that Calvinism can now deceive Zelotes, as easily as the tempter formerly deceived Aaron, David, Solomon, Demas, and Judas in the matter of the golden calf, Uriah, Milcom, and mammon?

I have prayed for thee, that thy faith fail not, Luke 22:49.
That Peter's faith failed for a time is

I know thy works, &c, thou holdest fast my name, and hast not denied my faith [as Peter did.] Having damnation evident from the following observations: (1.) "Faith without works is dead;" much more faith with lying, cursing, and the repeated denial of Christ. (2.) Our Saviour himself said to his disciples, after a far less grievous fall, "How is it that you have no faith?" Mark 4:40. (3.) His adding immediately, "When thou art converted, strengthen thy brethren," shows that Peter would stand in need of conversion, and consequently of living, converting faith; for as by destructive unbelief we depart from God, so by living faith we are converted to him. Hence it is evident that if Christ prayed that Peter's faith might not fail at all, he prayed conditionally; and that upon Peter's refusing to watch and pray, which was the condition particularly mentioned by our Lord, Christ's prayer was no more answered than that which he soon after put up, about his not drinking the bitter cup, and about the forgiveness of his revilers and murderers. But if our Lord prayed (as seems most likely) that Peter's faith might not fail, or die like that of Judas, i.e. in such a manner as never to come to life again, then his prayer was perfectly answered: for the candle of Peter's faith, which a sudden blast of temptation (and not the extinguisher of malicious, final obstinacy) had put out — Peter's faith, I say, like the smoking flax, caught again the flame of truth and love, and shone to the enlightening of thousands on the day of pentecost, as well as to the conversion of his own soul that very night. However, from our Lord's prayer, Zelotes concludes that true faith can never fail, in opposition to the scriptures which fill the opposite scale; yea, and to reason, which pronounces that our Lord was too wise to spend his last moments in asking that a thing *might not* happen, because they have cast off their first faith, Revelation 2:13; 1 Timothy 5:12. Which [a good conscience, the believer's most precious jewel, next to Christ] some having put away, concerning faith have made shipwreck, 1 Timothy 1:19. Without faith it is impossible to please God. The just shall live by faith, but if he draw back [i.e. if he make shipwreck of faith] my soul shall have no pleasure in him, Hebrews 11:6; 10:38. If any [believer] provide not for his own, &c, he hath denied the faith, and is worse than an infidel, 1 Timothy 5:8.

which, if we believe Zelotes, *could not* possibly happen.

God, even our Father, who hath loved us, and given us everlasting consolation, &c, stablish you in every good word and work, 2 Thessalonians 2:16, 17. He who establishes us with you in Christ, &c, is God, 2 Corinthians 1:21.

Christ shall also confirm you unto the end, that ye may be blameless, &c. God is faithful, by whom ye were called unto the fellowship of his Son, 1 Corinthians 1:8, 9.

If ye will not believe, ye shall not be established, Isaiah 7:9. God preserveth not the life of the wicked, &c. He withdraweth not his eyes from the righteous, &c. He showeth them their work, and their transgressions, &c. He openeth also their ear to discipline, and commandeth that they return from iniquity. If they obey and serve him, they will spend their days in prosperity, &c. But if they obey not, they shall perish, &c, and die without knowledge, Job 36:6-12.

Know ye not that ye are the temple of God? &c. If any [of you] defile the temple of God, him will God destroy, 3:16, 17. If thy right eye offend thee, pluck it out; for it is profitable for thee that one of thy members should perish, and not that thy whole body should be cast into hell, Matthew 5:29. Destroy not him with thy meat, for whom Christ died. For meat destroy not the work of God [in] thy brother, who stumbleth, or is offended, Romans 14:15, 20, 21. The Lord having saved the people, &c, afterward destroyed them that believed not, Jude 5. They did all drink, &c, of that spiritual rock which followed them, and that rock was Christ. But with many of them God was not well pleased; for they, &c, were destroyed of the destroyer, 1 Corinthians 10:4, 5, 10. They were broken off because of unbelief, and thou standest by faith, &c, continue in his goodness, otherwise thou also shalt be cut off, Romans 9:20, 22. Through thy knowledge shall thy weak brother perish, for whom Christ died, &c. Wherefore, if meat make my brother to stumble [and so to perish] I will eat no flesh while the world standeth, 1 Corinthians 8:11, 13. There shall be false teachers among you, &c, who, denying the Lord that bought them, shall bring upon themselves swift destruction. These shall utterly perish in their own corruption, and shall receive the reward of unrighteousness, &c. Cursed children, who have forsaken the right way, 2 Peter 2:1, 12, 15. See also the scriptures quoted in page 82.

He hath said, I will never leave thee, *nor forsake thee:* so that [in the way of duty] we may boldly say, *The Lord is my helper,* Hebrews 13:5, 6. (I add, *in the way of duty,* because God made that promise originally to Joshua, who knew God's breach of promise, when Achan stepped out of the way of duty. Compare Joshua 1:5, with Joshua 7:12, and Numbers 14:34.)

My people have committed two evils, they have forsaken me, &c. I will even *forsake you,* saith the Lord, Jeremiah 2:13; 23:33. The destruction of the transgressors and of the sinners shall be together, and they that forsake the Lord shall be consumed, &c, and they shall both burn together, and none shall quench them, Isaiah 1:28, 31.

Then the devil taketh him up into the holy city, and setteth him on a pinnacle of the temple, and saith unto him. If thou be the Son [or child] of God, cast thyself down: for it is written, He shall give his angels charge concerning thee, &c, [not only lest thou fall finally, but also] lest thou dash thy foot against a stone, Matthew 4:5, 6; Psalm 91:11, 12.

Jesus said, It is written again, Thou shalt not tempt the Lord thy God, Matthew 4:7. Neither let us tempt Christ, as some of them also tempted, and were destroyed of serpents, 1 Corinthians 10:9.

How wisely does the tempter quote Scripture, when he wants to inculcate the absolute preservation of the saints! Can Zelotes find a fitter passage to support their unconditional perseverance? It is true, however, that he never quotes it in favour of his doctrine: for who cares to plough with such a heifer? (*Fœnum habet in cornu.*) Therefore, though she is as fit for the work as most of those which he does it with; he never puts her to his plough, no, not when he makes the most crooked furrows. Should it be asked why the devil did not encourage Christ to throw himself down, by giving him some hints that a grievous fall would humble him, would make him

Who can tell how many have been destroyed by dangerous errors, which after insinuating themselves into the bosom of the simple, by means of their smoothness and fine colours, drop there a mortal poison, that too often breaks out in virulent expressions, or in practices worthy of — Mr. Fulsome?

sympathize with the fallen, would drive him nearer to God, would give him an opportunity to shout louder the praises of preserving grace, &c, I reply, that the tempter was too wise to show so openly the cloven foot of his doctrine; too decent not to save appearances too judicious to imitate Zelotes.

SECTION III.

What thoughts our Lord, St. John, St. Paul, and St. James entertained of fallen believers — A parallel between the backsliders delineated by St. Peter, and those who are described by St. Jude — A horrible destruction awaits them, for denying the Lord that bought them, and for turning the grace of God into lasciviousness.

IT is impossible to do the doctrine of perseverance justice, without considering what Christ and the apostles say of apostates. Even in their days the number of falling and fallen believers was so great, that a considerable part of the last epistles seems to be nothing but a charge against apostates, an attempt to reclaim Pharisaic and Antinomian backsliders, and a warning to those who yet stood, not to "fall away after the same example of unbelief and conformity to this present world."

Begin we by an extract from Christ's epistles to the Churches of Asia. Though the "Ephesians hated the deeds of the Nicolaitans," yet, after St. Paul's death, they so far inclined to lukewarmness, that they brought upon themselves the following reproof: — "I have somewhat against thee, because thou hast left thy first love. Remember, therefore, whence thou art fallen, and repent, and do thy first works, or else I will remove thy candlestick." The Church at Pergamos was not in a better condition; witness the severe charge that follows: — "Thou hast them that hold the doctrine of Balaam, who taught Balak to cast a stumbling block before the children of Israel, &c, to commit fornication. So hast thou also them that hold the doctrine of the Nicolaitans, which thing I hate. Repent, or else I will fight against thee with the sword of my mouth." The contagion reached the faithful Church of Thyatira, as appears from these words: — "Thou sufferest that woman Jezebel to seduce my servants to commit fornication. But unto, &c, as many as have not this doctrine, and have not known the depths of Satan, I will put upon you none other burden." In Sardis "a few names only had not defiled their garments;" the generality of Christians there had, it seems, "a name to live and were dead:" but the fall of the Laodiceans was universal. Before they suspected it, they had all, it seems, slidden back into the smooth, downward road that leads to hell. "I know thy works," says Christ, "I would thou weft cold or hot. So then, because thou art lukewarm, I will spue thee out of my mouth." Like those who stand complete merely in notions of imputed righteousness, "thou sayest, *I am rich, &c, and have need of nothing;* and knowest not that thou art wretched, and poor, and blind, and naked," Revelation 2:3.

Can we read this sad account of the declension and falling away of the saints without asking the following questions: (1.) If backsliding and apostasy were the bane of the primitive Church, according to our Lord's doctrine; and if he did not promise to *any* of those backsliders that victorious, almighty grace would *certainly* bring them back; what can we think of Zelotes' doctrine, which promises infallible perseverance, and insures finished salvation to every backsliding, apostatizing believer? (2.) If the primitive Church, newly collected by the Spirit, and sprinkled by the blood of Christ, guided by apostolic preachers, preserved by the salt of persecution, and guarded by miraculous powers, through which apostates could be "given to Satan for the destruction of the flesh," (witness the case of Ananias, Sapphira, and the incestuous Corinthian:) if the primitive Church, I say, with all these advantages, was in such danger by the falling away of the saints, as to require all those reproofs and threatenings from Christ himself; is it not astonishing that whole bodies of Protestant believers should rise in our degenerate days to such a pitch of unscriptural assurance, as to promise themselves, and one another, absolute, infallible perseverance in the Divine favour? And (3.) If the apostate Nicolas, once "a man of honest report, full of the Holy Ghost and wisdom," but afterward (it seems) the ringleader of the Nicolaitans; — if Nicolas, I say, went about to "lay a stumbling block before" Christians, by teaching them that fornication would never endanger their finished salvation; does Zelotes mend the matter, when he insinuates withal, that fornication, yea, adultery, and, if need be, murder, will do Christians good, and even answer the most excellent ends for them?

Consider we next what were St. John's thoughts of Antinomian apostates. He had such a sight of the mischief which their doctrine did, and would do in the Church, that he declares, "This is LOVE, that we walk after his commandments. This is the commandment, that ye have heard from the beginning, ye should walk in it. For many deceivers are entered into the world, who confess not [practically] that Jesus Christ is come in the flesh," to destroy the works of the devil; who deny Christ in his holy doctrine; and among other dangerous absurdities will even give you broad hints that you may commit adultery and murder without ceasing to be God's dear children. But believe them not. "Look to yourselves, that we lose not those things which we have wrought. Whosoever transgresseth and abideth not in the [practical] doctrine of Christ, hath not God, &c. If there come any unto you, and bring not this doctrine, receive him not into your house, neither bid him God speed," 2 John 1:6-10. Again: "He that saith, *I know him,* and keepeth not his commandments, is a liar, and the truth is not in him. These things have I written unto you, concerning them that seduce you, 1 John 2:4, 26. Little children, let no man deceive you: he that does righteousness is righteous, &c. He that committeth sin is of the devil, &c. In this the children of God are manifest, and the children of the devil," 1 John 3:7, &c.

When, in the text quoted above, St. John says, "They went out from us, but they were not all of us," what a fine opportunity had he of adding, "If they are elect they will INFALLIBLY come back to us." But, as he believed not the modern "doctrines of grace," he says nothing either for Calvin's reprobation, or Dr, Crisp's election. Nor does he drop the least hint about a "day of God's power," in which changeless love was *infallibly* to bring back *one* of all those backsliders, to make him sing louder the praises of free, sovereign, victorious grace.

Although I have frequently mentioned St. Paul's thoughts concerning fallen believers, I am persuaded that the reader will not be sorry to see them balanced with St. James' sentiments on the same subject.

I.
St. Paul's account of
BACKSLIDERS.

Alexander the coppersmith (who was once a zealous Christian, see Acts 19:33,) did me much evil; the Lord reward him according to his works. No man [i.e. *no believer*] stood with me; but all forsook me: I pray God that it may not be laid to their charge, 2 Timothy 4:14, 16. I fear lest, when I come, I shall not find you such as I would — lest there be debates, envyings, wraths, strifes, backbitings, whisperings, swellings, tumults; and lest my God humble me among you, and that I shall bewail *many* who have sinned already, and have not repented of the uncleanness, and fornication, and lasciviousness which they have committed, 2 Corinthians 12:20, 21. Not forsaking the assembling of ourselves together as the manner of some is, &c. For if we sin wilfully [as they do] there remaineth no more sacrifice for sin, but a certain fearful looking for of judgment, and fiery indignation, which shall devour the adversaries, &c, [especially him] who hath trodden under foot the Son of God, and hath counted the blood of the covenant, wherewith he was sanctified, an unholy thing, and hath done despite to the Spirit of grace, Hebrews 10:25, &c. Many [fallen believers] walk, of whom I have told you often, and now tell you, even weeping, that they are enemies of the cross of Christ; whose end is destruction, whose god is their belly — and who mind earthly things. For all [comparatively speaking] seek their own, and not the things which are Jesus Christ's, Philippians 3:18; 2:21.

II.
St. James' account of
UNFAITHFUL BELIEVERS.

My brethren, &c, if there come unto your assembly a man in goodly apparel, and also a poor man in vile raiment, and ye have respect to him that weareth the gay clothing, &c, are ye not partial? &c. But *ye have despised* the poor, &c. If ye have respect to persons ye commit sin, &c, for whosoever [of you] shall keep the whole law, and yet offend in one point, he is guilty of all. From whence come wars among you? Come they not even of your lusts? &c. Ye adulterers and adulteresses, know ye not that, &c, whosoever will be a friend of the world, is the enemy of God? James 2:1, &c; 4:1, 4.

The Epistle to the Hebrews is a treatise against apostasy, and of consequence against *Calvinian perseverance*. As a proof of it, I refer the reader to a convincing discourse on Hebrews 2:3, published by Mr. Olivers. The whole Epistle of St. Jude, and the second of St. Peter, were particularly written to prevent the falling away of the saints, and to stop the rapid progress of apostasy. The Epistle of St. Jude, and 2 Peter 2, agree so perfectly, that one would think the two apostles had compared notes: witness the following parallel: —

I.
St. Peter's description of
ANTINOMIAN APOSTATES.

They have *forsaken* the right way; following the way of Balaam, who loved the wages of unrighteousness, 2 Peter 2:15.

Spots are they and blemishes, sporting themselves with their own deceivings, while they feast with you, ver. 13.

They *walk* after the flesh in *the lust of uncleanness,* ver. 10.

They speak *great swelling words* of vanity, they promise them [whom they allure] liberty, while they themselves are the servants of corruption, verses 18, 19.

As natural brute beasts, &c, they *speak evil* of the things that they understand not, [especially of *the perfect law of liberty,*] and shall utterly perish in their *own corruption,* ver. 12.

Wells *without water,* clouds that are carried with a tempest — beguiling *unstable souls* — to whom *the mist of darkness is reserved for ever,* verses 14, 17. [How far was St. Peter from soothing any of those backsliders by the smooth doctrine of *their necessary infallible return!*]

[St. Peter indirectly compares them to] *the angels that sinned* [whom] God spared not, but cast down to hell, and delivered into *chains of darkness,* to be reserved unto *judgment,* ver. 4.

II.
St. Jude's description of
ANTINOMIAN BACKSLIDERS.

These be they who *separate* themselves. They ran greedily after the error of Balaam for *reward,* Jude 1:19, 11.

These are *spots* in your feasts of charity, when they feast with you; feeding themselves without fear, verse 12.

Filthy dreamers — *walking* after their own *lusts,* verses 8, 16.

Their mouth speaketh *great swelling words:* — creeping in unawares [i.e. insinuating themselves into rich widows' houses] having men's persons in admiration, verses 4, 16.

These *speak evil* of those things which they know not [especially of Christ's law.] But what they know naturally, as brute beasts, in those things they *corrupt themselves,* ver. 10.

Clouds they are *without water, carried* about of winds, trees whose fruit withereth, &c; *wandering stars,* to whom is *reserved the blackness of darkness for ever,* verses 12, 13. [How far was St. Jude from rocking any of those apostates in the cradle of *infallible perseverance!*]

[St. Jude compares them to] *the angels who kept not their first estate,* but left their own habitation, &c, reserved in everlasting *chains under darkness* unto the *judgment* of the great day, ver. 6.

From this remarkable parallel it is evident that the apostates described by St. Peter, and the backsliders painted by St. Jude, were one and the same kind of people: and by the following words it appears that all those backsliders really fell from *the grace of God,* and denied *the Lord that bought them.*

Even denying *the Lord that bought them,* and bring upon themselves *swift*

Ungodly men, turning *the grace of our God* into lasciviousness, and *denying* [in *destruction,* &c, whose &c, *damnation* slumbereth not, 2 Peter 2:1.

works at least] *the only Lord God, and our Lord Jesus Christ,* [as Lord, Lawgiver, or Judge,] Jude 1:4.

St. Peter more or less directly describes these backsliders, in me same epistles as people who have "forgotten that they WERE PURGED from their old sins" — who do not "give all diligence to add to their faith virtue" — who do not "make their calling and election sure" — who, "after they have ESCAPED the pollutions of the world through the KNOWLEDGE of our Lord Jesus Christ, [i.e. through a true and living faith,] are again entangled therein, and overcome; whose latter end is worse than the beginning — who, after they have KNOWN THE WAY of righteousness, *turn* from the holy commandment delivered unto them," and verify the proverb, "The sow that was WASHED is turned to her wallowing in the mire."

Here is not the least hint about *the certain return* of any of those backsliders, or about *the good* that their grievous falls will do either to others or to themselves. On the contrary, he represents them ALL as people that were in the high road to *destruction:* and, far from giving us an Antinomian innuendo about the final perseverance of all blood-bought souls, i.e. of the whole number of the redeemed, he begins his epistle by declaring that those self-destroyed backsliders "denied the Lord that BOUGHT them," and concludes it by this seasonable caution: "There are in our own beloved brother Paul's epistles things [it seems, about the election of grace, and about justification without the works of the law] which they that are unlearned (αμαθεις, *untaught in the Scriptures*) and unstable, wrest, &c, unto their own destruction. Ye, therefore, beloved, seeing ye know these things before, [being thus fairly warned] beware lest YE ALSO, being led away with the error of the wicked, fall from your own steadfastness. But grow in grace, and in the knowledge of our Lord Jesus Christ;" which is the best method not to fall from grace — the only way to inherit the blessing, with which God will crown the faithfulness and genuine perseverance of the saints.

I read the heart of Zelotes; and seeing the objection he is going to start, I oppose to it this quotation from Baxter: "To say that then their faith (which works by faithful love) *does more* than CHRIST did, or GOD'S GRACE, is a putrid cavil. Their faith is no efficient cause at all of their pardon or justification; it is but necessary, receptive qualification. He that shuts the window, causeth darkness; but it is sottish to say that he who opens it, *does more* than *the sun* to cause light, which he causeth not at all; but removeth the impediment of reception; and faith itself is God's gift," — as all other talents are, whether we improve them or not.

I should lose time, and offer an insult to the reader's understanding, were I to comment upon the preceding scriptures; so great is their perspicuity and number. But I hope I shall not insult his candour by proposing to him the following queries: (1.) Can Zelotes and Honestus be judicious Protestants, I mean consistent defenders of Bible religion, if the one throw away the weights of the second scale, while the other overlooks those of the first? (2.) Is it not evident that, according to the Scriptures, *the perseverance of the saints* has two causes: THE FIRST free grace and Divine faithfulness; and THE SECOND free will and human faithfulness produced, excited, assisted, and nourished, but *not necessitated* by free grace? (3.) With respect to the capital doctrine of perseverance also, does not the truth lie exactly between the extremes into which Zelotes and Honestus perpetually run? And (*lastly*) is it not clear that if Candidus will hold "the truth as it is in Jesus," he must stand upon the line of moderation, call back Zelotes from the east, Honestus from the west, and make them cordially embrace each other under the Scripture meridian? There the kind Father falls upon the neck of the returning prodigal, and the heavenly bridegroom meets the wise virgins. There free grace mercifully embraces free will, while free will humbly stoops at the footstool of free grace. There "the sun goes down no more by day, nor the moon by night;" that is, the two Gospel axioms, which are the great doctrinal lights of the Church, without eclipsing each other, shine in perpetual conjunction, and yet in continual opposition. There their conjugal, mysterious, powerful influence gladdens the New Jerusalem, fertilizes the garden of the Lord, promotes the spiritual vegetation of all the trees of righteousness which line the river of God, and gives a Divine relish to the fruits of the Spirit which they constantly bear. There, as often as free grace smiles upon free will, it says, "Be faithful unto death, and I will give thee a crown of life;" and as often as free will sees that crown glitter at the end of the race, it shouts, *Grace! free grace unto it!* a great part of our faithfulness consisting in ascribing to grace all the honour that becomes the FIRST CAUSE of all good — the ORIGINAL of all visible and invisible excellence.

Perseverance must close our race, if ever we receive the prize; let then the Scriptural account of it close my Scales. But before I lay them by, I must throw in two more grains of Scriptural truth; lest the reader should think that I have not made good weight. If I thought Zelotes to be a gross Antinomian, and Honestus an immoral moralist; and that they *maliciously* tear the oracles of God in pieces; I would make them full weight by the two following scriptures: —

I.	II.
The wrath of God is revealed from heaven against all ungodliness, and unrighteousness of men, who hold the truth [or a part of it] in unrighteousness, Romans 1:18.	I testify, &c, that if any man shall take away from the words of the book of this prophecy [much more if he take away from the words of *every book in the Old and New Testament*] God shall take his part out of the book of life, and out of the holy city, and from the things which are written in this book, Revelation 22:18, 19.

But considering Zelotes and Honestus as two good men, who sincerely fear and serve God in their way, and being persuaded that an *injudicious* fear of a Gospel axiom, and not a *wilful* aversion to the truth, makes them cast a veil over one half of the body of Bible divinity; I dare not admit the thought that those severe strictures are adapted to their case. I shall therefore only ask, whether they cannot find a suitable reproof in the following texts: —

I.	II.
I am against the prophets, saith the Lord, that steal my word [contained No. 2.] every one from his neighbour, Jeremiah 23:30.	Ye have made the word of God [contained No. 1.] of none effect by your tradition, Matthew 15:6. [Equally dismembering Christianity, ye still help the adversaries of the Gospel to put in

practice their pernicious maxim, Divide and conquer. And who requires this at your hands? Who will give you thanks for such services as these?]

SECTION IV.

A Scriptural plan of reconciliation between Zelotes and Honestus; being a double declaration to guard equally the two Gospel axioms, or the doctrines of free grace and free obedience — Bishop Beveridge saw the need of guarding them both — Gospel ministers ought equally to defend them — An answer to Zelotes' objections against the declaration which guards the doctrine of free obedience — An important distinction between a primary and secondary trust in causes and means — Some observations upon the importance of the second Gospel axiom — Which extreme appeared greater to Mr. Baxter, that of Zelotes, or that of Honestus — The author's thoughts upon that delicate subject.

I HAVE hitherto pointed out the opposite errors of Zelotes and Honestus, and shown that they consist in so maintaining one part of the truth as to reject the other; in so holding out the glory of one of the Gospel axioms as to eclipse the other. I now present the reader with what appears to me a fair, Scriptural, and guarded plan of reconciliation between themselves, and between all good men, who disagree about the doctrines of faith and works — of free grace and obedience. The declaration which the Rev. Mr. Shirley desired the Rev. Mr. Wesley to sign at the Bristol conference, (in 1770,) gives me the idea of this plan; nay, the first part of it is nothing but that declaration itself, guarded and strengthened by some additions in brackets.

IT IS PROPOSED:

I.

That the preachers who are supposed to countenance the Pharisaic error of Honestus shall sign the following anti-Pharisaic declaration, which guards the doctrine of faith and free grace without bearing hard upon the doctrine of obedience and free will; and asserts the free, gratuitous justification of *a sinner in the day of conversion* and afterward, without denying *the gracious, remunerative* justification of *a believer*, who, in the day of trial, and afterward, keeps the faith that works by love.

Whereas the doctrinal points in the Minutes of a conference, held in London, August 7, 1770, have been

II.

That the preachers who are supposed to countenance the Antinomian error of Zelotes, shall sign the following anti- Solifidian declaration, which guards the doctrine of obedience and free will without bearing hard upon the doctrine of faith and free grace; and asserts the gracious, remunerative justification of *a believer in the day of trial,* and afterward, without denying *the free, gratuitous* justification of a sinner in the day of conversion, and afterward.

Whereas the books published against the said Minutes have been understood to favour the present, inamissible, and understood to favour [the Pharisaic] justification [of a *sinner*] by works; now the Rev. John Wesley, and others assembled in conference, do declare that we had no such meaning; and that we abhor the doctrine of [a sinner's] justification by works, as a most perilous and abominable doctrine: and as the said Minutes are not [or do not appear to some people] sufficiently guarded in the way they are expressed, we hereby solemnly declare, in the sight of God, that [as sinners — before God's throne — according to the doctrine of first causes — and with respect to the first covenant or *the law of innocence*, which sentences all sinners to destruction] we have no trust or confidence but in the [mere mercy of God, through the sole righteousness and] alone merits of our Lord and Saviour Jesus Christ, for justification, or salvation, either in life, death, or the day of judgment: and though no one is a real Christian — believer, (and consequently, though no one can be saved [as a believer] who does not good works where there is time and opportunity,) yet our works have no part in [properly] meriting or purchasing our salvation from first to last, either in whole or part; [the best of men, when they are considered as sinners, being *justifed freely by God's grace, through the redemption that is in Jesus Christ,* Romans 3:24.]

eternal justification of all fallen believers before God, that is, of all those who, having made shipwreck of the faith that works by obedient love, live in Laodicean ease; and, if they please, in adultery, murder, or incest; now the Rev. Mr. **** and others do declare that we renounce such meaning, and that we abhor the doctrine of the Solifidians or Antinomians as a most perilous and abominable doctrine: and as the said books are not [or do not appear to some people] sufficiently guarded, we hereby solemnly declare, in the sight of God, that [as penitent, obedient and persevering believers — before the Mediator's throne — according to the doctrine of second, causes — and with respect to the second covenant, or *the law of Christ,* which sentences all his impenitent, disobedient, apostatizing subjects to destruction] we have no trust or confidence,* but in the truth of our repentance toward God, and in the sincerity of our faith in Christ for justification or salvation in the day of conversion and afterward; — no trust, or confidence, but in our final perseverance in the obedience of faith, for justification, or salvation in death, and in the day of judgment; because no one is a *real* believer under any dispensation of Gospel grace, and of consequence no one can be saved who does not good works, i.e. who does *not truly repent, believe, and obey,* as there is time, light, and opportunity. Nevertheless, our works, that is, our repentance, faith, and obedience, have

---

* I beg the reader would pay a peculiar attention to what precedes and follows this clause. I myself would condemn it, as subversive of the doctrine of grace, and Pharisaical, if I considered it as detached from the context, and not guarded or explained by *the words in Italics,* upon which the greatest stress is to be laid. If Zelotes has patience to read on he will soon see how the secondary trust in the obedience of faith, which I here contend for, is reconcilable with our *primary* trust in Christ.

no part in *properly* meriting or purchasing our salvation from first to last, either in whole or in part; the properly meritorious cause of our *eternal*, as well as *intermediate* and *initial* salvation, being only the merits, or the blood and righteousness of our Lord and Saviour Jesus Christ.

The preceding declaration, which defends the doctrine of free grace, and the gratuitous justification and salvation of *a sinner*, is founded on such scriptures as these: —

The preceding declaration, which defends the doctrine of free obedience, and the remunerative justification and salvation of *a believer*, is founded on such scriptures as these: —

I.

If Abraham were justified by works, he hath *whereof to boast*. To him that *worketh not*, but believeth on him that justifieth the ungodly, his faith is imputed, &c. God imputeth righteousness *without works*. Not by works of righteousness which we have done, *but of his mercy* he saved us. *By grace* are ye saved, through faith; and that *not of yourselves*, it is the gift of God; not of works, lest any man should boast. By the deeds of the law shall no flesh be justified, &c.

II.

Was not Abraham our father justified *by works?* Ye see how by works a man is justified and not by faith only. We are saved *by hope*. In *doing* this thou shalt save thyself. He that *endureth* unto the end, the same shall be saved. He became the author of eternal salvation to them that *obey* him. This shall turn to my salvation through your prayer. With the mouth confession is made to salvation. *By thy words* thou shalt be justified. *The doers* of the law [of Christ] shall be justified, &c.

And let none say that this doctrine has not the sanction of good men. Of a hundred, whom Zelotes himself considers as orthodox, I shall only mention the learned and pious Bishop Beveridge, who, though a rigid Calvinist in his youth, came, in his riper years, to the line of moderation, which I recommend, and stood upon it when he wrote what follows, in his "Thoughts upon our Call and Election." (*Third Edition*, page 297.)

"What then should be the reason that so many should be called and invited to the chiefest good, and the highest happiness their natures are capable of; yet so few of them should mind and prosecute it so as to be chosen or admitted to the participation of it? What shall we ascribe it to? The will and pleasure of almighty God, as if he delighted in the ruin of his creatures, and therefore although he calls them, he would not have them come unto him? No: that cannot be: for in his revealed will, which is the only rule that we are to walk by, he has told us the contrary in plain terms, and has confirmed it too with an oath, saying, "As I live, I have no pleasure in the death of the wicked, but that he should turn from his ways and live," Ezekiel 33:11. And elsewhere he assures us that he "would have all men to be saved, and come to the knowledge of the truth," 1 Timothy 2:4. And therefore if we believe what God *says*, nay, if we believe what he has *sworn*, we must needs acknowledge that it is his will and pleasure that as many as are called should be all chosen and saved: and indeed if he had no mind we should come when we are called to him, why should he call us all to come? Why has he given us his word, his ministers, his ordinances; and all to invite and oblige us to repent and turn to him; if after all he has resolved not to accept of us, nor would have us come at all? Far be it from us that we should have such hard and unworthy thoughts of the great Creator and Governor of the world; especially considering that he has told us the contrary, as plainly as it was possible to express his mind unto us."

Then the bishop mentions five reasons why many are called but few are chosen: and he closes them by these words, (page 310:) "The last reason which our Saviour gives in this parable, is because, of those who are called, and come too at the call, many come not aright, which he signifies by the man that came without the wedding garment: where, although he mentions but one man, yet under that one is comprehended all of the same kind, even all such persons as profess to believe in Christ, and to expect salvation from him, yet will not come up to the terms which he propounds in the Gospel to them, even to "walk worthy of the vocation wherewith they are called," Ephesians 4:1. And indeed this is *the great reason of all*, why of so many, who are called, there are so few chosen, because there are so few who do all things which the Gospel requires of them. Many, like Herod, will *do many things;* and are *almost persuaded to be Christians,* as Agrippa was, &c. Some are all for the duties of the first table without the second, others for the second without the first. Some [like heated Honestus] are altogether for obedience and good works without faith in Christ: others [like heated Zelotes] are as much for faith in Christ, without obedience and good works. Some [like mere moralists] would do all themselves, as if Christ had done nothing for them: others [like mere Solifidians] fancy that Christ has so done all for them, that there is nothing left for them to do: and so between both sorts of people [between the followers of Honestus, and those of Zelotes] which are the far greater parts of those who are called, either *the merits* or else *the laws* of Christ are slighted and contemned. But is this the way to be saved? No, surely."

Hence it is evident, that if Bishop Beveridge be right here, the saving truth lies exactly between the mistake of Zelotes and the error of Honestus. Now if this be the true state of the question, is it possible to propose a plan of reconciliation more Scriptural than that which so secures the merits of Christ as not indirectly to overthrow his laws, and so enforces his laws as not indirectly to set aside his merits? And is not this effectually done in the reconciling declarations? Do they not equally guard the two Gospel axioms? Do they not with impartiality defend free grace and free obedience? And might not peace be restored to the Church upon such a Scriptural, rational, and moderate plan of doctrine?

I fear that a *lasting* reconciliation upon any other plan is impossible: for the Gospel must stand upon its legs, (the two Gospel axioms,) or it must fall. And if Satan, by transforming himself into an angel of light, prevail upon good, mistaken men to cut off one of these legs, as if it were useless or mortified; some good men, who are not yet deceived, will rise up in its defence. So sure, therefore, as "the gates of hell shall never prevail against the Church of the living God — the pillar and ground of the truth," there shall always be a succession of judicious, zealous men, disposed to hazard their life and reputation in the cause of Gospel truth, and ready to prevent the mystical ark from being overset on the right hand or on the left. If a pious Crisp, for example, push it into the Antinomian ditch, for fear of the Pharisaic delusion; a pious Baxter will enter his protest against him: and if a Taylor throw it into the Pharisaic ditch, for fear of the Antinomian error; God will raise up a Wesley to counterwork his design. Nay, a Wesley is a match for a benevolent Taylor, and a seraphic Hervey; and I hope, that should Mr. Shirley ever desire him to sign an anti-Pharisaic declaration, he will not forget to desire Mr. Shirley to sign also an anti-Solifidian protest: every Gospel minister being an equal debtor to both axioms. Nor can I conceive why Mr. Shirley should have more right* solemnly to secure the first axiom, than Mr. Wesley has solemnly to guard the second.

But leaving those two divines, I return to Zelotes, who seems very much offended at my saying, "*We have no trust nor confidence* that any thing will stand us instead of repentance, faith, and obedience." An assertion this which implies, that (with respect to the second causes and secondary means) we place *a secondary trust and confidence* in the graces which compose the Christian character. But I ask, Wherein does the heresy of this doctrine consist? Do I renounce orthodoxy when I say that with respect to some second means, and some second causes, I have no *trust nor confidence* but in my EYES to see, in my EARS to hear, and in my THROAT to swallow? Should I not be fit for Bedlam, if I trusted to see without eyes, to hear without ears, and to swallow without a throat? If I had not a trust that my shoes will answer the end of shoes, and my hat the end of a hat; may I not wisely put my shoes upon my head, and my hat on my feet? And if I have not a confidence that my horse will carry me better than a broomstick, may I not as well get upon a broomstick as on horseback? What would Zelotes think of me, if I did not trust that bread will nourish me sooner than poison, and that fire will warm me better than ice? Is it not a branch of wisdom to trust every thing, just so far as it deserves to be trusted; and a piece of madness to do otherwise?

---

* Mr. Wesley is too judicious a divine to sign a paper that leaves the second axiom quite unguarded. Accordingly we find that axiom guarded in these words of Mr. Shirley's declaration: "No one is a believer, (and consequently cannot be saved,) who doth not good works where there is time and opportunity." Nevertheless, this clause does not by far form so solemn a guard as might have been demanded upon so remarkable an occasion. Mr. Shirley, and the clergy that accompanied him, might with propriety have been desired to remove the fears of those who signed the declaration which he had drawn up, by signing at least the following memorandum: "Forasmuch as Aaron, David, Solomon, Peter, and the incestuous Corinthian did not do good works when they, or any of them worshipped a golden calf, Milcom, and the abomination of the Zidonians, — denied Christ, or committed adultery, murder, or incest, we hereby solemnly declare, in the sight of God, that we abhor the doctrine of the Solifidians, who say that the above-mentioned backsliders had justifying, saving faith, while they committed the above-mentioned crimes; such a doctrine being perilous and abominable; because it absolutely overturns the twelfth article of our Church, and encourages all Christians to make Christ the minister of sin, and to believe that they may commit the most atrocious crimes, without losing their faith, their justification, and their title to a throne of glory."

If Mr. Shirley and his friends had refused to sign such a memorandum as this, the world would have had a public demonstration that Calvinism is the doctrine of Protestant indulgences; and that it establishes speculative, and consequently makes way for practical Antinomianism in all its most flagrant immoralities, as well as in its most winning refinements.

O ye admirers of Zelotes' gospel, come and I will explain to you all my supposed error. I trust only and solely in God as the first and capital cause, and in Christ as the first and capital means of my present and eternal salvation. But beside this primary trust, I have a thousand inferior trusts. Take a few instances: I have *a sure trust and confidence* that the Bible will farther me in the way to eternal salvation, more than the Koran: baptism more than circumcision: the Lord's Supper more than the Jewish passover: the house of God more than the play house: praying more than cursing: repentance, faith, hope, charity, and perseverance more, far more than impenitency, unbelief, despair, uncharitableness, and apostasy.

If I am a heretic for saying that something beside Christ is conducive to salvation, and of consequence may, *in its place and degree*, be trusted in for salvation; is St. Paul orthodox when he exhorts the Philippians to "work out their own salvation," assures them that his afflictions shall "turn to his salvation *through their prayers*," and writes to Titus, that "in DOING the work of an evangelist he shall SAVE himself and them that hear him?"

Again: will Christ stand to me instead of repentance? Has he not said himself, "Except YE repent, ye shall perish?" Will he be to me instead of faith? Did he not assert the contrary when he declared, that "he who believeth not shall be damned?" Will he be instead of an evangelical obedience? Does he not maintain the opposite doctrine, where he declares that he will bid them "depart from him, who call him *Lord, Lord,* and DO NOT the things which he saith?" Will he stand me instead of perseverance? Has he not said himself that he will "deny them that deny him;" that he will finally own us as his "disciples, *if we continue in his words;*" and that "he who *endureth to the end*, the same shall be saved?" Zelotes finds it easier to raise difficulties than to remove those which are thrown in his way. He comes, therefore, with his mouth full of objections, against my second declaration. Let us lend him an ear, and give him an answer.

OBJECTION I. "If, with respect to the doctrine of second causes, and second means of eternal salvation, you have no trust or confidence to be saved as a *penitent, obedient, and persevering believer,* but by true repentance, faith, obedience, and perseverance, you cannot repose your *whole trust* upon God alone; nor can you give Christ *all the glory* of your salvation."

ANSWER. To make God a second cause, and Christ a second means of salvation, is not to give them the glory: it is to pull them out of then throne, and make them stoop to an office unworthy of their matchless dignity. If the king gave you a purse of gold, could you not give him *all the glory* of his generosity, without supposing that he was the laborious digger of the golden ore, the ingenious coiner of the gold, and the diligent knitter of the purse? If you complimented him in *all* these respects, lest he should not have all the glory, would you not pour contempt upon his greatness? And do you not see, that by a parity of reason, what you call "robbing God and Christ of their glory" is only *refusing to dishonour them*, by ascribing to them a dishonourable office; I mean the office of a second cause, or of a secondary means of salvation? Can you not conceive, that to give a general the honour of a sergeant, under pretence of giving him *all* the honour, is to set him below an ensign, and rank him with a halberd bearer? Again: when you say, that in general, upon a journey, with respect to second causes and means, you have *no trust or confidence* but in your money, in the goodness of your horses and carriage, in the passable state of the roads, in the skill of your driver, &c, do you betray any mistrust of Divine Providence? On the contrary, does not your distinction of second causes and second means show that you reserve your primary *trust or confidence* for God, who is the first cause of your blessings; and for his providential care over you, which is the first means of your preservation? And if a pretender to orthodoxy charged you with Atheism or heresy for your assertion, would you not give him your vote to be an officer of the Protestant inquisition, — if the black tribunal, which totters in Spain, should ever be set up in England?

OBJECTION II. "Your first declaration indeed exalts Christ; but the second uncrowns him, to crown our graces — yea, to crown ourselves as possessed of such and such graces; which is the rankest popery, and the very quintessence of Pharisaism."

ANSWER. How can my crowning repentance, faith, and obedience, with a Scriptural coronet, rob Christ of his *peculiar crown?* Are we not indebted to him both for our graces and for the coronet with which he rewards our acceptance and improvement of his favours? Would it be right in you to represent me as an enemy to the crown and king of England, for asserting that barons, earls, and dukes have received from him, or his predecessors, the right of wearing coronets, or secondary crowns? Is it not the glory of our sovereign to be at the head of a crowned peerage? And would you really honour him, if, on a coronation day, you secured the glory of his imperial crown, by kicking the coronets off the heads of all the peers who come to pay him homage? Would he thank you for that ill-judged proof of your loyalty? Would he not reprove you for your unparalleled rashness? And think you that Christ will commend the Antinomian zeal, with which you set up the great image of finished salvation in the plain of mystical Geneva, upon a heap of the coronets, wherewith he and his apostles have crowned the graces of believers? Can you search the sacred records without finding there the doctrine which you represent as treasonable or heretical? Did you never read, "O woman, great is thy faith! THY FAITH hath saved thee?" And what is this but allowing believers to wear a *salvation coronet* — a coronet this, which they will justly "cast before the throne" of the grace that gave it them, and offered it all the day long to those who obstinately "put it from them?" Did you never read, "We are saved *by hope: be faithful* unto death, and I will give thee a crown of life: he is the author of eternal salvation to them that obey him: he will give the crown of life to them that love him," &c? Is not this a salvation coronet to the *hopeful, faithful, obedient*, loving believer? And if you throw my Scales away, and cry out, "Arminian* Methodism turned out rank popery at last!" think you there are no Bibles left in the kingdom? No people able to read such scriptures as these? "Let no man beguile you of your reward through voluntary humility — fair speeches — and deceivableness of unrighteousness. Hold fast that which thou hast, that no man take thy crown," on any pretext whatever, no, not on the most plausible of all pretexts, "Pray, give me thy crown, for it is not consistent with that of the Redeemer." Who could suggest to good men so artful and dangerous a doctrine? Who but the deceitful adversary that can as easily "transform himself into an angel of light," to rob us of our "crown of righteousness," as he formerly could transform himself into a serpent, to rob our first parents of their *crown of innocence?*

---

* The title of a Calvinistic pamphlet published against the Fourth Check.

OBJECTION III. "You may turn and wind as long as you please, but you will never be able to reconcile your doctrine with the doctrine of grace; for if you have *the least* trust and confidence in your graces, you do not trust *wholly* in the Lord; you trust *partly* in 'an arm of flesh,' in direct opposition to the scripture, 'Cursed is the man who trusteth in man, and maketh flesh his arm,' Jeremiah 17:5."

ANSWER. I grant that our doctrine can never be reconciled to what you call "the doctrines of grace," because your partial doctrines of grace are irreconcilable with the holy, free, and equitable Gospel of Christ. But we can as easily reconcile the primary trust mentioned in our first declaration, with the secondary trust mentioned in the second, as you can reconcile my second Scale with the first. Our secondary confidence, which arises from the testimony of a good conscience, no more militates in our breasts against our primary confidence, which arises from the love of Christ, than our regard for the queen excludes our respect for the king. In mystic Geneva indeed they teach, to the honour of the king, that the royal spouse is all filthy; but in our Jerusalem we assert that "she is all glorious," and that "the king greatly desires her beauty." To uncrown her, therefore, and load her with infamy, can never be the way of honouring and pleasing our Melchisedec.

With respect to the passage which you produce from Jeremiah, the sense of it is fixed by what immediately follows: — "And whose heart departeth from the Lord." These words show that the trust forbidden in that scripture is only *such a trust in man and things as makes our hearts depart from the Lord.* Now this can never be the trust and confidence mentioned in our second declaration: for in both declarations we secure to God, as the first cause, and to Christ, as the first means, all the glory which is worthy of the first cause, and of the first means: and, I repeat it, if you ascribe to the Lord any other glory, you insult him as much as you would do a prince, if you gave him the glory which belongs to his consort or his cook; — I mean the glory of bearing fine children, and of making good sauces.

Again: there is no medium between *some* degree of trust, and the *utmost* degree of distrust. Now if the scripture which you produce absolutely forbids *every degree* of inferior trust in man or things, it follows that the more full we are of distrust and diabolical suspicions, the more godly we are. And thus, for fear of putting any degree of secondary trust in man or in things, we must *mistrust* all our wives as adulteresses, all our friends as traitors, all our neighbours as incendiaries, all our servants as murderers, and all our food as poison. But if this fair consequence of your doctrine stand, what becomes of charity, which "thinketh no evil, but hopeth all things?" And if the words of Jeremiah are to be understood in your narrow sense, what becomes of Christ himself, who reposed a degree of trust in man — yea, in Judas, while he counted him faithful? That expression of Job, therefore, "He [the Lord] putteth no trust [that is, no *absolute trust*] in his saints," is to be understood so as not to contradict the words of St. Paul, "He [the Lord] counted me faithful, putting me into the ministry;" or the prophetic words of David concerning Christ and Judas, "Yea, mine own familiar friend in whom I trusted, who did eat of my [multiplied] bread, hath lifted up his heel against me."

To conclude: if England smiles yet at the imbecility of the king, who durst not venture over London bridge, and wondered at those who trusted that fabric as a solid bridge; shall we admire Zelotes' wisdom, who wonders at our having a Scriptural, inferior trust in the graces which form the Christian character? And shall we not count it an honour to be suspected of heresy, for "having a sure trust and confidence," that true repentance, and nothing else, will answer for us the end of *repentance?* That true faith, and nothing else, will answer for us the end of *faith?* That evangelical obedience, and not an imputed righteousness, will answer for us the end of *evangelical obedience?* And that final perseverance, and not whims about "finished salvation," will answer for us the end of *final perseverance?*

Having thus answered Zelotes' objections against the declaration which guards the second Gospel axiom, I shall now present him with some observations upon the importance of that axiom: —

(1.) The first axiom, or the doctrine of grace, holds forth chiefly what Christ has done; and the second axiom, or the doctrine of obedience, holds forth chiefly what we are to do. Now any unprejudiced person must own that it is as important for us to know our own work, as to know the work of another. (2.) In the day of judgment we shall not be judged according to Christ's works and experiences, but according to our own. (3.) Thousands of righteous heathens, it is to be hoped, have been saved without knowing any thing of Christ's external work; but none of them were ever saved without knowing and doing their own work, that is, without working out their salvation with fear and trembling, according to their light. (4.) Most of the Jews that have been saved have gone to heaven without any explicit, particular acquaintance with Christ's merits; (see *Equal Check*, p. 62;) but none of them was ever saved without "fearing God and working righteousness." (5.) To this day, those that are saved, three parts of the world over, are in general saved by the gracious light that directly flows from the second Gospel axiom, through Christ's *merits;* although they never heard of his *name.* (6.) England and Scotland, where the redeeming work of Christ is gloriously preached, swarm nevertheless with practical Antinomians; that is, with men who practically separate works from faith, and the decalogue from the creed. Now all these Gnostics follow the foolish virgins, and the unprofitable servant into hell, crying, *Lord! Lord!* and forgetting to do what Christ commands. (7.) We can never be too thankful for the light of both axioms; but, were I obliged to separate them, I had much rather obey with Obadiah, Plato, and Cornelius, than believe with Simon Magus, Nicolas, and "Mr. Fulsome."

These, and the like observations appeared so weighty to judicious Mr. Baxter, that, in the preface to his *Confession of Faith*, p. 29, he says, "The great objection is, that I ascribe too much to works. I shall now only say, &c, that I see many well-meaning, zealous men dividing our religion, [which is made up of the two Gospel axioms,] and running into two desperate extremes. One sort [at the head of whom is Zelotes] by the heat of opposition to popery do seem to have forgotten that faith and Christ himself are but *means,* and a way for the revolting soul to come home to God by; and thereupon place all the essence of their religion in *bare believing;* so making that THE WHOLE, which is but the door, or MEANS to better, even to a conformity of the soul to the image and will of God. Others [at the head of whom is Honestus] observing this error, flee so far from it as to make faith itself, and Christ, to be scarce necessary. So a man have God's image, say they, upon his soul, what matter is it which way he comes by it? Whether by Christ, or by other means! And so they take all the history of Christ to be a mere accident to our necessary belief; and the precepts only of holiness to be of absolute necessity. The former contemn God under pretence of extolling Christ. The latter contemn Christ under pretence of extolling God alone. He that pretending to extol Christ or faith, degrades godliness, thereby so far rejects God; and he that on pretence of extolling godliness, degrades faith, so far rejects Christ, &c. I therefore detest both these extremes — [that of Zelotes and that of Honestus.] But yet it being the former which I take to be the greater, and which too many men of better repute give too much countenance to, in their inconsiderate disputes against works in justification, I thought I had a call to speak in so great a cause."

It appears, from this excellent quotation, that judicious Mr. Baxter gave the preference to the second Gospel axiom, and thought the doctrine of Honestus less dangerous than that of Zelotes. For my part, though Zelotes thinks me partial, I keep my Scales even: and according to the weights of the sanctuary which I have produced, I find that Zelotes and Honestus are equally wanting. I thank them both for embracing one axiom; I check them both for neglecting the other; and if Zelotes deserves superior praise for maintaining the first axiom, I will cheerfully give him the first place in my esteem. I confess, however, that I am still in doubt about it, for two reasons: (1.) Zelotes preaches indeed the first Gospel axiom, for he preaches Christ and free grace: but, after all, for whom does he preach them? For *every creature*, according to the Gospel charter? No: but only for the little flock of the rewardable elect. If you believe his gospel, there never was a single dram of free, saving grace in the heart of God; or one single drop of precious, atoning blood in the veins of Christ, for the immense herd of the reprobates. Before the beginning of the world they were all personally appointed necessarily to sin and be damned. Thus, according to Zelotes' doctrine, free grace and the first Gospel axiom are not only mere chimeras, with respect to a majority of mankind, but free wrath lords it with sovereign caprice over countless myriads of men, to whom Christ may, with the greatest propriety, be preached as *a reprobating damner,* rather than as a gracious Redeemer. (2.) I could better bear with Zelotes' inconsistencies, if he only diminished the genuine cordial of free grace, and adulterated it with his bitter tincture of free wrath. But alas! he openly or secretly attacks the doctrine of sincere obedience: he calls them "poor creatures," who zealously plead for it: he unguardedly intimates that they are out of the way of salvation: and (O! tell it not among the heathens!) he sometimes gives you deadly hints about the excellence of disobedience; sin, he intimates, "works for our good: it keeps us humble: it makes Christ more precious: it endears the doctrines of sovereign, rich, distinguishing grace: it will make us sing louder in heaven."

"You wrong me," says Zelotes, "you are a slanderer of God's people, and a calumniator of Gospel ministers. I, for one, frequently enforce the ten commandments upon believers." True, sir; but how do you do this? Is it not by insinuating more or less, sooner or later, as your moral audience and your pious heart can bear it, that the decalogue is not now a rule to be judged by, but only "a rule of life," the breach of which will answer all the above-mentioned excellent ends in believers? And what is this but preaching Protestant indulgences, as I said before? When you do this, do you not exceed the popish distinction between venial and mortal sins? Yea, do you not make all the crimes of fallen believers venial? Nay, more, do you not indirectly represent their grievous falls as profitable? And to seal up the delusion, do you not persuade the simple, wherever you go, that our works have nothing to do with our eternal justification before God? That our everlasting salvation is finished by Christ alone; and that whoever believes fallen believers will be condemned by their bad works, is an enemy to the Gospel, an Arminian, a Pelagian, a Papist, a heretic?

If this character of Zelotes be just, and if Honestus be a conscientious good man, who preaches Christ every sacrament day, and who enforces spiritual, sincere obedience, (i.e. true repentance, true faith, true hope, and true love to God and man, in all their branches;) and who does it with sincerity, assiduity, and warmth, I cannot but think as favourably of him as I do of his antagonist.

I must however do Zelotes the justice to say, that an appearance of truth betrays him into his favourite error. If he do not lay a Scriptural stress upon the indispensableness of obedience, it is chiefly for fear of "legalizing the Gospel," and robbing God's children of their comforts. See that fond mother, who prides herself in the tenderness she has for her children. She will not suffer the wind to blow upon them; the sun must never shine on their delicate faces; no downy bed is soft enough; no sweetmeats are sweet enough for them; lest they should know weariness, they must always ride in the easiest of carriages; their tutor must be turned out of doors, if he venture to give them proper correction; all the day long they must be told what an immense estate they are born to, and how their father has put it out of his own power to cut off the entail. Above all, nobody must mention to them the duty they owe to him. *Duty* — that bad word *duty* must not abridge their privileges, and stamp their obedience with legal and servile meanness. In a word, by her injudicious, though well-meant kindness, she unnerves their constitutions, spoils their tender minds, and brings deadly disorders upon them. Her fondness for her children is the very picture of Zelotes' tender regard for believers. No duty must be pressed upon them as duty: no command insisted upon, no self denial ordered, lest the dear people should lose the sweetness of their Gospel liberty. And if at any time "Mr. Fulsome's humours call aloud for physic, it is given with so much honey, that the remedy sometimes feeds the mortal disease.

Honestus sees, and justly dreads the error of Zelotes: and to avoid it, he is so sparing of Gospel encouragements, that he deals chiefly (if not wholly) in severe precepts and hard duties. You may compare him to a stern father, who, under pretence of making his children hardy, and keeping them in proper subjection, makes them carry as heavy burdens as if they were drudging slaves, and threatens to disown them for every impropriety of behaviour.

Not so a Gospel minister, who reconciles both extremes. He knows how to use sweets and bitters, promises and threatenings, indulgence and severity. He is like a wise and kind father, who does not spare the rod when his children want it; but nevertheless wins them by love as much as possible; — who does not disinherit them for every fault, and yet does not put it out of his power to do it, if they take to a vicious course of life, and obstinately trample his paternal love under foot. Reader, who of the three is in the right, Zelotes, Honestus, or the reconciler?

SECTION V.

The doctrines of free grace and free will are farther maintained against Honestus and Zelotes by a variety of Scripture arguments.

I FLATTER myself that the harmonious opposition of the scriptures, produced in the preceding sections, demonstrates the truth of the Gospel axioms. But lest prejudice hinder Honestus and Zelotes from yielding to conviction, I present them with some Scriptural arguments, which, like so many buttresses, will, I hope, support the doctrines of free grace and free will, and render them as firm as their solid basis, — REASON and REVELATION. I begin with the doctrine of free grace.

1. How gladly would Honestus stoop to, and triumph in free grace, if he considered the force of such scriptures! "Without me you can do nothing. What hast thou which thou hast not received," in a remote or immediate manner? "We are not sufficient of ourselves to think any thing as of ourselves, but our sufficiency is of God. Who hath first given him, and it shall be recompensed unto him again? For of him, &c, are all things."

2. We cannot do an action that is truly good without faith and love; and the least degree of true faith and genuine love springs first from free grace; for "faith is the gift of God, love is the fruit of his Spirit:" and when the apostle wishes charity to his converts, he wishes it to them "from God the Father, who is the author of every good and perfect gift." Now if our every good thought, word, and work, spring from faith and love; and if faith and love spring from God; is it not evident that he is the first cause of our genuine righteousness, as well as of our existence?

3. When God says, "Ask and you shall have," does he not show himself the original of all that we want for body and soul, for time and eternity? And if God owes us nothing, if "the help, that is done upon earth, the Lord *originally* does it himself," is it not the height of ingratitude and pride to restrain from God, and arrogate to ourselves, the glory due to him and his infinite perfections?

4. We are commanded "in every thing to give thanks." But if grace be not the source of all the good we do or receive, does it not follow, that in some things the original glory belongs to us, and therefore we deserve thanks before God himself? And is not this the horrid sin of antichrist, who "sitteth as God in the temple of God," and there receives Divine honours "as if he were God?"

5. Does not reason dictate that God will not give his glory to another, and that even "the man who is his fellow," must pay him homage? Is it not the Almighty's incommunicable glory to be the first cause of all good, agreeably to those words of our Lord, "There is none good [i.e. self good, and truly self righteous] but God," from whom goodness and righteousness flow, as light and heat do from the sun? How dangerous then, how dreadful is the error of the self righteous, who are above stooping to Divine goodness, and giving it its due! If robbing a Church of its ornaments is sacrilege, how sacrilegious is the pride of a Pharisee, who, by claiming original goodness, robs God's grace of its indisputable honours, and God himself of his incommunicable glory!

Creeds and Scripture Scales

6. To show Christians how ridiculous and satanic the pride of the self righteous is, I need only remind them that Christ himself — "Christ the righteous" (as the Son of David) declined all self righteousness. Did he not call his works "the works that I do in my Father's name," or by my Father's grace? And did he not, as it were, annihilate himself, when he said, "Why callest thou me GOOD," without any reference to the Godhead, of which I am the living temple? "I can do nothing of myself. I speak not of myself, but the Father that dwelleth in me, he does the works. Learn of me to be lowly in heart?" What real Christian can read such scriptures without learning to disclaim all self righteousness, and to abhor Pharisaic dotages? If Honestus be a reasonable Christian I need say no more to reconcile him to free grace.

I know not which of the two extremes is the most abominable, that of the Pharisee, who, by slighting free grace, will not allow God to be the first cause of all our good works; or that of the Antinomian, who, by exploding free will, indirectly represents the Parent of good as the first cause of all our wickedness. This last error is that of Zelotes, to whom I recommend the following arguments:—

1. All rationals (as such) are *necessarily* endued with free will, otherwise reason and conscience would be powers as absurdly bestowed upon them, as persuasiveness upon a carp, and a taste for music upon an oyster. What are reason and conscience but powers, by which we distinguish right from wrong, that we may choose the one and refuse the other? And how do they reflect upon God's wisdom, who suppose that he gave and restored to man these powers, without giving him a capacity to use them? And what can this capacity be, if it be not free will? As surely then as wings and legs prove that eagles have a power to fly, and hares to run; whether they fly or run *toward* the sportsman's destructive weapon, or *from* it; so surely do reason and conscience demonstrate that men are endued with liberty, i.e. have a power to choose, whether they make a right or a wrong choice. Again:

2. What is a human soul? You justly answer, "It is a thinking, willing, accountable creature." And I reply, from the very nature of our soul, then, it is evident that we are, and ever shall be, free-willing beings. For the moment souls have lost their power of thinking and willing *freely*, they are no longer *accountable;* moral laws are as improper for them as for raging billows. None but fools would attempt to rule delirious persons, and mad men by penal laws. The reason is plain: people stark mad, thinking freely no longer, are no longer free willers; and being no longer free willers, they are no more considered as moral agents. So certain then as man is a reasonable, accountable creature, he is endued with free will: for all rationals under God are accountable, and all accountable beings have more or less power over themselves and their actions. "He [the Lord] himself made man from the beginning, and left him in the hand of his own counsel. If thou wilt keep the commandments, and perform acceptable faithfulness. He hath set fire and water before thee: stretch forth thy hand unto whether thou wilt. Before man is life and death, and whether him liketh shall be given him," Ecclus. 15:14, &c. The tempter therefore may allure, but cannot force us to do evil; and God himself so wisely invites, and so gently draws us to obedience, as not to turn the scale for us in an irresistible manner.

3. O the absurdity of supposing that "God has appointed a day in which he will judge the world in righteousness," if the world be not capable of making a right and wrong choice; and if Christ, Adam or the devil absolutely turn the scale of our morals for us! O the blot upon God's wisdom, when he is represented as rewarding

men with heavenly thrones, for having done the good which they could no more avoid doing than rivers can prevent their flowing! O the dishonour done to his justice, when he is represented as sentencing men to everlasting burnings, for committing sin as necessarily as a leaden ball tends to the centre!

4. If free grace do all in believers without free will, why does David say, "The Lord is my helper?" Why does our Church pray, after the psalmist, "Make haste to help me?" Why does St. Paul declare that "the Spirit itself* helpeth our infirmities?" Why did he not say, *I can do absolutely nothing,* instead of saying, "I can do all things through the Lord who strengtheneth me?" And when Christ had said, "Without me ye can do nothing," why did he not correct himself, and declare that we can do nothing with him, and that he alone must do all? Nay, why does St. Paul apply to himself and others, *when they work with God,* the very same word that St. Mark applies to God, *when he works with men?* "We are συνεργοι, workers together with God," 1 Corinthians 3:9. "The Lord συνεργουντος, working together with them," Mark 16:20.

5. Do not all the PROMISES, the performance of which is suspended upon some terms to be performed by us through Divine assistance, prove the concurrence of free grace with free will? When God says, "Seek, and you shall find. Forgive, and you shall be forgiven. Come unto me, and I will give you rest. Return to me, and I will return to you," &c; when God, I say, speaks this language, who does not see free grace courting and alluring free will? Free grace says, "Seek ye my face;" and free will answers, "Thy face, Lord, will I seek." On the other hand, unbelievers know that so long as their free will refuses to submit to the terms fixed by free grace, the promise miscarries, and God himself declares, "Ye shall know my breach of promise," Numbers 14:34.

6. As the promises, which free grace makes to submissive free will, prove the doctrine of the Gospel axioms; so do the THREATENINGS, which anxious free grace denounces, lest it should be rejected by free will. Take also two or three examples: — "I will cast them that commit adultery with her into great tribulation, except they repent of their deeds. Except ye repent, ye shall all likewise perish. He that believeth not shall be damned. If we sin wilfully, [i.e. obstinately, and to the last moment of our day of grace,] after we have received the knowledge of the truth, there remaineth [for us,] &c, a fiery indignation, which shall devour the adversaries," &c. Who does not see here that free grace, provoked by inflexible free will, can, and will act the part of inflexible justice?

7. There is not one reproof, encomium, or exhortation in the Old or New Testament that does not support the capital doctrines of free grace or free will. When Christ says with a frown, "How is it that you have no faith? O perverse generation, how long shall I suffer you? O generation of vipers, bring forth fruit meet for repentance. Have ye your heart yet hardened?" When he smiles and says, "Well done,

---

* The word in the original has a peculiar force: (συναντιλαμβανεται.) It expresses at once how God's Spirit does his part (συν) "with us," and (αντι) "over against us;" like two persons that take up a burden together and carry it, the one at one end, and the other at the other end; or like a minister and a congregation. who join in prayer by alternately taking up the responses of the Church.

good and faithful servant." When he marvels and cries out, "Great is thy faith." Or when he gives such gracious exhortations, "Be not faithless, but believing: come to the marriage: be faithful unto death: only believe." When Christ, I say, speaks in this manner, is it not as if he expressed himself in such words as these: "My free grace tries every rational means to win your free will. I reprove you for your sins, I commend you for your faith, I exhort you to repentance, I shame you into obedience, I leave no stone unturned to show myself the rational Saviour of my rational, free creatures?"

8. I may proceed one step farther, and say, There is not one commandment in the law, nor one direction in the Gospel that does not demonstrate the truth of this doctrine. For all God's precepts and directions are for our good; therefore free grace gave them. Now since God is wise as well as gracious, it follows that he gave his precepts and directions to free agents, that is, to free-willing creatures. Let a king, who has lost his reason, make a code of moral laws for trees or horses; let him send preachers into every mill in the kingdom to give proper directions to cog wheels, and to assure them that if they turn fast and right, they shall grind for the royal family; and, if they stop or turn wrong, they shall be cut to pieces and ground to saw dust. But let not the absurdity of a similar conduct be charged upon God.

9. Every humble confession of sin shows the various workings of free grace and free will: "I have sinned — I have done wickedly," &c, is the language of free will softened by free grace. To suppose that these acknowledgments are the language of free grace alone, is to suppose that free grace *sins and does wickedly*. And when we heartily join in such petitions as these, "Turn us, and we shall be turned: draw me, and I will run after thee: bring my soul out of prison, that I may praise thy name: save, or I perish," &c, do we not feel our free will endeavouring to apprehend free grace? Is this heresy? Did not St. Paul maintain this doctrine in the face of the Church, and seal it with the account of his own experience, when he said, "I follow after, if that I may apprehend that for which also I am apprehended of God?"

10. To conclude: there is not a damned spirit in hell that may not be produced as a living witness of the double doctrine which I defend. Why is Lucifer loaded with chains of darkness? Is it because there never was any free grace for him, and because free wrath marked him out for destruction, before he had personally deserved it? No: but because his free will "kept not the first estate" of holiness, in which God's free grace had placed him. Why is Judas gone to his own place? Is it because the Holy Ghost spake an untruth when he said that (till the day of retribution comes) "God's mercy is over all his works?" No: but because Judas' free will was so obstinately bent upon "gaining the world," that, according to our Lord's declaration, "he lost his own soul," became a "son of perdition," and, by "denying in works the Lord that bought him, brought upon himself swift destruction." Now, if Judas himself cannot say, "God's free wrath sent me to hell, and not my free will; I am here in Adam's place, and not in my own; I never rejected against myself the counsel of a gracious God; for, with respect to ME, the Father of mercies was always unmerciful-'the God of all grace' had never any saving grace:" — if Judas, I say, cannot justly utter these blasphemies, surely none can: and if none can, then every sinner in hell demonstrates the truth of the Gospel axioms, and is a tremendous monument of the vengeance justly taken on free will, for doing obstinately despite to the Spirit of free grace.

11. But leaving Judas to experience the truth of this awful scripture, "The backslider in heart shall be filled with HIS OWN ways," let your soul soar upon the wings of faith and reason to the happy regions where the spirits of just men made perfect shine like stars or suns in their Father's kingdom. Ask them, "To whom and to what do you ascribe your salvation?" and you hear them all reply, "Salvation is of the Lord. Not unto us, but to his name we ascribe glory. Of his own mercy he saved us, to the praise of the glory of his grace." What a noble testimony is this to the doctrine of free grace!

12. Nor does the Lord stand less for their free will than they do for his free grace. Prostrate yourselves before his everlasting throne; and, with all becoming reverence, ask the following question, that you may be able to vindicate God's righteous ways before unrighteous man. "*Let not the Lord be angry, and I will take upon me to speak unto the Lord.* Didst thou admit those happy spirits into thy kingdom entirely out of partiality to their persons? If they are raised to glorious thrones, while damned spirits are cast into yonder burning lake, is it merely because absolute grace and absolute wrath made *originally* all the difference? In a word, is their salvation so of thy free grace that their free will had absolutely no hand in the matter?"

Methinks I hear "the Judge of all the earth" giving you the following answer, which appears to me perfectly agreeable to his sacred oracles: —

"O injudicious man, how canst thou be so 'slow of heart to believe all that I and my prophets have said!' Am not I a Judge as well as a Saviour? Can I show myself a *righteous* Judge, and yet be *partial* in judgment? Nay, should I not be the most unjust of all judges, if from my righteous tribunal I distributed heavenly thrones and infernal racks out of distinguishing grace and distinguishing wrath? Know that 'all souls are mine,' and that, in point of judgment, 'there is no respect of persons with me.' In the great day 'I judge,' that is, I condemn or justify, I punish or reward 'every man according to his own work,' and consequently according to his free will; for if a work is not the work of a man's free will, it is not *his* work, but the work of him that uses him as a tool, and works by his instrumentality. So certain then as the office of a gracious Saviour is compatible with that of a righteous judge, my capital doctrines of free grace and free will are consistent with each other. If these, therefore, 'walk with me in white,' know that it is 'because they are WORTHY: for the righteous is MORE EXCELLENT than his neighbour. Like good and faithful servants, they occupied till I came; and lo, I come, and my reward is with me.' They have 'kept the faith;' and I have kept my promise. They have not finally forsaken me; and I have not finally forsaken them. 'They have kept the word of my patience; and I have kept them from the great tribulation.' They have 'made themselves ready,' (though some have done it only *at the eleventh hour,*) and I have admitted them to the heavenly feast. They have 'done my commandments, and they are entered by the gates into the New Jerusalem.' My free grace gave them their free will; their free will yielded to my free grace: and now my free grace crowns their faithfulness. They 'were faithful unto death, and I have given them the crown of life.' Thus my free grace and mercy, which began the work of their salvation, concludes it in conjunction with my truth and justice: and my free-willing people shout, *Grace! grace!* when they consider *the top stone,* as well as when they behold *the foundation* of their salvation. My free grace is ALL to them, and their free will is *so much* to me that 'I am not ashamed to call them BRETHREN,' and to acknowledge that 'as the bridegroom rejoiceth over the bride, so do I rejoice over them, because when they heard my voice, they knew the day of their visitation, and did not harden their hearts to the last."

If Honestus and Zelotes candidly weigh the preceding arguments in the balance of the "sanctuary, they will, I hope, drop their prejudices against free grace and free will, and consent to a speedy, lasting reconciliation. But Zelotes is ready to say that there can be no reconciliation between Honestus and himself, because he cannot in conscience be reconciled even to me, who here act the part of a mediator; though I come nearer to "the doctrines of grace" than Honestus does. Consider we then the capital objections of Zelotes: and if we can answer them to his satisfaction, we shall probably remove out of his way the strongest bars which the author of discord has fixed between him and Honestus.

SECTION IV.

Zelotes produces his first objection to a reconciliation with Honestus, taken from God's foreknowledge — Our Lord is introduced as answering for himself, and showing how his prescience is consistent with our liberty, and his goodness with the just destruction of those who obstinately sin away their day of initial salvation — The absurdity of supposing that God cannot certainly know future events, which depend upon the will of free agents, because we cannot.

WHILE Honestus says that he has no great objection to the doctrine of free grace, when it is stated in a rational and Scriptural manner, Zelotes intimates that he is still averse to the doctrine of free will; and declares that capital objections are in his way, and that, till they are answered, he thinks it his duty equally to oppose Honestus and the reconciler. Hear we then his objections, and let us see if they are as unanswerable as he supposes them to be.

OBJECTION I. "You want to frighten me from the doctrines of grace, and to drive into the heresy of the free willers, by perpetually urging that the personal, unconditional, and eternal rejection of the non-elect is inconsistent with Divine mercy, goodness, and justice: but you either deny, or grant God's foreknowledge. If you deny it, you are an Atheist: it being evident that an ignorant God is no God at all. If you allow it, you must allow that when God made such men as Cain and Judas he foreknew that they would *certainly* deserve to be damned; and that when he made them upon that foreknowledge, he made them that they might *necessarily* deserve to be damned. And is not this granting all that we contend for, namely, that God does make, and of consequence has an indisputable right of making 'vessels of wrath,' without any respect to works and free will? Is it not far better to say that we have no free will, than to rob God of his prescience?"

ANSWER. We need neither rob God of his prescience, nor man of his free will. I grant, God made angels and men, that if *they would not be eternally saved,* they might be damned. But what has this doctrine to do with yours, which supposes that he made some angels and men that they might *absolutely* and *necessarily* be damned? Is not our doctrine highly consistent with God's goodness and justice; while yours is the reverse of these Divine perfections? Again: —

Your argument, though ingenious, is inconclusive, because it is founded upon the common mistake of shifting the words upon which it chiefly turns. The flaw of it consists in substituting the clause "*necessarily* deserve to be damned," instead of the clause "*certainly* deserve to be damned," just as if there was no difference between certainty and necessity! But a little attention will convince you of your error. It is *certain* that I write this moment, but am I *necessitated* to it? May I not drop my pen, and meditate, read, or walk? The chasm which, in many cases, separates absolute certainty from absolute necessity, is as immense as that which stands between a point and infinity. Take notice of the insect that buzzes about your ears: does it not exist as *certainly* as God himself? But would it not be a kind of blasphemy to say that it exists as *necessarily*? Would it not at least be paying to a fly an honour which is due to none but God, the only supreme and *absolutely necessary* being? And when you support your doctrines of grace by confounding certainty with necessity, do you not support them by confounding two things, which, in a thousand cases, and especially in the present one, have no more connection than the two poles? Have not judicious Calvinists granted that although the prescience of God concerning Judas' destruction could not stand (*cum eventu contrario*) "with his salvation;" yet it stood perfectly well (*cum possibilitate ad eventum contrarium*) "with the possibility of his salvation?" And is not this granting that although God clearly saw that Judas *would not* repent, he clearly saw also that Judas *might* have repented "in the accepted time," which is all that I contend for? (See *Davenant's Animad. Cambridge edition*, 1641, p. 38.)

To be a little more explicit: let me again intreat you to fall with me before the throne of grace, where the Redeemer teaches mortals to be "meek, lowly, and wise in the heart." Spread your doubts before him in such humble language as this: "Thou light of the world, let not thy creature remain in darkness with respect to the most important question in the world. Am I appointed *necessarily* to continue in sin and be damned? Is my damnation finished? Hast thou *absolutely* ordained me to be a vessel of wrath, and irrevocably appointed my eternal rejection without any respect to my personal free will? Does thy foreknowledge *necessitate* my actions? Or may I choose life or death, and, through thy mercy or justice, have either the one or the other, according to my free, unnecessitated choice — my choice equally opposed to unwillingness and to necessity? Speak, gracious Lord, that if I am a *necessary* agent, I may, without any farther perplexity, yield myself to be carried by the irresistible stream of thy free grace, or of thy free wrath, to the throne in heaven, or to the dungeon in hell, which thou hast appointed for me from all eternity, according to the doctrine of the heathen poet: —

'Sovite mortales animos, curisque levate:
Fata regunt orbem, certa stant omnia lege.'"*

---

* "O ye mortals, dismiss your cares, and unbend your minds. Predestination rules the world: all things happen according to a fixed decree." (*Manilius*.)

Creeds and Scripture Scales

If Christ is the Logos; if he is reason and the Word — the eternal wisdom, and the uncreated Word of the Father; may we not get a satisfactory answer to the preceding question by considering, with humble prayer, his unerring word, and by diligently listening to the reason which he has given us? And shall I take an unbecoming liberty, if I suppose that he himself expostulates with Zelotes in such words as these?

"Son of man, if thou chargest the reprobation of the damned, or their *predestination to eternal death* upon my free wrath, my sovereignty, or Adam's sin, thou insultest my goodness and justice. That reprobation has no properly original cause, but their own personal free will. I would a thousand times have crushed thy primitive parents into atoms, when they forfeited my favour, rather than I would have spared them to propagate a race of creatures, most of whom, according to thy doctrines, are under an absolute necessity to sin and be damned. Thou hast a wrong idea of my word and attributes. With the wisdom and equity of a tender-hearted judge I condemn the victims of my justice, and I do it merely for their personal and obstinate contempt of my free grace. Be then no longer mistaken: my decree of reprobation is nothing but a fixed resolution of giving sinners over to the perverseness of their free will, if they resist the drawings of my free grace to the end of their day of initial salvation. And what can be more equitable than such a resolution? Is it not right that free agents, who to the last despise my goodness, should become monuments of *my despised goodness*, which is but another name for my vindictive justice?

"I foresaw, indeed, that, by such a final contempt of my grace, many would bring destruction upon themselves; but having wisely decreed to make a world of probationers and free agents, I could not *necessarily* incline their will to obedience, without robbing them of free agency: nor could I rob them of free agency without foolishly defeating the counsel of my own mind, and absurdly spoiling the work of my own hands. Beside, from the beginning my intention was not only to show my power and goodness in *creating*, but also to display my wisdom and justice in governing accountable creatures, to whom 'without respect of persons, I should render according to their works — eternal life to them who by patient continuance in well doing seek for glory; but tribulation and anguish to them that are contentious and disobedient.'

"I abhor extorted, forced, necessary submission in rationals: it suits the dastardly children of the devil, and not the free-born sons of God. I could not then in wisdom send upon this world such overpowering streams of light; or permit the tempter to spread such thick darkness upon it, as might invincibly or necessarily turn the scale of man's will for loyalty or rebellion. So unadvised a step would immediately have taken them out of the probation in which I had placed them.

"Again: had I directly or indirectly thrown into the scale a weight sufficient to turn it irresistibly, I should have acted a most unreasonable and detestable part: (1.) A most *unreasonable part*: for if I alone *completely* 'work out the salvation' of believers, according to what thou callest *finished salvation*, nothing can be more absurd than my appointing a day of judgment and rewards, to bestow upon the elect an eternal life of glory *according to their works*. (2.) A most *detestable part*: for if I earnestly invited all the wicked to choose life, after having absolutely chosen death for most of them, should I not show myself the most hypocritical of all tyrants?

"But thou stumblest at my foreknowledge, and askest why I bestow the blessings of initial salvation upon those whose free agency will *certainly* abuse my goodness, and do despite to the Spirit of my saving grace. Thou thinkest it is wrong in me to give them that *will perish* the cup of initial salvation, when I know they *will not accept* the cup of eternal salvation. Thou supposest it would be better to reprobate them at once, than to expose them to a greater damnation, by putting it in their power to reject the terms of eternal salvation, and by that mean to fall from initial salvation. But I shall silence thy objections by proposing some plain questions to thee, as I once did to my servant Job.

1. "Is it reasonable to suppose that I should pervert my nature, and act in a manner contrary to my perfections, to prevent free agents from perverting *their* nature, and acting in a manner contrary to *their* happiness? What wouldest thou have thought of my wisdom if I had appointed Lucifer to hell, and Adam to the grave, from eternity, for fear they should deserve those punishments by wilfully falling from heaven and from paradise? Is it not absurd to fancy that the Creator must bring himself in guilty of misconduct, lest his rational creatures should render themselves so?

2. "If thou thinkest it right in me to command the Gospel of my free grace to be preached to 'every creature,' although thou knowest that the neglecters of it will, like the people of Capernaum, fall into a deeper hell for their final contempt of that favour; why shouldest thou think it wrong in me to extend the virtue of my blood, and the strivings of my Spirit to those who will finally reject my free grace? When thou approvest the extensive tenor of my Gospel commission, dost thou well to be angry, or to fret, like Jonah, at the extensiveness of my mercy? Dost thou not see that if I were absolutely merciless toward *some men*, my commission to preach the Gospel to *every man* would be utterly inconsistent with my veracity?

3. "Have I not a right to create free agents, and to place them in a state of probation, that I may wisely reward their obedience, or justly punish their rebellion? 'Who art thou, that repliest against God? Shall the thing formed say to him that formed it,' *Why hast thou made me a free agent? a probationer for heavenly rewards, or infernal punishments?* May not I appoint that free-willing unbelievers, who do final despite to the Spirit of my free grace, shall be 'vessels of wrath, self fitted for destruction;' and that free-willing, obedient believers shall be 'vessels of mercy, afore prepared unto glory' by my free grace, with which their free will has happily concurred?

4. "In the nature of things must not free agents, in a state of probation, be free to fall, as well as free to stand? When thou weighest gold, if thou hinderest one scale from turning, dost thou not effectually hinder the free motion of the other scale?

5. "Does it not become me to show myself good and gracious, though my creatures prove wicked and ungrateful? Should I extinguish or restrain *my* light, because some people love darkness rather than light? If they will not do their duty by me, as obedient creatures, ought I not to behave to *them* as a gracious Creator, and to hold out the golden sceptre of my mercy, before I strike them with the iron rod of my vengeance? And should not the honour of my Divine attributes be considered more than the *additional* degrees of misery, which ungrateful free agents will *obstinately* bring upon themselves?

6. "When I had decreed to create a world of free agents, and to try their loyalty, in order to reward the obedient and punish the rebellious, could I execute my wise, just, and gracious plan without *suffering* sin to enter into the world, *if free agents would commit it?* Is permitting *the possibility of sin,* any more than permitting that *free will might, or might not* concur with my free grace? And could I ever have judged the world in righteousness, if I had not permitted such a possibility?

7. "If I had given the casting vote for Peter's obedience, and for Judas' disobedience, should I not have fixed an eternal blot upon my impartiality? Thinkest thou that I could be so unwise and unjust as to hold a universal judgment, to judge angels and men according to what they have done through mere necessity? Shall irresistible free grace, and omnipotent free wrath, force the human will? and shall I reward or punish overpowered mankind according to such constraint? Far be the thought from thee! Far be the iniquity from me! I judge the world in righteousness, and not in madness; according to *their own works,* and not according to *mine.*

8. "When I foresaw that sin would enter into the world, could I have been just if I had not decreed to punish sinners? Could I, with justice, sentence moral agents either to *non-existence,* or to *a wretched existence,* BEFORE they had done wickedly? — AFTER they had sinned, and I had graciously promised them a Saviour, could I, without showing myself full of dissimulation, partiality, and falsehood, condemn those that perish, BEFORE I had afforded them the means of recovery, by which many of their fellow sinners, *under the same circumstances,* attain eternal salvation? Must not, in the nature of things, those who work out their damnation be doubly guilty, or I be notoriously partial? Must they not appear without excuse before all; or I without mercy, long suffering, and truth toward them?

9. "Dost thou not see that although the ministration of righteousness and rewards 'exceeds in glory,' yet the ministration of condemnation and punishments 'is glorious?' Beside, are they not closely connected together? Has not the fear of hell, as well as the hope of heaven, kept thousands of martyrs from drawing back to perdition, when the snares of death compassed them about? Nay, is not 'the spirit of bondage unto fear' the beginning of wisdom, and, generally, of the conversion of the heart of man to me? And shall I act a deceitful part for thousands of years together, working upon my people by a lie, and making them believe that they have damnation if they disbelieve, or if they cast off their first faith, when yet (upon thy scheme) there is nothing but finished salvation for them?

10. "Will not the damnation of obstinate sinners answer as important ends in the world of rationals, as prisons and places of execution do in the kingdoms of this world? If incorrigible, free-willing rebels sin to all eternity, will it not be just in me to make the line of their punishment run parallel with the line of their wickedness? Does not thy reason dictate that an unceasing contempt of my holy law, and a perpetual rebellion against creating, redeeming, and sanctifying grace, will call aloud for a perpetual outpouring of my righteous indignation? And does it not follow that the eternal damnation of rebels eternally obstinate — of rebels who have *wantonly* trampled under foot the blessings of initial salvation, is as consistent with my despised goodness, as with my provoked justice?

11. "As I could not justly condemn *necessary* agents to infernal misery; so I could not delight in, and reward the obedience of *such* agents. And as thou hast more pleasure in the *free,* loving motions of one of thy friends, than in the *necessary* motions

of ten thousand pieces of clock work, let them move ever so regularly, so do I put more value upon the free, voluntary obedience of one of my people, than upon all the necessary revolutions of all the planetary worlds. Why then wilt thou, by thy doctrine of bound will, rob me of what I value most in the universe — the free obedience of my faithful servants — the unforced, spontaneous love of my mystical body, my spouse, my Church?

12. "With respect to my foreknowledge of sin, it had absolutely no influence on the commission of it. Thou thinkest the contrary, because thou canst not, in general, *certainly* foresee what thy neighbours will do, unless they are absolutely directed and influenced by thee: but the consequence does not hold. Short sighted as thou art, dost thou not sometimes *with a degree of certainty* foresee things which thou art so far from *appointing*, that thou wouldest gladly prevent them, if thou didst not consider that such a step would be inconsistent with thy wisdom, and the liberty of others?

13. "Again: may not my foreknowledge of a future event imply the certainty of that event with respect to me, without implying its necessity with respect to the free agent who *spontaneously* causes it? Suppose thou wert perfectly acquainted with the art of navigation, the force of every wind, the situation of every rock and sand bank, the strength and burden of every ship, the disposition and design of every mariner, &c: suppose again thou sawest a ship going full sail just against a dangerous rock, notwithstanding thy repeated signals and loud warnings to the pilot; mightest thou not foresee the *certain* loss of the ship, without laying the least *necessity* upon the pilot to steer her upon the fatal spot where she goes to pieces? And shall not I, from whom no secrets are hid, and before whom things past and to come meet in one immovable, everlasting NOW: — shall not I, 'who inhabit eternity,' where he 'that was, and is, and is to come,' shows himself the unchangeable I AM, — shall not I, I say, foresee the motions and actions of all my free-acting creatures, as certainly as a wise artist foresees the motions of the watch which he has made? Imperfect as the illustration is, it is adapted to thy imperfect understanding. For though thou canst not comprehend how I know future contingencies, thou canst easily conceive, that as no one but a watch maker can perfectly foresee what may accelerate, stop, or alter the motion of a watch, so none but the Creator of a free agent can perfectly foresee the future motions of a free agent. If 'hell is naked, and destruction hath no covering before me,' is it not absurd to suppose that the human heart can be hid from my all-piercing eye? And if thou, who livest but in a point of time, and in a point of space; — if thou, whose faculties are so shallow, and whose powers are so circumscribed; — if thou, I say, in that point of time and space which thou fillest, canst see what is before thee, why should not I, an all-wise and superlatively perfect Spirit, who fill all times, and all places, through an infinite NOW and a boundless HERE, see also what is before me? Perceivest thou not the absurdity of measuring me with thy span? Try to weigh the mountains in a balance, and to measure the seas in the hollow of thy hand; and if thou findest thyself confounded at the bare thought of a task so easy to my omnipotence, fall in the dust, and confess that thou hast acted an unbecoming part, in attempting to put the very same bounds to my omniscience, which I have put to thy foreknowledge. To conclude: —

14. "Thou art ready to think hardly of my wisdom goodness, or foresight, for giving a talent of saving grace to a man, who, by burying it to the last, enhances

his own destruction. To solve this imaginary difficulty, thou ascribest to me a dreadful sovereignty — a horrible right of making vessels to dishonour, and filling them with wrath, *merely to show my absolute power.* But let me expostulate a moment with thee. I foresaw, indeed, that the slothful, unfaithful man, to whom I gave one talent, would bury it to the last: but if I had kept it from him; if I had afforded him no opportunity of showing his faithfulness, or his unfaithfulness; what could I have done with him? Had I sent him to hell upon *foreseen disobedience,* I should have acted the absurd and cruel part of a judge who hangs an honest man to- day, under pretence that he foresees the honest man will turn thief to- morrow; — had I taken him to heaven, I should have rewarded *foreseen unfaithfulness* with heavenly glory. And, had I refused to let him come into existence, my refusal would have been attended with a glaring absurdity, and with two great inconveniences. (1.) With a *glaring absurdity;* for if I foresee that a man will *certainly* bury his talent; and if, upon this foresight, I refuse that man existence, it follows I foresaw that a thing which shall *never* come to pass, shall *certainly* come to pass. And what can be more unworthy of me, and more absurd, than such a foresight? (2.) The notion that my foreknowledge of the man's burying his talent should have made me suppress his existence, is big with two great inconveniences. For, *first,* I should have defeated my own purpose, which was to show my distributive justice by rewarding him, *if he would be faithful;* or by punishing him, *if he would continue in his unfaithfulness.* And, *secondly,* I should have broken, almost without interruption, the laws of the natural world, and nipped the man's righteous posterity in the bud. Had I, for instance, prevented the wickedness of all the ancestors of the Virgin Mary, by forbidding their existence, ten times over I might have suppressed her useful being, and my own important humanity. Nay, at this rate, I might have destroyed all mankind twenty times over. Drop then thy prejudices; be not wise above what is written for thy instruction. Under pretence of exalting free grace, do not pour contempt upon free will, which is my masterpiece in man, as man himself is my masterpiece in this world. Remember that hell is the just wages which abused free grace gives to free- willing, incorrigible sinners; and that heaven is *the gracious reward* with which my free grace, when it is submitted to, crowns the obedience of corrigible persevering believers. Nor forget that, if thou oppose the doctrine of free grace, thou wilt undermine my cross, and insult me as a Saviour: and if thou decry the doctrine of free will, thou wilt sap the foundation of my tribunal, and affront me as a judge."

To the arguments contained in the preceding plea, I add an extract from a discourse written, I think, by Archbishop King, with a design to reconcile the Predestinarians and the free willers.

"Foreknowledge and decrees," says that judicious writer, "are only assigned to God, to give us a notion of *the steadiness and certainty* of the Divine actions; and if so, for us to conclude that what is represented by them is inconsistent with the contingency of events or free will, &c. is the same absurdity as to conclude that China is no bigger than a sheet of paper, because the map that represents it is contained in that compass."

The same ingenious author proposes the argument that has so puzzled mankind, and done so much mischief in the world. It runs thus: — "If God *foresee,* &c, that I shall be saved, I shall *infallibly* be so; and if he *foresee,* &c, that I shall be damned, it is *unavoidable.* And therefore it is no matter what I do, or how I behave myself in this life." "If God's foreknowledge were exactly conformable to ours, the consequence would seem just; but, &c, it does not follow, because our foresight of events, if we suppose it *infallible*, must presuppose a necessity in them, that therefore the Divine prescience must require *the same necessity* in order to its being *certain*. It is true we call God's foreknowledge and our own by the same name; but this is not from any real likeness in the nature of the faculties, but from some proportion observable in the effects of them; both having this advantage, that they prevent any surprise on the person endowed with them. Now as it is true that no contingency or freedom in the creatures can any way deceive or surprise God, put him to a loss, or oblige him to alter his measures; so on the other hand it is likewise true that the Divine prescience does not hinder freedom: and a thing *may either be, or not be,* notwithstanding that foresight of it which we ascribe to God. When therefore it is alleged that if God foresees I shall be saved, my salvation is *infallible;* this does not follow: because the foreknowledge of God is not like man's, which requires necessity in the event, in order to its being *certain;* but of another nature consistent with contingency: and our inability to comprehend this arises from our ignorance of the true nature of what we call foreknowledge in God, &c. Only of this we are sure, that it so differs from ours that it may consist either with the being, or not being of what is said *to be foreseen,* &c. Thus St. Paul was a *chosen* vessel, and he reckons himself in the number of *the predestinated,* Ephesians 1:5. And yet he supposes it possible for him to miss of salvation: and therefore he looked upon himself as obliged to use mortification, and exercise all other graces, in order to make his calling and election sure; 'lest,' he says, 'that, by any means, when I have preached to others, I myself should be a castaway,' or *a reprobate,* as the word is translated in other places."

This author's important observation, concerning the difference between God's foreknowledge and ours, may be illustrated by the following remarks: — Hearing and sight are attributed to God, as well as foreknowledge and foresight. "He that planted the ear," says David, "shall he not hear? And he that formed the eye, shall he not see?" Now is it not as absurd to measure God's perfect manner of foreseeing and foreknowing, by *our imperfect foresight and knowledge*, as to measure his perfect manner of seeing and hearing by our imperfect manner of doing them? If Zelotes said, "I cannot see the inhabitants of the planets: I cannot see the antipodes: I cannot see through that wall: I can see nothing of solids but their surface, &c, therefore GOD cannot see the inhabitants of the planets, the antipodes," &c, would not his argument appear to you inconclusive? Nevertheless, it is full as strong as the following, on which Zelotes' objection is founded: — "I cannot *certainly foresee* the free thoughts and contingent intentions of the human heart, therefore God cannot do it: I am not omniscient, therefore God is not so." If I argued in this manner, would you not say," O injudicious man, how long wilt thou measure God's powers by thine? See, if thou canst, what *now* passes in my breast? Nay, see thy own back; see the fibres which compose the flesh of thy hands, or the vapour that exhales out of all thy pores. And if these near — these present — these material objects are out of the reach of thy sight, what wonder is it if future contingencies are out of the reach of thy foresight? Cease then to confine God's foreknowledge within the narrow limits of thine, and own that an omnipresent, omniscient, and everlasting Spirit, who 'is overall, through all, and in all,' and whose permanent existence and boundless immensity comprehend all times and places, as the atmosphere contains all clouds and vapours; — own, I say, that such a Spirit can, at one glance, see from his eternity all the revolutions of time far more clearly than thou canst see the characters which thine eyes are now fixed upon. And confess that it is the highest absurdity to suppose that an omnipresent, omnipotent, spiritual, and eternal eye, which is *before, behind,* and *in* all things, times, and places, can ever be at a loss to know or foreknow any thing. And what is God but *such an eye?* And what are Divine knowledge and foreknowledge, but the sight of such a spiritual, eternal, and omnipresent eye?"

I do not know whether this vindication of our free agency, of God's foreknowledge, and of the consistency of both will please my readers: but I flatter myself that it will satisfy Candidus. Should it soften the prejudices of Zelotes, without hardening those of Honestus, it will promote the reconciliation which I endeavour to bring about, and answer the end which I proposed when I took up the pen to throw some light upon this deep and awful part of my subject.

SECTION VII.

Zelotes' second objection to a reconciliation — That objection is taken from President Edwards' and Voltaire's doctrine about necessity — The danger of that doctrine — The truth lies between the extremes of rigid bound willers and rigid free willers — We have liberty, but it is incomplete, and much confined — The doctrines of power, liberty, and necessity, are cleared up by plain descriptions, and important distinctions — The ground of Mr. Edwards' mistake about necessity is discovered; and his capital objection against free will is answered.

ZELOTES has another specious objection to a reconciliation with Honestus. It runs thus: —

OBJECTION. "Honestus is for free will, and I am against it. How can you expect to reconcile us? Can you find a medium between free will and necessity? Now, that we are not free-willing creatures may be demonstrated from reason and experience: (1.) From reason. Does not every attentive mind see that a man *cannot help* following the last dictate of his understanding; that such a dictate is the necessary result of the light in which he sees things; that this light likewise is the necessary result of the circumstances in which he is placed, and of the objects which he is surrounded with; — and, of consequence, that all is *necessary;* one event being as necessarily linked to, and brought on by another, as the second link of a chain in motion is necessarily connected with, and drawn on by the first link? Thus, for example, the accidental, not to say the *providential* sight of Bathsheba, necessarily raised unchaste desires in David's mind: these desires necessarily produced adultery: and adultery, by a chain of necessary consequences, necessarily brought on murder. All these events were decreed, and depended as much upon each other as the loss of a ship depends upon a storm, and a storm upon a strong rare faction or condensation of the air. (2.) EXPERIENCE shows that we are not at liberty to act otherwise than we do. Did you never hear passionate people complain that they could not moderate their anger? How often have persons in love declared that their affections were irresistibly drawn to, and fixed upon such and such objects? You may as soon bid an impetuous river to stop, as bid a drunkard to be sober, and a thief to be honest, till sovereign, almighty, victorious grace makes them so. "The way of man is not in himself; it is not in man that walketh to direct his steps,' Jeremiah 10:23."

ANSWER. I grant that "the way of man is not in himself" to make his escape, when the hour of vengeance is come, and when God surrounds him with his judgments: and that this was Jeremiah's meaning, in the verse which you quote to rob man of his moral agency, is evident from the words that immediately precede: "The pastors are become brutish: therefore they shall not prosper, and all their flocks shall be scattered; behold the noise of the bruit [the hour of vengeance] is come, and a great commotion out of the north country, to make the cities of Judah desolate, and a den of dragons." Then come the misapplied words, "O Lord, I know that the way of a man [to make his escape] is not in himself, &c. Correct me, but with judgment, &c, lest thou bring me to nothing:" see verses 21, 22, 24. With respect to David, he had probably resisted as strong temptations to impurity, as that by which he fell; and he might, no doubt, have stood, if he had not been wanting to himself, both before, and at the time of his temptation. With regard to what you say about a storm; two ships of equal strength may be tossed by the same tempest, and without necessity one of them may be lost by the negligence, and the other saved by the skill of the pilot. And if we may believe St. Paul, the lives which God had given him would have been lost, if the sailor had not stayed in the ship to manage her to the last, Acts 27:31, 34. You appeal to experience: but it is as much against you as against Honestus. Experience shows that we have liberty, and thus experience is against you. Again: experience convinces us that our liberty has many bounds, and thus experience is against Honestus. As to your scheme of the concatenation of forcible circumstances and events, it bears hard upon all the Divine perfections. God is too wise, too good, and holy, to give us a conscience and a law which forbids us to sin; and to place us in the midst of such forcible circumstances as lay a majority of mankind under an absolute necessity of sinning to the last, and being damned for ever. We are therefore endued with *a degree* of free will. Through Him who "tasteth death for every man," and through "the free gift which came upon all men," we may "choose life" in the day of initial salvation; we may, by grace, (by "the saving grace which has appeared to all men,") pursue the things that make for our peace; or we may, by nature, (by our own natural powers,) follow after the things that make for our misery, just as we have a mind. "We cannot do *all*," says one, "therefore we can do *nothing*." "We can do

---

* This very passage was urged to a friend of mine by the obdurate highwayman who was hanged last year at Shrewsbury! He cited it on the morning of his execution, to excuse his crimes, and to comfort himself. He had drunk so deeply into the doctrine of necessity, bound will, and fatalism, that he was entirely inaccessible to repentance. What pity is it that Zelotes should countenance so horrid a misapplication of the Scriptures! Heated Austin is my Zelotes in this respect. Bishop Davenant saith of him, that "he did not abhor fate;" and to prove his assertion he quotes the following words of that father: — "If any one attributes human affairs [which take in all the bad thoughts, words, and actions of men,] to fate, because he calls *the will and the power of God* by the name of fate, let him hold his sentiment and alter his language. *Sententiam teneat, linguam corrigat.*" (Aug. De Grat. lib. 5, c. 1.) Is not this granting Mr. Voltaire as much fatalism as he contends for? and gilding the *fatal* pill so piously as to make it go down glib with all the rigid bound willers in Christendom?

something," says another, "therefore we can do *all.*" Both consequences are equally false. The truth stands between two extremes. Beside: —

The doctrine of bound will draws after it a variety of bad consequences. It is subversive of the moral difference which subsists between virtue and vice. It takes away all the demerit of unbelief. It leaves no room for the rewardableness of works. It strikes at the propriety of a day of judgment. It represents truth and error like two almighty charms, which irresistibly work upon the elect and the reprobates, to execute God's absolute decrees about our good or bad works, our finished salvation or finished damnation. In a word, it fastens upon us the grossest errors of Pharisaic fatalists, and the wildest delusions of Antinomian gospellers.

Having thus given a general answer to the objection proposed, I remind the reader that Mr. Edwards, president of New Jersey college, is exactly of Zelotes' sentiments with respect to necessity or bound will. They agree to maintain that *necessary* circumstances necessarily turn the scale of our judgment, that our judgment necessarily turns the scale of our will, and that the freedom of our will consists merely in choosing *with willingness* what we choose *by necessity.* Mr. Voltaire also at the head of the fatalists abroad, and one of my opponents at the head of the Calvinists in England, give us, after Mr. Edwards, this false idea of liberty.

To show their mistake, I need only to produce the words of Mr. Locke: — "Liberty cannot be where there is no thought, no volition, no will, &c. So a man striking himself, or his friend, by a convulsive motion of his arm, which it is not in his power by volition, or the direction of his mind, to stop or forbear; nobody thinks he has liberty in this; every one pities him, as acting by necessity and constraint. Again: there may be thought, there may be will, there may be volition, where there is no liberty. Suppose a man be carried, while fast asleep, into a room, where is a person he longs to see, and there be locked fast in beyond his power to get out; he awakes, and is glad to see himself in so desirable company, in which he stays so willingly; that is, he prefers his staying to going away. Is not this stay voluntary? I think nobody will doubt it; and yet being locked fast in, he is not at liberty to stay, he has not freedom to be gone. So that liberty is not an idea belonging to *volition,* or *preferring;* but to the person having the power of doing, or forbearing to do, according as the mind shall choose or direct." (*Essay on Hum. Und.* chap. 21.)

This excellent quotation encourages me to make a fuller inquiry into the mistakes of the rigid Predestinarians and rigid free willers, who equally start from the truth that lies between them both. It is greatly to be wished that the bounds of necessity and liberty were drawn consistently with reason, Scripture, and experience. I shall attempt to do it: and if I am so happy as to succeed, I shall reach the centre of the difficulty, find point out the very spring of "the waters of strife:" Honestus will be convinced that he has too high thoughts of our liberty: Zelotes will see that his views of it are too much contracted: and Candidus will learn to avoid their contrary mistakes. I begin by a definition of necessity and of liberty.

Moral philosophers observe that necessity is that constraint upon, or confinement of the soul, whereby we cannot do a thing otherwise than we do it. Hence it appears that, *strictly speaking,* there is no such thing as moral necessity. For could we be constrained to do *unavoidable* good or evil, that good were not *moral* good, that evil were not *moral* evil. Could we be necessarily confined in the channel of virtue or of vice, as a river is confined in its bed, without any power to retard or accelerate our virtuous or vicious motions as we see fit; our tempers and actions would lose their morality and their immorality. To speak with propriety, necessity has no place but in the *natural* world. Strictly speaking, it is excluded from the moral world; for what we *may* and *must* regulate or alter, cannot possibly be *necessary* or *unalterable*. Nevertheless I shall, by and by, venture upon the improper expression of moral necessity, to convey the idea of a strong, moral propensity or habit, and to point out with greater ease Mr. Edwards' mistake.

This ingenious author asserts that, by the law of our nature, we choose what we *suppose* to be, upon the whole, most eligible. I grant it is so *in most cases:* nevertheless, I deny necessity, because there is no necessity imposed upon us to *suppose* that, upon the whole, a thing is most eligible which at first sight appears to be so to the eye of prejudice or passion; our liberty being chiefly a limited *power* to attend either to the dictates of reason and conscience, or to those of prejudice and passion; — to follow either the motions of the tempter or those of Divine grace. I say *a limited power*, because our power is incomplete, as will appear by considering the particulars of which our liberty does and does not consist. And,

1. It does not consist, *in general,*[*] in a power to choose evil and misery as such. *Seldom* do men, who are yet in a state of probation; men, who are not degenerated into mere fiends, choose evil only as evil. When we pursue some evil, it is then *generally* under the appearance of some good; or, as leading to some good, which will sooner or later make us ample amends for the present evil. For God having made us for the supreme good, which is the knowledge and enjoyment of himself, he has placed in our souls an unquenchable thirst after happiness, that we may ardently seek him, the fountain of true happiness. It can hardly be said, therefore, that probationers are at liberty with respect to the capital inquiry, "Who will show us any good?" We naturally desire good, just as a hungry man desires food: although he may say, "I do not choose to be hungry," yet he is so, whether he will or not.

2. But although a hungry man is *necessarily* hungry, yet he does not *eat necessarily;* for he may *fast*, if he please: and when he chooses to eat, he may prefer bad to wholesome food; he may take more or less of either; he may take it now, or by and by; with deliberation, or with greediness, as he pleases. Apply this observation to our

---

* I use these limited expressions because, upon second thoughts, I do not absolutely assent to Mr. Edwards' doctrine, that the will *always* necessarily follows the last dictate of the understanding. I now think that in this respect Calvin's judgment deserves our close attention: — "*Sic interdum flagitii turpitudo conscientiam urget, ut non sibi imponens sub falsa boni imagine, sed sciens et volens, in malum ruat. Ex quo affectu prodeunt istæ voces, 'Video meliora proboque, Deteriora sequor.'*" (Inst. lib. 2, cap. 2, section 23.) Sometimes the horrid nature of vice so urges the conscience, that the sinner, no longer imposing upon himself by the false appearance of good, knowingly and willingly rushes upon evil. Hence flow these words, *I see and approve what is good, but follow what is bad.*

Since these sheets went to the press, I have seen Mr. Wesley's *Thoughts upon Necessity.* He strongly sides with Calvin against Edwards. For after asserting that sometimes our *first*, sometimes our last judgment is according to the impressions we have received; that in some cases we may or may not receive those impressions; and that in most we may vary them greatly; he denies that the will *necessarily* obeys the *last* judgment, and affirms that "the mind has an intrinsic power of cutting off the connection between the judgment and the will."

necessary hunger or thirst after happiness. All probationers necessarily ask, "Who will show us any good?" But although they necessarily aim at happiness, yet they are not necessitated to aim at it in this or that way; although they cannot but choose that end, yet they are not irresistibly obliged to choose any one particular mean to attain it.

Here then room is left for free will or liberty. We may choose to go to happiness, our mark, by saying, "What shall we eat? What shall we drink? Wherewith shall we be clothed?" Who will give us corn and wine, silver and gold, worldly honours and sensual gratifications? or we may say, Who will give us pardon and peace, grace and glory? "Lord! lift thou up the light of thy countenance upon us!" In a word, though we are not properly at liberty, whether we will choose happiness in general, that choice being morally necessary to us; yet in the day of initial salvation we may choose to seek happiness in ourselves, in our fellow creatures, or in our Creator; we may choose a way that will lead us to imaginary and fading bliss, or to real and eternal happiness: or, to speak as the oracles of God, we may choose death or life.

This being premised, I observe that our liberty consists, 1. In our being under *no natural necessity* with regard to our choice of the means by which we pursue happiness; and, of consequence, with regard to our schemes and actions. I repeat it; by *natural necessity* I mean an absolute want of power to do the reverse of what is done. Thus by *natural necessity* an ounce is outweighed by a pound; it can no ways help it: and a man, whose eyes are quite put out, cannot absolutely see the light, should he desire and endeavour it ever so much. Hence it appears, that when Peter denied his Master, he was under no natural necessity so to do; for he might have confessed him if he had pleased. When the martyrs confessed Christ, they might have denied him with oaths, if they had been so minded: and when David went to Uriah's bed, he might have gone to his own. There was no shadow of natural necessity in the case. We *may* then, or we *may not* admit the truth or the lie, that is laid before us as a principle of action. Thus the eunuch, *without necessity*, admitted the truth delivered to him by Philip; and Eve, *without necessity*, entertained the lie which was told her by the serpent.

2. Our liberty consists in a power carefully to consider whether what is presented to us as a principle of action is a truth or a lie; lest we should judge according to *deceitful appearances*. Our blessed Lord, by steadily using this power, steadily baffled the tempter: and Adam, by not making a proper use of it, was shamefully overcome.

3. It consists in a power, natural to all moral agents, to do acts of sin if they please, and in a supernatural or gracious power (bestowed for Christ's sake upon fallen man) to forbear, with some degree of ease, doing sinful acts,* at least when we

---

* I make these exceptions for two reasons: (1.) Because I am sensible of the justness of Ovid's advice to persons in love: —

Principiis obsta, sero medicina paratur, &c.

For if love, and indeed any other violent passion, is not resisted at its first appearance, it soon gets to such a height that it can hardly be mastered, till it has had its course. (2.) Because a habit strongly rooted is a second nature. It is far easier to refrain from the first acts than to break off inveterate habits of virtue or of vice. In such cases, powerful, uncommon impulses of grace or of temptation are peculiarly necessary to throw us out of our beaten track. Hence the strong

have not yet fully thrown ourselves down the declivity of temptation and passion; and when we have not yet contracted such strong habits as make virtue or vice *morally necessary* to us.

4. It consists in a gracious power to make diligent inquiry, and to apply in doubtful cases to "the Father of lights" for wisdom, before we practically decide that such a doctrine is true, or that such an action is right. Had Eve and David used that power, the one would not have been deceived by a flattering serpent; nor the other by an impure desire.

But, 5. The highest degree of our liberty consists in a power to suspend a course of life entered upon; to re-examine our principle, and to admit a new one, if it appear more suitable; especially when we are particularly assisted by Divine grace, or strongly assaulted by temptations adapted to our weakness. Thus, by their *gracious* free agency, Manasses and the prodigal son suspended their bad course of life, weighed the case a second time *for the better*, admitted the truth which they once rejected, and from that new principle wrought righteousness: while, on the other hand, Solomon, Judas, and Demas, by their natural free agency suspended their good course of life, weighed the case a second time *for the worse*, admitted the lie which they once detested, and from that new principle wrought damnable iniquity. Is not this account of our real, though limited liberty, more agreeable to Scripture, reason, conscience, and experience, than the necessity maintained by Calvinistic bound willers and Deistical fatalists?

I have already observed, (*Equal Check*, p. 50,) that the seemingly contrary systems of those gentlemen, like the two opposite half diameters of a circle, meet in natural necessity, a central point which is common to both; Mr. Voltaire, who is the apostle of the Deistical world, and Mr. Edwards, who is the oracle of Calvinistic metaphysicians, exactly agreeing to represent man as a *mere*, though *willing* slave, to the circumstances in which he finds himself, and to lead him from head to foot, and from the cradle to the grave, with the chains of absolute *necessity*, one link of which he can no more break, than he can make a world. Their error, if I mistake not, springs chiefly from their overlooking the important difference there is between *natural necessity*, and what the barrenness of language obliges me to call *moral necessity*. Hence it is that they perpetually confound *real liberty*, which is always of an *active* nature, with that kind of necessity in disguise, which I beg leave to call *passive liberty*. Clear definitions, illustrated by plain examples, will make this intelligible; will unravel the mystery of fatalism, and rescue the capital doctrine of *liberty* from its confinement in mystical Babel.

1. A thing is done by *natural necessity*, When it *unavoidably* takes place, according to the fixed laws of nature. Thus, by natural necessity, a serpent begets a serpent, and not a dove; a fallen man begets a fallen child, and not an angel; a deaf man cannot hear, and a cripple cannot be a swift racer.

2. A thing is done by *moral necessity*, (if I may use that improper expression,) when it is done by a free agent with a peculiar degree of readiness, resolution, and

---

comparison of the prophet, "Can the Ethiopian change his skin, or the leopard his spots? Then may ye also, that *are accustomed* to do evil, do good," — without a more than common assistance of Divine grace.

determination; from strong motives, powerful arguments, confirmed habits; and when it might nevertheless be done just the reverse, if the free agent pleased. Thus, by a low degree of *moral necessity*, chaste, conscientious Joseph struggled out of the arms of his master's wife, and cried out, "How can I do this great wickedness, and sin against God?" And, by a high degree of it, Satan hates holiness, God abhors sin, and Christ refused to fall down and worship the devil.

3. I have observed in the Second Check that Mr. Edwards' celebrated Treatise upon Free Will turns in a great degree upon a comparison between *balances* and the *will*. To show more clearly the flaw of his performance, I beg leave to venture upon the *improper*, and, in one sense, *contradictory* expression of "passive liberty." By *passive liberty* (which might also be called *mechanical liberty*) I mean the readiness with which just scales turn upon the least weight thrown into either of them. Now it is certain that this *liberty* (so called) is *mere necessity;* for two even scales necessarily balance each other, and the heavier scale necessarily outweighs the lighter. According to the fixed laws of nature it cannot be otherwise. It is evident, therefore, that when Mr. Edwards avails himself of such popular, improper expressions as these, "Good scales are *free* to turn either way; just balances are at *liberty* to rise or fall by the least weight," he absurdly imposes upon the *moral* world *a mechanical freedom or liberty*, which is mere necessity. His mistake is set in a still clearer light by the following definition:
—

4. *Active liberty* is that of living creatures endued with a *degree of power to use their faculties in various manners;* their prerogative is to have in general the weight that turns them, in a great degree, *at their own disposal*. Experience confirms this observation: how many stubborn beasts, for example, have died under the repeated strokes of their drivers, rather than move at their command! And how many thousand Jews chose to be destroyed rather than to be saved by Him who said, "How often would I have gathered you, &c, and ye would not!" Hence it appears that *active* liberty subdivides itself into *brutal* liberty, and *rational* or *moral* liberty.

5. *Brutal liberty* belongs to beasts, and *rational* or *moral* liberty belongs to men, angels, and God. By *brutal liberty* understand the power that beasts have to use their animal powers various ways, according to their instinct and at their pleasure. By *rational liberty* understand the power that God, angels, and men have to use their Divine, angelic, or human powers in various manners, according to their wisdom, and at their pleasure. Thus, while *an oak* is tied fast by the root to the spot where it feeds and grows, *a horse* carries his own root along with him, ranging without necessity, and feeding as he pleases, all over his pasture. While a horse is thus employed, *a man* may either make a saddle for his back, a spur for his side, a collar for his shoulder, a stable for his conveniency, or a carriage for him to draw: or, leaving these mechanical businesses to others, he may think of the scourge that tore his Saviour's back; call to mind the spear that pierced his side; reflect upon the cross that galled his shoulder; the stable where he was born; and the bright carriage in which he went to heaven: or he may, by degrees, so inure himself to infidelity as to call the Gospel a *fable*, and Christ an *impostor*.

According to these definitions it appears that our sphere of liberty increases with our *powers*. The more powers animals have, and the more ways they can use those powers, the more *brutal liberty* they have also: thus those creatures that can, when they please, walk upon the earth, fly through the air, or swim in the water, as some sorts of fowls, have a more extensive liberty than a worm, which has the freedom of one of those elements only, and that too in a very imperfect degree.

As by the help of a good horse a rider increases his power to move swiftly, and to go far: so by the help of science and application a philosopher can penetrate into the secrets of nature, and an Archytas or a Newton can

> Aerias tentare domos, animoque rotundum
> Transmigrare polum.[*]

Such geniuses have undoubtedly more *liberty of thought* than those sots, whose minds are fettered by ignorance and excess, and whose imagination can just make shift to flutter from the tavern to the play house and back again. By a parity of reason, they who enjoy "the glorious liberty of the children of God," who can in a moment collect their thoughts, fix them upon the noblest objects, and raise them not only to the stars, like Archytas, but to the throne of God, like St. Paul; — they who can "become all things to all men, be content" in every station, and even "sing at midnight" in a dungeon, regardless of their empty stomachs, their scourged backs, and their "feet made fast in the stocks;" they who can command their passions and appetites, who "are free from sin," and find "God's service perfect freedom;" these happy people, I say, enjoy far more *liberty of heart*, than the brutish men who are so enslaved to their appetites and passions, that they have just liberty enough left them, not to ravish the women they set their eyes upon, and not to murder the men they are angry with. But although the liberty of God's children is "glorious" now, it will be far more glorious when their regenerate souls shall be matched in the great day with bodies blooming as youth, beautiful as angels, radiant as the sun, powerful as lightning, immortal as God, and capable of keeping pace with the Lamb, when he shall lead them to new fountains of bliss, and run with them the endless round of celestial delights.

To return: innumerable are the degrees of liberty peculiar to various orders of creatures; but no animals are accountable to their owners for the use of their powers, but they which have a peculiar degree of knowledge. Nor are they accountable, but in proportion to the degree of their knowledge and liberty. Your horse, for instance, has power to walk, trot, and gallop: you want him to do it alternately; and, if he does not obey you, when you have intimated your will to him in a manner suitable to his capacity, you may, without folly and cruelty, spur or whip him into a reasonable use of his liberty and powers; for inferior creatures are in subjection to their possessors in the Lord. But if his feet were tied, or his legs broken, and you spurred him to make him gallop; or if you whipped a hen to make her swim, or an ox to make him fly, you would exercise a foolish and tyrannical dominion over them. This cruel absurdity, however, or one tantamount, is charged upon Christ by those who pretend to "exalt him" most. They thus dishonour him, as often as they insinuate that the children of men have no more power to believe, than hens to swim, or oxen to fly; and that the Father of mercies will damn a majority of them, for not using a power which he determined they should never have.

---

[*] Soar to the stars, and with his mind travel round the universe.

Creeds and Scripture Scales

Some people assert that man has a little liberty in *natural*, but none in *spiritual* things. I dissent from them for the following reasons: (1.) All men (monsters not excepted) having a degree of the human form, they probably have also a degree of human capacity, a measure of those *mental* powers by which we receive the knowledge of God; a knowledge this, which no horse can have, and which is certainly of a spiritual nature. (2.) The same apostle, who informs us that "the natural man" (so called) the man who quenches the Spirit of grace under his dispensations, "cannot know the things of the Spirit of God, because they are discerned" only by the light of the Spirit, which he quenches or resists, — the same apostle, I say, declares, that "what may be known of God, is manifest in them, [the most abandoned heathens;] for God hath showed it unto them; so that they are without excuse; because when they knew God, [in some degree,] they glorified him not as God," according to the degree of that knowledge; but became brutish, besotted persons; or, to speak St. Paul's language, "they became vain in their imaginations; they became fools; their foolish heart was darkened; wherefore God gave them up to a reprobate mind," and they were left in the deplorable condition of the Christian apostates described by St. Jude, "sensual, having not the Spirit:" in a word, they became ψυχικοι,* *mere animal men*, the full reverse of *spiritual men*, 1 Corinthians 2:14. Far from being the wiser for "the light that [graciously] enlightens every man that cometh into the world," they became "inexcusable, by changing the truth of God into a lie," and turning their light to darkness, through the wrong use which they made of their liberty.

When the advocates for necessity deny man the talent of spiritual liberty, which Divine wisdom and grace have bestowed upon him, they fondly exculpate themselves, and rashly charge God with Calvinistic reprobation. For who can think that an oyster is culpable for not flying as an eagle? And who can help shuddering at the cruelty of a tyrant, who, to show his sovereignty, bids all the idiots in his kingdom solve Euclid's problems, if they will not be cast into a fiery furnace? Nor will it avail to say, as Elisha Coles and his admirers do, that though man has lost his power to obey, God has not lost his power to command upon pain of eternal death: for this is pouring poison into the wound, which the doctrine of *natural* necessity gives to the Divine attributes. Your slave runs a sportive race, falls, dislocates both his arms, and by that accident loses his power or liberty to serve you: in such circumstances you may indeed find fault with him, for bringing this misfortune upon himself; but you show a great degree of folly and injustice if you blame him for not digging with his arms out of joint; and when you refuse him a surgeon, and insist upon his thrashing, unless he choose doubly to feel the weight of your vindictive hand, you betray an uncommon want of good nature. But in how much more unfavourable a light would your conduct appear if his misfortune had been entailed upon him by one of his ancestors, who lost a race near six thousand years ago and if you had given him a

---

* ψυχη is sometimes taken only for the principle of *animal life*. Thus, Revelation 8:9, "The third part of the sea became blood, and the third part of the creatures which were in the sea: and had ψυχχας [not *natural* but] *animal* life, died." Hence Calvin himself renders the word ψυχικος, *animal man*, though our translators render it "natural man," as if the Greek word were φυσικος. And upon their mistakes a vast majority of mankind are rashly represented as being absolutely destitute of all capacity to receive the *saving* truths of religion.

bond stamped with your own blood, to assure him that "your ways are equals" and that you are "not an austere man," that "your mercy is over all your household," and that punishing is your "strange work?"

God is not such a master as the Calvinian doctrines of grace make him. For Christ's sake he is always well pleased with the right use we make of our present degree of liberty, be that degree ever so little. For unconverted sinners themselves have *some* liberty. Fast tied and bound as they are with the chain of their sins, like chained dogs, they may move a little. If they have a mind they may, to a certain degree, come out of Satan's kennel. When they are pinched with hunger or trouble, like the prodigal son, they may go a little way toward the bread and the cordial that came down from heaven; and when their chains gall their minds, they may give the Father of mercies to understand that they want "the pitifulness of his great mercy to loose them." Happy the souls who thus meet God with their little degree of power! Thrice happy they who go to him so far as their chain allows, and then groan with David, "My belly cleaveth to the dust. Bring my soul out of prison, that I may praise thy name!" When this is the case, "the captive exile hasteneth that he may be loosed;" they that are thus "faithful over a few things," will soon be "set over many things;" they will soon experience an enlargement, and say with the psalmist, "Thou hast enlarged my steps under me:" my liberty is increased. "I will run the way of thy commandments."

The defenders of necessity are chiefly led into their error by considering the *imperfection* of our liberty, and the *narrow limits* of our powers: but they reason inconclusively who say," Our liberty is imperfect: therefore we have none. 'Without Christ we can do nothing:' therefore we have absolutely no power to do any thing." As some observations upon this part of my subject may reconcile the judicious and candid on both sides of the question, I venture upon making the following remarks: —

All power, and therefore all liberty, has its bounds. The king of England can make war or peace when he pleases, and with whom he pleases; and yet he cannot lay the most trifling tax without his parliament. The power of Satan is circumscribed by God's power. God's own power is circumscribed by his other perfections: he *cannot* sin, because he is *holy;* he cannot cause two and two to make six, because he is true; nor can he create and annihilate a thing in the same instant, because he is wise. Our Lord's power is circumscribed also: "Jesus said unto them, Verily, verily, I say unto you, *The Son can do nothing of himself, but what he seeth the Father do."*

If a *degree of confinement* is consistent with the liberty of omnipotence itself, how much more can *a degree of restraint* be consistent with our *natural, civil, moral,* and *spiritual* liberty! Take an instance of it: (1.) With regard to *natural* liberty. Although you cannot fly, you may walk, but not upon the sea, as Peter did; nor thirty miles at once, as some people do; nor one mile when you are quite spent; nor five yards when you have a broken leg. (2.) With respect to *civil* liberty. You are a free-born Englishman: nevertheless, you are not free from taxes; and probably you have not the freedom of two cities in all the kingdom. On the other hand, St. Paul is Nero's "prisoner, bound with a chain," and yet he swims to shore, he gathers sticks, makes a fire, and preaches "two years in his own hired house, nobody forbidding him." (3.) With respect to *moral* liberty. When Nabal is in company with his fellow sots, has good wine before him, and is already heated by drinking, he cannot refrain himself, he must get drunk: but might he not have done violence to his inclination before his blood was inflamed? Conscious of his weakness, might he not at least have avoided the dangerous company he is in, and the sight of the sparkling liquor, in which all his good resolutions are drowned?

Take one instance more of the *imperfect* liberty I plead for. Is not what I have said of *civil*, applicable *to devotional* liberty? You have not the power to LOVE God with all your heart; but may you not FEAR him a *little*? You cannot wrap yourself for *one hour* in the sublime contemplation of his glory; but may you not meditate for *two minutes* on death and judgment? St. Paul's *burning zeal* is far above your sphere; but is not the *timorous inquisitiveness* of Nicodemus within your reach? You cannot attain the elevations of him who has ten talents of piety; but may you not so use your one talent of consideration, as to gain two, four, eight, and so on, till the unsearchable riches of Christ are all yours? And, if I may allude to the emblematic pictures of the four evangelists, may you not ruminate upon earth with the *ox* of St. Luke, till you can look up to heaven with St. Matthew's *human face*, fight against sin, with the courage of St. Mark's *lion*, and soar up toward the Sun of righteousness, with the strong wings of St. John's *eagle*? Did not our Lord expect as much from the Pharisees, when he said to them, "Ye hypocrites, how is it that you do not discern this [accepted] time? Yea, and why even of yourselves judge ye not what is right?" Alas! how frequently do we complain of the want of power, when we have ten times more than we make use of! How many *slothfully* bury their talent, and *peevishly* charge God with giving them none! And how common is it to hear people, who are sincerely invited to the Gospel feast, say, "I *cannot* come," who might roundly say, if they had Thomas' honesty, "I *will not* believe!" The former of these pleas is indeed more decent than the latter: but is it not shamefully evasive? And does it not amount to the following excuse: — "I *cannot come* without taking up my cross; and as I *will not do that*, my coming is *morally* impossible?" A lame excuse this, which will pull down aggravated vengeance upon those who, by making it, trifle with truth, and their own souls, and with God himself.

From the whole I conclude that our liberty, or free agency, consists in a *limited ability* to use our bodily and spiritual powers right or wrong at our option; and that to deny mankind such an ability is as absurd as to say that a man cannot work, or beg, or steal, as he pleases; bend the knee to God, or to Ashtaroth; go to the house of prayer, or to the play house; turn a careless, or an attentive ear to a Divine message; disbelieve, or give credit to an awful report; slight, or consider a matter of fact; and act in a reasonable, or unreasonable manner, at his option.

Is not this doctrine agreeable to the dictates of conscience, as well as to plain passages of Scripture? And when we maintain that, as often as our free will inclines to vital godliness since the fall, it is *touched*, though not *necessarily impelled* by free grace: when we assert, in the words of our tenth article, that "we have no power to do good works acceptable to God, without the grace of God, by Christ preventing [not *forcing*] us that we may have a GOOD will;" do we not sufficiently secure the honour of free grace? Say we not as much as David does in this passage: "Thy people [obedient believers] shall [or will] be willing [to execute thy judgments upon* thine

---

* That this is the true meaning of Psalm 110:3, is evident from the context. Read the whole Psalm; compare it with Psalm 149:6; Malachi 4:1, 2, 3; and Revelation 19:19; and you will see that "the day of God's power," or "the day of God's army," is *the day of his wrath against his*

enemies] in the day of thy power," i.e. in the day of thy powerful wrath? Or, as we have it in the Common Prayer, "In the day of thy power shall the people offer free will [not *bound will*] offerings?" Do we not grant all that St. Paul affirms, when he says to the Philippians, "Work out your own salvation with fear, &c, for it is God that worketh in you both to WILL and to DO?" i.e. God of his own good pleasure gives you a gracious talent of will and power: bury it not: use it "with fear:" lay it out "with trembling;" lest God take it from you, and "give you up to a reprobate mind." And is it not evident that these two passages, on which the rigid bound willers chiefly rest their mistake, are perfectly agreeable to the doctrine of the moderate free willers which runs through all the Scriptures, as the preceding pages demonstrate?

THIRD OBJECTION OF ZELOTES, Rational and Scriptural as the doctrine of liberty is, President Edwards will root it up: and to succeed in his attempt, he fetches ingenious arguments from heaven and hell.

Superos, Acheronta movendo,

he musters up all the subtleties of logic and metaphysics, with all the refinements of Calvinism, to defend his favourite doctrine of necessity. To the best of my remembrance, a considerable part of his book may be summed up in the following paragraph, which contains the most ingenious objections of the Calvinists: —

The Arminians say that if we act *necessarily* we are neither punishable nor rewardable; because we are neither worthy of blame, nor of praise. But the devil, who is punished, and who therefore is blameworthy, is *necessarily wicked;* he has no liberty to be good. And God, who deserves ten thousand times more praises than we can give, is *necessarily good;* he has no liberty to be wicked. Hence it appears that the reprobates may be *necessarily* wicked like the devil, and yet may be *justly* punishable like him; and that the elect may be *necessarily* good like God and his angels, and yet that they may be, in their degree, *praiseworthy* like God, and *rewardable* like his angels. Therefore, the doctrine of the Calvinists is rational, as only supposing what is undeniable, namely, that *necessary sins* may *justly* be punished in the reprobates; and that *necessary obedience* may *wisely* be rewarded in the elect. And, on the other hand, the doctrine of the Arminians, who make so much ado about reason and piety, is both absurd and impious: *absurd*, as it supposes that the devil is *not worthy of blame*, because he sins *necessarily;* and *impious*, as it insinuates that God does *not deserve praise*, because his goodness is *necessary*.

This argument is plausible, and an answer to it shall conclude this dissertation. God is enthroned in goodness far above the region of evil; neither "can he be tempted of evil;" the excellence, unchangeableness, and self sufficiency of his nature being every way infinite. He does not then exercise his liberty in choosing moral good or evil; but, (1.) In choosing the various manners of enjoying himself according to all the combinations that may result from his unity in trinity, and from his trinity in unity. (2.) In regulating the infinite variety of his external productions. (3.) In appointing the boundless diversity of rewards and punishments, with which he

enemies: a day this which is expressly mentioned two verses after, and described in the rest of the Psalm.

crowns the obedience or disobedience of his rational creatures. (4.) In finding out different methods of overruling the free agency of men and angels; and of suspending the laws by which he governs the material world. And, (5.) In stamping different classes of beings with different signatures of his eternal power and Godhead; and in indulging, with multifarious discoveries of himself, the innumerable inhabitants of the worlds which he has created, or may yet condescend to create.

On the other hand, the devil is sunk far below the region of virtue and bliss; neither can he be *tempted of good*, on account of his consummate wickedness, and fixed aversion to all holiness. His liberty of choice is not then exercised about moral good and evil; but about various ways of doing mischief, procuring himself some ease, and trying to avoid the *natural* evils which he feels or fears.

This is not the case of man, who inhabits, if I may use the expression, *a middle region* between heaven and hell; a region where light and darkness, virtue and vice, good and evil, blessing and cursing, are yet before him, and where he is in a state of *probation*, that he may be rewarded with heaven, or punished with hell, "according to his *good or bad* works." It is then as absurd in President Edwards to confound our liberty with that of God and of the devil, as it would be in a geographer to confound the equinoctial line with the two poles.

A comparison may illustrate this conclusion. As the *mechanical* liberty of a pair of just scales consists in a power gradually to ascend as high, or to descend as low as the play of the beam permits; so the *moral* liberty of rationals *in a state of probation*, consists in a *gracious* power gradually to ascend in goodness quite to their zenith in heaven, and in a *natural* power to descend in wickedness quite to their nadir in hell; so immensely great is the play of the *moral* scales! God's will, by the perfection of his nature, being immovably fixed in the *height* of all goodness, cannot stoop to an inferior good, much less to evil: and the devil, being sunk in the *depth* of all wickedness, and daily confirming himself in his iniquity, can no more rise in pursuit of goodness. Thus the presence of all wickedness keeps the scale of the prince of darkness *fixedly sunk* to the nethermost hell; while the absence of all unrighteousness keeps the scale of the Father of lights *fixedly raise*d to the highest pitch of heavenly excellence. God is then quite *above*, and Satan quite *below* a state of probation. The one is good, and the other evil, in the highest degree of *moral* necessity. Not so man, who hovers yet between the world of light and the world of darkness — man, who has life and death, salvation and damnation placed within his reach, and who is called to "stretch forth his hand" to that which he will have, that "the reward of his hands may be given him."

Nor does it follow from this doctrine that God's goodness is not praiseworthy, and that Satan's wickedness is not worthy of blame: for although God is fixedly good, and Satan fixedly wicked, yet the goodness of God, and the wickedness of the devil are still of a *moral* nature; and therefore commendable or discommendable. I mean, (1.) That God's goodness consists in the perfect rectitude of his eternal will, and not in a want of power to do an act of injustice. And, (2.) That the devil's wickedness consists in the complete perverseness of his obstinate will, and not in a complete want of power to do what is right. Examples will explain this: —

A rock cannot do an act of justice or an act of injustice, because reason and free agency do not belong to a stone; therefore, the praise of justice and the dispraise of injustice; can never be wisely bestowed upon a rock. If a rock fall upon the man who is going to murder you, and crushes him to death, you cannot seriously return it thanks; because it fell without any good intention toward you; nor could it possibly help falling just then. Not so the "Rock of ages," the parent of rationals and free agents: he does justice with the highest certainty, and yet with the highest liberty: I say *with the highest liberty;* because, if he *would,* he COULD, with the greatest ease, do what to me appears inconsistent with the Scriptural description of his attributes. Could he not, for example, to please Zelotes, make "efficacious decrees" of absolute reprobation, that he might secure the sin and damnation of his unborn creatures? Could he not protest again and again that "he willeth not *primarily* the death of sinners, but rather that they should turn and live;" when, nevertheless, he has *primarily,* yea *absolutely* appointed that most of them shall never turn and live? Could he not openly "command all men every where to repent," upon pain of eternal death, and yet *keep most men every where* from repenting, by giving them up to a reprobate mind from their mother's womb, as he is supposed to have done by the myriads of "poor creatures" for whom, if we believe the advocates of Calvinistic grace, Christ never procured one single grain of penitential grace? Could he not invite "all the ends of the earth to look unto him, and be saved," and call himself *the Saviour of the world,* and *the Saviour of all men, though especially of them that believe,* (of *all men* by initial salvation; and *of them that believe and obey* by eternal salvation,) when yet he determined from all eternity that there should be neither Saviour nor initial salvation, but only a *damner* and *finished damnation* for the majority of mankind? Could he not have caused his only begotten Son to assume a human form, and to weep, yea, bleed over obstinate sinners; protesting that he "came to save the world, and to gather them as a hen gathers her brood under her wings;" when yet from all eternity he had absolutely *ordained* * *their wickedness and damnation to illustrate his glory?* In a word, could he not prevaricate from morning till night, like the God extolled by Zelotes, — a God this, who is represented as sending his ministers to *preach the Gospel* [i.e. to offer "finished and eternal salvation"] *to every creature,* when his unconditional, efficacious decree of reprobation, and the partiality of Christ's atonement, leave to multiplied millions no other prospect, but that of finished and eternal damnation? Could not God, I say, do all this *if he would?* Do not even some good men indirectly represent him as having acted, and as continuing to act in that manner? Now if he does it not, when he has full power to do it; if he is determined not to sully his veracity by such shuffling, his

---

* When Calvin speaks of the absolute destruction of "so many nations, which, (*una cum liberis eorum infantibus,*) together with their little children, are involved without remedy in eternal death by the fall," he says that "God foreknew their end before he made man;" and he accounts for his foreknowledge thus: "He foreknew it, because he had ordained it by his decree:" a decree this, which three lines above he calls "horribly awful." "*Et ideo præscivit, quia decreto suo sic ordinarat. Decretum quidem horribile, fateor.*" And in the next chapter he observes, that, "Forasmuch as the reprobates do not obey the word of God, we may well charge their disobedience upon the wickedness of their hearts; provided we add at the same time that they were devoted to *this wickedness,* because, by the just and unsearchable judgment of God, they were raised up to illustrate his glory by their *damnation.*" "*Modo simul adjicitur, ideo in hanc pravitatem addictos, quia justo, et inscrutabili Dei judicio suscitati sunt, ad gloriam ejus sua damnatione illustrandam.*" This Calvinism unmasked may be seen in *Calvin's Institutes,* third book, chap. 23, sec. 7, and chap. 24, sec. 14.

goodness by such barbarity, his justice by such unrighteousness; or, to use Abraham's bold expression, if "the Judge of all the earth does right," when, if he would, he *could* do wrong, to set off his "sovereignty" before a Calvinistic world; is not his goodness *praiseworthy?* Is it not of the *moral* kind?

The same might be said of the devil's wickedness. Though he is confirmed in it, is it not still of a *moral* nature? Is there any other restraint laid upon his repenting, but that which he first lays himself? Could he not confess his rebellion, and suspend some acts of it, *if he would?* Could he not of two sins, which he has an opportunity to commit, choose the least, *if he were so minded?* But, granting that he has lost all *moral* free agency, granting that he sins *necessarily,* or that he could do nothing better *if he would;* I ask, Who brought this absolute necessity of sinning upon him? Was it another devil who rebelled five thousand years before him? You say, No; he brought it upon himself by his *wilful, personal, unnecessary sin:* and I reply, Then he is blame-worthy for *wilfully, personally, and unnecessarily* bringing that horrible misfortune upon himself: and therefore his case has nothing to do with the case of the children of men, who have the depravity of another entailed upon them, without any personal choice of their own. Thus, if I mistake not, the doctrine of liberty, like the bespattered swan of the fable, by diving a moment in the limpid streams of truth, emerges fairer, and appears purer, for the aspersions cast upon it by rigid bound willers and fatalists, headed by Mr. Edwards and Mr. Voltaire.

SECTION VIII.

The fourth objection of Zelotes to a reconciliation with Honestus — In answer to it the reconciler proves, by a variety of quotations from the writings of the fathers, and of some eminent divines, and by the tenth article of our Church, that the doctrines of free grace and free will, as they are laid down in the Scripture Scales, are the very doctrines of the primitive Church, and of the Church of England — These doctrines widely differ from the tenets of the Pelagians and ancient semi-Pelagians.

OBJECTION IV. "You have done your best to vindicate the doctrine of moderate free willers, and to point out a middle way between the sentiments of Honestus and mine, or to speak your own language, between *rigid* free willers and rigid bound willers, but you have not yet gained your end: for, if you have Pelagius and Mr. Wesley *on your side,* the primitive Church and the Church of England are *for us:* nor are we afraid to err in so good company."

ANSWER. I have already observed that, like true Protestants, we rest our cause upon right reason and plain scriptures: and that both are for us, the preceding sections, I hope, abundantly prove. Nevertheless, to show you that the two Gospel axioms can be defended upon any ground, I shall, *first,* call in the Greek and Latin fathers, that you may hear from their own mouths how greatly they dissent from you. *Secondly,* to corroborate their testimony I shall show that St. Augustine himself, and *judicious Calvinists* have granted all that we contend for concerning free will and the conditionality of *eternal* salvation. And, *thirdly,* I shall confirm the sentiment of the fathers by our articles of religion, one of which particularly guards the doctrine of free will evangelically connected with and subordinated to free grace.

I. I grant that when St. Augustine was heated by his controversy with Pelagius, he leaned too much toward the doctrine of fate; meaning by it the overruling, efficacious will and power of the Deity, whereby he *sometimes* rashly hinted that all things happen: (see the note, page 185:) but in his best moments he happily dissented from himself, and agreed with the other fathers. Take some proofs of their aversion to fatalism and bound will, and of their attachment to our supposed "heresy."

1. JUSTIN MARTYR, who flourished in the second century, says: — *Si fato fieret ut esset aut improbus aut bonus; nec alii quidem probi essent nec alii mali.* (Apol. 2.) That is, "If it happen by fate (or necessity) that men are either good or wicked; the good were not good, nor should the wicked be wicked."

2. TERTULLIAN, his contemporary, is of the same sentiment: *Cæterum nec boni nec mali merces jure pensaretur ei, qui aut bonus aut malus necessitate fuit inventus, non voluntate.* (TERT. lib. 2, contra Marc.) "No reward can be justly bestowed, no punishment justly inflicted upon him who is good or bad by necessity, and not by his own choice." In the fifth chapter of the same book he asserts that God has granted man liberty of choice, *ut sui dominus constanter occurreret, et bono sponte servando, et malo sponte vitando: quoniam et alias positum hominem sub judicio Dei, oportebat justum illud efficere de arbitrii sui meritis:* "that he might constantly be *master of his own conduct* by voluntarily doing good, and by voluntarily avoiding evil: because, man being appointed for God's judgment, it was necessary to the justice of God's sentence that man should be judged according to [*meritis*] the deserts of his free will."

3. IRENÆUS, bishop of Lyons, who flourished also in the second century, bears thus his testimony against bound will: — *Homo vero rationabilis, et secundum hoc similis Deo, liber arbitrio factus, et suæ potestatis, ipse sibi causa est ut aliquando quidem frumentum, aliquando autem palea fiat; quapropter et juste condemnabitur.* (Lib. iv, adv. Hæret. cap. 9.) That is, "Man, a reasonable being, and in that respect like God, is made *free in his will;* and being endued with power to conduct himself, *he is a cause of his becoming* sometimes wheat and sometimes chaff;* therefore will he be justly condemned." Again: *Dedit ergo Deus bonum, &c, et qui operantur quidum illud, gloriam et honorem percipient. quoniam operati sunt bonum, cum possent non operari illud, Hi autem qui illud non operantur, judicium Dei nostri recipient, quoniam non sunt operati bonum cum possent operari illud:* "God gives goodness, and they who do good shall obtain honour and glory; because they have done good, *when they could forbear doing it.* And they who do it not, shall receive the just judgment of our God; because they have not done good, *when they could have done it.*" Once more: *Non tantum in operibus, sed etiam in fide, liberum, et suæ potestatis, arbitrium servavit homini Deus.* (Ibid. lib. 4, cap. 62.) "God has left man's will free, and at his own disposal, not only with regard to works, but also with regard to faith." Nor did Irenæus say here more than St. Augustine does in this well-known sentence: *Posse credere est omnium, credere vero fidelium:* "To have a power to believe is the prerogative of all men; but actually to believe is the prerogative of the faithful."

---

* According to the doctrine maintained in these pages, God is the first cause of our conversion, or of our "becoming wheat." But man is the first cause of his own perversion, or his "becoming chaff."

4. ORIGEN nobly contends for liberty: he grants rather too much than too little of it: he continually recommends καλην προαιρεσιν, "a good choice," which he frequently calls την ροπην του αυτεξουσιου, "the inclination of the powerful principle whereby we are masters of our own conduct." He observes that we are not at liberty to *see*, but (to κριναι — το χρησασθαι την ροπην,την ευδοκησιν)" to judge; to use our power of choice and our approbation." And in the solution of some scriptures, which seem to contradict one another, he refutes the sentiment of those who reject the doctrine of our co-operating with Divine grace, and who think ουκ ημετερον εργον ειναι το κατ' αρετην βιουν, αλλα παντα θειαν χαριν, "That it is not our own work to lead a virtuous life, but that it is entirely the work of Divine grace."

5. ST. CYPRIAN and LACTANTUS speak the same language, as the learned reader may see by turning to the seventh book of *Vossius' History of Pelagianism*. Nor did St. Basil dissent from them, if we may judge of his sentiments by the following passage, which is extracted from his thirty- seventh homily, where he proves that God is not the author of evil: — "What is forced is not pleasing to God, but what is done from a truly virtuous motive, and virtue comes from the will, not from necessity." Hence it appears that, in this father's account, necessity is a kind of *compulsion* contrary to the freedom of the will. "For," adds he, "the will depends on what is within us; and within us is free will."

6. GREGORIUS NYSSENUS is of one mind with his brother ST. BASIL. For speaking of faith, he says, that it is placed "within the reach of our free election." And again: "We say of faith what the Gospel contains, namely, that he who is begotten by spiritual regeneration, knows of whom he is begotten, and what kind of a living creature he becomes. For spiritual regeneration is the only kind of regeneration which puts it in our power to become what we choose to be." (*Greg. Catech. Disc.* chap. 36, and chap. 6.)

7. ST. CHRYSOSTOM is so noted an advocate for free will, that CALVIN complains first of him. Part of Calvin's complaint runs thus: — *Habet Chrysostomus alicubi, &c.* (Inst. lib. 2, cap. 2, sec. 4.) That is, "St. Chrysostom says somewhere, 'Forasmuch as God has put good and evil in our own power, (*electionis liberum donavit arbitrium*,) he has given us a free power to choose the one or the other; and as he does not retain us against our will, so he embraces us when we are willing.'" Again: "Often a wicked man, if he will, is changed into a good man; and a good man, through sloth, falls away[*] and becomes wicked; because God has endued us with free agency: nor

---

[*] I have advanced several arguments to prove that Judas was sincere, when Christ chose him to the apostleship. I beg leave to confirm them by the judgment of two of the fathers. St. Chrysostom, in his fifty- second discourse, says, Ο Ιουδα; Βασιλειας υιος πρωτον ην, &c. That is, "Judas was at first a child of the kingdom, and heard it said to him with the disciples, 'You shall sit upon twelve thrones;' but at last he became a child of hell." And St. Ambrose, upon Romans 9:13, has these remarkable words, *Non est personarum acceptio in præscientia Dei*, &c, That is, "There is no respect of persons in God's foreknowledge; for prescience is that whereby he knows assuredly how the will of every man will be, in which he will continue, and by which he shall be damned or crowned, &c. They who, as God knows also, will persevere in goodness, are frequently bad before; and they who, as he knows also, will be found evil at last, are sometimes good before, &c. For both Saul and Judas were once good." Hence it is, that he

does he make us do things necessarily, but he places proper remedies before us, and suffers all to be done *according to the will* of the patient," &c. From these words of St. Chrysostom, Calvin draws this conclusion: — *Porro Græci præ aliis, atque inter eos singulariter Chrysostomus, in extollenda humanæ voluntatis facultate modum excesserunt.* That is, "The Greek fathers above others, and among them especially Chrysostom, have exceeded the bounds in extolling *the power of the human will.*" Hence it appears that, Calvin himself being judge, the fathers, but more particularly the Greek fathers, and among them St. Chrysostom, strongly opposed bound will and necessity.

8. ST. AMBROSE, a Latin father, was also a strenuous defender of the second Gospel axiom, which stands or falls with the doctrine of free will. Take two proofs of it: — *Ideo omnibus opera sanitatis detulit, ut quicunque periret mortis suæ causas sibi adscribat; qui curari noluit cum remedium haberet quo posset evadere.* (*Amb. lib. 2, de Cain et Abel, cap.* 12.) That is, "God affords to all the means of recovery, that whoever perishes may impute his own destruction to *himself;* for-as much as *he would not* be cured when *he had a remedy whereby he might have escaped.*" Again, commenting upon these words of Christ, "It is not mine to give," &c, he says, *Non est meum qui Justitiam servo, non Gratiam. Denique ad Patrem referens addidit, " Quibus paratum est," ut ostendat Patrem quoque non petitionibus deferre solere, sed* MERITIS; *quia Deus personarum acceptor non est. Unde et apostolus ait, "Quos præscivit prædestinavit." Non enim ante prædestinavit.* (*Amb. de fide. cap.* 4.) That is, "It is not mine [to give the next seat to my person] in point of justice, for I do not speak in point of favour; and referring the matter to his Father, he adds, *To them for whom it is prepared,* to show that the Father also [in point of reward] is not wont to yield to prayer, but (*meritis*) to worthiness; because God [when he acts as judge and rewarder] is no respecter of persons. Hence it is that the apostle says, *Those whom God foreknew he predestinated.* For he did not predestinate to reward them before he foreknew them" [as persons fit to be rewarded.] From this excellent quotation it appears that St. Ambrose maintained the two Gospel axioms, or the doctrines of grace and justice, of favour and worthiness, on which hang the election of distinguishing grace, and the election of remunerative justice, which the Calvinists perpetually confound, and which I have explained, section twelfth.

9. ST. JEROME, warm as he was against Pelagius, is evidently of the same mind with the other fathers, where he says: — *Liberi arbitrii nos condidit Deus. Nec ad virtutes nec ad vitia necessitate trahimur. Alioquin ubi necessitas est, nec damnatio nec corona est.* That is, "God hath endued us with free will. We are not *necessarily* drawn either to virtue or to vice. For where necessity rules, there is no room left either for damnation or for the crown." Again, in his third book against the Pelagians, he says: — *Etiam his qui mali futuri sunt, dari protestatem conversionis et penitentiæ.* That is, "Even to those who shall be wicked, God gives power to repent and turn to him." Again, upon Isaiah 1, *Liberum servat arbitrium, ut in utramque partem, non ex præjudicio Dei, sed ex meritis singulorum, vel pæna vel præmium sit.* "Our will is kept free to turn either way, that God may dispense his rewards and punishments, not according to his own prejudice, but *according to the merits* [that is, according to *the works*] of every one." Once more: he says to Ctesiphon, *Frustra blasphemas, et ignorantium auribus ingeris, nos Liberium Arbitrium*

says, in another place, "Sometimes they are at first good, who afterward become and continue evil; and in this respect they are said to be written in the book of life, and blotted out of it."

condemnare. Damnetur ille qui damnat. That is, "You speak evil of us without ground; you tell the ignorant that we condemn free will; but let the man who condemns it, be condemned."

When I read these explicit testimonies of ST. JEROME, in favour of free will, I no longer wonder that Calvin should find fault with him, as well as with ST. CHRYSOSTOM. Take Calvin's own words: (*Inst. lib.* 2, *cap.* 2, *sec.* 4.) *Ait Hieronymus (Dial.* 3, *contra Pelag. &c.) Nostrum [est] offerre quod possumus; Illius [Dei] implere quod non possumus.* "Jerome says, (in his third dialogue against Pelagianism,) *it is our part to offer what we can. It is God's part to fill up what we cannot.* You see clearly by these quotations," adds Calvin, "that they [these fathers, upon the Calvinian plan,] attributed to man too much power to be virtuous." Such a conclusion naturally becomes Calvin. But what I cannot help wondering at is, that Zelotes should indifferently call all the advocates for free will, Pelagians, when St. Jerome, who, next to St. Augustine, distinguished himself by his opposition to Pelagianism, is so strenuous a defender of the doctrine of free will, in the books which he wrote against Pelagius.

10. EPIPHANIUS confirms this doctrine where he says, *Sane quidem justius a stellis, quæ necessitatem pariunt, pœnæ repetantur, quam ab eo qui quod agit necessitate aductus aggreditur.* (Epiph. advers. Hær. 50. 1.) "It would be more just to punish the stars, which make a wicked action *necessary*, than to punish the poor man, who does that wicked action by *necessity*." He expresses himself still more strongly in the same book. Speaking of the Pharisees, who were rigid Predestinarians, he says, *Est illud vero extremæ cujusdam imperitiæ, ne dicam amentiæ, cum resurrectionem mortuorum esse fateare, ac justissimum cujusque facti judicium constitutum, fatum nihilominus esse ullum asserere. Qui enim duo ista convenire possunt,* JUDICIUM *atque* FATUM! That is, "It is extreme ignorance, not to say *madness*, to allow the resurrection of the dead, and a day of most righteous judgment for every action; and at the same time to assert that there is a destiny; for how can these two agree together, a JUDGMENT AND A DESTINY?" (or necessity?)

11. ST. BERNARD grants rather more liberty than I contend for, where he says, *Sola voluntas, quoniam pro ingenita libertate aut dissentire sibi, aut præter se in aliquo consentire nulla vi nulla cogitur necessitate, non immerito justum vel injustum, beatitudine seu miseria dignam ac capacem creaturam constituit, prout scilicet justitiæ, injustitiæve consenserit.* (Bern. De Grat. et lib. Arb.) That is, "The will alone can make a man deservedly just or unjust, and can deservedly render him fit for bliss or misery, as it consents either to righteousness or to iniquity; forasmuch as the will, according to its *innate liberty*, cannot be forced to will or nill any thing against its own dictates."

12. CYRILLUS ALEXANDRIUS upon John, (book vi, chap. 21,) vindicating God's goodness against the horrid hints of those who make him the author of sin, as all rigid Predestinarians do, says with great truth: — "The visible sun rises above our horizon, that it may communicate the gift of its brightness to all, and make its light shine upon all; but if any one shut his eyes or *willingly* turn himself from the sun, *refusing* the benefit of its light, he wants its illumination, and remains in darkness: not through the fault of the sun, but *through his own fault.* Thus the true Sun who came to enlighten those that sit in darkness, visited the earth, that *in different manners and degrees* he might impart to all the gift of knowledge and grace, and illuminate the inward eyes of all, &c. But many reject the gift of this heavenly light *freely given to them*, and have closed the eyes of their minds, lest so excellent an irradiation of the eternal light should shine unto them. It is not then through the defect of the true Sun, but only

through their own iniquity," i.e. through their own perverse free will. And, (book i, chap. 11,)the same father, speaking on the same subject, says, "Let not the world accuse the word of God and his eternal light; but its own weakness: for the Sun enlightens, but *man rejects the grace that is given him*, blunts the edge of the understanding granted him, &c, and, as a prodigal, turns his sight to the creatures, neglecting to go forward, and through laziness and negligence [not through necessity and predestination] buries the illumination, and despises this grace."

13. CLEMENS ALEXANDRINUS is exactly of the same sentiment; for, calling "the Divine word" what St. Cyril calls "Divine light," he says, "The Divine word has cried; calling all, knowing well those that will not obey; and yet, because it is *in our power, either to obey or not to obey*, that none may plead ignorance, it has made a righteous call, and requireth but that which is according to the ability and strength of every one." (CLEM ALEX. *Strom. book* 2.)

14. The father who wrote the book *De Vocatione Gentium*, says, *Sicut qui crediderunt juvantur ut in fide maneant; ita qui nondum crediderunt, juvantur ut credant: et quemadmodum illi in sua potestate habent, ut exeant; ita et isti in sua habent potestate ut veniant.* That is, "As they that have believed are helped to abide in the faith; so they that have not yet believed are helped to believe; and as the former have it in their power to go out, so the latter have it in their power to come in."

15. ARNOBIUS produces this objection of a heathen: "If the Saviour of mankind be come, as you say, why does he not save all?" and he answers it thus: — *Patet omnibus fons vitæ*, &c. That is, "The fountain of life is open to all, nor is any one deprived of the right of drinking: but if thy pride be so great that thou refusest the offered gift and benefits, &c, why dost thou blame him [Christ] who invites thee," *cujus solæ sunt hæ partes, ut sub tui juris arbitrio fructum suæ benignitatis exponat?* (ARN. *Contra Gentes, lib.* 2,) "whose full part it is to submit the fruit of his bounty to a choice that depends upon thyself?"

16. PROSPER, although he was St. Augustine's disciple, does justice to the truth which I maintain. For speaking of some that fell away from holiness to uncleanness, he says, *Non ex eo necessitatem pereundi habuerunt quia predestinati non sunt; sed ideo prædestinati non sunt; quia tales futuri ex voluntaria prævaricatione præsciti sunt.* (PROSP. *Ad. Ob. iii, Gall.*) That is, "They did not lie under a necessity of perishing because they were not elected [to a crown of life;] but they were not elected [to that reward] because they were foreknown to be such as they are by *their voluntary iniquity*." The same father allows that it is absurd to believe a day of judgment, and to deny free will. *Judicium futurum, says he, omnino non esset si homines Dei voluntate peccarent.* (PROS. *ad. obj.* 10, *Vinc.*) That is, "By no means would there be a day of judgment, if men sinned *by the will or decree of God*." The reason is plain, if we sinned through any necessity laid on us by "the will of God," or by predestinating fate, we might say, like the heathen poet, *Fati ista culpa est; nemo fit fato nocens:* "It is the fault of fate: necessity excuses any one."

17. FULGENTIUS, although he was also St. Augustine's disciple, cuts up the doctrine of bound will by the root, where he says: — *Nec justitia justa dicetur, si puniendum reum non invenisse, sed fecisse dicatur. Major vero injustitia, si lapso Deus retribuat pœnam, quem stantem dicitur prædestinasse ad ruinam."* (FULG. 50. 1, *ad Mon. cap.* 22.) That is, "Justice could not be said to be just if it did not find, but made man an offender.

And the injustice would be still greater, if God, after having predestinated a man to ruin when he stood, inflicted punishment upon him after his fall."

18. If any of the fathers is a rigid bound willer, it is heated AUGUSTINE: nevertheless, in his cool moments, he grants as much free will as I contend for. Hear him: *Nos quidem sub fato stellarum nullius hominis genesim ponimus, ut liberum arbitrium voluntatis, quo bene vel male vivitur, propter justum Dei judicium ab omni necessitatis vinculo vindicemus.* (AUG. 1, 2, *contr. Faust.* c. 5.) That is, "We place no man's nativity under the fatal power of the stars, that we may assert the liberty of the will, whereby our actions are rendered either moral or immoral, and keep it free from every bond of necessity, on account of the righteous judgment of God." Again: *Nemo habet in potestate quid veniat in mentem; sed consentire vel dissentire propriæ voluntatis est.* (AUG. *De Litera et Spiritu, cap.* 34.) That is, "Nobody can help what comes into his mind; but to consent or to dissent from involuntary *suggestions*, is the prerogative of our own will."[*] Once more: *Initium salutis nostræ a Deo miserante habemus; ut acquiescamus salutiferæ inspirationi, nostræ est potestatis. (De Dogmatibus Ecclesiasticis, cap.* 21.) That is, "The beginning of our salvation flows from the merciful God; but it is *in our power* to consent to his saving inspiration." And what he means by "having a thing in our power," he explains in these words, *Hoc quisque in sua potestate habere dicitur, quod si vult facit, si non vult non facit.* (AUG. *De Spir. et lit. c.* 31.) That is, "Every one has that in his own power which he does if he will, and which he can forbear doing if he will not do it."

Agreeable to this is that rational observation, which, I think, is St. Augustine's, also: — *Si non est liberum arbitrium, non est quod salvetur. Si non est gratia, non est unde salvetur:* "If there be no free will, there is nothing to be saved: if there be no free grace, there is nothing whereby we may be saved:" a golden saying this, which is as weighty as my motto, "If you take away free grace, how does God save the world? And if you take away free will, how does he judge the world?"

So great is the force of truth, that the same prejudiced father, commenting upon this text, "Every man that hath this hope in him purifieth himself," 1 John 3:3, does not scruple to say: — "Behold after what manner he has *not taken away free will*, that the apostle should say, 'keepeth himself pure.' Who keepeth us pure, except God? But God keepeth thee not thus *against thy will*. Therefore inasmuch as *thou joinest thy will to God*, thou keepest thyself pure. Thou keepest thyself pure, not of thyself, but by him who comes to dwell in thee. Yet because in this thou *dost something* of thine own will, therefore is *something also attributed to thee*. Yet so it is ascribed to thee, that still thou mayest say, with the psalmist, 'Lord, be thou my helper!' If thou sayest, 'Be

---

[*] Dr. Tucker judiciously unfolds St. Augustine's thought, where he says, "There is a sense, in which it may be allowed on the semi-Pelagian, [semi-Augustinian] or Arminian plan, that grace is irresistible: but it is a sense that can do no manner of service to the cause of Calvinism. Grace, for instance, especially *prevenient*, or preventing grace may be considered as a precious gift, or universal endowment, like the common gifts of health, strength, &c, in which case the recipient must necessarily receive them; for *he has not a power* to refuse. But after he has received them, *he may choose whether* he will apply them to any good and salutary purposes or not: and on this freedom of choice rests the proper distinction between good and evil, virtue and vice, morality and immorality. Grace therefore must be received; but, after it is received, it may be abused: the talent may be hid in a napkin, and the Spirit may be quenched, or have a despite done to it."

thou my helper,' thou *dost something;* for if thou dost nothing, how does he help?" Happy would it have been for the Church if St. Augustine had always done justice in this manner to the second, as well as to the first Gospel axiom! He would not have paved the way for free wrath, and Antinomian free grace. Nor could Mr. Wesley do more justice to both Gospel axioms than Augustine does in the following words: — *Non illi debent sibi tribuere, qui venerunt, quia vocati venerunt: nec illi, qui noluerant venire, debuerant alteri tribuere, sed tantum sibi: quia ut venirent vocati in libera erat voluntate.* (AUG. *lib.* 83, *Quæstionum.*) "They that came [to Christ] ought not to impute it to themselves, because they came, being called: and they that would not come, ought not to impute it to another, but only to themselves, because, when they were called, it was in the power of their free will to come." *Deus non deserit nisi desertus:* "God forsakes no man, unless he be first forsaken." (Quæst. 68.) Here is a right dividing of the word of truth! a giving God the glory of our salvation, without charging him with our destruction!

Nay, ST. JEROME and ST. AUGUSTINE, notwithstanding their warmth against Pelagius, have not only at times strongly maintained our remunerative election; but by not immediately securing the election of distinguishing grace, they have really granted him far more than I in conscience can do. Take the following instances of it: —

ST. JEROME upon Galatians 1, says, *Ex Dei præscientia evenit, ut quem scit justum futurum, prius diligat quam oriatur ex utero:* "It is owing to God's prescience that he loves those who he foresees will become just, before they come out of their mother's womb." Again, upon Malachi 1, he says, *Dilectio et odium Dei vel ex præscientia nascitur futurorum vel ex operibus:* "God's love and hatred spring from his foreknowledge of future events, or from our works." Nay, in his very dispute with the Pelagians, (book iii,) he declares that God *eligit quem bonum cernit,* "chooses him whom he sees good:" which is entirely agreeable to this unguarded assertion of St. Augustine: — *Nemo eligitur nisi jam distans ab illo qui rejicitur. Unde quod dictum est, quia "elegit nos Deus ante mundi constitutionem," non video quomodo sit dictum, nisi de præscientia fidei et operum pietatis.* (AUG. Quæst. 2, ad Simplicianum.) That is, "Nobody is chosen but as he already differs from him that is rejected. Nor do I see how it can be said that "God has chosen us before the beginning of the world," unless this be said with respect to God's foreknowledge of our faith and works of piety."

I call these assertions of St. Jerome and St. Augustine "unguarded," because they so maintain the election of remunerative justice as to leave no room for the election of distinguishing grace, which I have maintained in my exposition of Romans ix, and Ephesians i: an election this, which the Pelagians overlook, and which St. Paul secures when he says that God chose Jacob to the privileges of the covenant of peculiarity," before he had done any good, that the purpose of God according to the election [of superior grace] might stand not of works, but of [the superior kindness of] him that calleth:" an important election this, inconsistently given up by St. Augustine, when speaking of Jacob he says, in the above-quoted treatise, *Non electus est ut fieret bonus, sed bonus factus eligi potuit:* "He was not chosen that he might become good; but, being made good, he could be chosen."

I shall close these quotations from the fathers, with one more from St. Irenæus, who was Polycarp's disciple, and flourished immediately after the apostolic age: — *Quoniam omnes ejusdem sunt naturæ, et potentes retinere et operari bonum, et potentes rursum amittere id, et non facere; juste apud homines sensatos, quanto magis apud Deum, alii quidem laudantur, et dignum percipiunt testimonium electionis bonæ, et perseverantiæ; alii vero accusantur, et dignum percipiunt darmnum eo quod justum et bonum reprobaverunt.* (IREN. *Adv. Hær. lib. iv, cap.* 74.) That is, "Forasmuch as all men are of the same nature, having power to hold and to do that which is good, and having power again to lose it, and not to do what is right; before men of sense, (and how much more before God!) some are justly praised, and receive a worthy testimony, for making a good choice and persevering therein; while others are justly accused, and receive condign punishment, because they refused what is just and right."

If I am not mistaken, the preceding quotations prove, (1.) That the fathers in general pleaded for as much free will as we contend for. (2.) That the two champions of the doctrines of grace, Prosper and Fulgentius, and their Predestinarian leader, St. Augustine, when they considered (*justum Dei judicium*) "the righteous judgment of God," have (at times at least) maintained the doctrine of liberty as strongly as the rest of the fathers. And, (3.) That St. Augustine himself was so carried away once by the force of the arguments and scriptures which support the remunerative election of impartial justice, as rashly to give up the gratuitous election of distinguishing grace.

Should any of the above-mentioned fathers have contradicted himself, (as St. Augustine has done for one,) I hope I shall not be charged with "gross misrepresentations" for quoting them when they speak as the oracles of God. If at any time they deviate from that blessed rule, let them defend their deviations if they can; or let Zelotes and Honestus (who follow them when they go out of the way) do it for them. I repeat it, like a true Protestant, I rest the cause upon right reason and plain Scripture; and if I produce the sentiments of the fathers, it is merely to undeceive Zelotes, who thinks that all moderate free willers are Pelagian heretics, and that the fathers were as rigid bound willers as himself.

II. Proceed we to confirm the preceding quotations by the testimony of some modern divines.

1. Calvin says, *Quasi adhuc integer staret homo, semper apud Latinos Liberi Arbitrii nomen extiTitus Græcus vero non puduit multo arrogantius usurpare vocabulum. Siquidem αυτεξουσιον dixerunt, acsi potestas sui ipsius penes hominem fuisset.* (*Inst. lib. 2, cap. 2, sec. 4.*) "The Latin fathers have always retained the word FREE WILL, as if man stood yet upright. As for the Greek fathers, they have not been ashamed to make use of a much more arrogant expression; calling man αυτεξουσιον, [*free agent*, or *self manager.*] just as if man had a power to govern himself." This concession of Calvin decides the question. I need only observe that Calvin wrongs the fathers when he insinuates that they ascribed liberty to man, "as if man stood yet upright." No: they attributed to man a *natural* liberty to evil, and a *gracious* blood-bought liberty to good. Thus, like our reformers, they maintained man's free agency without derogating from God's grace.

2. Bishop ANDREWS, a moderate Calvinist, says, "I dare not condemn the fathers, who *almost all* assert we are elected and predestinated according to faith foreseen; that the necessity of damnation is hypothetical, not absolute, &c. That God is ready and at hand to bestow and communicate his grace, &c. It is the fault of men themselves, that what is offered is not actually conferred: for grace is not wanting to us, but we are wanting to that." And this he confirms, by this passage from St. Augustine: — "All men may turn themselves from the love of visible and temporal things to keep God's commands, *if they will;* because that light [Christ] is the light of all mankind."

3. The doctrine of free will stands or falls with the *conditionality* of the covenant of grace. Hence it is that all rigid bound willers abhor the word *condition:* nevertheless, Mr. Robert, a judicious Calvinist, sees the tide of the contrary doctrine so strong, that he says, in his *Mystery of the Bible,* "Sound writers, godly and learned, ancient and modern, foreign and domestic, do unanimously subscribe to the *conditionality* of the covenant of grace, in the sense before stated:" a sense this, which Bishop Davenant clearly expresses in these words: — "Peter, notwithstanding his predestination, might have been damned, if he had *voluntarily* continued in his impenitency." And Judas, notwithstanding his reprobation, might have been saved, if he had not *voluntarily* continued in his impenitency. (*Animadversions,* p. 241.)

4. DR. TUCKER observes, that although Vossius and Norris (who have each written a history of Pelagianism) differ in some points, yet they "agree that St. Augustine's [Calvinian] positions were allowed by his warmest defenders at that very time to be little better than novelties, if compared with the writings of the most ancient fathers, especially of the Greek Church." (*Letter to Dr. Kippis,* p. 79.)

5. EPISCOPIUS, in his answer to Capellus, p. 1, says, "Augustine, Prosper, and all the other divines of that age, [*quin et priorum omnium seculorum Patres,*] and the fathers of all the preceding ages, have not represented the grace of regeneration so *special* as to take away free will. On the contrary, they unanimously agree that the full effect of regenerating grace depends in some degree on man's free will: insomuch that, this grace being imparted, the consent or dissent of the human will may follow. I say the *consent* or *dissent,* lest some people should think that I understand by free will nothing but a certain willingness." The same learned author says, in his answer to Camero, chap. vi, "What is plainer than that the ancient divines, for three hundred years after Christ, those at least who flourished before St. Augustine, maintained the liberty of our will, or an indifference to two contrary things, free from all internal or external necessity! &c. Almost all the reformed divines confess it, when they are pressed by the authority of the fathers. Thus Melancthon on Romans 9, says, *Scriptores veteres omnes, præter Augustinum, ponunt aliquam causam electionis in nobis esse.*" That is, "All the ancient authors, except St. Augustine, allow that the cause of our election [to an eternal life of glory] is in some degree in ourselves."

6. VOSSIUS, a divine perfectly acquainted with all the ancient Christian writers, says, in the sixth book of his *Pelagian History,* "The Greek fathers ALWAYS, and ALL the Latin fathers who lived before Augustine, are wont to say that those men are predestinated to life [eternal glory] whom God foresaw would live piously and well; or, as some others speak, whom God foresaw would *believe and persevere,* &c. Which they so interpret, that predestination *unto glory* is made according to God's foreknowledge of faith and perseverance. But they did not mean the foreknowledge of such things, which a man was to do by the power of nature, *but by the strength of prevenient and subsequent grace.* Therefore this consent of antiquity is of no service to the Pelagians or semi-Pelagians, who both hold, that a reason of predestination, in all its effects, may be assigned from something in us. Whereas the orthodox* fathers

---

* I desire the reader to take notice that this doctrine of the absolute freedom of prevenient grace, or initial salvation, is all along maintained in my first Scale; and that if Vossius' account of the semi-Pelagians is exact, Zelotes cannot justly charge us with semi-Pelagianism: and we have as much right to be called orthodox as the fathers themselves.

acknowledge that the first grace [i.e. initial salvation] is not conferred of merit [or works] but freely. So that they thought no reason, *from any thing in us,* could be given of predestination to *prevenient grace.*"

7. DR. DAVENANT, Bishop of Salisbury, and one of the English divines who were sent to the synod of Dort, (in his "Animadversions upon a treatise entitled, *God's love to all Mankind,*" Cambridge edition, 1641, p. 48,) sets his seal to the preceding quotations in these words: — "The fathers, when they consider that the wills of men non-elected do commit all their evil acts *freely,* usually say that *they had a power to have done the contrary.*" And he himself espouses their sentiment: for speaking of Cain's murder, Absalom's incest, and Judas' treason, he says, p. 253, "All these sinful actions, and the like, are committed by reprobates, out of their own free election, having a power whereby they might have abstained from committing them." Again, p. 198, he says, "They [God's decrees] leave the wills of men to as much liberty as the Divine prescience* does. And this is the general opinion of divines, though they differ about the manner of reconciling man's liberty with God's predestination." Once more, p. 326, &c: "The decree of preterition neither taketh away any *power of doing well,* wherewith persons non-elected are endued, &c. Neither is it a decree binding God's hands from giving them sufficient grace to do many good acts, which they wilfully refuse to do, &c. The non-elect have a power, or possibility to believe or repent at the preaching of the Gospel; *which power might be reduced into act,* if the voluntary frowardness and resistiveness of their own hearts were not the only hindering cause." Page 72, the learned bishop grants again all that we contend for, in these words: — "In bad and wicked actions of the reprobate, their freedom of will is not vain; because thereby their consciences are convicted of their guiltiness and misdeserts, and God's justice is cleared in their damnation. Neither is there any indeclinable or insuperable necessity domineering over free will, more than in the opinion of the remonstrants." Once more, p. 177: "Predestination (says he) did not compel or necessitate Judas to betray and sell his Master, &c. The like may be said of all other sinners who commit such sins upon deliberation, and so proceed to election, [i.e. to choose evil;] having in themselves a natural power of understanding, whereby they were able otherwise to have deliberated, and thereupon *otherwise* to have chosen. And we see by experience that traitors and adulterers, fully bent to commit such wicked acts, can, and oftentimes *do refrain* putting them in practice upon better deliberation. This is a demonstration that they can choose the doing or the forbearing to do such wicked acts."

From these quotations it appears that, when judicious and candid Calvinists have to do with judicious and learned remonstrants, they are obliged to turn moderate free willers, or fly in the face of the sacred writers, the fathers, and the best divines of their own persuasion.

Since the preceding pages were written, Providence has thrown in my way DR. WHITBY'S *Discourse* on the points of doctrine which are balanced in the "Scripture Scales." He highly deserves a place among the modern divines who confirm the

---

* This would be true if it were spoken of the predestination which I contend for: but it is a great mistake when it is affirmed of the doctrine of efficacious, absolute predestination maintained by Zelotes.

contents of this section, concerning the antiquity of the doctrine of free will, evangelically connected with the doctrines of free grace and just wrath. I therefore produce here the following extract from his useful book, second edition, printed in London, 1735: —

In the preface, p. 3, he says, with respect to the leading doctrines of election and reprobation, in which he entirely dissents from Calvin: "I found I still sailed with the stream of antiquity, seeing only one, St Augustine, with his two boatswains, Prosper and Fulgentius, tugging hard against it, and often driven back into it by the strong current of Scripture, reason, and common sense." As a proof of this, the doctor produces, among many more, the following quotations from the fathers, which I transcribe only in English; referring those who wish to see the Greek or Latin to the doctor's *discourses*, where the books, the pages, and the very words of the fathers are quoted: —

Page 95, &c, Dr. Whitby says, "They [the fathers] unanimously declare that God hath left it in the power of man 'to turn to vice or virtue,' says Justin Martyr: 'to choose or refuse faith and obedience, to believe or not, say Irenæus, Clemens Alexandrinus, Tertullian, and St. Cyprian: 'that every one, &c, renders himself either righteous or disobedient,' says Clemens of Alexandria: 'that God hath left in our own power to turn to, or from good; to be good or bad, to do what is righteous or unrighteous:' so Athanasius, Epiphanius, Macarius, St. Chrysostom, Theodoret, and Cyril of Alexandria: 'that our happiness or punishment depends on our own choice; that it is our own choice to be a holy seed, or the contrary; to fall into hell, or enjoy the kingdom; to be children of the night or the day: by virtue to be God's or by wickedness to be the devil's children:' so Cyril of Jerusalem, Basil, Chrysostom, and Gregory Nyssen: 'that we are vessels of wrath, or of mercy, from our own choice, every one preparing himself to be a vessel of wrath from his own wicked inclination; or to be a vessel of Divine love by faith, because they have rendered themselves fit for [rewarding] mercy:' so Origen, Macarius, Chrysostom, Æcumenius, and Theophylact."

Page 336, &c, the doctor has the following words and striking quotations: — "All these arguments [for the freedom of the will of man] are strongly confirmed by the concurrent suffrage, and the express and frequent declarations of the fathers. Thus Justin Martyr having told us that man would not be worthy of praise or recompense, 'did he not choose good of himself, nor worthy of punishment for doing evil, if he did not this* of himself,' says, 'This the Holy Spirit hath taught us by

---

* This good father, to guard the doctrine of grace as well as that of justice, should have observed that free grace is the first cause, and free will the second, in our choice of moral good; but that free will is the first cause in our choice of moral evil. Forgetting to make these little distinctions, he has given the Calvinists just room to complain, and has afforded the Pelagians a precedent to bear hard upon the doctrine of grace. Should some prejudiced reader think that this doctrine ascribes too much to man, because it makes free will a first cause in the choice of moral evil, I answer two things: (1.) To make God the first cause of moral evil is to turn Manichee, and assert that there is an evil as well as a good principle in the Godhead. (2.) When we say that free will chooses moral evil of itself, without necessity, and is, of consequence, the first cause of its own evil choice; we do not mean that free will is its own first cause. No: God made the free-willing soul, and freely endued man with the power of choosing without necessity. Thus God's supremacy is fully secured. If, therefore, in the day of probation, we

Moses in these words, *See, I have set before thee good and evil; choose the good.*' Clemens Alexandrinus says, 'The prophecy of Isaiah saith, If you be willing, &c, demonstrating that both the choice and the refusal, (viz. of faith and experience, of which he there speaketh,) are in our own power.' Tertullian pronounces them 'unsound in the faith, corrupter, of the Christian discipline, and excusers of all sin, who so refer all things to the will of God, by saying, *Nothing is done without his appointment,* as that we cannot understand that any thing is left to ourselves to do.' St. Cyprian proves, *Credendi vel non credendi libertatem in arbitrio positam,* 'that to believe or not, is left to our own free choice,' from Deuteronomy 30:19, and Isaiah 1:19. Theodoret, having cited these words of Christ, *If any man thirst, let him come to me and drink,* adds: 'Ten thousand things of this nature may be found, both in the Gospels and other writings of the apostles, clearly manifesting the liberty and self election of the nature of man.' St. Chrysostom speaks thus: — 'God saith, *If you will,* and *if you will not,* giving us power, and putting it in our own option to be virtuous or vicious. The devil saith, *Thou canst not avoid thy fate.* God saith, *I have put before thee fire and water, life and death, stretch forth thy hand to whether of them thou wilt.* The devil says, *It is not in thee to stretch forth thy hand to them.*' St. Austin proves, from those words of Christ, *Make the tree good, &c,* or *make the tree evil (in nostra potestate situm esse mutare voluntatem,)* 'that it is put in our own power to change the will.' It would be endless to transcribe all that the fathers say upon this head. Origen is also copious in this assertion: for having cited these words, *And now, Israel, what does the Lord thy God require of thee?* he adds: 'Let them blush at these words, who deny that man has free will. How could God require that of man which he had not in his power to offer him?' And again: 'The soul,' saith he, 'does not incline to either part out of necessity, for then neither vice nor virtue could be ascribed to it; nor would its choice of virtue deserve reward; nor its declination to vice punishment. But the liberty of the will is preserved in all things, that it may incline to what it will; as it is written, *Behold I have set before thee life and death.*' St. Augustine also, from many passages in which the Scripture saith, *Do not so, or so;* or *do this, or that,* lays down this general rule: that all such places sufficiently demonstrate the liberty of the will: and this he saith against them, *qui sic gratiam Dei defendunt, ut negent liberum arbitrium,* 'who so assert the grace of God, as to deny the liberty of the will.'"

Page 340. "They [the fathers] add, that all God's commands and prohibitions, &c, would be vain and unreasonable, and all his punishments unjust, and his rewards groundless, if man, after the fall, had not still the liberty to do what is commanded, and forbear what is forbidden. For, saith St. Austin, 'the Divine precepts would profit none, if they had not free will, by which they, doing them, might obtain the promised rewards, &c. These precepts cut off men's excuse from ignorance,' &c, But then, 'because others,' saith he, 'accuse God of being wanting in giving them power to do good or inducing them to sin:' against these men he cites that known passage of the son of Sirach, *God left man in the hands of his counsel, if he would to keep the commandments,* &c. And then cries out, 'Behold, here, a very plain proof

---

have the cast, when good and evil are set before us; our free will is not placed on a level with God by this tremendous power, but we place ourselves voluntarily under the rewarding sceptre of free grace, or the iron rod of just wrath. By this mean God maintains both his sovereignty as a king, and his justice as a judge; while man is still a subject fit to be graciously rewarded or justly punished, according to the doctrines of free grace and just wrath.

of the liberty of the human will! &c, for how does he command, if man hath not free will or power to obey? What do all God's commands show, but the free will of man? For they would not be given, if man had not that freedom of will by which he could obey them.' And therefore in his book, *De Fide*, against the Manichees, who denied that man had free will, and that it was in his power to do well or ill, he makes this an indication of their blindness: — 'Who,' saith he, 'will not cry out that it is folly to command him who has not liberty to do what is commanded; and that it is unjust to condemn him who has it not in his power to do what is required? And yet these miserable men [the Manichees] understand not that they ascribe this wickedness and injustice to God.' Clemens of Alexandria declares 'that neither praises nor reprehensions, rewards nor punishments are just, if the soul has not the power of choosing or abstaining: but evil is involuntary.' Yea, he makes this 'the very foundation of salvation, without which there could be neither any reasonable baptism, nor Divine ordering of our natures, because faith would not be in our own power.' 'The soul,' says Origen, 'acts by her own choice, and it is free for her to incline to whatever part she will: and therefore God's judgment of her is just, because of her own accord she complies with good or bad monitors.' 'One of these two things is necessary,' saith Epiphanius, 'either that there should be no judgment, because men act not freely; or if laws be justly made by God, and punishments threatened to, and inflicted on the wicked, and God's judgments be according to truth, there is no fate; for therefore is one punished for his sins, and another praised for his good works, because he has it in his power to sin or not.' 'For how,' says Theodoret, 'can he justly punish a nature [with endless torments] which had no power to do good, but was bound in the bonds of wickedness?' And again: 'God, having made the rational nature with power over its own actions, averts men from evil things, and provokes them to do what is good by laws and exhortations, but he does not necessitate the unwilling to embrace what is better, that he may not overturn the bounds of nature.' Innumerable are the passages of this nature, which might be cited from the fathers."

Page 361, &c, the doctor produces again many quotations from the fathers, in defence of liberty. Take some of them: "Justin Martyr argues: 'If man has not power by his free choice to avoid evil, and to choose the good, he is unblamable, whatsoever he does.' Origen, in his Dissertation against Fate, declares 'that the asserters of it do free men from all fault; and cast the blame of all the evil that is done upon God.' Eusebius declares 'that this opinion absolves sinners, as doing nothing on their own accord which was evil; and would cast all the blame of all the wickedness committed in the world upon God and upon his providence.' 'That men lie under no necessity from God's foreknowledge [which was of old the chief argument of the fatalists, espoused of late by Mr. Hobbes, and is still made the refuge of the Predestinarians] may be thus proved,' saith Origen, 'because the prophets are exhorted in the Scripture to call men to repentance, and to do this in such words, as if it were unknown whether they would turn to God, or would continue in their sins; as in those words of Jeremiah, *Perhaps they will hear, and turn every man from his evil way:* and this is said, not that God understood not whether they would do this or not, but to demonstrate the almost equal balance of their power so to do, and that they might not despond, or remit of their endeavours by an imagination that God's foreknowledge laid a necessity upon them, as not leaving it in their power to turn, and so was the cause of their sin.' 'If men,' says Chrysostom, 'do pardon their fellow men, when they are necessitated to do a thing, much more should this be done to men compelled by fate [or by decrees] to do what they do; for if it be absurd to punish them, who by the force of barbarians are compelled to any action, it must be more so to punish him who is compelled by a stronger power.' 'If fate be established,' says Eusebius, 'philosophy and piety are overthrown.'"

Page 364, the doctor adds: — "Though there is in the rational soul a power to do evil, 'it is not evil on that account,' saith Didymus Alexandrinus, 'but because she will freely use that power; and this is not only ours, but the opinion of all who speak orthodoxly of rational beings.' St. Augustine lays down this as the true definition of sin: — 'Sin is the will to obtain or retain that which justice forbids, and from which *it is free* for us to abstain.' Whence he concludes 'that no man is worthy of dispraise or punishment, for not doing that which he *has not power* to do; and that if sin be worthy of dispraise and punishment, it is not to be doubted, (*tunc esse peccatum cum et liberum est nolle*) that our choice is sin, when we are free not to make that choice.' 'These things,' saith he, 'the shepherds sing upon the mountains, and the poets in the theatres, and the unlearned in their assemblies, and the learned in the libraries, and the doctors in the schools, and the bishops in the churches, and mankind throughout the whole earth.'"

I conclude this extract by accounting for St. Augustine's inconsistency. He was a warm man: and such men, when they write much, and do not yet firmly stand upon the line of moderation, are apt to contradict themselves, as often as they use the armour of righteousness on the right hand and on the left, to oppose contrary errors. Hence it is, that when St. Augustine opposed the Manichees, who were rigid bound willers, he strongly maintained free will with Pelagius; and when he opposed the Pelagians, who were rigid free willers, he strongly maintained bound will and necessity with Manes. The Scripture doctrine of free will lies between the error of Pelagius and that of Manes. The middle way between these extremes is, I hope, clearly pointed out in section 20. Upon the whole, he must be perverse who can cast his eyes upon the numerous quotations which Dr. Whitby has produced, and deny that the fathers held the doctrine of the Scripture Scales with respect to free will; and that, if they leaned to one extreme, it was rather to that of the Pelagians, than to that of the rigid bound willers, who clothe their favourite doctrine of necessity with the specious names of invincible fate, irrevocable decrees, or absolute predestination.

III. Zelotes endeavours to hide his error under the wings of the Church of England, as well as behind the authority of the fathers, but with as little success. I design to show his mistake in this respect, in an "Essay on the Seventeenth Article." In the meantime I shall observe, that a few years before Archbishop Cranmer drew up our "articles of religion," he helped the other reformers to compose a book called, "The Necessary Doctrine of a Christian Man," and added to it a section upon free will, in which free will is defined "a power of the will joined with reason, whereby a reasonable creature, without constraint, in things of reason, discerneth and willeth good and evil; but *chooseth good by the assistance of God's grace, and evil of itself.*" "Wherefore," adds Cranmer, "men be to be warned, that they do not impute to God their vice or their damnation, but to themselves, which by free will have abused the grace and benefits of God. All men be also to be monished, and chiefly preachers, that in this high matter they, looking on both sides, [*i.e.* regarding both Gospel axioms] so attemper and moderate themselves, that neither they so preach the grace of God [with Zelotes] that they take away thereby free will; nor, on the other side, so extol free will [with Honestus] that injury be done to the grace of God."

I grant that in the book, from which this quotation[*] is taken, there are some errors which Cranmer afterward renounced, as he had done absolute predestination before. But that he never varied from the doctrine of free will laid down in the above-mentioned passage, is evident from the tenor of our articles of religion, which he penned, and which contain exactly the doctrine of the above-quoted lines.

Hear him and the Church of England publicly maintaining free grace and free will. In the tenth article on free will they assert, that "we have no power to do good works pleasant and acceptable to God, without the grace of God, by Christ preventing [i.e. first visiting] us, that we may have a good will." Let the article be thrown into the scales, and the judicious reader will easily see that it directly or indirectly guards the very doctrine which the fathers maintained, and which we defend, No. 1, against Honestus, and No. 2, against Zelotes.

I.	II.
"The condition of man after the fall of Adam is such, that he cannot turn and prepare himself by his own natural strength, &c, to faith and calling upon God."	The condition of man after the fall of Adam (and the promise made to him) is such, that he can turn and prepare himself to faith and calling upon God, although not by his own natural strength.

---

[*] Burnet's *History of the Reformation*, (second edition, part i, p. 291,) and a pamphlet entitled, *A Dissertation on the Seventeenth Article*, &c, furnish me with these important quotations. The last seems greatly to embarrass Mr. Hill. He attempts to set it aside, by urging: (1.) That in *The Necessary Erudition of a Christian Man*, "the doctrines of the mass, transubstantiation, &c, are particularly taught as necessary to salvation." (2.) That "Bonner and Gardiner, as well as Cranmer, gave their *imprimatur* to it." And, (3.) That "even in this book the doctrine of predestination is not denied, but the thing itself clearly admitted; only it is laid down in such a manner as not to, &c, supersede the necessity of personal holiness." To this I answer: (1.) That Cranmer expressly recanted the errors which Mr. Hill mentions, but instead of recanting the doctrines of free grace and free will, he proceeded upon that very plan, in drawing up our articles and liturgy, as I shall prove just now. (2.) That Bonner and Gardiner gave their *imprimatur* to this quotation, no more proves that it contains false doctrine, than their subscribing to the thirty articles some years after shows that our articles are heretical. (3.) We thank Mr. Hill for informing the public that the book called *The Erudition of a Christian Man*, "clearly admits the doctrine of predestination only in such a manner as not to supersede the necessity of holiness." This is just the manner in which we admit it after Cranmer in our seventeenth article. And we argue thus: — If the doctrine of free grace and free will, admirably well balanced by Cranmer in *The Erudition of a Christian Man*, be a false doctrine, because the book contains some Papistical errors; does it not follow that the doctrine of *a predestination consistent with personal holiness* is a false doctrine, since (Mr. Hill himself being judge) such a doctrine is clearly admitted in that very book? If Mr. Hill give himself time to weigh this short answer to his pamphlet, entitled, "Cranmer vindicated from the charge of [what he is pleased to call] Pelagianism, by the author of Goliath slain;" I make no doubt but he will see that Goliath, (if that word means our doctrine,) far from being *slain*, is not so much as *wounded*.

"Wherefore we have no power to do good works, &c, without the grace of God by Christ preventing us, [i.e. visiting us first,] that we may have a good will, and working with, [not without] us, when we have that good will."

Wherefore we have a power to do good works, &c, through the grace of God by Christ preventing us, (i.e. visiting us first,) that we may have a good will, and working with, (not without us,) when we have that good will.

Who does not see that there is not the least disagreement between these balanced propositions? And that, when Zelotes produces the tenth article of the Church[*] to prove us heretics, he acts as unreasonable a part as if he produced John 15:5, to show that St. Paul was not orthodox when he wrote Philippians 4:13.

I.	II.
Without me [Christ] ye can do nothing, John 15:5.	I [Paul] can do all things through Christ strengthening me, Philippians 4:13.

This supposed "heresy" runs, through our Common Prayer Book. Take one or two instances of it. In her catechism, she teaches every child whom she nurses, to "thank God for calling him to this state of salvation," *i.e.* to a state of initial salvation according to the Christian covenant. She informs him that "his duty is to love God with all his heart, and his neighbour as himself," &c, and then she adds: — "My good child, know this, that thou art not able to do these things of thyself, nor to walk in the commandments of God without his special grace, which thou must learn at all times to call for by diligent prayer," &c. Now every child, whose mind is not yet tainted with Calvinism, understands the language of our holy mother according to the doctrine of the Scales, thus: —

I.	II.
Of myself I am not able to love God with all my heart, &c.	By God's special grace I am able to love him with all my heart, &c.
I am not able to walk in the commandments of God without his special grace.	I am able to walk in the commandments of God with his special grace, "and, by God's grace, so I will."
I am in a state of initial grace, and I heartily thank our heavenly Father that	To have God's special grace, "I must learn at all times to call for it by

---

[*] The Rev. Mr. Toplady makes much ado in his Historic Proof of the Calvinism of our Church, about some dissenters whom he calls free willers, and represents as the first separatists from the Church of England. But they were rigid Pelagian free willers, and not moderate, Bible free willers, such as Cranmer was, and all unprejudiced Churchmen are. This is evident from the account which Mr. Toplady himself gives us of their tenets, page 54. Some of which are as follows: — "That children are not born in original sin: that lust after evil is not sin, if the act be not committed," &c. Honestus does not run into such an extreme: much less we, who stand with Cranmer on the line of moderation, at an equal distance from Calvinian rigid bound willers, and from Pelagian rigid free willers. I hope this hint is sufficient to show that though the simple may be frightened by the words free willers and separatists, no judicious Church-of-England man will think that he separates from our Church when he stands to the harmonizing doctrine of free grace and free will, which is maintained in our tenth article, and in these pages.

he has called me to this state of salvation.

diligent prayer," according to the help afforded me in my state of initial salvation.

This doctrine of free grace and free will runs also through the collects of our Church. Read one of those which Zelotes admires most: — "Grant to us, Lord, we beseech thee, the spirit, [*i.e.* the special grace,] to think and do always such things as be rightful; that we who cannot do any thing that is good without thee, may by thee be enabled to live according to thy will, through Jesus Christ our Lord." (*Ninth Sunday after Trinity.*) Divide the doctrine of this collect according to the two Gospel axioms, and you will have the following balanced propositions: —

I.	II.
We cannot do any thing that is good without thee, or thy Spirit.	By thee, or thy Spirit, we can think and do alway such things as be rightful.
We cannot, but by thee, live according to thy will, &c.	By thee we can live according to thy will, &c.

To bring more proofs that this is the doctrine of the Church of England, would be to offer an insult to the attention of her children. Nor can her sentiments on free will be more dearly expressed than they are in these words of the martyred prelate who drew up her articles: — "It pleaseth the high wisdom of God, that man prevented [*i.e.* first visited] by his grace, which, being offered man, he may *if he will* refuse or receive, be also a worker *by his free consent* and obedience to the same, &c, and by God's grace and help shall walk in such works as be requisite to his [continued* and final] justification." (Necess. Doct.)

However, lest Zelotes should object to my quoting "the *Necessary Doctrine of a Christian Man,*" I substitute for the preceding quotation, one to which he has indirectly subscribed, in subscribing to the thirty-fifth article of our Church: — "Cast we off all malice, and all evil will; for this spirit will never enter into an evil-willing soul [to bring there his special grace.] Let us cast away all the whole lump of sin that standeth about us, for he will never dwell in a body that is subdued to sin, &c. *If we do our endeavour,* we shall not need to fear. *We shall be able* to overcome all our enemies, &c. *Only let us apply ourselves to accept the grace that is offered us.* Of Almighty God we have comfort by his goodness; of our Saviour Christ's mediation we may be sure; and this Holy Spirit will suggest unto us that which shall be wholesome, and comfort us in all things." (*Homily for Rog. Week, part* 3.) How strongly are the doctrines of free grace and free will guarded in these lines! And who does not see that our articles, liturgy, and homilies agree to maintain the Gospel marriage of free grace and free will, as well as Mr. Wesley, Mr. Sellon, and myself?

The preceding quotations and remarks will, I hope, convince the impartial reader, that (some few unguarded expressions being excepted) Zelotes might as well screen his doctrines of narrow grace, bound will, and free wrath, behind the Scripture

---

* I add the words "continued and final," to guard the unconditional freeness of initial justification and salvation: because this justification is previous to all works on our part, and because all good works are but the voluntary (Zelotes would say *the necessary*) fruits of the free gift, which is come upon all men to justification, Romans 5:18.

Scales, as defend them by the authority of the primitive Church, and the Church of England.

IV. Should Zelotes think to answer the contents of this section by saying that my doctrine is "rank Pelagianism:" I reply, 1. That Vossius, who wrote the history of Pelagianism, entirely clears our doctrine of the charge of both Pelagianism and semi-Pelagianism, as appears by the passage which I have quoted from him, page 209: and in this cause the name of Vossius is legion.

2. PROSPER, in his letter to St. Augustine, gives us this account of the principles of the Pelagians: — *Prior est hominis obedientia quam Dei gratia. Initium salutis ex eo est qui salvatur, non ex eo qui salvat.* "Man's obedience is beforehand with God's grace. The beginning of salvation is from him that is saved, and not from him that saves." These two propositions are greatly Pharisaic and detestable: they set aside the first Gospel axiom; and, far from recommending them, I every where oppose to them the weights of my first Scale. It would not then be more ridiculous to charge me with Crispianity, than it is to accuse me of Pelagianism.

3. Bishop Davenant, in his "Animadversions," (pages 14 and 15,) calls Faustus Rhegiensis "one of the ancient semi-Pelagians," and lays down his doctrine in the five following anti-Calvinistic propositions, in which reigns a confusion equal to that of Calvinism: (1.) *Salus hominis non in prædestinatione factoris, sed in operatione famulantis collocata est:* "Man's salvation is not placed in the election of the Creator, but in the actions of the worker." This is absolutely false with respect to the election of distinguishing grace. What had the Ephesians wrought to deserve to be elected and called to share the blessings of the Gospel of Christ, which St. Paul calls "so great salvation?" Who can make appear that they merited so great a favour better than the Hottentots? (2.) *Non est specialis circa credentes Dei munificentia:* "God shows no special grace and favour to believers." This is absolutely false also with respect to all Jewish and Christian believers, to whom he gives that grace, and those talents, which he does not bestow upon the heathens who "fear God and work righteousness." (3.) *Prædestinatio adjustitiam pertinet:* "Election belongs to justice." This also is absolutely false, if it be understood of the election of distinguishing grace, whereby a man receives one, two, or five talents to trade with before he has done any thing. And it is partly false if it be understood of our election to receive rewards of grace and glory: for that election belongs to rich mercy as well as to distributive justice; it being God's mercy in Christ, which engaged him to promise penitent, obedient believers rewards of grace and glory, (4.) *Nisi præscientia exploraverit, predestinatio nihil decernit:* "Predestination appoints nothing, unless prescience has seen a cause for the appointment." This is false also, if this cause is supposed to be always in us. What foreseen excellence made God predestinate the posterity of Jacob to the old covenant of peculiarity rather than the offspring of Esau? And what reason can Honestus assign for his being called to read the Bible in a church, and not the Koran in a mosque? (5.) *Justitia periclitabitur, si sine merito indignus eligitur:* "Justice will be in danger, if an undeserving person is chosen without any worthiness." This is true with regard to the remunerative election of obedient believers to crowns of glory in the Church triumphant. Therefore, when Christ speaks of that election, he says, "They shall walk with him in white, for they are worthy:" but it is absolutely false with respect to the election of distinguishing grace, whereby the English and Scotch are chosen to the blessings of Christianity, rather than the Turks and Cannibals. I may therefore

conclude that, according to the accounts which Vossius, Prosper, and Bishop Davenant give us of Pelagianism and ancient semi-Pelagianism, our doctrine is just as far from those erroneous systems, as it is from fatalism and Calvinism.

SECTION IX.

The fifth objection of Zelotes against a reconciliation with Honestus — In answer to it the reconciler shows that the earliest fathers held the doctrine of the Scripture Scales, and that the Rev. Mr. Toplady's Historic Proof of their Calvinism is quite anti- historical.

THE preceding section seems to embarrass Zelotes almost as much as my second Scale; but, soon recovering his positiveness, he endeavours to set all the preceding quotations aside by the following objection: —

OBJECTION V. "I make no great account of the fathers, except those who may be called *apostolic*, as having lived in or immediately after the apostolic age. Therefore, if Barnabas, who was St. Paul's fellow apostle; if Clement, who was bishop of the uncorrupted Church at Rome; Clement, whom the apostle mentions not only as his 'fellow labourer,' but also as one 'whose name was written in the book of life,' Philippians 4:3; if Polycarp and Ignatius, who were both disciples of the apostle St. John, who filled the Episcopal sees at Smyrna and Antioch, and who nobly laid down their lives for Christ, the one in the flames, and the other in the jaws of hungry lions: if these early fathers, I say, these undaunted martyrs are for us as well as St. Augustine; we may, without endangering the truth, allow you that the generality of the other fathers countenanced too much the doctrine of your Scales. And that these fathers were for us, is abundantly demonstrated in the Rev. Mr Toplady's *Historic Proof of Calvinism.*"

ANSWER. It is true that when Mr. Toplady promises us "the judgment of the earliest fathers," concerning Calvinism, he says, (*Historic Proof*, page 121,) "I must repeat my question, which seems to have given Mr. Sellon and his fraternity so much disquiet: where was not the doctrine of predestination before Pelagius?" But nothing can be more frivolous than this question; since I myself, who oppose Calvinian predestination as much as Mr. Toplady does the second Scripture Scale, would put the question to a Pelagian, i.e. to a rigid free willer. To do the subject justice, and not to mislead his unwary readers into unscriptural tenets by the lure of a Scriptural word, Mr. Toplady should have said, "Where was not, before Pelagius, the Calvinian doctrine of the absolute predestination of some men to unavoidable, eternal life, and of all the rest of mankind to unavoidable, eternal death, without any respect to their voluntary faith and works?" For neither Mr. Sellon, nor any of his "fraternity," ever denied the predestination which St. Paul mentions. Nay, we strongly contend for it; see section 14. All we insist upon is, that the predestination, election, and reprobation taught by St. Paul, by the earliest fathers, and by us, are as different from the predestination, &c, taught by Calvin, Zanchy, and Mr. Toplady, as the Scripture Scales are different from *the Historic Proof.* (See our *Genuine Creed*, article 7.)

Creeds and Scripture Scales

We grant also that the ingenious vicar of Broad Hembury has filled a section with proofs that the early fathers were sound Calvinists; but what weight have these proofs? Are they not founded, (1.) Upon the words *our, we, us,* and *elect,* which he fondly supposes to mean us who are Calvinistically elected in opposition to our neighbours, who, from all eternity, were unconditionally and absolutely reprobated from eternal life? (2.) Upon some phrases, where those fathers mentioned the particular, applicatory redemption, or the particular election and calling of those to whom the Gospel of Christ is preached; a redemption of believers, an election and a calling these, for which I myself, who am no Calvinist, have strongly contended in my answer to Mr. Hill's *Creed for the Arminians?* (3.) Upon some sentences, which, being torn from the context, seem to speak in the Calvinian strain? (4.) Upon the harmless words will, purpose, requisite, decree, &c, which are fondly supposed to demonstrate the truth of Calvinian necessity and Calvinian decrees? (5.) Upon the words "brethren, the Church of saints, the new people, my people?" Which (such is the force of prejudice!) Mr. Toplady imagines *must* mean his Calvinistically elected brethren, &c, just as if people could not be brethren, form a Christian Church, be God's peculiar, new, Christian people, in opposition to his old people, the Jews, or to those who in every nation fear God and work righteousness, or even in opposition to unconverted people, without the chimerical election, which drags after it the necessary damnation of all the world beside!

The truth is, that the fathers, mentioned in Zelotes' objection, followed the very same plan of doctrine which is laid down in these pages, although they did not always balance the two Gospel axioms with the scrupulous caution and nicety which the vain jangling of captious, contentious, and overdoing divines obliges me to use. Mr. Toplady himself will hardly deny that the early fathers held the doctrine of our first scale. And that they held the doctrine of the second, I prove by the following* extracts from their excellent epistles.

Barnabas says, in his *Catholic epistle,* "Let us give heed unto the last days, for all the time of our life and faith *shall profit us nothing, if we do not* endure unjust things, and future temptations. Let us, being spiritual, be made a perfect temple to God, *as much as in us lies.* Let us meditate upon the fear of God, and endeavour to keep his commandments, that we may rejoice in his judgments: the Lord, accepting no man's person, judgeth the world; every man shall receive *according to his deeds.* If he be good, *his goodness goes before him;* if wicked, the ways of his wickedness follow after him. Take heed lest, at any time, being called, and at ease, we should fall asleep in our sins, and the wicked one getting power over us, &c, exclude us from the kingdom of the Lord. Understand a little more; having seen the great signs and wonders among the people of the Jews, and that the Lord does so leave them; therefore let us take heed, lest haply we be found, as it is written, 'Many called, few chosen.' That man shall justly perish, who hath knowledge of the way of truth, and yet *will not* refrain himself from the dark way." (Pages 6, 7, 8.)

---

* Not having the original, I extract what follows of Clement's, from Mr. Wesley's *"Christian Library,"* vol. 1. The quotations from the epistles of Barnabas, Polycarp, and Ignatius are taken from the translation of Thomas Elborowe, vicar of Chiswick. It is to be met with in his book, called "A Prospect of Primitive Christianity, as it was left by Christ and his Apostles;" printed in the Savoy, 1668.

The Works of John Fletcher

I grant to Mr. Toplady, that Barnabas says, p. 28, "Thou shalt not command thy maid or man servant with bitterness, especially those who hope in him, *lest thou be found destitute of the fear of God*, who is over both: for he came not to call men [to the blessings of Christianity] by their persons, [that is, according to the context, *he came not to call masters only*,] but those whom his Spirit prepared:" [whether they be servants or masters: for God called to Christian liberty the devout soldiers and servants who waited on Cornelius, as well as Cornelius himself; giving them equally" the Spirit of adoption," because they were equally prepared for it by "the Spirit of *conviction and bondage*," which they had not received in vain.] From the last words of this quotation Mr. Toplady fondly infers the Calvinism of Barnabas; whereas from the words which I have produced in Italics, it is evident that this apostle was as far from Calvinism as St. James himself: for they show that Barnabas thought a believer could be "found destitute of the fear of God," i.e. could so fall away into a graceless state, as to make shipwreck even of "the fear of God," only by "commanding a servant with bitterness."

This historic proof of Barnabas' Calvinism is so much the more surprising, as he says, a few lines below, "Meditate *to save a soul* by the word. And thou shalt *labour for the redemption of thy sins*. Give to very one that asketh of thee; but know withal who is the good Recompenser for the reward, &c. It is therefore an excellent thing for him who learns the righteous commands of the Lord, &c, *to walk in them*. For he who *does them*, shall be glorified in the kingdom of God; but he who chooseth the other things, shall perish with his works. Therefore there is a resurrection and a retribution. The Lord is at hand, and his reward. I entreat you, again and again, that ye be good lawgivers to yourselves, and that ye remain faithful counsellors to yourselves. Be ye taught of God, seeking out what the Lord requireth from you, and do, that ye may be saved in the day of judgment." I see no Calvinism in all this; but only the doctrine of the second Scripture Scale, which all Calvinists would abhor, as they do Mr. Wesley's Minutes, if consistency belonged to their system.

Nor was St. Clement more averse to that scale than Barnabas: for although, in the excellent epistle which he wrote to reconvert the wrangling Corinthians, he maintains the Protestant doctrine of faith, as clearly as our Church does in her eleventh article; yet he as strongly inculcates the doctrine of works, as she does in the twelfth. Nay, he so closely connects faith and its works, that what St. Paul calls faith, he does not scruple to call obedience. "By obedience, (says he) he [Abraham] went out of his own land." And again: "By faith and hospitality was Rahab saved." Hence it is that he guards the doctrine of obedient free will as strongly as that of prevenient free grace. "Let us remember (says he) the words of our Lord, *Forgive, and ye shall be forgiven*. Let them [children] learn how great power humility has with God; how much holy love avails with him; how the fear of him is good and great, and saveth all those who, with a pure mind, turn to him in holiness. Let us agonize to be found in the number of them that wait for him, [God,] that we may partake thereof:" that is, of the things which are prepared for them that wait for him.

His description of love is so highly anti-Calvinistic, that it amounts even to Christian perfection. "By love were all the elect of God made perfect: no words can declare its perfection — all the generations, from Adam to this day, are passed away;

but those who were made perfect in love, are in the region of the just, and shall appear in glory.* 'Love covereth a multitude of sins.' Happy then are we, beloved, *if we fulfil the commandments of God* in the unity of love, that so through love our sins may be forgiven us. Following the commandments of God they sin not."

So far was he from Calvinian narrowness and reprobation, that when he exhorts the Corinthians to repentance, he does it in these words: — "Let us fix our eyes on the blood of Christ, and see how precious it is before God, which, being shed for our salvation, brought the grace of repentance to all the world. Let us look diligently to all ages, and learn that our Lord has always given place for repentance to all who desired to turn to him. Noah preached repentance, and they who hearkened to him were saved. Jonah denounced destruction upon the Ninevites; yet they, repenting of their sins, appeased God by their prayers, and received salvation, although they were strangers to the covenant of God. Wherefore let us, &c, turn ourselves to his mercy."

In all this I see no more Calvinism than I do in Mr. Wesley's Minutes. However, Mr. Toplady's "Historic Proof" is gone forth; and it is now demonstrated that St. Clement was an orthodox and a sound Calvinist; while the author of the Minutes is a heretic, and almost every thing that is bad! O Solifidianism! is thy influence over those who drink of thy enchanting cup so great that they can prove, believe, and make people believe almost any thing?

By the same frivolous arguments Mr. Toplady attempts to evince the Calvinism of Polycarp, whose epistle, in some places, is rather too much anti-Calvinistical. Reader, judge for thyself, and say which of Calvin's peculiarities breathe through the following passages of his Epistle to the Philippians: page 2, "Who [Christ] shall come to judge the quick and the dead, and whose blood God will strictly require at the hands of those who do not believe on him. But he, who raised him

---

* By comparing these two sentences, it is evident St. Clement believed and taught that our charity not only causes us to cover the sins of others, but in a secondary sense *causes* also God's covering of our own sins: the first cause of pardon being always his free grace in Jesus Christ. Mr. Baxter exactly expresses St. Clement's sentiment in his comment upon these words of St. Peter: — "Above all things have fervent charity among yourselves; for charity shall cover the multitude of sins." "It is but partiality (says he) and jealousy of the cause of justification among the Papists, which makes some excellent expositors distort the text, so as to exclude from its sense *God's covering of our sins;* because they consider not aright, (1.) That pardon, as continued, and as renewed, has more for the condition of it required in us, than the first pardon and begun justification has. The first act of sound faith serveth for the beginning, but the continuance of it [of sound faith] with its necessary fruits [love, &c,] is necessary to the continuance of pardon. (2.) That the faith which is required to justification and pardon, is giving up ourselves to God the Father, Son, and Holy Ghost in the baptismal covenant; that is, our Christianity, which is not put in opposition to that love or repentance, which is still implied as part of the same covenant consent, or as its necessary fruit; but to the works of the law of Moses, or of works, or to any works that are set in competition with Christ and free grace. If prejudice hindered not men, the reading of the angel's words to Cornelius, and of Christ's, ('forgive and ye shall be forgiven,')and the parable of the pardoned debtor, cast into prison for not pardoning his fellow servant, with James 2, and Matthew 25, would end all this controversy." O Clement! O Baxter! what have ye said? Are ye not as heterodox as the author of the Minutes and their Vindicator?

from the dead, will raise us up also, *if we do his will, and walk in his commandments, &c,* remembering what the Lord said, teaching in this wise, 'Judge not, that ye be not judged: forgive, and it shall be forgiven you: be merciful, that ye may obtain mercy: in what measure ye mete, it shall be measured to you again,' &c. These things, brethren, I write unto you concerning righteousness."

Polycarp, far from recommending the Calvinian imputation of Christ's righteousness, openly sides with those who are reproached as perfectionists in our days; for in the next page he says, "If any man is possessed of these, [faith, followed by hope, and led on by love,] he hath fulfilled the command of righteousness. He who is possessed of love, is free from all sin. Let us arm ourselves with the armour of righteousness, and teach ourselves in the first place to walk in the commandments of the Lord:" "from whom," says he, in the next page, "if we please him in this world, we shall receive a [or the] future reward. For he has engaged for us, to raise us from the dead: and if we have our conversation worthy of him, we shall also reign with him, as we believe." Nor is he ashamed to urge the practice of good works from a motive which Zelotes would call downright popery. For after observing that "Paul, and the rest of the apostles, have not run in vain, but in faith and righteousness; and having obtained the place due unto them, are now with the Lord," &c, he adds: "When ye can do good, do not defer it, for *alms delivereth from death*." If Mr. Wesley said this, he would be a heresiarch. Polycarp says it; but, no matter, Polycarp is a famous martyr; and therefore he must be a sound Calvinist.

And so must Ignatius, who, from the same motive, is pressed into the service of the Calvinian doctrines of grace. To show that Mr. Toplady is mistaken, when he asserts that Ignatius was Calvinistically orthodox, I need only prove that Ignatius enforced the second Gospel axiom as well as the first. And that he did so, is evident from the following quotations. He writes to the Smyrneans: — "Let all things abound among you in grace, for ye are worthy. Ye have every way refreshed me, and Jesus Christ will refresh you. Ye have loved me, &c. God will requite you; and if ye patiently endure all things for his sake, ye shall enjoy him. Being perfect yourselves, mind the things which are perfect. For if ye have but a will to do good, God is ready to assist you." He writes to Polycarp: — "The more the labour is, the more the gain. It is necessary for us patiently to endure all things for God, that he may patiently bear with us. Ministers of God, do things pleasing to him, &c, whose soldiers ye are, from whom ye expect your salary. Let none among you be found a deserter of his colours. Let your baptism arm you; let faith be your helmet, love your spear, patience your whole armour, and your works your gage [your *depositum*] that you may receive a reward worthy of you. When ye shall have despatched this business, the work shall be ascribed to God and to you," according to the doctrine of free grace and free will. And, at the end of his letter, he exhorts the presbyters and Polycarp to write edifying letters to the neighbouring Churches, "that ye may all be glorified by an eternal work, as thou art worthy."

To the Ephesians, whom he calls "elect by real sufferings," as well as "through the will of God," he writes: — "Keeping the melody of God, which is unity, ye shall with one voice glorify the Father by Jesus Christ, that he may also hear you, and acknowledge you by what you do, to be the members of his Son. So that it is profitable for you to continue in immaculate unity, that ye may always be partakers of

God. Keep yourselves in all purity and temperance, both in flesh and spirit, through Jesus Christ."

To the Magnesians he says "All works have some end; two [ends] are proposed, DEATH and LIFE; and every man shall go to his proper place," through his works of faith or unbelief.

To the Trallians indeed he writes: — "Flee therefore evil plants [Atheists and infidels] which bring forth deadly fruit, which if a man tastes of, he dies presently. For these are not the plantation of the Father; if they were, they would appear branches of his cross, and their fruit would be incorruptible," or rather, *not rotten, not unsound.* Mr. Toplady depends much on the latter part of this quotation: but all we see in it is, that Ignatius believed none are actually plants of righteousness but they who actually appear such, by actually bearing good fruit, which he calls αφθαρτος, in opposition to rotten fruit: for if the word φθειρω means "to spoil, to corrupt, to rot," αφθαρτος means as well "not rotten" as "incorruptible." And that it means so here is evident from the motive urged by Ignatius in the context, to make the Trallian believers flee from those evil plants, these Atheistical apostates' "If a man," that is, if any one of you, believers, (for unbelievers being *dead* already, have no spiritual *life* to lose,) "if a man tastes their deadly fruit, he dies presently;" so far is he from being sure to recover, and sing louder in heaven if he apostatizes, and feasts for months upon their deadly fruit! This important clause renders the quotation altogether anti-Calvinistical, especially if we compare it to a similar caution which this very father gives to the Ephesians: — "Let no one among you be found an herb of the devil; keep yourselves in all purity," &c. That is, let none of you apostatize by tasting the deadly fruit of these evil plants, which have apostatized. Both quotations evidently allude to these words of Jeremiah 2:21, "I had planted thee a noble vine, wholly a right seed: how then art thou turned into the degenerate plant of a strange vine!" Both are strongly anti-Calvinistical; and yet the former is produced by Mr. Toplady as a proof of Calvinism! Need I say any more to make Zelotes himself cry out, *Logica Genevensis?*

From the whole, I hope that unprejudiced readers will subscribe to the following remarks: (1.) Barnabas, Clement, Polycarp, and Ignatius undoubtedly held the first Gospel axiom, or the godly, Scriptural doctrine of free grace; so far we agree with Mr. Toplady. But to prove them *fathers after his own heart,* this gentleman should have proved that at least by necessary consequence they rejected the second Gospel axiom, which necessarily includes our doctrines of moderate free will, of the works of penitential faith, and of the reward of eternal salvation annexed to the unnecessitated, voluntary obedience of faith. (2.) If Mr. Toplady dismembered the "Equal Check," and broke the "Scripture Scales;" taking what I advance against the proper merit of works, and in defence of free grace; producing my arguments for the covenants of peculiarity, and for the election of distinguishing grace; and carefully concealing all that I have written in favour of assisted free will, and evangelical morality: if Mr. Toplady, I say, followed this method, in those two pieces only, he would find a great many more proofs of Calvinism, i.e. of mangled, immoral, Antinomian Christianity, than he has found in all the writings of the earliest fathers, to whom he so confidently appeals. (3.) We must then still go down so low as the fourth or fifth century, before we can find *Calvin the First,* I mean HEATED St. Augustine. And how inconsistent a Calvinist COOL St. Augustine was, has already been proved. I therefore flatter myself, that Mr. Toplady's *anti*-historic proof of the Calvinism of the primitive Church will no longer keep Zelotes from a Scriptural reconciliation with Honestus. But I see that the time is not yet come; for he turns over two octavo volumes, and prepares another weighty objection, which the reader will find in the following section.

SECTION X.

Zelotes' sixth objection to a reconciliation with Honestus — The reconciler answers it by showing, (1.) That the evangelical marriage of free grace and free will reflects no dishonour upon God's sovereignty. (2.) That Mr. Toplady's grand argument against that marriage is inconclusive. (3.) That Mr. Whitefield's "inextricable dilemma," in favour of Calvinian election and reprobation, is a mere sophism. And, (4.) That Zelotes' jumble of free wrath, and unevangelical free grace, pours real contempt upon all the Divine perfections, sovereignty itself not excepted.

OBJECTION VI. "If you are not a Pelagian, are you not a secret Atheist? Do you not indirectly represent Jehovah as not God? You want me to meet Honestus half way: but if I meet him where you are, shall not I meet him on the brink of a horrible precipice? Are you not an opposer of God's sovereignty, which shines as gloriously among his other perfections, as the moon does among the stars? Is not a God without sovereignty as contemptible as a king without a kingdom? And can you reconcile your arrogant doctrine of free will, with the supreme, absolute, irresistible power, by which God 'works all things after the counsel of his own will?' Hear the Calvin of the day — the champion of the doctrines of grace: —

"'For this [Atheism] also Arminianism has paved the way, by despoiling the Divine Being, among other attributes of his unlimited supremacy, of his infinite knowledge, of his infallible wisdom, of his invincible power, of his absolute independency, of his eternal immutability. Not to observe that the exempting of some things and events from the providence of God, by referring them to free will, &c, is another of those black lanes, which lead, in a direct line, from Arminianism to Atheism. Neither is it at all surprising that any who represent men as gods (by supposing man to possess the Divine attribute of independent self determination) should, when their hand is in it, represent God himself with the imperfections of a man, by putting limitations to his sovereignty, by supposing his knowledge to be shackled with circumscription, and darkened with uncertainty; by connecting their ideas of his wisdom and power with the possibility of disconcertment and disappointment, embarrassment and defeat; by transferring his independency to themselves, in order to support their favourite doctrine, which affirms that the Divine will and conduct are dependent on the will and conduct of men; by blotting out his immutability, that they may clear the way for conditional, variable, vanquishable, and amissible grace; and by narrowing his providence, to keep the idol of free will upon its legs, and to save human reason from the humiliation of acknowledging her inability to account for many of the Divine disposals, &c. Who sees not the Atheistical tendency of all this? Let Arminianism try to exculpate herself from the heavy, but unexaggerated indictment, which if she cannot effect, it will be doing her no injustice to term her Atheism in masquerade.'" (*Rev. Mr. Toplady's Historic Proof,* p. 728, &c.)

ANSWER. If this terrible objection had the least degree of solidity, I would instantly burn the Checks and the Scripture Scales; for I trust that the glory of God is ten thousand times dearer to me than the success of my little publications. But I cannot take bare assertions, groundless insinuations, and bombastic charges for solid proofs. In a mock sea fight, cannons may dreadfully roar, but no masts are shot away, no ship is sent to the bottom. And that, in this polemical broadside, the weight of the ball (if there be any) does not answer to the noise of the explosion, will appear, I hope, by the following answers: —

I. (1.) This objection is entirely levelled at the second Scripture Scale, which is made of so great a variety of plain scriptures, that, to attempt to set it aside as leading to Atheism, is to endeavour setting aside one half of the doctrinal part of the Bible as being Atheistical. And if so considerable a part of the Bible be Atheistical, the whole is undoubtedly a forgery. Thus Zelotes, rather than not to cut down what he is pleased to call Arminianism, fells one half of the trees that grow in the fruitful garden of revealed truth, under pretence that they are productive of Atheism: and, by that means, he gives infidels a fair opportunity of cutting down all the rest.

(2.) Zelotes is greatly mistaken if he thinks that the free agency we plead for, absolutely crosses the designs of "Him who works all after the counsel of his own will:" for if part of this counsel be, that man shall be a free agent, that life and death, heaven and hell, shall be "set before him;" and that he shall eternally have either the one or the other, according to his own choice: if this be the case, I say, God's wisdom cannot be disappointed, nor his sovereign power baffled, be man's choice whatever it may: because God designed to manifest his sovereign wisdom and power in the wonderful creation, wise government, and righteous judgment of free agents; and not in overpowering their will, or in destroying their free agency; much less in subverting his awful tribunal, and in obscuring all his perfections to place one of them (sovereignty) in a more glaring light.

(3.) I grant that the doctrine of free will evangelically assisted by free grace, (not Calvinistically overpowered by forcible grace or wrath,) I grant, I say, that this doctrine can never be reconciled with the doctrine of an unscriptural, tyrannical sovereignty, which Zelotes rashly attributes to God, under pretence of doing him honour. But that it is perfectly consistent with the awful, and yet amiable views which the Scriptures give us of God's real sovereignty, is, I hope, abundantly proved in the preceding pages. To the arguments which they contain, I add the following illustration: —

If a king, wisely to try, and justly to reward the honesty of his subjects, made a statute, to insure particular rewards to thief catchers, and particular punishments to thieves; would it be any disparagement to his wisdom, power, supremacy, and sovereignty, if he did not necessitate, nor absolutely oblige some of his subjects to rob, and others to catch them in the robbery; lest he should not order the former for infallible execution, and appoint to the latter a gratuitous reward? Would not our gracious sovereign be injured by the bare supposition that he is capable of displaying his supreme authority by such a pitiful method? And shall we suppose that the King of kings — the Judge of all the earth, maintains his righteous sovereignty by a similar conduct?

(4.) We perpetually assert that God is the only first cause of all good, both natural and moral; and thus we ascribe to him a sovereignty worthy of the Parent of good. If we do not directly, with the Manichees, or indirectly, with the Calvinists, represent God as the first cause of evil, it is merely because we dare not attribute to him a diabolical supremacy. And we fear that Zelotes will have no more thanks for giving God the glory of predestinating the reprobate *necessarily* to continue in sin, and be damned, than I should have, were I to give our Lord the shameful glory of seducing Eve in the shape of a lying serpent, lest he should not have the glory of being, and doing all in all.

(5.) We apprehend that the doctrine of the Scales (i.e. the doctrine of free will, evangelically subordinate to free grace or to just wrath) perfectly secures the honour of God's greatness, supremacy, and power without dishonouring his goodness, justice, and veracity. It seems to us unscriptural and unreasonable to suppose that God should eclipse these, his MORAL perfections, (by which he chiefly proposes himself to us for our imitation,) in order to set off those, his NATURAL perfections. A grim tyrant, a Nebuchadnezzar, is praised for his greatness, sovereignty, and power; but a Titus, a prince who deserves to be called "the darling of mankind," is extolled for his goodness, justice, and veracity. And who but Satan, or his subjects, would so overvalue the praise given to a Nebuchadnezzar, as to slight the praise bestowed upon a Titus? Was not Titus as great a potentate as Nebuchadnezzar and Darius, though he did not, like them, make tyrannical decrees to assert his powers, and then execute them with wanton cruelty, or with absurd mourning; lest he should lose the praise of his sovereignty and immutability, before a multitude of mistaken decretists?

II. Having, I hope, broken the heart of Zelotes' objection by the preceding arguments, it will not be difficult to take in pieces his boasted quotation from Mr. Toplady's "Historic Proof;" and to point out the flaw of every part.

(1.) "Arminianism paves the way for Atheism by despoiling the Divine Being of his *unlimited supremacy.*" No: it only teaches us that it is absurd to make God's supremacy bear an undue proportion to his other perfections. Do we despoil the king of his manly shape, because we deny his having the head of a giant, and the body of a dwarf? (2.) "Of his *infallible wisdom.*" No: God wisely made free agents, that he might wisely judge them *according to their works;* and it is one of our objections to the modern doctrines of grace, that they despoil God of his "wisdom" in both these respects. (3.) "Of his *invincible power.*" No: God does whatever pleases him, in heaven, earth, and hell. But reason and Scripture testify that he does not choose to set his invincible power against his unerring wisdom, by overpowering with saving grace, or damning wrath, the men whom he is going judicially to reward or punish. (4.) "Of his *absolute independency.*" Absurd! when we say that the promised reward, which a general bestows upon a soldier for his gallant behaviour in the field, *depends* in some measure upon the soldier's gallant behaviour, do we despoil the general of his independency with respect to the soldier? Must the general, to show himself *independent,* necessitate some of his soldiers to fight, that he may foolishly promote them; and others to desert, that he may blow their brains out with Calvinian independence? (5.) "Of his *eternal immutability.*" No: when we assert that God justifies men according to their faith, and rewards them according to their good works; or when we say that he condemns them according to their unbelief, and punishes them according to their bad works; do we intimate that he betrays the least degree of mutability? On the contrary, do we not hereby represent him as faithfully executing his eternal, immutable decree of judging and treating men *according to their works* of faith, or of unbelief? (See "the *Genuine Creed*," article eighth.)

Mr. Toplady goes on: (6.) "The exempting of some things and events from the providence of God, by referring them to free will, &c, is another of those black lanes, which lead, in a direct line, from Arminianism to Atheism." This is a mistake all over. By the doctrine of moderate free will we exempt no event or thing from the providence of God: for we maintain, that as God's power made free will, so his providence rules or overrules it in all things. Only we do not believe that *ruling* or *overruling* implies "necessitating, overpowering," or "tricking," when judgments, punishments, and rewards are to follow. Our doctrine, therefore, is a lightsome walk, which leads to the right knowledge of God, and not one of those "black lanes which leads in a direct line" from Calvinian election to "Mr. Fulsome's" presumption; and from Calvinian reprobation, to Francis Spira's despair.

(7.) Arminianism "represents men as gods, by supposing man to possess the Divine attribute of independent self determination." Our doctrines of grace suppose no such thing: on the contrary, we assert that obedient free will is always dependent upon God's free grace; and disobedient free will upon God's just wrath: this charge of Mr. Toplady is therefore absolutely groundless. (8.) Arminianism "represents God himself with the imperfections of a man, by putting limitations to his sovereignty." This is only a repetition of what is absurdly said, No. 1, about God's "unlimited supremacy." (9.) It "supposes his knowledge to be shackled with circumscription, and darkened with uncertainty." It supposes no such thing: on the contrary, one of our great objections to Calvinism is, that it so shackles God's infinite knowledge as to despoil him of the knowledge of future contingencies, or of those events which depend upon man's unnecessitated choice: absurdly supposing that God knows what he absolutely decrees, and no more. "If events were undecreed," says Mr. Toplady, in his *Hist. Proof*, p. 192, "they would be unforeknown; if unforeknown, they could not be infallibly predicted. How came God to foreknow man's fall," says Calvin, [*nisi quia sic ordinarat,*] "but because he had appointed it?" Thus Calvin and Mr. Toplady, in one sense, allow less foreknowledge to God, than to a stable boy; for without decreeing any thing about the matter, a postilion knows that if the horse he curries gets into his master's garden, some of the beds will be trampled; and that if a thief has an opportunity of taking a guinea without being seen, he will take it. (See pages 283, 287.)

(10.) The Arminians "connect their ideas of God's wisdom and power with the possibility of disconcertment and disappointment, embarrassment and defeat." No such thing: we maintain that God, in his infinite wisdom and power, has made free agents, in order to display his goodness by rewarding them, if they believe and obey; or his justice by punishing them, if they prove faithless and disobedient. Whichsoever of the two therefore comes to pass, God is no more "disconcerted, disappointed, embarrassed," &c, than a lawgiver and judge, who acquits or condemns criminals according to his own law, and to their own works (11.) What Mr. Toplady says in the next lines about the Arminian "transferring independency to themselves in order to support their favourite doctrine, which affirms that the Divine will and conduct are dependent on the will and conduct of men;"and what he adds about their "blotting out God's immutability, and narrowing his providence, to keep the idol of free will upon its legs," is a mere repetition of what is answered in No. 4, 5, 6, 7. This elegant tautology of Mr. Toplady may make some of his admirers wonder at the surprising variety of his arguments; but attentive readers can see through the rhetorical veil.

What that gentleman says of "conditional, variable, vanquishable, and amissible grace," is verbal dust, raised to obscure the glory of the second Gospel axiom, to hide one of the Scripture Scales, and to substitute overbearing, necessitating grace, and free, unprovoked wrath, for the genuine grace and just wrath mentioned in the Gospel. Let us however dwell a moment upon each of these epithets: (1.) "Conditional grace:" we assert (according to the first axiom) that the grace of initial salvation is unconditional; and (according to the second axiom) we maintain that the grace of eternal salvation is conditional, excepting the case of complete idiots, and of all who die in their infancy. If Mr. Toplady can disprove either part of this doctrine, or, which is all one, if he can overthrow the second Gospel axiom, and break our left Scale, let him do it. (2.) "Variable grace:" we assert that grace, as it is inherent in God, is invariable. But we maintain that the displays of it toward mankind are various; asserting that those displays of it which God grants in a way of reward to them that faithfully use what they have, and properly ask for more, may and do vary according to the variations of faithful or unfaithful free will; our Lord himself having declared that "to him that hath *to purpose, more* shall be given;" and that "from him that hath not *to purpose, even* what he hath shall be taken away." (3.) "Vanquishable grace:" to call God's grace vanquishable is absurd; because Christ does not fight men with grace, any more than a physician fights the sick with remedies. If a patient will not take his medicines, or will not take them properly, or will take poison also, the medicines are not vanquished, but despised, or improperly taken. This does not show the weakness of the medicines, but the perverseness of the patient. Nor does it prove that the dying man is stronger than his healthy physician; but only that the physician will not drench him as a farrier does a brute. If Mr. Toplady asserts the contrary, I refer him to page 67 of this volume. And, pointing at Christ's tribunal, I ask, Could the Judge of all the earth wisely and equitably sentence men to eternal life, or to eternal death, if he first drenched them with the cup of finished salvation, or finished damnation? (4.) "Amissible grace:" why cannot evangelical grace be lost as well as the celestial and para-disiacal grace which was bestowed upon angels and man before the fall? Is a diamond less precious for being amissible? Is it any disgrace to the sun that thousands of his beams are lost upon the drones who sleep away his morning light? or that they are abused by all the wicked who dare to sin in open day? If Divine grace is both forcible and inamissible, what signify the apostolic cautions of "not receiving it in vain," and of not "doing despite to the Spirit of grace?" In a word, what signifies our second Gospel Scale, with all the scriptures that fill it up?

To conclude: if those scriptures clearly demonstrate the doctrine of a free will, always subordinate either to free grace or to just wrath; when Mr. Toplady calls that free will an "idol," does he not inadvertently charge God with being an idol maker, and represent the sacred writers as supporters of the idol which God has made? And when that gentleman says that we "keep the idol of free will upon its legs, to save human reason from the humiliation of acknowledging her inability to account for many of the Divine disposals;" does he not impose bound will and Calvinian reprobation upon us, just as the bishop of Rome imposes transubstantiation upon his tame underlings: that is, under pretence that we must humbly submit our reason to the Divine declarations, decrees, or disposals? Just as if there were no difference between popish declarations, or Calvinian decrees, and "Divine disposals!" Just as if the bare fear of regarding reason were sufficient to drive us from all the rational scriptures which fill our second Scale, into all the absurdities and horrors of free wrath and finished damnation!

And now say, candid reader, if I may not justly apply to the Calvinian doctrines of grace a part of what Mr. Toplady rashly says of "Arminianism?" "Let Calvinism exculpate herself from the heavy, but unexaggerated indictment, which, if she cannot effect, it will be doing her no injustice to term her" (I shall not say "Atheism in masquerade," but) an irrational and unscriptural system of doctrine.

III. "Not so, (replies Zelotes:) if you have answered Mr. Toplady's argument, you cannot set aside Mr. Whitefield's dilemma in his letter to Mr. Wesley. To me, at least, that dilemma appears absolutely unanswerable. It runs thus: — 'Surely Mr. Wesley will own God's justice in imputing Adam's sin to his posterity: and also, that after Adam fell, and his posterity in him, God might justly have "passed them all by," without sending his Own Son to be a Saviour for any one. Unless you do heartily agree in both these points, you do not believe original sin aright. If you do own them, you must acknowledge the doctrine of election and reprobation to be highly just and reasonable. For if God might justly impute Adam's sin to all, and afterward have passed by all, then he might justly pass by some. Turn to the right hand or to the left, you are reduced to an inextricable dilemma.'" (See Mr. Whitefield's Works, vol. iv, p. 67.)

ANSWER. We own God's justice in imputing Adam's sin seminally to his posterity, because his posterity sinned seminally in him, and was in him seminally corrupted. And we grant that, in the loins of Adam, we seminally deserved all that Adam himself personally deserved. So far we agree with Mr. Whitefield; maintaining, as he does, that, by our fallen nature in Adam, we are all children of wrath; and that, as soon as our first parents had sinned, God might justly have sent them, and us in their loins, into the pit of destruction; much more "might he justly have passed us all by, without sending his own Son to be a Saviour for any one." Therefore Mr. Whitefield has no reason to suspect that we deny the Scripture doctrine of original sin.

This being premised, we may easily see that the great flaw of the "inextricable dilemma" consists in confounding our seminal state with our personal state: and in concluding that what would have been just, when we were in our seminal state in the loins of Adam, must also be just in our personal state, now we are out of his loins. As this is the main spring of Mr. Whitefield's mistake, it is proper to point it Out a little more clearly. Let the following propositions form the pointer: —

(1.) "The wages of sin is death," yea, eternal death or damnation. (2.) The wages of sin personally and consciously committed, is damnation personally and consciously suffered. (3.) The wages of sin seminally and unknowingly committed is damnation, seminally and unknowingly suffered. (4.) When Adam had personally and consciously sinned, God would have been just if he had inflicted upon him the personal and conscious punishment which we call damnation. (5.) When we had seminally and unknowingly sinned in Adam, God would have been just if he had inflicted a seminal and unfelt damnation upon us for it; for then our punishment would have borne just proportion to our offence. We should have been punished as we had sinned, that is, seminally, and without the least consciousness of pain or of loss.

But is it not contrary to all equity to punish a sin seminally and unknowingly committed with an eternal punishment, personally and knowingly endured? For what is Calvinian reprobation but a dreadful decree that a majority of the children of men shall be personally bound over to conscious, necessary, and eternal sin; which sin shall draw after it conscious, necessary, and eternal damnation? Hence it appears that Calvinian predestination to death is horrible in its end, which is personal, necessary, and eternal torments consciously endured: but much more horrible in the means which it appoints to secure that end, namely, personal, remediless sin; sin necessarily, unavoidably, and eternally committed; and all this merely for a sin seminally, unknowingly, and unconsciously committed: and (what is still more horrible) for a sin which God himself had absolutely predestinated, if the doctrine of Calvinian predestination, or of the absolute* necessity of events be Scriptural. "It is true," Zelotes says, "that although reprobates are absolutely reprobated merely for the sin of Adam, yet they are damned merely for their own." But this evasion only makes a bad matter worse; for it intimates that free wrath so flamed against their unformed persons, as to determine that they should absolutely be formed, not only to be necessarily and eternally miserable, but also to be necessarily and eternally guilty; which is pouring as much contempt upon Divine goodness, as I should pour upon Phinehas' character, if I asserted that he contrived, and absolutely secured the filthy crime of Zimri and Cosbi, that, by this means, he might have a fair opportunity of infallibly running them both through the body.

An illustration may help the reader to understand how hard the ground of Mr. Whitefield's dilemma bears upon God's equity. I have committed a horrible murder: I am condemned to be burnt alive for it; my sentence is just; having personally and consciously sinned without necessity, I deserve to be personally and consciously tormented. The judge may then, without cruelty, condemn every part of me to the flames; and the unbegotten posterity in my loins may justly burn with me, and in me: for with me and in me it has sinned as a part of myself. Nor is it a great misfortune for my posterity to be thus punished; because it has as little knowledge and feeling of my punishment, as of my crime. But suppose the judge, after reprieving me, divided and multiplied me into ten thousand parts; suppose again that each of these parts necessarily grew up into a man or a woman; would it be reasonable in him to say to seven or eight hundred of these men and women, "You were all seminally guilty of the murder committed by the man whom I reprieved; and from whose loins I have extracted you; and therefore my mercy passes you by, and my justice absolutely reprobates your persons? I force you into remediless circumstances, in which you will

---

* Wickliff used to say, "All things that happen do come absolutely of necessity." (*Historic Proof,* page 191.) And Mr. Toplady, after taking care to distinguish, and set off the words *will, absolutely,* and *necessity,* says, in the next page, "I agree with him as to the necessity of events."

all necessarily commit murder; and then I shall have as fair an opportunity of unavoidably burning you for your own unavoidable murders, as I have had of absolutely reprobating you for the murder committed by the man from whom your wretched existence is derived." Who does not see the injustice and cruelty of such a speech? Who, but Zelotes, would not blush to call it a gracious speech, or a "doctrine of grace?" But if the persons, whom I suppose extracted from me, are reprieved as well as myself; if we are put all together in remediable circumstances, where sin indeed abounds, but where grace abounds much more, supposing we are not unnecessarily, voluntarily, and obstinately wanting to ourselves; who does not see that, upon the personal commission of avoidable, voluntary murder, (and much more upon the personal refusal of a pardon sincerely offered upon reasonable conditions,) my posterity may be condemned to the flames as justly as myself?

If this illustration exactly represents the deplorable case of Calvinian reprobates, who, barely for a sin which they seminally committed, are supposed to be personally bound over first to unavoidable perseverance in sin, and next to unavoidable and eternal damnation; will not all my unprejudiced readers wonder to hear Mr. Whitefield assert that the Calvinian doctrine of reprobation is "highly just and reasonable?"

"What!" replies that good mistaken man, "will not Mr. Wesley own that God might justly have passed all Adam's posterity by, without sending his own Son to be a Saviour for any man?"

ANSWER. God forbid we should ever imagine that God was bound to send his Son to die for any man! No: God was no more bound to redeem any man, than he was bound to create the first man; redemption as well as creation entirely flowing from rich, and every way undeserved grace.

"Then you give up the point," says Zelotes; "for there is no medium between God's refusing to send his Son to redeem a part of Adam's posterity, and his passing a sentence of Calvinian reprobation upon them. Now if he could justly refuse to send his Son to save *all*, he could justly refuse to send him to save *some*, and therefore he could justly reprobate some, i.e. predestinate them to a remediless state of sin, and of consequence to unavoidable damnation."

This sophistical argument probably misled Mr. Whitefield. But the "medium" which he could not see, the medium which spoils his "inextricable dilemma," the door at which we readily go out of the prison where *Logica Genevensis* fancies she has confined us, may easily be pointed out, thus: — If God had not entertained gracious thoughts of peace, mercy, and redemption toward all mankind; if he had designed absolutely and unconditionally to glorify nothing but his vindictive justice upon a number of them, for having seminally sinned in Adam, he might undoubtedly have passed them by; yea, he might have severely punished them. But, as I have observed, in this case he would have punished them equitably, that is, seminally: he would have crushed guilty Adam, and with him his Cainish, reprobated seed; contriving the birth of Abel, Seth, and others, in such a manner as to bring no man into personal existence, but such as had a personal share in his redeeming mercy. And this is the very plan, which, according to our doctrines of grace, and according to the Scriptures, God graciously laid down in eternity, and faithfully executed when "the Lamb slain from the foundation of the world tasted death for every man — gave himself a ransom for all" — and became an evangelical (not an Antinomian) "propitiation for the sins of the whole world."

A third flaw in Mr. Whitefield's dilemma is the supposition that Calvinian reprobation is only a harmless preterition: but a passing by, in some cases, is horrible cruelty. Thus if a mother Calvinistically passes by her suckling child for a week, she actually starves and destroys him. This is not all: Calvinian reprobation is a downright appointment to eternal death. "The [Calvinian] predestination of some to life," &c, says Mr. Toplady, "cannot be maintained without admitting the [Calvinian] reprobation of some others unto death," even unto eternal death, or damnation. But I ask, again, what can be more unreasonable and unjust than to appoint millions of unborn infants to personal, conscious, unavoidable, and eternal death, through the horrible medium of a personal, unavoidable perseverance in sin; and this merely for a sin which they never personally and consciously committed?

A fourth flaw in Mr. Whitefield's argument consists in confounding the Calvinian with the Scriptural imputation of Adam's sin. If God imputed sin to Adam's offspring in its seminal state, it was merely because Adam's offspring seminally sinned in him. God's imputation is always according to truth. When Adam had actually tainted his soul with sin, and his body with mortality, sinfulness and mortality actually tainted all his offspring then in his loins; and therefore God can truly impute sinfulness and mortality to all, that is, he could truly account them all to be what they really were, i.e. seminally sinful and mortal. How different is this righteous imputation, from the imputation maintained by Zelotes! a cruel, supposed imputation this, whereby God is represented as arbitrarily determining that numberless myriads of unformed men shall be so accounted guilty of a sin which they never personally committed, as to be personally and absolutely predestinated to eternal death, through the horrible medium of necessary, remediless sin!

If Zelotes reply: "God may as justly impute Adam's sin to the natural seed of Adam, as he does impute Christ's righteousness to the spiritual seed of Christ:" I reply, (1.) The case is not parallel. The king may justly give a thousand pounds gratis to whom he pleases, but he cannot give a thousand stripes gratis to whom he pleases, because free wrath is absolutely incompatible with justice. (2.) "Faith is imputed for righteousness;" or, if you please, God imputes righteousness to believers. Now, who are believers? Are they not men who have faith? men who have that grace which unites them to Christ the righteous, and by which they actually derive from Christ (in various degrees) not only a peculiar interest in his merits, but also the very righteousness, the very hatred of sin, and the very love of virtue, which were in the heart of Christ? Therefore when God imputes faith for righteousness, or when he imputes righteousness to believers, he only accounts that what is in believers is actually there; or, if you please, that believers are what they really are, that is, righteous. Hence it appears, that to support Calvinian imputation of sin, by Calvinian imputation of righteousness, is only to defend one chimera by another.

Mr. Whitefield's argument in defence of Calvinian reprobation appears to us so much the more inconclusive, as it is not less contrary to Scripture than to reason. Who can fairly reconcile that reprobation to the texts which intimate that "this proverb shall no more be used in Israel: — The fathers have eaten sour grapes, and *the case is remediless;* the children's teeth being *necessarily and eternally* set on edge?" that "the son shall not *eternally* die," or be reprobated to eternal death "for the sins of the father;" that "God's mercy is over all his works" till provoked free grace gives place to just wrath; that he "willeth not *primarily* the death of a sinner;" and that "God our Saviour will have all men to be saved," in a rational, evangelic way, that is, by freely working out their own salvation in subordination to his free grace.

From all the preceding answers, I hope I may conclude, that the "inextricable dilemma" is a mere sophism; and that the truly reverend Mr. Whitefield understood far better how to offer up a warm prayer, and preach a pathetic sermon, than how to follow error into her lurking holes, in order to seize there the twisting viper with the tongs of truth, and bring her out to public view, stripped of her shining, slippery dress, and darting in vain her forked and hissing tongue.

IV. Having answered the threefold objection of Zelotes, Mr. Toplady, and Mr. Whitefield, I shall now retort it, and show, that upon the plan of the Calvinian "doctrines of grace" and wrath — of unavoidable, finished salvation for a fixed number of elect, and of unavoidable, finished damnation for a fixed number of reprobates, all the Divine perfections (sovereignty not excepted) suffer a partial, or a total eclipse. I have, it is true, done it already in the Checks: but as my opponents do not seem to have taken the least notice of the passage I refer to, though it contains the strength of our cause with respect to the Divine perfections, I beg leave to produce it a second time. If in a civil court a second citation is fair and expedient, why might it not be so too in a court of controversial judicature? I therefore ask a second time: —

"What becomes of God's goodness, if the tokens of it, which he gives to millions of men, be only intended to enhance their ruin, or cast a deceitful veil over his everlasting wrath? What of his mercy, which 'is over all his works,' if millions were for ever excluded from the least interest in it, by an absolute decree that constituted them vessels of wrath from all eternity? What becomes of his justice, if he sentence myriads of men upon myriads to everlasting fire, 'because they have not believed on the name of his only begotten Son;' when, if they had believed that he was their Jesus, their Saviour, they would have believed a monstrous lie, and claimed what they have no more right to, than I have to the crown of England? What of his veracity, and the oath he swears that he 'willeth not *primarily* the death of a sinner; if he never affords most sinners sufficient means of escaping eternal death? if he sends his ambassadors to 'every creature,' declaring that 'all things are now ready' for their salvation, when nothing but 'Tophet is prepared of old' for the inevitable destruction of a vast majority of them? What becomes of his holiness, if, in order to condemn the reprobates with some show of justice, and to secure the end of his decree of reprobation, which is, that 'millions shall absolutely sin and be damned,' he absolutely fixes the means of their damnation, that is, their sins and wickedness? What of his wisdom, if he seriously expostulates with souls as dead as corpses, and gravely urges to repentance and faith persons that can no more repent and believe, than fishes can speak and sing? What becomes of his long suffering, if he waits to have an opportunity of sending the reprobates into a deeper hell, and not sincerely to give them a longer time to 'save themselves from this perverse generation?' What of his equity, if there was mercy for Adam and Eve, who personally broke the hedge of duty, and wantonly rushed out of paradise into this howling wilderness; while there is no mercy for millions of their unfortunate children, who are born in a state of sin and misery without any personal choice, and of consequence without any personal sin?

And what becomes of his omniscience, if he cannot foreknow future contingencies? if to foretel, without a mistake, that such a thing will happen, he must necessitate it; or do it himself? Was not Nero as wise in this respect? Could not he foretel that Phebe should not continue a virgin, when he was bent upon ravishing her? That Seneca should not die a natural death, when he had determined to have him murdered? And that Crispus should fall into a pit, if he obliged him to run a race at midnight in a place full of pits? And what old woman in the kingdom could not precisely foretel that a silly tale should be told at such an hour, if she were resolved to tell it herself; or, at any rate, make a child do it for her?

"Again: what becomes of God's 'loving kindnesses, which have been ever of old toward the children of men?' And what of his impartiality, if most men, absolutely reprobated for the sin of Adam, are never placed in a state of personal trial and probation? Does not God use them far less kindly than he does devils, who were tried every one for himself, and remain in their diabolical state, because they brought it upon themselves by a personal choice? Astonishing! That the Son of God should have been flesh of the flesh, and bone of the bone of millions of men, whom, upon the Calvinistic scheme, he never indulged so far as he did devils! What a hard-hearted relation to myriads of his fellow men does Calvin represent our Lord! Suppose Satan had become our kinsman by incarnation, and had by that mean got the right of redemption, would he not have acted like himself, if he had not only left the majority of them in the depths of the fall, but enhanced their misery by the sight of his partiality to the elect?

"Once more: what becomes of fair dealing, if God every where represents sin as the dreadful evil which causes damnation, and yet the most horrid sins work for good to some, and, as P. O. intimates, 'accomplish their salvation through Christ?' And what of honesty, if the God of truth himself promises that 'all the families of the earth shall be blessed in Christ,' when he has cursed a vast majority of them with a decree of absolute reprobation, which excludes them from obtaining an interest in him, even from the foundation of the world?

"Nay, what becomes of his sovereignty itself, if it is torn from the mild and gracious attributes by which it is tempered? If it is held forth in such a light as renders it more terrible to millions than the sovereignty of Nebuchadnezzar in the plain of Dura appeared to Daniel's companions, when 'the form of his visage was changed against them, and he decreed that they should be cast into the burning fiery furnace?' For they might have saved their bodily life, by bowing to the golden image, which was a thing in their power; but poor Calvinian reprobates can escape at no rate; the 'horrible decree' is gone forth; they must, in spite of their best endeavours, 'dwell,' body and soul, 'with everlasting burnings.'"

To these queries, taken from the Third Check, I now add those which follow: — What becomes of God's infinite power, if he cannot make free agents, or creatures endued with free will? And what of his boundless wisdom, if, when he has made such creatures, he knows not how to rule, overrule, reward, and punish them, without necessitating them, that is, without undoing his own work — without destroying their free agency, which is his masterpiece in the universe? Nay, what would become of the Divine immutability, about which Zelotes makes so much ado, if after God had suspended in all the Scriptures the reward of eternal life, and the punishment of eternal death, upon our unnecessitated works of faith and unbelief, he so altered his mind, in the day of judgment, as to suspend heavenly thrones, and infernal racks, only upon the good works of Christ, and the bad works of Adam; through the necessary medium of faith and holiness, absolutely forced upon some men to the end; and through the necessary means of unbelief and sin, absolutely bound upon all the rest of mankind? And, to conclude, how shall we be able to praise God for his invariable faithfulness, if his secret will and public declarations are at almost perpetual variance? And if Zelotes' doctrines of grace tempt us to complain with the poet,

Nescio quo teneam mutantem Protea nodo;[*]

instead of encouraging us to say, with David, "For ever, O Lord, thy word is *settled* in heaven:" "thy faithfulness is unto all generations."

If Zelotes cannot answer these queries in as rational and Scriptural a manner as his objections have, I trust, been answered; will not the Calvinian doctrines of unscriptural free grace and everlasting free wrath appear to unprejudiced persons as great enemies to the Divine perfections, and to "the sincere milk of God's word," as Virgil's Harpies were to the Trojan hero, and to his richly spread tables? And is there not some resemblance between the Diana and Hecate whom I unmask, and the petty goddesses whom the poet describes thus?

Sive[†] Deæ, seu sint diræ obscenæque volucres, —
Tristius haud illis monstrum, nec sævior ulla
Pestis et ira deum Stygiis sese extulit undis.
Virginei volucrum vultus, fædissima ventris
Proluvies, uncæque manus: — nec vulnera tergo
Accipiunt: ceterique fuga sub sidera lapsæ,
Semesam prædam, et vestigia fæda relinquunt.

---

[*] "He is like Proteus: I know not how to hold him:" whether by his *secret will*, which has absolutely predestinated millions of men to necessary sin and eternal damnation; or by his *revealed will*, which declares that he willeth not *primarily* that any man should perish, but that all should be *eternally* saved, *by* "working out their own salvation," according to the talent of will and power, which he gives to every man to profit withal.

[†] "'Tis hard to say whether they are goddesses or fowls obscene. However they are as ugly and dangerous appearances as ever ascended from the Stygian lake. They have faces like virgins, bands like birds' claws, and an intolerable filthy looseness! As for their body, it is invulnerable; at least, you cannot wound it, they so nimbly fly away into the clouds; leaving the food, which they greedily tore, polluted by their defiling touch."

SECTION XI.

Zelotes' last objection against a reconciliation with Honestus — In answer to it, the reconciler shows, by various illustrations, that the Scriptures do not contradict themselves in holding forth first and second causes — Primary and subordinate motives; and that the connection of free grace with free will is properly illustrated by the Scriptural emblem of a marriage; this relation exactly representing the conjunction and opposition of the two Gospel axioms, together with the pre-eminence of free grace, and the subordination of free will.

IF you compare the prejudice of Zelotes against Honestus to a strong castle, the objections which fortify that castle may be compared to the rivers which were supposed to surround Pluto's palace. Six of them we have already crossed; one more obstructs our way to the reconciliation, and, like Phlegethon, it warmly runs in the following lines: —

OBJECTION VII. "When King Joram said to Jehu, 'Is it peace:' Jehu answered, 'What peace, so long as the whoredoms of thy mother Jezebel are so many?' And what peace can I make with Honestus and you, so long as you adulterate the Gospel, by what you call the evangelical marriage, and what I call the monstrous mixture of free grace and free will? I cannot, in conscience, take one step toward a reconciliation, unless you call make appear that, upon your conciliating plan, the dignity of free grace is properly secured. But, as this is impossible, I can only look upon your Scripture Scales as a new attempt to set one part of the Scripture against the other, and to give infidels more room to say that the Bible is full of contradictions."

ANSWER. Exceedingly sorry should I be, if the Scripture Scales had this unhappy tendency. To remove your groundless fears in this respect, and to prevent the hasty triumph of infidels, permit me, (1.) To show that what at first sight seems a contradiction in the scriptures which compose my Scales, appears, upon due consideration, to be only just subordination of second causes to the first, or the proper union of *inferior* motives with leading ones. And, (2.) To prove what Zelotes calls "a monstrous mixture of free grace and free will," is their important concurrence, which the Scriptures frequently represent to us under the significant emblem of a marriage. Plain illustrations will throw more light upon the subject than deep arguments; I shall therefore use the former, because they are within the reach of every body, and because Zelotes cannot set them aside under pretence that they are "metaphysical."

I. May we not, on different occasions, use with propriety words which seem contradictory, and which nevertheless agree perfectly together? For instance: with respect to the doctrine of first and second *causes*, and of primary and secondary *means*, may I not say, "I ploughed my field this year," because I ordered it to be ploughed? May I not say, on another occasion, "Such a farmer ploughed it alone," because no other farmer shared in his toil? May I not, the next moment, point at his team, and say, "These horses ploughed all my field alone," if I want to intimate that no other horses were employed in that business? And yet, may I not by and by show Zelotes a new constructed plough, and say, "That light plough ploughed all my field?" Would it be right in Zelotes or Lorenzo to charge me with shuffling, or with self contradiction, for these different assertions?

If this illustration do not sufficiently strike the reader, I ask, May not a clergyman, without a shadow of prevarication, say, on different occasions, I hold my living through Divine permission; through the lord chancellor's presentation; through a liberal education; through my subscriptions; through the bishop's institution, &c? May not all these expressions be true, and proper on different occasions? And may not these causes, means, and qualifications, concur together, and be all essential in their places?

Once more: speaking of a barge that sails up the river, may I not, without contradicting myself, say one moment, The wind *alone* (in opposition to the tide) brings her up? And if the next moment I add, Her sails *alone* (in opposition to oars or haling lines) bring her up against the stream, would it be right to infer that I exclude the tackling of the vessel, the rudder, and the steersman from being necessary in their places? Such, however, is the inference of Zelotes. For while Honestus thinks him an enthusiast, for supposing that absolutely nothing but wind and sail [grace and faith] is requisite to spiritual navigation, Zelotes thinks that Honestus is hardly fit to be a cabin boy in the ship of the Church, because he lays a particular stress on the right management of the tackling and rudder; and both will perhaps look upon me as a trimmer, because, in order to reconcile them, I assert that the wind and sails, the masts and yards, the rigging and the rudder, the compass and pilot, have each their proper use and office.

II. With respect to primary and secondary *motives*, may I not say that Christ humbled himself to the death of the cross, out of obedience to his Father; out of compassionate love for a lost world; that he might put away sin by the sacrifice of himself; that whosoever believeth in him should not perish; that the Scriptures might be fulfilled; that he might leave us an example of humble patience; that through death he might destroy the prince of darkness; and that he might see the fruit of the travail of his soul, obtain the joy that was set before him, and be satisfied? Would Zelotes show himself a judicious divine, if he intimated that these motives are incompatible and contradictory? May not a variety of motives sweetly concur to the same end? May you not, for example, relieve your indigent neighbour, out of fear lest you should meet the fate of the inexorable rich man in hell? Out of pity for a fellow creature in distress? Out of regard for him as a fellow Christian? Out of a desire to maintain a good conscience, and to keep the commandments? Out of gratitude, love, and obedience to Christ? That the worthy name by which we are called Christians may not be blasphemed? That your neighbour may be edified? That you may show your love to God? That you may declare your faith in Christ? That you may lay up treasure in heaven? That, like a faithful steward, you may deliver up your accounts with joy? That you may receive the *reward* of the inheritance? That you may be justified by your works as a *believer* in the great day, &c? May not all these motives, like the various steps of Jacob's mysterious ladder, perfectly agree together? And if a good work "comes up for a memorial before God," winged with all these Scriptural motives, is it not likely to be more acceptable than one which ascends supported only by one or two such motives?

Zelotes frequently admits but of two causes of our salvation, and recommends but one motive of good works. The two causes of eternal salvation, which he generally confines himself to, are Christ and faith: and, what is most astonishing, Solifidian as he is, he sometimes gives up even faith itself: for if he reads that "*faith* was imputed to Abraham for righteousness," he tells you that faith is to be taken objectively for Christ and his good works; which is just as reasonable as if I said that when Sir Isaac Newton speaks of the eye and of a telescope, he intends that these words should be taken objectively, and should mean the sun and the moon. Again: as Zelotes frequently admits but one cause of salvation, that is, Christ's righteousness, so he often admits but one motive of sincere obedience, and that is, the love of Christ known by name. Hence he gives you to understand that all the good works of those who never heard of Christ are nothing but splendid sins. To avoid his mistake, we need only admit a variety of causes and motives: and to steer clear of the error of Honestus, we need only pay to the Redeemer the so justly deserved honour of being, in conjunction with his Father and Spirit, the grand *original cause*, and as he is the Lamb slain, the one *properly meritorious cause* of our salvation; representing a grateful love to him as the noblest and most powerful motive to obedience, where the Christian Gospel is preached. In following this reasonable and catholic method, we discover the harmony of the Scriptures; we reconcile the opposite texts which fill the Scripture Scales; and far from giving room to infidels to say that the Bible is full of contradictions, we show the wonderful agreement of a variety of passages, which, upon the narrow plans of Zelotes and Honestus, are really inconsistent, if not altogether contradictory.

III. With respect to the two *Gospel axioms* and their basis, FREE GRACE and FREE WILL, contrary as they seem to each other, they agree as well as a thousand harmonious contrasts around us. If Zelotes consider the natural world in a favourable light, he will see nothing but *opposition* in *harmony*. Midnight darkness, when it is reconciled with the blaze of noon, crowns our hills with the mild, the delightful light of the rising or setting sun. When sultry summers and frozen winters meet half way, they yield the flowers of the spring and the fruits of autumn. If the warming beams of the sun act in conjunction with cooling showers, the earth opens her fruitful bosom, and crowns our fields with a plenteous harvest. Reflect upon your animal frame: how does it subsist? Is it not by a proper union of opposite things, fluids and solids? And by a just temperature, of contrary things, cold and heat? Consider your whole self: are you not made of a thinking soul, and of an organized body? Of spirit and matter? Thus two things, which are exactly the reverse of each other, by harmonizing together, form man, who is the wonder of the natural world: just as the Son of God, united to the son of Mary, forms Christ, who is the wonder of the spiritual world.

I readily confess that the connection of the two Gospel axioms, like that of matter and spirit, is a deep mystery. But as it would be absurd to infer that man is an imaginary being, because we cannot explain how thought and reason can be connected with flesh and blood: so would it be unreasonable to suppose that the coalition of free grace with free will is a chimera in divinity, because we cannot exactly describe how they are coupled. We are, however, indebted to St. Paul for a most striking emblem of the essential opposition and wonderful union that subsist between the two axioms, or (which comes to be the same thing) between the Redeemer and the redeemed — between free grace and free will.

If the true Church is a mystical body composed of all the souls whose submissive free will yields to free grace, and exerts itself in due subordination to our loving Redeemer; does it not follow that free grace exactly answers to Christ, and holy free will to God's holy Church? "Now," says the apostle, "the husband is the head of the wife, even as Christ is the head of the Church: husbands, love your wives as Christ loved the Church: a man shall be joined unto his wife, and they two shall be one flesh: this is a great mystery, but I speak concerning Christ and the Church;" and upon the preceding observation I take the liberty to add: — *This is a great mystery, but I speak concerning* FREE GRACE *and* FREE WILL. If marriage is a Divine institution, honourable among all men, and typical of spiritual mysteries: if Isaiah says, "Thy Maker is thy husband:" if Hosea writes, "In that day, says Jehovah, thou shalt call me ISHI;" that is, MY HUSBAND: if St. Paul says to the Corinthians, "I have espoused you as a chaste virgin to one HUSBAND, even Christ:" and if he tells the Romans that they "are become dead to the law, that they should be *married* to another, even to HIM who is raised from the dead, that they should *bring forth fruit unto God:*" if the sacred writers, I say, frequently use that emblematical way of speech, may I not reverently tread in their steps, and in the fear of God warily run the parallel between the conjugal tie and the mystical union of free grace and free will? And, —

(1.) "If the husband is the head of the wife," as says St. Paul; or her lord, as St. Peter intimates; is not free grace the head and lord of free will? Has it not the pre-eminence in all things? (2.) If the bridegroom makes his address to the bride first, without forcing or binding her with cords of necessity, does not free grace also seek free will first, without forcing it, and chaining it down with necessitating, Turkish decrees? (3.) If the mutual, unnecessitated, voluntary consent of the bridegroom and of the bride, is the very essence of marriage; may I not say that the mutual, unnecessitated, voluntary consent of free grace and free will makes the marriage between Christ and the willing souls, whom St. John calls "the bride," and "the Lamb's wife?" (4.) The husband owes no obedience to his wife, but the wife owes all reasonable obedience to her husband. And does not the parallel hold here also? Must not free will humbly and obediently submit to free grace, as Sarah did to Abraham, calling him lord? (5.) The man is to "give honour to his wife, as to the weaker vessel:" and does not free grace do so to free will, its inferior? Is not its condescending language, "Behold, I stand at the door and knock: open to me, my sister, my love," &c. Yea, does not free grace, like St. Paul, "become all things [but sin and wantonness] to all men, that by any means it may gain *the free will of* some?" (6.) "If the unbelieving wife departs, let her depart," says St. Paul. And if unbelieving free will is bent upon eloping from free grace, may it not do it? Is it locked up as the sultanas are in Turkey? Although incarnate free grace compassionately mourned over the obstinate free will of the Jews, did it dragoon them into compliance? Was not its language, "I would and ye would not?"* "Thou hast been weary of me, O Israel. My

---

* Some Calvinists have done this great truth justice, and among them the judicious Mr. Ryland, of Northampton, A.M., who hath published an extract from Dr. Long, bishop of Norwich, descriptive of the resemblance that man bears to God. The first article of his extract runs thus: — "The soul is an image of the almighty power of God. God has a power of beginning motion: so has the soul. God's will acts with astonishing sovereignty, and absolute dominion and pleasure, where, and when, and how he will. The soul chooses or refuses, accepts or rejects an object, with an amazing resemblance to God. Even devils and the wicked refuse God with sovereign will and a most free contempt." Hence it appears that to rob man of free agency,

people would none of me; so I gave them up to their own hearts' lust, and they walked in their own counsel:" doing, as a nation, what Judas was judicially permitted to do as an individual. (7.) In case of adultery is it not lawful for the husband to put away his wife? And may not free grace repudiate free will for the same reason? When the free will of Judas had long carried on an adulterous commerce with mammon; and when he refused to return, did not our Lord put him away, giving him a bill of divorce, together with the fatal sop? And far from detaining him by fulsome Calvinian caresses, did he not publicly say, "Wo to that man! What thou doest, do quickly. Remember Lot's wife?" (8.) Can the husband, or the wife, have children alone? Can free grace do human good works without human free will? Did not our Lord speak a self-evident truth, when he declared, "Without *me ye* can do nothing?" And did not St. Paul set his seal to it when he said, "We are not sufficient, of ourselves, to think any thing [morally good] as of ourselves; but our sufficiency is of God. Not I, [alone or principally] but the grace of God, which was with me?" And, morally speaking, what can Christ do as the husband of the Church, without her concurrence? What beside atoning, inviting, pre-engaging, and drawing? Do we not read, that he could not do many works among the people of Nazareth, because of their unbelief? And for want of co-operation or concurrence in sinners, does he not complain, "I have laboured in vain: I have spent my strength for naught: all the day long I stretched forth my hands, and no man regarded?" LASTLY: may I not observe that as the procreation of children is the most important consequence of marriage; so the production of "the fruits of righteousness, which are by Jesus Christ," is the most important consequence of the harmonious opposition of free grace and free will, when they are joined together in that evangelical marriage, which the Scripture calls "faith working by love?"

Should Zelotes object here that "some good people produce all the fruits of righteousness, and do all the good works which St. Paul expects from believers, though they will hear of nothing but free grace, and perpetually decry their own good works:" I reply, that there are such persons is granted: nor are they less conspicuous for their unreasonableness, than for their piety. They may rank for consistency with a woman, who is excessively fond of her husband, and peevish with every body else, especially with her own children. Her constant language is, "My husband is all in all in the house; he does every thing: I am absolutely nobody, I am worse than any body, I am a monster, I bring forth nothing but monsters: my best productions are dung, dross, and filthy rags," &c, &c. A friend of her husband, tired to hear such speeches day by day, ventures to set her right by the following questions: — "Pray, madam, if your husband is all in all in the house, is he his own wife? If he does all that is done under your roof, did he get drunk the other day when your footman did so? Does he bear his own children, and give them suck? If you are absolutely nobody, who is the mother of the fine boy that hangs at your breast? And if that child is a *mere* monster,

---

under pretence of making free grace all in all, is to destroy the first feature of God's image in his living picture, man.

* Walking about my parish some years ago, I heard a collier's wife venting her bad humour upon somebody, whom she called "son of a b — h." I went into the house to make peace; and finding it was her own son, whom she thus abused, I expostulated with her about the absurdity of her language, so far as it offended God, and reflected upon herself. I might have added that

why do you dishonour your husband by *fathering* a monster upon him?" While she blushes and says," I hate controversy, I cannot bear carnal reasonings," &c, I close this parallel between marriage, and the evangelical union of free grace and free will, by some remarks, which, I hope, will reconcile Zelotes and Honestus to the harmonious opposition of the *seemingly* contrary doctrines of grace and justice, of faith and works, of free grace and free will, which answer to the two Gospel axioms, and are balanced in the two Scripture Scales.

Union without opposition is dull and insipid. You are acquainted with the pleasures of friendship: you would gladly go miles to shake hands with an intimate friend; but why did you never feel any pleasure in shaking your left hand with your right, and in returning the friendly civility? Is it not because the joining of your own hands would be expressive of a union without proper opposition; of a union without sufficient room to display the mutual endearments of one free will in harmony with another? For what I have all along called free grace, is nothing but God's gracious free will, to which the obedient free will of believers humbly submits itself. Why can you have no satisfaction in going to the fire, when a fever inflames your blood; or in drinking a cooling draught, when you are benumbed with cold? Is it not because in either case the pleasure ceases, or rather becomes pain, for want of proper opposition?

Is not opposition without union the very ground of infernal wo? When opposition amounts to downright contrariety, does it not end in fierce, destructive discord? And does not this discord produce the horrid concert which our Lord describes by "weeping, wailing, and gnashing of teeth," the genuine expressions of sorrow, anguish, and despair? On the other hand, is not opposition in union the very soul of celestial joys? And should I take too much liberty with the deep things of God, if I ventured upon the following query: — Is it not from the eternal, mysterious, ineffable opposition of Father and Son, in eternal, mysterious, ineffable union with each other, that the eternal love and joy of the Spirit proceeds to accomplish the mystery of the Divine unity, and form the very heaven of heaven?

But if that question appear too bold, or too deep, I drop it, and, keeping within earthly bounds, I ask, Does not experience convince us that the most perfect concerts are those in which a number of instruments, *soft* as the flute, and *strong* as the bassoon, *high* sounding as the clarion, and *deep* toned as the kettle drum, properly agree with *tenor, counter tenor, bass,* and *treble voices?* Is it not then that the combined effects of slow and quick vibrations, high and low notes, sharp and flat tones solemn and cheerful accents, grave and shrill, melting and rousing, gentle and terrible sounds, by their harmonizing oppositions, alternately brace and dilate our auditory nerves; or delightfully soothe and alarm, lull and ravish our musical powers? Such, and far more glorious, is the Gospel concert of free grace and free will: a sweetly awful concert this, in which prohibitions and commands, cautions and exhortations, alluring promises

---

if her child was *the son of a b--ch,* he must also be *the son of a d-g;* a circumstance this not less dishonourable to her *husband* than to *herself:* but I really forgot this argument [*ad mulierem*] at that time. However, I mention it here, in hopes that Zelotes, who, through voluntary humility, calls his good works as many bad names as the woman did her son, will take the hint, and will no more reflect upon Christ, by injudiciously loading the productions of his free grace with Antinomian abuse.

and fearful threatenings, gentle offers of mercy and terrible denunciations of vengeance, have all their proper places.

Now man is brought down to the gates of hell, as a rebellious worm; and now [by a proper transition] he is exalted to the heaven of heavens, as the friend of God. Now Christ hangs on an ignominious cross; and now he fills the everlasting throne: one day as a Saviour and a prophet, he gives grace, he offers glory; he calls, he entreats, he weeps, he bleeds, he dies: another day, as a rewarder and a king, he revives and triumphs; he absolves or condemns; he opens and shuts both hell and heaven. The treble in this doctrinal concert appears *enthusiastic* jar to prejudiced Honestus; and the bass passes for *heretical* discord with heated Zelotes: but an unbiassed Protestant "knows the joyful sound" of free grace; the solemn sound of free will; and the alarming sound of just wrath; and admitting each in his concert, he makes Scriptural melody to his Priest and Lawgiver — to his Redeemer and his Judge. As for the merry tune of Antinomian free grace, mixed with the reprobating roar of Calvinian free wrath, it grates upon him, it grieves his soul, it diffuses chillness through his veins, it carries horror to his very heart.

While a divine combines evangelically, and uses properly the two Gospel axioms, you may compare him to a musician who skilfully tunes, and wisely uses all the strings of his instrument. But when Zelotes and Honestus discard one of the evangelical axioms, they resemble a harper who peevishly cuts half the strings of his harp, and ridiculously confines himself to using only the other half. Or, to return to the Scripture simile of a marriage: when an unprejudiced evangelist solemnizes the doctrinal marriage which I contend for, he pays a proper regard to the bridegroom and to the bride; he considers both free grace and free will. Therefore when he sees Honestus perform all the ceremony with free will only, he is as much surprised as if he saw a clergyman take a gold ring from the right hand of a woman, put it on the fourth finger of her left hand, and gravely try to marry her to herself. And when he sees Zelotes transact all the business with free grace alone, he is not less astonished than if he saw a minister take a single man's right hand, put it into his left hand, and render himself ridiculous by pronouncing over him a solemn nuptial blessing.

If Zelotes be still afraid that upon the plan of an evangelical marriage between free grace and free will, the transcendent dignity of God's grace is not properly secured; and that *human agency* will absolutely claim the incommunicable honours due to *Divine favour;* I shall guard the preceding pages by some remarks, which will, I hope, remove Zelotes' groundless fears, and give Honestus a seasonable caution.

God's gracious dispensations toward man, (or which comes to the same,) the dealings of free grace with free will, are frequently represented in Scripture under the emblem of gracious covenants. Now covenants which are made between the Creator and his creatures; between the Supreme Being, who is absolutely independent, because he wants nothing; and inferior beings, who are entirely dependent upon him, because they want all things; such gracious covenants, I say, always imply a matchless condescension on the part of the Creator, and an inconceivable obligation on the part of his creatures. Therefore, according to the doctrine enforced in these sheets, free grace, which shines by its own eternal lustre, without receiving any thing from free will, can never, in point of dignity, be confounded with free will; because free will borrows all its power and excellence from free grace; just as the moon borrows all her light and glory from the sun.

We infer, therefore, that as the *moon* acts in conjunction with, and due subordination to the *sun* in the *natural* world, without supplanting or rivalling the sun: so *free will* may act in conjunction with, and due subordination to *free grace* in the *spiritual* world, without rivalling, much more without supplanting free grace. And hence it appears that Zelotes' fears lest our doctrine should pour contempt on the glory of free grace, are as groundless as the panic of the ancient Persians, who, when they saw the moon passing between the earth and the sun, imagined that the great luminaries which rule the day and the night were actually fighting for the mastery; and absurdly dreaded that the strife would end in the total extinction of the solar light.

Ezekiel, chap. 16, gives us an account of the glory to which God advanced the Jewish Church. From a state of the greatest meanness and pollution, he raised her to the dignity and splendour described in these words: — "I sware unto thee, and entered into a *marriage* covenant with thee, saith the Lord God; and thou becamest mine. I clothed thee also with embroidered work; I decked thee with ornaments: thou wast exceeding beautiful: thou didst prosper into a kingdom, and thy renown went forth among the heathen for thy beauty: for it was perfect through the comeliness which I had put upon thee, saith the Lord." However, the Jewish Church (such is the power of free will!) abused these glorious favours, as appears from the next words: — "Thou didst trust in thine own beauty, and playedst the harlot, saith the Lord God." But does this adulterous ingratitude of the Jews disprove the truth of Ezekiel's doctrine, any more than the adultery of Bathsheba disproved her being once Uriah's lawful wife? And can any consequence be charged upon the doctrine of the evangelical marriage maintained in these sheets, which is not equally chargeable upon the above- mentioned doctrine of the prophet?

We grant that free will too frequently forgets its place, as too many persons of the inferior and weaker sex forget theirs, notwithstanding their solemn promise of dutiful obedience till death; but does this show, either that the union of indulgent free grace and dutiful free will is a heretical fancy: or that free will is really equal to free grace? If imperious free will rises against free grace, and acts the part of a Jezebel, is not free grace strong enough to reduce it by proper methods, or wise enough to give it a bill of divorcement, if such methods prove ineffectual? Does Zelotes act a becoming part when he so interferes between free grace and free will, as to turn the latter out of the Church, under pretence of siding with the former? Has he any more right to do it, than I have to turn Queen Charlotte out of England, under pretence that bloody Mary abused her royal authority?

Why does Zelotes stumble at the doctrine of the evangelical marriage which I prove? And why is Lorenzo offended at the mystery of Christ's incarnation? Is it not because they overlook the noble original of free will? If you trace the free-willing soul back to its eternal source, you will find that it proceeds from Him, who "breathed into the nostrils of Adam the breath of life," that man might "become a living soul." And where is the absurdity of asserting that by means of the mysteries which we call redemption and sanctification, he reunites himself to that very spirit which came from him; to that very soul which he breathed into the earthly Adam? If man's dignity before the fall was such, that when St. Luke declares our Lord's human generation, and comes to the highest round of the genealogical ladder, he is not afraid to say that Christ was "the son of Adam, &c, who was the son of God," Luke 3:38, where is the absurdity of supposing that God in Christ kindly receives his son again, when that son returns to him like the free-willing, penitent prodigal?

Nor need free will be proud of this unspeakable honour: for, not to mention its creation, for which it is entirely indebted to free grace, does it not owe to Divine favour all the blessings of redemption? If free grace should say to free will, "When I passed by thee, and saw thee polluted in thy own blood, I said unto thee, Live;" would not believing free will instantly bow to the dust, and thankfully acknowledge the undeserved mercy? Why then should Zelotes think that free will will infallibly forget its place, if it be raised to the honour of an evangelical, conjugal union with free grace? If a prince raised a filthy, condemned, dead shepherdess from the dung hill, the dungeon, and the grave; graciously advancing her to princely honours, and a seat at his feet, or by his side; does it follow that she must necessarily forget her former baseness? or that his condescension must unavoidably rob him of his native superiority? For my part, when I hear St. John say, "Behold what manner of love the Father hath bestowed upon us, that we [who submit our free will to free grace] should be called the sons of God, — the wife of the Lamb," &c, far from being tempted to forget my wretchedness, I am excited to "fear the Lord and his goodness," and encouraged to "perfect holiness in *that* fear;" for "every man who hath this *faith and* hope, purifieth himself, even as God is pure:" so far is he from necessarily walking in pride as a vain-glorious Pharisee; or from exalting himself as a self-deified antichrist! Beside, to all eternity the glaring truth, maintained by the apostle, will abase free will, and secure the transcendent dignity of free grace: "What hast thou, which thou hast not [more or less directly] received" of *free*, creating, persevering, redeeming, sanctifying, or rewarding *grace?* "Who hath *first* given to it, and it shall be recompensed to him again?" "For of him," i.e. of God, the bottomless and shoreless ocean of free grace, "and through him, and to him, are all *good* things: to whom be glory, for ever. Amen!"

SECTION XII.

The author sums up the opposite errors of Zelotes and Honestus, whom he invites to a speedy reconciliation — To bring them to it, he urges strong and soft motives; and after giving them some directions and encouragements, he concludes by apologizing for his plainness of speech.

IF Honestus be not averse to the rational and Scriptural terms of peace proposed in the preceding pages; and if I have removed the objections which Zelotes makes against these terms, what remains for me to do but to press them both to be instantly reconciled? To this end I shall once more urge upon them two powerful motives, the one taken from the unspeakable mischief done by their unreasonable division, and the other from the advantage and comfort which their Scriptural agreement will produce.

Permit me, Zelotes, to begin by the mischief which you do, through your opposition to the moral truths maintained by Honestus. If reason and Scripture breathe through the preceding pages, is it not evident that, under pretence of exalting free grace, which is the first weight of the sanctuary, you throw away the *second* weight, which is the free will offering of sincere obedience; constantly refusing it the place of a weight before God, when the children of men are weighed for eternal life or eternal death, in the awful, decisive balance of election and reprobation? Does it not necessarily follow from thence that the personal election of some men to eternal salvation is merely of unscriptural free grace; while the personal reprobation of others from grace and glory is entirely of tyrannical free wrath? Is not this the language of your doctrine? "There is for the elect but one weight, bearing the stamp of Heaven and everlasting love; namely, *the finished work of Christ*, which is absolutely and irresistibly thrown into the scale of all who are predestinated to eternal life: and this golden weight is so heavy, that, without any of their good works, it will unavoidably turn the scale for their eternal salvation. And, on the other hand, there is for the reprobates but one weight, bearing the stamp of hell and everlasting wrath, namely, *the finished work of Adam*, which is absolutely and irresistibly thrown into the scale of all that are predestinated to eternal death: and this leaden weight is so heavy, that let them endeavour ever so much to rise to heavenly joys, it will necessarily sink them to eternal wo." Thus you turn the Gospel into a Calvinian farrago; whereas, if you divided the truth aright, you would do both Gospel axioms justice; asserting, that although the initial salvation of sinners is of free grace alone; yet the eternal salvation of adult believers, which is judicially as well as graciously bestowed upon them by way of reward, is both of free grace and of rectified free will; both of faith, and of its voluntary works; both of Christ living, dying, and rising again for us; and of believers graciously assisted (not despotically necessitated) to persevere in the obedience of faith.

The mischief does not stop here. To make way for your error, you frequently represent the second Scripture Scale, with the passages which it contains, as Pharisaical or Mosaical legality; distressing the minds of the simple by your unscriptural refinements, and hardening the Nicolaitans, — the practical Antinomians, in their contempt of morality and sincere obedience. I do you justice, Zelotes: I confess that, like Christ, you hate their deeds; but, alas! like antichrist, you love, you dearly love their spurious doctrines of grace; and this inconsistency involves you in perpetual difficulties and glaring contradictions. One moment Solifidianism makes you extol their immoral principles; the next moment your exemplary piety makes you exclaim against their consistent immoral practices. One hour you assure them that our eternal justification entirely depends upon God's absolute predestination, and upon the salvation completely finished by Christ for us; you openly declare that, from first to last, our works have absolutely no hand in the business of salvation; and you insinuate that a fallen believer is as much a child of God when he puts his bottle to his neighbour to make him drunk, or when he commits adultery and premeditates murder, as when he deeply repents and bears fruit meet for repentance. The next hour, indeed, you are ashamed of such barefaced Antinomianism. To mend the matter you contradict yourself, you play the Arminian, and assert that all drunkards, adulterers, and murderers are unbelievers, and that all such sinners are in the high road to hell. Thus you alternately encourage and chide, flatter and correct your Nicolaitan converts; but one caress does them more harm than twenty stripes or wounds; for instead of the precious balm of Gilead, you have substituted the cheap balm of Geneva: a dangerous salve this, which slightly heals, and too often imperceptibly poisons a wounded conscience. With this application they soon cure themselves; one single dose of unconditional election to eternal life, of inamissible, complete justification merely by the good works of another, or of "salvation finished in the full extent of the word," without any of our outward performances, makes them as hearty and cheerful as any Laodiceans ever were.

When they hear your Arminian pleas for undefiled religion, they wonder at your legality. If you will be inconsistent, they will not: they are determined to be all of a piece. You have inspired them with sovereign contempt for the preceptive, remunerative, and vindictive part of the Gospel: nay, you have taught them to abhor it, as the dreadful heresy of the Arminians, Pelagians, Pharisees, and free willers. And thus you have inadvertently paved and pointed out the way to the Antinomian city of refuge. Thither they have fled, by your direction, and having laid hold on the false hope which you have set before them, they now stand completely deceived in self-imputed and non-imparted righteousness. It is true that you attack them there from time to time; ashamed of the genuine consequence of your partial gospel, you call St. James to your assistance, and erect a Wesleyan battery to demolish their Solifidian ramparts: but, alas! you have long since taught them to nail up all the pieces of evangelical ordnance; and when you point them against their towers, they do but smile at your inconsistency. Looking upon you as one who is not less entangled in the law, than risen Lazarus was in his grave clothes, they heartily pray that you may be delivered from the remains of Moses' veil, and see into the privileges of believers as clearly as they do; and when they have briskly fired back your own shots, legality! legality! they sit down behind the walls which you take so much pains to repair, I mean the walls of mystical Geneva, singing there a Solifidian *Requiem* to themselves, and sometimes a triumphal *Te Deum* to one another.

Happy would it be for you, Zelotes, and for the Church of God, if the mischief done by your modern gospel were confined to the immoral fraternity of the Nicolaitans. But, alas! it produces the worst effect upon the moralists also. Honestus and his admirers see you extol free grace in so unguarded a manner, as to demolish free will, and unfurl the banner of free wrath. They hear you talk in such a strain of "a day of God's power," in which the elect are irresistibly converted, as to make sinners forget that now is the day of salvation, and the time to use one or two talents, till the Lord comes with more. Perhaps also Honestus meets with a soul frightened almost to distraction by the doctrine of absolute reprobation, which always dogs your favourite doctrine of Calvinian election. To complete the mischief you drop some deadly hints about the harmlessness of sin; or, what is still worse, about its profitableness and sanctifying influence with respect to believers. Neither height nor depth of iniquity shall separate them from the love of God Nay, the most grievous falls, falls into adultery and murder, shall be so overruled, as infallibly to drive them nearer to Christ, and of consequence to make them rise higher and sing louder in heaven. This Solifidian gospel shocks Honestus. His moral breast swells against it with just indignation; and supposing that the doctrine of free grace (of which you call yourself the defender) is necessarily connected with such loose principles, he is tempted to give it up, and begins perhaps to suspect that religious experiences are only the workings of a melancholy blood, or the conceits of enthusiastic brains. This, Zelotes, and more, is the mischief you inadvertently do by your warm opposition to the

Creeds and Scripture Scales

doctrines of *justice*, which support the second Gospel axiom, and are inseparable from the Scripture doctrines of *grace*.

And you, Honestus, if you lay aside the first weight of the sanctuary, are you less guilty than Zelotes? When you say little or nothing of the fall in Adam, of our recovery by Christ, and of our need of a living, victorious faith: and when, under the plausible pretence of asserting our moral agency, and pleading for sincere obedience, you keep out of sight the unsearchable riches of Christ, the wonderful efficacy of his atoning blood, and the encouraging doctrine of free grace; do you not inadvertently confirm Deistical moralists in their destructive notions, that scraps of moral honesty will answer the end of exalted piety, and of renovating faith? And do you not increase the prejudices of Zelotes; making him believe, by your sparing use of the *first* Gospel axiom, that all who represent morality and good works as an indispensable part of Christ's Gospel, are secret enemies to free grace, and stiff maintainers of Pharisaic errors?

O Zelotes, O Honestus, what have ye done? What are ye still doing? Alas! ye drive one another farther and farther from the complete "truth, as it is in Jesus." In your unreasonable contention, you break the harmony of the Gospel; ye destroy the Scripture Scales; ye tear in two the book of life, and run away with a mangled part, which ye fondly take for the whole. Ye crucify Christ doctrinally: Honestus pierces his right hand, while Zelotes transfixes the left; both pleading, as the scribes and Pharisees did, that ye only crucify a "deceiver of the people."

A skilful physician, by prudently mixing two contrary drugs, may so temper their effect as to compound an excellent medicine. Thus those ingredients, which, if they were given alone, would perhaps kill his patients, by being administered together, operate in corrective, qualifying conjunction, and prove highly conducive to health. Happy would it be for your spiritual patients, if ye imitated his skill, by evangelically combining the gracious promises, and the holy precepts, which support the two Gospel axioms! But, alas! ye do just the reverse, when ye indiscriminately administer only the truths of the first or of the second axiom. Thus, instead of curing your patients, ye sour their minds; Honestus with the poisonous leaven of the Pharisees; and Zelotes with the killing leaven of the Antinomians.

The practice of thousands shows what dangerous touches ye have, by these means, given to their principles: for your admirers, O Zelotes, are encouraged so to depend upon free grace, as not vigorously to exert the powers of free will. And it is well if some of them do not lie down in stupid dejection, idly waiting for an overbearing impetus of Divine grace, which, you insinuate, is to do all for us without us; while others cheerfully rise up to play, in consequence of the Laodicean ease which naturally flows from the doctrine of salvation Calvinistically finished. On the other hand, your hearers, O Honestus, are so taught to depend upon their best endeavours, and the faithful exertion of their free will, that many of them see no occasion ardently to implore the help of free grace, as depraved, impotent, blind, guilty, hell-deserving sinners ought to do. Trusting to what they will do to-morrow, they neglect and grieve the Holy Spirit, which is ready to help their infirmities to-day. And it is to be feared that many of them play the dangerous game of procrastination till the Sun of righteousness sets, with respect to them; till all their oil is burned, and their lamps, going out with a bad smell, leave them in the dreadful night when no man can work.

Who can tell the mischiefs which ye have already done by your mangled gospels? It will be known in the great day. But suppose ye had only caused the miscarriage of one soul; would not this be matter of unspeakable grief? If ye would esteem it a misfortune to have occasioned the loss of your neighbour's horse; think, O think, how sad a thing it must be to have caused, though undesignedly, the destruction of his soul! The loss of the cattle upon a thousand hills can be repaired; but if a man should gain the whole world, and through your wrong directions lose his own soul, what will he, what will *you* give in exchange for his soul?

In the multitude of those, whose salvation is thus endangered, I see Lorenzo — sensible, thoughtful, learned Lorenzo: his case is truly deplorable, and a particular attention to it may convince you of the fatal tendency of a gospel which wants almost one half of its proper weight. Although the dogmatical assertions of a preacher, if they be supported by the charms of a mellifluous eloquence, or the violence of a boisterous oratory, prevail with many; yet not with all. For while some greedily drink in the very dregs of error, through the weakness of their minds, the movableness of their passions, and the credulity which accompanies superstitious ignorance; others are tempted to doubt of the plainest truths, through the nicety of a keen wit, the refinements of a polite education, and the scrupulousness of a skeptical understanding. Lorenzo is one of this number. He is determined not to pin his faith upon any man's sleeve. And he sets out in search of religious truth with this just principle, that religion may improve, but can never oppose good sense and good morals. In this disposition Lorenzo hears Zelotes; and when Zelotes begins to play upon his numerous audience with his rhetorical artillery, Lorenzo examines if the cannon of his eloquence is loaded with a proper ball; if the solidity of his arguments answers to the positiveness, loudness, or pathos of his delivery. Zelotes, not satisfied to preach only the doctrine contained in the *first* Scripture Scale, takes upon himself warmly to decry the doctrine contained in the second; and at times he even explodes morality; unguardedly representing it as the cleaner way to hell. If this be the Gospel, says Lorenzo, I must ever remain an unbeliever; for I cannot swallow down a cluster of inconsistencies, whence the poison of immorality visibly distils.

He hears you next, Honestus; and he admires the rational manner in which you prove man's free agency, and point out the delightful path of virtue; but, alas! you mention neither our natural impotence, nor the help which free, redeeming grace has laid on Christ for helpless sinners. As this doctrine is not repugnant to the light of reason, Lorenzo prefers it to the Solifidian scheme of Zelotes. Thus reason stands him instead of Christ, free will instead of free grace, and some external acts of benevolence instead of the faith which renews the heart. And upon the same leg of this outward morality he hops along in the ways of virtue, till a violent temptation pushes him into some gross immorality. His wounded conscience begins then to want ease and a cure; but he knows not where to seek it. Honestus seldom points him clearly to the Saviour's blood; and when Zelotes does it, he too often defiles the sacred fountain with unscriptural refinements, and immoral absurdities, artfully wrapped up in Scripture phrases. Hence it is that Lorenzo does not see the remedy, or that he turns from it with contempt. Nor should I wonder if, while each of you thus keeps from him one of the keys of Christian knowledge, he remained a stranger to the Gospel, and began to suspect that the Bible is a mere jumble of legends and inconsistencies — an apple of discord thrown among men by crafty priests, and artful politicians, to awe the vulgar, and divert the thoughts of the inquisitive. In these critical circumstances he meets with Hume and Voltaire, whom he prefers to you both; and, renouncing equally free grace and free will, he flees for shelter to open infidelity and avowed fatalism. Thither numbers follow him daily; and thither your refinements, O Zelotes, and your errors, O Honestus, will probably drive the next generation, if ye continue to sap the foundation of the Gospel axioms. For the Gospel can no more stand long upon one of its pillars, than you can stand long upon one of your legs. Christianity without *faith*, or without *works*, is like a sun without *light*, or without *heat*. Such Christianity is as different from primitive Christianity, as such a sun is different from the bright luminary at whose approach darkness flies and winters retire.

Nor are Lorenzo, and his Deistical friends, only hurt by your doctrinal mistakes. Ye, yourselves, probably feel the bad effects of your parting the Gospel axioms. It is hardly possible that ye should take off the fore wheels, or the hind wheels of the Gospel chariot, without retarding your own progress toward the New Jerusalem. To say nothing of your spiritual experiences, may I not inquire if Honestus, after all his discourses on morality and charity, might not, in some instances, be a little more moral, or more extensively charitable, if not to the bodies, at least to the souls of his neighbours? And may I not ask Zelotes, if after all his encomiums upon free grace, he might not be a little more averse to narrowness of spirit, unscriptural positiveness, and self-electing partiality; a little less inclined to rash judging, contempt of his opponents, and free wrath?

Should ye find, after close examination, that these are the mischievous consequences of your variance; and should ye desire to prevent them, ye need only go half way to meet and embrace each other. You, Zelotes, receive the important truth which Honestus defends, and, in subordination to Christ and free grace, preach free will, without which there can be no acceptable obedience. And you, Honestus, espouse the delightful truth recommended by Zelotes. Preach free grace, without which free will can never be productive of sincere morality. So shall you vindicate morality and free will with less offence to Zelotes, and with more success among your own admirers. In a word, instead of parting the two Gospel axioms, and filling the Church with Gnostics or formalists; with Antinomian believers, or faithless workers; instead of tearing our Priest asunder from our King, and making Christianity a laughing stock for infidels by your perpetual divisions, admit the use of the Scripture Scales, contend for the faith once delivered to the saints; and, dropping your unreasonable and unscriptural objections against each other, seek, hand in hand, "Fulsome," the gross Antinomian, and Lorenzo, the immoral moralist; earnestly seek these lost sheep, which ye have inadvertently driven from the good Shepherd, and which now wander upon the dark mountains of immorality and skepticism. They may be brought back; they are not yet devoured by the roaring lion. If you will reclaim them, you, Honestus, calm the agitated breast of Lorenzo, and strengthen his feeble knees, by all the reviving, exhilarating truths of the first Gospel axiom. And you, Zelotes, instead of frightening him from these truths by adulterating the genuine doctrine of free grace, with loose, Solifidian tenets; or by slyly dropping into the cup of salvation which you offer him, poisonous drops of free wrath, Calvinian reprobation, and necessary damnation; recommend yourself to his reason and conscience by all the moral truths which spring from the fitness of things and the second Gospel axiom. With regard to Fulsome, remember, O Zelotes, that you are commanded to "feed the fat with judgment," and that Christ himself fed the ancient Laodiceans with that convenient food. Give therefore to this modern Laodicean *chiefly* the Gospel truths which fill the second Gospel scale. But give them to him in full weight. Let him have a good measure, pressed down, and running over into his Antinomian bosom, till he "hold the truth in unrighteousness" no more. And that he may receive the *"whole* truth as it is in Jesus," be you persuaded, Honestus, to second Zelotes. Enforce your moral persuasions upon Fulsome, by all the weighty, evangelical arguments which the first axiom suggests. So shall you break the force of his prejudices. He will see that sincere obedience is inseparable from true faith; and, being taught by happy experience, he will soon acknowledge that the doctrine of free will is as consistent with the doctrine of free grace, as the free returning of our breath is consistent with the free drawing of it. Thus ye will both happily concur in converting those whom ye have inadvertently perverted.

While, like faithful dispensers of Gospel truths, ye weigh in this manner to every one his portion of physic or food in due season, and in proper scales; our Lord, by lifting upon you the light of his pleased countenance, will make you sensible, that, in spirituals as well as in temporals, "a false balance is an abomination to him; but a just weight is his delight." Your honesty may indeed offend many of your admirers, and make you lose your popularity; but prefer the testimony of a good conscience to popular applause; and the witness of God's Spirit to the praise of party men. Nor be afraid to share the fate of our great Prophet, and of his blunt forerunner, who, by firmly standing to the Gospel axioms, lost their immense congregations and their lives. Christ fell a sacrifice not only to Divine justice, but also to Caiaphas' Pharisaic rage against the truths contained in the first Scale; and John the Baptist had the honour of being beheaded, for bearing his bold testimony to those contained in the second Scale, and against the Antinomianism of a professing prince, who "observed him, heard him gladly, and did many things." O Honestus, O Zelotes, think it an honour to tread in the steps of these two martyred champions of truth. Let them revive, and preach again in you. Shrink not at the thought of the Pharisaic contempt, and of the Antinomian abuse which await you, if you are determined to preach both the anti-Pharisaic and the anti-Solifidian part of the Gospel. On the contrary, be ambitious to suffer something for him, who calls himself the truth: for him, who suffered so much for you, and who, for the joy of your salvation, which was set before him, despised the shame, endured the cross, and now sits at God's right hand, ready to reward your faithfulness with a crown of righteousness, life, and glory.

Ye should wade to that triple crown through floods of persecution, and rivers of blood, if it were necessary. But God may not call you to suffer for your faithfulness. And if he do, he will reward you, even in this life, with a double portion of peace and love. While the demon of discord sows the tares of division, and blows up the coals which bigotry has kindled, ye shall inherit the beatitude of peace makers. "The peace of God, which passes all understanding," shall rest upon you as it does upon all the sons of peace. And the delightful tranquillity restored to the Church, shall flow back into your own souls, and be extended as a river to your families and neighbourhood, which your opposite extremes have perhaps distracted.

What a glorious prospect rises before my exulting imagination! A holy, catholic Church! A Church, where the communion of saints, the forgiveness of sins, and the foretastes of eternal life, are constantly enjoyed; where swords are beat into reaping hooks; and where shouts for controversial engagements are turned into songs of brotherly love! To whom, next to God, are we obliged for this wonderful change? It is to you, Zelotes, whose intemperate zeal is now rectified by the judicious solidity of Honestus; and to you, Honestus, whose phlegmatic religion is now corrected by the fervour of Zelotes. Henceforth, instead of contending with each other, ye amicably bear together the ark of the Lord. While ye triumphantly sustain the sacred load, and while Christian psalmists joyfully sing, "Behold how good and pleasant a thing it is for brethren to dwell together in unity; union is the refreshing dew which falls upon the hill of Sion, where the Lord has promised his blessing, and life for evermore:" — while they sing this, I see the thousands of Israel pass the "waters of strife," and take possession of the land of Canaan — the spiritual kingdom of God. Their happiness is almost paradisiacal! "The multitude of them that believe are of one heart and of one soul: they continue steadfastly in the apostles' doctrine and fellowship — in breaking of bread, and in prayers. They eat their meat with gladness and singleness of heart; neither says any of them that aught of the things which he possesses is his own: for they have all things common; *they are* perfected in one." Truth has cast them into the mould of love. Their hearts and their language are no more divided. They think and speak the same. In a word, Babel is no more, and the New Jerusalem comes down from heaven.

O Zelotes! O Honestus! shall this pleasing prospect vanish away as the colours of the rainbow? Will ye still make Lorenzo think that the *Acts of the Apostles* is a religious novel? And the Christian harmony there described a delusive dream? O God of peace, truth, and love, suffer it not. Bless the scriptures, bless the arguments which fill these pages. Give, O give me favour in the sight of the two antagonists whom I address. Make me, unworthy as I am, the mean of their lasting reconciliation. Remove their prejudices; soften their hearts; humble their minds; and endue me with the strength of a spiritual Samson; that, taking these two pillars of our divisions in the arms of praying love, I may bend them toward each other, and press them, breast to breast, upon the line of moderation, till they become one with the truth, and one with each other. When thou hadst prospered the endeavours of Abraham's servant, to the bringing about the marriage of Isaac and Rebecca, thou wroughtest new miracles. Thou didst melt angry Esau in the arms of trembling Jacob, and injured Joseph over the neck of his relenting brethren. Repeat, good Lord, these ancient wonders; show thyself still the God of all consolation. Let me not only succeed in asserting the evangelical marriage of condescending free grace and humble free will; but also in reconciling the contentious divines, who rashly put asunder what thou hast so strongly joined together.

O Zelotes! O Honestus! my heart is enlarged toward you. It ardently desires the peace of Jerusalem and your own. If to-day ye do not despise the consistent testimonies of the fathers, and of our reformers; if to-day ye regard the whispers of reason, and the calls of conscience; if to-day ye reverence the suffrages of the prophets, the assertions of the apostles, and the declarations of Jesus Christ; if to-day "ye hear the voice of God" speaking to you by the Spirit of truth, and by the Prince of Peace; "harden not your hearts." You, Zelotes, harden it not against free will, sincere obedience, and your brother Honestus. And you, Honestus, humbly bow to free grace, and kindly embrace your brother Zelotes. All things are now ready. Come together to the marriage of free grace and free will. Come to the feast of reconciliation. Jesus himself will be there, to turn your bitter "waters of jealousy" into the generous wine of "brotherly kindness." Too long have you begged to be excused; saying, "I have married a wife; I have espoused a party, and therefore I cannot come!" Party spirit has seduced you; put away that strumpet. Espouse truth; embrace love; and you will soon give each other the right hand of fellowship.

I have gently drawn you both with the bands of a man — with rational arguments. I have morally compelled you with the Spirit's sword, "the word of God." By the numerous and heavy weights, which fill these Scripture Scales, I have endeavoured to turn the scale of the prejudices, which each of you has entertained against one of the Gospel axioms. But, alas! my labour will be lost, if you are determined still to rise against that part of the truth, which each of you has hitherto defended. Come, then, when reason invites, when revelation bids, when conscience urges, yield to my plea: nay, yield to the solicitations of thousands; for although I seem to mediate alone between you both, thousands of well wishers to Sion's peace, thousands of moderate men, who mourn for the desolations of Jerusalem, wish success to my mediation. Their good wishes support my pen; their ardent prayers warm my soul; my love for peace grows importunate, and constrains me to redouble my entreaties. O Zelotes, O Honestus, by the names of Christians, and Protestants, which ye bear; by your regard for the honour and peace of Sion; by the blessings promised to them that love her prosperity; by the curses denounced against those who widen the breaches of her walls; by the scandalous joy, which your injudicious contentions give to all the classes of infidels; by the tears of undissembled sorrow, which God's dearest children shed in secret over the disputes which your mistaken zeal has raised, and which your opposition to a part of the truth continues to foment; by your professed regard for the sacred book, which your divisions lacerate, and render contemptible; by the worth of the souls, which you fill with prejudices against Christianity; by the danger of those whom you have already driven into the destructive errors of the Antinomians and of the Pharisees; by the Redeemer's seamless garment, which you rend from top to bottom; by the insults, the blows, the wounds which Christ *personal* received in the house of his Jewish friends; and by those which Christ *doctrinal* daily receives at your own hands; by the fear of being found proud despisers of one half of God's revealed decrees, and rebellious opposers of some of the Redeemer's most solemn proclamations; by all the woes pronounced against the enemies of his royal crown, or of his bloody cross; by the dreadful destruction which awaits antichrist; whether he transforms himself into an angel of light, artfully to set aside Christ's righteous law; or whether he appears as a man of God, slyly to supersede Christ's gracious promises; by the horrible curse which shall light on them, who, when they are properly informed, and lovingly warned, will nevertheless obstinately continue to weigh out, in false balances, the food of the poor to whom the Gospel is preached; and, above all, by the matchless love of him who "was in Christ reconciling the world unto himself," I entreat you, "suffer the word of reconciliation: be ye reconciled" to reason and conscience; to each other and to me; to all the Bible and to primitive Christianity; to Christ our King and to Christ our Priest. So shall all unprejudiced Christians meet and embrace you both, upon the meridian of moderation and Protestantism, which stands at an equal distance from Antinomian dreams and Pharisaic delusions.

Creeds and Scripture Scales

O Zelotes! O Honestus! mistaken servants of God; if there be any consolation in Christ; if any delight in truth; if any comfort in love; if any fellowship of the Spirit; if any bowels of mercies, fulfil ye my joy, and the joy of all moderate men in the Church militant; nay, fulfil ye the joy of saints and angels in the Church triumphant: "be ye like minded; having the same love; being of one accord; of one mind. Let nothing be done through strife or vain glory; but in lowliness of mind, let each esteem the other better than himself. Look not each on his own things, [on the scriptures of his favourite scale;] but look also on the things of the other," on the passages which fill the scale defended by your brother. Remember, that if we "have all faith," and all external works, without "charity *we are* nothing." "Charity suffereth long, and is kind: charity envieth not: charity seeketh not her own: charity rejoiceth not in iniquity and discord, but rejoiceth in the truth," even when the truth bruiseth the head of our favourite serpent — our darling prejudice. Let then charity, never-failing charity, perfect you both in one. Hang on this golden beam, and it will make you a couple of impartial, complete divines, holding together as closely, and balancing one another as evenly as the concordant passages which form my Scripture Scales.

My message respecting the equipoise of the Gospel axioms I have endeavoured to deliver with that plainness and earnestness which the importance of the subject calls for; if, in doing it, my aversion to unscriptural extremes, and my love of peaceful moderation have betrayed me into any unbecoming severity of thought, or asperity of expression, forgive me this wrong, which I never designed, and for which I would make you all possible satisfaction, if I were conscious of guilt in this respect. Ye are sensible that I could not act as a reconciler, without doing first the office of an expostulator and reprover; an office this which is so much the more thankless, as our very friends are sometimes prone to suspect that we enter upon it, not so much to do them good, as to carry the mace of superiority, and indulge a restless, meddling, censorious, lordly disposition. If unfavourable appearances have represented me to you in these odious colours, give me leave to wipe them off, by cordial assurances of my esteem and respect for you. Yes, my dear, though mistaken brothers, I sincerely honour you both for the good which is in you; being persuaded that your mistakes spring from your religious prejudices, and not from a conscious enmity against any part of the truth. When I have been obliged to expose your partiality, I have comforted myself with the pleasing thought that it is a partiality to an important part of the Gospel. The meek and lowly Saviour, in whose steps I desire to tread, teaches me to honour you for the part of the truth which you embrace, and forbids me to despise you for that which you cannot yet see it your duty to espouse. Nay, so far as ye have defended free grace without annihilating free will, or contended for free will without undervaluing free grace, you have done the duty of evangelists in the midst of this Pharisaic and Antinomian generation. For this ye both deserve the thanks of every Bible Christian, and I publicly return you mine. Yes, so far as Zelotes has built the right wing of Christ's palace, without pulling down the left; and so far as Honestus has raised the left wing, without demolishing the right, I acknowledge that ye are both ingenious and laborious architects, and I shall think myself highly honoured, if, like an under labourer, I am permitted to wait upon you, and to bring you some rational and Scriptural materials, that you may build the temple of Gospel truth with more solidity, more evangelical symmetry, and more brotherly love, than you have yet done.

God only knows what contemptible thoughts I have of myself. It is better to spread them before him, than to do it before you. This only I will venture to say; in a thousand respects I see myself vastly inferior to either of you. If I have presumed to uncover your theological sores, and to pour into them some tincture of myrrh and aloes, it is no proof that I prefer myself to you. A surgeon may open an imposthume in a royal breast, and believe that he understands the use of his scissors and probe better than the king, without entertaining the least idea of his being the king's superior. If I have made *a pair* of Scripture Scales, which weigh Gospel gold better than your *single scales;* it no more follows that I esteem myself your superior, than it follows that an artist who makes scales to weigh common gold esteems himself superior to the ministers of state, because he understands scale making better than they.

Horace will help me to illustrate the consistency of my reproofs to you, with my professions of respect for you. I consider you, Zelotes, as a one- edged sword, which cuts down the Pharisaic error; and you, Honestus, as a one-edged scymetar, which hews the Antinomian mistakes in pieces; but I want to see you both as the Lord's two-edged sword; and I have indulged my Alpine roughness, in hopes that (through the concurrence of your candour with the Divine blessing which I implore on these pages) you will be ground to the other edge you want. This, ye know, cannot be done without some close rubbing; and, therefore, while ye glitter in the field of action, let not your displeasure arise against a grinding stone cut from the neighbourhood of the Alps, and providentially brought into a corner of your Church, where it wears itself away in the thankless office of grinding you both, that each of you may be as dreadful to Antinomianism and to Pharisaism, as the cherub's "flaming sword, which turned, *and cut* every way," was terrible to the two first offenders. So shall ye keep the way to the tree of life in an evangelical manner; and instead of triumphing over you, as I go the dull round of my controversial labour, I shall adopt the poet's humble saying: —

Fungor vice cotis, acutum
Reddere quæ ferrum valet, exsors ipsa secandi.

Not that I dare to flaming zeal pretend,
But only boast to be the Gospel's friend;
To whet you both to act, and, like the hone,
Give others edge, though I myself have none.

Or rather, considering what the prophet says of the impartial hand which weighed feasting Belshazzar, and wrote his awful doom upon the wall that faced him, I will pray: "O God, be merciful to me a sinner; and when I turn my face to the wall on my dying bed, let not my knees smite one against the other at the sight of the killing word, 'TEKEL: thou art weighed in the balances and art found wanting.' Let me not be 'found wanting' either the testimony of thy free grace, through faith, or the testimony of a good conscience through the works of faith. So shall the Spirit of thy free grace bear witness with my free-willing spirit, that I am a child of thine, that I have kept the faith, and that in the great day, when I shall be weighed in the balances of the sanctuary, I shall be found a *justified sinner*, according to the *anti-Pharisaic* weights, which fill the *first* Scripture Scale; and a *justified believer*, according to the *anti-Solifidian* weights, which fill the *second*."

Apprehending Truth Publishers
Proclaiming Truth in the Age of Deceit
AD LEGEM MAGIS ET AD TESTIMONIUM

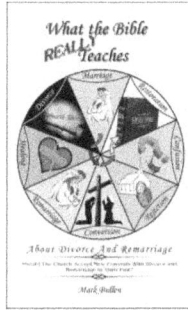

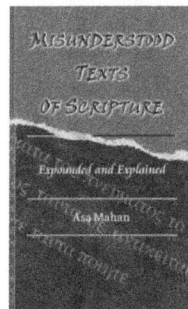

Coming Soon!   Coming Soon!

Also Published By Apprehending Truth:

DEFINING BIBLICAL HOLINESS

John Wesley, Asa Mahan

ed. Jeffrey L. Wallace

The Biblical doctrine of "Christian Perfection" has been denied even by those who call themselves by the name of Christ. "Defining Biblical Holiness" takes a look at this all important doctrine by casting our gaze into the past, and attempting to clearly define the truth presented in this doctrine. John Wesley and Asa Mahan both had a firm grasp upon a Biblical understanding of the teaching of holiness and Christian Perfection. Their two works on the subject, along with a new introduction, are here presented in juxtaposition in order to shed light on the current antinomian trend which continues unabated in the modern professing "Church".

- ISBN: 0615444040
- EAN13: 9780615444048
- Page Count: 296
- Binding Type: US Trade Paper
- Trim Size: 6" x 9"
- Language: English
- Color: Black and White
- Related Categories: Religion / Christian Theology / Ethics

Available at ApprehendingTruth.net and your favorite online book retailers. Ask your local bookstore to carry titles from Apprehending Truth Publishers.

www.ingramcontent.com/pod-product-compliance
Lightning Source LLC
Chambersburg PA
CBHW031229090426
42742CB00007B/124

9 780615 813370